A Man for All Seasons

A Man for All Seasons

THE LIFE OF
K.M. PANIKKAR

NARAYANI BASU

ebury

cntxt

Published by Context, an imprint of Westland Books, a division of Nasadiya Technologies Private Limited, in 2025

No. 269/2B, First Floor, 'Irai Arul', Vimalraj Street, Nethaji Nagar, Alapakkam Main Road, Maduravoyal, Chennai 600095

ISBN: 9789360455668

10 9 8 7 6 5 4 3 2 1

Typeset by Jojy Philip

Printed at Manipal Technologies Limited, Manipal

To my mother, who always believes that I can and who always ensures that I do.
To Bunny, this book wouldn't be real without you.
And
To Perky—the goodest girl who ever will be!

Contents

Preface

K.M. PANIKKAR WAS A NATIONALIST, AN ANARCHIST, A NOVELIST, A constitutional lawyer, an academic, a historian, a foreign policy mandarin, a journalist, a diplomat, an administrator and a poet.

He worked against an almost technicolour canvas—of world wars and princely states, independence movements, transnational anarchy and the Cold War. From 1915 to 1963, his career spanned the length of India's freedom movement and its first two decades as a postcolonial nation. He walked in the company of the legends of modern history: Jawaharlal Nehru, Mahatma Gandhi, Sardar Patel, Zhou Enlai, Chairman Mao and Gamal Abdel Nasser. He had audiences with Mussolini and the Pope, and encouraged Sir Aurel Stein to chart out forgotten sites of the lost Indus civilisation in Bikaner.

His literary career alone defies definition. Panikkar began writing when he was a student in college. He continued to write until the day he died, becoming one of modern India's leading public intellectuals. He wrote across different fields: from international relations to foreign policy, from constitutional law to history. From the 1930s to the 1940s, Panikkar was at his peak. As a member of the Chamber of Princes' legal team, he was the author of a tract that defined the future of a federal India, uniting princely states with provinces. In the same decade, he wrote a book which is still considered foundational: on post-colonial India's maritime policy. In those days, as India straddled the transition between colonialism and freedom, Panikkar was the man you called if you wanted an Asian perspective on history or foreign policy.

He also wrote fiction. In the world of Malayalam literature, there is not a genre that he did not touch. From poetry to drama, from satire to prose, Panikkar wrote so prolifically in his mother tongue that it warrants a book of its own.

In postcolonial India, Panikkar took centre stage during the Cold War with his controversial ambassadorship in China and as the diplomatic channel through which Chinese Premier Zhou Enlai communicated his views on the Korean war to the Americans as well as to the United Nations. He annoyed the CIA about as much as he annoyed his peers in the Ministry of External Affairs. He was Nehru's man in Cairo and France, besides being a quiet supporter of the Zionist cause. By the end of the 1950s, foreign offices across the world knew K.M. Panikkar—though their opinions of him were richly varied.

But despite the quantities he wrote himself, the reams that have been written about him over the years and the seminars that are still held about him, of Panikkar himself, one knows very little. Here is a man who has been inexplicably hard to pin down on paper. Various people have studied Panikkar in his various professional guises, but there haven't been many attempts to pull together a picture of the man as a whole.

Who was K.M. Panikkar? What was his real story? How did a young man from Kuttanad become one of India's founding fathers?

His close friend, the journalist K. Iswara Dutt, once remarked that Panikkar was one of India's 'impossible men'. As I began to write this book, I realised that no other phrase came close to describing Panikkar quite so well.

Panikkar exasperated diplomats and intelligence agencies, prime ministers and princes. He also earned their unwavering respect. His was a mind that troubled the Raj and provoked New Delhi. So fierce was his patriotism that, in his youth, security agencies from Britain to the Netherlands kept a sharp eye on his activities. As a member of the States Reorganisation Commission, Panikkar was co-author of a report that asked for the reorganisation of states on linguistic lines. Its recommendations were largely accepted. Between 1956 and 1966, cohesive states protecting the interests of Telugu, Tamil, Malayalam, Kannada, Marathi and Gujarati speakers came into being. It was yet another example of Panikkar's defining impact on the evolution of Indian nationhood.

At home, he was a charming, if unconventional, husband and father; a man who admired powerful women; a dutiful son, a loving brother and a loyal friend. He loved the finer things of life as much as he loved the traditional customs of home. Panikkar was a man capable of being as much at home in Kuttanad as he was in Paris. Those who knew him spoke of a roving spirit, strong opinions and forensic intelligence; a charming man who liked to provoke, and who possessed an impish sense of humour. You might disagree with Panikkar. But you could not ignore him.

This is his story.

Narayani Basu

New Delhi
May 2025

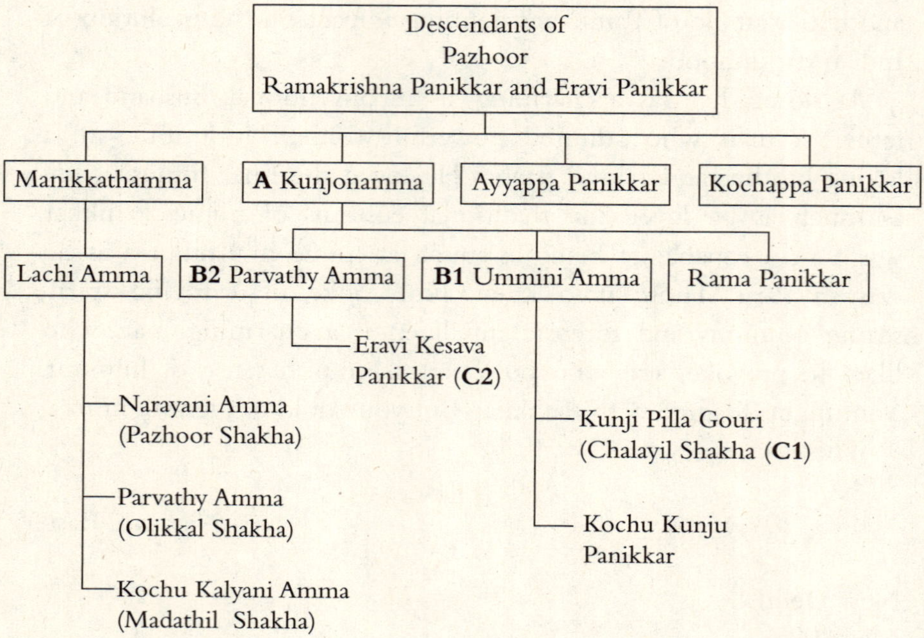
Descendants of
Pazhoor
Ramakrishna Panikkar and Eravi Panikkar
Manikkathamma
A Kunjonamma
Ayyappa Panikkar
Kochappa Panikkar
Lachi Amma
B2 Parvathy Amma
B1 Ummini Amma
Rama Panikkar
Eravi Kesava Panikkar (C2)
Narayani Amma (Pazhoor Shakha)
Parvathy Amma (Olikkal Shakha)
Kochu Kalyani Amma (Madathil Shakha)
Kunji Pilla Gouri (Chalayil Shakha (C1)
Kochu Kunju Panikkar

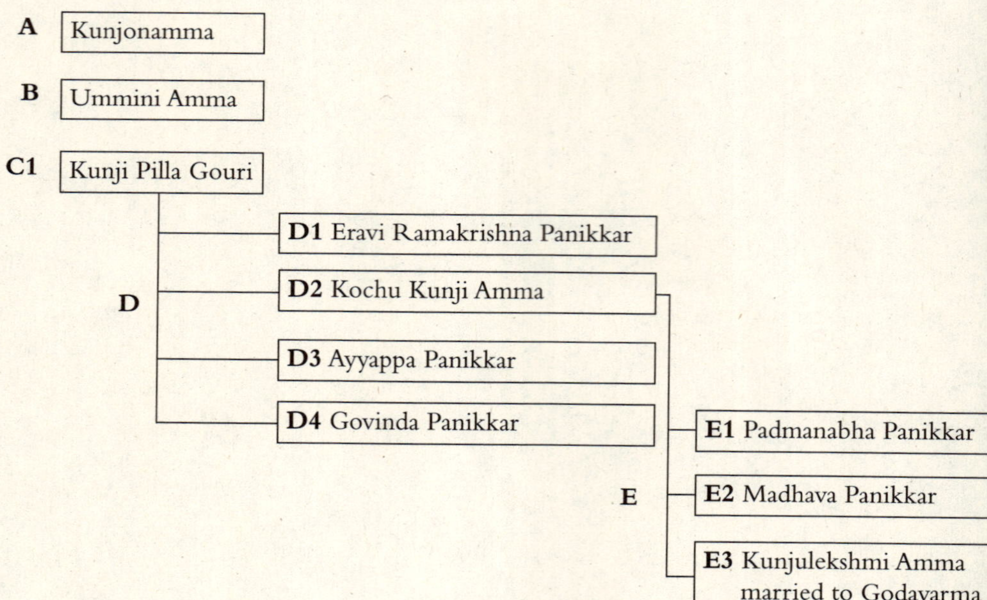
A
Kunjonamma
B
Ummini Amma
C1
Kunji Pilla Gouri
D
D1 Eravi Ramakrishna Panikkar
D2 Kochu Kunji Amma
D3 Ayyappa Panikkar
D4 Govinda Panikkar
E
E1 Padmanabha Panikkar
E2 Madhava Panikkar
E3 Kunjulekshmi Amma married to Godavarma

PART I

Beginnings (1894–1914)

Chapter 1

Home

THE KAINAKARY MAIN ROAD SNAKES THROUGH AN ENDLESS SEA OF GREEN paddy fields, bordered by the silver lakes so typical of Kuttanad, and indeed much of southern Kerala. It takes the curious visitor to the Kainakary jetty, from where you board a boat—still the only way to reach the small hamlet of Kavalam. Standing about seven feet below sea level, the village is irrigated by a finger of the Pamba River. It's quiet here, the sense of isolation palpable. Coconut trees bend over the silver-blue waters of Vembanad Lake, their fronds swaying in a warmly humid breeze. Every so often, the waters ripple as a boat chugs past. Sometimes, there is a lone fisherman, sailing languidly past with the silvery catch of the day glinting in the prow of his canoe. A laughing greeting is tossed to a passerby on the banks. Perhaps they know each other. Perhaps they will see each other later, after the day's work is done.

Fifty-eight years after his death, life has moved on in Kavalam, but at least on the outside, it all looks much the same. If K.M. Panikkar could see his native village, he would quite possibly agree. Marooned between snaking canals and waterways, as Panikkar's nephew, the great poet Ayyappa Panicker, wrote, at nights one sometimes had to hail a boat that seemed invisible in the thick darkness until 'the lone wick of the small lamp, at times, would reflect on the ripples as a long running line'.[1]

The Panikkar homestead, Chalayil, stately and dignified, was set against an expanse of land choked with flowers. Panikkar himself would describe it in rather bare prose thus:

> In the house itself only females live, while the male members of the family occupy rooms set apart for them, or, if they are rich, live in houses in neighbouring compounds. The Nayar house has always a large piece of enclosed ground in front of it, which is called *muttam*. Often it is used as an ornamental garden, and no man of the lower caste may enter it. There the children walk about and play in daytime, and the women have their dance and general merriment in the evening. Behind the house is a vegetable garden and a bathing tank, which is reserved exclusively for women. The dominant idea in the arrangement of the house is the proper separation of sexes in the family.[2]

Today, if you enter through an old weather-stained black iron gate that has *Chalayil* inscribed in flowing script on the mossy pillar beside it, you will arrive at the back of the tharavad. There is nothing much to see here. But if you walk around the back, you will come to the padipura, the main gateway. Beyond it lie two derelict buildings amidst a thickly weeded, marshy swamp—the ruins of what used to be the fertile canal system, 'a trellis of dykes' that once ran through the gardens that sloped down to the water's edge. There were crocodiles in these waters in Panikkar's time. P. Velayudha Panicker, Panikkar's nephew and the younger brother of the poet and historian K.N. Panikkar, remembered a pet crocodile that lived docilely in the tharavad pond.[3]

Even in those days, Kavalam was susceptible to regular and heavy flooding during the torrential Malabar monsoons. In 1923, a boat had to be dispatched from Alleppey to rescue members of the Panikkar family who had been forced to take refuge in the outhouse to escape the rising floodwaters. It was in this house that Kavalam Madhava Panikkar was born on 13 May 1894, the second son and the middle child of three children, to Chalayil Kochukunji Amma and Periamana

Puthiyillam Parameswaran Nampoothiri. He had an elder brother, Padmanabha, and a younger sister, Kunjulekshmi Amma. Of the three, only the brothers would survive.

When he was a grown man, Panikkar would often write that Kavalam was situated in the back of beyond. That may have been true then as it is now, but the Panikkar family was a prominent one. Derived from the Sanskrit word 'paninayaka', Panikkar (and its variant spellings) means 'warriors'. It is believed to have been a title bestowed on the teachers of a martial art known as Kalari that was used by warriors in the army. The roots of the community lay in the kingdom of Ambalapuzha Champakasseri. When Ambalapuzha was annexed by Marthanda Varma, the Maharaja of Travancore, its army was made redundant, though the art of Kalari and the men who taught it continued to flourish.

The Panikkars of Chalayil however were of a gentler bent, providing Kavalam for generations with a village teacher. They had of course also dispersed through searches for jobs or marriages elsewhere across Kuttanad. It was only in 1832 that young Madhava's grandmother, Kunjipilla Gouri, who lived in nearby Pazhoor-Valady at the time, moved there after she got wind of the fact that Chalayil was being mismanaged by the relatives then in residence there. Furious, she packed her bags and took herself and her brother, Eravi Kesava Panikkar—all of sixteen years old—off to take care of matters.

Madhava's childhood was dominated by Kunjipilla Gouri and her fiery brother. Eravi Kesava was an innovative, ambitious young man. He began the process of reclaiming land from the mighty Vembanad Lake to use for paddy cultivation. In the late nineteenth century, it was seen as a rare feat of engineering. Even before this impressive feat, Eravi Kesava had been known for his diversion of the course of a river at Chennamkary using entirely indigenous materials. This too was a technical marvel in those days, and it established him as an innovator of sorts in the locality.[4] His gamble paid off incredibly well, earning Chalayil the wealth and repute it needed to support itself as well as the other ancestral home in Pazhoor-Valady.[5] By the dawn of the twentieth century, the house of Chalayil was flourishing.

Young Madhava remembered Eravi Kesava as a grand old man with a fiery temper who inspired dread and awe in equal parts. He had a booming voice, went nowhere without a retinue of obedient servants and, unsurprisingly, had all the makings of a domestic tyrant. 'When he strode into the Chalayil house, striking terror into the lesser fry,' Panikkar recalled later, 'my grandmother used to tremble and withdraw into the inner court.'[6] If family memory serves, Eravi Kesava also liked his independence. He lived in a separate wing of the big house, breakfasting there before carrying on with his tasks for the day. This often involved regular meetings with residents and locals who came to discuss their problems with him, hopeful for an arbitration or a remedy. But to meet Eravi Kesava you had to be patient. He would interrupt his schedule for nobody. First, he would bathe in ice-cold water. Then his servants would solemnly hand him his daily pellet of opium, which he would swallow before eating his customary handful of roasted grain. Only after this would he appear before the assembled villagers to disburse justice and tend to the tasks for the day. His ideas of fairness and principles were even more terrifying than his personality, and the family lived in terror of his temper. He was known to have denied maintenance funds to an older branch of the family simply because they had dared to refuse his orders. In his adulthood, Panikkar recalled the incident of a young man who had been accused of drunken misbehaviour. Eravi Kesava sentenced him to being locked in a coconut store for a week, fed only once a day!

In time, the business of land reclamation passed to Panikkar's uncle—his mother's elder brother Eravi Ramakrishna Panikkar. Of this uncle, Madhava had fonder memories. Ramakrishna was Kesava's favourite, a stern-faced young man with a sharp, serious brain whose continuation of his uncle's efforts to reclaim land from the lake earned him the praise of the king, Moolam Thirunal Rama Varma. With more paddy required to feed a growing population, Rama Varma personally asked Ramakrishna Panikkar to expand his efforts. Ramakrishna's last effort in this direction was the Mathi Kayal. Thereafter, he turned his attention to setting up a school win the area. It is perhaps this school that Panikkar refers to when he talks of the Panikkars providing education to the village of Kavalam.[7]

A progressive man, well versed in local mythology and folklore, Eravi Ramakrishna's establishment of a primary school in Kavalam was a huge step forward for a village that did not, at the dawn of the twentieth century, have facilities even for the most basic kind of education. P. Velayudha Panicker recalled that Kavalam's topography, surrounded as it was by water, made it nearly impossible for modernity to reach the village.[8] Paper and pens were almost unheard of, and those who had the means hired tutors who taught students the Malayalam alphabet by inscribing the letters on damp sand.

Small wonder then that Madhava's education began at home. His father Periamana Puthiyillam Parameswaran Nampoothiri was a Brahmin from Kasaragod, whose family were managers of the nearby Palliyarakkavu Devi temple in Kavalam. When he visited the tharavad, special precautions had to be taken so that his caste status, superior to that of the Nairs, would not be contaminated. He remains a shadowy figure of whom we do not know much at all. Panikkar describes him dutifully in his memoirs as 'a devout and conscientious man, very attached to his children',[9] but since the man rarely makes an appearance thereafter, the reader is left to assume that Madhava and his siblings didn't have the easiest of relationships with their father.[10]

As chief priest of the temple, Parameswaran Nampoothiri was rarely home, leaving the running of the tharavad to Kochukunji Amma. Madhava's mother was a strong, quiet woman, calm, competent and as intelligent as any of her brothers. She had been educated and had a love for books and reading that stayed with her all her life. However, with the many duties that running an estate like Chalayil demanded, she was nearly always away from home, taking care of the agricultural side of things at Chalayil. Her son remembered her as a woman who preferred discipline to maternal warmth.

The home ran smoothly with Kochukunji Amma and her mother at the helm of affairs. In those days, there was no such thing as running water or pumps. Water was drawn from the tharavad well. Before the water was drawn, however, the women in the house would have arisen quietly and swept and cleaned the floors. The lobam (prayer lamp) would then be taken around the house and the foreheads of those who had woken for morning prayers were smeared with a mix of turmeric and powdered sandalwood. After this, the real work of the house began: feeding and milking the cows, churning boiled milk for butter, sending the children off to the fields or to school for the day. Later, coconuts and peppercorns would be ground for curries and mounds of vegetables would be chopped or boiled for the day's meals.

To read the Rev. Samuel Mateer's account of life in Travancore, written a decade before Madhava was born, is to gain the impression that the lot of the woman in Travancore—even a high-caste woman—was deeply unpleasant. According to Mateer, the woman was nearly always uneducated, her birth unwanted, her person unloved and her life devoid almost entirely of anything except domestic chores. 'A Brahmin gentleman was once asked, "What do you think a woman ought to know?" "She must know two things," was his reply, "First she must know the way to the bazaar to buy necessities for the house and secondly, she must know the way from the bazaar home again."'[11]

But Mateer was writing during a time of political and social reform. Political ideas were already beginning to take shape in the faraway eastern regions of India. In the south of the country, these ideas looked different. Travancore was, as Mateer observed, 'not a nation, but a congeries of artificially and widely separated for the most part, mutually opposing sections of population'.[12] By the time Madhava was born in 1894, Travancore was on the cusp of change.

As a boy, however, his earliest memories were those of his grandmother. Kunjipilla Gouri was a gentle, lovable woman who adored her grandchildren and was open with her affections. She was far softer than her daughter and was clearly the children's favourite. It was with her that they were almost always to be found. Madhava spent most of his days with her, learning his first tales of Hindu mythology and folklore. Kunjipilla Gouri had a satisfying store of appropriately adventurous stories from the Ramayana and the Mahabharata. It was she who played games with Madhava, who shielded him from the tempers of the adults in the house, who taught him how to read and write and 'practically brought me up until I was old enough for school'.[13]

When he was five years old, Madhava was deemed ready to officially begin learning the Malayalam alphabet. His precocity was evident, for he knew the alphabet already. His grandmother had secretly taught him the letters, a private little game for two to while away lazy morning hours together. Exasperated but indulgent, Kochukunji Amma did the next best thing and dispatched her son to the local school, a 'kalari' run by relatives of the Panikkars. There, in an open playground, nearly fifty children (including girls) sat dutifully every day. Their lot was to learn to write, first in the sand and then with a sharp stylus on palm leaves. They recited sentences in groups and learned arithmetic (which Madhava hated with a passion) and the story of Krishna (which everyone had to learn by heart). After school, Madhava spent the purpling, lamplit twilights listening to the murmur of his mother's voice as she read aloud from the Ramayana or the Puranas.

Kochukunji Amma was a deeply religious woman, disciplined about her reading of the scriptures, and this seems to have been a family ritual with the children automatically gathering around their mother's knee to listen to stories of duty, devotion and courage. It was from his mother that Madhava developed an abiding love for his mother tongue, for the rolls and cadences of Malayalam as it slid off the tongue. It was also from his mother and grandmother that the boy learned to connect deeply with his identity as a Travancorean, with Nair culture and custom, and with the land that gave him birth. Even when he was a grown man, Panikkar never forgot that sense of belonging. Nor would his forays into a wider, more Eurocentric world ever diminish that sense.

Six-year-old Madhava already showed definite signs of academic potential. His grandmother, whose favourite he was, longed for bigger and better things for him. An English education, for instance. But the closest one could get to a truly cosmopolitan education was in Travancore, and Madhava was far too young to travel so far. On the other hand, he had become downright rebellious. He loathed his mathematics classes and often refused outright to learn his sums. As

Kunjipilla Gouri began looking around for a suitable tutor, her eye fell on Madhava's uncle Ayyappa Panikkar, the quiet young man in charge of Chalayil's household accounts, not to be confused with the great poet. As choices went, this one had rather unfortunate consequences. Ayyappa may have been as intelligent as he was quiet, but underneath the surface ran a current of volatility. Madhava would soon learn that Ayyappa was capable of fits of sudden blind rage, often caning him for simple mistakes. This deterred the boy not one jot.

Classes began in Ayyappa's small single room above the portico of the family granary. In the mornings, Ayyappa would hand Madhava a sheet of paper and a pencil to copy the accounts and work on some rudimentary mathematics while the older man went about the estate doing his day's work. However, in the ways of small children from time immemorial, Madhava rarely sat obediently at his desk. Often, he slipped away to explore the jungle-like, overgrown estate, or as P. Velayudha Panicker wrote later, to tease the young girls in the village.[14] The story goes that the precocious Madhava once wrote a lyrical poem to a local girl's beauty. This was discovered by Ayyappa who promptly lost his temper on a grand scale. Seizing his errant nephew, he tied the boy to a pillar of the house and left him there in the sun to contemplate his mistakes. After Ayyappa had stormed off, Kunjipilla Gouri sneaked out to set her grandson free. But even she knew better than to cross Ayyappa. Before he came back from his rounds, Madhava was hastily tied up again. As methods to escape studying went, this seemed perfectly delightful. The two fell into a pattern. Every day, Madhava deliberately and slyly riled Ayyappa into tying him to the pillar in the sun and storming off. Kunjipilla Gouri then sneakily released him from his bonds so he could run around and play before Ayyappa returned. Unsurprisingly, this little charade was soon uncovered by Ayyappa, who disgustedly washed his hands of Madhava altogether. And so it was that mathematics went out of the window entirely.

This was just as well, for Madhava had discovered his next abiding love: poetry and reading. He began as precociously as ever with the thullals of Kuttanad's celebrated poet Kunchan Nambiar. This, combined with his mother's reading of the scriptures and his own natural love for poetry, ensured that Madhava was academically far ahead of the other students at Kavalam's local school.

Meanwhile, Kunjipilla Gouri was growing old and caring for her disruptive grandson would have been tiring for her. The family decided it was time to dispatch the boy to the faraway city of Trivandrum. In Eravi Kesava's opinion, Madhava would benefit from the company of his older brother, K. Padmanabha, who was already in the city, and of intellects equal to his own. This would be the first time that Madhava would leave the comforting confines of Chalayil. (To put things in context, a trip from Kavalam to Trivandrum was in those days fairly akin to a voyage overseas!) The decision to send Madhava to Trivandrum was also an acknowledgement of the changing times.

Travancore was a traditionally conservative state, where the rulers believed they were the descendants of gods and the guarantors of Hindu orthodoxy on earth. It was also teetering on the verge of bankruptcy, with a sorely mismanaged financial department. All that changed when the young Ayilyam Thirunal ascended the throne in 1860. With his progressive, far-sighted dewan T. Madhava Rao by his side, Ayilyam Thirunal implemented a series of administrative, economic and social reforms that transformed Travancore.[15] The first decade of Ayilyam Thirunal's reign saw Travancore's financial worries being quickly sorted out, a vast network of schools being set up and all kinds of new employment opportunities being created. Not surprisingly, with economic progress came social instability.

Panikkar remembered an episode from his childhood that, when read in today's light, reveals the socioeconomic fault lines emerging between the different communities, and the Nairs' desperate attempt to maintain the status quo. In an essay he wrote as a young man, Panikkar recalled an unnamed man arriving from Madras in Alleppey, travelling with his Christian friend. When the two men boarded their houseboat, the servant who would wait on them was still eating his lunch. In those days, the custom was that no food could be eaten in the company of or even in proximity to anyone from a lower caste. Christians were seen to belong to the latter. The upshot of this was that, by the time the boat docked in Kavalam, word had already spread that the Nair servant had eaten his food with a Christian man aboard the boat. The village was in a collective state of rage and only with great difficulty were the elders persuaded not to excommunicate the poor man.[16]

Communal fissures were harder to bridge than changes in social perception. Constant contact with the outside world meant that the ideas of the extended family were being challenged, as were the forms of collective property and matrilineal society. Young Nair men were beginning to question what the head of their family could or could not control and just how much of what a man earned could be passed on to his sisters' children.[17] From here, it was but a small step to challenging the forms of marriage and even the long-established matrilineal system. Much of this was already seeing legislative formalisation when Madhava was a baby, like the Malabar Marriage Act (1896) and the Travancore Wills Act (1899), the latter of which allowed men to divide their inheritance in half between the tharavad and their families. Panikkar's own family would see the first such division in 1909, while other branches would separate from Chalayil by 1921. There was none of the vicious pettiness that usually defined such occasions, with Eravi Kesava managing the transition with skill.[18] 'It is significant to point out that (the) Chalayil family was the last family to shed from the marumakkathayam (matriarchal) system.... in accordance to the changing needs,' noted P. Velayudha Panicker proudly.[19]

The new modes of education in Trivandrum were expensive. Only those from select elite families were able to send their boys to study there. Luckily for Madhava, Chalayil fell into that category. The Panikkar clan never had to answer the pressing question of *which* boy should be sent to an 'English' school. Govinda Panikkar, Ramakrishna's brother and Madhava's uncle, and Madhava's elder brother, K. Padmanabha, were already studying in Trivandrum and Madhava would join them there.

It was a vibrant time to be in the city. By the 1890s, the consort to the senior Maharani of Travancore, Kerala Varma had revolutionised primary schooling in Travancore. An acclaimed intellectual giant, he was a man of formidable talent, considered to be the state's Kalidasa for his facility with Sanskrit poetry and the father of Malayalam literature.

The new education system meant that youngsters like Madhava were the direct beneficiaries. Technically speaking, the government-run vernacular schools (Madhava would attend such a school a little later) were not really doing anything on the ground for the masses. Attendance was non-existent and teachers happily fudged figures to present a good picture to visiting inspectors. The syllabus was rough to say the least. But sarkari schools had team sports, debate clubs and dramatic societies, along with teachers of different castes, European missionaries and even a 'clever Cambridge atheist' by the name of H.N. Read, a Scottish science professor and later the principal of the Maharaja's College.

This was also a time when the conversation around caste discrimination was heating up, with Nair supremacy under attack and calls for the rights of marginalised communities like the Ezhavas. Things were changing even within the traditional ties of the sambandham—the prevalent marriage custom among Nair castes, which allowed marriage of women to ritually higher castes with the women having the capacity to end the marriage at will—all propelled by the new education system. Tharavads competed over which boy to send to Nagercoil, Kottayam or Trivandrum to study and possibly join government service. A new generation was growing up in Travancore, one that was increasingly disenchanted with the old ways of life and now aspired to government service instead.

Madhava would be among them.

On the occasion of Madhava's departure, Govinda Panikkar picked Madhava up from Chalayil, and the two left in the wee hours one morning in 1902. They travelled in style in their own covered country boats called kettuvallam, 'fully equipped with cooking facilities, bedding and all the rest'.[20] The journey lasted five days, and to the young, wide-eyed Madhava, it was a whole new world.

The forests of the Western Ghats were thick with teak and blackwood and teemed with wildlife. Low lying islands in the backwaters were blanketed with creepers, rattans and flowering shrubs. Across the quiet waters lay a strip of raised roadway. This little stretch of land was, in fact, a busy port. Boats or boatmen could be changed there and coasting steamers often docked to rest, drawing into the harbour alongside fleets of native vessels and the more advanced models of their European brethren. Overhead, clouds of parakeets screamed to each other, while in the trees, the kingfishers, brilliantly blue and unobtrusively tiny, watched the water for the gleam of fish. Stately cranes trod elegantly in submerged rice fields. Uncle and nephew reached Ambalapuzha around noon on the first day. This was the home of Madhava's favourite poet Kunchan Nambiar and of his favourite dessert, palpayasam. This was the first time that Madhava was visiting a place he had only read about, and it came vividly to life with all its sights, sounds and tastes. He spent a delightful day bathing in the temple pond that Nambiar had written of and eating payasam by the bowlful.

They set off again after lunch through the still backwaters to Thrikkunapuzha. The canals were busy thoroughfares during the day, with freight and passenger boats criss-crossing each other's paths. Dusk was falling when the boat entered the sleepy hamlet. The boat was moored and the servants who had accompanied the Panikkars leaped lightly on shore to begin preparing a simple meal of freshly caught fish and red rice. Crickets chirped through the twilight and waves lapped sleepily at the banks. It was a beautiful evening, bathed in the fading glow of the setting sun. Many other boats had glided to shore at various points, docking to collect provisions from nearby villages or to allow the boatmen to cook their meals. As night fell, so did a quiet calm. The silence was broken only by snatches of conversation from the boatmen and passersby, the distant barking of dogs from the villages, the fat croaking of frogs and the shrill chirps of cicadas in the trees. As much as Madhava would have liked to stay a while, they sailed on again, this time through the night to Ponmana where a quick breakfast at the government-run resthouse sufficed. They were more than halfway to Quilon by then. After lunch in Quilon, all that needed to be done was to forge the vast, serene expanse of the Ashtamudi Lake.

By lunch time on the fifth day, Madhava was tired and fractious. He wanted to stay awake to see everything and he wanted to go to sleep immediately. The last bit of their journey was the most exciting part, and it seemed to him too bad that he was quite so exhausted.

The boat would sail through Varkala, through the tunnel in the cliffs that had been commissioned by Dewan T. Madhava Rao. Madhava was determined to see this marvel of science and technology, but he fell asleep sometime close to lunch, awakening to the tinny splat of raindrops on the awning of the boat. Scrambling up to the deck, Madhava was met by his uncle who told him that they were finally sailing through the tunnel. What Madhava had assumed were raindrops was actually the drip-drip-drip of water from the roof of the tunnel. At the end of this tunnel, wide gates swung open, and they emerged onto the vast expanse of the Veli Lake. From here it was a brief journey to Trivandrum--and the beginning of a new life.

In his later years, Panikkar would travel the world in different kinds of transport and often in great style and ceremony. But this very first journey away from home, and through the backwaters of his beloved Travancore stayed vivid and clear in his mind to his dying day.

He would never again have the time for something so languid.

CHAPTER 2

A New World

MADHAVA AND HIS UNCLE MADE STRAIGHT FOR TRIVANDRUM. AS GOVINDA marshalled the servants and the luggage, Madhava looked about him with bright, curious eyes. Trivandrum was a city in the truest sense of the word. The streets were shut in by walls behind which lay houses. Some were two-storeyed buildings with balconies and verandas, tiled roofs and whitewashed fronts. There were clusters of shops selling all kinds of things from rice, grain and cotton seeds to English tinned meats and wines. On alternate Fridays, as Madhava would discover, the band of the Nair Brigade played in the bandstand at the city's public gardens. For a boy from an enterprising, erudite and deeply religious household in the rural backwaters of Kuttanad, this was a whole new world. His move to this urban landscape on the cusp of a new century would change young Madhava's life forever.

For the time being though, the focus was on getting back to his studies. Madhava didn't have much time in Travancore—only as long as Govinda was studying for his Bachelor's degree. Govinda and K. Padmanabha lived in a small house in the by-lanes of Thampanoor, to the east of the district court. Madhava was due to begin classes at the Maharaja's Free School, but before that he needed to learn the English alphabet. In his spare time, Govinda sat with his nephew to teach him the letters. Unfortunately, patience was not the older man's strongest suit. 'His affection for me,' Panikkar wrote acerbically later, 'was usually demonstrated through his cane.'[1] In Panikkar's memoir, the chapter about his school days in Trivandrum is almost entirely devoid of joy. These regular canings also impacted how an adult Panikkar came to view corporal punishment. 'One cannot be dogmatic about the extent of freedom to be given to young children,' he wrote rather pompously in his memoir. 'True, modern psychology commends freedom in play and extra-curricular activities as essential to development . . . but this is not the whole story . . . My own view is that children do benefit from punishment, if it comes from people who really love them.'[2]

If that were truly the case then Govinda Panikkar must have been loving to a fault because Madhava was caned almost daily, often as he himself admitted ruefully, 'for no apparent reason'.[3] The details of Panikkar's days in Trivandrum lose none of their starkness in the casualness of their recounting. Govinda Panikkar ran a tight ship at home. The boys had to go straight to school and come straight back home afterwards. There was to be no loitering or chatting to such friends as one might acquire along the way. At home, the brothers were expected to study quietly. 'Even my brother, soon to matriculate, enjoyed no greater freedom than I.'[4] If they played, it was usually Madhava who was hauled off by his collar for a whipping. Talking to other boys was a 'grave offence'.[5] Not unnaturally, Madhava took ages to make one lone friend, a boy by the name of Kesavan Panikkar. His uncle, predictably, didn't like that. Later, Panikkar would try to excuse Govinda on the grounds that it had been Panikkar's own mistakes that had led to constant beatings. 'I was a jealous, greedy, spoilt brat,' he would say. 'Of course I needed to be punished!'[6]

Whether this justification was warranted or not we shall never know, but thankfully, Madhava's torturous time there would soon end. He continued at the Maharaja's Free School up until what we call fifth grade today, but in those days was the third form.

School itself was harder than it had been in Kavalam. Whether it was the constant sense of being transplanted or the incessant canings, Madhava was prone to distraction. Still, he did excellently in history, though he compensated for that by failing miserably in mathematics (inexplicably, he failed to turn in his answer sheet). At no point did he impress his teachers and his peers with either promise or talent. He was a bookish boy whose preferred sport was reading and he did atrociously in all forms of physical activity. But an older Panikkar would have denied the fact that he was ever unhappy in the little house in Thampanoor.

For it was there that he was privy to the kinds of conversations that he could never have had at home. Govinda Panikkar may have ruled his home with an iron fist, but his public face was that of a staunch and erudite nationalist, deeply engaged in the eddies of political change that were rippling across Travancore at the dawn of the twentieth century.

In the Panikkar household in Trivandrum, journalists, writers, intellectuals and social reformers came and went all the time. Govinda had friends in nearly every field of life and vocation, and their discussions ranged across politics and music to religion and books. Both Padmanabha and Madhava were allowed to sit in on these discussions to at least listen if not participate. In this little house in Thampanoor then, rather than from any school curriculum, Madhava learned how to think for himself and form his own perspectives on the complex social, religious and political issues of the day.

In the early twentieth century, the Nairs were facing an internal upheaval, pitting the older, pro-establishment members against a newer, younger and more radical generation. The men who strolled in and out of the Panikkar household belonged to the latter category. They had no desire to participate in or propagate palace intrigues. For them, change could and would come only through extensive social and political reform. The campaign for this kind of change was reflected in the flourishing vernacular press of the day, such as the *Swadeshabhimani*. Started by Vakkom Moulavi, a quiet, astonishingly far-sighted man who campaigned tirelessly for modern education, the education of women and the need for Muslims to unite, the newspaper provided a platform for citizens to push for their rights at a time when the phrase 'civil rights' had not yet been coined. During Madhava's time in Trivandrum, the *Swadeshabhimani*'s editors were both Ramakrishna Pillai and the walrus-moustachioed C.P. Govinda

Pillai. Of the two, Ramakrishna Pillai was the angry young Nair man, something he made that clear in the slogan of the newspaper itself. 'Fear, crookedness and greed will not build a country,' was the line that ran under the *Swadeshabhimani*'s masthead.

By 1906, when Madhava was twelve years old, the newspaper was at the forefront of popular opinion in Travancore, unafraid to run feisty campaigns for change. Time and again, Vakkom Moulavi was told to rein in his fiery young editor. He refused outright. He was then asked to sell his press, an offer he refused as well. The subsequent crackdown of the state government on *Swadeshabhimani*—closing it down and deporting Pillai to Madras—is illustrative of the times in which young Madhava Panikkar was growing up and the kind of people he was now meeting.

There was, for instance, the erudite and influential Vaikom Narayana Pillai. He was a particular favourite of Madhava's, especially as he often intervened to save the boy from Govinda's cane. It was Vaikom Narayana Pillai who introduced young Madhava to the joys of Malayalam poetry and literature, and it was Vaikom Narayana Pillai's brother Pachu who introduced Madhava to national politics and names like Surendranath Banerjea, Pherozeshah Mehta and Gopal Krishna Gokhale. Madhava was also particularly attached to C.P. Govinda Pillai, who was excellent friends with his uncle. Pillai was often to be found at the Panikkar home, chatting to young Madhava, of whom he was very fond. In his memoir, Panikkar would recall how one day, Govinda Pillai dropped by to visit Madhava's uncle and found nobody except Madhava at home. Politely inviting him to wait, Madhava challenged the older man to a poetry reciting contest to pass the time. Pillai was not one for mollycoddling little boys and he gave the contest everything he had, only to be bested, much to his delight, by Madhava. When Govinda Panikkar returned home, Pillai told him approvingly that far more than Padmanabha, his young brother would be the one to watch.

After that, Govinda Pillai dropped in regularly only to meet Madhava. Sometimes, if they were bored of challenging each other to extempore poetry recitals, they sat and played solemn games of chess. His uncle also introduced him to the joys of bridge, and in both games, Madhava soon excelled.

Games, politics and poetry apart, the Panikkar home in Trivandrum was crammed with books, for all three inhabitants loved reading. Madhava borrowed the books either his brother or uncle were reading, fuelling a mind that was naturally curious and exploratory. Since both men were much older than he was, it was no surprise that, by the time he was fourteen years old, Madhava was reading far ahead of his age. By then, he had already read serious books like the scholar P. Govinda Pillai's *History of Malayalam Literature* and Kunjikuttan Thampuran's Malayalam translation of Kalidasa's *Vikramorvasiyam*. More than anything else, Trivandrum did much to expand Madhava's mind and broaden his horizons—though he was still an abject failure in mathematics.

In 1907, word came to Travancore of a split in the Indian National Congress. The power struggle between the moderates and extremists had reached a crescendo at a particularly ugly meeting in Surat, on the banks of the Tapti River, with chairs and shoes being hurled about with abandon. It was a reminder that modern politics, with its principles of popular agitation, participation and mobilisation, was new to India. But then, these were early days of resistance. Citizens were just realising that politics was the sanctuary of multitudes, rather than the preserve of a few. The partition of Bengal in 1905 had been one of the first instances where India had been united in a fury, the likes of which had not been seen before. From Dacca to Calcutta, the Bengal Presidency was on fire, with protests, speeches, petitions and meetings peopling the minutes between the hours. When it became clear that Lord Curzon, Viceroy of India, wasn't to be moved, the nationalists decided to press the accelerator. The Swadeshi movement was the first sign of an organised political movement in India, with its decision to boycott Manchester cloth and Liverpool salt nationwide. Now, in the face of this fresh crisis in Surat, historians, academics and journalists were beginning to ask themselves difficult questions. Was India capable of fighting the empire? What would that fight look like? Where would Indian bureaucrats stand vis-à-vis the Imperial Civil Services? How was political progress to be combined with social reform? As they grappled for answers, a new and dangerous style of politics was on the rise: revolutionary terrorism. For young men like Bhagat Singh and Chandrashekhar Azad who ascribed to this new method, it was a new way to mobilise and protest. But despite their presence, it was safe to say, as Aurobindo Ghosh morosely stated in 1909, 'A hush had fallen over the country.'[7]

A different kind of hush had fallen over the homestead in Thampanoor. Padmanabha had finished his intermediate degree and Govinda Panikkar was done training to be a lawyer. His brother was now bound for Madras, where he would study for his MBCM (equivalent to an MBBS today) degree. That meant more change for young Madhava.

He was moved to Thalavady High School, in the village of Thalavady Anaprambal in the neighbourhood at Upper Kuttanad. The choice of this rather ramshackle institution in the middle of nowhere, when Kottayam and even Alleppey were closer, was not as curious as it seemed, for it was an institution run by the extended Panikkar family. Run on locally collected funds, it was led by one Poonuthara Nilakanta Panikkar—not very well, because the English head of education in the district, Dr Mitchell, was about to order it to be shut down. But the matters of the Panikkar family had passed to the capable hands of Eravi Ramakrishna Panikkar (Eravi Kesava having died while the boys were in Thampanoor). Ramakrishna promptly designated his brother Govinda to take over the school.[8]

Madhava meekly followed his uncle to Kottayam, though every fibre of his being rebelled at the very thought. Still, given his dismal academic performance so far, he knew that it was a mercy he was being allowed to even continue his education. There had been agitated whispers over why he should be allowed to continue at all, given that his elder brother obviously had the greater potential. The prospect of repeating the third form was not an appealing one either.

Yet, the school itself was not appealing either. Nilakanta hadn't done a thing to improve it either from inside or outside. In fact, the memory of it provoked a much older Panikkar to biting sarcasm, writing that the school was a 'unique institution, with no parallel before or after'.[9] He describes it as decrepit, with a huge hall serving as a single classroom for all the students. There was no room to play and in the sheeting rains of the Malabar monsoon, the entire building would be flooded. The teachers knew little and the students couldn't have cared less. In comparison to Madhava's ordered, erudite life in Trivandrum, Kottayam was distinctly chaotic.

But even here, in a poorly run backwater school, Madhava encountered minds that were as wide open and curious as his own. There was the intense Kannan Nair who ran the political journal, *Nair Magazine*, and there were Kesava Pillai and Krishna Menon, two great lovers of literature. But Madhava's time there was short. Despite Govinda Panikkar's best efforts, Dr Mitchell ordered that the school had to be torn down and rebuilt if it wanted to continue.

Seeing no other way out, Govinda dispatched his young nephew to CMS College in Kottayam. Again, this was not a decision that thrilled the extended or immediate family. Even now, although he had cleared his examinations, Madhava wasn't seen as the brightest spark. Perhaps it would be best, said the family tactfully, if he was brought back home to help run Chalayil.

Madhava was keenly aware of these murmurs, and it seemed as though bad luck was trotting at his heels like a faithful dog. At CMS College, where he would attempt his matriculation examinations yet again, the meals were always late and the rice was unwashed. But the professors were excellent, particularly a warden by the name of Ambalapuzha Mahadeva Sarma, a lover of literature who had lately served Kerala Varma of Travancore. He prided himself on the quality of his poetry and translations, but as a warden he left much to be desired. The rooms were rarely clean and the rules were lax to say the least. If Madhava's mind hadn't been extremely well nourished, he might have had a reason to quit altogether. But he and Sarma struck up the kind of intellectual camaraderie that would come easily to Madhava as he grew older. Sarma was addicted to literary debates (even if they were all about his own work). He had a select literary circle, carefully handpicked, and into this ragtag book club he introduced Madhava. The boy quickly found that this was not so much a reading group as it was a research group, where participants exchanged views on the latest literary trends and thoughts on emerging or established writers.

It was at CMS College that Madhava, now well into his teens, began to exhibit more of his rebellious side. He had taken enough beatings from Govinda Panikkar to know who was allowed to beat him and who wasn't. Trivandrum had taught him that, wherever else he might lack or lag, his brain was his ultimate weapon. He could, if he so chose, talk or write rings around his opponents. He did this now when Sarma tried to force him to learn a poem he had written. In quick response, Madhava dashed off a biting little parody of that poem. It may not have been his finest literary moment, but it was clever enough to offend Sarma into stony silence for the next few days.

Two years passed in uneventful monotony before Madhava was judged ready to take his matriculation examinations one more time. But for all his quick wit and erudite literary skills, Madhava was still singularly horrible at science and mathematics. Unsurprisingly, he failed, more spectacularly than before. This time, the whispers in the family were not so quiet. They had sent him to every single one of the best schools a Nair boy of standing could be sent to. He had failed at each one. What, his aghast family wondered, were they to do with him now?

Guilty and despairing, Madhava took to wandering alone for hours along the banks of the canals, or sitting moodily in the shade of coconut trees, glaring sightlessly at the silvery waters. Eventually, his overwrought state caught up with him, causing a collapse so intense that he had to be rushed back home to recover in the comforting arms of his tharavad. Just how ill he was and what kind of illness he had have been lost to history, but we do know that Madhava lost one year of school. He spent much of his recovery period lying in bed with his books and his thoughts as company, watching shadows dance over the patches of sunlight on his bedroom walls. Downstairs in the main courtyard, his family conferred on the fate of its youngest son.

Kunjipilla Gouri in particular was sorely disappointed. Madhava had seemed so full of promise. His mother was equally mortified. It was no small thing to have a son who was so pathetically poor in his studies as to render him useless for any kind of future vocation. It seems that nobody thought to speak directly to Madhava, for if they had, they may have been able to prevent what he managed to do one day in the sleepy afternoon hours.

No one ever found out how he got hold of a bottle of chloroform, but Chalayil was thrown into a frenzy when Madhava was found lying pale and lifeless in his bed. When he came around eventually, he found himself being cradled by his distraught grandmother, tears running down her cheeks as she dabbed his face with a cool, damp towel. This praiseworthy attempt at ending his life was all it took to convince the softer members of his family that there was no need to pressure Madhava to study further. But it also meant that he couldn't, with this seemingly unstable temperament, be trusted to look after the tharavad.

This second possibility hadn't occurred to Madhava, who had rather naively hoped that he would now be allowed to live a life of quiet domesticity, filled with books and a little writing. Now, his brother Padmanabha wrote from Madras suggesting that Madhava be sent out to stay with him. Madras would be a clean slate, where he could attempt the examinations yet again.

The plan met with favour from the elders of the family—and with hot resentment from Madhava, who wanted no such thing. Nonetheless, Madhava was duly packed off to stay with Padmanabha and enrolled at St Paul's School in Vepery. It was a chance that even Madhava knew he didn't deserve. So he kept his head down and his nose firmly in his books, studying for hours in his chosen hideout in the golden-green bamboo groves in front of the school. He finally cleared his matriculation examinations in the summer of 1913.

Padmanabha Panikkar was pleased. The experiment in Madras had been perfect. He wrote to Govinda Panikkar that summer, letting him know quietly that he had begun the process of getting Madhava admission into Christ Church at the University of Oxford. There were six months before term began, but he would not, he promised his uncle, allow Madhava to spend those months in idleness. He would be joining Madras Christian College until he sailed for England.

There are no records of what Madhava did at Madras Christian College, but the six months passed sooner than he realised it. On a sunny spring morning at the docks in Bombay, Madhava boarded a crowded, dirty steamer bound for London. Photographs of the time show a thin young man, with a serious, unsmiling face and the beginnings of a moustache.

It was April 1914, just a couple of months before a single bullet changed the world.

PART II

Finding His Voice: The University Years (1914–1918)

Chapter 3

Rude Awakening

'London seemed to be having such a season, as it had not known for years,' wrote Lady Ottoline Morrell, wife of the Liberal Party member of parliament (MP), Sir Philip Morrell, in 1914, 'What fun it all was!'[1]

She was right about that.

From the first burst of fine weather early that spring to the last of the early court presentations in the first week of March, a certain class of London society was quite literally having a ball. The fashionable flocked to Hyde Park to ride in Rotten Row or to air their latest ensembles. Four balls were held on one night alone, each with a dinner party before the dancing began. Entire columns of London's society pages were given over to descriptions of balls (like the dance given by the Brunners at Harrington Square, where the rooms were festooned with carnations of every colour) or sightings of important personalities (like Lord Wellesley's arrival at the Hotel Lotti in Paris). For the wealthy, life was being lived in rich technicolour. As Stephen McKenna, the nephew of a Liberal Party cabinet minister, put it dryly, it was 'a new imperial Rome, in a new Silver Age'.[2]

But even in this gilded world, shadows were not far around the corner. French restaurateur D. Nichols Pigache, known for running Café Royal on Regent Street, recalled a regular customer who 'always ordered a wing of chicken in browned butter sauce for her Pekingese'. When it was nervously suggested to this lady that the leftovers be given to the poor people who hung around the restaurant's back door, she said coldly as she dabbed the corners of her mouth with a serviette, 'I hate poor people. They depress me.'[3] Depressing or not, the disparity in class and wealth could not be easily ignored. With migrants flooding the city from all corners of Europe in search of work, London was a divided city, seething with poverty, unemployment and overcrowding.

On 1 May 1914, the day Panikkar stepped off the steamer from India, thousands of workers struck work and marched instead to a great demonstration in Hyde Park.[4] That same month, the militant London and Provincial Union of Vehicle Workers threatened to strike over hours and wages. There was trouble in the trams, among shop assistants, and at Pink's Jam Factory in Southwark. Even more nightmarish was the possibility of an alliance between the miners, railwaymen and transport workers' unions. Calling itself the Triple Alliance—a tip of the hat to greater geopolitics—this united strike threatened to disrupt the entire country. In her diary entry for 23 April 1914, the economist Beatrice Webb noted approvingly, 'The talk was of civil war and revolution!'[5] On the other hand, David Lloyd George, then the chancellor of the exchequer, was an anxious man, writing later, 'From 1911 onwards, there was a steady development of strike action and in the summer of 1914, there was every sign that the autumn would witness a series of industrial disturbances without precedent.'[6]

Panikkar of course was oblivious to all this just yet. It was raining when the steamer docked at Dover, a steady, grey drizzle that he would later learn was typical of England. He had telegraphed his brother from Marseilles, asking him to come down to meet the boat, but there was no sign of Padmanabha. Panikkar didn't know that the cable had been delayed and so he waited miserably in the cold, his coat collar turned up fruitlessly against the dripping rain. All he knew about his brother's address was that it was somewhere in a place called Marchmont Crescent in Edinburgh. He had no idea how to get there or how to contact Padmanabha to let him know that he had arrived.

As evening drew closer and the gas lamps flickered to life through the mist, Panikkar knew he couldn't stand there all night. From a nearby porter, he managed to find out when and from where the night train would leave for Edinburgh and bought himself a ticket hastily for the eight o'clock train. By dawn the next morning, he was in Scotland—even colder and greyer than England had been the previous evening. Freezing, tired and hungry, Panikkar gathered his bags and set off for the Indian Students' Association. He knew his brother was a member and perhaps they would know where he could be found. Unsurprisingly, the members of this organisation were all fast asleep at that unearthly hour of the morning. By then Panikkar had had enough. He set up a din that woke everyone within earshot. Once he had his brother's address, he hailed a passing cab. The joy at seeing his brother was diluted considerably by the fact that there was hardly any time left to relax.

The entrance examinations for Oxford were around the corner and the next ten days had to be spent travelling between Edinburgh and Oxford. Panikkar decided to spend four days on campus, studying for and writing his examinations, which he later (very breezily) dismissed as 'not very formidable'.[7] In between he took some time to explore what would become his home for the foreseeable future. Christ Church was lovely, with its vast quadrangular courtyard, the beautiful Tudor staircase, its tinkling fountains and the rolling green meadows beyond. But idyllic as it all was, this brief interlude was enough to shake Panikkar up considerably. In those days, he was possessed of the slightly smug belief that, while science might be beyond his ken, he could comfortably hold his own in discussions on politics, literature and history. Oxford would teach him otherwise.

In the early years of the twentieth century, the University of Oxford had transformed into an institution meant to prep young elites to occupy key positions of colonial or government authority. Its dons were well aware of the duties that 'patriotic imperialism'[8] demanded of them, but even these enlightened men were staggered when Cecil Rhodes—that icon of imperialist values—left his formidable wealth to scholarships that would allow 'natives' from different corners of the empire an entrée to Oxford. As a result, there was no longer a sense of upholding or protecting the empire among its students. For Panikkar, this world view was wholly new.

In Travancore, despite his uncle's many political connections, the younger Panikkar had enjoyed his dips into Malayalam literature and poetry far more than literature of any other kind. So when he met a young man by the name of Asudomal Gidwani at Christ Church, and when Gidwani introduced him to some of the older scholars on campus, Panikkar was shaken out of his depth by their intellectual span. As he listened to their conversation, he was suddenly and sharply aware of the fact that he was small fry here. Worse, he was culturally inadequate and politically unaware. Of Travancorean politics and history, he could have told them a lot. But instead, these young men were discussing names he had never heard of: Ibsen, Bernard Shaw, Benedetto Croce. Matters of political and social concern were also being discussed and debated, the likes of which he had never really paid attention to at home: Home Rule, universal franchise—and war.

Of the three, Home Rule, though this topic applied at the time to Ireland's place in the British Empire, was the one Panikkar identified with the most. Annie Besant's ideas had not yet taken the shape they would during the war years, but self-governance for India (albeit *within* the empire) was a concept that was already being discussed at home. Here in England though Panikkar discovered that Home Rule had explosive connotations and consequences. The Home Rule Bill was due to be enforced later that year, but even so a civil war between Ulster and the south of Ireland seemed more than likely. The concept of Home Rule had torn families apart in England alone. It had also poisoned friendships, with some of Prime Minister Herbert Asquith's own government strongly opposed. As the third reading of the Bill approached, it seemed as though there was no other subject on people's minds—with the exception of the year's budget, which was due to be tabled in parliament. From conversations and newspapers, Panikkar learned that Chancellor David Lloyd George and his bête-noire Winston Churchill (then first lord of the admiralty) were locked in a bitter battle over the budget, which was in huge deficit due to Churchill's insistence that Britain's warships be converted from coal to oil.[9] For parliament, a 'good' budget was needed to tide over the considerable flap that the Marconi scandal, in which senior government members had been accused of insider trading around an impending government tender, had caused a couple of years earlier. Could that budget be granted this year? That was just one example of the many subjects of discussion in the common rooms at Oxford that spring.

Another topic that Panikkar pricked his ears up at was that of the suffragettes, who were by all accounts growing increasingly vicious. In the newspapers, he had seen photographs of an emaciated Emmeline Pankhurst on a hunger strike for equal voting rights. A few days on campus were enough to make him both startled by and aware of just how violent the fight for an equal vote was becoming. In March, for instance, Velasquez's beautiful painting of the Rokeby Venus, hanging in the National Gallery, had been viciously hacked by a young woman armed with a meat cleaver. Then there was the story of another young woman who had managed to inveigle her way into Buckingham Palace itself, where she had proclaimed loud solidarity for the movement before being unceremoniously thrown out.

All of these were subjects that Panikkar had not yet begun to think about, though they certainly set his brain to ticking furiously. Looming over all these conversations was the shadow of war.

Just over a year earlier, in 1913, Lord Esher, widely regarded as an expert in the realm of security and defence, had pooh-poohed the idea of a war to an audience of service officers, saying airily, 'War becomes every day more difficult and improbable.'[10] Indeed, H.G. Wells was to remember ruefully, 'Few of us realised in the earlier half of 1914 how near the crash was to us.'[11] But as Panikkar came to realise in his conversations with the Indians on campus, things were changing far too fast.

At the end of January 1914, Tsar Nicholas II had warned former French foreign minister Théophile Delcassé that he 'foresaw a perhaps inevitable and imminent collision between German ambitions and Russian interest'.[12] In Germany itself, tensions were running so high that the atmosphere seriously alarmed the American special envoy, Col. Edward House, who had come to Europe to try and broker a pact between the United States, Germany and Britain to prevent just such a war.[13]

Of all these brewing troubles, Gidwani and his cronies clearly had not just far more knowledge, but a wider perspective that was entirely unlike the men Panikkar knew in Travancore. They had, for instance, ideas on India's position within the empire, on universal franchise for Indians and on the nationalist movement. Panikkar, who had only recently prided himself on sailing through his university entrance examinations, now found himself speedily rethinking his academic worth and indeed his worth as any kind of contributor to the nationalist causes that Gidwani and his friends seemed so passionate about.

This wasn't easy for a young man who was already naturally sensitive about his own intellect. Nor would it be easy to speak to his elder brother about such a thing. Panikkar returned to Edinburgh considerably more miserable than he had been when he stepped off the steamer into a strange country. He had no idea how to approach the subject with his brother. Inadequacy and self-worth were not exactly masculine subjects of conversation, nor were they easy subjects to broach. The anxiety rendered him sleepless for a week before he finally clutched his courage in both hands and spoke to Padmanabha as honestly as he could.

From Panikkar's own account, Padmanabha appears to have been tolerant of, if not exactly sensitive to, a young man's natural fears of appearing intellectually inferior in the eyes of his contemporaries. Panikkar was permitted to buy as many books as he wanted to before he returned to Oxford. Gladly, over the next few days, he buried himself in the works of Ibsen and Shaw and began to learn as much as he could about English politics, global geopolitics and India's possible role in all this. It was the beginning of a tendency that would stay with him all his life. Whenever Panikkar felt as though he didn't know enough about a subject, he would seek piles of books and other research material and burrow into them. Knowledge would become his shield against a persistent feeling of inadequacy. He had always enjoyed reading, but university would give his choice of books a direction and purpose.

Two weeks later though, Ibsen and Shaw hardly seemed to matter. The world was at war.

It was a moment that Panikkar never forgot, for it kickstarted a process of nearly constant learning and re-learning of history and politics, and the way the two were often closely twined in the making of foreign policy decisions. India, for instance, was at war too. It was not a war of its choosing, nor was it a war in which it had any stake except to fight for an unknown king in a different country. What, Panikkar began to wonder, did war mean for India as a colony of an empire? What did war mean for the nationalist movement that Gidwani and the others were speaking of so animatedly? How did India seek to position itself in the empire *after* the war? Could this be the moment for India to ask for political and geopolitical equality within the empire?

So many questions, but for the moment Panikkar had a more immediate concern: his fate at Oxford. His results had arrived in a cream-coloured foolscap envelope early in the summer. He had cleared his entrance examinations. What was more, he had been granted the position of Dixon Scholar at Christ Church. He would be going up to university in September, 'ready to take on anyone'.[14]

CHAPTER 4

A Student at Oxford

PANIKKAR'S MEMORIES OF HIS FIRST DAYS AT OXFORD MAKE FOR interesting reading, given that he had only just admitted a few pages previously in his memoir that he felt intellectually inadequate about being there in the first place. He writes, for instance, nothing of the rooms he lived in, but doesn't forget to mention that they had been occupied 'a century earlier by Gladstone himself'.[1] Even less does he write of the difficulties—such as Gidwani and the others had told him of—that an Indian boy, irrespective of class and privilege, might have faced in adjusting to a European world and European way of life.

On the other hand, Panikkar doesn't forget to remind the reader that Oxford was 'the premier university of the empire'.[2] There may have been only sixty students in residence, but the Indians among them, Panikkar writes proudly, were 'the cream' of Indian scholarship, 'representing the best in intelligence, attainments and breeding'.[3] The single note in this lyrical introduction to university life is that of immense pride in the stature of Oxford and, one suspects, in himself at having attained a position in this elite institution. But as one progresses through this chapter in his autobiography, a biographer realises that without the controlling influence of his uncle or the disapproving murmurs of his family members, Panikkar was far more open to the idea of making friends and exploring campus politics.

Among the people he names as college friends and acquaintances are the Suhrawardy brothers, John Mathai, Dewan Chimanlal and B.K. Mallick. In those days, these were ambitious, privileged and vocal young men, unafraid to share and discuss their opinions. It was much the same atmosphere that Panikkar's uncle had encouraged in the little house in Thampanoor, just on a wider, grander scale. From the sounds of it, Panikkar seems to have been infatuated with H.S. Suhrawardy, a cultured polyglot. 'It was due to his deeply rooted patriotism' that Oxford had even earned its name as a training ground for Indian nationalists, Panikkar gushingly wrote of the elder Suhrawardy.[4]

Then there was Hasanand Datija, a young Sindhi intellectual prepping for the Imperial Civil Services or ICS (which he eventually failed to clear) and Dewan Chimanlal, the spoilt brilliant son of the Punjabi millionaire Dewan Daulat Rai. There were four Malayalis up at Oxford at that time, of whom two became good friends with Panikkar: V.K. Raman Menon, the son of the ruling Maharaja of Cochin, and V. Krishnan Tampi, brother-in-law of Moolam Thirunal, the maharaja of Travancore, who had arrived at Oxford to study Sanskrit. 'I never met a keener devotee of idleness than Tampi in those days,' wrote Panikkar acidly, though he soothed the sting somewhat in his assessment that as lazy as he might have been, Tampi was both brilliant and free of malice.

B.K. Mallick was a different kind of role model for Panikkar. He was more grown up in comparison to the other boys, already almost thirty years old, and at Oxford on scholarship for a varsity degree before taking up service with Nepal's Maharaja Chandra Shamsher. This bright resume was somewhat dimmed in Panikkar's eyes by a busy, fickle brain that seemed unable to fix on any single skein of thought. Mallick was as swayable as a reed in the wind. As a result, his planned thesis never saw the light of day, much to Panikkar's barely hidden scorn. But Mallick made up for these faults with his kindness and generosity in helping penurious young men out of a fix. The doors to his rooms were always open, allowing some of the finest minds of Oxford to gather and spend evenings discussing the more important subjects of the day in what Panikkar rather grandiosely called a 'salon of learning'.[5]

We do not really know when Panikkar decided that he'd had enough of preening about being at Oxford and the stature that these credentials brought him. But at some point not long after he arrived, a knack for supporting the right cause seems to have kicked into action. This instinct would serve him in more or less good stead for the rest of his life.

Oxford was a cosmopolitan stage, but in a world at war, it was also a stage where fraught and often conflicting interests collided. A dominating thought for Indian students was the question of India's political future. Panikkar knew that informal discussions went on about the subject constantly, but it wasn't until he met the Suhrawardy brothers that he was initiated into a more formal intellectual arena of debate.

Until the Suhrawardy brothers arrived on campus, the Oxford Majlis Society had been a quiet little student body that hung around the outskirts of campus life. Founded at the dawn of the twentieth century, its members, a mix of Indians, Burmese and Ceylonese, convened every Sunday night to debate the way forward for their countries. The meetings inevitably began with a vigorous singing of the Congress anthem *Vande Mataram* and ended with a hymn by the poet Iqbal. Among its members were hopeful aspirants to the ICS or those who were already ICS probationers. Did these young men feel any dissonance between their distrust of the British and their ambitions to enter the Raj's administration in India? Panikkar recalled that nobody felt anything of the kind.

K.P.S. Menon, who would be independent India's first foreign secretary, would arrive at Trinity College the same year that Panikkar left and note much the same in his own memoir. 'We went on studiously prepping for the ICS. The inconsistency between the making of anti-British speeches and the attempt to enter the ICS did not strike us.'[6]

Discussions on India's political future were driven by what was happening in India at the time. In 1914, the nationalist Bal Gangadhar Tilak had been released from prison in Mandalay. Severely diabetic but still fiery, Tilak joined forces with Annie Besant, the British socialist, theosophist and supporter of Indian nationalism, to launch the Home Rule League to spread the idea of self-governance within the empire. In 1915, Gopal Krishna Gokhale and Pherozeshah Mehta, both moderate members of the Congress Party, passed away, opening the doors for the extremist re-entry into the Congress fold. That same year, Mohandas Karamchand Gandhi stepped off a steamer from South Africa in Bombay. His arrival would change the course of South Asia's political history.

Meanwhile, a younger generation of Muslims was on the rise, represented by the brothers Mohammed and Shaukat Ali, both activists in the Khilafat Movement, and the young Abul Kalam Azad, who would be India's first education minister, among others. These people were beginning to feel alienated by British policies inside and outside India. For instance, the British government's 1911 annulment of the partition of Bengal had caused resentment among prominent Bengali Muslims who had benefited from the creation of a separate province in 1905.[7] The government's refusal in 1912 to accept a Muslim university at Aligarh without effective government control had angered several Western-educated Muslims in the United Provinces.[8]

On the international front, this newly prominent 'Pan-Islamic' section of Indian Muslim leadership was furious with Britain's tacit approval of attacks on the Ottoman Empire by Italy and the Balkan countries in 1911–1912 and with British (Christian) ministers making speeches approving the idea of partitioning the Ottoman Empire. The Muslim leaders saw themselves as part of a global Muslim community, with the Ottoman caliph as their spiritual head and the Ottoman Empire as the embodiment of a common Islamic civilisation. For some, paying allegiance to the caliph, a symbol of Islam, was simply a manifestation of their religious faith. These tendencies would bloom into fiery dissent soon enough, but for now, it was enough to ensure that Muslim leadership in India was favouring a reconciliation with the Congress and that Annie Besant had begun calling for a joint programme of reform from the Hindus and the Muslims. Meanwhile, it was enough for Panikkar that, in

Oxford, subjects like the internment by the British of the Ali brothers (the Majlis Society held meetings with Shaukat's portrait propped up on an empty chair) were argued upon.

The young men of the Oxford Majlis noted that, in India, the Muslim League had also taken up the objective of national government, creating a committee that would collaborate with the Congress to demand an agenda of post-war reform. This was the seed that would grow into the Lucknow Pact of 1916. Unsurprisingly then, discussions with speakers at the Majlis were no holds barred—some of them, like the one with Lala Lajpat Rai (who was speaking on 'India Today'), descended into full-blown shouting matches, ending with Rai storming out of the room in a rage.

No, these were not placid meetings.

S.W.R.D. Bandaranaike, Panikkar's friend and the future prime minister of independent Sri Lanka, would describe the Majlis meetings as enlivening an otherwise 'damp, grey, sunless winter'. These discussions took place a full decade before the young Jawaharlal Nehru called for purna swaraj, and the Majlis was acquiring a distinctly revolutionary character.

Revolution was the last thing the empire needed, considering it was already at war. The India Office, Home Office and Scotland Yard had been keeping a sharp eye on the activities of Indian students in England and Scotland long before the war. From the stories his brother had told him, Panikkar knew that at Edinburgh University, for example, officials sometimes expressed concern that the debates encouraged by the Edinburgh Indians' Association were more radical than desirable. In the same vein, the Cambridge and Oxford chapters of the Majlis had been under scrutiny almost since their inception in 1891 and 1896, respectively. On campuses known for their xenophobia, both chapters had had to constantly defend themselves from charges of sedition. But between 1905 and 1907, the temperature of these charges began to increase, primarily because of the activities at India House, which had become the epicentre of the radical Indian student movement in Britain. The story of India House is one for another day, but the arrival in England of the likes of

V.D. Savarkar and Shyamji Krishnavarma was a catalyst to the growth of militant Indian nationalism on English soil.

The empire acted fast to nip these dangerous tendencies in the bud. In 1905, the Defence of the Realm Act (DORA) was passed, followed by a slew of bad press against Indian students. A 1906 leader in *The Times* claimed that many of the Indian scholars in Britain were 'failures of the Indian education system sent off to merely get a degree and legal qualifications'. In 1907, things went a step further when the Lee-Warner Committee headed by the colonial administrator William Lee-Warner published its report[9] in which it made the patronising argument that since these were already discontented students from a discontented colony, 'it was not surprising'[10] that they should immediately feel that the methods of English politics were applicable to India. Truth be told, Indian students such as Jinnah and Nehru, albeit of a certain class and privilege, were no strangers to England, and over the years they had certainly enjoyed the freedom to organise into quiet political bodies, often disguised as debating clubs.[11]

Then there were those who had no illusions about the fact that racism and xenophobia stratified their experience in England. When they alighted at Plymouth or Dover, they were essentially on their own. It was up to them to find their own lodgings and establish themselves socially. Lodgings were far from cheap and landlords were racist, with vegetarian cuisine not always available. Given all this, and fired by news of what was happening in India, it wasn't at all surprising that Indian students acted very fast to create local associations and groups designed to support each other. Nor was it surprising that university authorities, in turn, looked askance at these groups.

In 1909, the Bureau of Information for Indian Students was set up, a surveillance watchdog. But it wasn't to stop revolutionary activities. On 1 July 1909, Madan Lal Dhingra entered history books by assassinating an India Office official.[12] The immediate result of this, as Panikkar would learn in short order, was a drastic change in the manner of British intelligence gathering.[13] It was now clear to the empire that the Indian diaspora, far from being helpful to the Raj, was a credible threat to its existence. If Indian colonies across the

Pacific Ocean, in the United States or further across western Europe were inspired by what had happened at India House, Britain could have a real crisis on its hands.

In 1912, the India Office set up an Indian Students Department, and the following year, it appointed local advisors to Indian students in Oxford and other universities. Officially tasked with assisting the latter, these advisors were seen by the students as watchdogs forced upon them to keep their political views in check. Meanwhile, Scotland Yard brought in the big guns: Superintendent John A. Wallinger was an old India hand, 'a brave officer with a talent for acquiring local native dialects and a flair for undercover criminal intelligence operations'.[14] Wallinger began sending agents down to Oxford and Cambridge and further north to Edinburgh to keep an eye on the Indian students there. He found them to be both nationalist and articulate, the latter being a quality he himself deeply admired.[15] The same couldn't be said for his agents, who were thoroughly annoyed, particularly by young K.M. Panikkar. 'He is said to have been given to seditious thought,' warned one agent primly.[16] Another file at the India Office declared that not only was he mixing with seditious Indians, but Panikkar had at one point been 'cautioned by the more moderate of these against being too outspoken'.[17] Speaking out against powers that control or oppress is almost always described as 'outspoken'. The word itself is a warning.

But the young members of the Oxford Majlis saw no other way forward than to exchange ideas about where India stood in the eyes of the empire and how that could change. 'In the Majlis, we made vehement speeches which we found patriotic and which the British thought seditious,' K.P.S. Menon would write later.[18]

For many, the war itself had begun a process of irrevocable change. India had responded obediently to the Raj's call for men and materiel, sending over 2,00,000 soldiers to support Britain in France, Egypt, Gallipoli and Mesopotamia. As the Raj approvingly noted India's stellar response to the war, hostility towards the Indian students reduced. But it was too little, too late. As the Congress leader Madan Mohan Malaviya told a session of the Imperial Legislative Council in 1917, the war had 'put the clock 50 years forward'.[19]

For Panikkar, it was the beginning of an irreversible process of intellectual and ideological development. He was not yet to know that the ultimate trajectory of his life and career would provide him with a ringside seat to history. But a year into attending university and participating in the revolutionary activities of the Oxford Majlis and a year into being watched by Scotland Yard as a person of interest, Panikkar was no longer the invisible nonentity he had feared he would be. By now, he had had the chance to meet and talk with students from different corners of India, from Calcutta to Punjab and from Aligarh and Sind, and was no longer a green young man unaware of the deeper political ramifications of being a colonial subject. His nationalist leanings were clearly established. Scotland Yard reported, 'During his stay in England he contributed strong nationalist articles to *New India*, *The Indian Review* and *The Hindustan Review*.... '[20]

He was developing opinions and finding his voice at last. There seem to have been mixed feelings about this: some police reports record that Panikkar was rather unpopular among his peers, but there are those who remember him as an excellent student, with a wide circle of friends.[21] He was not entirely brilliant at speaking on stage just yet, but it was at this time that Panikkar developed the gift that would stay with him all through his life, and for which he is still remembered today.

He began to write.

It was the beginning of a lifelong love of writing and an exploration of the mind that would develop into one of Panikkar's prime contributions to policy and politics in independent India. As India took its first steps down the rocky road to constitutional reform, the written word became both a means of articulating his opinion and a method by which he could contribute to not just the nationalist movement, but to charting an idea of post-colonial India. As Panikkar grew older, writing would become not just an intellectual pursuit, but an escape from deeper and more stressful emotions. He had not yet started writing the fiction or poetry for which he is known today. That would come with time, but from this time onwards Panikkar would never lay down his pen until the day he died.

Chapter 5

The Early Essays

BY THE END OF 1914, ONLY A HANDFUL OF STUDENTS REMAINED ON campus. It was the same across universities in England, with an article in St John's College magazine, *The Eagle*, noting, 'the conflict has turned the minds of those who are in residence in directions so different … and has seemed to diminish so much the relative importance of academic occupations.'[1]

Sporting activities, races, balls and college dinners were cancelled. Young men attended military lectures in the evening. With so many enlistments, rooms lay vacant and colleges began to lose money. With fears rising about potential air raids, some colleges hastily put their most valuable manuscripts and books away in storage. During the first confusing months when Britain was getting accustomed to being at war, Cambridge University's vice chancellor gave a speech in which he hoped that 'the fire of education, religion, learning and research shall outburn the flame of war'.[2]

Panikkar certainly took this well-meaning speech to heart. He spent much of the first year of the war studying the theoretical developments in imperialism and its impact on the rights of colonies. The subjects he began to write about tell the curious observer that Panikkar was no armchair activist, but a serious-minded young man with a strong desire to engage with the important ideas and concerns of the day. For example, listening to Hugh Egerton, the intensely pro-empire Beit Professor of History at Oxford at the time, on the merits of Britain's civilising mission in Asia and Africa, pushed an infuriated Panikkar towards learning as much as he could to combat and counter the existing colonial narrative.

As they had been before, books would be his salvation. Panikkar read now of the Boer War in faraway South Africa, which had prompted administrators like Sir Alfred Milner and Lionel George Curtis to begin piecing together a theory of imperial welfare in which race featured prominently. In fact, Curtis would play a significant role in promoting the idea of an imperial federation. After serving in the South African war, he became secretary to Milner, then the British high commissioner in South Africa. Curtis was part of 'Milner's Kindergarten', a group of young administrators who worked on the reorganisation of the Transvaal government. He would be instrumental in replacing the term 'empire' with 'commonwealth'. His work laid the groundwork for the transformation of the British Empire into the Commonwealth of Nations. Curtis's vision extended beyond the empire; he advocated for a federal world order and wrote extensively on the subject, including in his major work, *Civitas Dei*, where he proposed a world federation. In his ideas, Curtis was different from his mentor. Milner advocated for imperialism as passionately as Curtis pushed for self-governance within empire. This, then, was the beginning of the push and pull between different perspectives on the empire and its colonies. Panikkar didn't know it just yet of course, but federation and commonwealth would become the constitutional and legal concepts with which he would be associated professionally for most of his adult life.[3]

As the war moved into its second year, troops were billeted at universities across England, with officers dining with college dons and younger soldiers performing drills on the college lawns. Sometime in early 1915, Panikkar decided he wanted to take a stab at putting down his thoughts on where imperialism was taking India. He knew that, more than anything else, the war had put the question of different nationalities and identities at the heart of every political question being asked across the empire. Having following Milner's rise with interest, Panikkar was aware that Milner and his 'Kindergarten' were terrified of what the end of the war meant for imperialism. The dominions, which had risen to the occasion superbly during the war, would not 'endorse a peace which they will have no share in making and have never been consulted about'.[4] For Milner and his followers, the British way of life and the very soul of the empire was at stake. Every conflict thus far had only proved to them that it would be the 'strongest' culture and race that would survive. Given these new changed circumstances, the need of the hour was for Britain to establish itself as the trustee of all people and colonies in the empire before it was too late.

In July 1915, Milner spoke to the members of the United Empire Club in Piccadilly, where he said that he hoped an 'imperial cabinet' might be established. 'We should have a single British state embodying all the scattered portions of our race throughout the world … free and independent in their local concerns, but standing as one state among the nations.'[5]

What did this grand pronouncement mean for India?

Inspired, the twenty-year-old K.M. Panikkar began writing the essay that would become *India and the Imperial Cabinet*, while actively looking for a journal or a magazine that would carry it.

He was in luck.

The teens of the twentieth century were a time of active propaganda for causes the likes of which the empire had not seen before. It isn't surprising that Panikkar sent his essay to *The Commonweal*. Much like the *The Commonweal*'s founder, Annie Besant, Panikkar was already developing a brand of nationalism that didn't necessarily believe in the quietly constitutional. Prayers, petitions and memorials were, to his mind, outdated methods. The war had established that only radical change could get India what it wanted in the aftermath. Besant's ideological principles might have confounded a more peaceful soul, but she did believe—correctly—that the war would change the world forever. *The Commonweal* was her attempt to present a collective national consensus on economic, social and political reforms for the future.

Panikkar's first essay for *The Commonweal* was published on 13 August 1915. Even today, it reads as an exercise in rage against inequality and racism. Should Milner's suggestion for an imperial cabinet materialise, India would have no place in it, it said. 'It is universally understood and accepted that the ultimate authority on Indian matters is the British public, as represented in the House of Commons,' Panikkar wrote furiously. 'An Imperial Cabinet with full authority on all questions, transfers such rights from the British public to the white members of the Empire.'[6]

This would mean that voters of, for instance, Melbourne and Cape Town, would have a say in the governments of India and the colonies—unacceptable in Panikkar's eyes. India had responded to the empire's call for help during the war. Why then wasn't it to be recompensed for its help?

Panikkar's early essays reveal a young man's discovery of and rebellion against the empire's blatantly unequal ideas of race, citizenship and nationality. He would go on to write extensively on complex subjects like immigration, citizenship, international relations and diaspora rights. But even in the early days, his writing was incisive and insightful, emblematic of the kind of pen he was choosing to wield. 'Australia has shut her doors in our face; the position in South Africa is none too desirable and Canada has raised insidious distinctions of colour and race.'[7] What was worse, in Panikkar's eyes, was the fact that not a single English politician had deemed it necessary to look into the treatment of Indians in the colonies. It was the 'last desperate stand of "white-manity",' he warned. The more the Whites banded together, the more difficult it would be for India to meet its political salvation. 'India has to prepare for the fight,' he urged. 'One does not know from what point the offensive may come.'[8]

That much was clear, given what was happening in Europe that year. Panikkar's first essay on international relations—a field with which he would, though he didn't know it yet, go on to become intimately acquainted—was for the *Indian Review*. For him, it was a landmark. The *Indian Review* was a monthly periodical 'devoted to the discussion of all topics of interest' published out of Madras by the venerable publishing company G.A. Natesan and Co. More than the company itself, it was the allure of being acknowledged by Natesan, a staunch and serious nationalist known for his intellect, his ability to debate excellently and extempore on key social issues, and the integrity that he brought to his brand of journalism. The idea driving the *Indian Review* was to bring out a journal devoted to the welfare of India, staying independent enough to ensure that both Europeans and Indians could contribute without inhibitions. Natesan put much thought into the magazine's presentation. Its logo, for instance, had a European and an Indian standing side by side, with the rather obvious motto: *Away with Ill Feeling.*

By the early twentieth century, Natesan had established himself as a vocal supporter of freedom from colonialism. It helped that he was great friends with Gandhi, who had stayed at Natesan's little residence on Thambu Chetty Street in Madras and who introduced him to the importance of playing a direct role in local and national politics.[9] Panikkar would become good friends with Natesan, even if the friendship was tinged with more than a touch of awe on the younger man's side. The older man lent a much-needed Indian perspective to Panikkar's developing worldview by chatting easily to him about federation within the empire, the role that the colonies and dominions would and could play within that federation, and the importance of self-governance.

Natesan himself found Panikkar to have great intellectual promise, and invited the young man to write for the *Indian Review* on any topic he found interesting. Panikkar was thrilled because Natesan was notoriously picky about who he chose to write for his beloved magazine. Over the years, its contributors included Sir C.P. Ramaswami Aiyar, Srinivasa Sastri, V. Krishnaswamy Aiyer, C.A. White (then the chief justice of Madras), J.J. Cotton, Alfred Chatterton and the historian R.C. Dutt. To be published in the *Indian Review* at the age of twenty was a singular achievement.

Panikkar set about choosing the subject of his forthcoming essay with great care, eventually choosing to write a brief biographical sketch of the celebrated Hungarian political reformer and patriot Louis Kossuth. Kossuth had led the Hungarian Revolution of 1848, pushing back hard, albeit constitutionally, against the absolutism of the reigning House of Habsburg. He was elected governor of Hungary during the war of independence. Significantly, Kossuth envisioned a federation in the kingdom of Hungary in which all nationalities participated in a democratic system based on principles of equality and parliamentary representation. Kossuth would always advocate for Hungary's full independence, even though it would take decades before his cause truly saw the light of day.

The essay is no more than a page or two, but Panikkar's choice of Kossuth was perhaps the best indicator of what he thought about the war, about its implications for the international world order, and importantly, for India's place within the empire. It was, in its choice of main character, also a rather endearing insight into Panikkar's youthful admiration for a man like Kossuth and the kind of movement he was leading, which aimed to uplift an oppressed populace without forgetting their solidarity with other national movements. But Panikkar never forgot to underline the fact that nationalism, for him, was not a quiet attribute or an ideal. 'Prometheus can be imprisoned,' he wrote warningly, 'but the spark, once ignited, continues to burn.'[10]

That was true for Panikkar himself. Once he began writing, it seemed like he couldn't stop. Gone forever was the terrified, unsure youth of 1914, who had timidly confessed his insecurities to his elder brother. Here was a young man coming into his own at almost blinding speed, armed with a pen as sharp as it was intelligent. With his intelligence and wit, he was discovering that he could charm the ladies. He would enjoy that particular trait even more as he grew older. Scotland Yard files make oblique references to several love interests at this time, though who these ladies were has been lost to posterity.

The accolades pouring in were enough to turn any young man's head, and Panikkar was showing strong streaks of vanity and arrogance. Soon, he wasn't too popular among his peers. As his grand-nephew was to put it, he was 'downright insufferable'.[11] K.P.S. Menon would never tire of telling and retelling the story of how Panikkar's classmates once, to teach him a lesson, shoved him headfirst into the pool of the college fountain. If anything, these insults only hardened Panikkar's resolve to prove his worth to anyone who was watching him.

But he was far from friendless and alone. Panikkar, even then, was unforgettable. To those whom he liked, he was a wonderful friend, admitting them immediately and without inhibition or consideration of class or community to his inner circle. His close friend, the politician R.L. Mehta, would observe that this was a quality that lasted all his life. 'Among his friends are not only princes and princesses, cabinet ministers and diplomats, journalists and authors, but also actors and actresses, old as well as young, bankrupt schoolmasters and destitute scholars, unemployed young men and aspiring young women, M.P.'s [*sic*] and officials, both those who are struggling to find their feet and those who have reached the snug state of self-complacency when they see no other point of view except their own.'[12]

The Swarajist leader Dr P. Subbarayan who would work with Panikkar later and who knew him in university, remembered him as having 'a wide circle of friends'.[13] To his friends, he was both hospitable and fun, and he allowed his inner circle to see his most open self. His earliest friends remembered a peculiarly distinctive brand of humour based on an ability to observe people's behaviour and couple his insights with sharply apt phrases from literature. As his circle of friends expanded along with his reputation, Panikkar's pen grew louder and more radical with every essay he wrote. Given this tendency, it is curious to see that Panikkar also had strong streak of traditionalism. For instance, in his view, political issues were always linked to, and constrained by, social and cultural issues. So, for instance, he would argue many times in the years to come that, while it was important for India to modernise and push for full Home Rule, it was equally important to protect its unique culture and customs. All this while maintaining ties—hopefully, one day of equality—with the empire.

Panikkar's second essay for *The Commonweal* was on the thorny question of nationalism. Harking back to his first essay for the *Indian Review*, Panikkar reminded his readers that nationalism was a sacred ideal above everything else. The war had dealt that ideal a death blow. Thinkers like Karl Marx and George Bernard Shaw, for instance, no longer regarded nationalism to be the be all and end all of political life, but a stepping stone to 'a higher stage of political evolution'.[14]

In the twentieth century, Panikkar noted regretfully, nationalism had become reductive. 'If one strong nation reduces all other peoples to its own standards, there will be a dead uniformity in the world, which is manifestly against the full evolution of man.'[15]

The essay sees Panikkar attempting the first real answer to his own question of what nationalism meant to him and for him. True nationalism lay not in uniformity, but in the 'preservation of distinctive culture, ideals and life',[16] and the real role of political independence would be the preservation of that uniqueness. He was even then aware of the fact that he belonged to a country inhabited by different languages, customs, religions and ways of life. Whatever his ideas of freedom were, and however his views on India's place within the empire would evolve, he never lost sight of the fact that the country's plurality and diversity could not be divorced from nationalism. Where did nationalism fit into empire, particularly with an ongoing war? According to Panikkar, it was idealistic to think that any result could be achieved as a reward for India's contribution to the war effort. On the other hand, the war was demonstrating how important colonies were for Britain. The war had in fact brought the issue of nationality to the foreground.

As the world edged through the difficult autumn of 1915, Panikkar kept up a spate of writing. The act was both a response to the world as it was and the building of his own ideological and political framework. In *Some Economic Illusions*, for instance, he laid out a clear warning against dismissing a rising Germany and on being too complacent about Britain's naval supremacy. Though Germany had been blockaded, it not only had allies willing to help (Norway, Sweden, Denmark and Holland), but also the trade returns of neutral countries. It was in itself 'a self-sufficing nation'.[17]

What did that mean for the rest of the world and for the war in general? Panikkar answered this question admirably, proving his mettle as a keen observer of strategy and global geopolitics. For instance, he noted that Galicia had given Germany oil fields, while the conquest of Russian Poland had added to the resources of oil, iron and materiel. Panikkar pointed out that German statesmen had acknowledged and catered to the country's need for coal, which was why Germany's first act during the war had been the occupation of Belgium and Luxembourg which at the time contained some of the richest iron and coalfields in the world. He noted also that Germany had subjugated all else to military matters. In short, Germany had been preparing for a war for far longer than Britain had. In fact, Britain was trapped in a war that it did not necessarily want, primarily because all its neighbours were involved in the war. 'The great arguments of the pacifists,' wrote Panikkar sharply, 'thus proved to be great illusions.'[18]

They may have been illusions, but Panikkar himself was under no such delusion. He knew perfectly who his audience was and precisely what they wanted to hear. As a result, the end of the essay has a rather pleasing little paragraph on the fact that victory was with the Allies, despite Germany's menace. It is clear that, in his mind, the war had only served to shine a light on the chinks in Britain's military and economic armour. The war might be *won* by Britain, but the centre of global finance would shift to the United States.[19] How did all this tie in with the nationalist movement at home? Because a weak Britain would never relinquish India. If freedom had to be won, a 'moderate' policy, so to speak, would not do. India and Indians needed action.

It wasn't just geopolitics that kept Panikkar's mind active during these fraught war years at Oxford. In 1915, he made headlines back home in Travancore for all the wrong reasons. P.V. Krishna Warrier had invited him to write an essay for *Bhasha Vilasam*, the annual number of the magazine he owned called the *Kavana Kaumudi*, which was published in Kottakkal, Travancore. Panikkar knew immediately what he wanted to write about—he wanted to expand on a thesis he had proposed to *Nazrani Deepika* while he had been in India. That thesis had been more gauche and had been duly rejected, but Panikkar felt he was now able to present a more sophisticated version of the idea. The outcome of this was a formidable essay titled *Malayalam Poetry and Sanskrit Verses*. In the essay, he argued for the Dravidian metre instead of Sanskrit for Malayalam poetry, citing the works of the greats like Cherusseri Namboothiri, Kunchan Nambiar and the Niranam (Kannassan) poets. It was a daring call for change. Until the eighteenth century, there had been two parallel currents in Malayalam poetry: the Sanskrit and the Dravidian metres. The Dravidian metre had in fact held the upper hand, as Panikkar pointed out. But now, for the last two centuries, the proponents of the Sanskrit metre were legion and luminous, not least being the senior Prince Kerala Varma and the great Vallathol himself. The Dravidian metre was practically banished from the field. When an unknown young man, still a student and no known writer or poet, challenged the established Sanskrit metre, there was uproar.

In typical fashion, Panikkar downplayed the furore he had caused, writing in his memoir merely that 'eyebrows were raised'. But it was, in fact, nothing short of a scandal. Panikkar didn't care—he wanted to make a mark not just in geopolitics, but in the arts and the literature he loved, and he wasn't afraid of pulling strings to get where he wanted to go. In this case, for instance, he wrote to the great Vallathol himself, playing upon their connection from Thampanoor. Vallathol was used to Panikkar's daring arguments, and to his credit, he engaged with the younger man's scholarship on equal terms. But while affection often caused him to concede to Panikkar's blandishments, in this specific case, Vallathol felt challenged.

'Just see,' Panikkar begged. 'Even if one poem could work in the Dravidian metre.'[20]

Vallathol obliged by writing the poem 'A Picture' (in his collection of poems, *Sahitya Manjiri*). This is credited with being the first specimen of a Dravidian metre being used by a modern Malayali poet, and it began the trend of freely using the Dravidian metre in Malayalam poetry. For that poem, written in response to Panikkar's request, Vallathol is credited as having reformed the field forever.[21]

But that essay established Panikkar as a Malayalam literary scholar to reckon with. It is a largely overlooked facet of his erudition. When one thinks of him today, it is because of his contributions to foreign policy, to constitutional law and to strategic thought. But Panikkar would always be intricately involved with the evolution and writing of Malayalam poetry and literature. 'Nothing has given me that sense of contentment in times of difficulty and crisis as the writing of poetry,' he would recall later. 'There was never a period in my active life when I did not devote at least an hour a day to literary pursuits in Malayalam.'[22]

CHAPTER 6

A Scholar to Reckon With

'HOW COULD INDIANS CLAIM OR ASSUME OR EVEN RECOGNIZE THEMSELVES to be *citizens* of an Empire, when they were but subjects in their own motherland?'[1]

The question obsessed Panikkar.

As it would with countries and peoples alike, the war was changing his ideas of what it meant to be an Indian when so much of the world was defined by the empire. What rights did Indians hold? What rights *could* Indians hold? Were Indians entitled to the same rights as British citizens? Could a democratic political system fit India's aspirations for the future? These were but a few of the questions which Panikkar—and many young men and women like him—was grappling with at the time.

In retrospect, it is clear that, in 1916, the idea of citizenship was in flux. Indians across the world were beginning to demand their rights as subjects of the Crown even as they accepted the simultaneous liability of being citizens of an empire. This was not merely a question of constitutional codification, but of the *potential* of what the word 'citizenship' could and would mean.

As war raged across battlefields in Mesopotamia and Flanders, citizenship was emerging not just as a political right and a way of gaining social and cultural access; rather, it was a narrative in progress at a time when laws on the issue were decidedly nebulous. After all, the very existence of the empire proved that power could be exercised over subjects, not citizens (an emphasis that Lord Linlithgow would drive home admirably in 1939). In India, the concept was made even more complex by the fact that while equal citizenship continued to be promised by an urbane government, other dominions of the empire (led by the likes of Lionel Curtis) were shaping their own ideas of citizenship.[2]

Most Indians, especially those who were educated, were not unaware that the right given to Indians to move freely across the empire was just that—an *idea*. If it didn't want an uprising on its hands, the empire needed to take fairly hasty action. Since 1897, a flurry of imperial conferences had been held to show a veneer of unity across an empire with distant reaches and to codify claims of citizenship. In January 1915, a new passport design had been introduced in wartime Britain. The passport was just one example of how the Crown intended to uphold principles of territorial sovereignty over its colonies and dominions. A year later, predictably, the secretary of state for India suggested that the British Government of India do the same.[3] The inequality was glaring, for India was not a dominion yet, forcing the Imperial Conference in 1921 (where Srinivasa Sastri was a delegate) to issue a separate notice on the same issue. The problem was that it was all an eyewash.

The laws being passed in Britain, whether they were the British Nationalist and Status of Aliens Act (BNSA)[4] or even the DORA, which had incensed Panikkar when he first heard of it, only emphasised what every politically aware Indian already knew: they would always be subservient to the Crown.

For the *Commonweal*'s autumn 1916 issue, Panikkar focused on citizenship and identity. He asked the question with which this chapter opens, in an essay simply titled 'The Claims of Imperial Citizenship'. In retrospect, he was asking nothing new or particularly revolutionary. But what stands out in these essays is his use of Hinduism as a lens through which he could assess the rise of nationalism. This wasn't a remarkably new or unused lens, but it was one that Panikkar would evolve with age and time. For now though, the heart of his argument lay in the freedom to belong to an independent Hindu society without foregoing the right to political development. The twentieth century, according to Panikkar, was a period of culmination—a counter-reformation of sorts—after a century of cultural and ideological interactions. The nineteenth century had begun a process of qualitative change, introducing Indians to Western processes of thought. But that time had gone. 'The day when India stood dazzled by the splendour of Europe, when our thinkers believed in Herbert Spencer and [Auguste] Comte and our poets looked to London and Paris for inspiration has gone—never to return,' he wrote with the optimism of the very young in 1916.[5]

Panikkar's youth is still more obvious in the fact that this essay becomes progressively more agitated as one reads through it. He scorned the white man's view that education lay at the heart of democratic principles of equality. 'Education to read the Sunday newspaper is a thoroughly European ideal,'[6] he fumed. This was a view he would expand on later, for Panikkar was always interested in education as the foundation for progress. But at that moment in time, if someone had asked Panikkar if Indians were ready at all for democracy, he would have said that, as a political system, it was alien to India and not indispensable. He felt, rather interestingly, that India could govern itself without necessarily becoming or being a democracy. According to him, citizenship in a Hindu society did not mean universal suffrage, but the right to follow one's own religion. In fact, for Panikkar, the most important institution of the day was the Arya Samaj, with its militant responses to the empire and its militant beliefs not just in Hinduism but in sangathan (unity). Hinduism, then, was not just a religious philosophy. It represented a spirit of collective racial pride and nationalist self-belief. It was an argument that veered dangerously close to the Hindutva bone, but reading through Panikkar's youthful writing highlights just how much he was struggling to pull together the idea of a common 'Indian' political community or nation (in its modern nationalist sense, with connotations of self-government and statehood) with the idea of the plural communities that existed within its borders. He wasn't the only one struggling with these ideas, of course. The war years had thrown nearly every colonial intellectual into a morass of doubt. Panikkar wasn't old enough yet to mask his feelings when he wrote, but it would do a modern reader well to remember that his arguments were being made in a considerably fluid intellectual landscape. The Indian nation was being imagined and reimagined in those turbulent days. As far as India was concerned, considerations of religion, culture and politics often jostled with one another in an attempt to define what nationalism meant to Indians.

In retrospect, it is easy to see that the young Panikkar was anchoring many of his arguments in the 'Greater India' school of thought. In this, he was breaking no new ground. As an intellectual concept, 'Greater India' had been around since the 1880s. Developed primarily by Bengali educationists, journalists and scholars, this idea was connected with a Hindu revivalist nationalism that sought to establish a Hindu-inflected political order in India. The work towards this included the foundation of Hindustani associations outside India, the Arya Samajists' work abroad and within the country, and publications such as *The Modern Review.* The term was an abbreviated reference to 'Hindu' cultural influences in Southeast Asia over a period of about 1,500 years. From here, it was a hop and a skip to the argument that India had once been able to sustain a 'Hindu' colonial empire, signalling a cultural and geopolitical greatness in the past. In many ways, the idea was a uniquely Indian response to British, Dutch and French scholarship on the history, culture and arts in their colonies: British India, the Dutch East Indies and French Indochina (Vietnam).

At the period when Panikkar was writing in Oxford, a period when the world was at war and the colonies were rethinking their identities, the 'Greater India' concept came in incredibly handy as a propaganda tool to mobilise the Indian diaspora in America, Britain or Africa. Soft power, then, was already a weapon in the days before a term for it existed. The discourse around 'Greater India' was mostly in English, conducted primarily for international audiences. If by any chance vernacular scholarship on the subject was published, there was immense haste to translate it into English so that it could be read by a wider audience.[7] Panikkar's was just one voice—although a considerably young voice—in the cacophony of opinions at the time, though his ideas make for interesting reading today.

Race was another darkly cynical obsession that grew out of his thoughts at this time. In another essay, *Indian Home Rule and Imperial Federalism*, Panikkar maintained that it was easy to argue for Home Rule if you didn't know what it meant. Didn't those who called for Home Rule understand that race alone would ensure that the standard of imperial citizenship would be very different for Indians as opposed to white people? His tone in this essay borders on the belligerent, insisting that India's society, religion and pride was a citadel that could not be stormed by European culture.[8]

But youthful impatience aside, this essay is also the first in which Panikkar presented federation as the solution to India's political problems. It was undoubtedly a very nascent thought, a fact that is underlined by his insistence that India would *never* be part of the British Commonwealth (an argument that transfer of power turned on its head and one that Panikkar himself would backtrack on in a few years). He branched off from this argument to an even more succinct view that the only way forward lay in India becoming a self-governing federation in its own right, albeit *within the empire* (italics mine), based on the Austro-Hungarian model of dual monarchy that united the federation of the dominions on the one hand and the empire on the other.

With journalism like this, Panikkar entered the ranks of a community of writers and nationalists who were trying to make sense of nationalism, citizenship and identity at this point. But he was still too far away from home and too young. Often, he felt as though he was firing words and ideas into the void. At other times, his ego was bruised by readers who wrote in to refute some of his opinions. One reader, writing to the editor of the *Commonweal,* acknowledged that young Mr Panikkar's ideas were certainly 'thought compelling', but surely he was dismissing English education out of hand? After all, the reader remarked, wasn't it English education that had given Indians a previously unimaginable depth of thought?

The question considerably annoyed Panikkar, who didn't like his opinions being poked at. Still, he was undeterred, writing next about the Indian diaspora in the colonies and how, given the trajectories of migration, the nurturing of a national consciousness was critical. What might that national consciousness be based upon? The answer was simple: one that stayed loyal to Hinduism. The fealty to Hinduism was a telling indicator of the porous boundaries between communalism, secularism and nationalism in the early twentieth century. It is also a reminder that Panikkar, in this belief, stood at a deliberate distance from Hindutva. His ideas about India would evolve over the years, but he would never take the more extremist view (like Savarkar, for instance) of Hindu political supremacy. Panikkar was not an aberration in his ideas about Hinduism being the panacea to most of India's ills, but a product of his times.

That year, 1916, Panikkar's professional and intellectual life changed yet again with his decision to send an essay to a magazine called *Indian Emigrant*.

The issue of Indian emigration had come to the fore in national debates ever since anti-Asiatic laws had been imposed across Australia and other white dominions in response to the fear that a growth in the number of unskilled labourers would only deteriorate the living conditions of local and European labour.[9] Small wonder then that emigration was a political hot potato. Contemporary scholarship and chronicles on and around indentureship are both rich and colourful, but in his time, Panikkar was witness to the mobilisation of Indian society in a campaign to end indentureship. For the first time, grassroots organisations were created by Indians from various religious and political classes and backgrounds with the sole purpose of ending this scheme. These groups deployed pamphlets, serials, newspapers and lectures to disseminate information regarding indenture.

The *Indian Emigrant*, run by T.K. Swaminathan along with his excellent friend, Sir C.P. Ramaswami Aiyar, became a particularly important and hugely popular venture during this campaign. Within weeks of its first issue, it became the premier platform from which to disburse information on the experiences of Indians in the empire and those who had returned from the colonies. It allowed Indians everywhere to think about their status as citizens of the empire, as people deserving of equal rights. Its readership was vast, with copies being sent from Rajkot to Durban and from Ratnapura to Nova Scotia. Building on its popularity, the *Indian Emigrant* ran a full-page advertisement that year, announcing a prize essay competition for the best monograph/essay on the subject of Indian emigration. The princely sum of Rs 100 was being offered as a prize by Sir CP, then the high court vakil of Madras.

'It is the intention of the donor that a larger number of Indians should make a scientific study of this important imperial problem and this is intended only as an encouragement,' warned the ad. The essay needed to cover thirty to fifty pages of foolscap, typewritten only on one side of the page, with the deadline being 31 May 1916. 'Preference shall be given to original and practical suggestions for improving the condition and status of Indians throughout the world and the best means of bringing about better relations between Indians at home and abroad.'[10]

Panikkar had written often for the magazine, but this was the chance of a lifetime. To be brought to Aiyar's notice would truly be a fillip to Panikkar's career and standing in the eyes of his peers. Aiyar had a brilliant legal mind and was working almost fanatically hard to become one of India's greatest constitutional lawyers. And it was paying off, literally and metaphorically. He was one of the best paid lawyers in the country and the splendour of his lifestyle was the envy of Madras. He was the first in the city to own a motorcar, a Hudson. His wardrobe was vast and legend went that he regularly shipped batches of his shirts to be washed and pressed in a London laundry. Thanks to his legal brilliance and networking skills, it was very much the done thing to be seen at The Grove, his mansion at 1, Eldam's Road (now C.P. Ramaswami Aiyar Road), in Alwarpet, Madras. From Gandhi to Annie Besant, from Jinnah to Nawab Hamidullah Khan, everyone stopped by to see Sir CP. Panikkar was eager for Sir CP's approval. The subject therefore had to be perfect.

Panikkar decided that he would, for the first time, tackle the issue of emigration. His submitted essay was titled 'Problems of a Greater India'. It was his clearest and most persuasive argument for a 'Greater India'. Within its pages, he argued for ways in which to create a 'united Indian community' in the colonies: by providing scholarships at Benares Hindu University, by organising teachers from 'the Motherland' as he called India, and to ensure the ethos of the Indian civilisation that the Indian diaspora 'inherited in their blood'. His thesis framed 'Greater India' as part of a 'modern Indian expansion' based on emigrant waves of labourers since 1834.[11] He pointed to the communities of Indians 'in South Africa, Portuguese East Africa, Mauritius, F.M.S. [Federated Malay States], Fiji, Surinam, British Guiana and the British Islands of the West Indies.' Irrespective of where they were currently living, Panikkar claimed that they were bound together by Hinduism: its laws and customs.

'The Hindu society has withstood all foreign influences and is still a compact whole defying all the attacks on it. We justly pride ourselves on the fact that our society and our laws are not fabrics erected as temporary makeshifts, changing with every wind, but eternal institutions which, while permanent in their basis, grow on with the onward march of humanity,' he wrote. 'Wherever they go, the Hindus carry with them their social ideals and on this depends the greatness of Indian emigration ... Even the poorest and the meanest of them have definite conceptions and ideals as regards life, religion and society. They plant the Hindu community wherever they go and they live according to the Hindu ethical standard.'[12]

Panikkar's concern about Indian emigrants underlined (with some consternation) the possible loss of their 'Indianness' when they came in contact with different ways of life. This is an argument that leans heavily on the predominant intellectual tenets of Panikkar's time.

With remarkable blitheness, he bypasses both caste and ethnicity in this treatise, not to mention differences in religion and language. In his worldview, Hinduism was tolerant and universal enough to defend the unity of an Indian nation. He calls for a 'unification of the vernaculars', suggesting (surprisingly, given that he was from south India himself) the introduction of Hindustani as a mode of primary education in all the colonies: 'it will materially help to create a united Indian community in these Colonies'.[13] He insists, too, on the need for a 'national' system that could keep Indian youth firmly rooted in his own culture.[14]

Panikkar's tone is defiant, even angry. The primary concern for India and Indians across the empire, he argued, was to strengthen racially and culturally against the European civilisation. 'The challenge of the Colonies is not a challenge to our political life. *It is a challenge to our race: it is a challenge to our religion. It is a challenge to our culture* [italics mine].'[15]

Read in the light of present day, it is easy to attribute harder connotations to his arguments and even to take them out of context. In reality, 'Greater India' was a trans-imperial, Indo-centric research paradigm that drove the recovery of the ancient past in Central and Southeast Asia. Ancient India was an actor in world history, on par with ancient Greece and Rome. At its literal best, the Greater India movement was a scholarly quest for Indian identity, and it wasn't surprising that it was easily tied to anti-colonial, pedagogical, nationalist and Asianist agendas. That said, as a movement, it certainly also achieved the opposite: bolstering and energising militant Hindu nationalism, for instance. 'The Problems of Greater India' was fundamentally a twentieth-century product in that it was a response to colonial appropriation of history and culture and a defiant reminder that, against all odds, the idea of India had survived and would continue to do so.

The article itself is out of print and unavailable in any digitised form, but a copy dug up from the archives shows that Panikkar made some interesting acknowledgements and dedications in this tract. He acknowledged a Mr Dutt of Trinidad, for instance, who had supplied him with first-hand information about the plight of Indians in Trinidad and the British West Indies. The historian Feriel Nissa Kissoon points out that this exchange was the simplest example of the existence of a reciprocal but stealthy exchange of information between Trinidad and India with the sole intention of educating audiences about the problems of indentureship.[16] This was a mighty task in itself, considering how indentureship was talked about in the public discourse of the day. Still, Panikkar finished writing 'Greater India' in two weeks flat. He dedicated the monograph to one Monsieur Nakano.

Seigo Nakano was an obscure and deeply unconventional Japanese nationalist. Born in a time when Japan was a world of vanquished samurai, pan-Asian activists and political revolutionaries, Nakano studied the icons of the past as a boy, constantly seeking a role model for himself. Since nearly all those role models were leaders of various uprisings, and given that he came from a dysfunctional family, it is not surprising that Nakano became the neighbourhood bad boy long before he was ten. He was slim to the point of being scrawny; bellicose, with a tongue as sharp as a knife. At the age of fourteen, Nakano landed himself in hospital with a badly placed elbow in judo practice. Legend has it that this deterred him not a jot. He used the time to read and flirt with his nurse. It was during university that Nakano was drawn to a more unconventional career path, defined by anti-colonialism. He opted to study at the new Waseda University, where he learned of liberal democracy, parliamentary party politics, universal suffrage and gender equality. By the time he met Panikkar, Nakano had already worked for the *Tokyo Daily News* and *Tokyo Asahi News*, worked at the Osaka branch of the *Asahi Shimbun*, travelled through China, and witnessed a world war and a revolution in Russia. Over the course of his life, Nakano would continue with journalism while trying his hand (unsuccessfully) at politics. He did all this while writing over half a dozen books—a true role model for the aspirational young Panikkar.

The two men met in Oxford in the spring of 1915. Nakano lived up to the reputation that preceded him—arrogant, boastful and aloof. But in Panikkar's eyes, none of this took away from the fact that Nakano was a brilliant writer, capable of articulating political ideas with a pen that he wielded like a sword. Like all of Panikkar's choices, Nakano was interesting, considering that he is remembered today for his dabbles with fascism during his leadership of the Tohokai (Far East Society), his opposition to the totalitarian government of Tojo Hideki and his eventual suicide under extraordinarily murky circumstances. There are no records of the interaction between Nakano and Panikkar in Oxford, but Nakano himself was repulsed by the decadence of Western society. He left much earlier than he had intended to, firing off on his voyage back home an article condemning the hypocrisy of the West.

While Panikkar waited for his article to be judged by the *Indian Emigrant*, he began work on his next series of articles for *The Commonweal*. In 'The Illusions of Anglo-India, Pt. I: The Cult of Efficiency',[17] the reader sees a young Panikkar finally hitting his literary stride. This essay was the first of three parts on this subject, in which Panikkar spiritedly refuted the theories of those whom he called 'Anglo-Indians'. Here again the reader is reminded of the importance that Panikkar gave to a pluralist yet traditionalist version of nationalism. He wrote, ' … even in Nation-States, there are different and sometimes hostile nationalities … [This] is a historical fact that cannot be disputed.'[18] It was a prophetic sentence, given that years later he would head the States Reorganisation Commission and address just this point.

He also argued that if India were to progress in any form, it must do away with the line of thinking that without the Raj, India could never have built its own railway or postal system. In this specific piece, Panikkar railed against the 'ulsterisation' of the country by foreign bureaucrats and refused almost defiantly to acknowledge the role/rivalry of caste. For him, it seemed almost inconceivable that India would endure alien rule rather than 'Brahmin' rule. Yet again, he pointed to the fact that India didn't need the British to remain united. Hinduism, and its philosophy and culture, would keep India united, as it had for millennia. 'It is a question of fact … as to whether India was a cultural entity before the British Government … The whole point was, although we did not have political entity, there was behind and beneath the great diversity of her manner, customs and religion, the unifying fact of the geographical entity itself, and the permanent and remaining complex of Hindu culture which forms the broad basis of a synthetic Indian civilisation.'[19]

In between writing the first and second parts of this essay, he received word that he had won the first prize of Rs 100 as promised by Sir C.P. Ramaswami Aiyar, for his essay titled 'Problems of a Greater India'. Not only that but Aiyar had written a gratifying introduction for Panikkar's essay, in which he had endorsed his views: '... as in the past there was a greater India composed of the outlying countries and islands in the Southern Seas and in the Far East, so there will be inevitably in the future an outer India which will demand its place in the sun.'[20]

Spurred on by this encouragement, Panikkar wrote an even stronger second part to his essay series on 'The Illusions of Anglo-India', in which he lashed out at Christian missionaries. 'Most of the vilest insults that are daily heard in the west against us come directly from them.'[21] There is, in this essay, an almost blind need to defend India—Hinduism, Indian society and culture in particular—from an outsider's eyes. 'They have been, for us, lie-spreading agencies and nothing more.'[22]

In 'The Illusions of Anglo India, Pt. III: Hypnotism by Hypothesis', Panikkar launched a two-pronged attack on the critics of India and those who advocated the need for foreign rule as a 'civilising mission',[23] and on the moderates who had been so deeply 'hypnotised' by the promise of Anglo-India (here he meant the empire) that they would do anything to support and promote it. To remedy this, Panikkar called for what he termed an 'excavation' of prevailing political thought. He was bitter about the civil services and their aspirants, insisting that those within its portals knew that their supremacy depended on those who believed in it. The British, he insisted, needed any excuse to justify their reign in India, whether it was communalism or caste rivalry or even anarchy in the princely states. The goal of every political party that claimed to be nationalist must be, he argued, to do away with the idea that the empire equalled progress in any form. This was the kind of progress, he snapped, that India could do without.

By 1918, Panikkar was also writing for the *Modern Review*. Founded in 1907 by the venerable Ramananda Chatterjee, *Modern Review* quickly emerged as a vital forum for nationalist intelligentsia. It carried essays on politics, economics and society. But it was run by a Bengali, so it carried its fair share of poems, stories and sketches. Targeted at bilinguals across the subcontinent, *Modern Review* was published mainly in English and did not (quite deliberately) hold a brief for any political party. This meant that it automatically stood apart from the party journals that already existed in mainstream public discourse, such as those being brought out by the Congress, the Muslim League, the Hindu Mahasabha, the communists and the Scheduled Castes Federation. It also meant that it could, for the first time, act as a genuine all-India forum.

Chatterjee was one of the most influential editors of his day, known for his scholarly editorial notes and his obsessive penchant for anodyne statistical government reports. The literary historian Margery Sabin explored the questions that occupied this fiercely brilliant mind. Chatterjee, Sabin argued, sustained and sponsored fundamental and continuing questions about what constitutes the authentic Indian past. 'What foreign influences in the present should India welcome or shun? What directions for the future would allow India to become "modern" without betraying its own identity?'[24]

Right from the start, *Modern Review* was a fine platform for debate and discussion among some of India's finest minds. Within its pages, you might find anthropologist Verrier Elwin's first report from the Gond country or sociologist Radhakamal Mukherjee's earliest pioneering essays on environmental degradation in India. In *Modern Review*, Tagore debated with Gandhi on subjects as varied as the benefits of non-cooperation and the uses of the charkha. It was for this magazine, in 1937, that Jawaharlal Nehru would anonymously write and publish his now famously mocking review of himself.

In January 1918, K.M. Panikkar made his debut for *Modern Review* in an essay titled 'The Educational Problem of Indian Nationalism'. It was a return to Panikkar's abiding obsession with the question of Indian nationalism. He made the sharp point that education has always been used by ruling classes/castes to repress society. He argued that this could be said about Sanskrit as much as it could be said for English, but for India in the twentieth century, a time when politics was changing and nationalism was rising, the education system installed by the British was neither fair nor free. It was an instrument of the State. Now more than ever, he wrote, India needed an *educated nationalist*—one who was truly equipped to fight an alien Raj.

This is a brief essay in which Panikkar made some extremely loaded points. For instance, he argued against what he called 'educational servility' or being a slave in thought, word and opinion to the government of the day. He emphasised the institution of an independent system of education, for only then can society reconstruct and readjust to a new day and age. Interestingly though, Panikkar, like Sir Ross Masood and other leading educationists of the day, held to a vernacular idea of education. It was a curious but almost inevitable consequence of a mind caught between traditionalism and cosmopolitanism. A Western education, in Panikkar's mind, would certainly broaden young people's minds by bringing them into contact with ideologies like liberalism and individualism, but it would also make them that much more inclined to defect from the grand tradition of Hinduism. This line of thought has context if one considers the fact that the turmoil at the turn of the century had seen the foundation of universities and numerous educational institutions across India, some financed by princes, such as the universities of Mysore and Hyderabad, others by private individuals, such as Benares Hindu University or Muslim Anglo-Oriental College. According to Panikkar, lack of education in the colonies was due to the fact that the schools available were not suitable for the Indian community.

His assessment of the three great lacunae of Indian education was excellent: the lack of a common language; the education of women and a general policy. On the question of women's education, Panikkar's views seem more than a little dated even by the standards of his day, which saw some brilliant women holding their own. He did argue *for* women's education, but he insisted that it must not come at the cost of the Indian family system. Too much education could—horror of horrors—completely wipe out the differences between the sexes.

Then there was his protest against English ('a language in which to commit literary suicide', as he put it caustically), simply because he saw it as an instrument of an oppressor. 'It is most ridiculous for a man to say that an Indian child born a thousand miles away from his motherland but still adhering to Hindu customs and manners should first begin to study "I am"', he railed. 'There is no "I am" in any Indian language. The English language has no educational value for us.'[25] An English education would prevent youngsters from interpreting the very life of the culture they came from, he argued.

Tempted by Europeanism, young people would be more inclined to defect from the Hindu tradition.

But that of course posed a rather problematic question: *If not English, then what?* Having gone hammer and tongs at English, Panikkar wasn't entirely sure of what the alternative should be. Despite his previous insistence on Hindustani in 'Problems of a Greater India', he now sidestepped the issue, hoping to cover up the lack of a clear answer by simply pointing to the emergence of a new kind of Hindustani-Tamil mixed language among the emigrant communities. But he left a rather interesting question in the essay. 'Is the attempt to create a common language an attempt to create a uniformity of thought and expression?' he demanded. 'If so, it is treason to India.'[26]

Yet, even as he made extremely important points for India's political evolution, Panikkar never lost sight of his first love: Malayalam literature. As a student, he was trying his hand with poetry for the first time after his little face-off with Vallathol. His first poems appeared in P.V. Krishna Warrier's *Kavana Kaumudi*. Warrier and Panikkar would become close, but true delight would find Panikkar only later that year when Admiral Sir Roland Wilson gave his anthology of essays a fulsome review in *The Asiatic Review*. Delighted, Panikkar trotted along to the office of *The Asiatic Review* to get his personal copy to treasure. At the office, he ran into the editor, Dr John Pollan. Pollan was thrilled to meet him, and wringing his hand in a tight grip, asked whether he could write and read a paper on Indian education for the East India Association (EIA). This was a signal honour since the EIA was notoriously snooty. Its elders never asked a student, of all people, to read a paper in their august presence.

That paper would become the genesis for *Indian Nationalism: Its Principles and History*, Panikkar's first full-length book project. Honour it might have been, but he was made to defend it vigorously. The minutes of the meeting reveal a headstrong young man, unafraid to proclaim his views. 'Before I begin to read my paper,' Panikkar said firmly, 'I should like to say that I am a Nationalist, and a Nationalist of what some of you would call an extreme type. I believe India should have Home Rule, immediate and entire. Unless you understand that point of view of mine, I do not think you will be able to appreciate or follow the arguments I have advanced in my paper.'[27]

Picking up on Macaulay's famous *Minute on Education*, Panikkar noted that the system of education introduced in India had broken with its unique culture and civilisation. It was not, he argued, the best example of Western influence on Indian society. Careful listeners picked up on the critique of English and on the lack of an alternative in Panikkar's essay. He was publicly and stingingly criticised for his intellectual shortcomings. In several speeches made later, British orientalists ridiculed his arguments. How, they demanded, could India claim to rise above its existent chaos without either English or Western intellectual influence? Both, after all, were invaluable to those who wanted to govern themselves one day.[28]

Panikkar sought refuge in angry defensiveness. In India, he retorted indignantly, there was a common and very ancient cultural base, essentially rooted in Hinduism. India's past had seen plenty of other influences, but it had not altered the 'fundamental core' constituted by Hinduism.[29] Besides, he added rather cleverly, 'is it not arguable that any language which comes to be the spoken and written language of a great people will soon adapt itself to scientific thought and expression?'[30]

It was hard to argue with this and even harder to argue with a young man as self-assured as Panikkar was learning to be. Not all of his best-known theories were formed at this time. Some of them would require considerable rejigging as India's freedom struggle progressed and as Panikkar himself grew older and wiser. Indeed, he would leave some of them behind altogether as the world changed and as India changed. But his university years provide a rich treasure trove of literature that would prove foundational for Panikkar's intellectual evolution. It was at Oxford, driven by his contact with fellow Indian students and the ongoing war, that he began to search for and develop an idea of India. It was a complex one, for he was young and impatient, and his nationalism was, at the same time, both traditionalist and open to evolution, while his affinity for his home state allowed him to always lay emphasis on diversity and coexistence.[31]

All in all, Panikkar's academic track record at Oxford was, to put it mildly, spectacular, silencing even the strongest of the critics in his family. Moreover, the move abroad had introduced him to the kind of networks he would never have been part of in Travancore and opened his eyes to a whole new world of culture, art and literature. His reading and newfound love of writing had given him clarity on subjects that he had been terrified by when he first arrived in England. More importantly, his own individual political ideology was evolving at this time. Still, for all his developing thoughts and ideas, and beneath the arrogant exterior, there was a strain of insecurity about his own intellectual worth. 'My professors were kind to me and commended my work,' the first Indian recipient of the prestigious Dixon Research Scholarship wrote humbly in 1917.

In the summer of that year, a jittery Panikkar sat his final examinations. A first class seemed almost too much to hope for. After all, Indians had been at Oxford for over three decades by then, yet only Kuruvilla Zachariah had ever won a first class. Everyone else had managed only seconds. Panikkar's already fragile sense of self-esteem seems to have been under severe pressure at this juncture. He became hyper-sensitive about his academic and intellectual worth. 'Most of the Indians at Oxford in my time being graduates with honours degrees from India were inclined to look upon a raw matriculate with a certain amount of patronage and to emphasise the inadequacies of his background,' he recalled. 'Resenting this attitude I challenged one of the most aggressive of them and said that whatever the handicap I started with, I would do better than him in the final examinations.'[32]

On 6 July 1917, a delighted Panikkar saw his name up on the rolls of honour. He was one of only four students that year to gain the coveted first in history. Dr Thomas Strong, then the dean—and a paternal figure to Panikkar—sent him a personal note, bursting with pride. 'You have worked so well and covered so much ground that I had high hopes,' he wrote, 'but I know how hard it must be to do papers in a strange language. I think you are one of the first Indians to appear in the first class in history and I am sincerely glad that you have achieved this distinction as a Christ Church man; but I am also extremely happy at the success of a friend.'[33]

Panikkar's years at Oxford were officially over. He was now a young man with considerable academic merit and a polished exterior. Photographs of the time show an unsmiling and bespectacled young man with thick dark hair combed flat against his head. He was all of twenty-three years old and it was time for him to set foot in the real world.

But the war was not yet over and would not be for another year. It was just as well then that Panikkar chose to stay on in England for some more time. He sent word to Kavalam that he would be doing a short semester's study in anthropology and Indian history, and began working as an assistant to Sir Vincent Smith, the celebrated historian and orientalist. Panikkar wasn't quite ready to return. For a man capable of assessing and evaluating subjects with forensic erudition, Panikkar's low sense of academic self-worth is oddly touching. His defence mechanism was a simple one: to immerse himself in his work, to try and improve even further.

With Smith, he hoped to have that opportunity for self-improvement. Smith had retired from the ICS in 1900 and had both during and after his time in service written on Indian art and archaeology. Now he was putting together a comprehensive (and controversial) history of India.

While he settled into a routine of working and studying, Panikkar continued to attend meetings at the Majlis and chat with the many brilliant minds that were passing through Oxford from the subcontinent. For instance, there was the wise, principled Sir Baron Jayathilake. Already known as the Gokhale of Ceylon, Jayathilake was the president of the Ceylon Congress and was in England to speak out against British excesses in his country. Tempted by the atmosphere of Oxford, he stayed on to study philosophy. Panikkar and he became excellent friends and underneath the cosmopolitan veneer, the younger man found a peaceful, erudite mind. A conservative nationalist like Panikkar himself, Jayathilake was deeply interested in social reform and education, working earnestly for the Buddhists of Ceylon. He would go on to become Ceylon's first prime minister. He was an excellent contact to have and most suitable for a mind as sharp as Panikkar's. Aided greatly by their chats in Jayathilake's room on campus, Panikkar bent his powerful mind to the further study of Indian nationalism. When Panikkar finally departed for Kavalam, he left a finished first draft with his friend, who surprised him by arranging for its publication in England.

Then there was Dr T.M. Nair, the well-known physician, editor and civil administrator, upon whom, by the sounds of it, Panikkar had a bit of a crush. 'There was never a manlier Malayali,' he wrote rapturously, before going on to lyrically describe Nair as having 'a leonine face, a long curving moustache, a curving chest, a portly figure and powerful arms,' not to mention '[a] breathtaking intellect and unmatched raconteuring skills'.[34] Physical fineness aside, Nair was something of a connoisseur of wines, cigars and the best kind of company, and he chose his audiences (as one can see) well. As the leader of the non-Brahmin caste movement in Travancore, Nair was passing through England with the goal of lobbying against the Montagu-Chelmsford report, which was being typed that winter. Panikkar didn't really know where he stood politically as far as the report was concerned, but he clearly saw no harm in befriending this compelling man. The friendship would stand him in good stead.

As with all good things, Panikkar's time in England had to come to an end. He booked his passage back to India on the *SS Tasman,* which was due to sail from London to Calcutta on 11 September 1918. He was very ready to go home, but his new friends were deeply concerned. The theatre of war had shifted from the land to the sea by 1917. German submarines were attacking ships in the North Atlantic and around the British Isles. The immediate effect of this strategy was that the United States had been forced into joining the war in the spring of 1917. Slowly, but surely, the tide was beginning to turn in favour of the Allies. Germany was poised for defeat, but it was going down fighting. At Danzig, U-43 submarines were being built at the speed of summer lightning—including the *SS Emden*, which would terrorise Madras. By 1918, the Kaiserliche Marine (Imperial German Navy) had 329 submarines, many focused on the British Isles, where Allied and American vessels were being sunk with impunity. The underlying idea was to cut off Britain's supply lines and starve the island into submission.

Panikkar's friends were of the firm opinion that, with matters poised quite so delicately, he would do well to wait just a little bit longer. They warned him of torpedoes, of submarines that swam silently but lethally below the ocean's surface. But Panikkar was fed up of England by then. The news from Kavalam was not good. His beloved grandmother, Kunjipilla Gouri, had passed away just a month or so earlier. He hadn't been at her side to bid her farewell or to see her one last time. Grief-stricken, Panikkar blamed himself for staying on longer than he had intended to, and he was determined to leave England by hook or by crook.

Chapter 7

Capsize

DUSK WAS FALLING WHEN THE ROPES ANCHORING THE BIG STEAMER TO the docks at Tilbury fell away. Panikkar was on the crowded, dank decks, jostled against the railing by fellow passengers. He had hoped for a fine evening so he could watch the coastline of England falling away, inch by inch, bathed in the golden glow of the setting sun. After all, he had no idea when or if he would ever return to this country—this capital of the empire—that had taught him so much. But that evening was true to English form, miserably cold with dense fog as the *Tasman* tooted mournfully through the mists as it turned out towards the sea.

'I was not without qualms,' Panikkar confessed later. 'The voyage through the submarine infested Atlantic was risky.'[1]

That was one reason for his qualms perhaps. Another reason was a letter from the family astrologer who warned ominously of a disaster at sea should he risk leaving for India immediately. Panikkar wasn't one to turn down a challenge: 'I decided to take the risk.'[2]

It wasn't a pleasant journey. To begin within, the date of departure had kept changing from 4 September to 12 September and then to 11 September. Once on board and at sea, passengers had to present their passports and steamer tickets and surrender their ration cards and prayer books. With visibility near zero, the *Tasman* hugged the coastline on the way to Plymouth, harbouring in safe coves overnight, first in Colborough and then in Tor Bay.

Trouble had begun almost as soon as she had sailed out of London. For one, the *Tasman* was too small to serve as a passenger steamer, and was in a state of dirty chaos and loud confusion. The cabins and the deck were equally filthy, giving off the peculiarly ripe smell that one associates with decaying garbage. So dirty were some of the tiny rooms that many of the more fastidious passengers refused point-blank to take their luggage into the mess. The crew and the stewards were in thunderingly bad moods, the cause for which was soon discovered. The *Tasman* had sailed short of five stewards and those on board were sulking at being forced to man an understaffed ship. The irate passengers—there seem to have been no women or children aboard—went to talk to the cantankerous captain, who promised to take on five more men when the ship docked at Plymouth. 'We started,' noted the Rev. George Woodford gloomily in his diary, 'but there was a bad spirit present all the time.'[3]

There were some happy moments, however. In the Solent for instance, the lights on the water, combined with those onshore and the searchlights nearby, created a fairytale luminescence that made the exhausted, irritable passengers forget for a while that they were on a ship in perilous waters. The joy was short-lived. So excited was someone to watch the waters of the ocean glowing in the dark that they forgot to switch off the lights in one of the cabins, making the *Tasman* a sitting duck for a few dangerous moments. The chief steward appeared on deck after a while, highly agitated and shouting at passengers to switch off their lights. 'You know, the naval authorities here would think nothing of putting a shot through an unauthorised light in these waters,'[4] Woodford noted.

The reverend, who was on his way to India himself, was an observant man and, going by his diary, was fond of chatting to his fellow passengers. Panikkar is mentioned in the diary that survives as 'a young Indian, returning after some years at Oxford'.[5]

Later that night, when the lights in the ocean had faded and as the passengers filed below deck, they noticed that all the notices were written in Dutch, for the *Tasman* was a Dutch boat. More chaos ensued until a guesswork system of sorts was organised so that people didn't get confused. In the cabins themselves, the hot water system was non-existent, yielding only a few belches of steam. For safety reasons, all the lights on board were turned off by seven o'clock every evening. Nobody was allowed to turn them on again, so if you needed to go to the bathroom at night, you had to grope in the dark.

The *Tasman* had no escort on her journey, but at no time did the ship venture more than three or four miles away from the coast, an indicator of just how dangerous this part of the voyage was. Even less reassuring was the captain himself, 'a very elusive individual' whom the passengers rarely saw, except one night when he deigned to take his dinner with the rest of them. Even then, Woodford recalled, he barely spoke to his passengers. 'The discomforts of wartime travel were inevitable,' Panikkar wrote later, 'the constant threat of enemy action was an intolerable burden.'[6]

This was evident almost every day. At Plymouth Harbour, the ships lay quiet in the water, all of them so heavily camouflaged that they were difficult to spot. In addition to the 600 bags of mail and 100 tonnes of fresh water that were brought stealthily onto the *Tasman*, the passengers were considerably disconcerted to find the bloodied and bandaged survivors of a bombing being brought on board.

Agitated questioning yielded the knowledge that the *Galway Castle*, a destroyer that had been converted to a hospital ship, had been torpedoed by a German U-82 submarine two days away from safe harbour at Plymouth. The seas had been stormy that day, and in the panicked rush to abandon ship, several lifeboats had been swallowed by the mighty waves. The U-82 had slunk off after breaking the *Galway Castle* in half. No further submarines returned to attack and as Spitfires hovered anxiously overhead, the *Galway Castle* continued to wallow where she lay for another three days, until help arrived.

Now, as survivors filed on board the *Tasman*, Panikkar looked upon sights he had never seen before and hoped profoundly he would never see again. The *Galway Castle* had been carrying 400 walking wounded and 200 families. The survivors were mostly women and children, and for hours, the quiet morning air was ripped by the sounds of children screaming as they ran about searching for parents who were either lost or missing.

There was no time to wait, no time to search.

At dawn on 17 September 1918, the *Tasman* slipped out of Plymouth, making for the high seas, once again cloaked in thick mist. But this time, when the fog lifted, her passengers saw that they were no longer alone. They were now part of a thirteen-ship convoy escorted by Allied destroyers that sailed on the outer edges of the formation. If war had lurked in the background all this while, the events of the last few hours had wrenched it into the foreground. Fear was a palpable presence on board the *Tasman*. Panikkar was acutely aware of it, particularly as he remembered his family astrologer's agitated warning.

Somewhere during the middle of the day, the *Tasman*'s military escort slipped away, leaving them to sail on through ominously quiet waters. The silence lasted a handful of hours. Panikkar would recall that 18 September began as it ordinarily would have. At 3.30 p.m., the bell rang for tea. Many passengers, cold and hungry in the damp mist of the sea, went down to get themselves a hot cup of tea and a biscuit if they were lucky. Having had his tea, Panikkar went to his cabin to try and get some sleep. He had barely closed his eyes when a massive boom rocked the ship, shaking him awake. Chaos erupted as the *Tasman* tipped slowly and unmistakably to one side. It had been hit by a torpedo.

There was no time to think, no time to feel anything except cold terror and panic, no time to hear anything except shouts above the creaks of the dying ship. Panikkar managed to scramble out of his cabin and stagger up to the deck. The glass in the windows had shattered inwards, and shards carpeted the floor, slicing into the bare feet of those who had forgotten to wear their shoes. There was a sudden heave as Panikkar reached the upper deck, and the *Tasman* listed even more to her side.

There should have been even more chaos. But there was, as Woodford remembered, absolute silence. 'Nobody said a word. We all knew what had happened … I noticed how white and tense everybody's face was … I wondered if my face was like all the others.'[7]

As everyone scrambled towards the railings that would take them to the open air, the floor heaved under their feet and the air was rent with a shrieking, creaking sound.

The *Tasman* had broken in half.

The ship lurched again, flinging everyone hard against the wall. The incline of the stairs went from horizontal to vertical so fast that many people lost their grip and slipped. The silence of just a few minutes earlier shattered with screams. Panikkar managed to climb up to the deck, aware suddenly that he was freezing. In his panic, he had forgotten to put on anything save his thin shirt and pajamas. The wind was sharp, cutting through his clothes.

Rain was coming.

He could see it in terrifying slow motion in the skies. On deck meanwhile, lifeboats were being lowered. Half the ship was already under water and the other half was sinking fast. The captain, now very much in evidence, was shouting at the men left on board. Panikkar forced himself to listen—they were being ordered to jump off straight into the iron-grey, roiling waters below. The decks were flooding, slick with a dangerous mix of oil and water. Panikkar knew how to swim just as well as he knew that he stood no chance against the Atlantic Ocean. But there was no time to think. He had to leap overboard and try to strike out for the boats in the water. In those churning waters, slick with the oil leaking from the *Tasman*, people were clinging to the boats for dear life, 'like bloaters on a string'.[8] Panikkar never knew or understood the mix of blind terror and instinct that got him to the lifeboat. He was dragged out of the water by several pairs of hands. As his boat bobbed out into the water, there was a vast splintering sound. The *Tasman* had gone, sunk underwater.

He realised then, as he stared blankly at the spot where the ship had been just a few moments ago, that he was cold—colder than he had ever been before. He had nothing with him—his trunks, his books, his clothes, the letters he had kept from friends and loved ones over the years, all of that had gone to the bottom of the sea. The light was fading, rain was pelting down and there was no help in sight. The *Tasman*'s mast, rigging and wireless were still visible, bobbing through the waves, black silhouettes against grey skies. Someone would tell

Panikkar later that in total, it took four minutes for the ship to vanish. But in that space of time, there was an eternity of horror. Woodford recorded seeing the silhouette of a man—still alive, still trapped on board—his arms flailing against the porthole as the *Tasman* continued to sink. Trunks floated to the surface, bobbing uselessly in the water. Wailing and shrieking filled the air. Before long, darkness set in. The furious roar of the waves and the eerie whistle of the wind over the restless sea was something that Panikkar, even as he clung to the fast-fading hope that they would be saved, never forgot.

The *Colaba*—the main ship in the convoy—had vanished.

They were alone.

Soon, the lifeboat began filling with water. It was already crammed beyond capacity with thirty people in various stages of undress and terror, and barely able to float. The churning of the water, the bobbing of the boat, the screams of passengers for their loved ones, for help, all made Panikkar feel terribly sick. 'We rushed up one side of the waves,' recalled Woodford, '… hung for a giddy moment on their crests, and then down the opposite slope into a deep gulf, before we began the next ascent.'[9]

It seemed as though forever had passed before the waters began to calm and the rain began to slow. At some point the clouds parted to reveal a clear, full moon hanging over one end of the horizon. On the other side, Panikkar—who was steadily descending into hypothermia—remembered seeing a rainbow glisten brightly. The wind kept up, a stream of cold that chilled his bones. There was a desperate silence, the kind that falls only when there is no hope left. Then, sometime towards dusk, the waters parted yet again.

A submarine had surfaced.

Nobody knew whether this was the submarine that had torpedoed the *Tasman*. Everyone was beyond caring. Some passengers, beside themselves with fear, tried to hail the submarine and had to be forcibly prevented in case the U-82 renewed fire. She didn't, sinking silently instead below the surface of the sea. As the moon slid behind a thick bank of clouds, darkness fell, leaving the shivering passengers to try and steer by instinct alone. They had no food, save for one cask of water and one tin of biscuits per lifeboat. Tempers began to fray, with the Australian crew freely cursing everyone. By midnight, storm clouds began to scud overhead, pushed by the winds. Rain began to sheet down again.

It was altogether too much for Panikkar.

Frozen to the bone, soaked and hopeless, he passed out. He came out of his faint sometime later, covered in a wet rug, to shouts of 'A light! A light!' Struggling back to consciousness, he focused and saw the faint lights of a ship on the horizon. Nobody knew to whom the ship belonged, Germany or the Allies, but it was better than nothing. Panikkar sat up to watch, screwing his eyes up against the wind and the rain.

It was nothing: a passing submarine that left massive waves in its wake. Close to tears, Panikkar passed out again. When he awoke, it was morning, and the leaders of each boat were handing out one sip of water and one biscuit each.

The morning was clear, with calm blue waters and a gently shining sun, but no help in sight. Towards midday, hope awoke among the survivors again as smoke was spied on the horizon. One of the boats hoisted a boathook with handkerchiefs tied to it and another raised an oar. Yet again, it was nothing, 'leaving us all a bit sick', Woodford wrote in his diary.[10] Towards afternoon, when the sun was growing rather fierce, an American ship hove in sight. The nightmare was over.

Fifty-two survivors out of an estimated 273 passengers were taken back to England on board the *USS Talbot*, many of them ill and injured. Panikkar drifted in and out of consciousness. He didn't remember the journey back or the fact that the *Tasman* had sunk off Cape Villano on the west coast of Spain. His mind carefully blanked out his illness in England, an illness so severe that it was a full two weeks before he could summon the energy to write a letter to his family at home. In fact, the older Panikkar would rarely mention the episode at all—a measure of how much he had lost and how desperately it had affected him.

As soon as he was physically able, despite the advice of his doctors, he pulled himself out of bed and booked the next passage back to India.

He could stand to be here no longer.

PART III

Aligarh (1919–1922)

Chapter 8

Return

PANIKKAR RETURNED TO A COUNTRY THAT HAD BEEN IRREVOCABLY transformed by the tides of nationalism and war. He returned too to a home that had changed during his time away. His grandmother—his confidante and childhood saviour—was no longer there to welcome him. In England, he had managed to put away the grief as one folds clothes away into a cupboard. But coming back home only served for it to tumble out again. In the manner that would become typical of this new adult Panikkar, deep emotion would always be intellectualised. It was the best way he could deal with feelings that were otherwise better left unstudied. He turned his attention instead to the events that were taking place in Travancore and across the country.

The state at that moment was crippled by a famine. Panikkar would later lament the gap in public memory, saying that in the ordeal of the Second World War, one often forgot the damage caused by the First World War. 'To the unfortunate sufferers,' he wrote later, 'this was an ordeal indeed.'[1]

The famine was largely driven by natural geography, a change in occupations from agricultural to non-agricultural and developing trade networks. Besides, Malabar and Travancore repeatedly experienced flash floods due to excess monsoons, which destroyed standing crops, washed off food stocks and other belongings, and plunged the entire population into famine. After the British occupation, the state was increasingly handicapped in meeting its food demand even during years of better harvests as large areas of the surplus-producing Wayanad taluk, for instance, were converted into plantation estates. Despite attempts to salvage the situation, like the introduction of tapioca as a substitute for rice, things became worse after the arrival of European planters who began to plant coffee instead of rice. 'The price of rice has been mounting fearfully last week,' complained *The Hindu* on 19 December 1918. 'In view of the distress due to high prices, Dewan Krishnan Nair left yesterday on tour to meet food advisory committees ... to afford the people instantaneously such relief as may be suggested'.[2]

The Panikkar family's wealth and prestige in the community meant that the famine didn't touch them in the ways it did many other not so fortunate families. But for young Panikkar, it was the reality check he needed now that he was back on home ground. Living in England and writing about abstract (though important) concepts like citizenship and immigration was one thing, but being back in India and witnessing the changes the country was going through was quite another. In the aftermath of the war, Indian soldiers—sent to fight overseas for a king and another country—were returning in droves. Along with them came the dreaded Spanish flu, which would grip the country between 1918 and 1920. India was struggling under immense national debt, war loans and taxes, a fluctuating rupee-sterling exchange rate, import cuts and soaring inflation. Standards of living and consumption declined significantly, but at the same time, crises for some meant lucrative opportunities for others. For instance, there was no increase in real wages that corresponded to increased wartime production, even though the cost of living rose sharply. As India grew restless under these strains, Edwin Montagu, then the secretary of state for India, arrived in the country in the autumn of 1917. His predecessors had never visited the colony they were responsible for, but Montagu travelled the length of the land, from prince to province, interviewing politicians and kings so he could begin drafting the way forward for India's political future. This move laid the foundation for constitutional reform in India as well as administrative change and an increase in visibility on the international stage. In 1917, India was summoned to participate in the Imperial War Cabinet to discuss financing and administrative recruitment from the colonies, the issue of peace and the troubled matter of dominion status (which had been granted to Australia, New Zealand, South Africa and Canada but denied to India).[3]

India's representatives to the cabinet were the tall, flamboyant and urbane Maharaja Ganga Singh of Bikaner and the sharp Bengali barrister Sir Satyendra Sinha. Their presence at the cabinet meetings left a lasting impact on Whitehall. On the one hand, Bikaner paid attention to ceremonial protocols like the maharaja inspecting a royal guard of honour in London with Jan Smuts, the South African statesman soon to become prime minister of his country. On the other hand, Sinha expressed the startling hope that sooner rather than later India would be represented by an Indian rather than by an English secretary of state. Indeed, he went so far as to say that one day, he hoped to see an Indian prime minister at the helm of affairs in New Delhi.[4]

For Panikkar, this was a wildly interesting development, and he looked, quite naturally, for some kind of momentum reflected on the ground in his own home state. He was astonished to discover a distinct lack of interest in the national movement. Travancore was going through its own social and economic upheavals, which would result in not only the emergence of the state's first Leftist movement in the early 1920s, but also in the rise of organised local politics in a few years. The general feeling seemed to be that it had enough on its plate without also paying attention to what was happening in faraway New Delhi. Panikkar disagreed vociferously, convinced even then that the princes could be brought closer to the nationalist movement. Montagu's arrival and the eventual drafting of the Montford Report surely represented a moment for the princes to make a case for their position and place within the Indian political structure.[5]

His nascent thoughts on this, however, had to be temporarily abandoned. His mother wanted him, as mothers do, to marry and settle down as soon as possible. Padmanabha was already married to the solemn-faced, quiet Janaki, the daughter of their eldest uncle.

Panikkar's bride had been chosen: Eravi Ayyappa Panikkar's eldest daughter, Gouri Amma.

An early photograph of the brothers with their respective wives, taken in Madras in 1919, shows two young men, the elder one quite tall, the other of average height. Both are dressed in simple white kurta pyjama. The resemblance between the two is uncanny. Both have thick, dark hair and eyebrows and sport rather spectacular moustaches. Their wives, Janaki and Gouri, are seated side by side on a sofa in front of them. Janaki has long, thick, straight dark hair tied away from a heavy-browed face. Gouri is a small lady, quite obviously young, neat in her appearance, with dark crimped hair and a solemn face.

According to Panikkar, Gouri had lived at Kavalam since the age of ten. 'My grandmother and mother were especially attached to her.'[6] She was a quiet girl, preoccupied mostly with affairs of the kitchen and the garden. She spoke no English and had never been outside Kavalam. But by all accounts, she had been informed of her marital prospects much earlier than her prospective husband. When news of the *Tasman* being torpedoed had reached Kavalam, Gouri had offered prayers for Panikkar's safety at the local Devi temple along with the rest of the family. Theirs was a simple wedding, held quietly and without fuss. Panikkar acknowledged his young wife's gaucheness quite directly, betraying—whether he liked to admit it or not—a degree of confident sexism. 'I was not unaware that living abroad or in other parts of India with a wife lacking in English education would present difficulties.'[7]

There is also ambition in that single sentence. Panikkar may have done his familial duty by marrying according to his mother's wishes, but he had no desire to spend his life buried in Kavalam, attending to land reclamation and paddy cultivation like his uncles. There was, in his opinion, too much happening on the national and international front for that.

In June 1918, a month before the Montford Report was due to be published and some months before Panikkar returned to India, the Indian delegates to the Imperial War Cabinet had been getting truculent. Apart from the issue of the war's economic and human consequences, which the delegates felt needed to be addressed, there was the question of how much influence the dominions and India would have in shaping common imperial policy after the war. It was a decision that the empire visibly dithered over. India may have been slowly making its way towards self-government, but with its mix of religions and languages, Prime Minister Lloyd George doubted whether it would ever be able to manage on its own. The were no nationalist leaders in the Indian delegation to the cabinet—a factor that only made it rather more disappointing in Whitehall's eyes. Only on 4 December 1918 would the British prime minister finally agree to add India's name to the list of other dominions assembling for peace talks after the war.

In July 1918, the Montford Report was published. Along the lines of Lionel Curtis's thinking, the report advocated dyarchy: a programme of limited autonomy (subject to that convenient legal and legislative loophole of a 'review') to the provinces. Nobody knew whether dyarchy would work in India. Certainly, William Marris, colonial India's first reforms commissioner, felt it was highly unsuitable for India's unique political conditions. That same year, a Sedition Committee headed by Sir Sidney Rowlatt was set up to define terrorism in the colony. The results of that would be cataclysmic.

All that was some months in the future though.

For now, Panikkar had more pragmatic considerations. Gouri and he were currently in Madras, from where they visited Paliavaram, the cantonment town where Panikkar's brother was the head of the military hospital.

It wasn't exactly a honeymoon.

Panikkar needed to find a job, and his brother was ready with a potential appointment. It seemed that before his return from England, C. Ramalinga Reddy, Padmanabha's friend and then the inspector general of education in Mysore, had heard of Madhava, the brilliant younger Panikkar sibling. Known for his high sense of principles and integrity, Reddy had an excellent reputation in the world of education and to be on his radar at such a young age was no mean feat. Recognising this for the opportunity it was, Panikkar left Gouri in Madras with Padmanabha and Janaki and went post-haste to Bangalore to meet Reddy. The meeting was almost instantly fruitful, with Reddy informing the younger man helpfully that a crisis was developing at the prestigious Mohammedan Anglo-Oriental College (MOAC; now Aligarh Muslim University or AMU) in Aligarh. All the European professors had resigned in the aftermath of the war, primarily due to denial of tenure and charges that the authorities were interfering in their work. The university authorities declined to appoint Indians from European universities in their stead. If Panikkar was keen, Reddy suggested, he had already spoken to Sir Ross Masood to include his name as a possible professorial candidate.

Now, in those days, Panikkar had no idea of what MOAC represented, apart from its reputation as a 'leading private education institution in India'.[8] He had even less idea of who Sir Ross Masood was, but he *was* perfectly aware that in times such as these, to be selected as a Hindu to teach at a predominantly Muslim university was significant. He lost no time in agreeing to the post. Delighted, Reddy dashed off a letter of introduction so Panikkar could meet Syed Ross Masood, then director of education in Hyderabad state and a figure of some power in MOAC. Dutifully, Panikkar went next to Hyderabad.

It was his first visit to princely Hyderabad and he was simultaneously charmed and intrigued by its unique blend of mystique and modernism. In her classic account of the state, the travel writer Elizabeth Cooper described it lyrically as 'the most Eastern city in this most Eastern land'.[9] It was a city of zenanas, gold souks, marigolds and elephants, but it was also a state witnessing the last decades of the seventh nizam.

Osman Ali Khan had been twenty-one years old when he was anointed Mir Osman Ali Khan Asaf Jah VII in 1911. A quiet, serious young man, he had been greatly sheltered, by his mother, from his more flamboyant father, Mahboob Ali Khan. So little had he been seen in the days of his father that when he did emerge into the light of day, the Raj had no idea what to make of him. Little did it know that the young Nizam had some definite ideas of his own. He hadn't been allowed to participate in the activities of his state by his father, but he had been a keen observer. Aware of the extravagance defining his father's reign, Osman Ali Khan had grown up to be a pinchpenny worthy of Ebenezer Scrooge. But he was equally known for his progressive reforms, for breaking the power of the nobility and taking charge of his own administration, besides reorganising the revenue department and organising judicial reforms to bring the courts of Hyderabad in line with the rest of India.

In the aftermath of the Great War then, Hyderabad was a state on the cusp of modernity, staffed by officials who were as progressive as the Nizam himself. Panikkar was keen to meet Masood, about whom he had hastily read up, and sought him out almost immediately upon his arrival. The meeting was serendipitous, for Panikkar had only to lay eyes on Masood to adore him instantly.

Syed Ross Masood had returned to India from Oxford—after a passionate affair with the novelist E.M. Forster—in 1911. Born in 1889, he was the grandson of the famous reformer Sir Syed Ahmed Khan, who had founded MOAC in 1875. Its establishment was seen as the first organised response by the Indian Muslims to events in the wider world following the occurrences of 1857. Unsurprisingly, its mission statement was elitist. Sir Syed, for example, told the Hunter Education Commission in 1852 that the purpose of MAOC was to 'form a class of persons, Mohammedan in religion, Indian in blood and colour, but English in tastes, opinions and intellect'.[10] More than elitism though, the statement was revealing in its attempt to navigate two waters—the appeasement of the Muslim public and that of the Raj. For all the generations of Masoods, education was a vital instrument for the cause of Muslim nationalism, prompting the orientalist Sir Hamilton Gibb to describe MOAC as the first 'modernist institution' in India.[11]

After Sir Syed's death, Ross's father had suffered a mental breakdown, prompting Sir Theodore Morrison, MOAC's principal at the time, to adopt young Ross and dispatch him to England. It was also Morrison, then extremely friendly with the Forsters, who invited E.M. Forster to coach Masood in Latin. The relationship that ensued changed both men profoundly and is a story for another time and day, but by 1918, Masood was back in India, having abandoned a career in law for a much more successful one in education. That year, he became director of public instruction in Hyderabad, where he was instrumental in the founding of Osmania University and, after his recce trips to Japan, for pushing for the introduction of the vernacular as a medium of public instruction.[12] When Panikkar met him in the spring of 1918, Masood was at the peak of his powers and influence, charming everyone he met from Bombay to Hyderabad. 'This splendid young giant has stormed the citadel of the Arabian Nights by his charms and frank, breezy personality!'[13] Sarojini Naidu wrote enthusiastically to Syed Mahmud. He certainly stormed the citadel of Panikkar's emotions from the start. 'From the day we met to the day of his death, he was like a brother to me. I never had any friend who showed me so much affection.'[14]

Masood's intelligence and charisma won Panikkar's admiration, leading him to lyrically describe him in his memoir as 'a giant, physically and intellectually—six foot three and 290 pounds'.[15] With this rapturous beginning, there was no doubt that the visit to Hyderabad would have been anything but a tremendous success. For Panikkar, it was an eye-opening visit that gave him keen insight into how much power a long-sighted official could hold in a state if given the right headway. The visit ended in Masood writing enthusiastically to Nawab Mohammad Ali in Aligarh to finalise Panikkar's appointment at MOAC.

With their friendship firmly cemented, the two men returned to Madras together, travelling with Sir Akbar Hydari, then the finance minister in Hyderabad. The three men stayed for a couple of days with Sir Abdur Rahim, the then chief justice of Madras. A man with a serious face and an imposing moustache, Rahim was a successful barrister and educationist, eventually becoming an influential member of the Muslim League and the author of a critically acclaimed treatise on Muslim jurisprudence.

It was an interesting time to be in Madras, bringing Panikkar into close contact with the stream of political consciousness that was working to define a definite sense of Muslim nationalism. The Southborough Committee, a seven-member committee with three Indian members, Surendranath Banerjea, V.S. Srinivasa Sastri and Sahibzada Aftab Ahmad Khan, was in the city, working on delimitation and the question of franchise under the Montford Report. The committee ran headlong into lobbies it hadn't expected, such as the suffragettes, who had already petitioned the committee for equal rights (these weren't granted, even though members like Sastri were pro-rights, because it was felt there wasn't adequate demand). B.R. Ambedkar testified too, independently and cogently, that there must be representation for untouchables in the legal and constitutional process.

Staying with Hydari throughout the remainder of 1918, Panikkar met many interesting and prominent personalities, including the nationalist leader Surendranath Banerjea. He had heard much about Banerjea—he was the man who had fired the people of Bengal with patriotic fervour and shaken the cool Lord Curzon himself. At the height of his political influence, Banerjea had been a strong proponent of autonomy within a British Commonwealth, an academic with a somewhat chequered career, an effective orator, and a firm believer in representative government and progress by constitutional means. But Panikkar's first meeting with the older man appears to have been a disappointment. By 1919, Banerjea had left the Congress to found the Indian Liberation Foundation, and was effectively on the sidelines in terms of a political career.[16] Panikkar, who had heard what Banerjea had once been capable of, had rather naively been expecting a more charismatic person than this short, thin man, with his heavily lined face. But that initial disappointment was short-lived. Surendranath Banerjea was an old man now, but he was rarely without a gleam of wry humour in his eyes. He worked extremely hard and kept a tight schedule, getting up at four in the morning for a two-mile walk every day. Banerjea was a likeable man—patriotic and opinionated—but Panikkar didn't like was what he saw as the older man's persecution complex. 'I soon realised that he was the victim of an obsession.'[17]

Just what Banerjea was obsessing over and why, Panikkar does not tell us. Nor does he seem to have gone back to collect Gouri from his brother's home. Clearly there were other people to meet and places to go. One evening, when Masood and he were strolling down Mount Road, a short, erect figure came down the steps of Higginbotham's bookshop. Panikkar had never met Sir C.P. Ramaswami Aiyar in person, although the latter had written the foreword to Panikkar's *The Problems of Greater India*. This meeting stayed with Panikkar forever. Aiyar was still young at forty, but he led the kind of life that made for technicolour retelling. Apart from his sartorial fineness and his legal brilliance, Aiyar kept a fine stable and a bevy of Alsatians and Pomeranians whom he adored.

When Panikkar met him, Aiyar had just transitioned into politics, joining the Congress. As the nationalist B. Pattabhi Sitaramayya rapturously put it, Aiyar was 'the one star on the Congress firmament, flooding the horizon of Indian politics with his radiance'.[18] This may have been pushing the envelope a tad, but in truth, the meetings in Madras, from Aiyar to Banerjea, set Panikkar up with some crucial connections and political networks that would come in handy during his career. Somewhere towards February 1919, Panikkar seems to have decided that the stay in Madras had served its purpose. It was time to travel across the country for a while to see what else might be professionally on offer.

He went to Delhi, once again leaving Gouri behind to stay with his brother in Paliavaram. She seems to have made no demur at this. Their marriage was still far too fresh and with all his constant travelling, there had been little time to get to know her new husband. Nor was Panikkar keen to know his wife—at least just yet. He was far too fixated on getting himself some kind of professional foothold. As he stepped off the train in New Delhi, he was looking ahead to newer opportunities. The new imperial capital was nothing like Panikkar had envisioned it to be. Gone was its cosmopolitan bustle. As Whitehall tabled what would become the Rowlatt Act, which would give the police the power to arrest nationalists without any specific reason, Delhi was a city waiting for an inevitable blow. 'The atmosphere had the even temperature of set determination,' Panikkar would recall later. 'Hope had fled from both sides.'[19]

Just what the death of that hope would portend would be made clear in only a few weeks. Meanwhile, a letter arrived in the post. MOAC had written to him, asking him to come to Aligarh for his interview. It was a formality: everyone knew that, coming as he did with glowing recommendations from Sir Ross Masood himself, Panikkar's appointment was assured. Following the interview, he returned to Madras briefly to pick up Gouri and pack up the scattered, sketchy beginnings of their new home.

As the Panikkars stepped off the train onto the bustling platform at Aligarh, Gandhi launched a nationwide protest against the Rowlatt Act. The act, described by Gandhi to the Ali brothers' legal advisor O.S. Ghate as 'damnable',[20] sparked off the struggles that would end in bloodshed in a narrow street in Amritsar.

Chapter 9

Aligarh

PANIKKAR DAMNS GENERAL REGINALD DYER AS A 'MILITARY MANIAC'.[1] But though the massacre at Jallianwala Bagh left India horrified and furious, the British Empire and the world at large were too busy to pay much attention the slaughter of Indian 'natives'.

Internationally, the empire was looking at the rise of pan-Islamic power, a trend that would change the history of the world. Within India, the pro-Turkish and pan-Islamic movement had begun to develop an institutional basis with the formation of a Khilafat Committee in March 1919. The labour movement led by M.N. Roy was seeing popular leadership, with the All-India Trade Union Committee (AITUC) holding its inaugural session in 1920, even as the empire suspected a Russian hand dicing with the communists in India.

At the same time, the Great War had irrevocably changed the country. The Spanish flu had arrived on Indian soil, crops had failed, prices were soaring, famines had been declared in Bundelkhand and Travancore. Champaran's indigo farmers were restless—surplus wheat stocks had been seized under the Defence of India Act, and many villages, especially in Punjab, were mourning their dead and looking after their dying.

As different political ideologies and goals jostled for attention within the country, the Indian delegation to the Paris Peace

Conference arrived on the damp streets of Paris. Nearly every race was present except, as a German journalist wrote, 'the palest ivory yellow, coffee-coloured brow, deep black'.[2] The Indian delegation was represented by Edwin Montagu, Ganga Singh of Bikaner and Satyendra Sinha of Bengal and had a vision of limited autonomy. All three men wanted India to stay within the ambit of the empire. In fact Sinha, having been given a peerage just before the conference started, was subdued, unlike his belligerent self during the meetings of the Imperial War Cabinet.

But the conference was, in the eyes of those in India, a distraction. Much to Panikkar's rage, Jallianwala Bagh was barely mentioned in the war cabinet's *British Empire and Africa Report* for the week ending 15 April 1919. The report merely mentioned 'trouble' in Amritsar and laughably stated 'that troops had been called in to restore order'. There was no mention of a massacre.

In Paris, Jallianwala Bagh wasn't mentioned at all.

Given everything that was happening in India and the world at the time then, it is small wonder that Panikkar felt a strong sense of dissonance. He had not actively participated in any political meetings since he had arrived in Aligarh, nor had he written anything particularly riveting. But in May, he hadn't been able to resist going to Delhi to attend a private party meeting of the Home Rule League. 'The object of the meeting was to consider the advisability of fighting the new elections on a party basis,' he recalled later.[3] Nothing came of the meeting and Panikkar knew that to continue appearing at these political meetings and dinners would be fatal to his new job. He was a pragmatist at heart and he had a young wife to take care of, not to mention a career to establish.

But barely a month in, he was already dissatisfied.

On the face of it, Panikkar had nothing really to complain about. Life was pleasant enough in Aligarh. He was finally getting a chance to live the quiet dreams he had had when he was a boy in school, recovering from his suicide attempt. He had books, a room of his own, and ample time to write, read and think. The company and conversations at MOAC were erudite, the faculty members were paid well and had a few months' vacation each year. He was a naturally good teacher, bringing the informality and erudition of Oxford to the more formal, hierarchical world of Indian academia. 'We did not know till then that a professor could also be a personal friend and deal with his students not from an Olympian height—like a God condescending to rather inferior mortals!—but in a man-to-man relationship like a "normal human being",' marvelled one of his students.[4] Panikkar's manners were easy and he wore his own erudition lightly, making it easy for keen young students to approach him or to sit in his study and discuss politics, history and philosophy with him. His days began early and usually continued well into the evening. He had always liked the 'open doors' he had encountered in Oxford, and he kept the principle going during his days as a lecturer. Students found him both friendly and chatty, characterised by what Panikkar himself called his 'undergraduate flippancy',[5] but woe betide anyone who tried to push his boundaries. 'Anyone who ever tried to get round the rules or indulge in any kind of "hanky-panky" found him suavely blocking the way with chapter and verse!'[6]

In a manner that was rapidly becoming typical of the man, Panikkar involved himself almost immediately with every committee and council the university had to offer. This left him very little time to spend at home with Gouri. We don't know if he asked Gouri how she felt about leaving Kavalam for the first time in her life, but Radha Mohan, the sole surviving Panikkar child, recalled that in the early days in Aligarh, Gouri was uncomfortably out of her depth.[7] She was by nature a reserved young woman and her joy was in the kitchen and in manufacturing a garden for herself wherever she went. She spoke no Hindi or English in those days. Panikkar airily paid no attention to this. 'Women learn the art of housekeeping as birds take to the air and fishes to water,' he wrote breezily. 'I have never had a second thought about this problem since.'[8]

In this remarkably chauvinist statement (written in 1955 and at a time when he was the father of no fewer than four daughters), he spoke the truth. Panikkar rarely paid attention to matters of the kitchen and the home, as long as everything was running smoothly. In the early days of their marriage, he wasn't really interested in spending too much time with his young wife. Gouri was still very innocent in the ways of the world. She didn't read as widely as her scholarly husband (yet!) and if the Masoods hadn't taken her under their kindly wing, Gouri may well have been hopelessly adrift. But Mrs Masood gave Gouri the gentle training and direction she needed in order to be more polished. Panikkar seems to have left them to it, focusing instead on what he was more interested in at the time: writing and thinking.

The pen would always be Panikkar's first weapon of choice and in his years at Aligarh, he produced yet another trove of literature across subjects in politics and history. He wrote in the early hours of the morning and late into the night when the house was asleep and the world quiet. His days were preoccupied with navigating inter-departmental rivalries, the petty kind that are intrinsic to the world of academia. The politics at MOAC were bitterly fractious. There were ongoing spats, mostly over political ideology and professional commitments, between Aftab Ahmad Khan (described by the historian David Lelyveld as 'aloof and humorous but with a passionate moral intensity and a desire to be of service to AMU's goals'[9]), the more introverted Ziauddin Khan and the militant Ali brothers Mohammad Ali Jauhar and Shaukat Ali. Of the four, Ziauddin had not taken to Panikkar for reasons that have been lost to history, though one of his students recalled that Panikkar's colleagues felt 'slightly overshadowed by him'.[10] The upshot of all of this was that a current of friction buzzed under otherwise excellent friendships. Mohammad Ali and Panikkar in particular became great friends. Ali would play an important role in Panikkar's first steps into the wider political universe of the nationalist movement. But at MOAC, as Panikkar wrote, 'It was I, an "infidel" who stood as witness to the marriage of Nawab Mohammad Ali's son, Azad.'[11] Another kindly friend was the older, urbane Raja of Mahmudabad, then the vice chancellor of the MOAC.

Apart from everyday irritants, Panikkar acknowledged that his time at the university was useful. 'My stay at Aligarh extended over three years, but it covered a very important period in that institution's history,' he wrote later, 'as it witnessed the crisis arising from the Khilafat and the non-cooperation movement, and the transformation of the Mohammedan Anglo-Oriental College into the Muslim University.'[12]

Rising nationalism had an inevitable impact on the university's students. Panikkar had a glimpse of this when he asked the second-year students of the undergraduate class to write a paper on 'The Most Eminent Living Indian'. To his pleasant surprise, nearly every student (except two) wrote about Pandit Madan Mohan Malaviya, who had shot into the headlines that year for his investigation of the truth behind Jallianwala Bagh (which the British were trying to suppress) and the presentation of his report in the Imperial Legislative Council of Punjab (Lahore) in September 1919, in which he flatly contradicted the findings of the Hunter Commission that had been constituted to investigate the massacre in Amritsar. 'The young students had forgotten Malaviya's Hindu orthodoxy in the gratitude he had earned for his heroic and almost single-handed work in exposing the atrocities in the Punjab. At that time, one could almost sense the growing sense of independence.'[13]

On the other side of the campus was the new National Muslim University that would grow into the Jamia Millia Islamia, housed in a rented bungalow, where Muslim students debated pan-Islamist ideas and ideologies fervently.

With politics as febrile as they were, Panikkar quickly realised that the peace of an academic life was but an illusion. He was also fast coming to the conclusion that as much as he enjoyed the *thought* of being an academic, he had no desire to take it up as a profession, much less at Aligarh. The internal politics, he was discovering, was a little too fraught for his liking, especially as 'a Hindu professor in a Muslim college'.[14]

More importantly, he realised that he had no desire to bury himself in books and oblivion. 'My main problem was how to enter politics.'[15]

As a statement, this is revealing. Not for Panikkar the life of an ICS official or a powerful bureaucrat. No, he wanted an active say in Indian politics and the shaping of his country's future. He could see even then that the country was gaining some much needed international visibility. On 28 June 1919, the Treaty of Versailles had been signed in the Hall of Mirrors. There had been last minute panic about whether Ganga Singh or Satyendra Sinha should be allowed to sign. Eventually, the decision was made by the king. George V thought that the pen should be handed to his old friend and shooting partner, the Maharaja of Bikaner. And so it was that Bikaner, in his gold turban and British military uniform, signed the treaty that brought peace to the world—and laid the foundation for a much darker future. Six months later, India took its seat in Woodrow Wilson's League of Nations, based on Bikaner's strong advocacy: 'Where it is a question of securing the peace of the world, the important fact must be borne in mind that India represents one-fifth of the entire human race.'[16]

It was a milestone. For the first time, India's role and weight in the empire had been underlined—and it had been done by the ruler of a princely state.

Later, the League's members would be beyond disillusioned as it began to protect imperial interests rather than focus on self-determination. In the aftermath of the destruction of the Ottoman and Habsburg empires, the League established the mandate system and a commission to determine the fitness of former colonies to rule themselves.[17] India's status was complicated as well. The original Covenant of the League of Nations granted India full membership, equal in status with other sovereign nations and British self-governing dominions. The helpful caveat here was that the delegates to the League were known supporters of the Raj, cherry-picked by New Delhi and London. Still, there was no doubt that India's inclusion was a marker of its arrival on the international stage. The moment is celebrated in William Orpen's famous painting, *The Signing of the Peace in the Hall of Mirrors* (Versailles, 28 June 1919), which hangs in the Imperial War Museum in London. The painting is the most visceral representation of the importance of Bikaner's place in this historic moment. He stands by a pillar, dashing in his gold turban and the full regalia of a British army general. In front of him is Edwin Montagu, then the secretary of state for India. Bikaner stands above the actual stars of the show—David Lloyd George, the British prime minister, and the walrus-moustached president of France, Georges Clemenceau.

The moment fascinated Panikkar with its symbolism and potential. It also set him thinking about the princely states and their role in India's nationalist movement. He wasn't the only one who was thinking about this, but he was certainly one of the first to bend his mind to deconstructing complex concepts of imperial sovereignty and princely autonomy. In those early years of the twentieth century, studies on the princely states were coming to the fore, yet they were still barely understood. The prime work of the day was William Lee Warner's *The Native States of India*. The son of a Norfolk clergyman, Warner had had a rich and storied administrative career in India that left him intimately acquainted with the customs, laws and policies of various princely states. *The Native States of India* became, upon its publication in 1910, the cornerstone of the basis on which the princely states were understood in that time. It was a study of British policies toward princely states from 1757 to 1813, in which Warner argued that the object of the British, represented by the East India Company, was to avoid all intervention in the native states, hoping that eventually a consolidated bloc of states would emerge. Reading this, Panikkar was intrigued, but also critical.

That spring, as the country tried to pull itself together in the aftermath of Jallianwala Bagh, Panikkar sat down to write one of his last essays for *Modern Review*. In 'The Native States and Indian Nationalism', Panikkar pointed out the dangers of clubbing the princely states into one broad monochrome brushstroke, a statement that twenty-eight years later, V.P. Menon might have appreciated. He noted prophetically that the princely states would certainly cause some problems for India should the country attain independence sometime in the future. Perhaps, he argued, that was because most of them were ruled by kings who were slow to realise that political progress was no longer a possibility, but a reality.

This was a rather sweeping generalisation, and given Panikkar's own distance from the princely states at this time, it also overlooked the fact that nearly all the princely states in the 1920s were well aware of the impact that the independence movement could have on their own sovereignty. For many princes, then, it was necessary to gain political immunity and reassurance on that score from the viceroy.

Not all of them were the glittery cartoons they were made out to be in reputation and reportage. The Maharaja of Alwar, for instance, may have been a charmer and a paedophile, and a man capable of setting his polo pony on fire when it didn't perform as he wanted it to, but he was also acutely aware of his constitutional rights, based on the Government of India Act, 1919. Then, of course, there was Ganga Singh, who knew what his presence at Versailles meant for the princely states in India's political future. The simple fact was that the princes were not at all slow. As early as the 1920s, they were beginning to tire of advisory bodies with fancy titles. They wanted results.

Panikkar skated over that reality in his essay, though his views on the matter would change rapidly in the coming years. He also went on a slight rant about the Congress, which he scornfully dismissed as a 'bourgeois movement', and its inability to take the significance of the princely states into account as part of their manifesto for independence. Here, Panikkar contradicted himself. The princes were not men that the national movement could hope to sideline, he wrote. They carried local and popular links with divinity and greatness. If the Congress could get the princes to side with them, the national movement itself would gain a considerable sheen of prestige and history. It behoved the Indian people to think about how the princes could fit into the map of a united India.

But as yet, Panikkar wasn't ready to think of the princely states as independent of the British Crown. In his eyes, the suzerainty of the Crown was indefensible. He called the native states 'subordinate allies' of the British and argued that once central self-government was established, who else could the princely states acknowledge? 'Their governments are zenana ridden,' he sneered. 'Their politics are merely backstair intrigue.'[18] When it came to the question of how to deal with them, the young Panikkar was resolutely against the previous policies of annexation. 'The immediate annexation by the stroke of a pen of the native states … is bound to create dissensions, civil wars and interminable strife, which would leave the central government ineffective in every way.'[19]

With politics changing rapidly on the ground and with history serving as a sharp reminder, Panikkar argued that both the extremes of complete preservation and complete annihilation would not work. Any middle path would have to integrate the fact that the princes had to be gainfully employed in the vision of a truly united India, and their power guaranteed. After all, he argued, almost all of the larger states were well-run and free of corruption, while their leaders (shown by the presence of the maharajas at the Imperial Conference and the Versailles Conference) were aware of the importance and role of nationalism. Presciently, he suggested that the central government would look after imperial or diplomatic concerns, while leaving the states a fig leaf for their independence and allowing them freedom in their internal affairs. As for the smaller principalities, Panikkar appeared to not have any concerns about them whatsoever, arguing that they lost their sovereign rights in exchange for keeping their social status.

The hopscotch between arguments is revealing of a Panikkar who still wasn't too clear about the princes and their role in Indian politics. A few years of solid research and reading and a few more of personal experience with the princes would soon set him right on that score.

There was no doubt though that, in the early years of the twentieth century, there was a certain caricature of the royals of India. Critics portrayed the maharajas as relics of a bygone age, reduced to idiotic cartoons that could never be at par with their masters in the Raj.[20] To be sure, their behaviour helped nothing, nor did their ways of life. The novelist and explorer Rosita Forbes wrote of the 'white durbar' in Jaipur, which took place once a year during the full moon on the rooftop of a marble palace. The floors were carpeted in white, she wrote, and the walls were sheathed in it. The maharaja himself sat on a silver throne, upholstered in white brocade. Everyone was dressed in white, with jewels to match. 'Hems are stiff with pearls and the breasts of coats heavy with diamonds. Streams of the same precious stones drip from turbans … rivers of them pour across the silver tissue of the ceremonial dress'.[21]

In Patiala, the Moti Bagh Palace made Versailles, at least to the rapturous eyes of Lady Reading's private secretary Yvonne Fitzroy, 'look like a cottage'.[22] Bhupinder Singh, a maharaja who would figure quite prominently in Panikkar's life, was known for his eccentricities as much as his wealth. Miss Fitzroy recalled him arresting the eyes of an entire crowd by arriving at an investiture ceremony at Viceregal Lodge with one-fourth of his brocaded coat 'entirely concealed by diamonds'.[23] Then there was the Maharaja of Kapurthala—a valued client of Cartier—who established a fully functional tent city on the Punjab plains upon the occasion of the marriage of his daughter Brinda, complete with a post office and a barber.[24]

With royal behaviour like this on display, the parodying and infantilising of Indian rulers ensured the crystallisation of the claim that the native rulers were incapable of serious government. To give this theory some breathing room, it is important to remember that the prevailing understanding of history and politics adhered only to British India and excluded almost entirely this large slice of Indian-ruled India. As Panikkar began to work more and more both on and with the princely states, he would come to understand that within the national narrative, and given the many treaties they had signed with the Raj, the rulers of large, industrially and educationally progressive states often did not get their due. Their relations with the Raj were based on constant parleys, negotiations and a running undercurrent of mutual suspicion. That was why it was important to start by first seeing each state in the light of its own identity. The Raj had to stay on its toes to ensure no disturbance in the delicate balance of power. And these playboy rulers often had their own political calculations.

Panikkar would soon discover this for himself.

CHAPTER 10

A Sense of Waiting

THE VERY EARLY 1920S WERE A TIME WHEN PANIKKAR FELT AS THOUGH he was stuck in limbo. He wanted desperately to find a foothold in nationalist politics, but could find no way in.

To curb his frustration, Panikkar began a deep dive into the history of the Malayalam language and its classics, starting with the *Lilathilakam*—a treatise of unknown authorship written between the fourteenth and fifteenth centuries in the manipravalam style, a blend of Sanskrit and Tamil. Literature brought him the mental respite he needed.

By this time, Panikkar was well networked among a host of prominent Malayali writers and magazines. He went on to publish a critically acclaimed translation of *King Lear*, a play based on Noor Jahan, and a poem that recreated an episode from the life of Gandhari from the Mahabharata (*Premageethi*).

Poems like *Premageethi* would establish Panikkar as a fine poet in his own right. It also showcased a peculiarly romantic side to his personality, for in his poetry more than in his prose, Panikkar was both delicate and attuned to the finer human instincts. Writing poetry came naturally to him, probably as a result of his uncle's introduction to like-minded friends in Thampanoor. Like his novels, poetry was an escape for Panikkar, especially at times when his emotions were running high or he needed refuge from the stress of reality.

He observed the results of his literary endeavours with no small amount of smugness. For instance, of his novel *Dorassini*, he recalled that the literary critic A. Balakrishna Pillai had compared it with the works of Guy de Maupassant. But for all Panikkar's pleasure in his literary achievements, the fact that he had only been able to contribute intellectually to the independence movement so far was annoying. So when Gandhi and the Ali brothers visited Aligarh in October 1920 to try to convince the students to boycott the college (since MOAC, now Aligarh Muslim University, was affiliated to the government university in Allahabad, and was hence run on British funds), Panikkar seized the chance to meet the man who had taken India by storm.

The university was closed for a month. Mohammad Ali had come armed with a proposal to create a new Muslim National University to accommodate the students who chose the path of non-cooperation. Those students who elected not to join the non-cooperation movement were sent back home. It was the first time that Panikkar met Gandhi in person.

Gandhi was always on the lookout for new recruits to the cause of freedom, and he asked Panikkar to join as well. It was the chance Panikkar had been longing for, but he was forced to turn it down. Some instinct told him that he was not yet fully ready to make the leap from the sidelines to the middle of the action. What was more, he had already promised Ross Masood that with the ongoing faculty crisis at AMU, he wouldn't leave just yet. Panikkar apologised, couching it in terms that Gandhi would understand, saying he had given his word to Masood that he would see his tenure through. Gandhi was understanding, but he made note of Panikkar's reason. Loyalty was always important in politics.

So Panikkar decided to wait another year, despite the simmering religious tensions on campus and the resulting fissures in political opinion in the wake of the Khilafat movement. Gandhi's approach to him may have been politely put on hold, but everyone had noticed the conversation. Everyone also noted that following this conversation, Panikkar seemed to have become deeply inspired by Gandhian principles. Perhaps it was inevitable, perhaps at least in some part it was for effect. Either way, he now began to dress almost entirely in khadi, the attire complete with a Gandhi cap. Aligarh was collectively amused to see him driving around the campus in a phaeton and four, dressed in crisp cream khadi.[1] Once you coupled his remarkable sartorial choice with his continuing contact with the Ali brothers and his open sympathy to the cause of the creation of the Muslim National University, it is perhaps not surprising that snide whispers went around campus. Panikkar, it was whispered, was a 'concealed non-cooperator'.[2] But the truth was that, despite his own inner frustration, Panikkar was biding his time.

Aligarh was the perfect place to do just that.

Panikkar was now the head of the history department, a position that granted him the ability to reflect even more deeply on India's identity, its past and the role of religion in defining India's nationhood. The three years he would spend in Aligarh would be foundational in building his idea of India, one of his most significant contributions to the national movement. One particular 'lesson which struck me in the face at Aligarh was the integration of Islam as a single community in India', he wrote. It was at AMU that Panikkar realised the dangerous potential of organising as one religious community versus another, for it was here that he noted that 'Aligarh represented the united face of Islam in India'.[3]

In 1920, Panikkar published *Indian Nationalism: Its Origin, History and Ideals.* This was his first book-length manuscript but more importantly it was his first attempt to present his own history of the Indian national movement. The book was born from his readings of Vincent Smith and Verney Lovett.

Panikkar hadn't stayed in London long enough to see the publication of *An Oxford History of India*, Vincent Smith's enormous and seminal contribution to colonial Indian history, but he had recently read it and been thoroughly irritated by it. Forty years later, the historian A.L. Basham would criticise Smith for not bothering with 'the imaginative and intellectual effort demanded in order to see the world through the eyes of a people not nurtured on the Bible and the Classics'.[4] It wasn't just the way Smith told history that annoyed Panikkar. Smith lost no opportunity to lambast the Indian national movement, publishing a critique of the constitutional reforms of 1919 that served as proof of how outdated his views had become.

On the other hand there was Sir Verney Lovett, who had become a reader in Indian history upon his retirement but who had only recently served as a member of the Rowlatt Committee. Lovett's claims of being a historian were rather perilously based on his single book, *History of the Indian Nationalist Movement*, a Whitehall-authorised biography of the freedom movement. He was by all accounts grandiose and pompous, and he dismissed India's aspirations to independence with a scornful flourish.

The more Panikkar read work like this, the more he seethed with rage. Was this how the freedom struggle was being presented to the world, he wondered. The only way he could rectify that was to use his own pen in retaliation. *Indian Nationalism* is both Panikkar's answer to lofty orientalists and a presentation of his ideas of what the freedom movement was and what it represented. For India to demand freedom, for instance, the country first had to understand what it was. On what grounds could it unite? A review of Panikkar's writing before *History of the Indian Nationalist Movement* will remind a reader that, in his eyes, India had been a cultural reality since the age of the Vedas. In ancient times, the motherland was epitomised as a deity—Bharat Mata, for instance. One saw that reality in the spread of Hindu temples and customs across the land, from the Himalayas to Kanyakumari. One undertook its worship in pilgrimages to the four dhams. On a cultural and religious level, as much as on the political level then, it was Hinduism that unified India as far as Panikkar was concerned.[5] He argued that 'India and Hinduism are related organically as body and soul.'[6]

In so doing, he grounded Indian nationalism in a religious foundation. 'This unity of India has not been merely the ideal of a few thinkers here and there. It has been felt and prayed for by every devout Hindu.'[7] As arguments went, this line of thinking might well have represented a religious/purist tilt that would delight the early right-wing thought of the likes of the All-India Hindu Mahasabha. After all, the idea of an 'Akhand Hindustan' (an undivided

Hindu-oriented India) fit into a discursive pattern that dated back to the nineteenth century. Did that mean that Panikkar was drifting close to the supremacist ideologies of the likes of V.D. Savarkar, K.B. Hedgewar, B.S. Moonje or K.M. Munshi?

Traditionalist nationalism was focused not merely on a spiritual revival but a sense of realpolitik. In 1915, the Mahasabha—and in another five years, the Rashtriya Swayamsevak Sangh (RSS)—had emerged to counter what it saw as the Muslim menace. For Panikkar though, nationalism was always grounded in unity. His insistence on a Hindu identity was more along cultural lines, rather than an overtly political or divisively communal angle. In that sense, his argument for a 'Greater India' transcended any notion of territorial boundaries. He had no truck with Aryan notions of ethnic and racial exclusiveness and Hindu nationalist visions that anchored India in the geography of South Asia. For Panikkar, 'Greater India' was an abstract, open concept that could not be drawn on a map. Now, internal political and communal differences could be overcome with the common goal of swaraj, or self-government. The alliance between the Muslim League and the Congress was thus proposed as a culminating moment of political unity, albeit within the framework of the empire.[8]

The Montford Report, the Rowlatt Act and Jallianwala Bagh all contributed to what Panikkar saw as the discrediting of imperial unity. All this was underpinned by the racism and xenophobia that Indians were facing across the empire, from Australia to the Transvaal. One could see the after-effects in India as well, especially in Panikkar's own home state of Travancore. During the nineteenth and early twentieth centuries, the colonial state had radically transformed various land and labour relations across the subcontinent. On the Malabar coast, this intervention had produced a highly oppressive landlord system delineated along religious and caste lines. Upper-caste Hindus served as British-controlled property managers while Muslim peasants—the Moplahs—toiled under harsh conditions. Not surprisingly, simmering tensions boiled over into a massive uprising in 1921 to which the state responded with brutal force. For the Mahasabha, the Moplah rebellion and the Khilafat movement were political and geopolitical signs that there was a militant Muslim threat that had to be countered. The Arya Samaj, for instance, quickly dispatched Shuddhi (purification) activists to Malabar to reclaim Hindus who had allegedly been forcibly converted.[9]

Panikkar did not go as far as this, but it is obvious that for him, Hinduism played a foundational role in nationalism. Its 'generous vagueness ... allowed room for every sort of opinion'[10] and thus allowed all other elements to flourish within a single political tapestry. Unity then, was a process that had taken centuries, in which the British Empire represented but one phase. After all, every empire or ruler from Ashoka to Harsha and from the Mughals to the Marathas had aimed to achieve unity, despite the many religious and political elements within the country.

Having thus established that India could call itself a nation on the basis of the rich tradition of Hinduism, Panikkar identified the four elements that had pushed India along the path of nationalism: religious revival, Western education, the economic strain imposed on a colony by an empire and finally, the fact that the privilege of participating in governance or administration was denied to the Indians themselves.

Yet, it is in his argument in *Indian Nationalism* for the role of princely states within a larger national context, that Panikkar, despite his youth and inexperience in the ways of the states, now made some pioneering—if flawed—arguments. According to him, the princely states could not be addressed either collectively or on an equal footing to the provinces in British India. He came from a princely state himself, and his knowledge of its unique politics, history and geography informed his formulation. He was emphatic about the fact that any plan for constitutional and political reform for India's future had to take the princely states into consideration.

How? In his view, one had to start from the point that the states could not be seen as 'feudatory states'. Characterised though they might have been by what he called an 'imperfect sovereignty', they were self-governing entities. Panikkar had different ideas of how each state should be treated. The larger states like Kashmir or Travancore should be allowed to take their place autonomously in what he called an 'Indian Commonwealth'. Smaller states like Cochin could be merged or integrated into the nation. *Indian Nationalism*, then, presented the first steps that Panikkar took towards understanding federalism and the role of the princely states. It was also the first time that the word 'integration' entered the lexicon regarding the princely states.

In many ways, Panikkar's book was emblematic of the changing concept of the princely states at the dawn of the twentieth century. This was no longer the era of consolidation of colonial power that had begun during the eighteenth century, but one of indirect rule.[11] By the twentieth century, princely options like administrative and territorial boundaries had been limited by treaties with the crown. Political agents were in place to implement the Crown's control on the ground and concepts of royal legitimacy now included complex terms like suzerainty, paramountcy and chains of succession. By the time *Indian Nationalism* was published, princely troops from Kashmir to Mysore had served the empire in Africa, Haifa, Afghanistan and China. In October 1916, an informal conference of the princes and chiefs of India was held 'to level progress in the backward states to the British standard and to give to the ruling princes greater independence than they possess in internal affairs'.[12] The Raj didn't like it but the fact was that the princes could no longer be ignored. As Panikkar himself pointed out, the Maharaja of Bikaner was the only Indian signatory to the Treaty of Versailles, standing shoulder to shoulder with the likes of Woodrow Wilson and Lloyd George. This, he argued, gave the princes undoubted optics of power.

Given the way the Raj's mind was changing, both about the significance of Indian nationalism and about the princely states, Panikkar's writing at this time established him as a scholar to watch out for.

Was he aware of that fact?

By all accounts, Panikkar never lacked a degree of complacent self-awareness verging on arrogance. But in the early years of his writing, he was not yet sure of being read by a larger audience. To his credit, that never stopped him from putting his voice out there on subjects ranging from history to politics in the hope that it *would* perhaps be picked up. Sometime in 1920, he dashed off a quick monograph on education as well. *Educational Reconstruction* built on some of the essays that Panikkar had written while he was still at Oxford. It was dedicated affectionately to Ross Masood, written from a point of view that was extremely aware of the role of education in the spread of nationalism, a cog without which the overall machine could not move. Much as Masood did, Panikkar also called for a wholly Indian system of education, since the model that existed in India, based on the English way, was not only different from but 'hostile' to Indian conditions.[13] Considering Panikkar had reaped the benefits of an English education himself, this theory is slightly baffling until it is contextualised not only against the backdrop of the ongoing political resurgence in India, but his own developing ideas of nationalism. Only then do his thoughts come into sharp, even prescient focus.

'The powers that be,' Panikkar wrote, 'have always tried to "continue to be" by an effective control of opinion through the educational machinery.'[14] This maxim was no different under the British than it had been under the Brahmins. The one was racial supremacy and the other was caste supremacy. What was truly required was a 'new Indian nation breathing the old and sacred atmosphere of the Vedas'[15] while staying progressive in its commitment to modern literature, thought and science.

Panikkar repeated the questions he had asked some five years earlier: important questions, showing a young man highly aware of the problems of his country and intelligent enough to ask the kind of granular questions that needed to be answered. What language, for instance, did one teach in? How did one address the inequality between men and women in their access to education? These were revolutionary questions, and in repeating himself, Panikkar was ensuring that they would be heard—and hopefully answered—at some point in time. It was, he felt, the ideal time to be asking these questions.

He also had plenty of time to ask these questions now.

Gouri had left Aligarh early in 1920 when she discovered she was pregnant with their first child. She would stay in Chalayil for the births of the first three Panikkar children. Their eldest, a daughter they named Parvathy, was born in Kavalam in April 1920, shortly after Gouri's return from Aligarh.

In January 1921, the non-cooperation movement began to gain momentum. Dyarchy, as William Marris had gloomily predicted, was beginning to break down. Taking advantage of the teetering political situation, Gandhi and the Ali brothers toured the country, addressing gatherings and meeting political workers. Thousands of students inspired by the movement left schools and colleges, joining the 'national' educational institutions that were springing up all over India. This aspect of the non-cooperation movement saw immense success in Bengal, where students in Calcutta triggered a province-wide strike to force their alma maters to disaffiliate themselves from the government of India. The campaign was spearheaded by Subhas Chandra Bose (who had just resigned from the ICS) and his mentor in the Congress, C.R. Das. Across the country, the Swadeshi movement gained even greater momentum, with foreign cloth being boycotted by the bale. The writer Prabhudas Gandhi, who accompanied M.K. Gandhi during the first months of 1921, recalled scenes at small stations where their train would stop for a few moments. There would invariably be a crowd on the platform, since word had gone around that Gandhi would be on board. Gandhi would speak persuasively to the assembled onlookers and within moments a pile of caps, dupattas and turbans would be heaped on the platform. As the train pulled out of each station, Prabhudas recalled, flames would be leaping from the accumulated pile of clothes.[16]

Throughout 1921, the Congress worked to collect funds, recruit more members and distribute charkhas. Amid boycotts of foreign cloth and government institutions, the membership of the Congress leaped upwards. Khadi became the uniform of the national movement. What, it was demanded, would happen to those who couldn't afford khadi? Simple, Gandhi retorted: one would simply wear less of it! It was that day that he discarded his dhoti and kurta in favour of a simple loin cloth.

For the British, it seemed like the year would never end, with the combination of the Moplah rebellion and the non-cooperation movement shaking the edifice of the Raj like nothing had before. In

May 1921, the government attempted, through talks between Gandhi and Lord Reading, to persuade the Mahatma to ask the Ali brothers to withdraw speeches that contained suggestions of violence. The talks broke down, leaving the government at a loss. Amidst this crisis, Whitehall made the supremely poor decision of sending the Prince of Wales to visit India in November 1921. It was part of a highly staged tour of India and the colonies to acquaint him with more of his princely duties. But it could not have come at a worse time.

The tour was estimated to cost a spectacular Rs 2.7 million (USD 10 million today) at a time when India was struggling to recover not only from a war where it had lost more than it could have imagined, but also from famines and flu outbreaks and a depleted exchequer, not to mention bloodshed in Amritsar. The local press ridiculed the prince's speeches. Gandhi led the burning of foreign cloth in the suburbs of Bombay on the day the prince arrived in the harbour. Clashes took place on the streets between nationalist and Raj loyalists. Prince Edward was met with empty streets and downed shutters wherever he went, as the Indian Merchants' Chamber decided indignantly that the previous policy of 'running with the hares and hunting with the hounds will not do'[17] and that it was time to take a stand.

'The shadow of Amritsar has lengthened over the fair face of India,' the Prince of Wales reported to his father petulantly.[18] The Raj hit back and by the end of 1921, so many political prisoners clogged the jails that one newspaper remarked acidly, 'The question before the people now is not which of their leaders have been arrested, but which of them have not *yet* been arrested.'

It was the same story in Calcutta, where Congress volunteer corps took over the city, shutting down shops and stopping trains and taxis. In Madras, hartals exploded into violence. Annoyed, Prince Edward sought refuge in polo and tiger shoots, but he made his resentment clear in a letter to his father, in which he termed his trip 'rather a waste'. George V wrote back sympathetically, 'I can't understand why Gandhi, the man who is causing all the trouble, has not been arrested and deported. Are the government frightened of him or what?'[19]

As questions go, it was a massive indicator of just how much the empire was underestimating the nationalist movement in India, and indeed, its impact. There was a revolution underway in politics, a shift from the pomp of the monarchy to a more violent pageantry of boycotts, bonfires and hartals. No longer would the simple optics of a royal tour drown out cries for freedom. 'The Prince will … know how after remaining under a tyrannical government for more than 150 years and undergoing innumerable hardships, they [the Indian people] have been forced to follow the golden saying, "He who is oppressed will fight",' the Urdu newspaper *Nusrat* reported triumphantly on 10 November 1921.[20]

It was a shift of which Panikkar was well aware. But nothing could have prepared him—or the rest of the country—for the horrors of Chauri Chaura.

Perhaps they should have known. The indicators that there would be massive violence at some point had been far too many, even if they were sporadically located across the country. In Awadh, the farmers' movement melded with the non-cooperation movement so seamlessly that it became difficult to discern the difference between the two. In Malabar, non-cooperation joined hands (dangerously) with Khilafat propaganda, turning Muslim tenants against their landlords. In Assam, workers on tea plantations struck work and were fired upon. Railway workers and dock workers went on strike, and in Andhra, forest laws were defied. In Punjab, the Akalis were beginning to push to take back control of the gurudwaras from the corrupt mahants (priests). Across the country then, the spirit of defiance born from the non-cooperation movement fuelled local movements that did not always adhere to Gandhi's principles of non-violence.

Over the next two months, as 1922 dawned, nearly 30,000 people were behind bars. Public meetings were banned and newspapers were gagged, with the offices of the Congress and Khilafat seeing midnight raids. In desperation, the Congress appointed Gandhi as the arbiter of civil disobedience. Hoping to use this as a final bargaining chip, Gandhi wrote to Reading in January 1922, stating that unless the government lifted the ban on civil liberties and released political prisoners, he would be forced to go ahead with civil disobedience. Reading was singularly unmoved. His hand forced, Gandhi announced that the next phase of the non-cooperation movement would begin in Bardoli, a taluk in Surat.

Yet again, fate stepped in. On 4 February 1922, members of a Congress and Khilafat procession in Chauri Chaura, Gorakhpur, irked by the behaviour of local policemen, attacked them. The police opened fire, causing chaos to break out. The incident ended with the murder of twenty-two policemen and a police station on fire. Appalled, Gandhi put the brakes on civil disobedience and non-cooperation, bringing it to an official end on 11 February 1922.

This decision caused a momentous rift in the ranks of the Congress. Motilal Nehru and his son Jawaharlal recorded their bewilderment at this, along with Subhas Chandra Bose and C.R. Das. Why, they demanded, did the whole country have to pay the price for the actions of one district in the United Provinces? It was a question that would haunt the Congress for the better part of the decade.

In Aligarh, Panikkar watched the drama unfold with a jaundiced eye. He was getting closer and closer to the end of his tether. 'Aligarh,' he would recall later, 'was always a blind alley for me.'[21] This is a caustic way to look back at what was undoubtedly a rich period in his academic life; two years in which published two more books. The first was a slim little treatise on Harsha of Kanauj, which he casually acknowledged later had become 'a standard work of history'[22] over the years. Standard it might have been, but at the time it was written, the choice of subject was politically significant and Panikkar knew it.

Harsha's reign began after the crisis of the mighty Gupta Empire. Panikkar's brief sketch highlighted a period that showed the ancient origins of Indian territory. He argued persuasively that the period symbolised one that was attaining order after a time of fragmentation. He felt that Harsha was an enlightened ruler who shared his powers with a council of state and personally involved himself in the affairs of his subjects. Panikkar thus took on and debunked his old boss Vincent Smith's theory that the absence of political evolution in Indian history was inextricably linked to despotism. But most importantly, the monograph underlines the syncretism in Harsha's kingdom and court. 'In Harsha's time, the general tendency was so eclectic that toleration of all creeds would have followed as a natural result even if Hindu tradition had pointed to the other direction.'[23]

It was yet another hat-tip to Panikkar's definition of traditionalist nationalism, which rested on the shoulders of an open-minded, inclusive Hinduism. His 'Greater India' thesis persists in an article—*The Interpretation of History*—that he published in *The Hindustan Review* that year. This article essentially repeats all of Panikkar's ongoing arguments during the early 1920s, the gist being that a Hindu-Indian 'Greater India' was an 'empire of culture'[24] rather than a political entity with demarcated boundaries like the Roman Empire, and for those reasons, it was easy to see why Hinduism had found such a permanent home in Southeast Asia.

Apart from his ideas of India, Panikkar also, in the wake of Chauri Chaura and Jallianwala Bagh, had very definite ideas of imperialism. Yet another monograph was published in 1922 on the subject. *Imperialism: In Practice & Theory* holds up a mirror to a far more adult, more reasonable Panikkar. The first ten pages alone make it quite clear how deeply the bitterness of the bloodshed in Amritsar, the elusive promise of attaining 'dominion status' by gradual stages and the realisation that the empire functioned on racial supremacy had influenced him. The war had allowed Panikkar to expand his study of how imperialism worked, from Africa to Aden and from Burma to Asia Minor. Much had changed since the signing of the armistice. 'Today, there is no Indian who is an advocate of imperial connection, except on the basis of absolute equality.'[25]

The lack of equality was what infuriated Panikkar and the sentiment springs out at the reader in his explanation of how the principle of imperialism worked in India and how it worked for the Indian diaspora who lived elsewhere across the empire. 'The British Empire Co. Ltd, which like all other trade interests, is concerned only in giving maximum profit for its shareholders,' he raged.[26] Excellent and efficient though the civil service might have been, it functioned fundamentally on the basis of superiority and hypocrisy and on the creation of vested interests, whether based on religion or on separate electorates.

Panikkar wondered about the future of imperialism, whether it was permanent or a passing blip on the world's ideological radar. It was, in retrospect, perhaps a premature question, since imperialism would mutate into other hydra-headed chimera in the coming years. But again, the First World War had changed the geopolitical map to the point where Panikkar could argue prophetically that, from Syria to Turkey and from China to Egypt, with the rise of individual nationalist strains in the colonies, the days of imperialism were numbered. 'The growth of Asiatic resistance is a matter of the very highest significance in history and portents a revolution of no small magnitude.'[27]

For all the intellectual and political heft of these books, at a time when bloodshed was beginning to define the contours of the freedom movement, Panikkar knew that the time for words was over. In June 1922, he put in his papers at Aligarh, and together with Gouri, packed up the little house on campus and departed for Madras. Politics, he felt, was his next step.

Unsurprisingly, his brother and his uncles disapproved thoroughly of his plans. Panikkar didn't have much by way of savings and Gouri was already pregnant with their second child: Madhusudhan would be born later in 1922. Another daughter, Devaki, arrived in 1924.

In their earliest years, the children rarely saw their father except for a couple of months a year. He was bent on making a mark for himself in the wider world. When they *did* see him though, the children remembered an affectionate father who would always put aside his writing and papers for them. Still, given the fact that the family was increasing in size by the year, the elders at Kavalam were not quite sure that Panikkar should have left a job that guaranteed a steady income. But they said nothing just yet, perhaps hoping that this was a youthful passion that would ultimately pass. Those of a plainer bent of mind, like the Raja of Mahmudabad, were not so tactful. But the young Panikkar stood firm. 'I was never enamoured of security,' he would write grandly later. 'For myself, I preferred the rough seas to the haven … it was the tameness of academic life that bored me.'[28]

CHAPTER 11

Interlude

TODAY, TANGUTURI PRAKASAM IS REMEMBERED AS THE 'LION OF ANDHRA' or 'Andhra Kesari' for good reason. His serious, almost somnolently bespectacled gaze, belied the fiery rebel within. He was a former barrister who had renounced his profession in answer to Gandhi's call for non-cooperation. In Madras, this staunch Gandhian ran a newspaper entitled *Swarajya* (meaning self-rule, published in English, Tamil and Telugu) from his home at No. 155, Madras Broadway. T. Prakasam was known to be far too idealistic for a businessman, forever reduced to penury in pursuit of his ideals. His reputation would have given many people pause, but for Panikkar, journalism was a call to arms.

In the early twentieth century, being a journalist was an act of political patriotism. From there, there were several easy stepping stones to an active role in politics. Panikkar was delighted when he received an offer from Prakasam to join *Swarajya* as an assistant editor. It helped that his friend G.V. Krupanidhi (to whom he dedicated *Imperialism*) was then both the manager and editor of the paper. Krupanidhi would go on to become the last loyalist to stand by the paper until it finally ran its last edition long after Panikkar had moved on.

A delighted Panikkar wrote to Mahmudabad to let him know the news. 'Your decision to take up the editorship of a nationalist newspaper seems to me, in the case of a young man of your promise, to be a step of danger,' Mahmudabad wrote back with characteristic candour.[1] He warned his young friend of the inherent instability in the profession. 'I shall be sorry to think that you may find, after a few years, that you have exchanged an honourable career … for one in which your talents may not find ample scope.'[2]

His warnings fell on deaf ears. Panikkar was too overjoyed to find himself finally in a profession where his voice would make a difference—something T. Prakasam would discover too, much to his alarm.

Panikkar joined *Swarajya* at a rather delicate time in Madras politics. Gandhi had just been arrested on charges of sedition, but he had left behind a Congress riven by his decision to halt the non-cooperation movement. The Swaraj Party was formed by more radical leaders like C.R. Das who had decided to participate in the elections to the legislative councils, something Gandhi was firmly against, while the more conservative 'no-changers' remained faithful to Gandhi's recommendations. Within this debate, *Swarajya* maintained a strictly Gandhian line. Panikkar, however, was most distinctly *not* feeling Gandhian at the time.

Local politics did nothing to help the situation. In the early 1920s, the Justice Party was holding power in the presidency. Led by Swarajists like S. Satyamurti and S. Srinivasa Iyengar, the party would rule Madras until 1937, with an interlude during 1926–1930. Noting the significance of this victory, the *Official Review of the Government of India* (1921–1922) said, 'The first bulwark of caste dominance in political matters has been stormed as a result of the recent constitutional changes.'[3] Reservations were enacted, women were allowed to legislate and a mid-day meal scheme was introduced (a precursor to the free noon-day meal schemes of Kamaraj and MGR). It was the first political manifestation of the Dravidian movement, which had its origins in the struggle between the Brahmins and the non-Brahmins.

The demands for non-Brahmin political power in Madras had begun in the early years of the twentieth century, but it was now accelerating, with the establishment of associations like the

Madras United League in 1909, by men like C. Natesa Mudaliar (Panikkar's friend from Thampanoor days). In 1912, under Mudaliar's secretaryship, the League transitioned into the Madras Dravidian Association, the first time that the word 'Dravidian' had been used for a political entity. It aimed at non-Brahmin political power, hoping to be a 'Dravidian state under the British Raj'. With a '[g]overnment by and for non-Brahmins', that didn't go far, but it was taken forward in 1917 with the issuance of the Non-Brahmin Manifesto. The manifesto sought non-Brahmin advancement in the face of Brahmin monopoly by seeking reservations in legislative councils. This manifesto led to the formation of the Justice Party. The party drew its early leadership from the elite across linguistically contiguous regions (Tamil, Telugu, Kannada and Malayalam). These may have been anti-Brahmin but they were staunchly Hindu. In 1920, the Justice Party won a resounding victory during the first elections under the 1919 reforms, thus becoming the first real political body to function as a constitutional party in India because it had a majority in the Madras Council and enjoyed the government's support. In its rise and consolidation of political power, Panaganti Ramarayaningar (known popularly as the Raja of Panagal) was crucial.

Born in 1866, the raja was of aristocratic stock, his family being prominent landowners in Kalahasti (today a bustling temple town in Andhra Pradesh). In keeping with the practice among upper-class families, he was privately educated, displaying a remarkable intellect that would surprise even those who knew him, acquiring a degree in chemistry as well as one in law, besides a fluency in multiple languages. From the start, he was a man with his eye on politics and public service.

In 1912, the Raja of Panagal stood for the elections to the Imperial Legislative Council, Delhi, as the representative of the Madras Landowners' Association. Three years later, in 1915, he returned to the south to advocate the emancipation of non-Brahmins in Madras. When the Justice Party was established, the Raja gravitated to its echelons, followed by a number of zamindars and landowners from Andhra.

In the early days, this class's inclusion was beneficial for both clout and eyeballs, but eventually it was detrimental to Panagal's own cause which, he argued, was to interrogate and change the status quo. Today, Panagal is remembered for his historic leadership in taking the ideals of the Dravidian movement forward, including several far-sighted steps such as pushing for industrial development within the province and establishing a Hindu Religious Endowment Board to end the exploitation by Brahmins in Hindu temples. He is believed to have preceded Sir Maneckji Dadabhoy in taking up the cause of the depressed classes, resulting in a historic order in 1921 which reserved 44 per cent of jobs for non-Brahmins, 16 per cent for Muslims, 16 per cent for Anglo-Indians and Christians and 8 per cent for Scheduled Castes.

But Panikkar claims otherwise. In his memoir, Panikkar writes that he was the one who insisted that the Raja of Panagal take the measures that made him famous. 'My policy was to seek the support of non-Brahmins of nationalist views to weaken the Panagal ministry.'[4] The impression that a reader is left with after Panikkar's description of a 'perpetual struggle' is that Panagal was not as open to demolishing oppression and inequality as Panikkar seems to have been. There are no documents to prove this claim, but from a bare reading of Panikkar's memoir, it seems his short stint at *Swarajya* was tempestuous from the start.

For one, he trained his guns on Lord Willingdon, who had been appointed governor of Madras in April 1919, just a week before Jallianwala Bagh. Freeman Freeman-Thomas, the first marquess of Willingdon, was a man of stern resolve, with zero patience for the 'nonsense' of revolutionary dreams. He quickly put several key legislative reforms in place around urban planning, local government and education. But Panikkar had had his eye on Willingdon since the brutal handling of the Moplah rebellion and the implementation of dyarchy in the Madras Presidency. As assistant editor at *Swarajya*, he believed his job was to keep up a sharp attack on both his chosen targets: Panagal and Willingdon.

Panikkar's reports and editorials at this time were a constant source of agitation for Prakasam, ranging as they did from rants against religious conversion to frauds in the Imperial Bank to the excesses of rich landowners like Panagal's family to outright attacks on Willingdon's policies as governor of Madras. His journalism was militant against the excesses of the rich and the imperial, but this was hardly the place to begin firing on all cylinders. As it was, *Swarajya* was, financially speaking, a tanking establishment. The share capital was Rs 3,00,000, which was 'enthusiastically purchased' by investors.[5] Much of the paper was kept alive via donations and crowdfunding. Panikkar himself was paid Rs 700 a month. Given the bluntness with which he went about his journalistic career, it didn't seem as though he cared too much about financial or domestic stability, despite two children at home. He was bent almost entirely on making a mark for himself, at seizing the chance he had been given to step up to a political career. At this time, Panikkar's ambition had blinded him entirely to his domestic responsibilities, and if it hadn't been for the fact that Chalayil and the family were present to buffer the blows of reality, this might well have been a very different story.

But at the time, Panikkar was aided in his mission by the trouble blooming within the Justice Party.

Iyengar and the Swarajists shared Panikkar's dislike of the Raja of Panagal. Led by the feisty C.R. Reddy (Panikkar's old mentor and himself a dissident from the Justice Party), they took on the raja in November 1923, complaining of his 'dictatorial rule' and his 'insensitive policies'. Stung, the raja retorted on the floor of the house, 'I have with me reams of letters written by you, appreciating my deeds, but now you criticise them.' Quick as a flash, Reddy sprang up, 'In England,' he snapped, 'lovers return their correspondence when they quarrel!'[6] The no-confidence motion was unfortunately defeated by a margin of sixty-five to forty-four. The results did not please Panikkar, who was watching the outcome with a sharp eye.

Meanwhile, he had been cultivating people in Madras. Panikkar would always build and use powerful networks. His current network that involved politicians, journalists and writers had given him the leg-up he needed to start dabbling in local politics at the time.

Word already had it in fact that he didn't get on with Srinivasa Iyengar. Certainly, his memoir is not very flattering: 'Srinivasa

Aiyangar's *(sic)* main weakness was his egotism,' he wrote acidly. 'It seemed as if he was out to demolish everyone who did not concede his undisputed leadership in southern India ... It was said that he wished to be known as the Gandhi of Madras. He was in the habit of speaking but not of listening. '[7] He grudgingly acknowledged though, that there was none more patriotic or radical than Iyengar himself.

Of C. Rajagopalachari (affectionately known as Rajaji), another doyenne of contemporary Madras politics, Panikkar was more laudatory, acknowledging his ambition, erudition and 'extraordinary strength of mind'.[8] But as far as his own role was concerned, he swerved towards the disingenuous. 'My own activities were outside these two groups,' he wrote piously. 'Let leaders carry out politics!'[9]

The truth was of course that Panikkar himself began to 'carry out politics' not long after he joined *Swarajya*. In the middle of 1923, he took the first step that would allow him to cross the bridge between journalism and full-time politics. The context for it was provided by events in his home state of Travancore. In 1896, a petition to the maharaja had been signed by over 13,000 Ezhavas (traditionally tappers and purveyors of toddy, the first settled agriculturists in what would eventually become Kerala, often sub-tenants of Namboodiri, Nair or Syrian landlords). By the end of the nineteenth century, the Ezhavas had emerged as the most educated and organised Untouchable community in Travancore and India. By 1903, Sri Narayana Guru had set up the Sri Narayana Dharma Paripalana Yogam (SNDP Yogam) to push for socioreligious change. By 1919, the Ezhavas were seeking tax resistance and non-cooperation. An attempt was also on to access temple roads and gain temple entry, hitherto off limits for the community.

The movement for temple entry was led at the time by an Ezhava named T.K. Madhavan. Born into one of Travancore's wealthier families, Madhavan was one of the more educated Ezhava elite. His ability to take advantage of Travancore's Western-style education exposed him to the caste prejudices experienced by his community. 'My companion on my daily trip to and from the school was a Nair boy, whose poor mother was a dependant of ours,' he would recall later. 'He could go straight along all the roads, whereas I, in spite of being economically better off, had to leave the road now and then [so as not to 'pollute' the caste Hindus]. This used to cut me to the quick.'[10]

By the time he was twenty, Madhavan was a central figure in the political organisation of the Ezhava community, founding and becoming editor of the *Deshabhimani* in 1915. The newspaper publicised accounts of the achievements and injustices faced by the Ezhava community. His strategy from the start was smartly founded on the cooperation of progressive, educated Hindu upper castes, a stance greatly aided by Gandhi's rise on the political firmament. Indeed, Madhavan himself is usually remembered as dressing in white homespun, bearing a walking stick with a portrait of Gandhi in the handle. In Gandhi, Madhavan saw the light at the end of his tunnel. He was already frustrated by the more incremental approaches of organising petitions and appeals. Non-violence, particularly satyagraha, seemed to be a radical new strategy that could mesh the goal of the elimination of untouchability with the Indian national movement.

In November 1920, Madhavan became even bolder. He purposely ignored the 'theendal palakas' (discriminatory boards) on the roads near the Shiva temple in Vaikom, which indicated the obligatory distance to be maintained from the upper castes, and entered the prohibited area. To the magistrate before whom he was hauled, Madhavan loudly proclaimed, 'I am a Ezhava by caste. I came to Vaikom today and went to the temple there, past the notice board posted on the road.'[11] It was the beginning of a political and social juggernaut.

As non-cooperation rocked the rest of India between 1920–1921, Madhavan and his colleagues began to go from village to village in Travancore, holding public meetings and distributing literature on the subject. The state was on edge. The maharaja was a staunch Hindu and whatever else the Raj may have felt, it was aware that religion and caste were the kind of powder kegs it had no desire to ignite again. In 1921, Gandhi arrived in Travancore. His interest in untouchability had been mounting over the past few months. He saw it as a blot on the face of Hinduism and he was determined to make its removal part of the political agenda. His meeting with Madhavan convinced him that the Ezhava community was ripe to fight for its rights. But even as he gave Madhavan his blessing, he remained cautious.

According to the historian Mary Elizabeth King, Gandhi was, at this point, 'more concerned with protecting the relative political autonomy of the princely states under foreign rule in India'.[12] But more important was the fact that even as this meeting went ahead, the state was convulsing under the fire and bloodshed of the Moplah rebellion. If matters went astray at this juncture, the Indian National Congress would receive the blame. Still, the opportunity was too good to pass.

Gandhi advised Madhavan to seek the support of the Kerala Provincial Congress Committee (KPCC), which had been set up as the outcome of the Nagpur session—the same session that had accepted that untouchability had to go. Gandhi wanted this Vaikom movement to be seen as separate from that of non-cooperation (a point of difference between his ideas and that of Madhavan). 'I do not regard this campaign as part of the [non-cooperation] movement as such,' Gandhi would say. 'It is certainly part of a satyagraha, but it has no direct connection with the movement.'[13]

The Vaikom movement was an excellent if microcosmic example of how the Congress had begun to approach the question of the princely states in the 1920s. Gandhi believed that this was a local struggle, and it should not antagonise the maharaja. As a result, local Congress leaders were to keep mobilisation about upper caste temples within agreed parameters and avoid targeting the state's royal house and government. There was, in addition, too much work to do in terms of unifying the leaders and personalities from various provinces and regions into a coherent mobilisation. The Congress, according to Gandhi, was not yet ready to take on regional grievances. In short, the Vaikom movement must not, at any cost, give the impression that the Congress could or would lead by example in the 564 other princely states.

At the same time, the Congress Working Committee meeting of 1 January 1921 had given the people of the princely states the right to send delegates to annual meetings. It had also assigned princely states to contiguous provincial congresses based on linguistic homogeneity.

Travancore and Cochin for example, had been assigned to the KPCC. It was a policy of mixed signals, but it seemed to be the best way forward for the Congress, at least in states like Travancore.

But there was a caveat here, as there always is in politics. The party's abstention did not mean non-participation, said Gandhi. Congress members were free to work to 'influence' a state government. Local committees could help guide the efforts of oppressed people as long as they did not clash with the royal government. If they did, they would do so as individuals. In the context of Travancore, this would mean an attempt to change untouchability independent of the larger national movement.

The strategy would change in the coming years of course, but the Vaikom movement was an excellent insight into what Congress leaders like Gandhi were thinking as they chose to support certain political or social movements in princely states during the 1920s. Panikkar, who had gone home to Kavalam for his uncle's birthday, kept an eye on these developments, making a note of the Congress strategy as much as he did of the relevance of the Vaikom movement. He couldn't resist dashing off a quick piece on the imperial context of the Ezhava struggle, which he published in *Modern Review*.

In *Europe and Asia*, Panikkar traced the Ezhava problem back to the social intolerance and religious bigotry that had been born as a result of contact with British policies. It was, he argued, only as a reaction to missionary propaganda, social intolerance and the political use of religion—the paraphernalia of imperialism as it were—that society had split down sectarian lines.[14] Before the Europeans had arrived, India was a land of variety. But now, tradition and caste were defended blindly. This was an argument that he would stick to. In *A History of Kerala*, which he wrote years later in 1959, he declared, 'The absurdity to which caste oppression could go was best exemplified in Kerala where the gradations of untouchability were marked by distances of approach.'[15] In the context of Vaikom, however, Panikkar's arguments in support of the Ezhavas were undoubtedly political. Having seen what the Congress was capable of, he was convinced that the Congress would remain in the minority in Travancore until it had won the support of the non-Brahmin. The Vaikom satyagraha was a key moment and, for Panikkar, the Congress had to seize the opportunity it provided to gain a foothold in the south of India.

The essay came out in the summer edition of *Modern Review* just in time for Panikkar's views on the caste struggle in his home state to be made nationally public. Not surprisingly, T. Prakasam was aghast. He was at his wit's end with his fiery assistant editor, but with Panikkar's connections and the fact that he was strongly backed by his senior editor, Krupanidhi, there was little the older man could do just yet.

For a few days, Panikkar was away from Madras. It was a welcome break from the hubbub of politics and journalism and a warm reminder of what home and Kavalam meant to him. He put aside all thoughts of work and immersed himself in his family at Chalayil. He and his brother organised a ceremony at the tharavad to celebrate Ramakrishna's birthday, which was attended by a guest list that reads like a Malayali Who's Who—Vallathol to C. Sankara Menon. A boat race was organised. 'That they should have gathered at this remote and inaccessible village was indeed a compliment to us and a tribute to uncle,'[16] he noted proudly. It certainly was all of the above, but it was also a local community's method of acknowledging that the Panikkar family was not only an influential one, but growing ever more powerful as its youngest son took his first steps into politics.

Panikkar, Gouri and the children returned to Madras as soon as they could after the birthday celebrations were over. They were delayed somewhat by Eravi Ramakrishna's insistence that they stay behind to be part of the family's formal division of assets. Change was coming and Ramakrishna had got wind of it through his work with the Nair Service Society (established by the social reformer Mannathu Padmanabhan Pillai). The older man was dismayed to learn that moves were afoot to dismantle the system of marumakkathayam, the prevailing system of matrilineal inheritance. It would still take a couple of years before the Nair Regulation Act of 1925 was passed, but Ramakrishna had no desire to see his family's hard-earned wealth and reputation crumble. The division of assets was done quite painlessly by all accounts, leaving Panikkar finally free to return to take care of his friend Madhavan.

Madhavan wasn't thrilled with Gandhi's ambiguous plans for the Vaikom movement's integration with the national freedom struggle. But he could hardly rebel against the Mahatma. So he did the next best thing and sought Panikkar's help. It speaks volumes about the fact that Panikkar, for all his youth and inexperience in both politics and journalism, was well-established enough to offer the kind of backchannel assistance that Madhavan was looking for. In fact, Panikkar had just the plan.

That year's annual Congress session was scheduled to be held in Kakinada, a major town in Andhra's Godavari district, in December 1923. The main agenda would be to send a message of Hindu-Muslim unity and form constructive programmes to carry the national movement forward. If Madhavan managed to meet some local senior leaders, Panikkar mused, it would help give the Vaikom movement the publicity and legitimacy it needed. He wasn't averse to a challenge, but events were in his favour. That year's chairman was Panikkar's old friend Maulana Mohammad Ali, fresh out of prison.

Panikkar was pleased. Why yes, he told the anxious Madhavan, he knew just the thing.

It wasn't going to be easy.

The annual session of the Congress was in danger that year. The Raj suspected dissidence, though it had no idea when or where it might come from. The collector of Godavari was asked to put a stop to the session. He did his best, threatening everyone with arrest if they were found funding or volunteering with the Congress. Despite this brave attempt, nearly Rs 50,000 was donated voluntarily to the Congress. The Maharaja of Pithapuram defiantly provided a 120-acre venue, christened Gandhipuram for the occasion. A huge tent capable of accommodating over 12,000 people was erected, with 150 cottages for the more senior participants.

Ever resourceful, Panikkar asked Prakasam if he could report personally on the session as *Swarajya*'s assistant editor. Blissfully ignorant of his young editor's schemes, Prakasam agreed and Panikkar went off hastily before his boss changed his mind. He had already written a letter to Ali, asking if he could bring T.K. Madhavan to attend the session at Kakinada. Ali, never unsympathetic to a cause similar to his own, agreed readily, inviting Madhavan as a special guest who would introduce a resolution for the formation of an all-India committee to work towards the eradication of untouchability. The resolution carried at Kakinada also stated that 'temple entry was the birthright of all Hindus'.[17]

In the wake of the Kakinada session, the Vaikom Satyagraha kicked off in February 1924, though it would be another decade before the movement reached its full culmination. It was far more than Madhavan had got with Gandhi and it was due to Panikkar. Indeed, the year 1923 seems to have been a busy one for Panikkar. Even as he dealt with Madhavan and the Vaikom movement, he was asked to head the literary conference being held on the sidelines of the second Kerala Provincial Congress in May. It was the first meeting after the Moplah rebellion and undoubtedly a pivotal moment in state politics for the Congress. Originally slated to be held in Thalassery, the final destination of the conference was Palakkad. Sarojini Naidu was due to preside.

Panikkar was delighted to hear that Sarojini was coming down for it. He was already good friends with her fiery sister Mrinalini and this was a great chance to get to know this extraordinary family better. He had met Sarojini earlier during her travels to Oxford, but by now, in 1923, she was holding her own on the international and national stage.

The eldest of eight children, Sarojini had been born to a father who was a social reformer, alchemist, savant and scientist. Aghorenath Chattopadhyay was the first principal of the Nizam's university in Hyderabad, although he had twice been deported from the state for his unorthodox views. His wife Varada had been educated in a Brahmo home for women and was a skilled singer and storyteller. The pair of them unsurprisingly produced eight equally extraordinary children.

Sarojini was unconventional, open, without prejudice and precocious. She passed her matric examinations at twelve, composed thirteen hundred-line poems when she was barely in her teens and fell in love with a man from a different caste when she was fourteen. She went on to marry that man—Dr Govindarajulu Naidu—under the Special Marriage Act, one of the first such unions in Hyderabad at the time. A mundane existence wouldn't have done for Sarojini. By 1915, she had thrown herself, at the behest of Gopal Krishna Gokhale, into the national movement, stirring masculine audiences from Bombay to Kerala with her fiery oration. By 1919, she was an integral part of the movement for self-rule and women's suffrage. The suffragist Margaret Cousins described Sarojini rather beautifully, as 'a highly wrought, bejewelled clasp of finest gold, which held together the divided edges of Mother India's cloak of patriotism'.[18]

Panikkar's stay in Palakkad was a handful of days, but it was enough to renew his acquaintance with the woman who had become the fierce feminist voice of the Indian freedom movement. Sarojini and he would go on to become excellent friends, and she would become a powerful link in his political networks as he grew older.

On his return to Madras though, there was trouble.

T. Prakasam had finally reached the end of his tether. He had hired a young editor, trained in Oxford and Aligarh, known to be scholarly and erudite in his perspectives. He had hoped that that young editor would put his best foot forward to make *Swarajya* a dignified Gandhian newspaper with a wide circulation. Instead, he had on his hands a veritable revolutionary, unafraid to take on anyone from established politicians to the governor himself. Panikkar was playing politics in an extremely open manner, hoping to score an optical and political victory for himself by batting for the marginalised. This wasn't going down well with the local Congress leadership either.

The straw that broke Prakasam's back was a salvo against Willingdon. This time, Panikkar based his accusations on several letters, accusing Willingdon outright of shady dealings with a prominent local jeweller. Prakasam was livid. The last thing he wanted was to tempt the fury of Willingdon, who was not known to cavil at the use of repression. He asked Panikkar—not quite so politely—to leave.

PART IV

An Emissary and an Editor (1924–1925)

CHAPTER 12

Mission to Amritsar

PANIKKAR NOW HAD TIME—TIME HE NEEDED TO THINK AND PLAN HIS next move.

His foray into journalism had not gone to plan. He had harboured some rather romantic ideals about what he could accomplish, the kind of campaigns he could run, the ladder it could have been into politics. But over the last few months, tensions had been building between Prakasam and himself not just on ideological grounds, but on financial grounds as well. For the last couple of months that he had been working at *Swarajya*, Panikkar hadn't been paid despite repeated requests and follow-ups. There was only so long that he could rely on his family's financial aid and sheer bravado. Gouri was a remarkably patient woman, but even she had her limits. She had let him know in no uncertain terms that they could not afford to continue in this piecemeal fashion permanently. Now, Panikkar made it clear to Prakasam that he wasn't sorry to be leaving journalism.

As soon as he quit, Panikkar began reaching out to the connections he had made during his Oxford days to try to see what would work out. A few weeks later, an opportunity landed in his lap.

In February 1924, Gandhi was released from Yeravada Jail two years into his prison term. He had taken severely ill with appendicitis in January. Already weak, the resulting surgery left him so debilitated that his physicians and the government agreed that there was no need to cause further furore by having Gandhi die behind bars. It was declared that an unconditional release was necessary, followed by six months in the open countryside, either in the mountains or by the sea.

The news made headlines across the world, but Gandhi had no real intention of taking time off from the national movement that was, at the time, at a critical stage. His time in prison had allowed him ample opportunity to ponder India's political future. To the American journalist Drew Pearson, Gandhi said that he still hoped 'for the attainment of swaraj by non-violence'.[1] At this point, he was also clear that he was as opposed to council entry as he was to the obstruction of work in the councils.

But the brewing crisis within the Congress had to be resolved first. If the British government had hoped that there would be a Surat-like split between the Swarajists (those who wanted participation in legislative councils) and Gandhi, they were to be sorely disappointed. Gandhi didn't like the Swarajists' agenda, but realpolitik required continued cooperation with them.

Even as he tossed about ideas for the way forward, Gandhi was trying to see the bigger picture. Where, for instance, did India stand in the map of colonies of the British empire? We don't know whether Gandhi had had the time to read Panikkar's work on this question, but in his interview with Pearson, his answers are strikingly similar to Panikkar's ideas. For instance, Gandhi's views on India's political future vis-à-vis the empire were still defined as a 'full partnership' with other parts of the empire, similar to Canada or South Africa. He also argued for 'full citizens' rights throughout the British Dominions for all the king's subjects, irrespective of caste, colour or creed'.[2]

In the months following the suspension of the non-cooperation movement, nationalism was kept alive by Gandhi's many workers across India's villages, by the Swarajists in the legislative councils, by Koya tribals in Andhra who fought the armed might of the colonial state under Ramachandra Raju, the Akalis in Punjab, the satyagrahis who defended the honour of the flag in Nagpur, and the Vaikom satyagraha that had begun in the spring of 1924 in Travancore. To regain the momentum of the national movement, Gandhi had to choose wisely.

He chose, with unerring accuracy, the Akali movement in Punjab.

The Akali movement had developed as a purely religious issue with the objective of freeing the gurudwaras from the control of the corrupt mahants (priests). This was a century-old problem. The gurudwaras had been endowed with revenue-free land and money by Ranjit Singh during the eighteenth and nineteenth centuries. These shrines had come to be managed in the eighteenth century by Udasi Sikh mahants. The government had supported the mahants, using them to preach loyalism among the Sikhs and keep the community away from the rising national movement. But in 1920, this tidy little plan unravelled in the face of a popular agitation for the reform of the gurudwaras. Reformers organised groups of volunteers known as jathas to compel the mahants and government-appointed managers to hand control to local devotees. Symbolic of their early success was the control they gained over the Golden Temple and the Akal Takht. To manage this, a representative assembly of nearly 10,000 reformers met in November 1920 and elected a 175-member committee known as the Shiromani Gurudwara Parbandhak Committee (SGPC). To organise the struggle on a more central and systematic basis, the Shiromani Akali Dal was established in December 1920 as the chief organiser of the Akali jathas.

It was not long before blood was spilled. A violent stand-off between the mahant and jathas took place at Nankana, the birthplace of Guru Nanak, which brought the Akali movement into the national spotlight. National leaders from Gandhi to Shaukat Ali extended their support to the movement, causing the Akali jathas to change tack and integrate themselves with the national movement. Further impetus was provided by the Guru Ka Bagh movement, where peacefully protesting Akali jathas were beaten by government forces. C.F. Andrews, a missionary and Gandhi's close friend, described it as 'an inhuman, foul, cowardly, and moral defeat of England'.[3] National leaders and journalists converged on the scene and massive protests were organised across Punjab. The self-control exhibited by the Akalis was extolled in various sections of the Indian press as a 'triumph of

Gandhism'.[4] This is somewhat at odds with Panikkar's memories of the incident in his memoir, which describes the Sikhs as a 'militant people' who 'revelled in fighting'.[5]

But perhaps some context to this description can be found in a long-running bitter feud between the maharajas of Nabha and Patiala. Ripudaman Singh (Nabha) and Bhupinder Singh (Patiala) were ambitious, arrogant young men. It helped nobody that each attacked the other's claims to sovereignty, which led to boundary disputes between the two states. Both princes began to cultivate lobbies for support. Patiala began to look towards the British and Nabha looked towards the more radical members of the Sikh community in his state, who were assuming positions of power within Punjab politics. Inevitably, this led to divide and conflict—and a crisis where Panikkar would come in unexpectedly handy.

By 1923, matters were coming to a sharp head. Patiala was now insisting that the issue be referred to the Government of India for settlement, while the SGPC (which was pro-Nabha) was frantically attempting backchannel talks to salvage the situation. All of this makes for amazing archival reading, but the upshot of that tense summer was that Nabha was officially accused of maladministration and asked to step aside.[6]

Events now began to move very fast.

Nabha had initially been persuaded to abdicate, but by the end of June, he was rethinking this rather rash decision. At the beginning of July, the Raj, summering in Simla, received word that some extremist Akalis had wheedled Nabha into believing that they would support his cause if he refused to abdicate. Unsurprisingly, the government was appalled and responded by cracking down hard on Nabha. The state was taken over with some powerfully restrictive conditions. The maharaja would have to, for example, reside outside his own state. He could visit it only with the prior permission of the government. He also was required to compensate Patiala to the whopping tune of Rs 50 lakh. It was an agreement that, for obvious reasons, the Government of India did not want to become public. As a result, the official report on the abdication merely stated that the Government of India had definitive evidence of a 'perversion of justice' within the state, and for those reasons, Nabha's 'voluntary abdication' had been accepted.[7]

Nabha emerged from the resulting controversy glorified among his supporters as a Sikh nationalist leader. Patiala acted swiftly in retaliation, issuing a statement in support of Nabha's abdication and the Government of India's stand on the matter. As historian Barbara Ramusack put it, 'Once the premier Sikh prince of the Punjab openly approved of Nabha's abdication, a united Sikh front on the matter was no longer possible.'[8]

The Akalis—and indeed, much of the population of Punjab—were up in arms in support of Nabha. On 24 August 1923, an Akali agitation was held at Jaito, a Nabha village close to British Punjab. The protests boiled over into nearby villages in Faridkot and Patiala, forcing the British Resident, A.B. Minchin, to request that the states begin to crack down hard against any jatha-related violence within their borders. It was fast becoming clear that this was a dangerous case of politics bleeding into religion and at its special session in Delhi, the Congress decided that it was now time to step in. Three observers were sent to Nabha—Jawaharlal Nehru, K. Santanum and Panikkar's friend, the Congress leader A.T. Gidwani. Nehru and his companions had quite likely hoped to effect some kind of Congress–Akali alliance in an area where the Congress presence was weak. Panikkar confirmed as much in his memoir later: 'The Congress deputed a reliable person to give them proper advice ... This was my old contemporary and friend, Gidwani.'[9]

Unfortunately, not only was the jatha stopped in its tracks, but police orders were issued, asking Nehru to abandon his plans of entering Nabha.[10] The Congress observers disobeyed the orders and found themselves clapped behind bars.[11] It took some weeks to release them, wrapping up what Nehru bitterly called a 'farcical process' and sending the three Congressmen back to Delhi.[12]

A second chance for the Congress to establish contact with the Akalis came some weeks later. At the end of September, the SGPC voted to send a jatha of five hundred Akalis to protest the government's interruption of the Akhand Path (the Sikh tradition of uninterrupted reading of the Guru Granth Sahib). By doing so, the SGPC was positioning itself as champions against state interference in religious affairs. The British cracked down, declaring the SGPC as an unlawful organisation. This was the turning point. Quietly, the Congress began reaching out to Akali leaders yet again. An Akali Sahayak Bureau was set up in Amritsar to assist with publicity, and Congress funds began to be diverted to the Akalis in early 1924.

While the Congress had been working to build an organisational foundation, the Government of India had been working equally hard to subvert its attempts. The government was now adept not only at propaganda, but skilled at using Indian princes and politicians as a front for its own schemes. The Congress had also not factored in local religious and political dynamics. Locally speaking, Nabha's abdication was a source of considerable confusion for the SGPC. Religious-minded Sikhs were alienated by Akali support of such a political cause as the abdication of a maharaja who was hardly noted for his virtues as an orthodox Sikh. Furthermore, its flirtation with the Congress—an avowedly political, secular, Hindu-dominated organisation—only served to tarnish the credentials of the SGPC in the eyes of the more conservative Sikhs. The original programme had been to reform gurudwaras. Why were the Akalis getting involved in politics? Conservative Sikh lobbies had no desire to get involved with the larger nationalist movement. This was the crisis brewing in Nabha and Amritsar that Panikkar would be sent to resolve as Gandhi's emissary in 1924.

His illness and subsequent operation had rendered him too weak to travel just yet, but Gandhi knew he needed reliable eyes and ears on the ground to report back to him so he could devise plans for the way ahead. Given what had happened to Gidwani and Nehru, the emissary would have to be intelligent, perceptive and politically neutral as an observer. This was when Panikkar arrived in Bombay to meet C.F. Andrews, an old friend from Oxford days.

Panikkar was in the city to check up on the credentials of the *Indian Daily Mail*. He was wary of journalism now. Another stint in a badly paid, irregular job wasn't what he wanted at all. He said as much to Andrews, but the other man was listening with only half an ear. Andrews knew that Gandhi was keeping his eyes peeled for a suitable emissary to sort out the crisis in Punjab. Could Panikkar be the man for the job?

Andrews wrote immediately to Mohammad Ali, then serving as the Congress president, to find out what he thought of Panikkar. Ali responded very favourably. Yes, Panikkar was just the man Gandhi needed for the job. He would, Ali had no doubt, be perfect for this delicate mission. So it was that Panikkar was summoned to Juhu, to the Gujarati industrialist Narottam Morarjee's attractive cottage, nestled in coconut groves by the Arabian Sea, to meet Gandhi.

Gandhi was duly prepped for the meeting, though he did remember young Panikkar from Aligarh. He asked forthrightly if the younger man was prepared to face arrest upon arrival in Amritsar. Panikkar readily assented, though this was hardly a point of nobility as much as it was the awareness that this, finally, was his make or break moment. He stayed with Gandhi for a few days, walking with him in the mornings on the beach, to gain instructions for his mission to Amritsar.

Gandhi was remarkably clear. The Congress had established an office in Amritsar, discreetly named the Akali Sahayak Bureau, where Panikkar would be based. His duties, apart from investigating incidents of violence, would be to disseminate propaganda on behalf of the Sikhs, handle the press and send dispatches to Delhi on the state of relations between the religious communities in Punjab.[13] Based on their discussions, Gandhi issued a statement in which he made it clear that he wanted the Akalis to divorce their struggle from the issue of Nabha's abdication. He also stated that he wasn't entirely convinced by the maharaja's case, since Nabha's writings alone had made it 'practically impossible' to support any agitation in his favour. Only if the maharaja was publicly willing to face the consequences of his actions would Gandhi think of supporting his cause.[14]

Would Panikkar be open to taking up this assignment?

Panikkar most certainly was: 'Failure to discharge the high responsibilities devolving on the representative of Gandhiji and the Congress would disgrace me, while success in my mission would establish my reputation.'[15] On 12 March, he told Gandhi that he would be ready any time the mission was green-lit.

Gandhi wrote that night to Nehru, telling him about the man he had chosen to head the Sahayak Bureau in Amritsar. If he had expected Nehru to be delighted, however, he was mistaken. Nehru had already been working on getting his own replacement. In fact, he had been in touch with the Sanskrit scholar Sampurnanand, briefing him about his potential duties at the Sahayak Bureau. 'All this work must be done in Amritsar as quietly as possible without any fuss or show.'[16] Sampurnanand, from the looks of it, had seemed ready to take on the job. Nehru had already written to Mangal Singh, the SGPC president, letting him know that the scholar would be arriving in Amritsar to head the bureau. Now Gandhi was telling him something completely different.

Swallowing what must have been a keen amount of embarrassment, Nehru wrote hastily to the SGPC officials again, letting them know that Sampurnanand would no longer be coming to Amritsar. Panikkar was the man deputed personally by Gandhi to take over. To Gandhi himself, Nehru was encouraging (not that he had a choice). 'I have known Panikkar by repute for several years and met him for a short time in Coconada *(sic)*. I am sure his presence will be very useful in Amritsar,' he wrote. 'His ignorance of Hindustani will be a drawback, but this will be more than compensated by his other achievements. He will be an excellent man for publicity work. Perhaps, owing to his language difficulty, he might be very helpful in bringing the Sikhs and Hindus nearer to each other. But on the whole, Panikkar will be an acquisition in Amritsar.'[17]

What terms of compensation, Nehru inquired, had Gandhi in mind for Panikkar?

The question took the Mahatma aback, for in true Gandhian fashion he hadn't dreamed of suggesting anything as worldly as a salary. Amused, Nehru tactfully suggested that perhaps it would be suitable to let Panikkar know that this would not be a mission without monetary recompense. 'As regards terms, anything that you consider reasonable will surely be agreed to by all others.'[18] Considerably embarrassed by this reminder of his material duties, Gandhi retorted, 'I have not intended, nor do I intend now to form any decided opinion about making appointments, fixing salaries etc.'[19] But he wasn't quite as other-worldly as all that. He had taken the time to get to know his young emissary and he knew that Panikkar was still in debt from his time at *Swarajya*. Giving him the salary that Nehru suggested was one way to ensure Panikkar's loyalty. He proposed a six-month stint in Amritsar, with Panikkar to return if matters could be wrapped up earlier than that.

On 16 March, Panikkar departed for Amritsar, clutching a letter of introduction to Mangal Singh. For Gouri, left behind in Kavalam with the children, it was the beginning of a pattern that would last for the rest of their married lives. She would acidly tell one of her daughters later, 'My dear girl, with your father I could never tell when he would just jump up, throw everything over and stomp off.'[20] As a husband, Panikkar was both a man to be proud of and a man who would infuriate the most patient of wives. For large swathes of time, Gouri would be left on her own, looking after a growing family. They already had three children, two more would follow. Gouri would be patient with this lifestyle for a while. For her generation, this was not an unusual marital situation, particularly if you were married to a man with considerable drive and ambition. But Gouri, as Panikkar would discover, was not a typical woman.

For now, though, he was thinking only of cementing a position for himself on the political landscape.

'I have told him that he is to give the public an unvarnished and impartial statement about all the happenings in connection with the movement of the SGPC,' Gandhi told Nehru, warning, 'While he must necessarily be sympathetic in his consideration of the situation as it presents itself to him … he must not hide shortcomings if he notices any.'[21]

From here, Nehru took over as the person to whom Panikkar would be reporting from Amritsar. It was the beginning of a long working relationship between the two men. From Amritsar to Peking, Panikkar's dispatches would become an equal source of insight and frustration for Nehru. There was, in these first letters between the two, a note of authority from Nehru as he set the tone for the younger man: 'You need not send frequent reports. All your communiques should be sent to me . . . you might also from time to time send me a personal letter, giving any special news which has not appeared in the press.'[22]

Along with that letter and a brief to see if he could broker an informal conference between the Sikhs and the Hindus, Panikkar received a lengthy sketch of the legal circumstances of Gidwani and Nehru's detainment in Nabha.[23] It was best, Nehru felt, if the man on the ground was in full possession of the facts. Only then could Panikkar carry out his public relations effectively. In this arena, Nehru deferred to Panikkar courteously. 'You are a journalist. I can hardly give any tips as to how to carry on the publicity work most effectively.'[24] If he wanted, Nehru added, Panikkar could assume charge of *Onward*, the official magazine of the SGPC. That would be the best way to front his propaganda mission in Punjab and achieve the purpose of blunting the magazine's otherwise aggressive tone.

Panikkar was thinking fast on his feet. His inquiries, when he arrived in Amritsar, told him that though the grievances of the Akalis were very real, they weren't quite as piously sanctimonious as they claimed to be. Nor did he get much help from local SGPC officials, many of whom were certainly not prepared to face a smooth-talking Malayali with little understanding or knowledge of the local language, or even of Hindustani. Nor was Panikkar particularly prepossessing physically. Photographs of the time show a slight, swarthy man, with round spectacles in the style favoured by Gandhi, a mop of thinning black hair and a vague attempt at a toothbrush moustache. But in terms of enthusiasm, persuasiveness and intelligence, the Congress couldn't have chosen their man better. As the public relations officer (so to speak) of the Akali Sahayak Bureau, he devoted his time to writing articles, sending out press releases by the dozen and using his wide network of contacts in the press to get extended coverage of the issue to give maximum publicity to Gidwani's arrest.[25] In all these endeavours, he met with little to no cooperation from the SGPC itself.

That he was not particularly welcome on the ground doesn't seem to have fazed Panikkar. He was bent on reporting the truth as he found it to Gandhi and Nehru. He reported that the language being used by magazines like *Onward* and by the local press was 'inflammatory and untrustworthy'.[26] This was important because violence in language or motive would automatically distance the Sikhs from Gandhian principles. Since his own persuasion was failing, Panikkar decided to get Gandhi involved directly. Compiling a report based on his assessment and adding a copy of the *Onward Special* (issued on 17 March), he sent copies to Nehru and Gandhi. Mincing no words, his report absolved the Sikhs of violence. 'The crowd [jathas] was unarmed and not in the possession of lathis.' Nehru was incredulous. Surely the crowd had held *some* weapons, like kirpans? Wasn't Panikkar being too sweeping in his assessment?

Panikkar replied swiftly that the Hindus were to blame. They were 'narrow-minded'. But Nehru retorted, 'The Sikhs have been largely to blame ... There could have been a word or gesture which would have won over the Hindus ... but they did not care to make it.'[27]

For Nehru then, the bitterness of the Hindus was clearly not without foundation. It was 'chiefly due to the realisation of his [a Hindu man] utter weakness ... and being narrow-minded and bigoted, this bitterness, instead of urging him to better himself or make himself stronger, turns to hatred and curses'.[28] Nehru noted that in comparison to the Hindu majority, the Sikhs had no one to turn to, and 'in this respect, one can sympathise with the Sikhs'.[29] Sympathy or not though, the Congress general secretary wasn't too pleased with the SGPC either. 'Their treatment of the Congress Bureau, their secretiveness and their desire to not get mixed up in any way with the Congress is not very courteous to the Congress,' he wrote crossly to his colleague, Dr Saifuddin Kitchlew. 'It almost appears that we are thrusting ourselves and our help where it is neither appreciated nor wanted.'[30]

Gandhi was appalled by what Panikkar was reporting. He lost no time in debating with Panikkar on the merits of his assessment, writing instead to Mangal Singh straight away, berating him about what he was reading in the *Onward Special*. 'If the *Onward* is to be run as the official organ, you should have a sober and truthful editor.'[31] Writing separately to Panikkar, Gandhi was in despair. 'How is it possible to issue any statement after reading the *Onward Special*?' he demanded irately. 'It is impossible for me to throw myself heart and soul into a struggle which, claiming to be religious, requires to be supported by inflammatory and untruthful writings.'[32]

This was going too far for Panikkar who, while he certainly had his doubts, felt that the Gandhian programme had met with some amount of success in Punjab. Quickly, he dashed off yet another report, letting Gandhi know that to a large extent, the Sikhs had implemented his principles. They wore swadeshi khadi, had abolished untouchability and there was a wide emphasis in the community on the prohibition of alcoholic beverages. But he admitted that, for the majority, non-violence was still a strategy rather than an end in itself. It didn't, for instance, stop every village from forming 'semi-military bodies of Sikh youth under local commanders and these were linked to district commanders. This Akali Dal formation was intimidating Hindus and Muslims in the villages.'[33]

But he was even then keenly aware of just how to report the truth to those in power. In a nicely tempered report written in April to Gandhi, Panikkar explained, 'The (Sikh) community, as a whole, has understood non-violence merely to mean abstention from actively assaulting their opponents. Perhaps that idea is, to some extent, inevitable, among the uncultivated rustics who constitute the *jatha* but what I consider a fundamental weakness in the whole Sikh position is that even the Shiromani Gurudwara Prabhandak *(sic)* Committee does not understand the implication of non-violence.'[34] In addition, he hastened to reassure Gandhi that it wasn't as though he didn't get on with *anyone* in the SGPC. Indeed, the one Sikh leader who he felt had the principles to support satyagraha was Mangal Singh himself. With him, Panikkar told Gandhi, he had managed to build a close working relationship and a closer friendship.[35]

The truth of course was that that Panikkar wasn't sure of the waters in which he was swimming. He knew he was mistrusted by the majority of the SGPC leaders, just as he knew they were polite to him because they felt they needed to be civil to Gandhi's emissary. So he was not as yet sure of how far he could broker a midway between the Sikhs and the Hindus.

For one, he knew that once his report to Congress headquarters was made public to the SGPC, there would be uproar. He was right on that score. The Akalis were outraged that Panikkar had in a sense blown their cover, and Gandhi's emissary received a flood of death threats from the Dal's more extreme members. It was a rapidly escalating situation, and would have slipped out of a lesser man's control, but Amritsar was the first time that Panikkar demonstrated his skills in walking a very tight rope. On the one hand, he had to bring Gandhi around from his position of horrified reluctance as far as supporting the Sikhs was concerned. On the other hand, Panikkar had to balance Nehru's more pragmatic view of affairs, which was that it was still necessary to make gestures of détente, wherever possible.[36]

Throughout that summer, tensions ran high.

Panikkar was not in Amritsar for very long, but it changed not only how he thought of his career, but how senior Congress leaders perceived him and his potential for both the party and the freedom movement. It was Panikkar's controlled reporting from Amritsar that, along with Lala Lajpat Rai's influence, changed Gandhi's initial reluctance to support gurudwara reform into a mood of thoughtful acceptance, and it was Panikkar's balancing of Nehru's insistence on rationality that saw the eventual carving out of a resolution for the Akali problem.[37]

CHAPTER 13

Summer in Punjab

AS SPRING EDGED INTO SUMMER, PANIKKAR FOUND HIMSELF DEALING with fast boiling political hot water. If he had to get Gandhi *and* Nehru's stamp of approval on his time in Amritsar, he needed to resolve the Akali issue quickly.

It was the first time he was involved directly not just in the negotiation of a politically advantageous position, but a diplomatic negotiation of sorts as well. His style of functioning is, in retrospect, interesting to observe. Once he had drawn up an outline of his plan, he went not to Jawaharlal, the man running his operation in Amritsar, and not to Gandhi, the man who had personally vouched for his deployment to Punjab. He went instead to Motilal Nehru, a known and vocal Swarajist, and to Malcolm Hailey, then the governor-designate of Punjab. According to Panikkar's plan, the Congress would support the Sikh claim to control their own gurudwaras and not even the provincial government would oppose this claim. In return for this concession, the Sikhs would have to work towards a settlement of their dispute with Congress leaders. In his eyes, this meant a break-up of the Akali Dal. 'I think that in any peaceful solution of the question of our acceptance of the (Sikh) case as a national one, one must insist on the break-up of this force,' Panikkar wrote to Gandhi. 'Even non-Akali Sikhs have many times spoken to me about this, and they are afraid that when once the fight with the Government in the Gurudwaras is over the forces of the Khalsa would have to be turned against someone else.'[1]

Truth be told, Panikkar was also worried about what he was seeing on the ground as far as the spread of ultra right-wing forces were concerned. The Shuddhi (purification) and Sangathan (unity) movements launched by the Arya Samaj at this time had an obvious anti-Islamic impetus and it wasn't surprising that local Muslims, led by the fiery Dr Saifuddin Kitchlew, had banded together in defence. 'Dr. Kitchlew is very busy here with his sanghathan movement,' Panikkar reported to Gandhi. 'He is organising the Muslims on the lines of Sikh *jathas.* I have once written to you at length my objections to this system of armed peace, of each community organising itself into semi-military bodies. I am much afraid that, if Sikhs, Muslims and Hindus are to have *jathas* in the Punjab, the peace of the province would not be worth a day's purchase.'[2]

The only means that Panikkar could think of to get around this problem was if the Congress supported the claims for the control of the gurudwaras while avoiding other overtly political issues. Gandhi acted on this suggestion as fast as possible, sending Mangal Singh a memorandum to that effect. The provincial government, with the benedictions of Sir Malcolm Hailey, seemed willing to reach an agreement as well, one that would entrust the SGPC with the management of the gurudwaras on the condition that the committee would not interfere in the dispute over Nabha's abdication. Left with no option, the SGPC agreed reluctantly, prompting Gandhi to send a jubilant telegram to Panikkar, 'My congratulations on jatha's peaceful surrender!'[3]

For Panikkar, it was a big step forward in gaining Gandhi's trust and esteem, ingredients vital to furthering a potential career in the Congress. But in typical fashion, he was not fully content until he took on two birds with one stone. Having waited a while, Panikkar now dared to write to Gandhi about a cause that was still dear to his heart: the newly begun Vaikom satyagraha.

On 30 March 1924, the Kerala Pradesh Congress Committee (KPCC) had made a start in its fight against untouchability. That day, a Nair, a Pulaya and an Ezhava activist, followed by thousands of khadi-clad others, attempted to walk on the barricaded roads leading to the Shiva temple at Vaikom.[4] They were promptly arrested by the Travancore police. More Congress activists, repeating the same act, were jailed immediately. With most of the KPCC languishing behind bars, the harried barrister George Joseph desperately sought directions from Gandhi and C. Rajagopalachari on what to do next. While he waited for a response, Joseph dashed off a letter to Periyar, the president of the Tamil Nadu Congress Committee, pleading with him to lead the satyagraha. Periyar handed over temporary charge to Rajaji before arriving hastily in Vaikom on 13 April 1924.

The Vaikom satyagraha commanded national attention. Demonstrators marched each day to the barricades set up by the state police. They blocked roads, sat before the police lines at each of the temple's four entrances, sang patriotic songs and fasted.[5] On 24 April 1924, in a show of support, a Sikh jatha arrived in Travancore, travelling all the way from Amritsar. Panikkar wrote to Gandhi about this jatha, letting him know that the Sikhs would be opening free kitchens in Travancore.[6]

Gandhi, who would take another year before going to Travancore himself, wasn't quite ready to take the leap. He was still physically frail and after the horrors of Chauri Chaura, and wanted to take things step by step. He told Panikkar as much, even though he conceded 'that is a most important movement that has been launched in Travancore'.[7] But he called for the closure of the Sikh kitchens and warned local Christians in Travancore to keep away from 'a Hindu affair'.[8] Having done this, Gandhi politely sent his best wishes to K.P. Kesava Menon, the nationalist founder of the daily Malayalam newspaper *Mathrubhumi* and one of the leaders of the satyagraha in Vaikom.[9]

Panikkar remained unfazed at Gandhi's noncommittal attitude, reminding him tactfully that untouchability was a cause worthy of integration into the national movement. He had seen enough of Gandhi's tactics to know that there was in this seemingly neutral stance a far cannier logic. The situation on the ground in Vaikom was complicated by the fact that Travancore was a princely state. For

Gandhi to endorse the struggle would mean an acknowledgment of popular resistance against the maharaja. He had already publicly stated in an interview to the *Hindu* that the rulers were 'trustees of their peoples'.[10] Like Amritsar then, this issue would have to be purely religious without relying on external support or aid. Only then could Gandhi step in.

It speaks volumes about Panikkar's savviness that he lost no time in aligning with Gandhi's positions. Unsurprisingly, this called down a hailstorm of criticism. Panikkar was accused of opportunism, if not outright betrayal, of a cause that could never succeed without political involvement from the Congress high command. 'The so-called *satyagrahi* press in Travancore has been ... saying that I have expressed those opinions because the Travancore Durbar has bribed me, and that I am anxious to get into Government favour by expressing opinions favourable to them,' Panikkar wrote ruefully to Gandhi.[11] The vernacular press in his home state was even more savage, openly saying that Gandhi had blocked the possibility of Congress support because the facts had been misrepresented by Panikkar.[12] It would take another year for the satyagraha to be resolved, but in Punjab, there was faster progress.

Throughout the summer of 1924, Panikkar's hands were full with the maharaja of Nabha. Following SGPC's agreement to Panikkar's plan, Gandhi had asked him to meet the disgruntled prince and find out what he wanted. After all, the Nabha issue was now the only thing blocking the resolution of the Akali problem as well as the way forward for ties between the Akalis and the Congress.

In the middle of April 1924, Panikkar went obediently to Dehra Dun where the maharaja had been externed. The full report of the conversations between himself and Nabha are not available, but Panikkar has quoted part of the conversation in his memoir.[13] Once Nabha granted him an audience, Panikkar lost no time in opening with the tantalising gambit that Gandhi would like to get better acquainted with the details of the case. The maharaja, always keen to enjoy the limelight, was delighted.

'What details does he wish to know?'

'You have issued a proclamation that you abdicated voluntarily,' Panikkar explained tactfully. 'If this is true, then how does any inquiry arise at all?'

'The proclamation was signed under duress,' Nabha protested indignantly, 'I was in fact externed!'

If that was the case, Panikkar said, Gandhi would be willing to raise the subject directly with the government, but if the government continued to press charges, then Gandhi would be forced to make a public inquiry into the issue. Would Nabha agree to that?

Predictably, the maharaja was incensed. 'Who are they to sit in judgement over me?' he demanded irritably. 'Who is Gandhiji to ask for an inquiry?'

Panikkar scented blood in the water. 'No one wants an inquiry,' he reminded the maharaja gently. 'But unless he is convinced that you have been treated unjustly, Gandhi will not take any step. Hence, it is in your own interest to establish the justice of your case ... Otherwise how can there be a restoration?'[14]

The maharaja was cornered.

Clearly on the backfoot, Nabha made the mistake of asking Panikkar to wait for his lawyer Durga Prasad to arrive from Allahabad. He would not, he said, say anything further without his lawyer present. This answer gave Panikkar a certain grim satisfaction. By now, he had had enough conversations with the maharaja to draw his own conclusions, none of which were favourable to Nabha. 'The more I heard, the more certain I became that the Congress should disassociate itself from him.'[15]

Durga Prasad's arrival the next day yielded the answers Panikkar was expecting. Nabha was not prepared to deny in writing that his abdication had been voluntary, nor was he prepared to agree to a public enquiry on his conduct of state affairs as maharaja. Nobody in the Congress would be delighted with this outcome, but Panikkar had been thinking rapidly about contingency plans. The seed of an idea had been planted during his stay in Dehra Dun and it would ultimately culminate in the bifurcation of religious and princely interests in Punjab.

The next day, Panikkar left the cantankerous Nabha and set off to meet Jawaharlal Nehru in Allahabad. It was the first time he would be meeting the man he had been reporting to for so many weeks, and he was pleasantly surprised. Nehru at this time was thirty-five years old, buried somewhat crossly in administrative duties with the Congress. He was already the president of the Allahabad Congress Committee and heavily involved in provincial party work. On top of all that, he was also the general secretary. This made him, as he described rather bitterly to the lawyer Abdul Majeed Khwaja, 'a kind of Pooh-Bah'.[16] But Nehru was aware that gaining Sikh support for the national movement was not just important, but easier said than done. He also was aware of the fact that despite his lack of language skills and his greenness at dealing with political issues, Panikkar had done far more than Gandhi and he himself had expected. As a result, when he met Panikkar in the book-lined library in palatial Anand Bhavan, Nehru was quite cordial.

Panikkar on the other hand very nearly forgot why he was there in the first place. Anand Bhavan even today is a grand sight, and in its heyday, it really was quite something. 'Motilal Nehru was fonder of luxury than most maharajas,' Panikkar recalled snidely later, though Jawaharlal went up several notches in his eyes for his simplicity and his aversion to glamour. 'He lived there almost like another guest.'[17]

The two days and nights that Panikkar spent in Anand Bhavan taught him much about how the freedom movement was being run behind the scenes. More importantly, it laid the foundations for a much closer friendship with Nehru. With Motilal's son, Panikkar found it easy to be frank. He minced no words therefore when Nehru asked for his opinion on the Nabha affair. There was no reward, Panikkar said, to be found in supporting the maharaja's cause for he was 'by nature vicious and as a ruler, arbitrary and inhumane'.[18] Still, he repeated, if the Sikh community's religious problems were separated from the political affairs of Nabha, then the gurudwara issue could easily be settled. It was a far-sighted suggestion and would result in the Sikh Gurudwara Act of 1925, with Nehru's approval.[19]

For Panikkar, this moment was the fillip his career had been seeking. So when Nehru suggested that they both meet Gandhi to run Panikkar's plan for the resolution of the Akali problem by him, he was only too delighted. A personal meeting with the Mahatma would, he felt, guarantee his political credentials and gain him another stab at getting Gandhi more closely involved with the unfolding events at Vaikom. He hadn't paused in his campaign to keep Gandhi apprised of what was happening on the ground. For instance, when he heard that George Joseph was planning to lead the satyagraha, Panikkar wrote immediately to Gandhi, suggesting rather insidiously that a non-Hindu had no business participating in such a movement. Gandhi agreed as Panikkar had known he would, though this little move would cost the younger man some friends.

But here was a chance to meet Gandhi in person and perhaps have a longer, more fruitful discussion with him. Panikkar and Nehru travelled the next day to the ashram at Sabarmati, where Gandhi was resting. Though he was still recovering from his illness, Gandhi was very much at the centre of several political developments at this time. It was at Sabarmati for instance that the Congress held a rather momentous meeting to try and thrash out the differences between the no-changers and the Swarajists. It wasn't the first time they had attempted to find a middle path, but just as the other times, when the issue of council entry was raised, Motilal and other dissenters walked out, leaving the frustrated Gandhi close to tears.[20]

There were more meetings after this. Panikkar watched how politely and deftly the older man dealt with the many groups and cliques who flooded the ashram every day. There were Hindus complaining bitterly that the Aga Khan's followers were insulting them; Punjabis with the allegation that Dr Kitchlew was damaging the interests of Hindus and Maulvis who were livid at the forced conversion of Muslims to the Hindu fold. Apart from local groups, there were hundreds of Europeans in Sabarmati wanting to meet the mystic fakir, the legend of whom had taken the West by storm. It was a 'wonderful spectacle', wrote Panikkar later, but there were so many people that he began to fret quietly about Vaikom and the Akali movement. Were they both now on the backburner as far as Gandhi was concerned?

Here though, Panikkar severely underestimated Gandhi's willingness to devote time to a cause he considered both politically and socially worthy. On the evening of 29 April, Gandhi told Panikkar politely, as he went in for his nightly meditation, 'Exactly at midnight, I shall come out and then we can decide everything.' Panikkar was taken aback by the suddenness of this pronouncement. Gandhi hadn't had the time to even think about Vaikom or Punjab so far. However, he was too well mannered to betray shock. So he went obediently for dinner, and at midnight precisely, he went and stood outside Gandhi's bedroom door. He was wondering whether to knock or not when the door opened and the Mahatma strode out, nearly knocking him down in the process. 'You may return to Amritsar on the morning train,' Gandhi told a delighted Panikkar. 'The Sikh leaders have not only accepted your suggestions, but have agreed to carry them out. They have agreed to drop the Nabha affair.'[21]

Panikkar was thrilled. This had been his first political assignment and to have completed it to the satisfaction of both Nehru and Gandhi was beyond gratifying. He left for Amritsar the next morning, just missing Nehru who was coming back to Sabarmati to meet Gandhi. The Congress general secretary was pleased at how events were moving, and receptive, thanks to Gandhi's interventions, of the fact that the Congress could have prevented the Akali issue from becoming a problem. 'I feel that we are to blame partly for allowing the situation to drift and not taking steps earlier to define our position,' he wrote thoughtfully to Panikkar.[22]

But Nehru was also wondering how best the Congress could further utilise Panikkar. He had had Panikkar investigated by then and had also pulled together a selection of the younger man's work to read and assess. He obviously liked what he read, for he lost no time in asking Panikkar to begin putting together a history of the non-cooperation movement. Nehru had clearly thought the plan through in his head. One idea, he suggested, was to edit a collection of essays on different aspects of the movement and the other—the one he was leaning towards—was a straightforward biography of the movement. Gandhi was markedly disinterested in this project, but for Nehru the main goal was always the bigger public relations picture: getting India's story and struggle out into the wider world. In Panikkar, he sensed a worthy pen.

When Panikkar read through Nehru's offer, he was sorely tempted. It was not journalism, but it was not academia either. It would also be a big step towards establishing his credentials as not just a representative and emissary of the Congress, but as its spokesperson as well. The only problem was that there was far too much ambiguity around Nehru's suggestion and around the events on the ground in Amritsar.

The resolution of the Akali problem had brought Panikkar recognition within the pillars of the Congress and by the end of July that year, he was able to successfully report to Gandhi that even the most recalcitrant SGPC leaders were now determined to drop the Nabha issue.[23] But once the mission ended, what would be next? He didn't know whether Congress headquarters intended to shut down the bureau once his mission was over. He was also uncomfortably aware that the British had cottoned on to the real activities of the Sahayak Bureau and the reasons behind his presence in Amritsar.[24] What, in that eventuality, would become of him? When he wrote anxiously to Nehru about it, the Congress general secretary's response was disconcertingly airy. 'I think it is very unlikely. But there is no knowing and everything that happens is perhaps for the best, *n'est-ce pas*?'[25]

The letter was a shower of cold water for Panikkar. He had his pride, and not unnaturally, he felt that the least the Congress general secretary could have told him was what he might expect in Amritsar next. In swift response, he stopped reporting to Congress headquarters. So cold was his silence that Nehru was betrayed into equal frustration, addressing Panikkar as 'sir' in a formal telegram.[26]

But to no avail.

For over a month, there was radio silence from Amritsar. Panikkar was occupied otherwise—this time in plotting his next move.

Chapter 14

'Alone, I Did It!'

FOR A WHILE, THE SIKHS HAD BEEN PUSHING TO SET UP AN ENGLISH daily to gain a wider outreach for their political problems. A key mover behind this idea was one of the founding fathers of the Akali Dal, Sunder Singh Lyallpuri.

Lyallpuri was Mangal Singh's son-in-law, a proud young man who wanted nothing to do with the British and who wanted, at a time when Sikhs were joining the Arya Samaj fold in large numbers, to revive an awareness of Sikhism and its rich history. He was a sharp organiser and knew that one of the best ways to disseminate information was to start publishing.

In many ways, Lyallpuri was a far-sighted reformer. Between 1906 and 1908, he had worked closely with Nabha on a draft of what would become the Anand Marriage Act in 1909. It was under the aegis of both the Akali Dal and Lyallpuri that the Shiromani Akali Dal (SAD) came to be in December 1920. An undaunted propagandist, Lyallpuri was pursued by the British for his provocative political stance. And yet he pursued his goal of an English-language mouthpiece for the Sikh cause. In this ambition, he was egged on by Madan Mohan Malaviya. A gifted educationist, orator and politician, Malaviya had already participated in debates on issues ranging from education to the nationalisation of railways. In 1915, he had helped found the Hindu Mahasabha. As Lyallpuri's friend, he believed that an English newspaper would gain the Sikhs far greater reach. Both men took Panikkar into their confidence. He was educated, intelligent and articulate. Could he write for them as he had written for *Modern Review* and *Commonweal*?

If they had expected any kind of visible delight at their proposition, they were mistaken. Panikkar had been burned by his experience with the Congress. He had no desire to remain in Amritsar all his life, nor did he desire any longer to relegate himself to a position that was largely behind the scenes. He told Lyallpuri and Mangal Singh politely that 'to base an English daily in a district centre would lead to disaster'.[1] Delhi at the time didn't have an English daily, he pointed out. If the Akalis were willing to consider Delhi as a base, he would be prepared to assist.

For a time, there was a deadlock.

Lyallpuri and Mangal Singh couldn't understand how or why Delhi rather than Amritsar should be representative of Sikh interests. But Panikkar stuck to his guns. For him, it was Delhi or nothing. He also insisted to the considerable alarm of the Sikhs that the paper, if it went ahead, could not become a bias tool for Nabha. It would deal with national politics, rather than the communal interests of the Sikhs.

Singh and Lyallpuri took the offer home to ponder it, but they could see the sense in what Panikkar was suggesting. Talks began to move ahead for a potential new daily, possibly titled *Hindustan Times*, known briefly as *The Hindustan*. If this worked out, it would be a splendid opportunity for Panikkar, bigger and more dynamic than the backroom role that Nehru had envisioned for him. If it came down to getting Gandhi on board, that wouldn't be a problem either. Panikkar knew enough of the Mahatma by now to understand that Gandhi would see it for the political opportunity it was. Still, he saw no reason to tell Nehru directly about anything just yet. Instead, he allowed the rumour mills to begin spinning. By June, word had reached Delhi of his intentions. Nehru wrote agitatedly to Mohammad Ali, 'Panikkar has evidently decided to leave the Akali Sahayak Bureau and take to editing *The Hindustan* … He has not written to me anything definite about his plans but I take it he cannot continue in Amritsar.'[2]

Once he was sure that Nehru would have heard *something*, Panikkar wrote pleasantly to the Congress general secretary, reestablishing contact after a month in the most neutral fashion possible. Deliberately, he mentioned not one word about the *Hindustan Times*, keeping his letter to a perfectly polite report of events on the ground in Amritsar. Nehru was unsurprisingly miffed. 'Your letter came as quite a surprise,' he responded stiffly. 'I thought you had forgotten us and our office.' He then ruined the effect of this superb coldness by asking plaintively, 'Is there any truth in the report that you are soon going to take charge of a daily in Delhi?'[3]

To this, Panikkar never replied.

Even in retrospect, this is a little astounding. Jawaharlal Nehru was not really a person to ignore, especially if you were a young man trying to make it in the world of politics. Panikkar had only just embarked on a career that he clearly wanted to be political. Being deliberately rude to those holding the reins of power was a risky gamble to take. But, if a gamble it was, it paid off excellently. It showed both Nehru and Gandhi that Panikkar, despite his youth and inexperience, didn't really *need* either of them. He could make big moves on his own. On 30 July 1924, Nehru was staggered to receive a printed notice about the launch of *Hindustan*, which would go on to become *Hindustan Times*. 'I wonder if you are too busy to write to me about it,' he wrote to Panikkar in natural confusion. 'What is going to happen to the Sahayak Bureau? When do you intend leaving Amritsar? … Also, what happens to the great history?'[4]

There was no reply to this either.

Whether Nehru liked it or not, matters were out of his hands. He never really forgot that moment. The year 1924 was when K.M. Panikkar gained Jawaharlal Nehru's reluctant and permanent respect.

The decision to jump ship yet again, from politics back to journalism, had an insuperable advantage in Panikkar's eyes: he would no longer be reporting to anyone. Both Lyallpuri and Singh had promised him that he would run the show as he saw fit. That said, Panikkar had never run or started a paper from scratch. He would soon discover that naming a newspaper was the simplest part. He chose *Hindustan Times* simply because in north India, 'the country was better known as Hindustan, than either India or Bharat'.[5]

On a daily basis though, there were administrative annoyances to handle, such as long discussions on whether *Hindustan Times* should be a morning or an evening paper. Everyone decided that it was best to fit in with the reigning model of the day, which was to publish it as an evening paper. Then there was the question of how many pages it ought to be, and how *Hindustan Times* would be priced. That took even longer to answer; eventually, Lyallpuri, Singh and Panikkar decided to fix on twelve pages with a price point of six paise. The one point on which they foundered was the decision of funding. Many years later, in 1974, Mangal Singh ruefully admitted, 'Like me, Panikkar was totally ignorant of the business side of the newspaper and thought rupees one lakh should be sufficient to run it.'[6] The money was eventually organised by the Sikh diaspora in the United States who were keen to find other ways to fund the movement in Punjab in the aftermath of the Ghadar movement. Unfortunately, Singh and Panikkar couldn't meet their ambitious goal of a lakh of rupees, making do instead with a paltry Rs 25,000, including some money that Panikkar himself managed to scrape together.

Next was the question of location. Singh and Lyallpuri had agreed reluctantly to let Panikkar investigate the potential of setting up a press in the capital. Panikkar duly went to Delhi, where he was aghast to discover that there was no printing press in the entire city. If this project, on which he had staked a fair bit of his reputation and personal finances, had to take off, he would have to start from scratch. To his credit, that is exactly what he did, though with what funds we do not exactly know.

He spent a few weeks in Delhi in the sticky monsoon of 1924, visiting and exploring potential office spaces across the city. Ultimately, Panikkar chose to rent a building on Burn Bastion Road, off Lahori Gate, now known as Shraddhanand Bazaar. It was a three-storey building colonnaded in the style of Connaught Place, not far from the Old Delhi railway station. Inside this imposing building, a Dawson Payne hand-fed stop cylinder press and a Miele Press, the only makes available in Delhi at the time, were crammed into two rooms measuring twenty-four by twenty-four feet on the ground floor. The top two floors, furnished plainly with wooden benches and chairs, were reserved for editorial staff. It was simple but it was better than nothing at all. Panikkar bent his mind to the task of finding two deputies who would help him in the day-to-day running of the paper as well as administrative work. He chose his friend, the journalist G.S. Raghavan, and Dr Ambadi Krishna Menon, one of his best friends from college.

All seemed to be set.

The only thing that seemed suitable now was to get Gandhi's blessing on this new venture. Panikkar hoped fondly that they could convince him to inaugurate the first edition.

As it turned out, this was the last thing Gandhi wanted to do. A few weeks earlier, some Muslim water-bearers had beaten up a Hindu boy in Queen's Park, then a small park on the outskirts of Delhi. A riot had inevitably erupted, lasting three days. On 15 July—Bakr Eid—communal hostilities had increased when the British administration banned the passage of sacrificial cows. The army was called in to restore order, but peace continued to elude the city. The Congress president, Maulana Mohammad Ali, was uneasy as he watched peace unravel. He suggested to Gandhi that it was best to leave 'the maintenance of peace to the guns and bayonets of the police'. The Congress, he wrote, was currently 'the object of everybody's wrath'.[7] When Gandhi himself reached Delhi in September, things were palpably tense. Trouble had spread to Lucknow, Shahjahanpur, Jabalpur, Gulbarga, Allahabad, Calcutta and Kohat. Under the circumstances, Gandhi was in no mood to think of such mundane things as inaugurating a printing press. But he had promised the Akalis that he would do this. And so on the sunny morning of 15 September 1924, he addressed a solemn little group in the *Hindustan Times* building. He spoke briefly but honestly, letting the assembled crowd know that it was not without hesitation that he was there at all. Under the present conditions of the country, Gandhi said, he would stop all papers if he could, except *Young India*. But this new venture must, he warned, abide by truth and integrity. 'There should be not only be no untrue statements, but no *suggestio falsi* or *suppressio veri*.'[8] In other words, no false suggestions and no suppression of the truth.

Perhaps it was an omen of things to come that the first issue of the *Hindustan Times*, expected to roll off the presses that evening, had to be postponed by a week.

The printing presses had broken down.

The first edition of *Hindustan Times* rolled out on 23 September 1924 with a lead article titled 'Ourselves', in which the newspaper summarised its policy as standing for nationalism without giving in to partisan views. In so doing, it branded itself right away as the 'only nationalist paper in north India'. But its front page was a vibrant testimonial of Panikkar's network of contacts, with messages from Sarojini Naidu to Rabindranath Tagore; from C.F. Andrews to Lala Lajpat Rai and from both the Nehrus to Mohammad Ali. Their messages, more than anything else, cemented *Hindustan Times* as a mouthpiece for the national movement.

As its editor, Panikkar plunged into his task with vim, taking on peers, foreigners and viceroys as well as communalism and loyalists of the Raj. The early issues of the newspaper were largely devoted to the maintenance of religious harmony, which was the foundation on which Gandhi was carrying his Unity Conference in September 1924. On its opening day, *Hindustan Times* ran a powerful editorial, stating, 'India has again become the cockpit of warring factions and creeds … The choice before them is clear. It is whether they want India to be a united and prosperous nation taking her place among the civilised communities of the world, or whether she is to remain not only in bondage, but the distracted prey of disunited factions and creeds.'[9]

The editorials that Panikkar ran during his time at *Hindustan Times* are a surprising mirror into his changing views of nationalism. He was no longer the traditionalist boy that he had been at Oxford. He had watched how the wheels of politics turned, and he had seen how deeply communal fault lines were carved into India's social and political fabric. Unity as a concept was all very well, but organisationally and structurally speaking, it could not be realised until the various communities sorted themselves into cohesive and separate bodies. One editorial, running in April 1925, stated the case quite bluntly, 'The relation of one community to another and of all the different communities to each, in a country constituted like India, can only be on the basis of independent organisation, as the existence of the Muslim League, the Khilafat Committee, the Central Sikh League and other communal institutions amply demonstrates.'[10]

Apart from current politics, Panikkar also kept an eye on the princely states, a subject that had intrigued him since his college days.

His style as an editor—and indeed, as a journalist—hadn't changed since his time in *Swarajya.* Editorials may have been erudite, but there was always room for the scandalous and salacious at the *Hindustan Times.* The front page was often devoted to the sensational case of Mr A., more popularly known as Maharaja Hari Singh of Kashmir. This was a particularly juicy tale: the profligate young maharaja was having an exuberant affair with a beautiful Englishwoman named Mrs Robinson. Unfortunately for Hari Singh, this beauty was also the wife of one of London's most prominent bookmakers and was, unknown to her royal lover, in cahoots with a gang led by the maharaja's own aide-de-camp. Late one night, as the couple relaxed in bed in Paris, a gang member burst in, demanding £125,000 in hush money. Terrified, Hari Singh paid on the spot. Later, when he had managed to pull himself together, he called his bank to put a stop on the cheque. But to his shock, the robbers were undaunted. The maharaja was audaciously sued for the recovery of the money, to which he responded (rather foolishly) with a blackmail suit. At the request of the Government of India, the presiding judge allowed Hari Singh to give evidence under the pseudonym of 'Mr. A'. The British press remained politely discreet, but their fellows across the English Channel saw no such compunction. To Hari Singh's vast humiliation, the scandal hit the Indian, French and American newspapers, becoming common gossip within a matter of days.

Apart from these enjoyable stories, *Hindustan Times* also addressed the problem of corrupt state governments and the intrusiveness of British policy. More significantly, with Panikkar at the helm, it began to push the Congress actively, urging it to develop its own policy towards these states. The princely states were not autocracies and should not, *Hindustan Times* stated, be seen as such. Based on what he had seen at Vaikom, Panikkar insisted that social and religious reforms had to come from within the state itself rather than from outside it. 'At the not very distant future, the place of the Indian states in our polity will have definitely to be decided … It should be made perfectly clear to the princes that the people of British India have no desire and do not put forward any right to interfere in their affairs, constitutions or peculiar customs,' he warned. 'But it must be made equally plain that on no account whatever can it be possible to allow them external independence.'[11]

It was the first time since 1919 that he had made an argument for what would become one of the foundation stones of his future dealings with the princely states. Everything that he had lived through until now was forcing him to rethink the arguments on nationalism that he had laid out in his university days and in his days at Aligarh. Panikkar never stopped engaging with his ideas about the past and how India's past was reflected in its present. His was not a static mind, nor were his ideas fixed or rigid. Now, for instance, he was thinking seriously about nationalism.

'The national feeling which is prolonged backwards in attempting to see in the past a golden age is such an inflation of the ideal of nationalism,' he wrote in yet another essay for *Modern Review,* which was reproduced as a *Hindustan Times* editorial. 'For our weaknesses of the present we satisfy ourselves that the past was a glorious one.'[12] In the essay, Panikkar pondered that there had never really been a time in India's history when progress had been stymied, not even during Mughal rule. Only the introduction of the English education system had blocked India's constant evolution, simply by breaking radically with past methods of learning and knowledge. But now, he took that with a pinch of salt, in contrast to his previous indignation. A renewal in society was necessary for progress. The past had to be critically understood at all times if unity had to be achieved.[13]

Here then was the change in Panikkar's thinking. His experience with the national movement at a time when it was prone to political and religious fissures had taught him that, above all, progress was possible only with unity. That was why, when the Congress gradually overcame its internal divisions and an agreement was reached between the Gandhians and the Swarajists, *Hindustan Times* ran a celebratory editorial.[14]

As India moved towards the mid-1920s, the Swarajists began to enjoy a degree of visibility and influence. They were now described in *Hindustan Times* as the defenders of national interests, as in the case of their opposition to the railway budget in the Central Legislative Assembly.[15] Panikkar's editorials approved of the increased space being given to the functioning of the provincial councils and the Central Legislative Assembly, but he remained clear and firm on the fact that India (and Indians) could not rely on Westminster. They must unite and rely on their own strength to do so.[16]

While the archives of the *Hindustan Times* provide an insight into Panikkar's changing mind about what nationalism meant to him, he wasn't destined to be at the newspaper for much longer. Journalism was never the right choice for him. He was far too outspoken about the causes that mattered to him. He had no patience for lies, corruption or scandal. In early 1925, the *Hindustan Times* attacked the powerful C.H.C. Cotton, the corrupt British Resident of Travancore. With Panikkar's green light, a series of articles exposed Cotton's meddling in state affairs under the title 'Cotton Epidemic'. Not surprisingly, Panikkar's uncle was seriously alarmed by his nephew's rampaging search for the truth. The state government issued a formal denial of the reports, and family friends began to write to Chalayil, warning the family that attacking Cotton would be harmful for the whole Nair community. Thoroughly horrified, Eravi Ramakrishna reached out to his nephew, telling him to drop this dangerous new pastime and return to Kavalam immediately. The warning was enough. Journalism, whether one ran a paper or reported for it, was subject to certain conditions. Not for Panikkar these conditions and endless strictures on which line could be crossed and which must be toed. He promised his irate uncle that he would indeed resign in another six months—in the end, it would take another year.

Meanwhile, Gandhi arrived in Delhi yet again. He was deeply disturbed by the rioting that was continuing across north India. He knew that the Congress offered little support here—they too were a house divided. Gandhi spent some time wondering what to do since he had no wish to fight either side. But he had certainly kept his eye on the events at Nabha. Word had reached him of Nabha's supporters led by the young barrister and independence activist Asaf Ali arriving at the Swarajist conference in Calcutta to present a resolution in support of the maharaja. This would have scuppered the hard work that Panikkar had done in Amritsar. Hastily, Gandhi dispatched Panikkar to Calcutta, where he used every atom of his glib diplomacy to speak directly to both Motilal Nehru and Swarajist leader Chittaranjan 'Deshbandhu' Das and persuade them that supporting Nabha was the last thing anyone should do. Panikkar stepped off the train in Calcutta to find himself in the cheery company of Asaf Ali. The meeting was a cordial one, with Panikkar smugly aware that he had what Ali clearly lacked—Gandhi's approval. To his credit, Ali recognised this immediately, laughingly teasing, 'My friend, you have won!'[17]

Pleased, Panikkar returned to Delhi the next day, delayed only slightly by a detour to the beautiful Jorasanko, the Tagore household in south Calcutta. By all accounts, Rabindranath Tagore wanted Panikkar to come and teach at his newly established university in Shantiniketan, Visva-Bharati. 'The poet found in the young man a veritable store-house of knowledge,' recalled the Malayalam writer Parayath E. Raman Menon.[18] 'You are one of the few Indians whose articles and assistance I require for my Viswa Bharati! *(sic)*' Tagore wrote to Panikkar.[19] It wasn't surprising that Tagore thought Panikkar suitable as a teaching candidate, since they shared many similar ideas about India.

Visva-Bharati was an educational institution founded on Tagore's principles of internationalism and his ideas of pan-Asianism. The poet was, from the start, a pioneering proponent of the notion of India as a syncretic and peaceful civilisation. According to Tagore, India's historical mechanism for coping with ethnic, religious or cultural differences was an intricate social and cultural matrix that created a perfect and harmonious atmosphere. As he put it, it was 'the realisation of unity in diversity, the establishment of synthesis amidst variety—that is inherent, the Sanatan Dharma of India.'[20]

Panikkar never took Tagore up on his offer to teach at Visva-Bharati, but we do know that Tagore, who was leaving for Japan, charged him with giving Gandhi the somewhat cryptic message: *This is what I have to say to India now: don't be misled by personalities and forget the truth.*[21] There are no records of any such conversation, but as an anecdote it certainly feels prescient.

By the dawn of 1925, it seemed as though Panikkar's luck was beginning to run out. *Hindustan Times* was beginning to rack up losses. Under Panikkar's leadership it had achieved national attention, but now the Akalis were steadily losing interest in the paper. Their political demands had been met and with the paper incurring heavy financial losses, it was a millstone around their necks. Sardar Mangal Singh saw the *Hindustan Times* as a 'white elephant'.[22] Panikkar soon heard the worst of the rumours that were circulating—that the *Hindustan Times* would likely be sold to either Lala Lajpat Rai or Madan Mohan Malaviya, both of whom were pushing the right-wing agenda of Hindu sangathan. He was appalled. For Malaviya, he had no real dislike. He even approved of Malaviya's motto of 'service to Hindus and to Sanatana dharma'.[23] Rai was another story. 'I had no respect for Rai. This self-styled icon of the Punjab was the embodiment of egoism, a scheme with a deceptive appearance of simplicity.'[24]

At a loss for what to do, Panikkar decided to bide his time. Luckily, he didn't have long to wait. There came a day when Malaviya gave his sub-editor 'certain instructions about the contents of the paper'.[25] Panikkar hauled up the junior in question for not consulting him, triggering an argument with Malaviya.

It was the end.

On 19 February 1925, newspapers began reporting that the *Hindustan Times* had changed hands. Malaviya was now its chairman and a new board of directors had been put in place. One of the new directors was a young businessman by the name of G.D. Birla. On 18 March, a rather snide note in the *Hindustan Times* assured its readers, 'It is hardly necessary to say that every effort will be taken to improve the paper.'[26]

Panikkar stepped down in the early months of 1925. He felt no real sense of anguish or rage as he had done in the aftermath of his time at *Swarajya*. With the establishment of the *Hindustan Times*, he had learned invaluable things about founding and running a newspaper and also about how propaganda could influence an entire political movement if it was done right. More than at *Swarajya*, his position at the *Hindustan Times* had given him the ability to speak far more openly on political issues and to develop a more refined sense of nationalism. His contributions at the paper were recognised by everyone across the political spectrum. Mohammad Ali wrote indignantly in his own journal, *Comrade*, 'We do not know any important daily newspapers, which owe practically everything—finance of course excepted—to the labours of one man and yet, with regard to the establishment of the *Hindustan Times*, K.M. Panikkar could well say like Coriolanus, *Alone I did it.*'[27]

PART V

Interlude: Rebels and Royals (1925–1927)

Chapter 15

Starting Over

HE WAS BACK IN KAVALAM, DEPRESSED AND UNCERTAIN.

At the age of thirty-one, Panikkar had tried academia and journalism and, briefly, politics. Nothing had worked out. Journalism had proved to be steered by the winds of political bias. As for academia, he was at heart a scholar but not a teacher. He had tried his hand at politics, but he hadn't been retained by the Congress. What else could he do? He had no desire to borrow money from home. The Panikkars were broke now, and it was only generational wealth that ensured they didn't feel unduly pinched.

Panikkar was emotionally and mentally at his lowest at this point. He was aware that he needed to start over, but how did one do that and where did one go? In this wistful frame of mind, he dropped in for tea and a chat with his friend Dr Krishnan Pandalai, then the presidency magistrate of Madras. Over coffee, the older man told him kindly that all was not lost. Why not, he asked, try for the bar? The advice seemed good to Panikkar. He had never considered the occupation, but felt he had no real choice in the matter now. In addition, it would give him some distance from India at a time when the national movement was undergoing yet another transition. There was, for instance, currently a lull in the working class movement, which would stay until the rise of a powerful Left Bloc at the end of the 1920s. The Swarajists were beginning to crumble, with the death of C.R. Das in June 1925 proving to be a major blow. Nationalist fervour was running on empty. It needed a period of rest and recovery.

On the other hand, this was a period of rising violence as well. Many young men who had been enthusiastic participants in the non-cooperation movement were thoroughly disillusioned. These young men from Punjab, the United Provinces, Bengal and Bihar were inspired by the Russian Revolution, keen to learn from the young Soviet state and its ruling Bolshevik Party. Some of their names have passed into legend—Sukhdev, Bhagat Singh, Chandrashekhar Azad. But to overthrow the Raj as they intended, they would need to unionise and organise funds. The Hindustan Republican Army (HRA), the result of this organisation, soon put its plans into motion. On 9 August 1925, ten men held up the 8 Down train at Kakori, an obscure village near Lucknow. The train, which had been carrying cash, was looted. The government hit back so hard that, for a brief while, the revolutionary movement was dazed.[1] All in all, it was a vaguely disorienting time to be in the country, with very little to do.

But once Panikkar decided that he would move to London, he had no time to pay attention to shifting political currents. For one, he had to take Gouri back home to Kavalam. His time away from her would be a turning point in their marriage. There was the emotional tug of leaving his wife and children behind for the next couple of years, but Panikkar had no time to process that emotion just yet. There were other things to do. The police had denied him a fresh passport. Backed into a corner, Panikkar contacted V.T. Krishnamachari, then the law secretary to the Madras government, to get his paperwork in order.

On 27 September 1925, Panikkar stepped off a ship to England for the second time in his life. But this was a much more confident young man, bolstered by the awareness of his own intelligence and charm, and aware of the importance of networks. Unlike a decade earlier, he now had the contacts he would need to pave his way.

This was a new and international stage at a critical juncture in his life and career. It meant a world of possibilities. To Panikkar's credit, despite the many setbacks to the career and life he had imagined for himself, he had managed to stay open-minded, willing to put in the work it would take to build the kind of reputation he needed.

As soon as he was settled in his lodgings, he marked off time on his calendar to pursue research on a subject he had been thinking about for a long time—the Dutch occupation of his home province of Malabar. But Panikkar's mind was restless and always inquisitive, perennially seeking answers to difficult questions, and he was usually writing or researching two or three widely varying subjects simultaneously. 'His mind seems to me to consist of a number of vaults,' remarked someone who knew him closely. 'When he has done with business in one vault, he slams its door shut and opens another.'[2] Put simply, Panikkar enjoyed a good intellectual challenge.

He had contacts in *The Daily News* and the *Daily Herald*, and also began writing columns for them straightaway. Then, shortly after learning that he was living in London, the Civil Service Commission of England got in touch, asking Panikkar to serve as an examiner in Indian history for the outgoing civil service candidates. It was, he noted, a signal honour, but even more delightful was the annual fee of £150.[3] The money was welcome and meant that he was settled financially for the moment. He could also send money back for Gouri and the children, assuaging some of the guilt he felt about being away from them for so long. Once these details were taken care of, he could think of other things—such as engaging with his understanding of imperialism and working on the manuscript he had begun when the *Hindustan Times* began running into the ground.

This manuscript had nothing to do with Malabar history. In fact, it was new ground for Panikkar. For at least the last couple of years, he had turned his scholarly attention to the Indian princely states. At the time, Panikkar was just a scholar looking to fill a gap in academic and political literature on an aspect of Indian politics that, in his eyes, had not been studied enough.

In retrospect, it was a carefully chosen subject. There was a definite lack of international and—Panikkar shrewdly suspected from his ringside view of the way Gandhi had approached Vaikom—national understanding about the role the princely states could play in the achievement of India's independence. The war had changed life as the princes knew it. They had supported the war effort with both men and materiel, and expected returns on their investment, whether in the form of reduced interference or as concessions regarding disputed territories. The Raj recognised their restiveness and threw the princes a crumb: a Chamber of Princes was inaugurated in 1920, with consultative powers to the viceroy.[4]

Composed of 109 princes with a salute of eleven guns or more, and twelve princes who were selected to represent 127 other states, the chamber did nothing to fulfil expectations. The viceroy was the presiding official, which meant the princes could rarely discuss what they really wanted. There were also debilitating differences between the princes, of course. For example, prominent princes such Hyderabad, Mysore and Travancore did not want to participate in a group venture that they viewed as an encroachment on their territorial sovereignty. Still, the chamber proved to be an important means through which the princes could pursue their objectives, one of which was the (re) definition of the relationship between the states and the Crown. The creation of a collective forum expanded discussions between the princes and the British from narrow individual cases to broader issues of political reform.

Despite these slim advantages, attendance at the initial meetings was rather low. The princes were suspicious and most tended to keep their distance. This resulted in the emergence of rival factions within the chamber, factions in which Panikkar would find himself inextricably embroiled in the very near future. But there *was* a small group of princes who were committed to understanding their role in national politics. In the years to come, the names of states like Bikaner and Patiala would mean far more than they did in 1925. At the moment though, there wasn't enough international attention to merit an entire book. Panikkar's publishers advised him kindly not to publish.

Feeling familiar pangs of dread, he took the manuscript to a friend of his.

Frank Brown is dismissed in Panikkar's memoir as 'the sub-editor of *The Times*'.[5] But in reality, he was far more than that. Born to a vicar in Norfolk, Brown had come out to India at the dawn of the twentieth century. He worked at the *Bombay Gazette* for five years as a lead writer and assistant editor, witnessing the assassination of Curzon Wylie in 1909. Then he shifted to the *Indian Daily Telegraph* before a combination of malaria and failing eyesight forced him to return to London. Despite his illness and impairment, his mind remained as sharp as a knife. In 1917, Brown was one of a group of expert advisors on India who worked with Edwin Montagu, along with Thomas Bennett and Sir Valentine Chirol. After all these years, he was still closely linked to both sides of the national movement, and as a contact, he was invaluable. Brown, who liked Panikkar's forthright ways and keen mind, agreed to have a read of the manuscript on the princely states.

He wasn't disappointed in what he read, and told Panikkar that he would be sending it on to the publishing firm of Martin Hopkinson, where he had friends. It was two months before Panikkar heard back—a letter of acceptance, providentially signed by his old Oxford tutor John Murray, who had recently become a director at the firm. The letter was the assurance Panikkar had been seeking. This meant that his academic future, at the very least, was assured.

Now, in between his legal studies, he could breathe a little. Perhaps he could even think about travelling abroad? The idea held appeal, though truth be told, Panikkar was more than a little nervous. He hadn't travelled through Europe alone before, and he was beginning to wonder if it was a good idea to do so, when a letter arrived from Madras. His friend V.K. John, a brilliant young lawyer, had written that he would be arriving in England soon for a short holiday on the continent. Would Panikkar, he asked, care to join him?

Panikkar was thrilled. He wrote back immediately, assenting to John's plans. In the winter of 1925, the young men left for Portugal to travel across Lisbon and Port Belam. It was nothing like he had hoped to see. Whatever John might have felt, Panikkar was certainly suffering from considerable disillusionment. Portugal's history was rich and somewhat chequered. A century earlier, it had had the wealth to give the island of Bombay to King Charles II as part of Catherine of Braganza's dowry. Now, in the twentieth century, it was poor and bedraggled, teeming with people and poverty. Still, it was there, wandering on the beaches at Belam, the same coastline from which Vasco de Gama had set sail for India, that Panikkar decided to explore Europe's history with Asia and closer to home, Malabar's history with the Portuguese.

Malabar and the Portuguese would become yet another landmark book when it was published three years later, in 1929. Panikkar's time in Europe was spent in acquiring as much material for it as he could, for the academic in him rarely took a day off. When he had a moment to spare, he spent it sitting at his desk and writing busily. It helped that he was in the very land about which he was writing, for it gave him a unique sense of flavour, nuance and understanding. A reading of *Malabar and the Portuguese* tells a curious observer that Panikkar was also tracing the history of Malabar. The Zamorin of Calicut is more or less the main character, a ruler trying to consolidate his power and politically unify the Malabar region. During the Zamorin's rule, trade was flourishing, religious tolerance was absolute, and life was thriving and happy, albeit politically isolated and 'primitive'. Into this scenario erupted the Portuguese.

Panikkar gave no real emphasis to the voyage of Vasco Da Gama. In his eyes, trade networks had existed between Malabar and the West for centuries, since the time of the Phoenicians, and the ancient Greeks and Romans. In fact, as he argued, by the time the Portuguese arrived, long-distance trade was controlled by Egypt and Venice. The real importance of the discovery then, was not in establishing trade contact—which already existed—but in *breaking* previous monopolies and, for India, entering into a direct relationship with a major European maritime power.

On the whole, Panikkar's assessment of the Portuguese arrival in Malabar is emphatically negative. But two crucial points he *did* make were Portugal's technological superiority and the importance of naval power. Accustomed to considering only land-based threats, the Indian potentates would have underestimated the Portuguese danger. In particular, Panikkar's emphasis on naval power would become one of his key contributions to postcolonial India's maritime and foreign policy.

For the time being, he packed up the draft he had written to revisit later. He and John were now bound for Paris, another city he had heard much about but never visited.

Chapter 16

'The Capital of the Men Without a Country'

THESE WERE THE *ANNÉES FOLLES*—THE CRAZY YEARS.

Panikkar and John arrived in Paris in the bitingly cold January of 1926. His first stop was at 17 Rue de Sommerard, before they shifted to 36 Rue des Ecoles. John had letters of introduction to the Indian students' association at the Sorbonne. The association was the obvious first stop for newly arrived Indian students in Paris, providing practical advice on how to navigate not only a different academic system, but a new city. Once they had settled in, it was time to explore the city they had heard so much about.

In the 1920s, Paris was the 'moveable feast' that Ernest Hemingway wrote of. Panikkar had never seen anything like it. Paris would live in his memories as a city soaked in culture, art and history, not to mention the veritable 'Congress of thinkers' at the Sorbonne alone.[1] So much did Panikkar come to love it that he would, in later years, refer to it as his 'spiritual home'.[2]

Truly, the city was witnessing its golden era in those years. You could find Hemingway drinking whisky with Ezra Pound and W.B. Yeats in the smoky cafés around the intersection of Boulevard

Montparnasse—Raspail, le Jockey, le Dome and la Rontonade. Paris was the home and studio of artists from Pablo Picasso to Alberto Giacometti and to musicians like Igor Stravinsky. George Gershwin came to Paris in 1928, where he stayed at the Majestic Hotel and composed *An American in Paris*, capturing the horns of the Paris taxis as they circled the Place de l'Etoile. Just a year before Panikkar arrived, the beautiful dancer Josephine Baker had taken Paris by storm, appearing nude on stage, wearing only a skirt of bananas.

Underneath the glitz, the city was the unlikely underbelly of empire. The civil rights activist Roger Nash Baldwin stayed in Paris on a stopover, following the Brussels Congress of the League Against Imperialism in 1927. In the city, he found 'the headquarters of agitation of the French colonial peoples, where black, brown and yellow men can argue their case for freedom'.[3] In those days, Paris was one of the few European cities where political refugees, dissidents and exiles could easily find accommodation and livelihood. For young Indian scholars, the bustling French capital was, unlike England, free of prejudice or bias. Panikkar's contemporary in Paris, the historian Kalidas Nag, mused that in London, he was always conscious of the humiliation of being a colonial subject. In Paris, he was delighted to discover that one 'was not judged merely according to [one's] political status but as a human being coming from the cradle of Asian humanism.'[4] Panikkar noted the same, observing, 'Everyone knows that the British look down on coloured people. The reverse was true of Paris. Negro or Mongol, Hindu or Briton, each man was respected according to his education and status.'[5]

It was a cosmopolitan anti-imperial metropolis that provided a safe haven for activists and minority communities from Blacks to Jews to women. Dissidents who straddled empires were at home here. Vietnamese activists took inspiration from their Chinese peers, West Africans met Antilleans, and Algerians engaged with Syrian nationalists. It did not seem to matter to any of the young men and women from India that France was a colonial power in its own right. All that mattered was that France played no role in subcontinental politics. Panikkar's discovery of Paris came via an introduction to the Sorbonne's brilliant young Orientalist, Prabodh Chandra Bagchi.

At the time, the twenty-eight-year-old Bagchi was the secretary of the Hindustan Samaj, an organisation of the Indian diaspora in Europe, and was in France on a government scholarship. His academic career provided excellent cover for the kind of dissident activities he was really engaged in. When Panikkar met him, he was an acclaimed Indologist and had worked with the greats in Indology and Sinology from Sylvain Lévi to Louis Finot and from Henri Maspero to Jules Bloch. Heavily influenced by Tagore and Lévi, Bagchi subscribed to the 'Greater India' theory: that ancient Indian history could only be understood through the web of cultural, religious and economic relations that spanned Central Asia via South Asia to China and Southeast Asia. It was through Bagchi and Kalidas Nag that Panikkar discovered that Asia and India were subjects that many gifted French scholars were discussing. There were lectures and talks on Asian history, art and culture. The Central Asian explorer and noted Sinologist Paul Pelliot, for instance, lectured on the spread of Indian artistic influences in 'Serindia'; Lévi delivered a series of talks on ancient India's maritime relations ('L'Inde et la mer') and the French linguist and scholar of religion Jean Przyluski discussed the architecture of ancient Angkor. Bagchi and Nag, in particular, were invited by Lévi to join the sittings of the Société Asiatique. Together with Panikkar, the Indian scholars also attended talks at the Musée Guimet where one 'could soak [one's] soul into the art of the Far East, Tibet (Backot collection), Serindia (Pelliot collection), China, Japan, Indonesia and above all the grand relics of Champa and Cambodia'.[6]

Apart from history, art and culture, Panikkar was also introduced to the wider transnational anti-imperialist movement in Europe. It was here that Panikkar made the connections that would establish him firmly on the international geopolitical scene. At one meeting of the samaj, for instance, he met the attractive young Germain Merlange, her lover Arnold Wilson Mononutu of Indonesia (who would go on to become the information minister when his country was decolonised) and a slim Chinese by the name of Ho Ying-chin (later a senior general) who was an official with China's nationalist party, the Kuomintang. These were, among many others, the young men and women who formed the vibrantly anti-imperialist networks in interwar Europe.

Panikkar had encountered Southeast Asia before in his academic reading and writing, but it was the first time that he was seeing it as a region hopeful of decolonisation, much like India. This was because many of his friends now were Southeast Asian freedom fighters and dissidents. Talking to them brought the region alive for Panikkar as no book ever had. It was in Paris, sitting at the coffee shops with 'Chin', as everyone called Ho Ying-chin, or Mononutu, that Panikkar learned of the history and politics of Southeast Asia, shaped as the region was by colonialism, capitalism, nationalism and international relations.

The end of the war had done much to galvanise Southeast Asia, from Burma to Indochina. Thousands of young radicals emerged to form the web of the Asian underground that spread across vast distances, attacking officials, organising strikes, plotting coups and disseminating propaganda. Recruits for the underground came from the villages of Punjab and Bengal, from the Kampongs of Sumatra and Java and from the cities of China. They organised strikes across Asia from the Dutch sugar factories in Java to the British tea plantations in Assam. These young men and women were defiantly modern, united in their belief that the colonial age was over. To achieve their goals, to meet colleagues and fellow dissidents across borders, they drove across the Gobi Desert and slept in steamers across the Baltic Sea. They slipped in and out of Weimar Germany, Tokyo, Shanghai, Canton, Paris and New York. In Malaya, they were known as the *orang-orang pergarakan*—the 'movement people'. Many of them studied or worked in Europe to get a taste of the very civilisation and system whose terms they sought to challenge.

To be at the heart of this kind of anarchist environment was something Panikkar hadn't expected. It came at a time when his ideas of nationalism, of how to achieve freedom for his country, were shifting from traditionalism to something more radical. At a time when the Indian national movement seemed to be at a loss, Paris was the place to be. None of these students, whatever their nationality, seemed to pay much attention to their studies. As Nag put it in his

Memoirs, 'degree or diploma was secondary to me; human contact and international relations were my primary passions, for through them I realised my personality, and propagated the ideals of India to the west'.[7] It was the same for Panikkar.

For the Indians and Indonesians, life bustled around the Latin Quarter, a rough university district dotted with bars, cafes, and cheap lodgings. Students lived in the Hôtel du Progrès at 50 Rue Gay-Lussac, or the Hôtel Soufflot at 9 Rue Toullier, just around the block from the Jardin du Luxembourg. Their discussions with each other and their critiques of the existing imperial order enhanced their political knowledge and spawned what the historian Michael Goebel has called 'shadow diplomacy'.[8] From Saigon to Washington, Tokyo to Paris, this was a new generation of young intellectuals who sought to weave together seemingly irreconcilable ideologies and doctrines—anarchism, nationalism, religious revival and communism—in the name of unity and collective opposition to Western imperialism. For now, they travelled light, often with banned literature or illegal currency in their baggage, often under false papers or, like Panikkar, as young students of global affairs. For all of them, Paris was the ideal venue, dotted as it was with quiet cafes or opportunities for walks along the Seine.

Mononutu took Panikkar to his favourite haunt, Taverne Pascal, a small two-storey bar that had been a typical old cafe before its new owner turned it into a Chinese restaurant called the Wan Houa Wsieou Leou at the beginning of the 1920s. Here, Panikkar, Mononutu and his friends debated the latest political events, sometimes stopping behind the bar to pick up pre-sale tickets for interesting shows or conferences. If you looked closely, Panikkar discovered, there was more for sale at the Taverne Pascal than a pint. You could, if you wanted, pick up a suitable companion for the evening for the right price. If you were not inclined thus, you merely paid your tab and stepped back out into the lights of Paris and found your way back easily to the Association des Étudiants Hindous de France (to which Panikkar belonged) or the Association Mutuelle des Indochinois, the Khana Ratsadon/Thai People's Party, the Association des Étudiants Chinois and the Leftist faction of the

Chinese Kuomintang nationalists. Some of these addresses were no more than post box offices or shady Chinese diners, but often they were fronts for dissident organisations, a fertile breeding ground for transnationalism—common ground beyond the Asian, the pan-African, pan-Arab and Muslim spheres. It was a mirror to what decolonisation would truly come to mean for each of them.

Panikkar learned that each of his friends had experienced politics and history through a different lens, a different sense of time and place. In 1925, Mononutu was a quiet and scholarly young man. He hardly left the immediate impression of being a firebrand, inclined more towards silent observation and behind the scenes organisation, with a special taste for the artistic and intellectual.[9] Later of course, he would become famous for organising the Bandung Conference in 1955. But in 1925, he was in Paris ostensibly on a scholarship to study at the prestigious Institut d'Études Politiques. He didn't enrol at the institute, however. He had other plans. Documents of the time show Mononutu approaching prominent periodicals and political societies, looking to establish a network of underground anti-colonial resistance. Eventually, as he met and fell in love with Germaine Merlange, Mononutu established the Association pour l'Étude des Civilisations Orientales (Association for the Study of Oriental Civilisations or AECO). He took a board position there, working to bring together students and intellectuals from various colonies across the Orient. In this attempt, he was aided by Merlange who had by now become his lover. In later interviews and in Mononutu's authorised biography, it is suggested that Merlange and Mononutu were engaged, though the relationship didn't ultimately culminate in a marriage.

In Paris to study Oriental influences in silk and other textiles at the Musée Guimet, Merlange was highly intelligent, demurely attractive and extremely efficient. She was a woman of charm and immense resourcefulness, networked across the city with influential journalists, writers, historians and intellectuals—just the kind of people Mononutu needed to get the word out about the AECO. She was a great help when it came to organising meetings and recruitments for the AECO. It also helped that Merlange had a rather soft spot for Indonesians in general. One of the Indonesian recruits at the

AECO, a young man named Soepardi, would write to a friend in the Netherlands that Merlange liked to flirt with the Indonesian students in Paris, often exclaiming coquettishly, '*Vous Indonésiens, vous devenez dangereux pour les Parisiennes!* (You Indonesians, you're dangerous for Parisiennes!)'[10]

Together, Mononutu and Merlange were a formidable team, speaking with great passion and knowledge about the anti-colonial cause to those in the city who were interested. It was an inventive application of what 2025 recognises as soft power: introducing the West to Oriental art, politics, history and culture. The idea seems to have come from Tjeng Yin Chang, a visiting professor from the University of Peking, and Xia Ting, a communist Chinese worker in Paris. The AECO was successful in attracting a wide range of students, academics and activists from across Asia, from Syria to Japan, and from Russia to the Dutch Indies.[11]

Intrigued and delighted at these new possibilities to challenge the empire and to make his voice heard, Panikkar joined the AECO immediately, as did his friend Duong Van Giao. A lean, tall, serene man from Indochina, Duong taught criminal law when he wasn't practising at the Cour d'appel de Paris, the highest appeal court in France. Another good friend of Panikkar's, the Siamese student Prayun Phamonmontri, founded the Khana Ratsadon/Thai People's Party in Paris in 1927. The party would launch a daring coup against the absolutist Thai monarchy in 1932, and Prayun would eventually become his country's deputy prime minister. Then there was the Cambodian prince Areno Yukanthor, who had forfeited his rights to become monarch of Cambodia when he expressed his criticism of the corrupted Francophile elite of his country. Among people like these, Panikkar began to understand a melange of nationalisms.

Politically, the character of the AECO was diverse to say the least, with anti-Bolshevik and Francophile elements existing next to moderate nationalist demands, 'extremist' Chinese nationalists, and possibly more radical culturalist Pan-Asian theories. Only a sense of cultural pride and a passionate wish for Asian autonomy bound these very different young men and women together, introducing Panikkar to a more Asia-centric line of thinking. Where did Southeast Asia, as a specific example, stand in the empire? What were the ways in which the region could think about its independence? How could one compare the struggles of, say, Azerbaijan—so recently invaded by the Soviet Red Army—with British India? How did one study Siam's struggles as it tried to navigate French Indochina and the British Empire? How would all these individual voices begin to speak as one in the course of their work with AECO? It was clearly a matter that required further research.

Panikkar's instinctive reactions to questions like these, questions that were far bigger than he, were always academic. His first thought was always that he needed to read more on the subject in order to form an opinion and contribute to ongoing debates. It was a habit that had begun long ago in Thampanoor, that had been honed and built in Oxford, and would last for the rest of his life.

Spurred on by his new friends' radically anti-imperialist ideas, Panikkar took to sitting for hours in the Sorbonne's beautiful library, poring over history books and making endless busy notes. Reading more about other countries and talking to their residents helped Panikkar understand that much of Southeast Asian politics was inspired by wider historical events, like the reform in the Islamic world, Indian nationalism, China's civil war and Japanese militarism. More currently, Southeast Asia had not been fought over in the Great War, nor had it been repartitioned in the Paris Peace Conference, but it *had* gained new importance as Britain's position in the post-war world order changed.[12]

As more and more literature on resistance and anti-colonial movements in different countries came his way, Panikkar began to see for the first time the role being played by the Soviet Union. It was clear—and fascinating—to see that the Soviet Union and the colonies did not really belong to one particular bloc. If anything, the alliance was a strictly functional one. As an author of the Indonesian journal *Indonesia Merdeka* put it, 'Provisionally, our roads run parallel to each other and our goals are the same: to liberate our People from brutal oppression.'[13]

It was the first time that Panikkar had thought of freedom and nationalism on such a wide scale. He was no stranger to revolutionary ideas, but now he was aware of the fact that this was a bigger struggle and that not many of his generation would live to see the freedoms for which they would fight.

But Panikkar and his friends were watched.

All the time.

The pressure and surveillance on British Indians was almost twice as much as on other nationalities. After the First World War, Scotland Yard joined hands with the Direction de la SÛreté in France to keep a close eye on groups and associations that were, in security parlance, 'of interest'. The Indians in Paris were of considerable interest. A 1925 French police report stated that in contrast to the poor colonial workers from Indochina or Algeria, Indians in Paris were either traders in jewellery or 'for the most part, young, wealthy people who have come to study in our faculties *(sic)*'.[14] The same report added (incorrectly) that people like this were 'generally disinterested in politics'. It was difficult, the report stated unctuously, to see 'the interest of an agitation carried out in this environment for the emancipation of the Hindu people'.[15]

This was off the mark by a mile or ten.

The truth was that the arrival of Indian migrants in Paris after 1919 was due in part to the political and geographical factors that made the city a global hub for revolutionary activity, and also due to Paris's reputation as a sympathetic home for Indian nationalists. Of particular interest to London, for instance, was the Indian Association in Paris—the same Hindustan Samaj where Panikkar and John were staying. The India Office had had its eye on Bagchi who had arranged to hire a room at 17 Rue de Sommerard for the Samaj. The room served both as a reading room and a meeting place, not to mention a temporary residence for Indians who were looking for rooms in Paris. The fact that Panikkar and Bagchi were active in a 'secret club' of which representatives of various Eastern countries 'agreed that the salvation of the East lies in the casting off of the yoke of foreign domination' was reason enough to warn Western secret services about the AECO.[16] So, when Panikkar and John shifted to the more discreet 36 Rue des Ecoles, it was likely because they had detected the police on their heels. Even as they dodged the authorities, Panikkar found himself thinking of how best he could contribute to an international understanding of the Indian independence movement among all the other interests at the AECO. His pen, as always, was his best weapon, but he was stymied by his lack of skill with French. Here he was saved by Merlange.

In his memoir, Panikkar discreetly references her as 'de Gaulle's secretary during the [Second World] war', but as we've seen, she was a lot more than that. Later in life, Merlange would distinguish herself during the Nazi occupation of her country, giving valuable aid to the Allied forces as part of the French resistance. When Panikkar met her, she was at the height of her influence and power in the transnationalist network. As Mononutu's lover, she had only added prestige to her already formidable reputation. When Panikkar approached her for help, she suggested that he could write and she would translate his work into French and have it translated into Indonesian and other languages as well, so that it would be read across a wide spectrum. It was the start of a longstanding professional association that allowed him to write on Indian affairs for an interested audience in Europea. 'I had only to write the articles,' he would remember later. 'Germaine undertook to meet the editors, fix the remuneration and correct the proofs.'[17]

With her help, Panikkar began writing about the ideas and questions that were filling his mind during these stimulating days in Paris. One of these pieces, written for the *Indonesia Merdeka*, is fairly frank about Panikkar's awareness of and frustration with the fact that they were constantly watched by Western secret services. How was it possible, he railed, to establish any sense of pan-Asian unity if they were so constantly censored and followed? 'Asian students in Europe need to establish that unity,' he wrote, 'because it is possible in the European capitals to meet each other and to find common ground. Also because these Asian students will later become leaders of their suppressed peoples.'[18]

In addition to journals, Panikkar continued to earn a flourishing living by writing and selling articles on Indian culture and politics to French newspapers. In the middle of all this vigorous journalism, he and Germaine became flagrantly involved in a romantic affair.

This was a relationship that is rarely written about, though it was an open secret among Indonesian dissident networks, made even more scandalous by the fact that Merlange was still also involved with Mononutu. There is no sign that Mononutu minded this, for his own personal track record is rather spicy, with one scornful police file suggesting (wrongly) that he also had 'homosexual leanings'.[19]

Be that as it may, Merlange's relationship with Panikkar was as brief as it was torrid.

This was Panikkar's first affair outside his marriage (it wouldn't be the last), and while it occurred under fairly heady circumstances of revolution and secrecy, he had his eye on bigger things. He needed Germaine's help for introductions to people of influence, her sharp editorial eye and her skill at translating his words into French. He also had a point to prove to himself and hopefully to those in positions of power back home in India who might be watching.

Germaine introduced Panikkar to Felix Valyi, the Hungarian historian of the Near East, and together the two men oversaw a multilingual journal, *Revue des Nations*. Panikkar also wrote across other journals, like *Europe* and *Europe Nouvelle.* In all of these, he tried to familiarise European readers with the unique challenges that Indian nationalism faced.[20] He had long been annoyed with the communalism that plagued Indian politics, and in the many articles he wrote now, he highlighted the responsibility of India's separate communal organisations.[21] Other pieces dealt with racial discrimination in India and the other colonies of the British Empire[22] or with the negative effects of colonialism on European countries in terms of the rise of militarism and other practices that were in direct contrast to Western moral values.[23]

At last, this was the kind of journalism that, in his days at *Swarajya* and *Hindustan Times*, Panikkar had truly longed to do: the perfect intersection of angry politics and academia. As he knew perfectly well, his own nationality unlocked doors that were closed to his friends. Much of this privilege was because of his perceived link, by sheer virtue of being Indian, with Gandhi.[24]

The Mahatma's emblematic value as a man who was putting the brakes on colonialism was beyond quantification. Panikkar had a glimpse of just what he meant to certain French intellectuals in his relationship with the maverick lawyer Juliette Viellier-Duray. Born in 1899 in Fresnes to a father who worked as a prison director and a mother who was a housewife, Juliette was raised a staunch Catholic. The family seems to have been inclined towards academia, with Juliette's sister Lucienne becoming a professor of literature and her brother Maurice entering the world of banking. After earning herself a law degree from the Paris law faculty and a degree in literature, Juliette left first for Oxford and then for the United States. She returned a handful of years later with a Bachelor of Law degree. In 1922, Juliette joined the Paris bar while she continued to study for her doctoral degree. She had her eye set on higher things for herself. In the days when women were strongly discouraged from taking on something like a law degree, Juliette was determined to prove detractors wrong. In 1924, she entered the Berryer Conference oratory competition, a contest designed to train candidates (with considerable rigour) for the Paris Bar Association. By 1925, Juliette was the second secretary of the Conference of the Internship and awarded the signal honour of making a speech at the start of the bar in 1926.

She had already met Panikkar at this point in time. The two had hit it off almost immediately. Panikkar was by now extremely aware of his appeal to women of a certain intellect and style, and there is nowhere that he seems to have flaunted this redoubtable aptitude more than in Europe. In short order, he was invited to watch Juliette speak at the magnificent Palais de Justice. She had chosen her subject daringly, as she chose always to do through her life. She was speaking on Gandhi and his civil disobedience movement among other things.

Panikkar never forgot that moment—or the woman herself.

It was a packed house that morning. Nobody had ever witnessed a woman speaking to a house of men before. Viellier-Duray rose to speak, tall, thin and bright-eyed. She spoke in a resonant, beautifully modulated voice of feminism, of women daring to make the world a more equal place. 'Today, we women lawyers have the same difficulties in our careers as men,' she said to an enthralled audience. 'We must, through our work, ensure an honourable place for ourselves ... We will be able to see later, if the proportion of women who succeed is lower than that of men. But I doubt it in advance. I tell you again: it's all a question of individuality of vocation. Why not believe in us?'

Juliette's speech made headlines in France and across the Atlantic. *La Jeune République* reported exultantly, 'It is not only the friends of beautiful language who will have felt pleasure, but also, above all, the idealists, those who believe against all odds, as Miss Juliette Veillier so aptly put it, "that in the world, there must be a little less machinery and a lot more soul."'[25]

Panikkar was among the fervent hundreds who believed in Juliette Veillier-Duray with all his heart that morning. As he watched her, after the speech, being mobbed by colleagues and seniors trying to shake her hand, and as he listened to the shouts and cheers that rose to the ceiling, he was captivated. He wasn't going to lose the opportunity of getting to know this 'extraordinary woman' a little more.[26] Whether that friendship remained platonic is a matter of vivid question since, according to the Panikkar family, there was much more than that between the two.[27] This was a longer affair than his with Merlange had been.

In his memoir, Panikkar acknowledges that he and Viellier-Duray became extremely close and remained so for the rest of his days in Paris. They took to spending every moment they could together. Photographs show a tall and angular woman with a long, patrician nose, crimped dark hair and a pair of compelling dark eyes. For Panikkar, it was a meeting of the minds. Viellier-Duray was a passionate defender of her ideals and principles. She was also a far more intelligent woman than Merlange, with a quicksilver mind that matched Panikkar's own. Her legal career was a rich and storied one, underlined always by her belief in equality for women. Panikkar would spend his days in the city, working on his books, articles and essays and on developing ideas for transnational resistance. They would meet for coffees and dinners after work.

But on the weekends, he would slip out of Paris to Juliette's family villa on the outskirts of the city. There, they would spend their days together, chatting or lazing in the sun. It was the first time that Panikkar had met a woman like this.

What of Gouri, a reader might justifiably wonder at this point. In all honesty, Gouri was the exact opposite of both Germaine and Juliette, at least at this moment in time. She was entirely devoted to family life, to the children, to her readings of the Gita or to tending the kitchen garden. In Juliette, on the other hand, Panikkar found a woman with whom he could discuss and debate erudite ideas. While his tendency was to analyse and reflect, her mind was faster and more agile, making conversations with her a delight. Her peers noted it too, with a colleague who watched her in court remarking, 'She knows how to improvise, to take advantage of all the incidents in court with a superior skill that many ... could envy.'[28] And she was warm, fearless and great fun.

Being with Juliette was not only a novelty; it was, in many ways, a refuge from reality.

The authorities were extremely interested in Panikkar by this time.

Apart from writing considerably inflammatory articles, he had also established contact with Chaim Weizmann, a leading figure on the Zionist scene. It was the first time Panikkar had encountered Zionism up close. He would never fully step away from it, though he prudently kept those leanings undercover.

The Indian National Congress had already made its first statement in strong support of Palestine in the aftermath of the Balfour Declaration and the establishment of the British mandate over Palestine in 1922.[29] As Panikkar knew, the Congress was thinking about what the struggles across Egypt, Syria and Palestine meant, and how solidarity with these struggles could factor into its definition of imperialism and possibly a postcolonial foreign policy. The Muslim League, on the other hand, had taken the exact opposite stand. While the Congress tried to maintain a pro-Arab approach without being hostile to the Jews, the Muslim League was explicitly pro-Arab and pro-Islamic.

As long as India was subjugated, so was the region known then as West Asia. Anti-colonialist movements were intertwined in the aftermath of the war, and India had a chance to take the leadership role. Despite this opportunity, nothing much happened until Jawaharlal Nehru took on a more central role in the Congress in the late 1920s.

He was in Europe around the same time as Panikkar and it was here on the continent that the two men would develop very different ideas about Palestine and a potential Israel.

That, however, would come much later, as India moved towards its freedom. For now, any kind of contact with Indian nationalists, both Congress and Muslim League, was enough for Zionist leaders. When Panikkar met him in 1926, Chaim Weizmann was at the peak of his diplomatic powers. By 1917, his energy and ambition had catapulted him to the head of the World Zionist Organisation in Europe. The historian Jehuda Reinharz terms him 'the best known Jew of the day' in the 1920s. In England, he was received by the king himself, had the blessing of the prime minister and foreign minister, and was cosily cocooned at the very top of British diplomacy. There was no door in Whitehall that would not open for Weizmann.

Short and bald, with twinkling dark eyes and a sudden, charming smile, Weizmann was possessed of that consummate gift of a born diplomat: the ability to forge and maintain relationships from all walks of life.[30] So charming was he that one always managed to look past his less charming qualities—a distinctly autocratic and suspicious personality, prone to intense jealousy, pettiness and impatience. For many in England, he was a dignified spokesperson for Zionism, capable of speaking both honestly and credibly about his cause. Panikkar, introduced to Weizmann by the progressive (and Zionist) member of parliament Josiah Wedgwood (great-grandson of the man who founded the famous pottery firm), was struck by his intelligence and passion for his cause. 'Weizmann was undoubtedly one of the most remarkable men I met,' he would write later. 'I felt in his presence the kind of reverence and humility which I used to feel in the presence of Mahatma Gandhi.'[31]

Panikkar couldn't help his admiration for the Zionist cause or for Weizmann himself, but even then, he knew it would be controversial to display it publicly. The Zionist policies that Weizmann advocated were running into troubled waters in the years after the war. Confronted by mounting problems and unrest caused by nascent Arab nationalism, Britain was retreating from its previous commitments to foster a Jewish national home. Weizmann ploughed on regardless, but the going was far tougher at the end of the 1920s than it had been during the First World War. Official enthusiasm, despite former British prime minister Arthur Balfour's Zionist leanings, was waning towards the cause.

From Britain's perspective, the question of Palestine was a tricky one, tied uncomfortably tightly to India. The empire had Muslim unrest to think of as well as strategic and financial valuations from India (by way of the Suez Canal). Government ministers like Curzon and Andrew Bonar Law (then the chancellor of the exchequer) made it clear that the principal drive was imperialist rather than Zionist. Their aims, they argued, related to the security of the Suez Canal and continued access to India as the prime overseas support of British economic and military power around the world.

In the face of this, Weizmann was furious and frustrated. But in Panikkar, he sensed a worthy diplomat for his ideas. During their initial conversations, Weizmann spoke to him about where the Zionist movement currently stood and its recognition of the Indian Muslims as a crucial factor in delaying a Jewish homeland. The nature of the problem in Palestine was Islamic, something the grand mufti of Jerusalem, Hajj Amin al-Husseini, had recognised. In the early 1920s, al-Husseini had sent a three-member delegation to India to raise funds for the restoration of the dilapidated al-Aqsa Mosque, much of which had come from the Muslim rulers of India. The Nizam of Hyderabad alone had contributed over £7,000. While seeking Indian support, the delegation projected the prevailing political climate in Palestine as an anti-colonial struggle. The British, said the mufti, were the enemies of the Arabs *and* the Indians. This struck a chord of sympathy with Nehru, who saw him as a genuine nationalist fighting for Arab liberation—much to the horror of the Zionists, who fervently hated the mufti and were furious that his strategy of presenting himself as a pan-Islamic leader with a base beyond Palestine was paying off. With so much hinging on Muslim opposition, senior officials in the India Office were naturally opposed to Jews being given special privileges in Palestine. They feared that this could result in widespread opposition from the Indian Muslims and lead to disaster. So the Zionist movement was stuck.

Weizmann spread his hands persuasively.

Did Panikkar see the problem, he asked.

Panikkar did.

There was nothing concrete he could offer right now, but he promised to build Weizmann's networks within Congress circles where he had access to Nehru and to Gandhi.

For now, apart from studying for his law degree, Panikkar remained active on the secret dissident circuit with Merlange, Mononutu and several others. The AECO's membership had ballooned to some thirty members, citizens of Indochina, Java and China. Its members, dodging their surveillance every morning, would meet at the Chinese students' secretariat to discuss the business for the day. They often bumped into each other by accident or design at public lectures on Asian or colonial affairs. Their main goal was to counter what they considered to be fake propaganda by advocates of colonialism. In the evenings, they sat around in what Panikkar has recalled as 'Domago coffee house', which was in all likelihood the Café Les Deux Magots, a famous and very popular bar in the Saint-Germain-des-Prés area that also attracted members of the Paris literary and Surrealist art scene of the moment.

A look through the archives leaves one in no doubt that Mononutu, a member of the executive committee of the AECO, was the leader of this little gaggle of students and dissidents. For him, it was a clear and exciting opportunity to introduce the rest of the world to the Perhimpoenan Indonesian (PI) students' movement, a nationalist progressive movement established by overseas Indonesian students. The purpose was, as with most such movements, to establish connections with foreign political groups and associations working for the same cause. He invited friends to come and speak to the PI, to open discussions on colonialism and anti-imperialism. On 6 June 1926, for instance, Panikkar lectured at the general meeting of the PI in Leiden about 'the necessity of Asiatic unity',[32] a theme that had interested him since he first met Mononutu and his new friends in Paris. Significantly, he didn't speak about Gandhi for he was learning the ways and interests of different audiences. If the French were enamoured by Gandhian techniques of resistance, the Indonesians were not. They were aware certainly of Gandhi's principles of non-cooperation and civil disobedience, but they were not entirely enthusiastic about the more spiritual elements of Gandhian resistance such as non-violence or self-sacrifice.

But even as he wrote and lectured on subjects carefully tailored for international audiences, Panikkar hadn't forgotten his own research interests. In the summer of 1926, he travelled to the Netherlands to stay at the Hague in Mohammad Hatta's house. He was there for a month, researching what would become *Malabar and the Dutch* a handful of years later. His activities were innocuous enough, but since he was already a 'person of interest' for the British and the French, and a known AECO activist, it's not surprising that he was of equal interest to the Dutch intelligence agencies. While Panikkar dug about in the archives of the Hague and the university in Leiden, frantic messages were ricocheting between surveillance agencies in India, Britain, France, Holland and the Dutch Indies. Panikkar returned to Paris in due course, fully and smugly aware that he had been trailed and his activities in the Netherlands noted.

In his memoir, Panikkar is almost bland about his time in Paris, but in reality the keen perspectives on foreign policy and geopolitics for which he is remembered today were acquired over low-voiced conversations in the popular cafes and shady side-alleys of the city. These were the days when he was thinking hard and long about Asian nationalism, ideas that he would soon articulate to a wider audience.

CHAPTER 17

Bierville and Beyond

IT WAS DURING A CONVIVIAL EVENING AT THE CAFÉ LES DEUX MAGOTS, that Duong Van Giao announced to his friends that he knew some people who were organising an international pacifist conference in Bierville, a small village 120 kilometres northwest of Paris. Grandly titled Congrès Démocratique International pour la Paix and run at the initiative of the peace activist, educationist and ardent Roman Catholic Marc Sangnier, the conference would take place between 14 and 23 August 1926.

Panikkar and Mononutu sat up straighter, their attention caught. Pleased at this reception, Duong explained that this was usually an annual event hosted by the Ligue de la Jeune-République, a small but progressive Catholic party that was advocating peace through diplomacy across the world via the League of Nations and the Locarno Treaties of 1925.[1] Usually, Duong said, this conference focused primarily on Europe and was taken seriously enough for countries to send their top diplomats. How about the AECO register for this and raise the question of colonialism and peace *outside* Europe?

Panikkar and the others looked at one another, hardly able to contain their excitement. If they could get in, it would be an undoubted coup. The only problem was that the face and voice of their group, Mononutu, would not be in Paris. He would be going instead to the the Peace Palace summer school at the Hague. The

PI scratched its head for a while and finally decided to send young, serious Mohammad Hatta as a representative of the Indonesian youth. A student of economics in the Netherlands, Hatta was already devoted to the cause of Indonesian independence. He would become independent Indonesia's first prime minister, guiding his country through a crucial period of transition from a federal to a unified state.[2]

Hatta arrived in Paris at the end of July and was introduced by Mononutu to the rest of the delegation. They were a mixed lot. Apart from Panikkar himself and Duong, there was the sixty-seven-year-old Alimardan Bey Topchubachev, an Azeri exile who in 1918 had founded the independent Azerbaijan Democratic Republic and was now in Paris working to secure his country's freedom.[3] There was also a Chinese representative, a quiet, elusive young man by the name of Tung Meau. In preparatory meetings, this motley crew agreed upon forming an 'Asian bloc' and writing a joint manifesto, which Panikkar would present on behalf of the others.[4] They would then, Duong instructed, 'talk about the politics of the Orient'.[5]

Panikkar set off for Bierville two days before the conference was scheduled to begin. He found a small village with all of 100 inhabitants labouring to accommodate the flood of foreign visitors. Five thousand delegates from thirty-three countries were in attendance that year. The conference enjoyed patronage from high-level French politicians and even from the French foreign minister Aristide Briand.[6]

From the start, it had been Sangnier's wish that this congress take place 'in peaceful and calm environs, under the great pacific trees, near to the pure and moving springs, that you might know one another, love one another'.[7] Bierville was Sangnier's own country estate, some forty hectares of parkland, woods and prairies, in the Juisne valley of the Beauce region between the Seine and Loire rivers. It had been bought in 1922, thanks in part to his wife Renée, who had lately come into her own mother's estate. On its usual days, Bierville was the Sangnier family weekend home, and had its own separate guesthouse.

For the congress, the delegates were accommodated in three large campsites, one for men, one for women and one for the clerics, in large army tents provided, ironically for a pacifist event, by the French war ministry. From where the tents were situated, delegates had a wonderful view of the many religious symbols that littered the Bierville estate, from Le Calvaire de la Paix (Calvary of Peace) to nicely located grottoes of St Francis of Assisi, and even a large crucifix made of wood from the German Schwarzwald. Panikkar had expected it to be pompously official but Bierville was more like a cosmopolitan jamboree, with Boy Scouts as volunteers. The accommodation was a little cramped—Hatta complained about sleeping on a stretcher seventy-five centimetres in width and a metre away from his neighbour[8]—but Panikkar had a pleasurable feeling of anticipation in his stomach.

He had written his position paper already, in which he had chosen to argue that British rule in India was responsible for 'mortgaging the freedom of Asia'.[9] His turn to speak came on the seventh day of the ten-day conference. He warned of the dangers of a superficial peace across the empire's colonies—repression would only instil hatred in the hearts of the colonised, and sooner or later, that dam would burst. He spoke as an Indian nationalist, emphasising the importance of the future of British India. As long as the British empire stood in India, he argued, the freedom of other Asian countries and peace across the world was endangered. Indeed, a truly global idea of peace couldn't be a Eurocentric one. You couldn't simply discard Asia or Africa in your understanding of peace. Colonialism was no answer either. It implied what he called a 'shadowy peace', keeping civilisations subdued at the point of the bayonet.[10] 'A progress which excludes the vast majority of human beings and affects only a fraction can never be permanent,' Panikkar insisted. Across the world, he argued, the most dangerous tensions were to be expected in the colonised world. You only had to look at the ongoing wars and conflicts in the Hejaz and China and their potential for conflagrating the whole empire to understand the depth of the danger. If India, on the other hand, was quiet right now, that peace was a deceptive one, reinforced as it was by colonial repression.

It was the first time that he had publicly addressed the geopolitical position of India in the empire. It would be India, he prophesied, that would determine the future of Asia—and that of the British

Empire. Only once there was true freedom and peace for the Indian people could the 'spirit of Asia', which was 'essentially pacifist' be strengthened. 'In India we have rediscovered—after many centuries—the great doctrine of Ahimsa or non-violence of which Mahatma Gandhi is the Apostle. [. . .] Help to liberate that spirit and you would have achieved your object.'[11]

The speech highlighted two resolutions: one underlining the right to self-determination for *all* nations and the other confirming that universal peace was only possible with the liberation of the suppressed peoples of the East. 'Let China, India and the rest of Asia be free,' he said, looking around the room. 'Then you would have built up a family of free people willing to live together in co-operation, and more than that you would have eliminated the most potent causes of war.'[12]

Panikkar sat down to thunderous applause. His had been the opening salvo for the Asian delegation, and he had fired brilliantly.

The next day, on 21 August 1926, Mohammad Hatta spoke, keeping his speech aligned to the common Asian manifesto, but taking a slightly more militant tone than Panikkar had by warning that, if colonial powers did not pay attention to the aspirations of the Indonesian people, nationalism could well turn violent. The other Asian delegates, Tung Meau, Topchubachev and Duong Van Giao, gave speeches as well, with Giao repeating Panikkar's words, stating that it was the task of all pacifists to let freedom and justice reign in the whole world without regard to nations or races.

The final position paper was signed not just by Panikkar but by all the Asian delegates at the conference, from China to India and from Azerbaijan to Indonesia. As a moment, it was a remarkable one, bringing transnational resistance to imperialism onto the world stage where it could be seen and where, Panikkar hoped, their voices would be heard.

Looking back at Bierville in an essay for *Indonesia Merdeka*, Hatta wrote: 'For the first time the Western pacifists saw Asia being represented at their congress. And for the first time they heard Asia's voice, which declared in clear language that no lasting peace is possible as long as the oppressed peoples are not free of the foreign yoke.'[13]

But within this clear language, there existed different timbres and tones. There is no real evidence that suggests open disagreement among the Asian delegation, in itself a remarkable achievement. But there *were* differences in perspective, many of which are naturally beyond the story of Panikkar himself. To give only one example, one might focus on a rather visible difference of opinion on the issue of peace itself.

At Bierville, the question of peace and war was generally seen as a matter between states and armies. With the emphasis being on the importance of international diplomacy, the subject of peace between colonised and coloniser was one to be carefully navigated, especially since the ultimate end was liberation for the colonies. With regard to this, Panikkar and Hatta moderated their statements differently. Panikkar, perhaps tempered by his friend, Duong Van Giao, stressed the peaceful character of the Asian peoples, influenced as they were by Buddhist culture. Supporting Asian movements for independence, he said, implied supporting peace. But this temperate view belied the tone of his essays and articles published across Indonesia and Europe at the time. In one of them, Panikkar refuted moderate and cooperative attitudes towards the English as impotent and naïve. 'The guarantee against the repetition of incidents [such as the Massacre of Amritsar in 1919, when English troops opened fire on peaceful protesters] lay not so much in parliamentary acts as in the power of the people to enforce respect. It was with this that the non-cooperation movement of Mahatma Gandhi was started,'[14] he wrote in an essay for *Indonesia Merdeka*, also warning: 'While the moderates are *constitutionalists* believing only in the parliamentary action, the nationalists believe also in direct mass action, either by civil disobedience or by passive resistance as a means of enforcing national demands.'[15]

This essay had been met with delight by Indonesians, including Hatta himself. In an essay written in July 1930, Hatta referred to Panikkar's essay. 'Who has taken the article of K.M. Panikkar to heart, will not discover mere passivity in Mahatma Gandhi's non-cooperation without violence, but a great revolutionary spirit ... Superficial readings of Gandhi have put too much emphasis on passivity, which in essence is only a *preliminary* action, and they overlook the fact that when Gandhi considers that the time has come, he does not reject violence as well.'[16]

It is safe to say then that Bierville was a turning point in Panikkar's thinking, not just about India, but about India's place in Asia.

With the conference done and dusted, Panikkar bade goodbye to Merlange, Bagchi and the other friends he had met and made in Paris. He also met Juliette one last time. We don't know if they kept in touch through the years, but it is certain that Panikkar never saw Juliette again. It was the beginning of a pattern that would develop through his years of travelling the world. He had always enjoyed the company of women and as he began to advance in his career, he actively sought their presence in his life.

It was not difficult to say yes to Panikkar. He was not a particularly prepossessing man; photographs show a heavy-browed, serious face, with the goatee beard that would become his trademark and a waistline that was beginning to slide towards stockiness. But he more than made up for what he lacked in the physical department in terms of charm and intelligence. A first meeting—especially if it was a professional one—might lead you to think that he was cold and businesslike, even hard. But Panikkar was capable of great tenderness and gentleness. He was also a wonderful conversationalist, at ease with discussing anything under the sun with verve, intelligence and humour. His travels would lend a depth to all these qualities that did not come from mere bookishness. Small wonder then that women found him particularly attractive. For all that his eye roved gladly, Panikkar's family was his foundation. He would always return to Gouri and his children. But it is debatable whether they were uppermost on his mind in these years in Europe. There was simply too much happening around him in terms of intellectual, sexual and political stimulation.

He would never forget Paris, nor would his way of looking at the world ever be the same again. But now that his bags were packed, he was looking firmly ahead to his next destination—Berlin.

Berlin was bleak. The 'roaring twenties', so alive in Paris, had almost entirely passed the average German by. The Treaty of Versailles had imposed conditions and reparations that were difficult, if not impossible to bear, and in the mid-1920s, Weimar Germany was looking to get back on its feet again. The Treaty of Locarno, signed in 1925, had been the catalyst it was desperately seeking, the economic engine behind which Germany gathered steam. Ideologically speaking, the country was trying (and beginning to fail) to balance communist and sectarian politics. If there were the avant-garde productions at the Kroll Opera and if some of Berlin's fanciest nightclubs saw gin and dancing until the crack of dawn, there were also marching bands, a 'red district' in the heart of Berlin and processions of clean-shaven young men who wore brown shirts and were members of the National Socialist German Workers' Party. The party's name exhausted the traveller Emily Pollard, but she was grateful to notice that, over time, the name was 'mercifully shortened to Nazi'.[17]

The one similarity between Paris and Berlin was the buzz of underground politics. For South Asians in particular, Berlin eclipsed other European cities as a haven for politically active expatriates and exiles. With the existing conditions of inflation, soaring wartime debts and a politically weak centre, Germany was a hotbed for socialists, anarchists and communists, and they operated in the same secretive ways that Panikkar had seen in Paris.

Here though, communism painted the town red. Moscow encouraged anti-colonial nationalists from the colonies to join the common struggle against capitalism and imperialism. Berlin was ideal for collaborations between anti-colonialists and communists. Panikkar was aware of their presence. He was, after all, carrying letters of introduction to, among others, the known revolutionary and communist Virendranath Chattopadhyaya (Sarojini Naidu's younger brother, known colloquially as Chatto). In his memoir, Panikkar is dismissive, writing, 'Since I had no desire to involve myself with revolutionaries … I kept my distance during my stay there.'[18] This is a bit rich coming from a man who had arrived in Berlin fresh from vividly anarchist activities in Paris, though it makes better sense if one remembers that Panikkar wrote his memoir in the middle of his diplomatic career and right after he'd finished a contentious ambassadorial posting in China. Given his circumstances then, it was hardly politically correct to write that he had actually thoroughly enjoyed the radical atmosphere of interwar Europe. In reality, he didn't think twice about taking Chatto's help to get himself published in Berlin so he could continue making an Indian voice heard on the international stage.

The heavy-browed, moustachioed Chatto had led a stormy life. He had first travelled to London in 1902 to take the civil service examinations. After failing them spectacularly, he began studying law, with his mind drifting steadily towards politics. Chatto found some succour at India House until Curzon-Wylie's assassination forced him out of England to Paris and thence to Berlin. Here, to the considerable embarrassment of his sister Sarojini, Chatto emerged as the chief agent of the German foreign office during the First World War by attempting to incite rebellion and mutiny among Indian soldiers stationed in Baghdad, Kabul and the Suez Canal. When Nehru and Panikkar separately met him in Berlin, Chatto was one of the most carefully watched men in Europe.[19] He had been working extensively with German communists, especially Willi Münzenberg, a propagandist who ran a Berlin-based relief organisation with communist ties, the Workers International Relief (WIR).[20] His sister Sarojini had been forced to renounce him publicly in order to save face as a leader of the national movement in India. Meanwhile, Chatto's other sister, Suhasini, was in Berlin too, married to A.C. Nambiar, then a budding journalist and anti-colonial activist. Chatto had just organised an anti-colonial conference in Brussels when Panikkar arrived in Berlin. The conference interested Panikkar since he had attended just such a one in Paris. This effort by Chatto would lead to the formation of the League Against Imperialism, to which Nehru would be the official delegate in Brussels in February 1927.[21]

Nehru was already in Europe, travelling much as Panikkar had done, albeit more widely between Germany and France and the Netherlands and Britain. He was also doing much the same work as Panikkar—writing extensively across newspapers and journals to ensure that international audiences didn't forget that India existed. It was perhaps also an exercise in his own passion for the national movement's goals. The year 1927 was a difficult time in the history of the Congress Party, which was riven with fissures and factions.

Gandhi had done his best to bring the Swarajists and the no-changers together, but the party still lacked cohesion and direction. When Nehru left India, as he wrote in his memoir, he was thankful for the break. 'I wanted an excuse to go out of India … My mind was befogged, and no clear path was visible; and I thought that, perhaps, if I was far from India I could see things in better perspective and lighten up the dark corners of my mind.'[22]

The Brussels Congress was just the remedy his tired mind sought. His position on India was exactly the same as Panikkar's had been in Bierville. Nehru argued, 'India is a world problem, and as in the past so in the future other countries and peoples will be vitally affected by the condition of India.'[23] There was no way to overstate how central India was to the empire, as well as to the future of the world. 'What it will be in the future, if and when India becomes independent, I cannot say,' Nehru declared, 'but certainly the British Empire would cease to exist.'[24] And when it did, a free India would be the catalyst for a world free from the shackles of imperialism and capitalism.

Panikkar, who had immersed himself so deeply in politics in Paris, watched all this from afar. He continued to write in Berlin, following the same themes as he had in Paris, but his time was cut short by a telegram from his publishers in London. The book that would become *An Introduction to the Study of the Relations of Indian States with the Government of India* was ready to go to press. Martin Hopkinson wanted Panikkar back in London to correct the proofs. To be embroiled in anarchism and transnational resistance at this point was not something Panikkar, sorely tempted as he was, could afford to do. He left Berlin very quickly, avoiding any attempt from Chatto to make him stay on and work for the underground resistance in Germany.

By March 1927, Panikkar was back in London, his mind sharply focused on the task at hand. It was time to sit down with his book and see where it took him.

Chapter 18

Enter Haksar

PANIKKAR DIDN'T KNOW IT THEN, BUT HE WAS HOLDING HIS FIRST MAJOR contribution to India's constitutional history in his hands. The proofs of *An Introduction to the Study of the Relations of Indian States with the Government of India* were hot off the press, and Panikkar was convinced that he couldn't have chosen a more politically relevant subject.

These travels across Europe in the last couple of years had only reinforced his convictions that the time was coming for the states to join hands with the national movement. It was a prescient understanding of the fact that global geopolitics, as much as national politics, had thrown the concept of sovereignty into flux. To Panikkar's mind, the participation of princes like Bikaner and Patiala in international and imperial conferences had brought them into contact with the construction of new political and global orders. These new negotiations for their expanded sovereignty were but a natural fallout of the war and the national movement.

Yes, Panikkar had big plans for this new book of his, and he had been keeping a keen eye on who had been coming and going between India and England that year. He had his sights set on one Colonel Kailash N. Haksar. Scholarly and urbane, with gold-rimmed spectacles and bushy eyebrows, Haksar had begun his career as private secretary to the Maharaja of Gwalior before serving as the Dewan of

Bikaner. He was currently serving in Kashmir as prime minister for the moody profligate Maharaja Hari Singh, and he was in London on a mission.

In 1926, Kashmir had been elected to the Standing Committee of the Chamber of Princes. This was a year that was particularly tumultuous for the states' body. Jealousies and rivalries, particularly between Bikaner and Patiala, had riven the chamber internally. The princes were rarely able to find common ground on important issues. To top it all, 1926 was also the year in which the Nizam of Hyderabad provided the Raj with a much-needed chance to remind the princes who was boss. His state was much bigger than the rest and commanded a sizeable army, not to mention its own (small but feisty) vassal state, Berar. Since the Nizam's ego rivalled the geographical size of his kingdom, he had decided to let the British know that he would be pushing for Berar's inclusion within his dominion. He chose the simple expedient of bypassing the viceroy altogether and going straight to Whitehall with an extraordinary document advocating this desire, in which he even pushed for the creation of a popular constitution.

The audacity of the Nizam rendered Whitehall speechless until Nizam Osman Ali Khan declared that Hyderabad was internally independent and in that respect was the equal of the Government of India. This was going far too far. It was an attack on the heart of paramountcy and Britain wasn't having it. Lord Reading, then the viceroy, struck back sharply. 'The sovereignty of the British Crown is supreme in India and therefore, no ruler of an Indian state can justifiably claim to negotiate with the British government on an equal footing.'[1]

It was a single sentence, but it did two things. First, it struck cold terror into royal hearts across India. Second, it redefined the constitutional relationship between the British Crown and the princes.

Unsurprisingly then, an official government note assessing the royal mood across the country reported, 'The princes are afraid of the future ... Democracy has swept away others before their eyes. The reflections that it may end in dictatorship brings them no balm. Such a dictatorship would mean their downfall.'[2]

Events moved fast after Reading's castigation. A proposal to constitute a committee that would study the workings of paramountcy was greenlit, and the names of its members released. Known as the Indian States Committee (the Butler Committee for short), it was to be chaired by the round-faced erudite Sir Harcourt Butler, the same man who had scripted the laissez-faire policy of 1909—the policy that had claimed to guarantee royal autonomy while keeping the Raj's hand on the reins of political power.[3] The other two members of the committee were Sir Sidney Peel, a former financial advisor to the British government, and William Holdsworth, an eminent legal historian and a close friend of the then secretary of state for India, Lord Birkenhead. The Butler Committee would arrive in India in the spring of 1928.

The princes were delighted. Butler was a 'very old and true friend' as Jai Singh of Alwar told his colleagues enthusiastically.[4] Their ministers and advisors, on the other hand, were not quite so enamoured of the idea. The Butler Committee's deadline for arrival left them with very little time. Within a handful of months, the Standing Committee of the Chamber of Princes had to arrange for and brief legal counsel, collect documentation from member states on alleged abuses of paramountcy and infringement of treaty rights, and build a case (which had the chamber's support, another task in itself!) to present before the Butler Committee. This was going to be easier said than done.

The chamber decided that the best way to go about things was to delegate tasks to a full-time body dubbed the Special Organisation, which would function as a new executive arm of the chamber. The running of the Special Organisation was deputed to Haksar and to Lawrence Rushbrook-Williams, then the foreign minister of Patiala, even as the chamber continued to debate over the ways in which they could build their case.

There was deadlock over this question. Some saw merit in a defensive plan, dependent on the Butler Committee's report. Others leaned a toward a more offensive strategy based on extensive public relations targeting politicians and journalists and domestic reform. As Bhavnagar's dewan, Prabha Shankar Pattani, cryptically put it,

'You must take your subjects with you.'[5] Not everyone was thrilled with such a public relations-centric strategy. Yadavendra Singh of Panna wrote morosely to Patiala that he strongly felt that '[W]estern methods are not necessarily the best that can be devised to suit our environments'.[6] In the midst of this chaos, Haksar was in despair.

It was not that the princes were unaware of their constitutional rights or that they harboured no ambitions for the progress of their respective houses. But the differences prevailing within the chamber didn't help—nor did the public perception of them. The way the princes were talked about in the international press, for example, was still marked by a certain hilarity. Patiala's stay at the Savoy during the League of Nations assembly was remarked upon for his love for his pearls and diamonds, the installation of two wireless sets in his suite and his specific desire for a meal of quail. The last request had caused a veritable bombardment of cables across Europe for the elusive fowl. The ultimate haul was six birds from, oddly, Egypt. As long as the princes were dismissed in this manner, Haksar knew that he had his work cut out for him.

As the princes continued to debate and discuss their options, Haksar sailed for England, travelling with Rushbrook-Williams. Their aim was to secure the services of a reputable English barrister, knowledgeable in international and constitutional law, to represent the chamber before the Butler Committee. The two men had first visited the delightfully named chambers of Coward, Chance and Company. The law firm had asked them to enlist the services of Sir John Simon, who had already served England as both solicitor general and attorney general (the last with the unusual extra of a seat in the cabinet). But when Haksar and Rushbrook-Williams approached him, they found he had accepted the much more prestigious job of heading the Statutory Commission (the Simon Commission) that would be arriving in India in the winter of 1927. So it was that Simon wistfully passed up 'the biggest fee I have ever seen in my professional life'.[7]

The brief to represent the princes ultimately went to Sir Leslie Scott, a Tory member of parliament, an old friend of the secretary of state for India, a privy councillor and also a former solicitor general.

Scott was delighted. It wasn't just the fat fee that was attractive. He was a brilliant lawyer who loved his work and this seemed to be a challenge perfect for his mind and abilities. Rushbrook-Williams and Haksar arranged that Scott should fly out at Christmas to meet the princes and begin preparing his arguments.

With the logistics suitably arranged, the two men began a flurry of public relations, cultivating influential journalists like Panikkar's friend, Sir Frank Brown at the *Times*. Rushbrook-Williams's wife helped them meet some conservative members of parliament socially. Haksar and Rushbrook-Williams also threw lavish dinners in their suite at the Ritz Carlton to better engage with senior officials of the India Office. This frenetic publicity drive was the talk of London in those days, and being friends with Brown made it easy for Panikkar to track down where Haksar was staying. Without hesitation, Panikkar mailed the proofs of his manuscript to the Ritz, with a polite covering letter introducing himself and the main argument of his book.

Haksar had heard of K.M. Panikkar, but to his knowledge, the young man hadn't written very much on the subject of the princely states. He flipped idly through the first few pages before sitting up in considerable interest. Panikkar had noticed what no outsider had—that this was a phase in which power dynamics were being redefined. *An Introduction to the Study of the Relations of Indian States with the Government of India* insists that the states were of paramount importance to Indian politics for two reasons. One, they were purely Indian, and two, they were excellent case studies for self-governance because they were *already* self-governing. They were, if taken seriously, excellent laboratories in which to examine an Indian capacity for administration. Above all, Panikkar wrote, the states had been key in preserving local and regional identity, a factor which would come in handy during an era of undoubted modernisation. The Chamber of Princes was a step forward in this direction. 'By belonging to it, no state loses its independence or right of direct negotiation and the internal affairs of no state can be discussed unless the ruler himself desires it.'[8]

Panikkar's voice was the first to directly engage with India's climb to federal constitutionalism, but in all fairness the very air of the 1920s in India buzzed with thoughts on the subject. The federal argument was a real step forward on the royal road to constitutional reform. As early as 1923, the Bengali historian Brajendranath Seal had prepared a federal constitution for Mysore at the behest of Sir Albion Banerji, who would eventually be Panikkar's colleague in Kashmir, and he was just one of a close-knit group of historians, philosophers and political scientists who had already begun to argue that the predominant form of the state in India had always been federal.

More significantly (and unlike Gandhi), these political scientists argued that popular government in its truest form could exist only through participatory citizen councils at the local level. A federal structure was the only way for direct democracy (swaraj) to exist over a territory as vast as that of India. Seal, for example, refined this broad perspective into a federalist state (specifically Mysore) with a monarchical central government coordinating self-ruling citizens assemblies in every jurisdiction.

Seal's plan remained a draft, but it was a beginning. Panikkar had built upon this both fluently and persuasively. Not all states could be considered in the same way in his view, given their profound historical, political and geographical differences. Some, for instance, had been defeated into submission, some were vassals or subordinate allies. This automatically led to differentiated relationships with the empire. Some bigger states might hold complete legislative and executive independence within their borders. Others might be smaller states that only enjoyed some concessions from the Crown. For Panikkar, the two groups had to be treated differently. He suggested that the ideal political structure for India was a federal one. After all, that was the path down which history was leading the country. The British may have created a central government, but they hadn't been able to eliminate local authorities. A federation, Panikkar argued, was the only way in which British India could be united wholly with the states.

Haksar was convinced.

In his memoir, Panikkar wrote later that one day he was passing the hotel in which Haksar was staying. Upon noticing him passing by, Haksar sent a messenger to call him back. Whether this is how it happened or not, the upshot was that Haksar asked Panikkar 'point blank' if he would like to accept an official posting in Kashmir.

Not for nothing had Haksar served the princely states so long and so well. He knew exactly what to say to whom. 'I know almost all about your past career,' he coaxed the flattered Panikkar. 'I am not inviting you to take up an ordinary job. A committee will soon be set up to study the relationship between the Indian states and the British government. Work connected with it should suit you very well. Don't think that you will be asked to go as just another official.'[9]

It was exactly the right thing to have said. Panikkar was thirty-two years old and he was acutely aware that he had to get back home soon. He had a wife and three young children to take care of. There was a limit to how long he could continue travelling across the continent, speaking at conferences and congresses and writing long essays on the Indian freedom movement. He wanted, as he admitted baldly to himself, a 'fixed residence, freedom from financial worry'.[10] More than that, he wanted action—to feel as though he were really contributing to the change that he dreamed of for India.

He knew this was a better prospect than any he had got thus far. If he could succeed in Kashmir, then there was no telling the number of doors that could and would open. Politics was still his ambition, and this was the biggest step up he had had in recent years.

In addition, he had the undoubted advantage of having secured his law degree. He had been called to the bar from the Middle Temple in August 1927. With a combination of that and Haksar's job offer, Panikkar felt he finally had a chance to begin again. Still, he felt several pangs of regret when he thought of the numerous foreign tours lined up that he would now have to cancel, including a very promising study tour of Russia. But there was one thing that he could not cancel, nor did he wish to.

Telling the astonished Haksar that he needed time to think about the job, Panikkar said airily that he would report back with an answer on 17 September 1927.

Then, shortly thereafter, he departed England yet again. His destination: the Democratic International, a peace congress in the small town of Wurzburg in Germany, taking place between 4 and 7 September 1927.

Of this, in his memoir, Panikkar conspicuously makes no mention.

Still run by Sangnier, this was a much smaller congress than Bierville. The years between 1926 and 1929 were quiet years for Germany. Not only was it a signatory to the Treaty of Locarno, but it had recently joined the League of Nations. The economy had improved, under the aegis of Gustav Streseman, the Nobel Prize-winning foreign minister at the time, and in another couple of years, Germany would become party to the most dramatic gesture of post-war reconciliation, the Kellogg-Briand Pact, which promised to outlaw aggressive war. The Nazi Party was rising, albeit slowly. It would only become a major player in German politics in 1933. These were the golden years of the Weimar Republic, and as a result, Würzburg was a disappointment in terms of attendance. But it *was* the first to include a Race Commission, following on from the head-turning presence of several non-European delegates at Bierville.

Along with his friend Duong Van Giao of Indochina, Panikkar led a fresh charge at Würzburg against colonialism. It was the last time that he could speak quite so freely. Once he was working officially for the court of Kashmir, he would have to, of necessity, adopt a more tempered and diplomatic approach.

The Würzburg Congress repudiated ideas of race inequality while colonial delegates like Panikkar went further and called, separately, 'in the name of morality and democracy, for the peace of our consciences and for material peace: No More Colonies!'[11] The Race Commission showed just how much the world was changing and how global anti-imperialism was being defined by non-European elites such as Ho Chi Minh of Indochina and Gandhi of India. Panikkar's speech at Würzburg was set against the communist-associated unrest in the French and Dutch colonies in Southeast Asia and a ferment of discontent in Europe's colonies in the interwar years. In it, he linked imperialism with capitalism and war and called for the abolition of League of Nations mandates (such as that France enjoyed in Syria). The last point in particular was perhaps the most open he would ever be when it came to his opinions on British mandates and what their abolition could mean for regions like Palestine. As a whole though, Panikkar's speech infuriated many of the listening French delegates, who raged that his proposal was 'extreme' and 'impractical'.

He didn't stay long in Würzburg. Panikkar departed almost as soon as the congress was over, heading back to London, where he met the waiting Haksar at the Ritz-Carlton and accepted the job in Kashmir. After shaking hands with Haksar, Panikkar left for his own more modest lodgings at the other end of the city, feeling a deep sense of satisfaction. His time on the continent had finally come to an end, and this time, when he went home, he had something to show for it.

For now, he had to settle affairs in Kavalam.

By the end of 1927, Panikkar was on the *SS Amjer*, steaming homewards. His fellow passengers were a motley crew—such as the scandalous Tukoji Rao III of Indore, who had only lately abdicated his throne following his sensational involvement in the murder of a prominent businessman in Malabar Hill. Panikkar had heard of the case (there was nobody in the country and on both sides of the ocean who hadn't!), and it was hard to keep a straight face in the presence of the suave maharaja. Holkar was no stranger to controversy—his ascension to the throne following his father's abdication was steeped in controversy.

When Panikkar encountered him, he was on his third marriage, this with the American socialite Nancy Miller who had taken the rather unctuous name of Sharmistha Devi. Nancy was an unhappy young woman. In 1925, her charming, roving-eyed husband had fallen in obsessive lust with a beautiful young nautch girl by the name of Mumtaz Begum. It was not long before Mumtaz fled, seeking succour from Holkar's purported abuse. She sought refuge with a businessman named Abdul Kadir Bawla. One golden evening in 1925, Mumtaz and Bawla were shot at in a hit that left him dead. News headlines exploded, implying that the maharaja's hand was behind it all. Forced to act against a ruling prince whose position they had sworn to uphold, the Government of India hastily suggested a private commission of inquiry. Insulted, Holkar abdicated wholesale, retiring with his long-suffering wife to a villa near Paris.

That story did not shock Panikkar as much as it shocked him to learn that Holkar had not married Nancy.

'It is never wise to marry a European,' Panikkar sniffed. The cultures, he argued later in a tone not unlike that of elders in contemporary Indian society, simply did not *match*. He was even sniffier when Nancy disembarked quietly at Port Said. 'Perhaps,' he wrote nastily, 'she disembarked midway to avoid scandalising people in India by arriving in his company.'[12]

All of this is rather amazing—not to mention hypocritical—from a man who had deeply enjoyed his own affairs with European women while in Paris.

Also on board were Jawaharlal Nehru and his wife Kamala, with their little girl, Indira, and Panikkar's old friend, K.K. Pillai. Nehru was on his way back to India after his travels across Europe and the Soviet Union and his attendance at the Brussels Congress against Colonial Oppression and Imperialism and for National Independence. Nehru was as profoundly affected by what he had learned in Europe as Panikkar was. In his autobiography, he remembered it as a time of great transformation. 'The old world I knew had expired in the blood and horror of the War and a new world awaited me.'[13]

The war had done more to change the world than either Nehru or Panikkar had expected it to. It had birthed new weapons and toppled powerful empires. It had served as the catalyst for the overthrow of the Tsar in Russia as well as the world's first communist revolution. Now, despite the League of Nations and the many treaties that had been signed since the armistice, there was still an exhilarating sense that more was to come. Nehru's observations in Europe had imbued him with a sense of radical purpose and driven home the importance of a wider, more intricately linked anti-colonial struggle. If countries smaller than India could aspire to be free, then why not India itself?

In asking that question, he and Panikkar were in agreement, though neither of them mentioned it just now. There was Indira to look after and Kamala, greatly weakened by tuberculosis, to tend to. The evenings were spent taking turns in the kitchen—though the lot of cooking often fell to Pillai—while stories of foreign lands and politics were told to the wide-eyed Kamala. But much as Panikkar liked keeping one eye on the latest goings-on, he had no time on his hands. He had another book to write, and spent the voyage pleasurably engaged in reading and writing (when he wasn't casting catty aspersions on his fellow passengers).

Though he had plenty of research material on the Portuguese and the Dutch, Panikkar ignored it for the time being. He was of the opinion that a more politically timely book was necessary, considering that the Simon Commission was due to arrive in early 1928. By his own admission, *The Working of Dyarchy in India*—more of a quick monograph than at book at 160 pages—was written in two weeks, primarily as a method of hedging his bets. After all, he had no idea what to expect in Kashmir. As a result, *Dyarchy* was written under the rather facetious pseudonym of Kerala Putra, one Panikkar would speedily discard as he gained more confidence.

Dyarchy is not just a judgement on the Montagu-Chelmsford Report, but an exhibition of Panikkar's political and journalistic knowledge and experience. He had watched the councils in action during his days as a journalist and he argued that, their limitations and inconsistencies notwithstanding, the councils were a good foundation for popular governance. They had shown definite results in terms of education and social legislation, with the elections becoming a good instrument for political participation. The problems lay elsewhere: in the communal electorates and in the barriers that language posed, or rather the problem of the lack of a common language of public participation. More importantly, there were issues with the implementation of dyarchy as a principle. The Government of India Act, 1919, instituted what Lionel Curtis had named 'dyarchy', a twofold division of the powers of government. This was between, first, central and provincial governments, and second, between provincial subjects reserved for administration by the governor and his council and those transferred for administration by elected Indian ministers. 'The division of functions, therefore, was not made in such a way as to give the transferred departments autonomy within their own sphere.'[14]

From every angle, Panikkar wrote acidly, the promise of 'responsible government' had failed to materialise. Why? Because dyarchy, as it was formulated for India, did not postulate, promise or make room for the potential of a party system. Dyarchy had come too quickly. Ministerial responsibility was denied from the start, the viceroy's emergency powers of intervention were a constant reminder of imperial autocracy and the councils themselves had little effective power. Panikkar argued that too much time had passed for India to return to the traditions and precedents of a time before empire. 'Village government, caste panchayats, and ancient republics are all undeniable facts,' he insisted. 'But it is not possible to go back to them so as to develop an Indian constitution, as it is to make the Ganges flow back to the Himalayas.'[15] What was required, he wrote, was to assimilate what England had shown India. That is to say, a government by an executive responsible to and removable by a parliament consisting of elected representatives of the nation. Anything less than that would be a 'disaster fraught with the gravest consequences for the future'.[16] This was not the age of Harsha or Chandragupta Maurya, after all, but the twentieth century.

'No one who has studied the Indian movement can deny that, in the realm of ideas, more than in the realm of politics, the assimilated tradition of England has become the basis of Indian thought,'[17] he wrote. Indians had—in the councils and in the princely states—shown themselves to be capable of the kind of self-government that Britain advocated. The next natural step was the ceding of further powers. At the central level, an Indian government accountable to the legislative assembly had to be created. This needed to be free from London's influence, except for those matters that affected the whole empire. At the provincial level, the distinction between transferred and reserved matters was to be abolished, with ministers fully responsible to the councils.

Panikkar refuted the idea of dividing electorates communally and pushed for a voting system that aimed for universal adult franchise. Freedom for India was different from the Western idea of it. For Panikkar, it meant that all Indians would be able to follow the rules of their caste, religion or sect without government interference. 'The future Constitution must be based on principles which unite the past with the future and not separate them ... The unification of India through political institutions, a common language and an administrative machinery, is the greatest movement set on foot by the British contact with this country.'[18]

A few fundamental questions remained to be answered, such as to what extent the Government of India could be made responsible to a parliament without Whitehall's control. Panikkar also dodged the thornier issue of reservation. You could awaken different communities to their rights, certainly, he argued, but in all honesty, only the vote could make them truly aware of their rights and duties. How exactly this would work once they were suitably awake, Panikkar did not explore.

Taken together though, *An Introduction to the Study of the Relations of Indian States with the Government of India* and *The Working of Dyarchy in India* formed Panikkar's first formidable contribution to Indian constitutional history, establishing him as a leading scholar and a mind to reckon with. By the time the *Amjer* docked in Bombay in January 1928, word had already spread that K.N. Haksar had pulled off the professional coup of the year by hiring K.M. Panikkar to work for Kashmir—and for the future of the princes of India.

PART VI

'Ye Gods! These Reforms and These Princes!' (1929–1939)

CHAPTER 19

Where It All Began

'IT WOULD BE TRUE TO SAY,' PANIKKAR WROTE IN HIS MEMOIR, 'THAT I had entered a totally different world.'[1]

In retrospect, that would turn out to be a vast understatement.

He had sent a letter to Gouri from London, letting her know that he had a new job, and that the family would be moving lock, stock and children to Kashmir.

As soon as he landed, Panikkar went straight to Kavalam. In excited anticipation, Gouri had already packed their trunks.

It was a joyful reunion.

Gouri had no idea of her husband's extracurricular activities in Paris, at least not just yet. Their quietly happy days in Kavalam marked a rare but brief period of stability on the domestic front. Home life would be rarely conventional for the family, given the nature of Panikkar's chosen career, but for now they enjoyed having him at home. Parvathy was nine, Madhusudhan was nearly six and Devaki a cheerful three-year-old. 'He was a very kind and gentle person,' Panikkar's youngest daughter, Radha, recalled. 'Always full of good humour.'[2] Gouri was clearly the disciplinarian in the household; Panikkar, by all accounts, never lost his temper with his children.

As he settled back into the routine of everyday life, Panikkar was happy to put memories of Juliette, Germaine and the excitements of Europe behind him. The letters he was already receiving from his friends across Southeast Asia and Europe told him that the rise of Soviet communism was doing more to debilitate transnational networks of resistance than anything else could have done. It was as well, Panikkar mused, that he had decided to avoid getting involved in the political quarrels between the communists (through Chatto) and the 'conservatives' (through Chempakaraman Pillai) in the German capital.[3]

Yes, it was time for him to begin focusing on his family, particularly on his children's schooling. Having spent his own schooldays mostly away from Chalayil, he was perfectly happy to consider sending his children away from home to study. For the moment, though, they could all accompany Gouri and himself to Kashmir, and be tutored at home while potential schools were considered. With this decision, Gouri was perfectly happy.

The separation of two years seems to have shifted something for her. From now onwards, she would rarely be apart from her husband unless she absolutely couldn't help it. Panikkar needed to travel to various states and countries, and clearly Gouri was now of the view that if she didn't travel with him, she would always be left behind. Seeing Panikkar jaunty and self-assured after his time away from home convinced her that she needed to keep up with her husband. It would mean adapting to all kinds of climates, company and postings. It would also mean not seeing her beloved home again for long stretches of time. It was a wrench, but she'd adjust.

For Panikkar, too, this made sense. He was now entering a world that demanded tradition and propriety, at least on the surface. Having his wife with him completed the picture of a happy young couple rising upwards in their chosen world.

It is also true that Panikkar had come home to find that Gouri had not just been busy taking care of their kitchen garden and children. She had been growing up as well. She was no longer the diffident child he had married, no longer the quiet little housewife and mother he remembered. She was a bright, intelligent young woman with a keen mind, a dry wit and a curiosity about life beyond Kavalam that delighted her more worldly husband. 'She was a remarkable woman . . . her own independent woman,' remembered her granddaughter, Ambika Nair.[4]

And so it was that from deepest south India, the young Panikkars arrived in the beautiful reaches of north India. Their arrival was watched with some dismay by the Government of India's foreign and political department. British intelligence officials knew perfectly well that Panikkar was not the suave, harmless, erudite young official that he presented himself to be. The dossiers on him, spanning both the French Sûreté and Scotland Yard, were rather thick by now. They knew that he was, in colonial parlance, a 'dissident' and that he had been involved heavily in activities that were at least radical and quite possibly subversive.

Now he was arriving in Kashmir, a state that was never peaceful, and which, geopolitically speaking, was a crucial frontier for the Raj in India.[5] The political secretary, Sir Bertrand Glancy (who would play critical roles in the politics of Punjab and Kashmir in the years to come), was torn between the need to keep this dangerous subversive away and a natural fascination with Panikkar's views on the princely states.[6] It was a telling insight into the fact that Panikkar, wherever he went, was capable of perturbing and intriguing those in power, which is how he is remembered to this day.

Panikkar of course had no idea that his arrival had elicited quite so much anxiety. He had much to absorb in his first few days in Kashmir. Maharaja Pratap Singh had died three years earlier, a sad, courteous 'tho' opium-sodden old gentleman'.[7] In his lifetime, the maharaja had placed his state's troops at the disposal of the empire during the First World War. The aftermath of the war provided the ideal opportunity to beg for the restoration of his full powers, of which he had been neatly divested in 1889. But even the restoration of his princely privileges did nothing to heal the festering communal rifts in his state. In the twilight of his years on the throne, Pratap Singh was faced with the spectre of popular nationalism as more and more Kashmiris began seeking rights for themselves. In 1924, the year before he died, workers at the government-run Reshamkhana silk factory in Srinagar struck work, demanding better wages and working conditions.[8] The strike was suppressed, but it was a turning point in the state's political history. That same year, when Lord Reading (then the viceroy) visited Kashmir, leading Muslims of the state presented him with a bitter, seventeen-point memorandum in which they asked for an improvement of their 'utterly deplorable' conditions.[9] Their demands included, memorably, property rights for peasants, greater Muslim representation in the administration and legislature, a Muslim governor for Kashmir (or an Englishman, if no suitable Muslim was available) and better education. For their pains, they were either jailed or exiled, but there was still no peace for the harassed Pratap Singh.

Shortly after this spirited attempt at rebellion came the 'Kashmir for Kashmiris' agitation inspired by the non-cooperation movement and against the court's employment of educated Punjabi Hindus in local administration, politics and trade.

When Hari Singh ascended the throne, his people—oppressed and suppressed until then—watched with a cautious optimism. At thirty years old, he was a young ruler, and with his membership of the Jammu and Kashmir State Council, he had administrative experience as well. He was also known to be more liberal than his religious and drug-addled uncle, scandalising half of Kashmir with his philandering. The new maharaja was also rich—so rich that a British newspaper described him sardonically as a man 'whose wealth is so great that even he cannot compute it'.[10] Ostentatious to a fault, Hari Singh decided to brazen out the gossip that surrounded his ascent to the throne by organising a lavish coronation, not the first monarch to make that particular mistake.

Angry mutterings against the maharaja were heightened by the presence of 'outsiders' in government service, soon leading to the reemergence of the Kashmir for Kashmiris movement that had haunted his uncle's dying days. Hastily, Hari Singh passed the Hereditary State Subject Law in 1927, forbidding the employment of non-state subjects in public services. But to widespread displeasure, the top positions were filled by people from Jammu, particularly from the ruling class of the Dogra Rajputs. As the lives of the Dogras and the Pandits began to improve, the Muslims became unsurprisingly aggravated, driven by low wages, unemployment and their sidelining along with other minorities.

When the Panikkars arrived, the atmosphere crackled with tension.

Panikkar called on Hari Singh on his first day in the state. This was protocol, but it was also an opportunity to take stock of the young ruler. It would be a few days before he discerned that the maharaja was a man with a 'permanent chip on his shoulder'.[11] An excellent rider and polo player with a strong tendency to gamble, Hari Singh in those days was a meticulous, aloof man with a beautiful, gentle wife. His son Karan was not born yet, but years later, he recorded in his memoir that he thought of his father as 'formidable'.[12] Hari Singh was careful to move in a 'chosen circle' of courtiers and possessed—probably due to the formidable nature, his son noted—very few friends.

Apart from Haksar himself, there were three key advisors to the state of Kashmir. There was Sir Albion Banerji, then the foreign and political minister, of whom Panikkar had heard much. Hailed as the first Brahmin baby to be born in Britain and technically Hari Singh's seniormost advisor, Banerji was the son of the famous Brahmo Samaj reformer Sasipada Banerji. When Panikkar met him, Banerji was a seasoned administrator. During his recent service in Mysore, he had led a negotiating team in 1924 for the Cauvery Waters Agreement. He had also tested the waters for a new federal constitution for Mysore, albeit unsuccessfully.

Pyari Krishna Vattal was in charge of internal affairs, and as Panikkar was to discover, 'apt to be jealous and scheming'.[13] Last but not least, George Wakefield was an experienced ICS officer who had served across India for years and had been in the service of Pratap Singh since 1921. He would become the prime minister of Kashmir between 1929 and 1931, before being ousted on mysteriously trumped-up charges.[14] Panikkar dismissed him scathingly as 'an illiterate European … proof of the theory that Europeans who serve Indian princes usually display the defects of both races'.[15]

Panikkar's brief in Kashmir was simple: to assist Vattal (and ultimately Haksar) in preparing a report on the maharaja's constitutional rights, which would then be presented to the Butler

Committee that was due to arrive in the state in April. But he was also quick to notice the hierarchy of power among the administrators. Banerji may have been the man with the greater experience, for instance, but Haksar ruled the roost.

The maharaja himself was not unaware of the power the colonel wielded over him and his court. 'My father, I suspect, was a trifle scared of him,' Karan Singh would write later. 'Though he joked about him with us in his absence, he was discreet when "Colonel Sahib" was in the room.'[16] The maharaja's son recalled Haksar telling him acidly as they drove away from a meeting with Hari Singh, 'Tiger, look very carefully, so that when you grow up, you will know what *not* to do.'[17]

Panikkar himself noticed that Haksar didn't adopt the usual obsequiousness to the maharaja that one might expect. That self-assurance quickly made him realise that he had done well to choose Haksar as his mentor and advisor, for here was a man who held the real keys to power and was singularly unafraid to use them. Knowing he had Haksar's backing was a layer of professional security that Panikkar was not yet accustomed to. Once he got used to that comfortable sense of power, he would actively seek it out over the course of his career.

While his mandate appeared to be simple enough, presenting a suitable report to the Butler Committee was not going to be easy. Of Sir Harcourt Butler, Panikkar had heard and read enough to be slightly anxious. In the aftermath of the revolt of 1857, the British had realised that the princely states would have to be incorporated into the imperial scheme of things, so as to consolidate colonial control. Naturally, this could not be put to the princes so crudely. They had to be cultivated as allies, *while* being kept as subordinates. The more polished phrase that Butler used was 'non-interference in the internal affairs of States'.[18]

Like everything else the Raj said or did, this pronouncement came with a convenient caveat: the Government of India had the right to interfere when there was misrule in the states. Of course, the degree of that misrule was based on the merits of each case. States were subject to 'imperial concern' and the protection of 'imperial interests'. Butler had laid that out nicely in 1909, with subjects spanning from the employment of Europeans, Americans and Australians by the states to mining concessions, coinage, military cooperation, communications, railways and opium cultivation—all vital imperial concerns indeed.[19]

All this of course had been a world war ago.

Now, everything was different.

Panikkar's time in Oxford and Europe had taught him to think about what it could mean to be a citizen of the empire, rather than a subject. More importantly, it had taught him the importance of being a self-governing citizen in his own country. For this, the First World War had been largely responsible. With its placement in the League of Nations, India's own role in the empire had already changed. Its admission into this international club had given it visibility and, to nationalist eyes, some credibility as well.

Meanwhile, nationalist leaders had been pleased to note Secretary of State for India Edwin Montagu's announcement on the floor of British parliament that imperial policy towards India after the war would be the 'gradual development of self-governing institutions with a view to the progressive realization of responsible government in India as an integral part of the British Empire'.[20] That magical phrase—self-governing—would frame politics in 1920s India, but it would, unfortunately, turn out to be a mirage for decades to come.

As the war came to an end, the Raj first dangled the concept of federation in the Montagu-Chelmsford Report. Then, the Government of India Act (1919) introduced the concept of dyarchy. Panikkar noticed that all of these definitions were vague and their timelines were hazy to say the least. Despite a constant back and forth between nationalist leaders, princely states and Whitehall, no definite date was set to any promise, and there was no clarity around *what* status India could actually aspire to and how it might possibly hope to get there. Unsurprising, for India was too commercially and strategically valuable to the empire.

Put crudely, the Raj was giving a little, while giving nothing at all. An excellent example was in the form of Sir Malcolm Hailey, Home Member in the Executive Council of the Governor-General, who declared in 1924 that responsible government need not mean dominion status. Indian nationalists began to grow naturally and increasingly irritated.

What of the princes in all of this?

In addition to proving themselves as 'natural leaders' through military service, princes such as Ganga Singh of Bikaner, Bhupinder Singh of Patiala and Ranjitsinhji of Nawanagar had become imperial and international players by participating in imperial war conferences and later by representing India at the League of Nations.[21] Unsurprisingly, stages like these—as well as the concepts of dyarchy and federation—had introduced the princes to the need for the right language to use in order to challenge British paramountcy.

But in Sir Harcourt Butler, they could well meet their match. He had redefined the crown's relationship with the princely states at a time of crisis before, and his experience alone meant that he had the upper hand. Given Butler's vast experience, Panikkar's presentation of Hari Singh's constitutional rights would have to be well played.

The Panikkars, meanwhile, were allotted a spacious bungalow on the banks of the Dal Lake, with a spectacular view of the snow-capped Himalayas in the misty distance. If you ignored the simmering tensions, Kashmir in the late 1920s was a place of serene beauty. For first-timers like the Panikkars, there was much to see. Panikkar and Gouri spent much of their free time exploring the state together. They came from a place of incredible natural beauty themselves, but they both agreed that there was nothing quite like Kashmir in summer. 'The prospect as one enters the valley through the Baramullah Pass is dazzling,' recalled Panikkar dreamily. He remembered looking down at verdant greenery, with carpets of flowers on the mountainsides and saffron fields stretching away as far as the eye could see. 'The perpetual snows of the mountain tops glow in radiant colours at dawn and dusk as if touched by a magician's wand.'[22]

Dreamlike beauty aside, Kashmir was a traveller's delight. Enterprising Englishmen leased houseboats for the summer season and these drifted peacefully on the silver-blue waters of the Dal. Active travellers often used them not just for transport but for entertainment, with many of the fancier ones being equipped with sitting rooms, bathrooms and a separate cook-boat for the servants.

For travellers unwilling to spend the summer in a tent pitched in verdant Munshi Bagh, or in a houseboat on the Dal, there was always Nedou's Hotel in Srinagar, open all year around.[23] For members of the court or the English populace in the state, the entertainment never stopped, with balls, parties and picnics continuing through the changing seasons.

Gouri accompanied Panikkar on their social rounds, and he noticed that she was beginning to pick up broken bits of English and Hindustani. Back in Aligarh, the Masoods had taught her to speak both in Urdu and Hindustani. But a decade in Kavalam, surrounded by her own family, meant that Gouri had happily let her skills slide. Seeing her try again now encouraged Panikkar to engage a tutor for her. Perhaps, he reasoned to himself, she could spend her days learning some new languages. It would keep her mind occupied and away from home.

But he was in for a bit of a shock. Gouri refused any attempt to train her. If there was going to be any training, it was going to be on her own terms and through her own will.[24] There was no need, she told her husband stiffly, to engage any tutor for her. She would sit with the children when they learned their Hindustani and English, and learn alongside them. Panikkar knew better than to argue with her. Gouri's temper was as quick and fiery as his own, and when she set her mind to something, there was little that could budge her.

Her hands were very full at the moment. She was an experienced mother, though it was difficult to look after three active young children and a new home in a state that she had only heard of. The court had provided staff—a luxury she was not used to—but they only spoke Hindustani. Here and at social occasions, she was hampered by her inability to communicate fluently in English, or even in the more prevalent Hindustani. If she had to find her footing in Kashmir, she knew she needed to start at home. So she sat for hours during the day with the same tutor who came to coach the children in their language lessons. At first it was slow going, but Gouri discovered to her delight that once she truly applied herself, she was actually very good at picking up languages.

Both husband and wife noticed little things about each other in these early days in Kashmir. Panikkar noticed that Gouri had grown into a young woman who was rarely fazed by what life—or her husband—presented her.[25] It was a sterling quality that would last all her life, much to the delight of her children. On her part, Gouri noticed that, though Panikkar was attentive and kind at home, he was very rarely as happy or as at peace as he had been when he had returned from Europe. There was too much to do and much to learn.

Though the beautiful valleys and hills of Kashmir were quiet for now, Panikkar was not unaware of what was happening across India. On 3 February 1928, the haughty John Simon and his men stepped off the *RMS Mooltan* in Bombay to a sea of black flags. The rage they were met with took them aback. Seven white men had arrived to determine the country's fate. There was not a single Indian to represent national views. It was beyond tolerance and India was united in fury. The roars at the harbour were deafening.

Simon, go back!

The Simon Commission found it hard to travel across the country. Strikes brought cities and villages to a halt. Rallies choked streets from Calcutta to Vijayawada. New ways to show anger and defiance were devised. In Lonavala, a group of enterprising young men took advantage of the fact that the railway tracks ran parallel to the main road. Waving black flags, they drove a lorry all the way to Poona alongside the train that carried the embarrassed members of the commission. Even the mercurial Jinnah refused to meet Simon and his men. As he told the cheering members of the Muslim League, 'Jallianwala Bagh was a physical butchery, the Simon Commission is a butchery of our souls. By appointing an exclusively white Commission, Lord Birkenhead has declared our unfitness for self-government … I welcome the hand of fellowship extended to us by Hindu leaders from the platform of the Congress and the Hindu Mahasabha. For, to me, this offer is more valuable than any concession which the British Government can make.'[26]

This display of unity was calculated to infuriate Birkenhead, the secretary of state for India, and Simon. Birkenhead was provoked to a storm of rage. 'It does not do to take these people seriously!' he snarled in a letter to the viceroy.

In Kashmir, Panikkar was beginning to feel the same about the princes. Leslie Scott, the chamber's legal counsel, was due to arrive in April to begin his defence of the royal case before the Indian States Committee. But in the first week of February, chaos reigned in the Chamber of Princes. For one, Patiala's nervous hope that Hyderabad, Mysore and Baroda—three notoriously aloof states—would agree to be represented by the chamber's legal team was dead in the water. More embarrassingly, some princes let it be publicly known that they hadn't even been consulted about Scott's appointment. They had no desire, they said petulantly, to pay an *English* lawyer, of all people. As a result, Patiala's plans to crowdfund Scott's gigantic salary was shot to smithereens. Panicking, the maharaja appealed to the members of the standing committee for help. If Scott arrived and found nothing ready and nobody willing to pay him for his pains, that would be the end of this royal bid for sovereignty. The softer-hearted princes, many of whom were friends of Patiala, loosened their purse strings. But the amount collected was not enough. Patiala was forced to borrow from Nawanagar (luckily an excellent friend) to cover the balance.

Then there was the little matter of historical records. Princely advisors faced the same problem that modern researchers across the world face today: prising records out of the durbars, some of which had no proper archives. If there was no paper trail, Scott would be hard pressed to present any evidence.

Yet another problem was how to get the princes to answer the official questionnaire being circulated to understand their opinions on the issues that the Butler Committee would discuss. There was no consensus on anything, with different princes pulling in different directions and states like Hyderabad insisting on responding individually. As a result, when the Indian States' Committee finally arrived a week before the Simon Commission at the end of January, there was bedlam.

Much to his embarrassment, Patiala had to meet Sir Harcourt Butler to request more time to get things ready (and scramble some funds together). Luckily, Butler agreed amiably, touring the states to personally meet their rulers in the meantime. He and his team already had a plan in mind. They were going to collect written responses[27] from the states (yet another questionnaire!), and later, oral hearings would begin in London. In Kashmir, Butler met Hari Singh, Haksar and Panikkar. He read through the file of recommendations Panikkar presented and was impressed enough to ask that Panikkar be brought on board the Special Organisation. Haksar and Panikkar were delighted. Hari Singh, it might be said, was not quite so pleased to have two of his top officials away from India—and Kashmir—for such long stretches of time. His state was never peaceful, and he was far too weak to keep order.

While the maharaja worried about his state, Panikkar was worrying about something else. As he read through Scott's proposals to take negotiations forward, he realised that it was just as well he would be travelling with the Special Organisation.

The chamber's legal counsel had built his case based on the material that Rushbrook-Williams and Haksar had given him in London, and he had decided that all royal rights and obligations would be defined by existing individual treaties with the British. 'Paramountcy,' he argued, would not give the viceroy or his political agents 'any general discretionary right to interfere with the internal sovereignty of the states'.[28] Now this might have been very good news to states who had signed treaties that guaranteed internal autonomy. But what about bigger states like Mysore and Travancore that had signed treaties that definitely allowed for imperial intervention? And what happened when paramountcy lapsed? Finally, what about small states (or principalities) that hadn't signed any treaties at all?

The states were even more alarmed when, in a paper cryptically titled 'Document 4', Scott proposed the creation of an executive 'States Council', consisting of three princes nominated by the Chamber of Princes, two English politicians nominated by the Crown and the political secretary. This council was meant to advise the viceroy on issues of paramountcy and to discuss issues of common concern to the states and provinces on their 'merits'. Scott also wanted to set up a common supreme court to deal with legal disputes. The Chamber of Princes, reading through these proposals, was thoroughly alarmed.

These resolutions did nothing to bring the states into closer contact with the central or provincial legislatures.

Scott's conservative leanings had always been a risk, and now it looked as though Document 4 had been deliberately drafted in an attempt to further the Conservative Party's agenda of maintaining a grip on India. Looking at the documents that Scott had prepared, Panikkar was incensed. With the Butler Committee already in India, there was no time to change legal counsel. 'None of us felt that Leslie Scott's arguments would help to establish the rights of the Indian states,' Panikkar wrote scathingly in his memoir.[29] As Chancellor of the Chamber of Princes, Patiala agreed with him. Recognising danger and the need to band together to ward off a brewing crisis, he hastily sent word to a few select rulers to meet Scott and try to talk him down from his position. The meeting was scheduled to be held at Moti Bagh on 28 March 1928, but so fractured was princely consensus at this point that only a handful of invitees bothered to show up. Beside himself with worry, Patiala tried again, calling for another, bigger conference in April. Yet again, his attempt met with disaster. No sooner had the invitations been dispatched than 'Document 4' was leaked—quite possibly by some enterprising soul on the standing committee—to the press.

Unsurprisingly, the leak caused a sensation, incensing the viceroy into snapping that Scott was either dreaming of his hefty fees or 'the feeling that he has been called upon by a wise providence to save the Indian Empire'.[30] In the wake of this public relations fiasco, the conference Patiala had called was a damp squib, with several states, led by Junagadh, walking out.

There was no hope for it but to present a legal case before the Indian States Committee. It was then that the limelight fell on the advisors and prime ministers of the princely states, a motley crew that would define the debates around the role and position of the princely states in India. Apart from Haksar, Scott and Panikkar, this team included Rushbrook-Williams, the man with whom Haksar had travelled in London.

A propaganda department was set up in London to begin projecting the royal point of view even as the four men began putting together the documents they would need during their arguments. None of them knew it then, but their papers would become the legal foundation of debates on princely sovereignty. These papers included a tract weightily titled *The British Crown and the Indian States: An Outline Sketch Presented to the Indian States Committee on Behalf of the Standing Committee of the Chamber of Princes*. It had no listed author, but everyone knew it was written by K.M. Panikkar—a written submission, much as a lawyer would write, which he dashed off in fifteen days and which earned him a delighted telegram from Haksar, who was the first to read it: 'You are a wizard!'[31]

This tract now became the main basis on which the team would present its arguments. With a section written by the economist Austin Robinson, Panikkar laid out the historical context of British expansion to describe the origins of paramountcy. In doing so, he wanted to show that during the days of the East India Company, the relationship between the Crown and the states had been one between sovereign and independent entities. As time passed, the nature of this relationship changed. There was growing British interference in the affairs of princely states, with many kingdoms being forced to hand over sovereignty over key concerns like transport, salt and coinage. Paramountcy, then, was based on a historical fallacy, Panikkar argued. The twentieth century was no place for a feudal relationship between the Crown and the states. Legally, after all, the princes had retained powers that had not been explicitly alienated in the treaties. For all these reasons, Panikkar argued, it was exactly the right time for a federal system to be built from the ashes of the old system of subordination.

While his battle for federation would be frustratingly star-crossed, Panikkar genuinely believed it was the only instrument that the princes could use to become a force to reckon with on the national scene. In his perspective, it would prevent the dangers of political fragmentation and shore up national unity after the Raj stepped away from India. 'He was no apologist of the princely order, though a defender of princely interests,' observed the journalist K. Iswara Dutt. 'At no time had he allowed his historical insight to be dimmed by the fierce controversies of the fleeting day.'[32]

The British Crown and the Indian States was a plausible, reasonably argued treatise, and the team rightly felt that it was an excellent backup to Scott's written legal opinions and oral arguments before the committee itself. Panikkar wrote this tract during a decade defined by the Balfour Declaration of 1926. The words 'dominion status' set the seal on a period marked by the rise of new nationalisms across China and Turkey and presented a whole new possibility for frustrated Indian nationalist leaders. It essentially meant that self-governing dominions could be defined as 'autonomous communities within the British Empire, equal in status, in no way subordinate, one to another, in any aspect of their external affairs, though united by a common allegiance to the Crown and freely associated as Members of the British Commonwealth of Nations'.[33] This definition of dominion status appealed greatly to Indian nationalists of the time, despite its ambiguity. To date, it puzzles legal scholars and historians alike, one of whom demanded, 'How did a style signifying subordination take on the meaning of complete self-rule?'[34]

Be that as it may, dominion status shone as a welcome north star for the radical young nationalist leaders of the late 1920s. Jawaharlal Nehru and his colleagues had suffered a decade of progressive annoyance, capped in 1925 by Lord Birkenhead, who smirked that the Indian nationalist movement talked a big game without actually pulling together any constructive proposal for constitutional reform.

On 19 May 1928, a committee was set up by the All Parties' Conference (organised by the Congress) to draft the constitution. Members of the committee ranged from Motilal Nehru (its chairman) to Subhas Chandra Bose, and included lawyers like Tej Bahadur Sapru and M.R. Jayakar. Jawaharlal Nehru was appointed secretary to the committee. Its brief was simple: to consider and draft the principles of the Constitution of India. In August 1928, the committee submitted its report.

The Nehru Report is an optimistic document, full of talk of communal harmony. The Congress leader M.C. Chagla told the *Hindustan Times* exultantly that the decisions laid out in the report were far more momentous than even those of the Lucknow Pact of 1916. It defined dominion status and universal adult franchise along with equal rights for women and the freedom to form unions. Within its pages is a separate chapter on the princes of India, authored by the moody, brilliant Tej Bahadur Sapru, and calling for federation much like Panikkar had.[35] The report set dominion status as the goal for India, which would mean full provincial self-government and responsible government at a centre that would inherit the Crown's suzerain rights over the princely states. The Central Legislative Assembly would be directly elected on a universal adult franchise, and Muslims would receive reserved seats in joint electorates, but not separate electorates in provinces where they were a minority.

But as is often the case in draft-work, the fine print was the report's undoing.

For one, Jawaharlal Nehru, Bose and others were pressing for purna swaraj (complete independence) as the only goal for the Indian National Congress. This was very much the mood of the nation, but it was also to the consternation of the older, more staid Congress leaders who felt that after finally managing to scrape some kind of consensus together, it was not the right time to shift goalposts.

Once again the Congress witnessed a rift from within, this time so wide that the younger Nehru felt despairingly that 'it was best to break' into two. Still, out of loyalty to Motilal Nehru, Gandhi suggested some kind of compromise. The Congress would support the Nehru Report for a year. After that, the party would resort to non-cooperation once again.

More damagingly, the abolition of the constitutional guarantees for Muslims—previously enshrined in the Lucknow Pact—incensed Jinnah, who called it a 'Hindu betrayal'.[36] It was a dangerous step, one of many, taken down the road to hard communal politics. Until then, many leaders and politicians in India often shifted airily between different wings of the Congress and the League and even into regional political organisations. The membership of one party had never implied the rejection of another. The Muslim League had, however, been pushing for a federation with powers residing in the provinces, not a (Congress-dominated) centre, separate electorates and a third of central legislature seats reserved for Muslims.

By the winter of 1928 it was clear that the Muslim League was going to support neither the Nehru nor the Simon Report, which was due to be published the following summer. It was also clear that the Congress was tired of open-ended British promises. The party had given the Raj a year to grant dominion status. Otherwise, they would start another campaign of civil disobedience.

Equally, the promptitude and clarity with which the Nehru Report had been produced severely alarmed the Raj, which had yet to release the Simon Commission's official report. True to form, Whitehall responded by shuffling its feet.[37] It is important to understand the role played by the Nehru Report here, for it was enough to alarm the princes as well.

Running their eye down the report, the Chamber of Princes knew that it was now or never. They had to try and present their own case for sovereignty, especially since collectively, they had no desire to have the Congress inheriting the Crown's rights at all. It was a known fact that the nationalist leaders—particularly those like Jawaharlal Nehru—were no admirers of the princely states. Now led wholly by Panikkar's explanation of federation, the princes argued that their rights and privileges were safeguarded by treaties and engagements signed independently with the British.[38] The focus on treaties ensured that they could argue that their relationship was with the Crown rather than the Government of India. Their aim, as always, was to minimise British control while retaining a link with the Government of India to defend themselves against the 'anti-colonial nationalists'.[39]

Rather than challenging the entire edifice of paramountcy, the states chose to rely on the division of sovereignty between themselves and the crown to limit imperial control. The states had 'absolute rights' that were 'based on contract with the Crown', which made their relationship more legal than political. The difference meant that paramountcy could be defined at will on the basis of sovereignty.[40] Bhupinder Singh, for instance, argued that 'paramountcy had in its origin a definitely circumscribed ambit, and should be equally defined in its operation'.[41]

Again, opinions were divided. Not all the states pulled together. Mysore, for instance, was happy to have the issue mediated and

Hyderabad pushed for a political relationship with the Crown.[42] The arguments lasted for the better part of the summer and autumn of 1928. In addition to Panikkar's arguments, Scott—in his written submission and oral arguments—tried to present a definition of paramountcy that would satisfy princely aspirations. He argued that the relationship between the Crown and the state meant a legal agreement 'by which the State cedes to the Crown certain rights in consideration of its accepting certain liabilities in connection with the foreign relations and security of the State'.[43] Those were the only areas in which the Crown's rights were paramount, Scott insisted. There was 'no justification for saying that the rights of the Crown in its capacity as Paramount Power extend beyond these matters'.[44]

But this was also precisely the point where matters became stuck, mired in legal quicksand, the eddies of anti-colonial nationalism, Whitehall's panic and its desperate attempts to stall progress as far as possible. In December 1928, faced with this dilemma and midway through the Simon Commission's tour, Irwin began to think fast. The Nehru Report stood in danger at the moment, considering Jinnah was never going to agree with it. Political India had put in its case for postcolonial independence, and princely India, represented by Scott, Panikkar and Haksar, was winding up its own presentations for the same cause. Might it not be simpler, he quietly suggested to Simon, that the Simon Commission and the Butler Committee discuss their individual reports together with the Indian stakeholders? Possibly, he added musingly, at a conference in London.[45] This would also mean, the viceroy added, that Whitehall would need to hand out greater assurances that Edwin Montagu's 1917 pledge would be honoured, now in the form of dominion status.

Even as Irwin and Simon began to volley and parley over the pros and cons of a round table conference, Panikkar boarded the ship back to India. For now, the oral hearings on behalf of the Chamber of Princes were over. All four men were justifiably exhausted, but until the Butler Committee chose to release its report, there was nothing to do but return to India.

Chapter 20

Limbo

PANIKKAR ARRIVED IN BOMBAY ON THE MORNING OF 9 DECEMBER 1928. He had been away for the better part of a year, unable to attend to his family or his personal affairs. Between himself and Gouri there had been a steady flow of letters and he knew, thanks to her, that his uncle—her father—was critically ill. He had thought of little else on the way home. Ayyappa Panikkar lived in his memory as the man who caned him for playing truant as a boy, but he was a shrewd, humorous old man and as Panikkar grew to adulthood, he found that they both liked each other much better. The exigencies of the career he had chosen for himself meant that he hadn't been home as much as he would have liked, and he hadn't been able to spend as much time with the old man as he would have wanted. Now, Gouri informed him that Ayyappa was on the verge of death.

The stress of it would have driven him mad on the voyage to India, if he hadn't picked up his pen and begun to write. It is around this time that Panikkar's tendencies to escape into an imaginary world by writing poems or novellas took root. For the rest of his life, anxiety, anger and other extreme emotions would be the catalysts behind some of his finest contributions to classical Malayalam literature and poetry. So effusive would his writing in this field be that the poet P. Kunhiraman Nair would once laughingly liken Panikkar to 'a

KSRTC bus, refusing sides for other vehicles to overtake'.[1] Now, he was working on drafts of two books—*Malabar and the Portuguese* and a novel in Malayalam titled *Punarkottuswaroopam*, a historical fiction based on the Portuguese in Malabar since the theme was fresh in his mind. By the time the ship docked in Bombay, he had two nearly full drafts—and a letter waiting for him on shore.

It was from Gouri, asking him to come to Chalayil immediately. There was, she said, not much time left. Panikkar left Bombay almost instantly, but it still took him two days to get back home. When he reached Kavalam, he was distraught to find that Ayyappa had already been dead two days. Never an openly emotional man, he focused instead on the practicalities of how he could help his family, particularly his grieving wife. He sent word to Kashmir that he would be delayed on personal grounds and spent some time at Chalayil, sorting through his uncle's papers with Gouri. It was a difficult time. 'I had a special esteem for this shrewd and utterly good man, and he in turn had a special affection for me,' Panikkar remembered.[2]

The loss of Ayyappa was a blow to the entire family. He had been indispensable to Eravi Ramakrishna in all affairs of agriculture and the estate at Chalayil. As Panikkar helped to get the family back on track, memories of Ayyappa were everywhere. 'Fair-minded, unaggressive and compassionate … uncle never liked to move out of the house,'[3] he wrote later, remembering a simple, good-hearted man whose moral compass remained unbendingly upright. Despite the weight of this loss, Panikkar knew he couldn't stay long. Once the formalities of death had been taken care of, it was time to get back to work.

Leaving Gouri behind in Kavalam for the time being, Panikkar arrived in Srinagar in the early months of 1929 to find the court of Kashmir, never a peaceful one, in an uproar. Sir Albion Banerji, always in favour of reform and progress, had tried to put in place some social and economic reforms that he felt were needed, since Hari Singh had done little on that front. According to Panikkar's memoir, the duo of Haksar and Vattal forced Hari Singh to take action against a man they both disliked. Banerji's measures were never popular in a court so raddled with intrigue. He was a straightforward, honest man, the kind that often comes to grief in the world of politics, and he was really no match for the schemes of Haksar and Vattal or for the weakness of the maharaja he served. Hari Singh was predictably useless with his back against the wall, and his only reaction to this fresh uproar in his court was to sack Banerji on the spot. This was a grievous tactical error.

For years, Banerji had kept quiet about the potholes in his job. Now he finally lost his temper. In a statement to the press, Banerji said roundly, 'Jammu and Kashmir State is labouring under many disadvantages with a large Mohammadan population, absolutely illiterate, labouring under poverty and very low economic conditions of living in the villages and practically governed like dumb-driven cattle ... There is not much touch between the Government and the people,' Banerji raged, 'no suitable opportunity for the representation of their grievances and the administrative machinery itself requires overhauling from top to bottom to bring it up to modern conditions of efficiency. It has, at present, little or no sympathy with the people's wants and grievances.'[4]

It was a searing indictment of not just Hari Singh, but of the officials in his administration, many of them Banerji's friends or former colleagues. The court made haste to issue a counterstatement, but it was too little, too late. For as many years as Banerji had kept quiet, the youth of Kashmir had grown steadily angrier. Political organisations and newspapers had sprung up and were flourishing as new dissident voices began to gain credence and attention. Among them was tall, young Mohammad Abdullah who was deeply stirred by Banerji's rant. Here at last, he felt, was someone who could give voice to the suffering of the Kashmiri people. Inspired, Abdullah dashed off a letter which was published in the *Muslim Outlook* in response to the court's counterstatement. It was the young man's first foray into politics, and it set the tone for his rise as one of the most influential leaders in modern Kashmiri history.

Today, he is popularly known as Sheikh Abdullah.

In all, it was a turbulent time to be in Kashmir, especially as an administrator. Panikkar spent the spring and early summer of 1929 in the valley, skilfully evading a personal role in the boiling tensions of Hari Singh's court. Despite the unease in the state and an ominous sense that change of some kind was in the air, there was not much to do except routine file work.

Meantime, Gouri had returned to Kashmir bearing the happy news that she was pregnant again. Despite Panikkar's coaxing and cajoling, she refused to return to Chalayil. She would have the baby here, in Kashmir, she insisted. It was the first pregnancy that she would go through away from the safety and comfort of Kavalam. With Gouri pregnant, there was no way that she could look after the other three children as well as run the house and learn her language lessons (which she refused to give up, even temporarily). Kashmir was not the safest place to send children to school, so Panikkar decided to send Parvathy and Devaki to Calcutta, to the recently established Gokhale Memorial Girls' School. Madhusudhan was dispatched to Delhi, to the equally recently established Modern School.

The year 1929 was one of preparation, protest and unprecedented events. The viceroy was trying to convince a furious Simon to include the round table conference in his official report. He was also trying to convince equally annoyed Congress leaders to attend the conference, even as he tried to cobble together an official definition of dominion status. In July 1929, Irwin travelled to Britain to discuss his plans with the new Labour government, where he found Ramsay MacDonald as prime minister and William Wedgwood Benn as secretary of state for India supportive of both a 'free' conference and India's quest for dominion status.

Meanwhile, back in India, in February 1929, Ruttie—Jinnah's beautiful, depressed young wife—died of heartbreak, loneliness and a possible addiction to drugs. Jinnah would never be the same man again. Locked up in a flat in New Delhi, obsessed with memories of his dead wife, Jinnah began to put together an alternative memo to the Nehru Report. In March, he proposed what came to be known as his 'Fourteen Points': a manifesto of points for a federal Indian constitution with various safeguards for Muslim culture and religion. It was badly timed. The country was in the mood for unity, not communal disharmony. Jinnah was consigned to the political wilderness, bitter, aloof and disillusioned with the Congress's brand of politics.

On 8 April, two young men by the names of Bhagat Singh and Batukeshwar Dutt created an even greater sensation by flinging smoke bombs and red flags into the pit of the Central Legislative Assembly in Delhi from their perch in the visitors' gallery. Even as chaos reigned, the Butler Committee decided to release its report on the princely states.

Whatever the princes had been expecting, this was not it. To be sure, the committee's report kindly endorsed the rulers' pleas that their treaties were with the Crown, not with the Government of India, but it dismissed Scott's argument that, as a result of that, the power of paramountcy would be defined by what was said in those treaties. In sterling legalese, the report said outright that the states had no international or independent status. Clearly, the focus was on keeping paramountcy intact, especially in view of changing global conditions and imperial interests.

The last two words became vital in the definition of the Crown's relationship with the princely states. 'Imperial interests', a vague, sweeping phrase, meant the Raj could use any excuse to tighten control over the states as and when it willed.[5] As Panikkar noted in some outrage, the rights of the princely states remained largely undefined so that the balance of power was tilted in favour of the British.

In short, as he grimly described it, 'Paramountcy must remain paramount.'[6]

The Hindu summed it up eloquently: 'What the princes bargained for was complete internal sovereignty; but what they were granted under the report was unqualified slavery, dressed up though it was, in glittering robes of royalty.'

Unsurprisingly, the states were in an uproar.[7]

Scott was furious, as was Panikkar. But in retrospect, there was no real way the Crown would have given ground to the princes at this stage in constitutional reform. In addition, the entire process, despite Panikkar's detailed arguments for federalism, had been a bureaucratic steeplechase. Despite being the chamber's counsel, Scott had been denied access by both the darbars and the Butler Committee to crucial documents that may have helped build a more formidable case for the defence. The darbars, as mentioned earlier, had not been exactly forthcoming with important papers or records. In the same way, the Butler Committee also prevented Scott from accessing papers that he could have used in his arguments for the chamber. Cross-examination of witnesses was not allowed by the Butler Committee, preventing the Chamber of Princes from contesting the government's submissions. It was an exercise weighted by bias and it would have never worked to the chamber's favour, particularly since elections were looming in Britain that summer.

But these are retrospective statements. In the moment, nobody could have predicted such an outcome. In the end, the coals of blame were heaped upon Leslie Scott's hapless head.

At a conference in June 1929 to deliberate upon an official response to the Butler Committee report, an agitated group of princes led by Bikaner shouted that Scott had defrauded the chamber of a large sum of money.[8] So enraged were the princes that even Scott's desperate appeal to publish a critique of the report never made it past the stage of suggestion. As he bitterly put it, 'My draft ultimatum was put in the wastepaper basket.'[9]

Discussions were once again in abeyance. They would hang in limbo for the better part of a year. There is no doubt that the princes were collectively worried about their future. With very few exceptions, the princes were deeply patriotic. Deep into the federal debates, Hamidullah Khan, the young Nawab of Bhopal, would state that sentiment publicly: 'I personally have always held it to be the first duty of all Indian princes that he should also be an Indian nationalist.'[10] But they still had to contend with the rapidly growing popularity of the Praja Mandals, which were lobbying persuasively for constitutional reform. Members of the All India States' Peoples' Conference (AISPC), which had been established in 1927 with a view to represent popular political interests both in princely states and provinces, had already petitioned the League of Nations, demanding inquiries into labour malpractices within the states.[11] Leaders of the states' people's movements, like P.L. Chudgar and G.R. Abhayankar, had written acclaimed tracts, highly critical of the way things were run in the states.[12] Small wonder then that, in the late 1920s, the states were feeling the heat.

In 1929, Bikaner and Kashmir joined the Nehrus, Jinnah and other political leaders at a working tea hosted by the Congress leader, Vithalbhai Patel, in the Central Legislative Assembly. A series of teas, lunches and dinners dotted the first half of 1930 as well, with guests ranging from the princes to politicians like Jawaharlal Nehru and to Hindu Mahasabha leaders like B.N. Moonje. These form a curiously civil contrast to Patel's rather coarse statements, making no bones about his thoughts on the princes and their ambitions. In 1929, for instance, at the fifth Kathiawar Political Conference, a grassroots organisation set up to give voice to the people of the region, Patel scoffed, 'For the princes to claim the Empire's friendship is sheer nonsense, like friendship between a lion and a jackal!'[13]

In August 1929, at Motilal's invitation, the Standing Committee of the Chamber of Princes conferred with a delegation from the All Parties' Conference to study and discuss the political ramifications of the Nehru Report.[14]

Equally, all the states were worried by Sardar Vallabhbhai Patel's hardening stance against them. The Congress was still keeping to its official line that the princes' future was for the princes themselves to resolve—but opinions like Patel's gave the game away. 'The red and yellow colours on India's map have to be made one,' Patel declared angrily, referring to the colours used to distinguish princely India (yellow) from British India (red).[15]

Small wonder, then, that the princes were unsure whether they wanted to be left to the tender mercies of Congress-led Indian nationalists, should the Raj eventually depart. They began to look for an alternative ally, and the Hindu Mahasabha stepped into the picture.

The coming decades would be marked with a growing engagement between the Mahasabha and the states. The Mahasabha, which had had less than impressive political successes in British India, decided to try its luck in princely India. In speeches and writings, Mahasabha spokespersons began to flatter the princes just as the Congress grew critical of them. V.D. Savarkar, then a prominent Mahasabha leader, promised that the Mahasabha would 'defend' the states from

'Congressites', Communists and Muslims.[16] Across India, Mahasabha meetings were hosted in states as far south as Mysore, though it was northern states like Alwar and Gwalior that engaged seriously with the idea of an alliance, allowing the Mahasabha official and financial patronage. The Mahasabha's entry into the princely fray would be yet another headache in the future, but fortunately for Panikkar, he had happier distractions at the moment.

In September 1929, Gouri gave birth to their fourth child, another daughter, whom they named Himavathy (known to the family affectionately as Haima). It was the first time that Panikkar had been home during the birth of a child, and the experience brought husband and wife closer together.

Professionally too, these last months of 1929 were satisfying for Panikkar. He was as close to content as he ever would be, with no desire to leave the state or this job that kept him so satisfyingly engaged with political and constitutional reform. Academically, it was a rich time too—he had had the gratification of learning from his friend K. Iswara Dutt that his little anonymous tract on dyarchy had been read with interest by Sir Samuel Hoare, who was now making inquiries as to the identity of 'Kerala Putra'.[17]

Watching events across India and within the states unfold, Panikkar felt that this was a moment that deserved a wider, more nuanced understanding of Indian history. Between 1928 and 1930, he wrote and lectured steadily. In 1929, he published his book *Malabar and the Portuguese* to critical acclaim. To his delight, the eminent historian Jadunath Sarkar reviewed his work, writing that, while the book would have benefited from a more 'elaborate quarrying' in Portuguese archives, too much information would have 'killed the book'.[18] Panikkar had wisely chosen to stick to a short, clear historical narrative, in which he insisted that India was not a mess to be rescued by the British (or any other European power). Its history showed that there were personalities, in this case, the Zamorin of Calicut, who were able to pull their states or kingdoms together to modernise and centralise, and in so doing, defend the country from external interference. In Malabar, the Zamorin had been working on politically integrating the region. Trade had flourished, as had religious tolerance. When the Portuguese arrived, the Zamorin opposed the newcomers with all his might.

In the book, Panikkar downplayed the significance of the discovery of a sea route to the Indies, and more specifically, the voyage of Vasco da Gama. In his view, trade already existed between Malabar and faraway lands like Egypt and Venice. So the real importance of the 'discovery' was not in establishing trade contact—which already existed—but in breaking previous monopolies and, for India, entering into a direct relationship with a major European maritime power. If anything, he wrote, the Portuguese brought with them only cruelty and bigotry, draining the region of its wealth. The theme of naval power that he touched upon here would become central to his geopolitical ideas as he progressed through his career.

The book, Sarkar wrote, was characterised 'with a surprising degree of freshness of outlook and independence of judgement, which will secure his readers' assent as to the truth of his conclusions'.[19] The review and the book's success established Panikkar as a rising young revisionist historian and a foreign policy mandarin.

It was true that he was now looking at and thinking of Indian history very differently. As he began to work on his drafts for *Malabar and the Dutch*, Panikkar continued to centralise the fact that local issues were strands of a broader national fabric. Those local issues were almost always driven by *people*. Who, he wondered, had made India great simply through their ability to stand up to extraneous forces like 'foreigners'? It wasn't an entirely new question, rather one that often dogged Panikkar's thoughts at various points in his career.[20] If one reads Panikkar's monograph on Harsha, which had been written in Aligarh, one might find striking parallels between that and these new histories that he was now writing. The themes were largely the same: a ruler/leader/figure of power who united a fractious, fragmented territory or curbed the power of overlords/aristocracy. But considering the wider context against which he was writing these books and the fact that he was by now both older and considerably more experienced, his arguments are more nuanced. *Malabar and the Portuguese* served to establish him as not just a bureaucrat, but as a revisionist historian. It was also the beginnings of the perception of Panikkar as a foreign policy mandarin.

In all of Panikkar's work, what is particularly fascinating is the clarity with which a reader can see his thought process evolving over the years. He didn't always have the answers to everything, and there are some books—such as his biography of Gulab Singh, Hari Singh's grandfather[21]—in which his ambivalence on some questions is clear. As with most of his biographies of rulers from Bikaner to Patiala, Panikkar presented the erstwhile ruler of Kashmir as an intelligent, dynamic man, one who expanded India's borders with his conquest of Ladakh, Baltistan and Western Tibet, and who was aware of the strategic need to maintain an equal relationship with the British Raj. But what of the Raj itself? How did nationalism reconcile itself to standing under an umbrella of imperialism? Panikkar's answers to these questions, written in the late 1920s, don't hold too much water in the light of modern day. In his biography of Gulab Singh, for instance, he grappled somewhat unconvincingly with the question of who *was* a foreigner.[22]

Many courts, after all, relied on 'foreign' bureaucrats for their functioning (Panikkar himself was one). Similarly, when one state attacked another, such as Mysore attacking Malabar, did that constitute a 'foreign' threat? If so, were alliances with colonial powers an act of realpolitik or cowardice? Panikkar presented no real answer to these questions, and at best this biography can be read as a transitional work, written by a man whose ideas were not fully formed as yet. Still, these were important concepts contributing quietly to a fresh-eyed understanding of Indian history at a time when the country stood at a crossroads.

Then, fate threw another spanner in the works. Facing a tanking stock market (which would trigger the Great Depression of 1929) and an Indian problem it had no idea how to deal with, the newly elected Labour government in Britain authorised Lord Irwin, then the viceroy, to announce eventual dominion status for India. According to this new proposal, British control would be restricted to viceregal and military power in the short term and provincial government within British India would pass into Indian hands. This was the policy that would launch Winston Churchill on his vicious parliamentary opposition to India's independence movement, an opposition that was to change the empire's history forever.

On 31 October 1929, two days after Wall Street crashed, the viceroy reported Whitehall's message to India and also promised the convening of a round table conference as soon as the Simon Commission was done preparing its report. Here again, British disingenuity was on fully display. Despite his announcement during November meetings with leading Indian nationalists, Irwin insisted that, with a free and fair conference on the cards, the presence of many political stakeholders would mean that dominion status could *not* be the only goal. After all, the Muslim League had disagreed with the Nehru Report's demands for dominion status. That was just one example of the kind of dissent that was bound to arise. Perhaps federation, the viceroy suggested tactfully, would be a better goal. After all, it would unite province and princely state and bring different yet important interests on board the same bandwagon.

Furious, on 2 November 1929, two days after the announcement, a conference of national leaders led by Gandhi, Sapru and the Nehrus convened to issue the Delhi Manifesto. Despite its grandiose name, it was essentially a request for details. The manifesto demanded that the main purpose of the round table conference should be the immediate realisation of dominion status. Its drafting marked the establishment of an angry radical youth leading the political charge. Further ire was caused in May 1930 when the Simon Report was published, absent of any mention of dominion status. Gandhi, reading the mood, handed the presidency of the Congress immediately to Jawaharlal—in the teeth of older leaders who felt that the younger Nehru might not be ready for this. Motilal himself felt that it was unfair to foist his son on the party and people against their will. But his protestations came to nothing.

At a landmark session of the Congress on the banks of the Ravi in Lahore, a cheering audience of thousands watched young Jawaharlal Nehru canter up on the back of a white horse, tall and upright in the saddle, to take over the presidency of the party. 'We have now an open conspiracy to free the country from foreign rule,' he told the crowds, his voice ringing out scratchily over the microphone, '[Y]ou, comrades, and all our countrymen and countrywomen, are invited to join it'.[23] As he spoke, fireworks lit the night sky behind him, silhouetting Jawaharlal, a slender figure in white, against the darkness.

To loud roars of *Inquilab! Zindabad!* the Indian flag was unfurled for the very first time.

India was awakening.

Chapter 21

Round Tables

INDIA MIGHT HAVE BEEN AWAKENING, BUT THE PRINCES WERE STILL concerned about the ramifications of the Butler Committee's report.

Panikkar, reading and re-reading the report, found himself both comforted and anxious. The report had worrying clauses, but it had also left several doors conveniently ajar. Any constitutional reform that took place from here onwards would always involve or affect the princely states. At least, he thought, they could derive some comfort—however cold it might be—from that.

As he waited for the princes to pull together their representative delegation for the Round Table Conference, Panikkar found himself invited to lecture at the University of Calcutta in the winter of 1929. Hari Singh approved the invitation and, leaving Gouri and Haima behind, Panikkar went to Bengal.

He was there for a week and in between meeting his excited daughters, he demonstrated to the students of the University of Calcutta that despite his lawyer's robes, he could and did practice as a historian as well. Largely, he stuck to the basis of his thesis for federalism. During its day, the East India Company's foreign policy was defined by its treaties with the princely states. The eventual British attempts to pull political and princely forces together as it built its empire outside Bengal was the result of 'the pressure of irresistible currents of history'.[1] Published as a monograph, the lectures sweep through a vast expanse of time: from the beginning of the policy of annexation to the age of the Marathas to finally the establishment of paramountcy and the sovereignty of the Crown.

They also marked Panikkar's legal and historical coming of age. His previously published books on nationalism and imperialism are fine transitional examples of his political ideology, but in his arguments before the Indian States Committee and then in Calcutta between 1928 and 1929, it was clear that he was at an intellectual turning point. In lucid, fluid language, Panikkar demonstrated the evolution of colonial political practices within a legal framework. During these lectures he developed the core of what would become a later book on inter-statal law, where he would study the jurisdictional independence of the states vis-à-vis the Crown and each other.

He returned to Kashmir at the end of 1929 after a short break, and immediately found trouble in the air.

The dawn of the 1930s saw the return of the first batch of Muslim graduates from Aligarh and other universities: young men equipped with progressive ideas, seeking democracy and a dominant place in local political and religious leadership. They found, to their outrage, that not much had changed in their home state. 'Had those at the helm of affairs been capable of a little foresight and imagination,' lamented Prem Nath Bazaz, a contemporary Kashmiri observer, 'they would have gladly and readily provided good jobs for those young men who were the first among the Kashmir Muslims to receive higher education.'[2] But the court wasn't inclined to give way or space.

In time, the graduates began to form small groups to discuss their grievances. In 1929, for instance, Ghulam Abbas, a Muslim from Jammu, organised the Anjuman-i-Islam into the Young Men's Muslim Association of Jammu to work for the betterment of Muslims. In Srinagar, the Reading Room Party was established with graduates from Aligarh Muslim University. By the early 1930s, Kashmir was witnessing a spate of violence between Dogras and Muslims. Hari Singh was once again anxiously aware that his state teetered on the edge of yet another abyss.

But so did the rest of the country.

The Simon Commission's omission of dominion status had highlighted unexpected differences between New Delhi and Whitehall. Horrified at the backtracking, Irwin reiterated his government's commitment to dominion status in May and July 1930. On 4 July, Stanley Baldwin, the leader of the Conservative Party, was permitted by Prime Minister MacDonald to telegraph Irwin, outlining his party's displeasure with the Conservative viceroy's approach. It was too sudden, Baldwin insisted. In response, Irwin wrote back that while full dominion status was certainly not a practical outcome, now that he had declared the purpose of the Round Table Conference, he could hardly backpedal. This was the line Irwin held until the Government of India's dispatch outlining their stance on constitutional reform was published on the eve of the conference. The dispatch was reported as committing the government to working, through the conference, to place the 'first but definite impress of Dominion status' upon India.[3]

Meanwhile, the constant vacillation over dominion status and its various meanings and implications had infuriated the Congress to a point where, it was felt, action was needed. Gandhi reverted to his tried and tested method of a civil disobedience movement, for which he was given powers at a secret meeting of the Congress Working Committee in February 1930. The plan was the boycott of the salt tax and the modus operandi would be a long walk—a kind of mass pilgrimage—to Dandi, some 240 miles away. There, Gandhi and his marchers would collect handfuls of muddy salt and boil it to purify it for use.

The Dandi march would become the most iconic moment of the Indian freedom movement. Its greatest strength lay in the simplicity of its appeal to all classes, castes and religions and its non-violent core, and in the publicity blitz that Gandhi conducted skilfully for word of the march to spread far and wide. The march and the subsequent breaking of the salt laws set India on fire. During the march itself, one-third of all Indian officials serving along its route resigned. Nearly every state, from the North-West Frontier Province to Karnataka, witnessed agitations around local issues. In Sholapur, textile workers took over the city to protest low wages. In east India, there were public refusals to pay the chowkidar taxes, as well as the rather aggressive Chittagong armoury raid in which the fantastically named 'Indian Republican Army' seized weapons from a local armoury and issued an independence proclamation. In Kheda and Broach, the peasants pushed back against unjust landlords in a determined no-taxation movement. Gandhi watched chaos reign from his specially built palm leaf hut. 'The Government's plight,' he noted a little complacently, 'is that of the serpent which has swallowed a rat. It would find it hard to resort to either course of action: allowing me to remain out or putting me behind bars.'[4]

The government, as it turned out, had no qualms about resorting to action. The violence of the repression that ensued made headlines across the world. Nearly 20,000 protestors and leading members of the Congress Working Committee were slammed behind bars. Gandhi himself was arrested in the dead of night, taken to Bombay by train and thence to Yeravada Jail in a yellow Studebaker. Unrest in India was the last thing the British Empire needed at this moment. The Great Depression was beginning, and its impact would wash over India as well. Unemployment soared, bringing popular enthusiasm in politics to a grinding halt. Meanwhile, the princes were summoned to Simla in July 1930 by Irwin to confer on the suitability of an all-India federation.

It was music to Panikkar's ears, but he could see that the way ahead would not be an easy one. Hyderabad and Mysore pulled their brakes, and several others muttered mutinously among themselves at the prospect. But Haksar and Panikkar continued to weigh the pros and cons of these developments. By this time, Panikkar was fairly clear that there were two roads the princes could take: in one, they would remain external to a British India poised for greater Congress influence, which was generally critical of the princely states. In the second, the princes could surrender *some* sovereignty by positioning themselves beneath a federal centre as well under the British Crown, but retaining enough power to defend their quasi-sovereignty. Both Haksar and Panikkar were equally clear in their minds that the only viable future for the princes was the second option. The question was: *how?*

The unenviable task of prepping this motley crew had gone to Haksar and Panikkar, with the older man in the lead as the more seasoned bureaucrat. As the director of the expert committee, Haksar would be lobbying the princes to come together and stay together. But he needed a deputy to put research, evidence and data together to shore up the royal case. That task fell to Panikkar, who stayed in Srinagar, putting together a preliminary report for the princes.

By October 1930, most people had no real desire to participate in hartals or processions. As a result, the declaration of a Round Table Conference didn't thrill the political leadership of either India or Britain. But the princes were pleased. It would be, as Panikkar wrote later, 'an international stage on which to reaffirm their influence'.[5]

A broken front at this juncture would be fatal to any semblance of progress, and as a result, work behind the scenes had to be both swift and persuasive. These weeks marked the superimposition of federation over the erstwhile goal of dominion status. From here onwards, the Round Table Conference would be marked by the struggle for and ultimate failure to achieve federation.

For the princes (led by Panikkar), time was of the essence. Patiala went to work on the Nizam, trying to persuade the irritable Osman Ali Khan to throw in his lot with the Chamber of Princes. The Nizam was not an easy man to lure, but Bhupinder Singh was not without his own charm and persuasive skills. Eventually, he wrangled a sulky agreement to allow Sir Akbar Hydari, the Prime Minister of Hyderabad, to visit Delhi and continue Hyderabadi funding for the Chamber of Princes. Next, Haksar asked Patiala for his permission to speak to Mysore (under charge of Sir Mirza Ismail, the progressive, courteous Iranian who would bring civic revolution to the city) and Hyderabad (presided over by the weak bluff-master that was Sir Akbar Hydari). Haksar's plan was that if Mysore and Hyderabad could join hands, a common front might be built between these two powerful southern states and the rest of the Chamber of Princes.

Panikkar watched Haksar, a whirlwind of charm, tact and careful diplomacy, deal with royal egos of varying sizes. It is testament to Haksar's fine negotiating skills—and no doubt, his ability to charm and blandish—that both these difficult states grudgingly agreed to send observers to the chamber's session in Delhi. The Colonel even got Nawanagar—a notoriously slippery customer—to agree with the idea of joining hands with the political forces of provincial India.

From here, the next step was to see whether the Indian National Congress could be brought on board the princes' mission of achieving federation. This was not entirely motivated by nobility. Haksar was, after all, Tej Bahadur Sapru's brother-in-law. He was also closely related to S.N. Haksar, then the secretary of the Delhi Congress Committee. It stood to reason that he would support an alliance between prince and politician. But despite these very personal motivations, getting the Congress to agree to anything was going to be far easier said than done.

After all, the party had already abandoned dominion status in January 1930. Its leadership hadn't reached a conclusion about federation either. Gandhi, for one, was reportedly still pressing for dominion status to be discussed at the RTC in his absence, despite the strength of Tory and Liberal opposition.[6] Nehru dismissed the Round Table altogether as an 'assembly of vested interests'.[7] Nor did it seem like the Conservatives were fully on board with the idea of federation, decrying it as 'dangerously progressive.'[8]

For Haksar and Panikkar, then, obstacles lay everywhere they looked. There was nothing for it but to focus on crossing one bridge at a time. By November 1929, months before the delegation of the Chamber of Princes sailed for England, Haksar was gleefully reporting to Sapru, 'I think I have induced the princes not to come in the way of British India's advance.'[9]

The real inducement lay not in Haksar's charm, but in 'the artfully deceitful pen'[10] of K.M. Panikkar. This description of his penmanship belongs to the historian Ian Copland, though the line between deceit and disingenuity is a fine one. In his memoir, Panikkar presents federation as being his sole idea, born from the draft that the viceroy showed a group of princes including Patiala, Bikaner, Kashmir, Bhopal, Alwar, Dholpur and others at Viceregal Lodge, Simla. The princes roundly rejected the draft at first, wrote Panikkar, a circumstance that 'deeply dejected and depressed' him.[11] But the idea of federation was not Panikkar's alone. As a concept, it had been around at least for a decade, though it was not a popular one. The Montagu-Chelmsford Report had hinted at federation, but almost as though it were a landmine to be approached with great caution. Haksar himself had raised the idea to the standing committee before he had met Panikkar, only to be categorically shot down.[12]

But importantly, the princes themselves didn't need much deceiving. They had never been entirely aloof from the nationalist project, simply because of popular political movements, such as the AISPC, within their respective states. There were plenty of factors to persuade them that working *with* the national movement was the only viable way for success.

In this context, the Round Table Conference was seen by royal eyes to be a means to drive this point home for those of the brother princes who still resisted the idea. It is at this point that ministers and administrators like Panikkar and Haksar became unlikely diplomats and politicians behind the scenes. These men had to deal with events that would have tried the patience of a saint. Hyderabad, for instance, threw a spanner in the works by informing the astounded Patiala that it would not only be discontinuing its generous stipend of Rs 50,000 to the Chamber of Princes, but also sending its own separate delegation to the Round Table Conference.

Yet another glitch to Patiala's plans came surprisingly from Irwin himself. The viceroy liked his princes, but he liked them better when they were pliant. He didn't like this new obsession with legal reforms. He pinned the blame for it squarely on the 'directions of the Standing Organisation'.[13]

In February 1930, Irwin dealt out his first hard reminder of who was in charge when he told the chamber that there was no way that the standing committee could be consulted in cases where internal intervention in stately affairs was concerned. None of the matters laid out in the Butler Committee Report would be allowed to be questioned at the Round Table.[14] It helped nobody when, that same month, a bombshell hit Patiala from which he never really recovered. The AISPC published a book titled *The Indictment of Patiala* in which the authors went for the jugular, accusing the maharaja outright of rape, murder, torture and kidnapping.[15] The scandal was instant and full-blown, knocking Bhupinder Singh into a cocked hat. Ultimately his friendship with the King of England and his undeniably stellar work with the Chamber of Princes saved him, giving him the pretence of an enquiry commission designed to let him off the hook. But the Raj lost no time in heavily censuring him for his lax morals and extravagant ways, warning him that if he continued down this path, he would be financially hamstrung in the manner of the Nizam.[16]

The controversy spanned the summer of 1930, an inauspicious start to an important year in India's constitutional history. Though not one to buckle easily, Bhupinder Singh was shaken to his soul. His moods fluctuated wildly and he spent even more lavishly than before, half in defiance, half in despair, plunging his treasury into vast debt. He couldn't bear the dissonance of having been simultaneously exonerated and shown his place. Small wonder that when Panikkar and Haksar came to talk to him about the idea of federation that June, he gave them short shrift. Much to their shock, he dismissed their careful plans as 'an exercise in star gazing'.[17] Later, he went a step further, hauling the aghast Haksar over the coals for even thinking of such an idea and accusing him (incorrectly) of trying to hijack the Simla Summit with the viceroy.[18] Caught between terror and fury, Patiala tightened his control over the chamber, causing Bikaner to remark caustically, 'If things develop along certain lines, the Chancellor might, in days to come, assume the functions and role of a dictator.'[19]

Haksar and Panikkar were frustrated and worried. It was now August 1930, and there were but a handful of weeks left before the royal delegation departed for London. As part of the propaganda campaign to solidify opinion in favour of princely participation in the national movement, Haksar bade Panikkar to draft a memorandum for the standing committee. The draft became the seed for *Federal India*—the seminal work that defined Panikkar's contribution to Indian constitutional history.

Though now lost to history, the draft became a solid foundation on which to present the princely case. Panikkar claimed in his memoir to have dashed off *Federal India*, which was published at around this time, in a matter of two weeks. Despite its weighty import and its constitutional vision for postcolonial India, the monograph is a simple document, some 200-odd pages all told. To ensure that everyone came on board, Panikkar highlighted that the Butler Committee had confirmed that the princely states were theoretically free to bind themselves to the Government of India or to maintain their ties with the Crown. If they gave consent to the idea of dominion status for India, and from there if they transferred their existing ties to the Crown to the newly formed dominion of India, they could set the conditions they wanted.

To tempt the princes, Panikkar argued, they had to be given two guarantees. First, the existence of a federation was not to imply a central power that could interfere any more than the Crown already did. After all, British assertion of power had already created some semblance of federal government in that the central power exercised foreign policy, control over defence and powers of coercion over the states. All that was needed now was a constitutional set-up that guaranteed their internal sovereignty. His main argument centred around the need to restructure the relationship between the states, the Crown and British India by limiting paramountcy to ensure that the princes were treated on par with the government of British India.

The argument found its supporters in Whitehall, helpfully across party lines. Labour was already considering it as a 'speedy and consensual solution' of Indian affairs.[20] Among the Tories, federation was seen as 'an opportunity to avoid democracy in the central government'.[21] As it was, the Conservative Party was riven internally over the Indian question, with 'Die Hard' opinion, championed by Winston Churchill and the *Daily Mail* press baron Lord Rothermere, resisting any substantial move towards self-government. Whether either Labour or the Conservatives even remotely considered that the Chamber of Princes would actually come up with a feasible idea, considering the disaster of the States Committee hearings, is debatable. But Panikkar wasn't going to take a chance. Once he was done with the manuscript, he knew what he had to do next.

'I fully understood,' he wrote shrewdly, 'that the princes would not accept the views of an unknown and obscure young man.'[22] Instead, he sent the manuscript to Haksar with a cover letter in which he wrote sanctimoniously that it would be best if the manuscript were to be published with both their names on it. Haksar read the book in two days flat. He was thrilled. Indeed, so thrilled was he that over time, he assumed ownership of a document that became central to the debates on federation in India. Eventually, Panikkar's blueprint would come to be known as Haksar's plan. *Federal India* was, even at the time of its writing, an excellent example of transnational constitutionalism. It modelled itself on Germany's imperial constitutionalism, advocated classic federalism and kept the sovereignty of the Indian states central to its thesis.

With the manuscript circulating among the princes and their advisors, everything seemed to be in train for London.

CHAPTER 22

Curtain Raiser

BHUPINDER SINGH WAS ANYTHING BUT GUNG-HO WHEN HE BOARDED the *SS Macedonia* in Bombay. The Maharaja of Patiala was a broken man that summer. He was massively in debt, his blood pressure was out of control and his kidneys were on the verge of collapse. Worse, he had no idea what to expect at St James' Palace, much less from his brother princes.

Even more worrying was the mercurial delegation from Hyderabad. It was sailing separately on the *SS Narkanda* and was led by Sir Akbar Hydari who had recently developed cold feet about the idea of a federation. Truth be told, Hydari was under pressure from several extraneous factors: his daughter was a paid-up member of the Congress Party and his brother was a prominent lawyer associated with the Congress. When the civil disobedience movement broke out, Hydari felt torn. On board the *Narkanda*, he dithered wildly over whether he was doing the right thing, considerably alarming Hyderabad's fiercely pro-federation British resident, Sir Terence Keyes.

Keyes couldn't afford to let Hydari's anxious hand-wringing scupper his carefully laid plans. Before the delegation boarded the *Narkanda*, Keyes had gone to formidable lengths to persuade the suspicious Osman Ali Khan that, in a federation, it would be the ruler who would hold supreme power. In reality, of course, he wanted a federation to 'neutralise' the princely dissidence within India.[1]

From Bombay to Aden, the British resident worked around the clock to persuade Hydari of the joys of federation. He wasn't the only one. Sapru was on the *Narkanda* as well, and he was also coaxing the petrified Hydari on board the federal bandwagon. So persuasive was Sapru that Mirza Ismail, the Dewan of Mysore and yet another waverer, also steadied his anxious heart. For the historian Ian Copland, Keyes's successful lobbying marked federation's arrival into practical politics.

But when the *Narkanda* and the *Macedonia* finally docked at Plymouth, Hydari would be the least of Keyes's problems. On the voyage to London, sharp differences had begun to develop between even the pro-federation ministers. The basic structure of it was agreed upon: the demarcation of state, federal, imperial and international spheres by dividing the exercise of sovereign powers among the Crown, the federal centre, and provincial and state governments.[2] But nearly every princely advisor from Hydari to Mirza to Panikkar had different conceptions of what that meant, as well as motivations for it.

Unsurprisingly, almost as soon as everyone disembarked, there was bedlam.

Hydari and Mirza fell out spectacularly. The Maharaja of Patiala was warned sinisterly by the Nizam to 'be careful' when he dealt with the likes of Hydari and Keyes. They were, Osman Ali Khan said ominously, 'traitors and servants of the Government of India'.[3] Worse, Patiala was told straight off by British ministers that 'he had no position at all and was just a member of the delegation'.[4] Furious at the insult (he had been told this in the presence of women stenographers), and already physically unwell, Patiala threated to resign on the spot.

With fractures and fissures beginning to split the chamber's delegation apart, Panikkar was overworked from the start. Every ounce of his natural persuasion and suavity went into the intense lobbying that took place behind the scenes. He knew that, for the princes, this was as high as the stakes would ever be.

But British politicians and officials also had an equally diverse range of opinions on federation. The Labour Party, which formed the minority government in Britain at the time, was in favour of federation in principle. Several in the Conservative Party—known as the diehards—considered federation to be a useful tool for the maintenance of colonial control over South Asia; prominent among these supporters was Samuel Hoare, the party's delegate to the Round Table Conference and soon to become secretary of state for India.

For Hoare, federation was ideal for 'avoiding democracy in the central government', thereby providing a means to 'retain in our hands the realities and verities of British control'.[5] If the princes were brought within a federal framework, it would be all the better for the Raj, since they could act as a buffer against the rising tides of anti-colonial nationalism in India. With the establishment of a national government dominated by the Conservatives in Britain in 1931, Hoare's views would become government policy in London.

The weeks before the Round Table Conference were marked by frenetic activity. Many of the important political contingents were set up in hotels across the city. Patiala was staying at the Savoy, along with Haksar and Panikkar. Mayfair Hotel housed Kashmir, Dholpur and Rewa. Alwar, Baroda and Sir Akbar Hydari were at the Hyde Park Hotel. Dinners and informal chats were the beating heart of royal diplomacy. The India Office hosted a welcome dinner at the Park Lane Hotel and a reception at Lancaster House. Bikaner invited everyone for dinner at the Carlton Hotel, with dancing and champagne. On 28 November, the young Maharajadhiraja of Dhrangadhra celebrated his twenty-third birthday at a massive party for over 200 guests. Everyone tipsily sang *For He's a Jolly Good Fellow* after they had consumed copious quantities of wine and been garlanded with strands of gold by liveried servants. The Maharaja of Alwar—arrogant, cruel and convinced he was the incarnation of Lord Rama—could be found at the society hostess Nancy Astor's bejewelled parties at St James' Square. In between rounds of discussions either at the Ritz Carlton or at Sir Cowasjee Jehangir's house at Stanmore Court, advisors and delegates wandered off to get a meal at 112 Gower Street, where the YMCA Indian Students' Hostel offered subsidised dal chapati. Panikkar and B.S. Moonje shared a meal of koftas, chicken curry and rice at Shafi's, one of the cheaper Indian restaurants.

A commemorative volume published in 1972 on his birth centenary describes Moonje as 'the first and foremost character of the great hymn of militarisation of Hindus'.[6] The holder of a medical degree, in the early twentieth century he was engaging with the Congress. From the mid-1920s, his loyalties switched from the Congress to the Hindu Mahasabha, the presidency of which he was holding when Panikkar met him in London.

Moonje's goal in London was quite simple. He was not only still clinging to the idea of dominion status, but pushing for a greater recognition that Muslims were the real threat to Hindus. For Hindus to protect themselves, he advocated military training, and he was in London with the explicit intention of blocking Muslim demands for further safeguards in provincial legislative chambers. Moonje's diaries are housed in the archives at the erstwhile Nehru Memorial Museum and Library, and they present a picture of a man who was deeply insecure, condescending about his peers and caustically judgemental about women's freedom. He made no attempt to hide these qualities in person either. Panikkar was perfectly aware of Moonje's proclivities, and he began straight off by flattering the older man, describing him ingratiatingly as a 'Maratha fighter and diplomat'.[7] If he thought obsequiousness would get him anywhere, Panikkar was sorely mistaken. Moonje was gracious enough, but in his diary entry that night, he noted nastily that Kavalam Madhava Panikkar had no personality and would never excel in executive positions. Still, Moonje noted as a kind afterthought, he might make a good clerk.[8]

Even with so much archival material available across both India and Britain, it is hard to fathom the number of serious discussions, both open and secret, that went into crafting this moment in India's constitutional history. Up until its opening plenaries, many delegates, politicians and commentators still expected dominion status to be the main conference object. In fact it was apparent, in these tense weeks before the conference actually opened, that dominion status still meant very different things to the Government of India, the British government and the Indian delegates, and even within these groups.

The more the princes thought about it, for example, the more opinions they had. The Maharaja of Alwar wrote a fluid essay in the

Asiatic Review in January 1930, in which he insisted that dominion status was the logical end of Montagu's declaration of 1917, though in his opinion, that could only come about 'by mutual consent between the Government of British India and ourselves ... '[9] Maharaja Sayaji Rao Gaekwad III of Baroda summed up the princely position best in terse bullet points:

1. The need for the complete autonomy of the states in internal affairs;
2. The strict observance of our treaties, both in letter and in spirit;
3. The establishment of an independent court of arbitration, to which both sides can appeal, as of right;
4. The devising of some means, whereby the states will be able to speak with weight, in all matters that are common between them and the rest of India.[10]

Among the delegates from British India, on the other hand, there was also growing ambivalence about the utility of dominion status as a demand at the Round Table Conference. The Congress was notable in its absence, furious over British non-commitment to dominion status and ambivalent about federation. Jinnah, in an interview with Conservative delegation secretary Robert Stopford on 4 November, made it clear that he was avoiding the use of the term dominion status due to its meaning different things to different people.[11] Behind the scenes of it all, Whitehall and the India Office were working hard to superimpose federation on top of dominion status.

Benn had heard of Panikkar and Haksar and their plans for federation. He knew that though the chamber was divided in its support for federation, there were enough royal houses supporting the cause for it to be achievable. The challenge for Benn was to honour Irwin's declaration at the conference without committing to the full definition of dominion status, which Baldwin and others in the Conservative Party had so vociferously opposed. In a briefing document from November 1930 outlining the cabinet's position before the conference, dominion status was described as having 'strong sentimental value' but fundamentally implied internal self-government.[12] Keeping all of this in mind, the secretary of state for India wrote to the viceroy on 14 November 1930, the week before the conference opened, suggesting judiciously that this 'new idea [federation] is much greater than the old and would make it easier to develop in all branches that Dominionhood which India already possesses in her representation at the League of Nations and at the Imperial Conference.'[13]

If the question of dominion status was raised, Benn suggested, it was important to convince the Indian delegates that circumstances had now changed. And so it was that federation and its achievement for India became the new lodestar at the Round Table Conference.

The princes were at the forefront, and with their cartoonish reputations, it was hard to take them seriously. The British press coverage of the conference focused breathlessly on the princes' eccentricities, extravagance and glamour—from the veiled Maharanis of Alwar to the size of the diamonds in Patiala's turban. Indeed, the princes were not really expected to contribute to the discussions at all. A report in the *Daily Telegraph* claimed that the princes had only a 'watching brief', and would only intervene if their positions were suitably threatened.[14]

A caricature in the *Evening Standard*, done by the cartoonist David Low, is a delightful mirror to the agonies regarding etiquette and prejudice suffered by the India Office and Whitehall as the Round Table loomed ever closer. In it, Low charted a series of imaginary blunders from the Maharaja of Patiala's hair to the Maharaja of Bikaner's formidable moustache. There was even a jibe about the jungles ('If you miss the jungles, Sahibzada, just look in at the House of Commons!'). The cartoon was an excellent example not just of the empire's awareness of optics in colonial diplomacy, but of the kind of unintentional slights that often cut Indians to the quick. They were often denied access to restaurants, dance halls and lodgings due purely to the colour of their skin. A report in *United India* from the summer of 1930 declared crossly, 'Every Indian during his stay in England feels the full force of race and colour prejudice existent in this country.'[15] Benn was naturally anxious, writing to Irwin, 'At times, one comes across the prejudice against entertaining Indians, a prejudice which, in so many hidden and subtle ways poisons the relations between our race and theirs.'[16]

From administration to logistics, the gremlin of failure dogged the heels of the first Round Table—an irony when one realises that it was actually organised to *prevent* failure. Nobody knew which way the dice would fall in the run-up to the conference.[17]

As the Round Table loomed ever closer, last-minute changes were made to the venues for the event. A specially made oval table was brought in for the conference itself and a special electric supply was laid in at St James's Palace to keep the draughty rooms warm as winter set in. Backchannel talks continued apace as the delegation from the Reforms Office in New Delhi (with a young V.P. Menon in attendance) arrived in London. Led by Sir Hawthorne Lewis, they would sit on the sidelines to minute meetings and send official reports of the proceedings to Delhi. To paraphrase the Canadian constitutional expert Frank Scott, the dominions were growing up. This, then, was no time for 'higgle-haggle'[18] to quote a cross B.S. Moonje, though the phrase was an excellent way to describe the latter months of 1930. Words and phrases like 'dyarchy' and 'dominion status' were being lobbed about like so many conceptual tennis balls. By early November, weeks before the conference began, the Government of India's special observer Harry Haig triumphantly cabled New Delhi with the welcome news that the 'states as a whole are considering seriously the possibilities of some immediate federal union with India', adding that if this was true, it would 'largely transform the central problem'.[19]

Through it all, personalities and egos dominated the stage as much as politics. Patiala, already insecure and greatly piqued that he wasn't (as he thought) being paid enough attention, tried the time-honoured tactic of seeking attention. Complaining loudly of a sore throat, he retired to his top-floor suite at the Hyde Park Hotel. A couple of days later, still complaining loudly, he departed for Paris. As tactical errors went, it was huge. With the chancellor missing in action and with the playing-field wide open for all kinds of machinations, it was not until 10 November, hours until the conference actually kicked off, that the text of the states' speeches was approved by their advisors.[20]

On the morning of 12 November, King-Emperor George V inaugurated the Round Table in the Royal Gallery of the Palace of Westminster. The *Illustrated Weekly of India* carried an exceptional cartoon of the proceedings by Mrs E. King, which made note of Bikaner, Jinnah, Sapru, Reading, Patiala, the Aga Khan and the governor of the United Provinces (and advisor to the conference) Sir Malcolm Hailey. Remarkably, the cartoon portrayed the figures of Gandhi, Nehru and Patel as odd caricatures of Banquo, wafting overhead and haunting the conference by their absence. It was an astute observation of a moment of missed opportunity, though Sapru did much to make up for it by giving the speech of a lifetime during the plenary session.

To read that speech is to understand the scope of Sapru's lawyerly brilliance since it displayed—to borrow the constitutional historian Stephen Legg's phrase—'a mastery of the ambiguity' that had built up around the concept of dominion status.[21] Sapru suggested that not only was the phrase 'forbidden', but that whenever he used it, British statesmen would inquire politely what it meant. Had the same question, he demanded irritably, been asked of Canada in 1865 or South Africa in 1909? All India wanted was equality in the Commonwealth and a government responsible to its legislature. That wasn't possible from the Simon Commission's recommendations without a responsible central government and a constitution that was federal. Sapru looked around the huge oval table at the princes. 'The Government of India … vaguely speaks of a far-off Federation,' he said. 'With us, it is a real live issue now. If we can come to some solution of that, I frankly think that nothing better can be achieved at this conference.'[22]

In response, Bikaner rose to his feet and in a stunning moment of constitutional theatre, proffered his support for federation. It was a volte-face from dominion status, and he was followed by Sayaji Rao of Baroda, Hari Singh of Kashmir, Akbar Rao Hydari of Hyderabad and Sir Mirza Ismail of Mysore. All of them pronounced themselves ready to join an all India federation 'occupying a position of honour and equality in the British Commonwealth of Nations'.[23] The Maharaja of Alwar repeated his previously stated position of a 'United States of India', which he suggested was 'the shortest and quickest' way to dominion status.[24]

With federation being unanimously spoken for, the resultant Federal Structure Committee (FSC) came to be the driver of the conference. Moonje's efforts to keep dominion status on the agenda ended in failure and his attempts to introduce an amendment that backed dominion status came to grief as well.[25]

On 20 November, Lord Reading spoke for the Liberals, and in a smart speech, took the ambiguity that Sapru had mentioned head-on. If the term was that vague, he said, it just meant that the need of the hour was to defer dominion status until its meaning was clearer. For now, he conceded, it would mean a status equal to the empire's other dominions. 'It has never been defined,' he stated. 'No lawyer has ever attempted to put it into definition, but I do not suppose anyone will doubt that that is what in truth is meant by it. Keep that meaning clear in your minds, because if you do, I think you must see that there are very many questions to be considered and discussed before you can get, quite, to the ultimate goal you naturally strive to attain.'[26]

It was a warning as much as it was a stalling tactic and it was aptly timed, for behind the scenes, trouble persisted. Benn described the idea of dominion status as being imbued with 'strong sentimental value',[27] and in this assessment, he hit the nail on the head. So strong was its value that Bikaner and Patiala were at fraught (and very vocal) loggerheads about the viability of federation. At one point, Bhopal had to step in to cool things down, and reports of the incident provoked the viceroy into lamenting to his father that he doubted if the princes realised what they were doing.[28] 'Possibly some face-saving formula might be devised,' Benn mused, adding rather unnecessarily, 'This is important.'[29] Just what that formula could be would require further meetings, since it was by now fairly obvious that the answer would not be attained within the space and time of this Round Table.

Still, Panikkar and Haksar had done some sterling work. 'Slowly … the intensive lobbying and the frenetic shuttle diplomacy of the pro-federation ministers (and especially of the suave Panikkar) began to bear fruit,' observed the MP Robert Stopford. 'As regards the princes, what had at first seemed strange and threatening began to appear, as the mechanics of federalism were explained to them by the ministers, logical and compelling.'[30] In all of this, *Federal India*, which had been put into official circulation on the day of the opening session of the conference, played a huge role. The reasoning and logic in *Federal India* were so soundly explained that when the Indian States' Delegation met on 11 October in London, its members agreed on the hypothesis of an All India Federation.[31]

But this was a sham, even if it was a remarkably good one. *Federal India*, for all its merits, had also succeeded in antagonising plenty of powerful players in this game. One of them was the influential Jam Sahib of Nawanagar who would become one of Panikkar's most dangerous enemies in the months to come. Matters were not helped by Leslie Scott, sympathetic to the diehard Conservative cause. He chose this moment to write a polite but fluent memo explaining that the federal scheme was not only dangerous for the states but fatal for British imperial interests in the subcontinent. The note is an excellent example of just how well a fine lawyer can play on human insecurities to make his case. Scott avoided attacking federation on its merits. Instead, he went for the jugular of princely fears about paramountcy. 'If they (the princes) are controlled by an undefined and unlimited paramountcy,' he wrote smoothly, 'if they are subject to unknown "residuary" powers, as claimed by the Government of India, they are not free men and the part which they can play in the moulding of the future constitution will be rendered to a great extent ineffective.'[32]

Scenting blood in the water, Scott pushed harder, suggesting that a 'carefully worded diplomatic letter' be sent to the British prime minister (the chairman of the Round Table Conference), demanding a judicial inquiry into paramountcy, failing which the princes would have no alternative but to withdraw from the conference and hold the government responsible for its breakdown.[33]

The letter hit home. On 19 November 1930, Bikaner was wondering, 'How can we federate until we know what rights and duties we bring to the federation?'[34] When Panikkar and Haksar beheld the contents of the letter, they were livid. Calling an emergency meeting of the Indian States' Delegation, they tabled the letter without preamble. The meeting ran for hours, with Panikkar and Haksar taking turns to frantically persuade the princes not to listen to a 'lawyer-cum-politician's opinion' that was plainly intended to dupe them into being pawns in a 'retrograde policy'.[35] They were interrupted by Patiala, who burst in dramatically, having rushed back from Paris as soon as he had heard the news of Scott's memo, and they were hampered by Rushbrook-Williams, who argued glibly in favour of Scott. But in the end, Panikkar and Haksar managed to prevail, securing the delegation's rejection of Scott's memo as a desperate attempt to derail their interests.

It was only a temporary breather.

The Round Table Conference was beginning to tank and everyone who was present in London in those tiring days knew it. India might want dominion status, Tej Bahadur Sapru wrote in some frustration to his daughter, but it did not yet have 'dominion status mind', primarily due to its failures on the communal front.[36] On 25 November 1930, Panikkar reported the same to Robert Stopford. The communal discussions were nosediving, he said bitterly, because the Muslim delegates were refusing to give up major representations in Punjab and Bengal. So hard were the lines drawn now that Sapru and Moonje nearly came to blows on the subject.

In London, at a dinner with Sapru and other Hindu delegates at the Savoy Hotel on 21 October, Moonje insisted that he would only negotiate with Jinnah if dominion status was granted and the British agreed to enforce the new constitution. The Aga Khan snapped at the exhausted Ramsay MacDonald that unless a government declaration contained adequate safeguards for the Muslim community, they would dissociate themselves from the conference proceedings. Meanwhile, Jinnah made it icily clear that *four* main parties were involved in these talks—the British, the princes, the Hindus and the Muslims. It was the first time he had presented the Muslims of India not as minorities with special interests but as a distinct group in their own right.

Unsurprisingly, the British were incensed. Sir Malcolm Hailey, the Government of India's senior consultative official at the conference, stormed angrily (and insultingly), 'Jinnah, of course, was always the perfect little bounder and as slippery as the eels which his forefathers purveyed in the Bombay market.'[37]

Eventually, a meeting that ran from 6 p.m. to midnight resulted in the signing of a compromise on 16 November. But even then, as Harry Haig reported morosely, the 'Hindu-Muslim conversations are believed to have reached something like a deadlock'.[38] Lord Sankey, chair of the Federal Structure Sub-Committee, was furious. 'The Hindus are v. insistent and unreasonable,' he wrote angrily to the viceroy. 'They are children. I much prefer the Mohammadans who are much more reliable.'[39]

Communalism was the fault line along which much of political and constitutional progress foundered and would continue to founder for the rest of the nationalist movement. As much as everyone tried, and no matter how many rounds of talks were held, no common ground or midway could be attained. Sir Reginald Glancy, the advisor to the Hyderabad delegation, ruefully wrote that the princes were, at this point, hoping that 'nothing will come of this Conference and that they will be able to continue their sheltered existence while the Hindus and the Muhammadans wage communal war in British India'.[40]

By the end of that year, disillusionment was rife. Nowhere was it clearer than at the badly timed banquet thrown by the Maharaja of Alwar on 17 December 1930 to celebrate the twenty-eighth year of his reign. With the communal crisis overshadowing the outcome of the conference and tempers and patience fraying at the seams, the last thing anyone wanted was to attend a banquet. But one could hardly refuse Alwar's invitation. The double-page spread in that week's *The Graphic* featured uncomfortably candid photographs of distinctly sullen guests. Malcolm Hailey had had the good sense to opt out, and later wrote sympathetically about the 'overwrought PM' being forced to listen to a meaningless speech for an hour until the clock struck midnight.[41] Panikkar was thoroughly annoyed at the way things were going, telling Stopford that *Federal India* was a 'deceitful book' and that it had been written in an attempt to persuade the princes to accept federation. As he put it, it 'emphasised all the sweets and omitted the sacrifices'.[42]

To be fair, this was disenchantment talking. Panikkar had always been deeply committed to the idea of federalism, but when he saw the intricacies of the egos and politics at play during the Round Table Conference, he was forced to rethink his own ideas. It speaks volumes about his belief in federalism that he stuck to his guns until there was no other choice.

CHAPTER 23

Storm Warning

IN THE WINTRY JANUARY OF 1931, PANIKKAR RETURNED TO INDIA.

He was emotionally exhausted. His involvement at the frontlines of the national movement this time had been weightier than his previous assignment as Gandhi's envoy in Punjab. The First Round Table Conference had not exactly been an unmitigated success, but it had opened the doors for further discussion, which was more than anyone could have asked for. Nor was it over in the strictest sense of the word. Rather, it had been adjourned, so that its work could continue in London and Delhi. As the Reforms Commissioner Hawthorne Lewis explained, 'While each R.T.C. was in session, London was the arena. In the intervals between each conference, the centre of gravity was back again in India, with successive investigations of particular problems by *ad hoc* committees and exploration, scrutiny and review by the Government of India of each aspect of the Federal scheme as it has developed.'[1]

So federation was very much in play in the spring of 1931, although the Chamber of Princes was still trying to figure out which version worked best for its ambitions. As Patiala put it, 'We can only federate with a British India that is self-governing and not with a British India government as it is presently ... We want to enter the federation as equal partners in a great and honourable enterprise, under conditions which will safeguard the internal autonomy of our states and secure our people all the advantages of citizenship in a mighty country.' They were fine words, but they came at the end of a fraught chancellorship. Patiala was not a man for the long haul—he threw a tantrum and resigned his post, frustrated that others were, as Bikaner wryly put it, 'taking the lead'.[2]

If he had thought his brother princes would rally around him at this dramatic gesture, he was sorely mistaken. The princes had wanted a leader during the conference, not a spoilt man-child. Worse still, there were whispers that much of the funds given to the Special Organisation had been hived off to pay Patiala's ballooning debts. Nobody wanted tantrums. They wanted youth, decisiveness and action. Almost as soon as the princes were back on native soil, the Chamber of Princes chose the young, urbane Hamidullah Khan, the Nawab of Bhopal, to be their new chancellor. In the same breath, they appointed a new secretary: K.M. Panikkar.

It was an appointment that would bear heavily on Panikkar's career, especially since it underscored princely belief in his knowledge and expertise. He was no longer the unknown young man who had had to lean on Haksar's name to carry the draft of *Federal India*. But if his memoir is to be believed, it was an appointment against the odds. He was, he averred, not quite liked within the Chamber of Princes, with quite a few princes (like the Jam Sahib of Nawanagar) thinking that he was too 'radical'.[3] But Panikkar's supporters within the chamber—a powerful lobby that included Patiala and Bikaner—outweighed his critics. In between the Round Tables then, Panikkar embarked on what would be his closest association with constitutional reform as well as princely politics.

For the new job, the Panikkars had to pack up their beautiful bungalow in Srinagar and move southwards to Bhopal. In many ways, the state was the perfect foil for Panikkar's intellect, his love for literature and his forward-thinking political mind. Situated in the Malwa region of central India, Bhopal had been founded in 1709 by the Afghan adventurer Dost Mohammad Khan, who first acquired the lease of a village named Bairasia, which served him as a base. From 1819 until 1926, the state was successively ruled by four incredibly powerful, erudite women who styled themselves as 'nawab begums' and practised feminism long before there was a word for it. A passage in *Night of the New Moon*, a book by the journalist and author Anees Jung, encapsulates their era almost perfectly: 'In the heart of every Muslim woman in Bhopal survives a magical island. She traces it back to a vision of four women who ruled and guided the destinies of the state for more than a hundred years. They ruled like men, rode horses and elephants, wore no veil and were referred to as Nawabs.'[4]

Bhopal's Begums were emblematic of the state that Hamidullah inherited. Each of the four administered a state mired in feudal male privilege with courage and fairness. Their battles were not fought on the battlefield: they worked largely behind the scenes to educate the women of their state, to uphold the tenets of Islam and patronise the arts. They were connoisseurs of literature, proficient authors and poets in their own individual rights; they encouraged modernity and were excellent (if deeply unconventional) diplomats. On her first trip to England, Sikander Begum shocked King George V and his queen by appearing majestically before them clad in a dressing gown. Jahan Begum annoyed Edwin Montagu by talking only of educational reforms when he met her in 1917. 'She jabbered about nothing else,' the secretary of state for India noted crossly in his diary. They were, to the last woman, excellent with the sword, notable polo players and perfectly capable of commanding their standing armies.

Hamidullah inherited a throne that required considerable upkeep in terms of stature. Older than Panikkar by a few months, the new nawab was the youngest son of Sultana Jahan Begum, the state's thirteenth ruler and the fourth consecutive Begum of Bhopal. Her granddaughter Abidaa would recall that, in her prime, Jahan Begum ruled with justice, humanity and piety, earning unswerving loyalty from her people. In 1926, following a bitter succession struggle that defined Bhopal's modern history, Jahan Begum abdicated in favour of Hamidullah. Many years in the future, Lord Wavell would exasperatedly liken the young nawab to a 'mischievous boy with a catapult',[5] but even as a teen, Hamidullah was a thorn in the Raj's side. He was known for his affiliations with the Ali brothers and the Khilafat movement, and the Raj was wary of his staunch nationalism as he grew older. Several words of caution were dropped in his worried mother's ear, but Jahan Begum could do nothing to rein in her son. The only thing she *could* do, she decided sensibly, was ensure that she trained him well enough to take over the throne. As a result, Hamidullah was the first of Bhopal's scions to receive a university education. Jahan Begum trained him in the art of public administration as well by appointing him as her chief secretary.

When Panikkar encountered him, he had grown into a suave, charming young man, a brilliant polo player and a man who exhibited a peculiar kind of blind courage, such as in his penchant for stalking and killing tigers on foot. In the mould of his mother, Hamidullah was progressive and democratic, ensuring that his state had all the latest amenities and infrastructure from electricity to running hot water. But he also enjoyed his social life. His daughter and heir Abidaa described her father's early years in power as the 'carefree years'.[6]

The Panikkars were soon part of a swirl of gaiety from regattas on the beautiful lake to shooting weekends at Chicklode. Gouri was delighted. She was doing well with her language lessons and had gained enough confidence to begin speaking fluently in English and Hindustani. She was far more vocal than she had been when Panikkar first met her, and beginning to read as voraciously as he did. Together, they read the classics when he was home in the evenings, and he would listen while she read the Gita to herself at night after baby Haima was asleep. Gouri always kept a copy of the Gita with her wherever they were in the world. She liked to end her days by reading a chapter or two. She still loved her kitchen garden and her cooking, but now there were new intellectual challenges to fill her days with, apart from their social engagements in the evening. Through it all, she continued running the home with the smooth efficiency that Panikkar enjoyed. The stability and ease that had grown between the two of them when he had first returned from Paris continued to flourish, and shortly into their stay in Bhopal, Gouri was pregnant again.

But outside the happy walls of their home, there were undercurrents of tension.

Panikkar knew he had no time to lose. For the first time in its modern history, India was not in the position of a supplicant demanding justice. 'The most powerful instrument of change,' noted Rushbrook-Williams, 'was the procedure of the Round Table Conference itself'.[7] That procedure had seen Indians sitting down with their British counterparts as responsible statesmen armed with a mandate that nobody questioned. They had not been expected to argue in defence of their rights. Their rights, so far as the Raj would or could admit, had been tacitly accepted. Now, India had to demonstrate how (or, indeed, if) those rights could be reconciled with its existent status as a colony of the British Empire. To think of it in these terms was almost overwhelming, exhilarating even. The archives present a picture of a delegation that was pleased with its work in London, despite the deadlock. 'The Indian states ... held the future of India ... in the hollow of their hands,' exulted Haksar in a confidential memo.[8]

He was to regret those words.

Within weeks of their arrival back in India, Panikkar and Haksar discovered that the enthusiasm for federation was rapidly waning. A public meeting summoned by Mirza Ismail in Mysore to explain the implications of federation was attended only by a trickle of disinterested people. A questionnaire to test the waters about federation was circulated among 109 respondents in the Chamber of Princes. Only fifty-five bothered to answer, of whom nine were downright hostile. In Hyderabad, Akbar Rao Hydari found that the Nizam, possibly repenting his decision to trust the persuasive Terence Keyes, was suddenly and stubbornly recalcitrant and no blandishments would move him.

By April 1931, it was clear that a storm was brewing. It helped nothing that Panikkar was increasingly isolated within the Chamber of Princes at this time. As brilliant as he was and as persuasive as his pen might be, he was no match for an array of intimidating opponents including the Jam Sahib, Panna and Dholpur. Of all of these, Nawanagar presented the greatest threat.

Sir Digvijaysinhji Ranjitsinhji Jadeja was a progressive ruler, a superb cricketer and soldier, and he held immense influence over his brother princes as did his advisor, Rushbrook-Williams. Described scornfully by Panikkar as an 'arch intriguer',[9] Rushbrook-Williams was smarting from having achieved pretty close to nothing (as he saw it) at the end of the first Round Table, all thanks to the communal troubles in the country. In an essay he wrote for *Foreign Affairs* at around this time, Rushbrook-Williams lamented, 'It is indeed among the tragedies of that situation that there seems almost no possibility of coming to satisfactory terms with one party in India, without bitterly offending another.'[10] As words went, they were an excellent summary of the majority opinion in political India. Nobody was more acutely aware of this than the harassed viceroy himself. Irwin was due to return home that summer, his time in India at an end. With his back to the wall, he now tried the dramatic tactic of attempting to loosen the deadlock through open negotiations.

For this, he needed Gandhi.

In late January 1931, the Mahatma had been released from jail. With his disciple Mirabehn (an admiral's daughter formerly known as Madeleine Slade), Gandhi visited Irwin to discuss the way forward. The two men talked for hours as Mirabehn prepared dates and milk for her guru on the marble floor outside the viceregal study. It took eight meetings, but by 5 March, there seemed to be some kind of agreement. Gandhi announced that he would end civil disobedience, including the boycott of British goods. Crucially, he would go to London at the end of the year to attend the next Round Table Conference. In return Irwin would recognise the virtues of the swadeshi movement and release thousands of imprisoned freedom fighters. On paper, the Gandhi-Irwin Pact was a triumph for both men.

Predictably, it was hit by controversy almost immediately. The younger, more radical members of the Congress felt Gandhi had been too weak and had agreed to the vaguest of British promises. Across the seas, the Tories were furious at what they saw as an outrageous surrender in the face of anarchy. There was more trouble coming—and it was coming fast.

On 29 March, a month after Panikkar had assumed secretaryship of the Chamber of Princes, the Congress met at Karachi to endorse the Gandhi-Irwin Pact. It was six days after the executions of Bhagat Singh, Sukhdev and Rajguru, and the atmosphere was electric with fury. Why, people muttered, was Gandhi signing a pact with the Raj when it had killed three of their own? Black flags fluttered along Gandhi's route to Karachi, a sign that the people were tired of everything changing yet staying the same. The Karachi session, however, became known for its resolution on fundamental rights and its definition of what swaraj would actually mean in terms of freedom and equality. It called for the protection of the rights, cultures and languages of the minorities and put in place a basic economic blueprint. The resolutions at Karachi would be the political and economic model of the Indian National Congress in the years to come.

But for every step forward, there were always two steps backward. 'Nothing can be done until some sort of *modus vivendi* is arrived at between the Hindus and the Mohammedans,' Rushbrook-Williams noted anxiously. 'The danger of delay is emphasised by the fact that communal spirit is spreading.'[11]

Irwin's successor, the haughty, repressive Lord Willingdon, knew he had inherited a colony that was growing steadily more restive. With two Round Tables stretching ahead of him and a national movement fissured with communalism, the best the new viceroy could do was to hold the line. Still, he moaned to his son, 'I rather wish Irwin had been here to sweep up the mess he left behind him.'[12]

It was a mess indeed.

The royal acceptance of federation, always unsteady to begin with, was beginning to slip. Panikkar's mandate was to keep the federal ship from capsizing, but this was not going to be easy. The atmosphere within the chamber was heavy with dislike, suspicion and fear. The smaller states were worried about their future. Bikaner and Patiala had never liked or trusted each other and it was clear that they weren't about to start now. Bhopal's election to the post of chancellor, backed shrewdly by Bikaner, had triggered a massive sulk from Patiala, who stormed to the other end of the federal spectrum to seek revenge. On 15 June 1931, to Panikkar's consternation, Patiala published a pamphlet called 'Federation and the Indian States'. In this simple but devastating tract, Bhupinder Singh trashed federation as a 'radical innovation' that 'subverts the very basis of the well-tried and time-honoured political institutions of the states'.[13] Even more alarmingly, Patiala was not alone in suddenly taking this stand.

Hyderabad was also cooling to the idea of federation, as were smaller states like Rewa, Dholpur, Rampur and Bahawalpur.[14] How, they wondered, would they survive as independent polities? How would a federation chamber encompass over five hundred princely states?

Patiala, his ears pricked to these concerns, decided the time was ripe to lay out an alternative scheme. The timing was certainly not the greatest, but to be fair to Bhupinder Singh, this was not an 'electioneering stunt', as Bikaner scornfully described it.[15] He had read Scott's memo and he feared the lack of safeguards for the princes and what that meant, given the trajectory of the nationalist movement. Displaying uncharacteristic thoroughness, Patiala even wrote to senior Congress leaders to find out what they thought of it all. He was told unequivocally that the princes' participation in an all India federation, along the lines of what had been proposed in London, was not in national interest.[16]

Patiala knew it was now or never. His draft on the subject makes for masterful reading. It draws on Australian and Canadian precedents (with a dash of German jurisprudence) to argue that federation would limit internal autonomy, extinguish international rights and subvert the existent autonomy of the states. In Patiala's opinion, a confederal scheme was the perfect alternative to this knotty problem. His new plan suggested that states would first enter a union with *each other*, before entering an agreement with British India. This way, Patiala argued persuasively, 'It will be a case of two interests seeking a relationship for the settlement of questions of joint interest and simultaneously preserving their internal sovereignty.'[17]

To be sure, the note is vague on the legal specifics. Patiala wasn't aiming for constitutional brilliance. He pegged his idea on the loose idea of equality between British India and the union of states, an idea inspired from the principles of the League of Nations whose meetings he had attended as an Indian representative. As with the federal scheme, this new plan revolved not just around the principle of sovereignty, but how that sovereignty would be implemented and how it would feature in bilateral relations with British India. He refuted the assertion that federation would limit British interference in the states' affairs while permitting the states to participate in decision making on issues of common concern. In short, federation, he concluded was 'fraught with the greatest dangers'.[18] It was an undoubted crisis in the ranks.

Confederation was a curveball that no federal supporter had been expecting. Haksar was incensed, calling the Maharaja of Patiala a 'tool of the Political Department' in a furious letter to Tej Bahadur Sapru.[19] Given that he had been at the forefront of the frantic lobbying and ceaseless diplomacy that it had taken to persuade everyone to come on board the federal bandwagon, Haksar's rage was not surprising. He ranted at length to Sapru, calling confederation 'idiotic' and 'manifestly absurd'.[20]

On the whole, the summer of 1931 was a fraught one, irrespective of whether you were a politician, a prince or a stressed advisor. Many saw Patiala's sudden volte-face as an attempt to sabotage federation. Others saw it as the wiles of the political department, attempting to keep the states under their control.[21] Then there were those like Nehru, to whom Patiala had written, asking for his opinion on federation, and who wrote back, saying that federation would only be acceptable if it took the form of a union of peoples based on democratic principles.[22] From yet other corners, there were whispers of Patiala having been influenced by the forthright Dewan of Bhavnagar, Sir Prabhashankar Pattani.

A farsighted man with a magnificent beard and a keen eye for economics, Pattani was one of the first prime ministers of a princely state to write off debts for the state's beleaguered peasants. He was a skilled administrator as well and to be fair to both Patiala and Dholpur (the maharaja's lead henchman), Pattani had recommended confederation at the first Round Table Conference on the grounds that it would enable the states to 'perpetuate' their existence as a collective body. If, Pattani argued in a note he sent to the viceroy, the states had to federate individually, it would only result in the individual state being 'swallowed up'.[23]

Pattani was known to work for the underdog, and it wasn't surprising that the smaller states (like Sangli and Sarila) were greatly swayed by this. These smaller states were painfully aware of the fact that, given their size, they would never gain individual representation in an all-India federation. Confederation, for them, seemed to be the most feasible plan to continue their existence. Seeing the support Pattani's ideas were getting, word was that Patiala had thrown in his lot with the Dewan of Bhavnagar. Whatever the truth, the floating of the confederal scheme was a mark of not just political and constitutional fluidity, but just how much political and constitutional milestones could turn on a dime purely because of ego and personalities.

Supporters of federation continued to try and persuade the nay-sayers and sudden ditherers. Hamidullah Khan was nearly frantic, trying to reassure his brother princes that far from constraining them, the federal scheme would secure their sovereign rights and would guarantee that 'British India and the States will be co-equal partners and the present position in which the States are placed in practical subordination to the present Government of India would cease'.[24] Likewise, Ganga Singh of Bikaner did his best to explain to anyone who would listen that in no way would princely rights or equality be limited. His prime minister, Manubhai Mehta, agreed. 'Federation,' he said righteously, 'would prick the bubble of undefined paramountcy.'[25]

Hamidullah Khan and Panikkar would have to work fast if they were to counter Patiala's confederal plan, which was getting an uncomfortably wide support base. As one of the main players on the constitutional stage at this point, Panikkar's role was key. Yet his memoir oddly makes no mention of the scale and scope of the crisis that would eventually upend federation forever.

These were months when Panikkar was almost never at home. He left very early in the morning and was awake long into the nights, writing and rewriting drafts and clauses. Even through this, he always had time for little Haima and ensured that he came home during lunch hours to eat with Gouri. There was nothing he enjoyed more than a good Malayali lunch and a cup of filter coffee before leaving for work again, though Gouri was beginning to try her hand at other cuisines. Nor did he cease his writing on the academic and literary fronts.

Malabar and the Dutch was published in 1931, in between Panikkar's bureaucratic swordplay in the Chamber of Princes. The book continues exploring the themes that Panikkar had picked up in his book on the Portuguese, although the Dutch are receive a less abrasive treatment. Panikkar's thesis is that these were essentially merchants in possession of far less than Portugal or Britain. Their invasion was less aggressive than that of the Portuguese, and they certainly contributed to the development of Malabar. But Panikkar doesn't shy away from holding the Zamorin—such a hero in *Malabar and the Portuguese*—responsible for betraying the national cause.

In all these works of history that he was producing now, spanning Kashmir to modern Kerala, Panikkar seems to be searching for a more coherent understanding of the Indian nation. His experience with different aspects of political and public life had revealed to him that there were several forces at play, not all of which even he could understand.

In Oxford and Paris, he had subscribed to the 'Greater India' school of thought. It had seemed the right answer for a lot of questions then. But now, just a handful of years after Paris, India was changing yet again, and there were different questions to answer. How did one fit princely states into a single Indian union? How did one explain the existence of so many languages, histories and religions within one geographical body? How did India currently define itself in a world dominated by empire? How did it bridge its storied past to its present? Where did his own state stand in all of this?

To the end of his days, Panikkar was profoundly influenced by the fact that he came from a coastal state, a peripheral state (given its place on the map) and one that was going through a time of profound social and political change.

All of these inner duels reflected in his writing, in the themes and subjects he chose to write about. It also reflected in his personal emphasis on continuing to study and write in Malayalam, in encouraging his wife and children to read the classics in the vernacular in which they were written, and never forgetting the customs and traditions of India, no matter where they lived in the world. All the Panikkar children were trained in ancient Indian root languages, encouraged to read the scriptures and classics, and constantly engaged in intellectual debates. So thoroughly was Devaki, for instance, trained by her father in the classics that when she was a young girl, she could recite a chosen text backwards.[26]

At home, meanwhile, the happy times were coming to an end. Their youngest and last daughter, Radha (known to her family as 'Chhoti'), was born in Bhopal during the autumn of 1931—a time of joy and bonding between Gouri and Panikkar that wasn't to last. Nobody knows how Gouri found out about Juliette Veilliers-Duray and how deeply Panikkar had been involved with her in Paris, but the resulting quarrel was legendary.

Panikkar discovered that his cheerful little wife had a blazing temper and was unafraid to pull her punches. 'That French woman' would always be a reference point in the more serious of their quarrels. There seems to have been a son born of that involvement, though how Gouri discovered that, or if Panikkar supported that child, or indeed, if there *was* a child at all is lost to posterity.[27] For Gouri, the wound cut deep and it marked yet another turning point in her life.

As strong as she was feisty, Gouri now sought complete independence. She would never stray from the marriage herself, nor change how she conducted herself as a good wife and mother. But in between taking care of Radha and Haima, she began to channel more and more energy into building herself up, into making herself into an almost new woman. New hobbies came into being, including (rather extraordinarily) carpentry, which she continued to persist with until the end of her days. Gouri began smoking at this time as well, buying herself a long cigarette-holder, which was all the fashion in those days. She also began to pay attention to fashion, taking to wearing beautiful sarees in strong jewel colours and buying herself sunglasses to wear during lunches outside.

If Panikkar was remorseful or repentant, we do not know. But he threw himself almost entirely into work. While we cannot know if it was an emotional reaction, it certainly was a necessary one. Things were moving far too fast on the princely front. Ahead of the meeting of the chamber in Bombay at the end of June, the Nawab of Rampur denounced federation. He was followed quickly by Bahawalpur, Limbdi, Sachin, Cutch, Indore, Bhavnagar and Talcher (on behalf of the Orissa states). With Panikkar's help, Hamidullah put out a statement, reassuring the princes that the federal scheme would secure the rights of their states and guarantee equality.[28] It was of little use. On the opening day of the Bombay session, Bhopal and Bikaner were heckled viciously, while Patiala looked on smugly.

Panikkar, meanwhile, put his pen to work and wrote a confidential memo entitled *An Alternative Scheme*, in which he explained that the failure of the federal project would leave the content and spirit of the treaties with the British as the only basis for princely claims. This would not stop the gradual ceding of powers to British India, he warned. The princes would only be able to safeguard those rights that were explicitly enshrined in the treaties.[29]

Eventually, the idea was put to the vote. Within minutes, Panikkar and Bhopal could breathe easy. Despite the support of nearly thirty states, Patiala was outvoted at a conference of the Chamber of Princes in Bombay in the sticky summer of 1931.[30]

The only way out was now to cross the seas once again for the Second Round Table Conference in London. 'The real trouble is,' Willingdon wrote in a grumpy letter to his son, 'Gandhi looks upon himself as equal and parallel with me, in working the administration of the country.'[31] The new viceroy was, as the historian Patrick French describes him, 'a standard-issue, top-ranking bureaucrat', who liked to do things by the book.[32] But though he had arrived in India just when the country's political trajectory was poised on the edge of a constitutional precipice, even Willingdon had to admit that Gandhi's self-assurance was 'not without reason'.[33]

Aboard the *SS Rajputana*, the Mahatma sailed for London at the end of August at the Dewan of Bhavnagar Prabhashankar Pattani's urging. 'I know this conference might not be successful. But your going there will not be futile as you can share details about the current state of affairs in India.' Whether anyone would be listening was another matter. Still, a motley crew was assembled to make sure that the stage looked presentable for this second round of talks.

On their way to London was the usual selection of Sikh politicians, Muslim League representatives, British officials and princely advisors. Gandhi's own entourage was larger than everyone else's, spanning his secretaries Pyarelal and Mahadev Desai, his financier G.D. Birla, the faithful Mirabehn and various other admirers. Among the princes, Patiala, Palam, Holkar and Dholpur formed the confederationist band, looking eagerly forward to presenting their ideas to the India Office. So many different interests at play, yet a look at the archival correspondence between Delhi and London and between both English and Indian bureaucrats highlights a single common factor: deep despair over rising communalism. In principle, the first Round Table had opened the doors to further negotiations, but communal deadlock, India's economic and commercial importance for the empire, as well as changing political leanings in Britain made it easy to stall talks on constitutional reform. In an India Office note, Benn confirmed what Panikkar had told Stopford in 1930 that the major problem facing this particular Round Table was not the princely states or even the federal question, but the communal issue.[34]

Gandhi's own potential as a negotiator was straitjacketed by the tight remit he had been given before his departure by the Congress Working Committee, which insisted on purna swaraj. He was further hampered by the presence of Dr Bhimrao Ramji Ambedkar. A Mahar untouchable by birth, the balding, bespectacled Ambedkar had been educated both in the trenches of poverty and in some of the best universities of the world. Brilliant, forceful and forthright, this was a man unafraid of taking on either privilege or power. He had been at the first Round Table Conference as well, to present his views on the Dalits and their position in Indian politics and society. But it was in August 1931 that Gandhi encountered Ambedkar for the first time, setting in motion one of the greatest political rivalries of pre-independent India. That rivalry accompanied them overseas to London, where their angry and eloquent ripostes on caste and untouchability brought the Second Round Table Conference to an absolute impasse.

On the sidelines of this drama were the princes. 'The problem as such is not that of the Indian states,' Nehru had told Patiala caustically. 'The problem is with the Indian princes.'[35] To the advisors and ministers desperately trying to salvage federation from the sinking constitutional ship, Nehru's words would have rung bitterly true.

Anyone reading through the vast archive of material that forms the foundation of the constitutional debates of the 1920s and 1930s may justifiably be both staggered and bewildered at the technicality and minuteness of the details involved. In essence though, the real duel was simple. The federal lobby wanted to establish greater legal protections for the states in a written constitution, a stronger judicial process and distance from the Crown. The confederal lobby wanted a closer relationship with the Crown.

On 30 November 1931, the Prime Minister of Patiala, Sir Liaqat Hayat Khan, along with Pattani, the flamboyant Yashwantrao Holkar of Indore and Udaibhan Singh of Dholpur, presented a detailed version of Bhupinder Singh's confederal proposal. The scheme proposed that the states first constitute themselves into a single unit, which would then collectively federate with British India 'for purposes of specific matters of common interest only'.[36] The plan pushed for a constitution that provided for the 'maintenance and preservation of the traditional and time-honoured relations between the States and the British Crown'.[37]

Gandhi promptly threw a spanner in the works. He explained that, from the Congress's point of view, the accession of the states to a federation should be made conditional first upon a guarantee being given of the fundamental rights of their subjects, safeguarded by a supreme court, and secondly, the representation of the states in the federal legislatures on an elective basis. However, if the princes chose not to accept these terms, Gandhi went on, 'we suggest that the consideration of the question of the States be postponed for the moment and the future of what is known as British India may be discussed with the British Government … In case a settlement is reached between British India and the British Government, the question of the States can be taken up afresh.'[38]

Unsurprisingly, the princes refused to even consider such a thing and though Gandhi sensibly didn't push the matter, the ensuing weeks in London were a nightmare for Panikkar as he tried to pull his delegation towards finding some kind of workable midway.

This was easier said than done.

Against the princely delegation's wishes, the Federal Structure Committee decided for a moderately sized upper house of 200, with only 40 per cent of the seats reserved for the states. There was an uproar, with the Raja of Morvi registering his alarm to Sankey in a personal cable and cries of outrage from Udaipur, Lunawada, Cambay and Dharampur. Much of the princes' future, particularly their financial prospects, was left vague. As Robert Stopford put it, 'British India is asking the States to take a leap in the dark.'[39]

Not surprisingly, the states had no desire to do any such thing.

As the arguments against federation began to stack up, prince after prince moved into the confederal camp, including Kolhapur and the big Rajputana states of Udaipur, Jodhpur and Jaipur. States such as Hyderabad, Mysore, Baroda and Gwalior remained ambivalent, splitting the princely order down the middle.[40]

Meanwhile, Patiala was putting his undoubted influence over his fellow princes to work. Support was canvassed regularly and weekly bulletins were sent out to encourage dithering states. Hamidullah, a young chancellor with no experience of the chamber's politics and no time to accumulate the kind of respect his mother had commanded, was at a loss. Even Ganga Singh, that redoubtable maharaja, was beginning to doubt whether they would ever succeed at selling federation. 'The split among the princes was weakening the position … at the Second Round Table Conference,' Panikkar noted despairingly.[41] Something needed to be done quickly.

Pulling all his negotiating experience from Amritsar to the fore, Panikkar sought out the prime minister of Patiala, Liaqat Hayat Khan. The son of a Punjabi police officer and elder brother to the brilliant Unionist Party leader Sikander Hayat, Liaqat was at the peak of his career at the time. He was adept at crisis management (an excellent skill to have when serving Bhupinder Singh) and was a superb administrator, known for his patient diplomacy and his superbly curled moustache. So excellent was he that he had often been lured by offers of higher pay and rich treasures by Patiala's fellow princes. But Liaqat was a faithful man and he served the maharaja until the end of Bhupinder Singh's days. He was also a staunch federationist, as Panikkar knew, and though he had been forced to present the confederal plan out of loyalty, he was secretly and bitterly against what Patiala was trying to do. There was, in Panikkar's mind, nobody better to turn to for help.

His talks with Liaqat were predictably successful since the prime minister needed no real convincing. The two men decided that what was needed at this moment was a 'committee of umpires'[42] to mediate between the rival camps. Sir C.P. Ramaswami Aiyar was named the chairman of this committee and its members were Sir Akbar Rao Hydari, K.N. Haksar, Manubhai Mehta, the Yuvaraja of Limbdi, Liaqat himself and Panikkar. Having decided their course of action, there was nothing to do but to wait until they got back to India to bring their royal masters around.

In the winter of 1931, a depressed Indian delegation was back on home soil. Gandhi had returned with nothing to offer those awaiting him at home. Worse, his political standing had taken a hit thanks to Ambedkar's brilliance. Now there were only more questions than answers. What should be done about the question of politically protecting and representing the Dalits? It was a fresh and uncomfortable perspective for the nationalist elite, and as national leaders wondered what to do, Dalits across the country united to lobby for their rights. The Raj was ready this time.

It might not have foreseen Ambedkar bringing the Second Round Table to a halt, but it had prepared for Gandhi's old tactics of resorting to mass struggle in the face of repression. In no way could it allow Gandhi to be set up as a rival to its authority. Quietly, the Government of India began to prepare plans for martial laws to crack down against the slightest sign of protest. In a few days, it had reason to put the plans into action. The Congress launched a no-rent, no-revenue campaign in five districts in the first week of December. The government hit back sharply, arresting Jawaharlal Nehru and Khan Abdul Ghaffar Khan. On 31 December, Gandhi asked Willingdon if they could meet and talk. The offer was rebuffed—the first of many such rebuffs over the next five years. A week after, as the new year dawned, Gandhi was arrested. Willingdon was taking no chances. Using the ordinances it had recently drafted, the Government of India outlawed the working structures of the Congress and arrested its leaders once more.

A dangerous stand-off had been reached.

Chapter 24

Middle Ground

THE YEAR 1932 WAS ONE OF DAMAGE CONTROL—AND OF GREAT DAMAGE as well. Gandhi began it behind bars in Yeravada jail, where he was ministered to affectionately by Sardar Vallabhbhai Patel (the new Congress president) and his special concoctions of baking soda, lime, honey and warm water. Outside the walls of the prison, Indians were furious at this cavalier treatment of their political leaders. In the first four months of the new year, over 80,000 Indians were jailed, while lakhs took to the streets, picketing shops selling liquor or foreign cloth. Non-violent or violent, each protest met with the same reaction: brutal repression. Nearly every Gandhian ashram was occupied by the police. Peaceful protesters were lathi-charged or beaten. Prisoners in jail were either shot or tortured. Whipping became an almost mundane form of punishment. No-tax campaigns in rural India were met with confiscations of property. The press was gagged and any kind of writing that was seen to be 'nationalist' was banned outright. It was too harsh a crackdown to endure for long. As monsoon clouds rolled over the country, the pushback against the Raj began to fizzle out in despair.

It is remarkable to think of debates on federation and confederation continuing apace against this turbulent backdrop, but that is what was happening both within the walls of the Chamber of Princes and overseas in the India Office. Patiala had been stymied in his efforts for now by Panikkar's skilful backchannel diplomacy. Nothing could succeed, as he well knew, without the support of big states like Mysore and Travancore, and those eluded the frustrated Bhupinder Singh.

Some time had been bought, but it was not enough.

For the India Office, the series of royal defections from the federal idea had been highly disturbing. In October 1931, the Conservatives romped to power in the general elections in England. For the Tories, there *had* to be federation in India—and with heavy princely participation at that.[1]

Samuel Hoare, the new secretary of state for India, was distinctly agitated. 'On no account must the Princes be allowed to give a negative to All-India Federation,' he wrote frantically to Lord Lothian, who was sailing for India as the head of the Franchise Committee. 'If they say no, all the fat in the world will be in the fire here.'[2]

Unfortunately for Hoare, the fat was already merrily crackling in the fire. In the spring of 1932, the princely order was staring down the barrel of an existential crisis, one that seemed far removed from the happenings across the country. The 'committee of umpires' met to try and devise a way forward as soon as they were back in India and several convoluted plans were drawn up. One of them, drafted by Panikkar, ran along the lines of a federation of the provinces of British India that would be joined by a confederation of princely states. Panikkar added that the two parties would then merge into a single entity with limited powers concerning only a few defined subjects, with federal legislation being ratified by individual states. The latter would collectively elect their representatives to the federal parliament. Their subjects would not acquire a new federal citizenship.[3] Ideas like this were tossed back and forth between the princes and their advisors throughout February until finally, an exhausted compromise was hammered out. On 11 March 1932, at a meeting at Patiala's residence in Delhi, Bikaner, Bhopal and Patiala came face to face for the first time since their fracas had broken out.

For a moment, there was an awkward silence.

Then Ganga Singh stepped forward and embraced Patiala. 'My dearest bhai,' he said emotionally. Always a lover of good drama, Bhupinder Singh bent to touch Bikaner's feet, ready tears in his eyes. With harmony temporarily restored, the three rulers agreed to the distribution of posts in the Chamber of Princes and set up a committee of princes, which Panikkar joined, to reconcile the federal and confederal projects as much as possible. This committee was headed by Sir C.P. Ramaswami Aiyar (and immediately became popularly known as the Aiyar Committee) and would report on the feasibility of the confederation scheme and the safeguards needed to protect the states in a federation. The interests of the larger states were aligned with the fears of the smaller states in a wide institutional blueprint that merged confederation with the Federal Structure Committee's scheme, studded with safeguard clauses.[4] Panikkar and Haksar were violently opposed to this, but were voted down by those present. The Delhi Pact was formally signed on 1 April 1932 as a mark of the new-found solidarity around the idea of federation, in exchange for more guarantees of autonomy and protection of their rights and sovereignty.[5]

'The princes have nearly killed me with all the work they've given me,' Willingdon sighed to his son. 'But it's been worthwhile, for they are now definitely committed to Federation.'[6]

Were they though?

Legally, the Delhi Pact provided only a qualified endorsement of federation at best and an awkward mix of confederation and federation at worst. It was the same problem: a consensus about protecting sovereignty and wide rifts about *how* to do that. Richard Glancy at the India Office was more honest than the viceroy when he said, 'We are none of us, I should imagine, convinced that [federation] will work … but we … are pledged to try the experiment.'[7] For Panikkar, there were other problems. One of the conditions of the Delhi Pact was to opt, in cricketing terms, for a third umpire: a new chancellor who would take over from 1932 to 1933. That was, rather unfortunately for Panikkar, the Jam Sahib of Nawanagar. Even worse, Haksar had withdrawn his services and left for Gwalior shortly after the signing of the pact.

Panikkar was now very much on his own. Without friendship or support within the chamber, Panikkar 'realised early enough that the Jam Sahib … would … be in head-on conflict with me.'[8]

Sure enough, the Jam Sahib lost no time in breaking with the chamber's policies, denouncing federation as being dangerous to the states. His views were endorsed by a conference of some fifty Kathiawar princes who assembled at Rajkot that same month. Rushbrook-Williams came into play almost immediately as well: in both his roles, as the Jam's legal advisor and an agent (unknown to the Jam Sahib, of course) working for the Conservative cause in England. In a private letter to Hoare, Rushbrook-Williams explained with insidious clarity that the reason for the Jam's decision was that many of the smaller states had only just begun to realise that princes like Bikaner and Bhopal were unilaterally committing them to arrangements they wanted no part of. Federation, Rushbrook-Williams informed Hoare, would mean the extinction of the smaller states and they would naturally recoil from an 'embrace which they fear might be octopus-like in its effect on them'.[9]

He wasn't to know of course that Hoare was never going to agree to such a statement and that Bikaner had already been warned by British officials sympathetic to the chamber's worries that nothing could be more disastrous than even inadvertently letting anyone in Whitehall know that 'on the one hand, they were dilatory or on the other, that agreement between themselves is never likely to be reached'.[10]

Ranji and his foreign minister were abetted in their machinations by Leslie Scott, who explained conveniently that the safeguards the government planned to insert were likely to be 'paper safeguards only'. The only sure protection, Scott said, was 'an absolute right of appeal' against both the new federal government as well as the Crown.[11]

Emboldened by this, Rushbrook-Williams dashed off a circular that Nawanagar could put out, which stated that the princes 'were not willing to federate', irrespective of the new constitution, until the 'doctrine of paramountcy' was replaced by the doctrine of 'the sanctity of treaties'.[12]

Patiala and Bikaner were appalled at this letter. By now, nearly everyone knew that Nawanagar was being manipulated by his foreign minister and both Bikaner and Patiala implored the Jam Sahib not to be blinded by his own biases. Negotiations to redraft the letter failed and in August 1932, Nawanagar was taken aback to receive what he thought was a rude letter, signed by Bikaner and Bhopal, that warned him bluntly to have 'no truck' with the likes of Leslie Scott.[13]

The Jam Sahib was not a man who liked to be ordered about and he demanded that Rushbrook-Williams (who was only too happy to comply) put out yet another circular, reiterating his stand on paramountcy. Every member of the Chamber of Princes received it, as did the secretary of state for India and the viceroy.

Nobody was fooled.

'The Jam Sahib, I am afraid, has got into the hands of that horrid little fellow, Rushbrook-Williams,' remarked Willingdon wearily.[14]

Caught unawares by the suddenness of Nawanagar's actions, the Chamber of Princes went into damage control. Bikaner, Bhopal and Patiala hastened to reassure the viceroy that the Jam Sahib's stand had nothing to do with them. In London, ahead of the third Round Table, Panikkar issued an official press release outlining the official royal policy and refuting Nawanagar's position. With the authority of the chamber behind him, he included an official rebuke in the same press release.[15]

When the Jam Sahib read the curt statement in the newspapers, he was not only caught off guard but deeply embarrassed. The embarrassment found refuge in rage, the flames of which were fanned by Rushbrook-Williams who said with great saintliness that Panikkar had puppeteered the entire situation. Acting on blind instinct, Nawanagar summoned the secretary and subjected Panikkar to a blistering tongue-lashing that lasted for the better part of an hour, allowed not a word in edgewise and left the younger man seething with humiliated anger.

The showdown was the official end of relations between Nawanagar and Panikkar. For months afterwards, Panikkar couldn't bring himself to speak to the Jam Sahib.[16] But the events also put paid to Nawanagar's machinations at least for the time being. Under the laws of the chamber, the chancellor had to comply with the directives of the standing committee whether he liked it or not. He grudgingly agreed to issue no more startling circulars without the chamber's permission. In September 1932, Nawanagar departed London for the sunny beach town of Aix-les-Bains in the south of France, where he could lick his wounds in peace.

But it wasn't the end.

In the meanwhile, Panikkar's own thoughts were going through a rather radical transformation. Popular movements within the states were taking on a life of their own. The official position of the Congress party was still one of non-intervention, but there was no doubt that the national movement was beginning to affect the internal politics of the princely states. Panikkar was aware that the newer and younger leaders of the Congress were critical of princely autocracy. Taken together, it was clear that, not just the politicians of British India, but the people of the princely states themselves were becoming players in the political game.

As was his nature, Panikkar turned back to studying the situation as he found it. That year, he published *Indian States and the Government of India*, a revised and expanded version of *Federal India*. The revised text highlighted the shift in his thinking. He now represented public and popular opinion within the states as a pivotal catalyst. Citizens of these princely states now saw themselves as citizens of India. To Panikkar, this was a momentous change, because the states could no longer project themselves as separate entities. They were part of British India and had to see themselves as such. That was, after all, why popular movements were spreading so fast within their borders. Democracy was now a vital part of constitutional and political progress.[17]

Yet another factor to consider was indubitably caste, particularly the protection of the marginalised and oppressed. Ambedkar had made that clear in his representations at the first two Round Tables. However, thanks to Gandhi's time-honoured tactic of fasting unto death, he was forced to sign the Poona Pact in September 1932, which provided for reservations in joint electorates rather than the separate electorates that Ambedkar had called for—a decision he would regret and resent for the rest of his life.

As always, Panikkar's keen observations of what he was living through at the time influenced his non-fiction. In *Indian States and the Government of India*, he writes of how the Raj had achieved the oddly ironic result of unifying the citizens of India against its existence.

The balance had thus shifted significantly and now federation was also described as a way of responding to the demand for political unification by the peoples of the states. It was yet another mark of his changing views.

He was also writing widely in Malayalam at this point. Between 1929 and 1932, he wrote two novels, *Dhumakethuvinte Udayam* and *Parangkipadayali*, as well as a plethora of poems. When it came to poetry, Panikkar was not, according to the diplomat A.K. Damodaran, a poet per se, but a 'versifier'[18] In this role he was seminal, for he represented the personification of the crossroads between the 'old verse means of communication and the new prose means of communication'.[19] As a result, he was able to bring a new depth and meaning to Malayalam poetry, which made him a pioneer in the field. 'There is hardly any branch—except Kathakali, I think—in Malayalam Literature to which Panikkar has not made a contribution,' wrote Dr C. Achutha Menon, head of the department of Malayalam at the University of Madras and himself an eminent writer. 'Fiction, poetry, short story, criticism, drama, farce, champu, *Sandesakavya*—in all these Mr. Panikkar is equally at ease.'

To go into Panikkar's literary achievements in Malayalam is to write wholly another book, and for the sake of space, comprehension and sanity, this book will refrain from doing so. But it *is* important to acknowledge that at the heart of both poetry and prose, his themes are common: history, Malabar and love. Panikkar is at his emotional and eloquent best when he is describing his home, or when he writes of love as a tender emotion that can lift one to untouched heights just as easily as it can shatter a heart to pieces. A look at his literary career is always a mirror to the facets of Panikkar's personality that he kept hidden from his political life. Here, he gave free rein to the gentler side of him, to the humour and the 'naughty little imp',[20] as Damodaran characterised it, in his nature.

Many of his literary achievements run hand in hand with important moments in his personal life. At this point, in the early 1930s, it was the rocky stretch in his marriage. To the outside world, there was no hint of the troubles behind the scenes. Both husband and wife continued to attend social scenes as vivaciously as they had always done. But Panikkar *was* under great stress both at home and at work during this time. The fight for constitutional reform, he knew, had just begun.

It would continue for years to come.

CHAPTER 25

'In Spite of the Attitude of Some of Our Friends'

THE VICEROY WAS ANNOYED.

Willingdon was no fan of the princes and he was irritated at how easily the chamber had made its endorsement of federation conditional upon a list of safeguards. Over the years, he had become a reluctant convert to the idea of federation, but as the months progressed, it became clear to Willingdon that Conservative political opinion in Britain would not tolerate the question of constitutional progress in India without federation. As a result, when he met the princes informally in September 1932, he was of the distinct opinion that 'too rigid a definition of paramountcy' would only weaken the Crown's ability to 'protect the States'.[1] Their best hope, he told them sanctimoniously, was 'the personal discretion of the Viceroy'.[2]

This was a profoundly sketchy assurance, since Willingdon had begun (rather foolishly) to meddle behind the scenes to 'break up the Bikaner Party'.[3] The viceroy stitched together a band of rulers from 'the states that really count'[4] (Mysore, Hyderabad and Travancore among them) to see if they could form a counterweight to the rest of the chamber. Given the indecision prevailing in the chamber, this transparently underhanded strategy worked.

At a summit in Simla between the viceroy and the Standing Committee of the Chamber of Princes, Hydari said Hyderabad wanted paramountcy to remain uppermost. Hamidullah Khan, listening to this speech in growing disbelief, jumped up to ask, 'Does this mean that the Nizam accepts the propositions contained in the Viceroy's letter of 1926?' Hydari flushed hotly, muttering something about 'certain unfortunate generalities'. It was clear that Bhopal had caught him off guard for it took him a full ten minutes to recover enough to state, in a rather high-pitched voice, 'Hyderabad does not accept Lord Reading's letter.'

A low ripple of laughter ran through the assembly, and though Hydari said little for the rest of the day, his expression was black. But Willingdon had set the cat among the pigeons. Others soon picked up on Hydari's main points, with Rewa's Gulab Singh unctuously saying that what really mattered in politics was the 'human touch'.[5] It was a summit wracked with disagreements and coldly personal sniping, so much so that towards the end of it, Hyderabad's Mehdi Yar Jung, a minister in the Nizam's government, leaned across to murmur mockingly to Panikkar, 'This … might be considered to be the funeral of the Chamber of Princes.'[6]

On the last day, Hamidullah Khan informed the viceroy angrily that the princes would no longer hear of federation without a satisfactory understanding of paramountcy. In the closing of an ironic circle, matters had come back to Nawanagar's position when he had been chancellor. Recognising danger, Hoare cabled Willingdon frantically, asking him to mend bridges immediately.

But it was too late.

At the end of 1932, the final session of the Round Table Conferences kicked off in London. It was a draggled end to what should have been an excellent beginning to India's constitutional progress. The princes were once again on the backfoot, though their advisors, led from the fore by the loyal Liaqat Hayat Khan, did their best to promote the safeguards they had agreed upon. Khan and his colleague, Sir Manubhai Mehta, did excellent work in a difficult situation, managing 'in spite of the attitude of some our friends',[7] to get the Delhi Pact adopted as a common basis for negotiation by the princely team. They made some headway in gaining official backing for confederation, and managed to wrangle several important financial concessions and a decision that the states should not be liable for direct federal taxation. All in all, they played a good game, but much of their victory was rendered void by the reappearance on the scene of the Jam Sahib.

Asserting his rights as chancellor, Nawanagar lost no time in wreaking havoc on any progress that had been made until then. He took over the meetings at the Metropole Hotel and invited Leslie Scott to attend as an observer (in deliberate defiance of the standing committee's instructions that he have nothing to do with Scott).[8] Nawanagar repeatedly pressed for an ultimatum on paramountcy. He got exactly nowhere with all this posturing, but for the rest of the chamber, it created hurdles so insuperable that eventually, minister after minister began meeting each other separately.

In December, Nawanagar delivered another bombshell when he gave an interview to Reuters in which he recited the lines given to him by Rushbrook-Williams and Scott: 'The states' best defence against the dangers of aggressive democratisation by British India inside the federation, lie in the united abstention of all.'[9] He followed up this staggering statement by writing to the standing committee, asking to be released from his mandate to support the Delhi Pact. It was a rebellion everyone could have done without, considering that Nawanagar had immense influence within the chamber. Weeks after his revolt, forty Kathiawar rulers voted at Jamnagar to reject federation.

There was nothing anyone could do but wait for the British government to release its white paper on reforms for the princes and hope that no revenge would be taken therein. As the chamber held its breath, Sir C.P. Ramaswami Aiyar came to see Panikkar.

There was worse trouble afoot.

According to Aiyar, the Jam Sahib had just returned from a hunting trip with the viceroy, during which he had made it clear that, as long as Panikkar continued in his position as the secretary of the Chamber of Princes, there would be no accord within the princely order. 'It was clear that the Jam Sahib's wrath would only be quenched with my dismissal,' Panikkar would write later.[10] It was not a comforting thing to look forward to upon return to India.

To distract his mind from spiralling into anxiety, Panikkar began to toy with the idea of another novel. Every morning, he would sit at his desk at home for an hour before the day began. He knew that the heart of this as yet untitled novel would be a love story, but he was undecided about the period. One morning, as he sat at breakfast with his daughter Parvathy, then home from school, he asked her what period he should set his new novel in. She replied that it should be set during the reign of the Mughals. And so, *Kalyana Mal*—the love story of a young Rajput couple and the rivalry of a Mughal princess in the court of Akbar—came to be written. It was published in 1934, but it was written during that spring of high tension when Panikkar was wondering whether he would lose his career.

When the white paper was eventually published, the chamber heaved a sigh of relief. It was a substantial improvement on the conference drafts. First, it raised the states' share in the upper house to 100, a number that guaranteed most medium-sized states an individual place. Second, it confined the states' fiscal responsibilities to the payment of corporation tax, phased in over ten years. Third, it handed powers of protection to a governor-general in the event a state was threatened by the federation. Fourth, it excised all mention of fundamental rights on the plea that a federal constitution should be a compact between units rather than ruler and subject.

Reading through the changes, Liaqat and Mehta were pleased. There would be no better outcome than this and given the way the national movement was going, the states would do well to take a realistic view of the future. In their report to the standing committee, they strongly urged the princes to accept the white paper.

Haughtily dismissing the white paper on the grounds that it delivered none of the safeguards considered essential, Nawanagar wrote that he could 'not advise our Order to join an All-India Federation'.[11]

The Chamber of Princes was set for another stormy spring session.

A week before the chamber was due to sit in March 1933, Nawanagar sent a confidential circular to the members of the Aiyar

Committee, proposing Panikkar's immediate removal from the post of secretary. In his memoir, Panikkar wrote coyly that he had only a 'rough idea' of what was afoot, but truth be told, he had plenty of willing informants within the chamber.[12] He was perfectly aware, for instance, that Rushbrook-Williams, Patiala's foreign minister Maqbool Mohammad and Baroda's dewan D. Madhava Rao ('who were not even on speaking terms!' Panikkar expostulated indignantly later) had joined forces against him.

The influence of 'the three evil planets', as Panikkar called them, was widespread and malevolent, but Panikkar had little idea of how to counter them. Haksar was still in Gwalior, though he wrote angrily to Sapru that 'Rushbrook-Williams is responsible for much mischief!'[13] Panikkar's old friend V.T. Krishnamachari was unavailable for comment. Even the maharajas of Patiala, Bikaner and others usually friendly to him 'appeared for some reason to have temporarily deserted me!'[14] Eventually, the Aiyar Committee put on the brakes, despite heavy pressure from Nawanagar. They would not sack Panikkar, they said firmly, unless there was definite proof of his working against the welfare of the princes.

Furious, Nawanagar turned to his cousin Panna, pulling him in to lobby the members of the committee before the chamber opened for business. Panna did so, pleading that Panikkar needed to be dismissed, 'otherwise the Jam Sahib would be disgraced'.[15]

Pressurised beyond tolerance, prince after prince agreed, and eventually word reached Panikkar that, at the next meeting of the chamber, he would be sacked.

He was in despair. Months of his life had been spent in pulling princely egos together, in drafting and redrafting the concepts of federation for India's constitutional progress. Had it all been for nothing?

A week before the chamber was due to sit in judgement on his career, Patiala came to see him. It wasn't the first time the two men had spoken of course, but on this occasion, Panikkar was struck anew by Patiala's handsomeness and height. 'The poet's description of Duryodhana—"in looks and hauteur, the equal of Indra"—might have been written of Bhupendra Singh.'[16]

Patiala sat down, light glinting off the diamond buttons on his coat. His pleasant, rather jowly face was serious. Bhopal had dropped out of the forthcoming meeting, Patiala said quietly, citing a toothache. Bikaner was miraculously also ill with a stomach ache. Kutch (who was Bikaner's uncle) had sent a polite message, saying he had been unfortunately called away on business. But even with these three major dropouts, nothing could be done.

Panikkar would be sacked.

Shame and rage washed over Panikkar. He had found a career that had showed him the kind of potential no other avenue had. And this was how it would end—through the wily, wicked machinations of a ruler who despised him.

Silently, he bowed to the Maharaja of Patiala. There was nothing else to be said.

The events of that year's session of the Chamber of Princes would stay in the minds of every ruler and minister who was present. The first shock came on the penultimate day of the session when the Jam Sahib stood up to read a text penned for him by Rushbrook-Williams.

He went off script instead, in a wild attack on federation, describing it as 'dangerous to the states and the British connection'. As his brother princes gaped at him, Nawanagar turned to the white paper and proceeded to verbally tear it apart. 'For my own part, I feel that it is very unfortunate that the realisation of British Indian political ambitions should have been made contingent upon the acceptance of a particular type of federation by the Indian states, and I do not see that there is any logical connection between these two matters ... I cannot help feeling that the constitution, as it has emerged from the white paper, will inevitably work as to destroy the very principle of Indian kingship.'[17] At that moment, the viceroy interrupted. Willingdon knew perfectly well that Nawanagar's words were not his own, but those of that 'damned little scoundrel, Rushbrook-Williams',[18] but he couldn't bear to hear anymore.

'You are out of order, sir!' he thundered, rising to his full height.

There was sudden, deafening silence.

Never in the chamber's history had any viceroy publicly castigated its chancellor. It was a brutal display of power and reduced any pretence of parity between the Crown and the rulers to ashes. Under Willingdon's blazing eye, the colour drained from Nawanagar's cheeks. Slowly, he crumpled back into his seat, folding up his papers.

He said nothing for the rest of the day, his face pallid, staring blankly ahead of him as the chamber stumbled through its day's agenda. The Jam Sahib would never recover from the blow to his honour and his biographer would attribute the cause of his death (which was to occur in just under two weeks) to a broken heart.[19]

Despite the viceroy's crude intervention, however, the seeds of doubt had been sown and they didn't take long to flower. Patiala was the first to stop short of endorsing the white paper. There was a need, he felt, for further safeguards. Most of the princes who spoke after him said the same thing.

Which way this would have gone is anyone's guess, but on 26 March, Nawanagar decided to make one last strike, despite being obviously unwell. This time, he chose Panikkar as his very public target. Using the budget debate, the Jam Sahib accused Panikkar of disloyalty, graft and financial mismanagement. Whatever Panikkar had been expecting, it was not this.

He was not a corrupt man by any stretch of the imagination, much as he enjoyed the finer ways of living that his work afforded him. He watched aghast as a chorus of cheers erupted from the floor of the chamber in support of the Jam Sahib. Patiala surged to his feet, his diamonds winking brightly under the lights, shouting in favour of Panikkar. But for once, even the powerful Patiala was ignored.

As the chamber broke for lunch, Nawanagar looked at Panikkar in the eye. 'You are dismissed,' he said curtly.

There was not a man present who was not shaken by the morning's events. Hastily, the standing committee, working through lunch, put together a resolution commending the general thrust of the white paper but tying the entry of the states to the 'inclusion in the Constitution and treaties of accession of essential safeguards'.[20] The Nawanagar camp had one last trump card, moving another amendment which made accession to federation on condition of an equitable and satisfactory settlement of paramountcy.[21] The Jam

Sahib pushed both amendments through, ruling that they were not contradictory.

It was his last act as chancellor.

The morning of 29 March 1933 dawned bright and sunny, with a sky cloudlessly blue. Panikkar awoke and dressed for the day, his jaw set. There was nothing left to lose now. So far, he had tried and failed to sustain a grand total of three different careers—as a teaching academic, as a journalist, and now, as a legal advisor to the princely states.

Any semblance of a reputation would be shattered today.

Leaving his breakfast uneaten, he went straight to the chamber, where the princes were gathering slowly. That morning's work was simple since everyone was now just going through the motions: to elect a new chancellor and to sack the secretary.

The election of the chancellor was simple enough. The princes were tired of the haughty, truculent Jam Sahib. They wanted to give the charming Maharaja of Patiala another chance. Bhupinder Singh came in as chancellor with a sweeping majority, a welcome second chance after a first term that had nearly broken him. Panikkar, seated in front of him, turned around to say quietly, 'Congratulations, Your Highness.'

Patiala nodded graciously and leaned forward in his seat. 'I want to speak to you later, Panikkar,' he said, just as quietly. 'See me outside later.'

Puzzled but willing, Panikkar bowed his head.

When the chamber broke for lunch, Panikkar waited until the rest of the princes had filed out, then went to the empty corridor to await Bhupinder Singh. It wasn't long before the maharaja appeared. He no longer looked quite so careworn, a new air of confidence mantled him and his eyes twinkled.

'Ah, Panikkar,' he said affectionately, 'I have reappointed you as the secretary of the Chamber. At the meeting of the new executive this afternoon the earlier resolution will be revoked, but don't tell anyone just now.'[22]

Panikkar's jaw dropped.

Here it was—a new chance and the possibility of starting over, but more crudely, it was a chance 'to enjoy the discomfiture of my enemies'.[23] He knew perfectly well that Patiala, in keeping this piece of news a secret, was playing his own game. Later, he would write that Patiala's 'stratagem was not to allow me to go to Bikaner, but to draw me ultimately to Patiala and the offer to continue me as secretary to the Chamber was only a means to this end'.[24] Whatever the game was, Panikkar was ready to play yet another round.

At the end of the session, as he was packing away his papers and pen, a shadow fell across his desk. Looking up, he beheld Ganga Singh, the maharaja of Bikaner. He knew immediately what was coming—Bikaner would do anything to undermine Patiala. Panikkar was offered a job as dewan of Bikaner. It was a fine up-and-coming state, and to be fair to Ganga Singh, he had no idea that Patiala had asked Panikkar to stay. Politely but firmly, and much to Bikaner's shock, Panikkar refused the job offer.

He had made his own choice.

But he was not quite noble enough to rise above the satisfaction of taking a last (rather vicious) shot at the Jam Sahib. He checked his watch. It was five o'clock, and just about time for the train bound for Nawanagar to arrive. Panikkar picked up his bag and hastened to the railway station. As he had expected, the Jam Sahib was on the platform, chatting with Rushbrook-Williams and Prabhashankar Pattani. He smiled at Panikkar pleasantly. 'Well, Panikkar,' he said heartily, 'since we are both relinquishing our offices with the Chamber, there needs to be no disagreement between us hereafter.' Taking his cue from the Jam Sahib, Rushbrook-Williams stepped forward to shake hands with Panikkar.

Panikkar nodded and shook hands with everyone, then grinned cheerfully at the Jam Sahib.

'Your Highness is right as always,' he said sweetly. 'But while *you* are no longer the Chancellor, *I* have again been appointed Secretary.'[25]

He waited just long enough to see the expression of blank shock transform the Jam Sahib's face before he turned on his heel and walked away. As he did so, he passed Pattani, whose face was inscrutable but for the ghost of a smile.

Chapter 26

Patiala

THE PANIKKARS TOOK A MUCH-DESERVED BREAK BEFORE THEY LEFT FOR Patiala. They were due in Patiala on 4 April, so they had barely a week, but Gouri, seeing how worn and tired Panikkar was looking, insisted that they take some time to recover at a health resort outside Bhopal. There, he relaxed and went on long walks with his son and daughters, and did what he loved best and began writing the first drafts of what would become *Balika Matham*, a long poem written in dialogue form that takes the reader through the myriad moods of a lovelorn and lonely girl. He also began work on a more scholarly contribution to Malayalam poetry, which he had already tentatively titled 'Kavita Tatwa Niroopanam'. After sending the elder children back to school, on 4 April 1933, the Panikkars arrived in Patiala.

Bhupinder Singh had appointed him as a minister, in addition to his duties as secretary to the Chamber of Princes. The maharaja had breathed new life into his career. Panikkar would always be grateful to Patiala and his loyalty, like that of Liaqat Hayat Khan, would be unfailing right to the end. But he knew he had his work cut out for him. The Chamber of Princes' credibility had taken a severe hit after the debacle of the last session. Kolhapur had stalked out, fed up of being consistently passed over for a place on the standing committee. Bhopal and Jodhpur had followed suit after seeing Nawanagar in full cry against federation. By the end of March, Kashmir, Travancore, Kapurthala and Rampur had all tendered their resignations. Negotiating constitutional reform would now be supremely complex.

Then there was the question of his new boss.

Baron Jean Pellanc, a traveller across much of princely India in the 1930s, described Patiala perfectly: 'None could embody more superbly the eastern prince of our fairy tales, the hero of our childish dreams, none could more aptly illustrate the magnificent and despotic power of the last absolute monarchs.'[1] Bhupinder Singh was a man of many facets, 'an admirable example of Punjabi manhood', as Panikkar rapturously described him.[2] He was a prince and a polygamist, a patriot and a soldier, a statesman and a scholar, an adoring father and a terrible husband. His son-in-law Natwar Singh would write enviously, 'He was a confirmed epicurean and a practicing hedonist. Endowed with exceptional sex appeal, his virility was every woman's dream.'[3]

Of Bhupinder Singh's vivid personal life, reams have been written. One book written in 1930 averred sarcastically, 'The Englishman begins on bacon and eggs, the German on sausages, the American on grape nuts. His Highness prefers a virgin.'[4] His jewels came from Cartier, his watches from Rolex, his silver from Garrad's and his suits from Savile Row. Everything about him was larger than life, but within Patiala was a deeply insecure man, riddled with complexes. He was lazy but brilliant, lonely but never alone, generous to a fault and exceptionally well-versed with governance and politics. He was also far from tactful and given to tantrums, and his attempts at political intriguing were, as Panikkar already knew, disastrous.

More worryingly, Patiala's position on federation and its feasibility was now nearly perpendicularly opposite to Panikkar's ideas. Navigating this appointment was going to be hellish to say the least, especially since Panikkar had been delegated to travel to Britain later that spring. He would be speaking on behalf of the chamber to the Joint Select Committee elected by the British Parliament that would be sitting between April 1933 and October 1934 to evaluate reforms.

How, he wondered, would he navigate the divergence in views between himself and the prince he worked for?

He did not yet know.

A day or so after the Panikkars reached Punjab, Patiala sent for him. Panikkar arrived to find Bhupinder Singh, glittering in his customary pearls and diamonds, sitting with his aide-de-camps (ADCs) on the sunny veranda. He was welcomed and given a cup of tea to drink before Patiala began his day's duties. As the men chatted, an ADC appeared, bearing a telegram. Still responding to what Panikkar was saying, Patiala ran his eye across the paper and abruptly stopped talking.

Respectfully, Panikkar waited. It was clearly a cable of some import, for after reading it, Patiala handed it silently to Panikkar and then leaned back in his chair, his eyes closed. The cable was brief, stating simply that Ranjitsinh of Nawanagar was dead.

His son, Digvijaysinh, was the new Jam Sahib.

Panikkar had never liked Ranjitsinh, but for Patiala; Nawanagar had been like a brother. Not only had Bhupinder Singh attained his state's gaddi thanks to Ranji's father Rajendra, but during Ranji's exile from his own state, the nawab had been Bhupinder Singh's ADC. Patiala sat in silence for a while, gazing vacantly into space as tears coursed down his heavy cheeks. Uncomfortable and embarrassed, Panikkar waited quietly to be told what to do. After a moment, Patiala sat up a little straighter and called out for his secretary, Radha Raman Das, to bring his almanac.

Panikkar had heard of this almanac. Compiled for Patiala by the famous astrologer Lahori Ram, the almanac, which reposed under Bhupinder Singh's pillows, ran from April to April, citing the major events of that astrological year. When the almanac, in its plain red cover, was brought, Patiala seemed suddenly unsure, turning it over in his hands for a while before he opened it to a particular page. He read it out to Panikkar, in a voice rendered dull with grief, 'The main events of this month are the deaths of two princes: one in South India and the demise of the Maharaj of Jamnagar.'[5]

Panikkar was so sceptical that he forgot where he was for a moment. He seized the almanac from Patiala's hands and flipped through its pages. That month's list of events had just one more significant occurrence: the Badshah of Afghanistan, Nadir Khan, would meet a violent end, it said. His son would peacefully accede to the throne.

Panikkar was astounded and not a little incredulous. Nadir Khan had survived and repressed several violent insurrections, managing to subdue Afghanistan into some kind of peace in 1931. Currently, his reign was peaceful and progressive, with a new constitution and thriving commercial and diplomatic links with the outside world. A violent end to his reign looked wildly unlikely in the spring of 1933. But Patiala seemed to take the almanac at its word. When Panikkar showed the lines to him, he simply nodded. 'Yes,' he said, 'I know.'[6] It was the oddest start to a career in one of the most politically active states in the princely order.

Towards the end of that month, Panikkar sailed yet again for England. As with most momentous events in his life, his memoir is silent about that visit. But it was one of the last rounds of constitutional negotiations for India. Most of the Joint Select Committee's concessions were favourable to the states: their membership of British India was to be voluntary and take place through negotiations with the Crown, a large upper chamber was in place to allow individual representation and a tax structure was approved that left a large share of customs revenue to the states. This was a reversion to the model that had been laid out during the First Round Table, but it was, as Panikkar wrote to Patiala from England, the best the princely order would get.[7]

It was a truthful assessment, but it was cold comfort. The snail-like pace of the committee's deliberations over the next eighteen months would jangle the already frayed nerves of the princely states. Panikkar's best efforts couldn't dissipate the effects of the Old Boys' Club atmosphere that prevailed during the committee's meetings, which left the Indian ministers feeling excluded and frustrated. Worse, the duration of the committee's deliberations coincided with upheaval in many states, with Kashmir, Alwar, Bharatpur, Bahawalpur, Kapurthala and Jind all experiencing agrarian revolts and bloody communal clashes.

Political intriguing between and within the princely order did nothing to help matters. In Alwar, Jai Singh was deposed and exiled, causing widespread fury in the chamber. Alwar was not the most well-liked ruler, but he had brains which were respected. Then there was the inevitable tug of war between federal and confederal forces. In May 1933, Delhi concluded the settlement of the Berar issue that had kicked off the whole crisis some five years earlier. Osman Ali Khan was given an extremely generous deal that established his right to stamp his authority on Berar. In early 1934, the Aga Khan toured Rajputana and Punjab to promote the cause of federation. The report of the Joint Select Committee was due to be published in the winter of 1934, and with constant bickering and internal rebellions disrupting the work of the chamber, Panikkar could do nothing more than wait it out. He was still in London and so had the time, which he had not had before, to observe some rather dangerous new trends in English politics. It was no longer Tory versus Labour. There was a new party on the scene.

The British Union of Fascists (BUF) was led by the dangerously charismatic, unscrupulous Oswald Mosley. English fascism was not (in the early 1930s) the same as fascism under the Third Reich. Larger geopolitical and economic contexts were weighing heavily on Britain at the time. In Geneva, the Disarmament Conference ground slowly on; in London, the pacifist movement was growing. Britain was still in the grip of the economic depression, preoccupied with its own woes and politically inward-looking. Unemployment was still skyrocketing. Panikkar was meeting and hearing of many newly returned travellers from Germany. All of them spoke of a country given new heart and life again, of a mood of unusual optimism in a country led by the charismatic Adolf Hitler. So it was in England.

For Mosley, fascism blended the Utopian ideal with the Nietzschean concept of the Superman—the individual striving to raise himself above the common clay of humanity while working for the good of the community. He believed that the goal of a better society could be achieved by willpower, expressed through action, backed up where necessary (he didn't mind violence at all) by a cadre of suitably muscular, disciplined and dedicated young men clad in black shirts. By the time Panikkar left England, the fascist movement was beginning to unite under Mosley, with meetings often beginning with arrogant fascist salutes and songs and ending in riots. The rise of the BUF caused horror and dismay among those who abhorred the early portents of fascism, but it added much needed context to Panikkar's rather curious pitstop on the way home: Germany.

The Weimar Republic had died just a month before Panikkar arrived. On 30 January 1933, shortly after noon, the new Reich Chancellor, Adolf Hitler, had sworn to uphold the constitution, to respect the rights of the presidents, and to maintain parliamentary rule. Exactly fifty-two days later, on 23 March 1933, the Enabling Act had been passed, marking the end of the Weimar Republic and giving Hitler the right to rule without the Reichstag. It was a landmark moment in Germany's modern history.

In the summer of 1933, when Panikkar visited, the formal process of *Gleich Shaltung* (to bring society in line with Nazi ideals) had not fully begun, but brutality was on the rise. The first concentration camps were up and running. Into them went those whom the Nazis considered undesirable: Jews, communists, Jehovah's Witnesses, gypsies and homosexuals. Flights and expulsions were beginning as repression moved into the arts and sciences. Jewish conductors such as Otto Klemperer and Bruno Walter were deprived of their batons. Teachers had to join the National Socialist Teachers' Union (Jews, of course, were excluded) and Jewish students as well as Jewish professors were driven out of universities. The experimental physicist James Franck, a Nobel laureate, was forced to take a 'voluntary' leave of absence because he was a Jew. At the University of Berlin, there was the Burning of the Books—all those by Jewish authors, including Albert Einstein, were thrown into the flames.

But little of this was seen by most visitors to Germany. Those like Panikkar were shown the new housing and the spanking new maternity clinics where smiling blonde mothers brought healthy, flaxen-haired babies for treatment. Visitors were told about the praiseworthy social welfare schemes, the new hope and happiness of the people. The Nazis understood the importance of tourism as propaganda. Even more did they invest in ensuring that any negative image of their politics be countered. Life in the Third Reich, for all intents and purposes, was happy and normal. Geopolitically speaking, it was best to posit Germany as the only reliable bulwark against that dangerous threat: communism.

Panikkar was in Berlin thanks to an introduction to Franz von Papen, then Hitler's vice chancellor, and his description of von Papen in his memoir is suitably anodyne. 'Papen was one of the foremost European statesmen,' he wrote, 'he was the chancellor of Germany before Hitler. Papen was very friendly and thanks to him, I was able to understand the drift of events in Germany.'[8]

These simple lines erase an entire swathe of who Papen really was. The scion of a wealthy Catholic landowning family, Papen had begun his career as a professional soldier, marred somewhat by charges of espionage and sabotage in the United States, where he had been posted as military attaché in the First World War. After the war, Papen entered politics. He had links with German monarchists, former aristocrats, big businessmen and the army, but he had no real political following. His elevation to the chancellorship, engineered by President Paul von Hindenburg's advisor General Kurt von Schleicher, took everyone aback. When Panikkar met him, Papen had proved more than capable of navigating the slippery slopes of Nazi politics, achieving the cancellation of Germany's war reparations under the Treaty of Versailles and persuading Hindenburg to appoint Hitler as chancellor.[9]

Since this was only 1933 and the Nazi mask had still some years left before it slipped entirely, it is most likely that Panikkar returned home with more questions than answers. Was the implementation of socialist principles inspired by idealism or dictatorship? Were the labour camps part of a genuinely philanthropic agenda or were they forerunners of something far more sinister? Were the marching bands and swastikas an expression of national pride or a warning of forthcoming militaristic aggression? His biography says nothing on the matter.

Mulling over these knotty questions, Panikkar was handed a telegram from Ganga Singh of Bikaner when his ship docked at Marseilles. But if Bikaner was hoping to lure him away from Patiala's service, this was a failed shot.

Panikkar was perfectly aware that if he had a job today, it was due to Patiala. Loyal as he was, he was nobody's fool. To annoy Bikaner was to alienate a powerful prince, something that, Panikkar knew by now, was a foolhardy thing to do. Haksar, with whom Panikkar consulted when his ship docked in Bombay, agreed. So off Panikkar went to Bikaner, feeling somewhat steadier in his mind. 'I consider it a great honour to serve your Highness,' he told Bikaner, 'but I am already committed to the Maharaja of Patiala. If and when he permits me, I shall be glad to come to Bikaner.'[10]

Having given Bikaner his answer and secured his future in Patiala, Panikkar trotted off to brief Bhupinder Singh, then holidaying at Eagle's Nest, his summer palace in Chail in modern Himachal Pradesh. In those days, there was nothing there except the palace and its attendant buildings for the ladies and gentlemen of the court, nestled among thick deodars. If you were bored, you could play a game of tennis or cricket on the property, which stretched over seventy-five acres of woodland. It was a brief respite from the heat of politics down in the plains.

On 1 September 1933, Panikkar was appointed foreign minister in Patiala, concurrently with his position as secretary of the Chamber of Princes. It was a delicate time to assume this position. Patiala's machinations behind the scenes to scupper federation would continue throughout 1933 and 1934, but the maharaja's hot-headedness was the least of Panikkar's problems.[11] Winston Churchill and his diehards were keenly following the trouble within the Chamber of Princes, fanning any flame they could to serve their cause. Meanwhile, across British India, the Raj was activating every law and ordinance it could think of to keep a chokehold on power. In his memoir, Jawaharlal Nehru would write disgustedly that 'India was the ideal police state, and the police mentality pervaded all spheres of government. Outwardly all non-conformity was suppressed, and a vast army of spies and secret agents covered the land.'[12] The last sentence was hyperbole obviously, but there was no doubt that Willingdon had cast a wide web of informants and spies.

All the webs in the world though couldn't put the brakes on the momentum of the 1930s. It was a time of agitation among the people of the princely states, many of whom were furious at how they had been dismissed by Gandhi during the Second Round Table Conference. The lawyer and politician N.C. Kelkar took Gandhi roundly to task in June 1934: 'It will be well to refer to the apprehensions that have arisen in the minds of the Indian States people by passages in your speeches at the Round Table Conference,' he said indignantly. 'You pleaded earnestly in this Conference with the rulers of the Indian States for allowing the States' representatives in the federal legislature to be chosen by election and for allowing the fundamental rights of the States people to be written into the federal constitution and placed under the protection of the federal court. But your pleadings on this occasion have given rise to an impression that if the Princes did not agree, as they did not and do not agree, you would accept a constitution in which provisions of the kind that you suggested did not find a place.' Kelkar pulled no punches: 'If this impression is well founded, we cannot help saying, and saying it straight out, that you have done a grave wrong to the States people.'[13]

It was a clear sign to the Congress that the Praja Mandals demanded their rightful say in national politics. Kelkar appealed for a clear statement of policy to the effect that the Congress would support 'all legitimate movements for the establishment of popular government' in the Indian states. The people of the states were tired of the Congress Party's ambiguity.

The 1930s also saw the idea of a separate homeland for Indian Muslims being seriously considered. 'Pakistan' would take another handful of years to become a goal to strive for, but its origin story remains vague. It all began in 1858 when the radical English MP John Bright suggested that the Indian empire be broken up into several smaller states. From here, the dots are varied and numerous, from Sir Syed Ahmed Khan to the Punjabi barrister and Urdu poet Muhammad Iqbal. This last man proposed the 'two nation theory'—that India was fundamentally divided between Hindus and Muslims. But even he did not envisage the creation of two independent states, rather the 'creation of a Muslim India within India'.

The next, most recent step was from Choudhry Rahmat Ali. Of Ali not much is known. Some say he came from the North-West Frontier Province. Others say he was a Bengali. In truth, he was a Punjabi, a brilliant young man born in a modest home, who eventually secured a scholarship to study law at Cambridge. While he was in London (on the upper deck of a bus), the vision of 'Pakstan' flashed through Ali's mind. After much tweaking and tuning, he finally settled for 'Pakistan', which means 'land of the pure' while helpfully doubling as an acronym of Punjab, Afghan (meaning the people of the North-West Frontier Province), Kashmir, Sind and Baluchistan. These were the areas of northwest India where Muslims were in a majority. Bengal, it must be noted, didn't feature in this equation.

In 1933, Ali published his controversial pamphlet 'Now or Never'. Within its pages was the first conception of total national separation, 'the release of our nation from the bonds of Minorityism'.[14] It was the first direct political challenge to the Indian National Congress, and while Ali never got a chance to present his ideas to Jinnah, Pakistan would quickly become the most dangerous bargaining chip of those fraught days.

In 1934, Jinnah himself returned to India. Like the instinctive leader he was, he sensed a change in the air. He was right about that. But if there was a new momentum among the Muslims of India, there was another, more dangerous kind of momentum on the other side of the world.

In Germany, nearly 4,00,000 Nazi Party members converged on the tiny town of Nuremberg, brought from all over the country in 400 special trains. There were 80,000 Hitler Youth alone—a smallish proportion of the three and half million boys aged twelve to eighteen already enrolled. Hitler would be speaking at Nuremberg, his ominous subject being 'The State is the Party and the Party is the State'. Great Britain, France, Poland, Russia, Spain, Czechoslovakia, Holland had all refused invitations to send an official representative. Bunting fluttered in the breeze and blood-red Nazi banners emblazoned with black swastikas streamed down the front of buildings. The streets rang with the sounds of marching feet and military bands. It was part theatre and part muscle-flexing. When Hitler spoke, the air seemed to explode with thunderous cheers, waves of reverberating Seig Heils. There was no mistaking the rise of Nazi Germany and there was no telling where it would end.

For now, the international community pretended to look the other way. Great Britain had a royal headache on its hands. The report of the Joint Select Committee was finally published in December 1934. The findings of the report gave the green light to the chamber's plans for confederation. It stressed that no state could be compelled to federate against its will; that each acceding state could define its extent of participation by negotiating a legally enforceable Instrument of Accession with the Crown.[15]

Reading through the report, Akbar Rao Hydari and his new Committee of Ministers, which included Sir Mirza Ismail and Sir C.P. Ramaswami Aiyar, gave it their guarded blessing.[16] Bikaner and his friends finally had a chance to hope for victory, although they were ready to fight a 'great and uphill fight'.[17]

When the draft Government of India Bill based on these numerous ruminations was published in January 1935, it left princes and advisors alike aghast. Crucial provisions differed from the positions that had been agreed upon during earlier meetings between the states' legal representatives and the India Office.[18] The nervous Hydari was particularly appalled at Clause 6 of the Bill, which made the entire Act applicable to an acceding state. Acting on a sharp warning instinct, Hydari made his team check their records where they discovered to their fury that the draft Bill departed on several crucial points from what had been agreed upon earlier.

In plain terms, everything in the Act had become binding for the states rather than (as earlier agreed) permitting the rulers to accept only *specific* provisions of the Act through an Instrument of Accession.[19] Bhopal was scathing in his assessment of the draft bill, saying that it fell 'far short of many of our vital demands'. Bikaner was equally furious, describing the Bill as 'a profound surprise and disappointment'. The sudden crisis in the ranks brought the feuding princes together as nothing else could.

Distraught, Patiala, Bikaner and Bhopal wrote a joint letter to the viceroy, trying to pull the focus back to their original points. They sought a realignment of views on treaties, insisting on entering the federation through the bilateral treaties between their states and the Crown, rather than through unilateral Instruments of Accession. It was a weighty letter, made weightier still by the luckless decision to attach a verbatim record of every royal speech made on the subject.

To receive this screed on top of his viceregal duties of running a restive colony was not exactly pleasant. 'Ye Gods! These reforms and these princes!' Willingdon shouted, flinging the letter down on his desk. 'After all the work we have done, it seems too damnable that they should try and run out at this moment!'[20]

But the division of sovereignty had always been the thorn in princely India's flesh. It would now become the basis on which the states tried to negotiate their way to protecting their interests, vis-à-vis the Crown.[21]

The princes—and India—were back to square one.

Chapter 27

Crisis

NOT SURPRISINGLY, THERE WAS BEDLAM.

When the Chamber of Princes met again in Bombay in January 1935, Patiala stood up before them, a sheaf of papers in his beringed hands. In his ears rang the words of Dr Rajendra Prasad, the Congress president, who had delivered a stinging address in Bombay just weeks earlier in which he had come down heavily on any idea of reform that allowed the princes to continue their 'autocratic rule'.[1] Having been coached the night before for seven hours by Madhava Rao, the wily Indian correspondent for the *Morning Post*, the maharaja was in fine form, reviewing the federal experiences of Canada and the United States which, according to him, showed that no constitution was immutable. He went on to hit out at the Raj: 'While the princes of India have always been willing to do what was best for their peoples and ready to accommodate themselves and their constitutions to the spirit of the times, we must frankly say, that if British India is hoping to compel us to wear on our healthy body politic the Nessus shift of a discredited political theory, they are living in a world of unreality.'[2]

In the same breath, he then delivered lines which led both his prime minister and his foreign minister to sit up in horror: 'The benefits of a federal scheme to the Indian states are, in any case, not so overwhelming that … it would be in our best interests to join it.'[3]

Liaqat Hayat Khan and Panikkar were speechless with rage and consternation at this fine example of Patiala's mercurial temperament. 'The Maharaja was, in some respects, like Ravana, whose ten heads and twenty hands pursued contradictory or at any rate incongruous aims,' Panikkar wrote with diplomatic understatement years later, though he added the pithy rider, 'Everywhere, he was accustomed to having his own way.'[4]

But Patiala met his match in both Willingdon, who chastened him with icy displeasure, and Bikaner, who moved that the chamber should endorse the general thrust of the report, despite Hydari's strong protests against it.

For weeks, confusion prevailed.

The resolution put and carried in Bombay that February stopped short, thanks to Hydari's logic and calm, of rejecting federation point-blank. Still, the princes made their displeasure apparent. The tone of the resolution and the speeches in support of it were outspokenly critical. Travancore predicted 'calamitous results'[5] if the Bill were to be passed in its current form. Patiala called it a 'counterfeit scheme'[6] that had nothing to do with the outline accepted at the First Round Table Conference. To drive home the message, Patiala, Bikaner and Bhopal sent a curt summary of the proceedings to Willingdon with a brusque covering letter in which they stated clearly that unless the Bill was drastically revised, it would be 'difficult for a very large number of Princes to accept (the) federation scheme'.[7]

This is an excellent example of how matters had perforce come full circle. The states were united in demanding as much autonomy as possible. They wanted clear constitutional provisions outlining their powers versus those of the federal government. They sought to refocus on treaties, demanding that any new constitution explicitly recognise the sanctity of the states' treaties with the Crown, rather than unilateral 'instruments of accession'. These were, if the reader remembers the duels of a few pages ago, the same concerns that had been raised by the princes before the Indian States Committee in 1928 and 1929, and repeatedly on other occasions in the interwar period.[8] Divided they may have been on their method, but their broad aims were similar: they all wanted to preserve their states as separate and sovereign political entities *within* a federal framework, connected to both British India and the Crown. Now, they were making it clear beyond doubt.

The crisis terrified Hoare in his last days as secretary of state for India into demanding of the viceroy whether it was worth proceeding with the Bill at all.[9] He had reason to be petrified. Through the offices of the *Morning Post* correspondent Madhava Rao, Patiala had managed to inform Churchill of the princes' decision before official confirmation had even reached the India Office.

On 26 February, Churchill informed the astonished House of Commons that the decision represented an outright rejection of federation from the princes of India. Hoare was aghast. To satisfy parliament, he would have to produce an additional white paper to explain the basis of the princes' objections and lay out just how far the government was willing to go to modify the Bill and the draft Instrument of Accession.[10] The diehards, on the other hand, were thrilled. Long had Churchill been fighting for this moment. Standing on the floor of parliament, he had denounced the India Bill memorably as a 'gigantic quilt of jumble crochet work ... built by the pygmies'.[11] Now, gleefully watching the princely order implode, he wrote enthusiastically to his wife, Clementine, 'It wrecks the federal scheme against which I have been fighting for so long.'[12]

He exulted a little too soon.

The Bill lived to tell India's tale. The Bombay resolution had never been anything more than a bluff as Hydari happily told Hyderabad's lawyers, Coward & Chance.[13] After talking to some of the rulers at a post-conference party at the Aga Khan's palace, M.R. Jayakar had come away with the impression that the princes had discovered that Samuel Hoare was the weak link at the India Office, apt to buckle under the slightest pressure. They were determined to test him to see if this hypothesis was true, which it was.[14]

But they hadn't reckoned that Whitehall would cotton on to this game of blackmail. The India Office lost no time in doubling down, this time uncaring if 'it gave Churchill a chance to "torpedo" the Bill.'[15] Willingdon was furious, ranting to his son that Patiala should 'get it in the neck' for what he had done.[16] In Delhi, he gave each of the princes a severe dressing-down, following it up (much like a strict governess) by warning them that with this unruly behaviour, they would not be welcome at the silver jubilee celebrations of King George V's reign in England that summer. In London, Lord Linlithgow, then the chairman of the Joint Select Committee, summoned Hamidullah Khan and gave him 'a very unpleasant ten minutes', leaving the young nawab white-faced and stammering.

The pressure worked.

By the time the summer of 1935 edged around, Patiala was visibly ill and downcast—a pleasant improvement, the India Office felt.[17] But for those who served him, it was an anxious time. For Panikkar in particular, it was a time of immense professional strain. Patiala was not doing well physically or mentally, and being chancellor of a fractious chamber was hardly helping matters. Panikkar sought refuge as always in writing, and though his time in Patiala saw the usual prodigious literary output, he tried now to divert his mind by spending more time with his children.

The Panikkar children were growing up to be very much like their father. They loved reading and learning, they loved writing and poetry, and they were all old enough now to observe their parents in the curiously insightful way that children have.

They saw their mother, for instance, as a deeply religious woman, simple in her ways and views of the world. She was capable of a sharp temper, of a dry, acidic wit and of immense strength and feistiness. She had taught herself to be independent, to pick up several languages and skills. Their father they universally adored. They had vociferous disagreements with him, because he was the figure who challenged them the most in intellect and authority. He had been patient and kind when they had been little, but now that they were growing up, they discovered that he was capable of a temper on occasion. Devaki, for instance, was known to be a careless child. Once, when he thought she had mislaid a particularly valuable piece of jewellery, Panikkar lost his temper and struck her across the face. But that was a rare instance. Mostly, he was indulgent and attentive, discussing books, politics, history, religion, culture and the world with them as his equals. All the children acknowledge Panikkar's roving eye, but put it aside as a personality quirk of their deeply loved father.

Panikkar was also cultivating friendships outside politics and the palace. This was not entirely easy to do, since Patiala was essentially a small town where everyone knew everyone else. But in the summer of 1935, Panikkar seems to have become great friends with the new gynaecologist to the Maharanis of Patiala. Dr Parvati Nair was a young widow who had transferred to Patiala from Bombay where she had been posted. Originally hailing from Alleppey, she was a brilliant, feisty woman with a curious mind and a certain charming reserve. Her husband had passed away early in their marriage, leaving her with two children, a girl and a boy roughly the same ages as Devaki and Radha. Nair had brought her sister to live with her in the house she had been allotted in front of Lady Dufferin Hospital.

Nair was a strong woman, known to all of Patiala simply as 'Doc'. She and her family were the only other Malayalis in Patiala at around this time and the Panikkars lost no time in getting to know them very well. It was a relief to be able to discuss home, to finally have someone who knew and loved Travancore and Malabar as much as he did. Then, in the spring of that year, yet another distraction presented itself.

For a while now, Patiala had been considering getting his handsome son and heir Yadavindra married. If anything happened to him, it was vital that he leave his state in good hands. In March 1935, as discussions around confederation and federation ebbed and swelled, celebrations began in the state of Patiala. Yadavindra's bride was the beautiful Hem Prabha Devi of the Chota Nagpur state Saraikela. It was a spectacular time and was richly documented. 'All Patiala was on holiday,' observed the French traveller Jean Baptiste Pellanc who had been invited for the wedding.[18]

Bhupinder Singh had left no stone unturned to ensure that the guests' approach to the wedding grounds would be a memorable one. Triumphal arches had been erected and festooned with flowers, special electric lamps were installed, the bridges spanning the local canals were draped in thick crimson damask and gold braid. Every official institution was festively hung with banners, from the post office ('All Happiness to Our Beloved Crown Prince!') to the fire station ('Long Life to Our Maharaja!'). The trees and flowerbeds had been swathed in golden fairy lights. On the wide state roads, elephants in royal paraphernalia jostled with gleaming Rolls-Royces and Daimlers for space and attention. As Pellanc's own vehicle drove swiftly down the highways, he noted that in many of these cars, 'gold apparelled princes lolled in the back seats, their aigrettes flashing in the breeze'.[19]

Archival film of Yadavindra's wedding, left by the British philologist R.M. Wilson, shows Bhupinder Singh smiling and regal with his diamonds and pearls, greeting guests, while the solemn-faced young Yadavindra is bestride a purebred bay gelding, five rows of flat-cut diamonds glittering on his brocaded chest. The official who came to collect Pellanc informed him proudly that the number of guests at the wedding numbered over 6,000. But the baron was visibly unmoved by the extravagance of it all. There was jewellery and luxury on display, enough to overawe anyone, but there was, as Pellanc noted disdainfully, no soul. When the nautch girls, the evening's entertainment, were brought in, Pellanc noted that 'the atmosphere was all wrong'.[20] There was no conversation or laughter despite Patiala's own excellent repartee.

'How long, O Lord?' he groaned to himself, 'How long?'

That wedding, spectacular though it was, was a curiously sad omen of what was to come. It was clear that the princes were in the twilight of their existence. How long would evening last in such a world? 'What if anything would come of all the whirlwind pledges bandied in this netherworld of spectral blue, this mirage of drinks and music, drifting smoke-wraiths?' Pellanc asked plaintively.

As it turned out, very little.

By May 1935, London felt confident that the back of the Chamber of Princes had broken. Buckingham Palace was told that the ban on Indian princes attending the jubilee could be lifted. At the end of that month, Panikkar sailed for London with Manubhai Mehta, a week ahead of the Maharaja of Patiala. Gouri stayed behind in Patiala. Radha—very much Panikkar's favourite—and Haima needed to be sent to school. Chhoti was a bright four-year-old by now, and Haima was six. At a friend's suggestion, the two children were sent to Simla to study at the Convent of Jesus and Mary. As soon as they had gone, Parvathy arrived home, an intelligent, serious-faced sixteen-year-old who was preparing to go to Delhi to study for her intermediate degree at Indraprastha College. She adored her father and Panikkar allowed her to look at many of his half-written stories and poems so that she could give him her opinions about what he was writing.

Thirteen-year-old Madhusudhan was still away in Delhi, where he would stay for the next five years or so, bidding fair to become as fluidly intelligent as his father. He was undeniably Gouri's favourite—her 'oray oru magan', her one and only son. For her, he could do no wrong. With his father, however, it was a fraught relationship from the beginning. The details of this are unfortunately hard to come by.

Devaki was about eleven at this point in time, on the cusp of her teenage years, full of fun and bright energy. A great favourite with the youngest siblings, she was full of zany stories of how she had learned to tie a saree at the tender age of four, helped by her Armenian school warden who used to put spit on her bushy eyebrows to smooth them. 'She never put on any airs with us,' recalled the youngest sibling, Radha. 'She was full of fun.'[21]

But it was also a relief for Panikkar to be away from home for a while. Murmurs in the personal archives suggest that this was a time of some strain in his marriage, a time marked by quarrels and silences, though what—or who—exactly was the cause remains a mystery.

What we do know is that the Patiala entourage stopped for some days in Rome where they met King Victor Emmanuel III. Panikkar was singularly unimpressed by his first encounter with European royalty, describing the hapless king with cruel accuracy as 'a small, unimpressive man, living in the shadow of Mussolini'.[22]

In 1922, the flamboyant, self-assured Mussolini had announced that the fascists would march on Rome 'to take over by the throat the miserable ruling class'. A singularly spineless ruler, Victor Emmanuel III first tried to dodge out of participating in what was clearly a fascist coup. When he discovered that his fate was inevitable, he overruled his horrified cabinet, forced his prime minister to resign and installed Benito Mussolini instead.

By 1935, Italy was openly fascist. Il Duce was funding Oswald Mosley's British Union of Fascists in England,[23] had invaded Ethiopia and begun Italy's colonisation of East Africa. Bhupinder Singh's son-in-law and biographer Natwar Singh is silent on what Patiala did in Italy, beyond quoting a letter to Whitehall from the British ambassador to Rome, Eric Drummond, in which the ambassador had written, 'Signor Mussolini has asked to see His Highness. If the Duce raises the Abyssinian question, the Maharaja will tell him that India stands behind HMG—and the Abyssinian adventure is highly unpopular to Indian public opinion.'[24]

On the other hand, a deliciously gossipy account is provided by Dewan Jarmani Das, a minister in the court of Patiala. Das was never known to be reliable, but from him we learn that the maharaja used his friendship with Signor Amadeo Scarpa, then the Italian consul general in Bombay, to gain an audience with Mussolini—a route Panikkar would eventually follow as well. One does not know Patiala's use for Mussolini, but Das alleged that Il Duce wanted to understand 'the help which the Maharaja would give him to conquer India'.[25]

At the entrance of the Palazzo Venezia, Patiala, Das and Panikkar were received by Mussolini's chief of protocol. The Patiala entourage walked through several spaciously airy rooms before entering the wide hall where Mussolini awaited them. Il Duce was seated on a dais, deliberately higher than the two chairs in front of him. The entourage was to enter according to pecking order, which meant that Panikkar had to wait his turn nervously in an anteroom. Das and Patiala went first, approaching Mussolini who watched them approach with smiling insolence, making no attempt to get up. An initial discussion lasted all of a quarter of an hour, though Das would recall several other discreet meetings between Patiala and Mussolini 'without any formalities and conventions'.[26]

Das would later make the sensational claim that Patiala had informed Mussolini that 'if El *(sic)* Duce invaded India, his services would be at his disposal', especially since, as chancellor of the Chamber of Princes, 'all the princes of India were at his beck and call'.[27] Of the veracity of this claim, there is much doubt, especially since Panikkar himself has stayed silent on the subject.

His own musings on Mussolini, as he waited his turn, read rather as though he admired the man. It must be remembered that in 1935, men like Mussolini and Hitler commanded a mix of curiosity, respect and repulsion. Fascism had not yet begun to bare its fangs. The real horrors of it still simmered below the surface of the prosperity and the power. Governments, diplomats and aristocrats all preferred to look the other way for now. It was convenient to pretend that Germany was the model that all downtrodden countries should base themselves upon. In Italy, fascism was milder than the German or the British version, and for many people, Il Duce, for all his comical strutting and his flamboyance, was a man who knew how to wield power. Mussolini had built his reputation and party based on his life's story—a man from nowhere, who now held the attention of the world.

Small wonder that Panikkar, never blind to being present in the eye of history, 'considered it my good fortune to have this opportunity to meet him personally'.[28] Seen in the light of present day, there is a natural recoil of horror, particularly since Panikkar wrote his memoirs some twenty years after he had met Mussolini, when he would have known exactly how repulsive fascism was. Even so, his memoir is honest about what a much younger Panikkar almost certainly *would* have felt in 1935, when the Second World War had not yet begun and when Nazism had not yet begun its death march across Europe.

When Panikkar was finally summoned, he appeared with some trepidation, though the towering presence of Patiala gave him some kind of courage. Again, in his memoir, Panikkar skirts the issue of what exactly was discussed, preferring to describe it as a half hour discussion on 'various matters'.[29] From Rome, the Patiala entourage travelled to the Vatican, where Panikkar had the opportunity to pay his respects to the Pope.

He left for London shortly thereafter. 'My mission was to secure amendments to the India Bill for protecting the interests of the Indian princes.'[30] His work was made easier by the fact that Whitehall had held out some olive branches disguised in the garb of 'hard-won discussions' to mollify the princes. Most importantly, Hoare proposed to amend the Bill in ways that would accord the rulers greater freedom to impose reservations on the power of the federal legislature to make laws for their states and which would clarify the Crown's continuing obligation to the states in the non-federal sphere. The princes' legal team was on board with this suggestion, handing the pro-federal ministers of the Indian delegation the hook they needed to argue that, with these amendments in place, the India Bill was now acceptable. 'When I say that after three months' work we were able to secure changes in nearly 40 sections of the Bill, the enormity of our efforts can be estimated,' Panikkar wrote later.[31]

In the summer of 1935, as crowds gathered on the Mall to celebrate King George V's silver jubilee, the Government of India Act emerged, battle-scarred from five years of conferences, haggling, debates and deadlocks. It set out the constitutional structure for federation and became law after receiving royal assent on 2 August 1935.

To outside observers of the Indian political scene, the passage of the Act was a milestone in India's constitutional history. Those closer to the action, like Panikkar, knew differently. On paper, it didn't look bad. The Act established, at a federal level, a Legislative Assembly and a Council of State. One-third of the members of the latter would be elected by the princely states. The viceroy would rule with the help of ministers representing the parliamentary majority, but would continue to be answerable to the Crown, enjoy special powers in matters of finance, defence, foreign and religious affairs and in case of emergency, and would be able to dissolve the Chamber of Princes. An Instrument of Accession would manage the relations between the princely states and the Government of India, but the Raj would have to convince the princes that it was worth their while to join the federation.

In plain words, political and economic power remained concentrated in British hands. As Lord Linlithgow put it, 'We thought that was the best way … of maintaining British influence in India. It is no part of our policy, I take it, to expedite in India constitutional changes for their own sake, or to gratuitously to hurry the handing over the controls to Indian hands at any pace faster than that which we regard as best calculated, on a long view, to hold India to the Empire.'[32]

Panikkar however was a worried man that summer. The princes would remain centre stage thanks to a major caveat in the Act: it would only come into force with the accession of a significant proportion of the princely states. This was the last task before the British government. Sir Walter Monckton, appointed legal advisor to the Nizam of Hyderabad in October 1935, observed that few princes recognised even the most basic principle that federation implied a loss of sovereignty. Therefore, he mused (correctly), most princes would double down on preserving their sovereignty during negotiations over the Instruments of Accession.[33]

What would the nationalists make of this Act? What if the princes chose to cavil?

Yes, Panikkar knew they were still a long way away from the end.

CHAPTER 28

Interlude

THIS HAD BEEN PATIALA'S SEVENTH FOREIGN TOUR AND IT WOULD BE HIS last.

Photographs of the summer of 1935 show an ageing Patiala, dissolute and sullen on a sunny carriage ride down the Mall. He had already terrified Panikkar by having no fewer than three heart attacks while in London. While his agitated ministers returned home, Patiala stayed for several weeks in France, receiving treatment for his heart, high blood pressure and his kidneys. He wrote to Colonel W.G. Neal, the political secretary to the secretary of state for India, that he wanted to tour a bit of Europe before he left for India. He wanted to stop over in Paris, Brussels and Belgium. 'There is also that rising Dictator, Herr Hitler,' he wrote casually, 'and it would afford me so much pleasure to see him and thus allow me to judge him on his merits or otherwise.'[1]

It was an unsettling time to have chosen to meet the Fuhrer. In Germany, anti-Semitism was becoming steadily more brutal, and in September that year, the Nuremberg Laws were enacted, giving constitutional authority to repression that was already being practiced. It became a crime to marry anyone with Jewish blood; Jewish names were erased from war memorials. The most basic rights were wrenched from the Jews.

So what was Patiala doing in Germany? Nobody seems to know. But on record is the fact that the maharaja badgered the Fuhrer for some time. Reluctantly, and quite possibly only because Il Duce had met Patiala recently too, Hitler granted Patiala a bare fifteen minutes.

'One thing led to another,' recalled Patiala's grandson, Raja Malvinder Singh. 'Fifteen minutes became thirty, and then sixty minutes. The Fuhrer asked my grandfather to stay on for lunch and then asked him to come back the next day and then a third day.'[2]

On the third day, Patiala was given a cache of German weapons, including Walther and Luger pistols, and a magnificent custom-made cream Maybach Mercedes. It was quite the gift. In those days, there were only six cars of that model. The Maybach was a monstrous vehicle that ran three miles on a gallon of petrol and used a 12 Zeppelin engine that made the bonnet enormous. The car had a drophead and maroon leather upholstery. It could seat the driver and one more in front and three at the back, with two jump-seats in the boot for servants.

The Fuhrer was certainly not in the business of giving gifts to leaders of smaller kingdoms. The only others who had been recognised with this personal touch were King Shamsher Rana of Nepal and King Farouk I of Egypt, both of whom were deemed to be easily swayed to fascist influence given their antagonism toward British colonialism. For Patiala to be recognised quite so publicly was a source of rather great concern, though he kept the subject of his conversations deliberately vague in case they were picked up by official censors. 'I will always recall to myself with real pleasure the most interesting conversations that I had the privilege to have with your Excellency in Berlin,' ran one demure missive, written after Patiala's return to India.[3]

At home, the tensions had not abated.

Willingdon, in his last days as viceroy, had armed himself with some dangerous new allies: Sir Harold Wilberforce-Bell was the new political resident in Patiala and Sir Francis Gauntlett was the new finance minister. Panikkar, who had not accompanied the maharaja to Berlin, was aghast to find that, for the first time, Bhupinder Singh was more or less isolated. Liaqat Hayat Khan was extremely ill and thus out of action. The viceroy meanwhile was seething over several nasty pieces against him in the *Morning Post* and in the *Hindustan Times*, and had written to coldly inform Patiala that he knew the stories had been planted.

The maharaja might have been sick and desolate, but he was never one to run from a fight. He decided (with rather poor timing) to impose his authority on this situation, replacing Gauntlett with his preferred candidate, the milder Colonel Van Ellis. It was the wrong move to have made.

Francis Gauntlett, a man after the viceroy's own heart, was outraged. He despatched a note to Willingdon promptly, in which he charged Bhupinder Singh with corruption, maladministration and extravagance. Panikkar got a copy of the letter and was struck dumb at the lies it contained. The maharaja was certainly a natural profligate, but of late he had been doing his best to listen belatedly to his more concerned advisors. For Gauntlett to have sent a note like this smacked of meanness and disloyalty.[4]

For a time, there was real concern among Patiala's advisors and ministers. The Raj was not known to forgive erring princes, and Panikkar himself had seen what had happened to the unfortunate Ripudaman Singh of Nabha. Could history be repeated here? Could Patiala too be forced to abdicate?

Almost paralysed with stress, Panikkar took to spending long hours at his desk, or wandering about the grounds at Moti Bagh, wrapped in thoughts of poems and possible scripts for a drama. *Pankeeparinayam*, *Chinthatharangini* and *Mandodari* are products of this anxious time—books that range from satire to a study of deep emotions like ambition.

In truth, he had no real reason to worry. Patiala was far more powerful than Nabha, and the Raj, however angry it was, could not afford to alienate a prince who had just befriended Hitler. Still, Panikkar was not about to take any chances. He pressed Patiala urgently to send him back to London, this time as an emissary. Feathers had been ruffled at Whitehall, he said; it would be wise if Panikkar went to smooth them down personally.

In terms of public relations, it was a good move and well-timed. He arrived in England just as Gauntlett's cable reached the India Office. Almost immediately, he was summoned by British officials to discuss the matter with them one on one. From Hoare to Halifax, everyone was concerned, not just about Patiala's extravagance but about his attempts to undermine federation. It was a short visit, studded with meetings, most of which ran along the same lines: worry from the British and reassurance from Panikkar. It ended successfully. Whitehall had no desire to stir up trouble just as the viceroyalty was set to change hands. 'I may claim that the Maharaja's regard and confidence in me increased,' Panikkar noted with satisfaction.[5]

His gratification would have cause to shrivel almost instantly. Between the passage of the Act and the official exit of Lord Willingdon as viceroy, there was enough time for more confusion to develop between Delhi and London. The new secretary of state for India, Lord Zetland, was in no rush to consummate the federal scheme. The archives in India and England are full of papers attributing this to reasonable delays: the draft Instrument of Accession was taking a while to draw up, he didn't want to rush the rulers into anything that might 'frighten them off' and, rather delightfully, 'the market of federation' was against the government in Britain at the moment.[6] If they waited just a bit, perhaps things would improve.

Zetland's predictions would fall flat as time wore on. The princes had assembled their legal team by now. Apart from the usual suspects—K.N. Haksar, C.P. Ramaswami Aiyar, Akbar Hydari, Manubhai Mehta and Panikkar—there would no doubt be a battery of foreign lawyers. The India Office awaited the list of names with smug complacency, sure that some of those names would be Englishmen of the Old Boys' Club. Certainly, the first draft of names bore out that complacency: Sir Walter Monckton and Alexander Fachiri (acting for Hyderabad, Cutch and Bhavnagar) and Sir Wilfred Greene and C.J. Colombos (acting for the Chamber). Monckton had been to school at Harrow with Zetland and Greene was held in the 'highest regard' in government circles.[7]

But what the India Office had reckoned without was the capricious temperament of the princes. In the winter of 1935, Patiala was enraged by rumours that Greene had spoken in an offhand way about him to officials at the India Office. He sacked the unfortunate Greene on the spot and proceeded to hire his own counsel: an American lawyer he had once met in Paris, the semi-retired Judge W.H. Wadhams.

At first, the India Office was taken considerably aback. Wadhams had begun his career as a sessions court judge in the city of New York and though he had been a delegate to the Paris Peace Conference in 1919, he had no experience with Indian constitutional reform. Still, he was pleasant, a keen federalist, knowledgeable about international law and willing to learn about Indian law. As Francis Wylie observed dryly, 'If we had to have an American lawyer in this business, we could have done worse than the Judge.'[8]

The drafting process would be slowed down considerably by his presence, since he was at the time wholly unfamiliar with the Government of India Act. All was well until Dholpur decided to fling a spanner into the works. Acting in concert with the busy Madhava Rao, he unearthed John Hartman Morgan, the abrasive, brash legal counsel of the *Morning Post*.

Panikkar was aghast. He knew Morgan was a Conservative stooge. If he was allowed anywhere near the deliberations around the Instrument of Accession, catastrophe was certain. Hastily, he leaped into the fray, persuading the standing committee to take on Wadhams *and* Morgan as legal counsels. Coming as they did from such different backgrounds, he argued with superb persuasiveness, surely the chamber would benefit from their complementary skills? The chamber pondered and agreed.

Losing not a minute, Panikkar personally drafted the telegram that was shot off to the chamber's solicitors in London, informing them of the decision that Wadhams was chief counsel and Morgan was his junior. It was the best way he could think of to minimise Morgan's capacity to make mischief.[9]

As it was, mischief was already afoot.

The Chamber of Princes was but a shadow of what it had once been. Disgusted by the politics and factionalism that rent it apart internally, some major rulers had dropped out over the years, leaving it nearly bankrupt in 1935. This year's session, opening in January, had seen only thirty-three rulers in attendance, barely enough for a quorum. Decision making, as Panikkar noted angrily, was practically at a standstill.[10] That only meant that not a second could be wasted. Pushing Patiala hard, Panikkar managed to ensure that the Chamber of Princes formed a committee to evaluate the Instrument of Accession for each state.[11]

A postal ballot in February 1935 brought Patiala in again with a comfortable majority, but Bhupinder Singh was nobody's fool. He knew that the chamber was currently stuck between a rock and a hard place: it could not progress until it changed, but it could not change until its members were forced to admit that reform was necessary. He had to do something drastic and it had to be done immediately.

What Patiala did next could certainly be called drastic, but whether it had the right effect was another matter altogether. In cahoots with his newfound allies Bikaner and Bhopal, Patiala told the standing committee that both he and Ganga Singh had decided that they could no longer serve the Chamber of Princes as it stood. They would be asking the viceroy to issue a writ calling for fresh elections.[12]

Willingdon, on his way out, and with nothing to lose, saw this as an excellent chance to strike back at Patiala, against whom he had long nursed a grudge. He calmly accepted Bikaner and Patiala's resignations. Then, ignoring Patiala's request for fresh elections, he authorised Dholpur (a deliberate and Machiavellian choice under any circumstance) to stand in as chancellor until the next annual session in February 1937. Panikkar, still in London on behalf of the standing committee, was in despair. Dholpur was the wrong man to be chancellor at this delicate stage. He was capable of undoing all of Panikkar's careful plans, or worse, bring in Morgan as sole counsel.

This is exactly what Dholpur did.

At its first meeting on 16 April 1936, the new standing committee chaired by Dholpur terminated the hapless Wadhams, recalled Panikkar from London and debited Wadhams's fees—an amount estimated at over £5,000—from Patiala state. Shortly thereafter, Dholpur instructed Herbert Smith & Company, a firm of solicitors that had acted for Churchill just recently, to take over the chamber's case and to brief Morgan as sole counsel.

All was in train for disaster.

Chapter 29

Downhill

THAT SPRING, THE WILLINGDONS BOARDED A STEAMER BACK TO ENGLAND. In their stead came the tall, haughty Victor 'Hopie' Hope, second Marquess of Linlithgow and Knight of the Thistle. A Scottish landowner born to power and status, Linlithgow had no strong qualifications for the job of viceroy apart from having chaired a royal commission on Indian agriculture and the parliamentary committee on Indian constitutional reform in 1933–1934. Yet circumstances would dictate that he would spend longer in the chair than any other viceroy since Lord Dalhousie a full ninety years earlier.

His reforms commissioner H.V. Hodson described him excellently: 'Though impressive in stature and manner, he was neither handsome nor graceful, nor had he any gift for light conversation or emotional oratory, for the words that disarm hostility, move crowds or sway assemblies. He was forbidding to many, not easy with strangers, nor given to bonhomie or quick friendships.'[1]

If anything, Linlithgow banished any pretence at bonhomie when he told the Indian nation over the wireless that, if in doubt, he would prefer suppression to dialogue. 'Amongst the manifold duties of the Viceroy, none is more vital than that of the maintenance of peace and good order throughout India,' he intoned. 'Believe me, my friends, that I can do you no greater service than by the vigilant and effective discharge of this duty.'[2]

Over time, Linlithgow would come to be heartily disliked and mistrusted. His time in India was marked by caution, a lack of imagination and a blend of repression and cynicism. Hodson would write coyly that his understanding of India's political ambitions was not high, though that was being far too kind to the new viceroy, who felt that India and Burma were only part of the British Empire because they were 'conquered countries which have been brought there by force, kept there by our control, and which hitherto it has suited to remain under our protection'.[3]

Unsurprisingly, his views towards the Indian political leaders were along the same lines. The Indian National Congress, for instance, was instantly disliked. Linlithgow staunchly believed that Nehru and Gandhi existed primarily to orchestrate 'the overthrow of the government, by organisation of agrarian mischief on a grand scale.'[4]

But the new viceroy's ultimate goal in India was the birth of federation. He had championed it for a while now and to him there was no better dream than leaving India a federal dominion. To do this, he revived an earlier plan of his: an exploratory tour of the states to be undertaken by two or three political officers. The idea was to glean some kind of understanding of the courts across the land—what they thought, how they functioned and more importantly, what they expected of federation.

Unfortunately for Linlithgow, a number of factors would hamper the smooth sailing of his plan. The first (and possibly the most important) was that not very many of the rulers really understood what federation under the Act would mean. Added to this was the fact that Linlithgow had arrived in India at a time when the national movement was seeing one of its sporadic forward momentums. Politically and ideologically, the national movement found itself a new Leftist orientation in the mid-1930s. But correspondingly, there was a divergence in terms of strategies to be used against the Raj. When civil disobedience movements had failed, when political leaders were jailed, how did one elevate the national movement out of its paralysis?

The answer to that question, at least as far as the Congress was concerned, was the Government of India Act. It was condemned across the political spectrum and rejected wholly by the Congress. In an article for the *Bombay Chronicle*, Nehru characterised it as a 'monstrosity'.[5] There was chaos within the ranks of political India as well. Nobody liked the new constitution, as Nehru said crossly, but it was the reality they had to contend with. The question was, as ever, how to go about it? Everyone within the Congress agreed that the upcoming elections should be fought on the basis of a detailed political and economic programme. But what was to happen after the elections? If the Congress got a majority in a province for instance, should it agree to form the government or not?

Those who opposed office acceptance (and therefore the Act's working) included Subhas Chandra Bose, Jawaharlal Nehru, the Congress socialists and the communists. Nehru presented his arguments with passionate conviction in Lucknow. To accept office, he said, was 'to negate our rejection' of the Act. If the Congress did participate, it would be cooperating 'in some measure with the repressive apparatus of imperialism, and we would become partners in this repression and in the exploitation of our people'.[6] Did the people of India, he demanded, want revolutionary changes or petty reforms? As a long-term strategy to oppose the Act, Nehru suggested entering the assemblies with the sole objective of creating deadlock and making the functioning of the Act impossible. This would be done by increasingly relying on workers and peasants and working to integrate these classes with the Congress, thereby kicking off a mass movement at the grassroots.

Those who opposed Nehru and his colleagues included Rajendra Prasad, who argued with disarming simplicity, 'So far as I can judge, no one wants to accept offices for their own sake. No one wants to work the Constitution as the Government would like it to be worked. The questions for us are different. What are we to do with this Constitution? Are we to ignore it altogether and go our way? Is it possible to do so?'[7]

The pro-office acceptance leaders admitted that pitfalls involved notwithstanding, the answer was not to abandon office. If the

Congress did that, there were other groups and parties who might form ministries and use them to weaken nationalism and strengthen communalism. What then?

As arguments went, this was persuasive. Over the year, the Congress finally decided to fight the elections in 1937. The decision to take up office was postponed to the post-election period. As election campaigns—the first in colonial India—kicked off, the princely states were negotiating their future on a parallel stage. At the end of April, the senior political official Sir Arthur Lothian arrived in Simla.

In 1935, Lothian had been interrupted on a pleasurable and much needed tour around Southeast Asia and the United States by a telegram summoning him back to England. He was considerably annoyed, particularly since the cable gave no reason why he should return quite so quickly. When he arrived in England, he was told briskly that he needed to catch the next boat out to India as soon as the ongoing debates over the Government of India Act were over. He spent a couple of weeks in London listening in fascination to speeches of princes, advisors and British officials. 'It interested me to see the different procedure followed in the Home Civil Service, as compared with the Indian [Civil Service],' he wrote later. 'The Home method of dealing with important issues affecting other departments by round table conferences is more expeditious, but not so thorough and it seems to me doubtful whether it would be so easy to bring responsibility home to the proper quarter.'[8]

An accurate assessment, but Lothian was a man of considerable experience. By 1935, he had served as resident or political officer in nearly every important Indian princely state, from Bharatpur to Kashmir and from Hyderabad to Alwar. There was nobody more seasoned than he to lead Linlithgow's charge across the princely states. With him would be Sir Courtenay Latimer and Sir Francis Wylie.

TIME magazine, which covered this entire effort, described the trio in inimitable prose: 'Respectively the three are an Englishman, an Irishman and a Scotsman, namely: handsome, epigrammatic Sir Courtenay Latimer, crusty Agent to the Governor General in the States of Western India, who will get potentates to sign in Baroda, the Deccan, the Gujarat Agencies and the Western India Agencies; astute and charming Francis Verner Wylie, the Resident at Jaipur, who must cope with the rulers of Jammu & Kashmir, Rajputana Agency and the Punjab States Agency; and scholarly, muscular Arthur Cunningham Lothian of the Political Department of the Government of India who must obtain the signature of "The Richest Man in the World" in Hyderabad, as well as those of the native rulers of Mysore, Travancore, Cochin, Central India and the Eastern States Agencies.'[9]

With the division of labour delineated among the Political Department, the ball was in the royal court. Unfortunately, this was in sheer disarray.

Panikkar had been put hastily on 'special duty' to negotiate the special exceptions that Patiala was demanding, including rights to coin its own money, set up its own communications systems, water treaties and territory agreements.[10] But before long, he was firefighting across several other matters as well. There were fissures now within the Chamber of Princes that were too deep to bridge or bandage.

It all went back to the treaties. The unsettled nature of the princes and their treaties was the basis of the royal hesitation to accede to federation. More specifically, there were concerns over financial matters, over jurisdiction, over transport and business licenses and, in many cases, with the formidable reach of the Intelligence Bureau. As Sir Kishen Pershad, the president of Hyderabad's Executive Council, put it, 'It is a matter of profound satisfaction to Your Exalted Highness's loyal subjects to know that the aim resolutely pursued by our Government has been that our State shall not join the Federation unless and until it is satisfied that by joining the Federation, it will not forfeit a particle of its present source of revenue and that internal autonomy and the special privileges hitherto enjoyed by it will remain absolutely unimpaired.'[11]

Small wonder that by the time Linlithgow's emissaries were touring the states, some princes were obstinately of the opinion that they should 'bide their time' before joining any federation. Only if they waited, they believed, could they see how it functioned and if indeed it would impact their sovereignty and autonomy.[12]

Meanwhile, at the India Office, the arrival of John Morgan caused consternation. He was not only rude but so unpleasantly brash in his style of working that even the British government's legal advisor, Sir Maurice Gwyer, seriously considered quitting.[13] Worse, Wadhams and Morgan not surprisingly hated each other. They had never met before, but their reputations preceded each other. Wadhams was obviously livid that Morgan was trying to undermine his work as the chamber senior counsel. Morgan in turn was annoyed by Wadhams's condescension and by Zetland's refusal to treat him as anything more than Wadhams's junior. The terms of the Instrument of Accession were up for debate, but the chamber's two lawyers spent their entire time feuding. Later, the exhausted Wadhams was to liken the experience to 'taking part in an Olympic Games—legal section'.[14]

The summer stretched on and soon the old debates over the appropriate relationship between the states, the federal government and the Crown resurfaced. The archives of this period make for eye-crossing reading, for many of the points are hashed and rehashed in new language. The princes were still keen to retain as much of their sovereignty as they could. They hoped to limit the powers of the federal government by acceding only on a narrow list of federal subjects and to push for the recognition of their treaty rights even after they acceded. As always, they differed on *how* to achieve all of this. Different camps and committees emerged within the fracturing chamber. Federationists from Bhupinder Singh to Ganga Singh, from Manubhai Mehta to Panikkar himself sat on the constitutional committee and argued that the division of sovereign powers in the Government of India Act would enable the princes to achieve an appropriate balance between autonomy and participation. Anti-federationists, on the other hand, argued outright that the states would be destroyed if federation came to pass.

Back and forth the ball of federation was lobbed, driving advisors like Panikkar close to madness with sudden changes in position and stance and equally sudden deadlocks.

The months passed in agonising limbo until Zetland—the same man who had asked Linlithgow to take things slow—suspended negotiations indefinitely, to the bitter disappointment of the pro-federationists and the secret satisfaction of the Dholpur faction. But the viceroy had no intention of easing the pressure on the princes.

Putting his finger on the trigger, he announced that his emissaries from the political department would be kicking off their tour soon.

The bluff worked.

An aghast Dholpur was jerked into action. Hastily, a questionnaire inviting member states to list their doubts about the Instrument of Accession was issued. He asked the Committee of Ministers to report to a general meeting of princes and ministers in Bombay in October 1936 about the type of reservations they considered essential. It was to his mind one way to get them all on the same page. If he had to avoid the wrath of the viceroy and the scuppering of his own plans, Dholpur knew he had to work fast. He lobbied the smaller states urgently, knowing they would soon be running shy of federation. Finally, he begged Linlithgow to give the durbars more time to prepare. The viceroy, with provincial elections looming in just a couple of months, agreed, putting the date of the tour back to November.

Time had been bought, but was it enough?

Running his eye down the responses of the states on the questionnaire, Dholpur saw that most rulers were prepared to federate only with extensive reservations. The report of his Committee of Ministers had also found that the safeguards in the Act were not watertight. At the meeting in Bombay, the chamber endorsed the recommendations of the Committee of Ministers but baulked at passing a firm resolution to that effect. Instead, two committees were set up, one under Patiala (constitutional), and one under Bhopal (financial). To the Patiala committee were elected Patiala, Dewas Junior, Panna, Rampur, Limbdi, Hydari, Bhopal, Jaipur, Indore, Mayurbhanj, Baroda, Travancore, Cochin and Udaipur. The bulk of Bhupinder Singh's committee were ardent federationists and they soon went public (led by Panikkar, Manubhai Mehta and the Dewans of Sangli and Mandi) with accusations of factual incorrectness against Dholpur.

Recognising that he was in for a long, hard fight, Dholpur sent for Morgan. But the younger lawyer was smarting over his ouster at the hands of Patiala. He was also keenly conscious that Dholpur no longer held the kind of power he had held just months ago. In a bid for power, Morgan upped his fees—and found himself promptly stalled from returning altogether. Patiala and Bikaner began strong backchannel campaigns to prevent him from coming back. He was too expensive, they insisted, and he was useless to boot. As a result of their pressure, Morgan was kept hanging until 5 November 1936, three weeks before he was due to leave for India.

Once he arrived, seething with rage at the delay, he was even more incensed to find that Wadhams was back as well. To add insult to injury, a thirty-four page screed landed on his desk shortly after his arrival. It was anonymous, but in truth it had been authored jointly by Panikkar and Wadhams. To Morgan's shock, it argued that the essential and negotiable proposals of the Chamber of Princes had been 'substantially incorporated in the Act'.[15]

Morgan was livid. He brought the memo to a meeting the next day and made no bones about his fury. He tore the memo apart, accusing its author of misreading the Act, of misunderstanding the law and ignoring international precedents. 'I do not quite know who is the "counsel" responsible for this highly original opinion,' he declared icily, looking straight at Wadhams, 'but I find it impossible to believe that he was an *English* counsel.'[16]

Over the next few days, Morgan presented his own case to the chamber, claiming that the Government of India Act, far from protecting princely interests, would lead to the autonomy of the states being 'considerably impaired and wholly transformed'.[17] Such safeguards as the Act contained were illusory. If, he argued, the federal legislature were allowed to directly legislate for the states, the allegiance of the states' subjects would be 'divided between the ruler and the Federation'.[18] He also took issue with the use of the term 'instrument of accession', claiming that the British government had deliberately refused to use the term 'treaty' so as to exclude the application of principles of treaty interpretation.

By now it was early 1937. India went to the polls that February. The Congress had gone all out to win the elections to the provincial assemblies, based on a manifesto that affirmed its rejection of the Government of India Act (1935), that promised the restoration of civil liberties and the release of political prisoners, that called for the transformation of the agrarian and land revenue systems, the right to form trade unions and to remove disabilities on the grounds of sex or caste.

The Congress campaign received the kind of support that politicians can only dream of, with Congress President Jawaharlal Nehru's nation-wide tour capturing the imagination across generations. He travelled nearly 80,000 km in less than five months, addressing more than ten million people on the basic issues of the day. The Congress swept to power in nine out of eleven provinces, with an absolute majority in six of them. It was a stunning, powerful moment in India's modern political history, but it ran parallel to growing unrest among railway and jute workers across the country and political stagnation within the princely states, which did not vote that year. Within the Congress, there were sharp voices of criticism, insisting that these elections could not be considered progress 'as long as there are over seven crores peoples in the States, under a discredited feudal system'.[19]

Within the Chamber of Princes, there was such rabid confusion about what to do in the face of this undeniably democratic moment in India's political progress that Lothian and his team were able to report to Linlithgow that most of the rulers had no clear idea of what federation meant. 'They were happier being inside the house, out of the rain, than outside, under their own umbrellas,' was how Lothian memorably put it.[20] It was not, he said, just the rulers who were clueless, but even the ministers, who were curiously out of date.[21] This claim is overstretched, since among the ministers, there was a recognition that the sand in the royal hourglass was running out.

Pro- and anti-federation factions clashed at meetings in the early months of 1937, forcing Panikkar to circulate a memo urging the princes to come to a decision fast. 'The problem has been clear of many misunderstandings and irrelevancies that had crept into the discussion, as the result of uncoordinated decisions by different groups.'[22] He asked that the princes defer to negotiations with Government of India representatives.

It was a pragmatic suggestion, considering that Morgan was doing himself no favours currently. He was in fact behaving just as Panikkar had felt he would. He kept personally attacking poor Wadhams with pointed insults that did not endear him to the other princely advisors. A livid Haksar raged to Panikkar that Morgan was 'positively abusive' and that he had 'not yet met anyone who had a good word to say for him!'[23]

Legally speaking also, Morgan was on the backfoot, fighting with the desperation of a cornered animal. He interpreted the Government of India Act very differently, arguing for instance that a federation would give the federal government power over the states rather than enable them to maintain their status and autonomy. Panikkar was able to counter him here by simply pointing to the opinions of other well-respected lawyers, notably Sapru, who had explained lucidly that, far from undermining sovereignty, the Instrument of Accession reinforced it. It left the states to decide which powers to concede. In Sapru's point of view, Panikkar explained, the Government of India Act (1935) was unique since it envisaged that the Indian states would enter federation through the means of Instruments of Accession that would not be overridden by the Act.[24]

On the basis of Sapru's opinion, the Constitutional Committee of the Chamber of Princes dismissed Morgan's arguments, concluding that the 'safeguards have been substantially met'.[25] In February 1937, as the rest of India went to the polls, Patiala staged a comeback as chancellor of the Chamber of Princes. His first action was to fire the hapless Morgan and bring the delighted Wadhams back.

It was not just a victory for federation or Patiala, but for Panikkar himself. Writing to him from England, his old friend, Sir Frank Brown was thrilled. 'You turned the Morgan bombshell into a mere damp squib!' he wrote triumphantly.[26]

Wadhams himself was over the moon, but he knew that none of this would have been possible without Panikkar's excellent diplomatic and legal skills under immense pressure. He sent a note of warm congratulations. 'I must add my congratulations to the many which you have received on the results so far achieved. Your prophecy has been fulfilled and your statesmanship justified. India is most certainly to be congratulated upon your most valuable contribution in the development of the Federal Plan and in your services to the rulers of the Indian States.'[27]

It was a landmark in India's constitutional history. But in a matter of four years, it would cease to exist.

Chapter 30

Derailment

IN MARCH 1938, BHUPINDER SINGH OF PATIALA PASSED AWAY.

He had suffered for months, a slow decay brought on by a life of unbridled hedonism. The best doctors from France, Germany and Calcutta had been flown in to treat him, but as Panikkar recorded despairingly, 'he seemed to rely more on sanyasis and astrologers'.[1]

With the end so near, Panikkar rarely left Moti Bagh.

His mind was almost overwhelmingly full with memories of the last few years. Patiala was a difficult man, flawed and insecure, and over the last year or so, he had nearly driven Panikkar wild with rage and frustration. Often had his faithful foreign minister wondered at the maharaja's jewels, his libido and his ability to eat twenty-five quails in one sitting, 'much as we munch on banana wafers!'[2] But he had been immensely kind and loyal to Panikkar. It was due to Patiala that Panikkar had the job and reputation that he did. In his later years, much as he railed against the other rulers he worked for, Panikkar never said a word against Bhupinder Singh.

To prevent himself from being altogether lost in grief, Panikkar flung himself into writing, working on plays that reminded him of an age that was on the verge of passing. The play that was written now was *Bhishmar.* He wrote in Sanskrit, a choice he later intellectualised as an excellent medium for sentiment. 'I do not recollect having written anything during days of happiness,' he admitted wistfully. 'Let psychologists explain why I could not achieve the concentration needed for authorship when free from strain or worry.'[3]

Three days before Patiala finally died, an aide came to find Panikkar. Having eaten a hearty breakfast, that included, if Panikkar is to be believed, a ten-egg omelette, Patiala was asking for him.[4] Panikkar knew instinctively that this was the end. Bhupinder Singh was (with good reason) very particular about whom he allowed in his personal space. When Panikkar nervously entered the royal boudoir, he found the maharaja lying back on his divan, surrounding by his weeping queens. He was white-faced and weak, but even then he had taken care to adorn himself with his customary pearls and earrings. A wand, given to him by a sanyasin in Travancore, lay very close to hand. Panikkar hadn't seen the maharaja for days, and he was shaken to see how deathly ill he looked. There are no records of what Patiala said to Panikkar in his dying moments, but when he finally left, the younger man had tears in his eyes.

'It was the last time that I would see him alive.'[5]

The passing of the Maharaja of Patiala was the end of an era. Much had already changed in Indian politics. Congress rule in British India had begun, with Nehru as president. Not everyone saw Nehru as the instant leader to reckon with. British intelligence officials observed rather nastily, 'Nehru's part is incidental. He is the high grade tool in the hands of the skilled craftsman.'[6]

Incidental or not, there was no doubt that the Congress victory was an omen of great promise. Using their newfound platform of power, Congress chief ministers reformed tenancy laws, regulated moneylenders, expanded education and introduced public health measures. Almost inevitably, ideological tussles began to emerge as did uncomfortably autocratic tendencies. With the parallel creation of a new Congress Parliamentary Board, Sardar Vallabhbhai Patel now emerged as another pivotal force in Indian politics. He ruled the ministries with an iron hand, removing anyone who refused to submit to his will, sacking the incompetent and throttling rebels and backsliders. As later members of the Indian Civil Service half-jokingly, half-seriously said, if the dead body of the Sardar were stuffed and placed on a chair, he would still rule over them all.[7]

By 1937, Patel was in control of the mechanics of the party, using the experience in mass organisation he had gained in the 1920s. But even as ideological and autocratic differences between the leaders within the Congress emerged, no elections had been held in the princely states with the curious exception of Mysore. During the election campaign itself, leaders like Nehru had demanded the establishment of a popular constituent assembly, rather than a federation that would be hamstrung by the presence of 'backward' elements like the princely states.[8] In May 1937, for instance, Nehru declared, 'There is a great deal of talk of the independence of the states and of their special treaties and the like. But the thing that is going to count in the future is the treaty that the people of India make with others ... So I would ask the princes to consider this matter from this point of view and not to rush in where wiser people fear to tread.'[9]

In a similar vein, Sardar Patel had already announced that the Congress Parliamentary Board would insist on being consulted in advance by provincial governments intending to use their discretionary powers. Such a convention, wrote Panikkar in an anxious report to the Chamber, would 'render many of the safeguards of the states nugatory'.[10]

Apart from keeping the chamber informed about political developments on the ground, Panikkar continued writing fluently on subjects in which he was gaining expertise. Nearly a decade of being the spokesman for federalism lent a richness and depth to his insights on kingship, which found utterance in his next book, *Origin and Evolution of Kingship* (1938), based on a series of lectures he had given in Baroda just a couple of years earlier. In it, he asked a question that was relevant given the current political situation: how did monarchy reconcile itself with the demands of the modern nation state? His answer was based, as many of his answers were, on a historical context.

Before the formation of a state, the law of fish had been applied, according to which the bigger fish would eat the smaller one. The state was founded for the protection of society. As a result, it was duty of the sovereign to protect his people. If he failed, the subjects had the right to rebel. Another check on royal power was the maintenance of dharma, which no ruler had the power to alter. Dharma—and its adherence—was a separate sphere removed from state power. By itself, it was a barrier to monarchical absolution.

Some of the stances Panikkar took in this book were surprising and almost certainly would have annoyed the men he worked for. For instance, he denied that Hindu political theory was based on the principle of divine right. He also rejected the theory that kings were considered deities and opposed the idea that their authority had a divine source. From Travancore to Udaipur, this argument coming from a prominent minister of the states would have been infuriating. But taken seriously, these are arguments based on realpolitik. The time for fanciful lineages and divine rights had gone. In so many words, this was both Panikkar's warning and wake-up call to the princes. It was a book written against the backdrop of an era that was dying. Panikkar was aware of that. He had been aware of it since Patiala's death. 'The maharaja's death was a great blow to me,' he would write later. 'I have never grieved so much even at the death of my relations.'[11] For six or seven years, his life and indeed his life's work had focused on and around Patiala. 'I felt that a chapter of my life had ended with his death.'

It certainly had.

The worry that was beginning to bloom in royal hearts was given momentum by the fact that communalism was as undeniable a factor in Indian politics as anti-colonialism. The Muslim League had done well in some key places like the United Provinces, but the Congress had gained a popular mandate, albeit without Muslim votes. For all its non-sectarianism, the Congress was simply not attracting enough Muslim voters. Nor, for all Jinnah's efforts, had the League been doing so—until now.

In the late 1930s, Jinnah transformed the party into a serious political force by recruiting and motivating wealthy, intelligent young Muslims like Liaquat Ali Khan and the Raja of Mahmudabad. None of these men were outright communalists, but they *did* believe in using religious nationalism as a means of safeguarding the Muslim community. As the Congress built its own position in the provinces, so too did the League. It became more stridently outspoken. In October 1937, Jinnah stood before an audience of thousands, dressed for the first time in a sherwani. He made a militant speech, demanding for the first time 'the establishment in India of full independence in the form of a federation of free democratic states, in which the rights and interests of the Mussulmans are paramount'.[12] The *Pioneer* reported that the motion was carried unanimously amidst roars of 'Allah ho Akbar!' and 'Islam Zindabad!'[13]

Nehru refused to see this as a warning of any kind, continuing to believe romantically that 'such opponents of the Congress ... have nothing to do with the masses'. It was an unwise statement riding on the back of the recent victory in the elections, and it was made even worse by Nehru's provocative question, 'May I suggest to Mr Jinnah that I come into greater touch with the Muslims masses than most of the members of the Muslim League?'[14]

By the end of the 1930s, the struggle for freedom was supplanted by the battle between political leaders claiming to represent Hindus and Muslims. For the Congress, if this movement was to see success, the states would have to play a big role. A resolution passed at the annual Congress session in February 1938 called for a 'full responsible government and guarantee of civil liberty' in the states.[15] It marked a major shift in policy because, even though the resolution maintained the current Congress position of non-interference in the states, it left a clever loophole. Congressmen from British India could participate in these agitations in their individual capacity. To back this resolution up, Gandhi directly warned the princes that the Congress might just abandon its policy of non-intervention altogether if the rulers failed to cultivate friendly relations with the organisations he claimed would soon replace the paramount power.[16]

Thoroughly shaken, princely support for federation began to decline even among enthusiasts like Mirza Ismail of Mysore and Ganga Singh of Bikaner. A last-ditch attempt, almost wholly characterised by terror, was made. At a November 1938 session of the Chamber of Princes in Bombay, the princes requested the inclusion of the following passage in the Instrument of Accession: 'Nothing in this instrument affects my sovereignty in and over the State and save as otherwise herein provided, all powers, authority and rights of the Ruler in and over this State and the exercise thereof are reserved to the Ruler of this State.'[17]

The clause in its entirety is a desperate final act in what the princes knew was inevitable. There was no way the India Office would even consider such a thing.[18] Royal concerns were no doubt being triggered even more by popular agitations instigated by the Congress across the princely states, beginning with Mysore in October 1937 and culminating in satyagrahas across Rajkot (1938–1939) and Jaipur (1939). It was yet another attempt by the Congress to impose democratisation on the states and it dovetailed fatally with the British refusal to back down on increasingly shrill requests from the princes.

At the forefront of it all, Panikkar was consumed by a sense of resigned gloom. He had long watched the anti-federationists trying to derail the federal project. With the victory of the Congress in the provincial elections, federation was a doomed ship. Writing wearily to Ganga Singh in the winter of 1938, Panikkar explained that the people of the states were being called upon to organise themselves to force the rulers through the instrument of civil disobedience to agree to their political demands. 'The right to rebel is therefore exalted as a fundamental right,' Panikkar warned, 'the object which the people of the states should work for is nothing short of responsible [government]—that is the surrender of the power of the ruler to the people.'[19] It was the best he could do to explain that all hope was now lost. The only alternative to the Indian federation, he felt, was the eventual collapse of princely rule in India. 'While I knew it was a personal defeat, it was even more the folly of the princes, cutting their nose to spite their face, as it were, that made me despair.'[20]

Folly, it seemed, was the flavour of the season.

In 1938, Gandhi's power was challenged across the spectrum. Within the ranks of the Congress, the dare came from the moon-faced Subhas Chandra Bose. Back in India after his travels across Europe (as 'the Ambassador of India in Bondage'), Bose had built up a formidable power base within the party. He was elected, on Gandhi's orders, president of the party that year, memorably arriving at the Haripura session on a chariot pulled by fifty-one bulls. It was a presidency that would be marked by endless spats between Bose and Gandhi. At the end of the year, wearied by the constant quarrelling, Gandhi asked Bose to stand down—and was staggered by his refusal to do so.

This refusal came on the heels of an unfortunate trip by Gandhi to Jinnah's palatial house on Malabar Hill for a meeting that went precisely nowhere and only confirmed the growing schism between the Congress and the Muslim League. Jinnah was now coming into his own as a politician, driven by a new furious edge to prove himself. Overtures from the Congress were rejected outright. The League maintained that no dialogue was possible until it was recognised as the 'one authoritative body' representing India's Muslims. To his followers, Jinnah ranted that the Congress wanted the Muslims to be 'mere foot-pages' and expected them to accept what they got. He wanted rights, he said forcefully, not favours. 'I have no hesitation in saying that it is Mr Gandhi who is destroying the ideal with which the Congress was started … His ideal is to revive the Hindu religion and establish Hindu Raj in this country and he is utilising the Congress to further this object.'[21]

He was also now confident that at least in New Delhi, the Raj was racing against a clock that the Chamberlain government was resolutely refusing to acknowledge. On 12 March 1938, Hitler had annexed Austria—the Anschluss. By August, as talks in Malabar Hill fell apart, Nazi troops began to mobilising against the shrill background of the Fuhrer's demands that the Sudetenland be detached from Czechoslovakia and incorporated into the Reich.

In August 1938, Jinnah took his chances and travelled to Simla where, together with the urbane Sir Sikander Hayat Khan, he indicated to the viceroy that in the event of war, the League would offer support to the British in return for a postponement of federation, which was against Muslim interests. Strategically speaking, it was an excellent move to make in the monsoon of 1938 when the viceroy was running out of time to start the federal project, Chamberlain was hellbent on looking the other way in Europe and Hitler was beginning to tighten his grip on the continent.

On 6 September 1938, the Nuremburg rally marked Nazi Germany's arrival on the scene as a terror to reckon with. 'The fatal hour for Europe had struck,' wrote Colonel Truman Smith, a US intelligence officer based in Berlin. Still, Europe's major powers made a last lunge at stopping the inevitable. At the end of September, the flags of Britain and France flew alongside the swastika on a beautiful, warm autumn day. 'It's Hitler weather,' remarked people as the Munich Pact was signed.[22]

If Chamberlain refused to see it, Linlithgow at least was under no illusions that there would soon be no time for the Indian federal project. He was of the view (with notes provided by Panikkar) that he could haggle over the finer points in the Instrument of Accession. Accordingly, he pushed for some concessions and some sharpening of otherwise ambiguous legalese and met with obstinate pushback. Whitehall was out of patience. Backed into a corner, the desperate viceroy played his last trump card and threatened to resign.

All this got was a lukewarm shrug of sorts.

In the autumn of 1938, a constitutional package was approved. It was certainly more generous than the original, but the political department read it with growing dismay. There was, they knew, nothing in the package that the durbars would agree to. But the cabinet was already distracted by events in Europe and each time the Bill went back and forth, it took longer than previous attempts. By the time the final offer was ready, there were still annoying crinkles in red tape to be ironed out. How long should the rulers have before they responded? Should a draft Instrument of Accession be published when the offer was sent out to the states? By the time everything was suitably hashed out, Christmas had come and gone.

Whitehall's final offer to the princes was mailed out in the early weeks of 1939. By now, three and a half years had passed since the passage of the Government of India Act (1935). The princes were given six months to respond.[23]

To a man, they were appalled at what they read. They had somewhat trustfully been relying on their rights to insert specific limitations in the Instruments of Accession to protect their sovereignty. But a note that accompanied the offer stated flatly that they would not be able to do any such thing. Instead, they discovered to their horror, they would have to rely on representation in the federal legislature to prevent any legislation inimical to their interests.[24] Even if they voted together as a bloc, they would form only a minority in the federal legislature. Their fears were confirmed by Linlithgow's March 1939 address to the Chamber of Princes, after which he briefed the standing committee with this reassuring phrase: '[T]he fact is, the old order has gone forever.'[25] Nobody had expected it to be phrased so baldly. As the historian Ian Copland put it, 'Having beaten off their enemies, the rulers felt they were about to be mugged by their friends.'[26]

In April 1939, the Hydari-led States' Ministers' Committee met in Bombay. They still considered (despite Bikaner's growing antagonism to the idea) the most viable answer to their problems to be federation, but they wanted negotiations.[27] However, was Whitehall willing to listen?

'There was never the slightest chance of getting rulers representing 50% of the population of the princely states to sign instruments of accession before World War II broke out in September 1939,' recalled Francis Wylie later. 'The only way, so far as the British government were concerned, if they genuinely wanted to expedite the creation of federation, would have been to take the princes by the neck and compel them to come. This is what Sardar Vallabhbhai Patel and VP Menon did later on.'[28]

Writing some two decades after independence and integration, and long after the federal dream was dead, this was disingenuous of Wylie. Federation hinged on much more than the princes. They were certainly made the fulcrum around which the scheme would operate. But politics in India was a wide and messy canvas even in the mid-1930s. It stood to reason that the Congress, for instance, would never agree to a political (or democratic) future which was yoked to the princes. Similarly, the League would never agree to a future without safeguards for itself. Communal deadlock as much as princely obstinacy would be the rocks on which the ship of federation would wreck itself.

The writing on the wall was clear to Bikaner, who now began fiercely lobbying his brother princes to drop the idea of federation. As he wrote furiously to Linlithgow, 'I trust I shall not be misunderstood … when I say that some of us feel … that we have been—I will not use the term "let down" but not supported by the authorities in England and left to fend for ourselves.'[29] The Maharaja of Bikaner was not a political statesman for nothing. His first convert was Dholpur (never a fan of federation), followed by Dewas and the Jam Sahib of Nawanagar. Alarmed by the speed at which the princes were allying themselves to Bikaner's flag, so to speak, Linlithgow did try to organise a counter-propaganda campaign, but it was too late. For better or for worse, the princes had turned their faces against federation.

It was a nightmare come to life.

The Chamber of Princes was split down the middle yet again, with many meetings ending in angry heckling from those outraged at the sudden volte-face. Panikkar had never seen such chaos in his life. But it speaks volumes for the tenacity with which he clung to the idea of federation that, as the world edged toward war, he continued to quietly push for it. Working behind the scenes with Gopalswamy Aiyengar and V.T. Krishnamachari that summer, he persuaded the standing committee to add a clause to their new resolution to commit the princes to negotiations. It was the closest he could come to keeping the federal door ajar.

It was too little, too late.

In a meeting of the chamber on 14 June 1939, most rulers abstained from voting. Despite this, the motion was reflected (in a brazen cheat) as having been carried and won. Then, in yet another stunning twist, Ganga Singh outrightly ignored Panikkar's carefully crafted open-door clause. Instead he stood up, declaring the meeting to have come to a 'final rejection of the federal offer'. Over furious shouts of 'No! No!' from an aghast V.T. Krishnamachari, Bikaner said calmly that the members of the Chamber of Princes were now morally bound by that decision.[30]

Livid, 'sorely disappointed at the failure of ten years' work',[31] Panikkar resigned immediately.

He would carry the bitterness of the failure of federation all his life.

PART VII

'The Puppets Have Walked Out!' (1939–1947)

CHAPTER 31

Storm Clouds

'MORE THAN ONCE, I ... ASKED MYSELF THE QUESTION: WHAT HAVE I done with my life so far? But I am not satisfied with the answer.'[1]

Panikkar was more tired and dejected than he had been in a long time. The last decade had been one of almost frenetic activity. With war in the air and the political future of India uncertain, it seemed as though all his labour on the constitutional front was in vain. Panikkar was glad to be in Bikaner, away from the noise and anger around the future of the princely states.

Here at least he could focus on contributing something of substance to a princely state. Working for Ganga Singh was a fillip to a suddenly sagging career, but Panikkar was a wary man now, unable to trust any ruler fully. His work in the Chamber of Princes had shown him that the princes, ultimately, served no man but themselves. No amount of loyalty would buffer an advisor against an unseemly fall from grace.

Even with Bikaner, his guard was up. He had seen Ganga Singh for years now and he knew that here was a ruler given to ego and powerplays. 'It was open knowledge that if Bikaner asked you to work with him, you wouldn't last long.'[2]

Gouri had heard the rumours as well. When Panikkar brought home the news of his appointment, she sighed, 'How long do you propose to stay in Bikaner?'

'Why do you ask?' Panikkar inquired, puzzled.

'Both the maharaja and you have terrible tempers,' answered his wife equably. 'That is why I ask.'

Annoyed, Panikkar demanded to know what she meant.

'Nothing,' Gouri replied. 'All I want to know is whether I should unpack our baggage as soon it arrives from Patiala.'[3]

Annoyance turned to amusement. Panikkar told her teasingly that she didn't need to unpack at all. Who knew, he agreed, how fickle Ganga Singh would turn out to be?

And so the Panikkars packed their bags and their home and made preparations to start afresh. The furniture and kitchen utensils were dispatched to Bikaner, with Gouri thanking her stars that she had started the practice of keeping two of every utensil with her.[4]

Panikkar accepted the job offer—Foreign and Political Minister of Bikaner—for a contract of a minimum of six months and a maximum of two years. He did not know then that this would be his last assignment in the princely state and that it would last for considerably longer than two years.

Ganga Singh, tall and handsome, was a strong man who had ascended his throne in 1898 at the age of eighteen. Despite his youth, he made it immediately clear to his nobles that he was far from being a boy. He was, he told them, a king. 'I want you to know that I am saying what I really mean ... and not what I have been told by other people to say.'

In the early days of his reign, the state of Bikaner was insignificant, quiet and prone to famine. Young Ganga Singh flew low on the Raj's radar until the Boxer Rebellion broke out in China in 1901. For a 'prince with the traditions of the Mughals', as Panikkar described him, this was a great opportunity to show the Raj his mettle. He hied himself to Calcutta, taking with him his prized Camel Corps, which he would take to China as a dismantled unit. In so doing, he became the first Indian prince to go overseas to fight under the British flag.

On his return, Bikaner was feted by an approving Curzon, who recommended him to the notice of the new King-Emperor, Edward VII. An invitation to Edward's coronation in England followed. Bikaner attended and was soon the talk of the town, with his suave good looks and his charming urbanity. Edward was especially pleased at this handsome example of princely India and soon Bikaner was appointed as an aide to the young Prince of Wales, the future George V. He would hold that position until the king's death in 1936.

'It is an open secret that between them there was established a bond of friendship,' wrote Panikkar later. Shrewdly, Ganga Singh realised that if there was a connection to build upon, this was it. When the First World War broke out, he cabled the king, begging to be of service. The empire obliged, sending him to France where he served on the staff of the 7th Division of the British Indian Army, though he was kept firmly away from the frontline. This would not do for the hot-blooded young ruler, who chivvied Lord Kitchener, then the secretary of war, to let him see active service against the Turks in Egypt. In this campaign, Bikaner had the joy of putting a battalion of Ottoman troops to retreat. He would have continued fighting had his daughter not fallen seriously ill at home, forcing him to hasten back to her side. More than pleased, the Raj invited him to participate in the Imperial War Cabinet and subsequently at the Paris Peace Conference in 1919. His was a strong and intelligent voice speaking for India's rightful place in the world. As the then prime minister Lloyd George rapturously put it in his memoir, 'More and more did we come to rely on his advice, especially on all questions that affected India.'[5]

From a personal point of view, Ganga Singh's role in the negotiations for India's constitutional reform appealed to Panikkar—or at least, it had before the prince decided to override his hard work in 1939. But by then it was too late to back out of working with the Bikaner prince. The official notice of Panikkar's appointment was issued on 2 May 1939. Along with the crucial portfolio of foreign and political affairs, he was also handed the health and education departments in a gesture that was both a marker of Bikaner's trust and a mollification for what had happened with federation.[6] This bouquet of portfolios would give Panikkar no time for anything else. But before they could catch their train for Bikaner, the Panikkars received word that Eravi Ramakrishna Panikkar had died.

It was a grievous blow. Panikkar's entire childhood had been lived in Ramakrishna Panikkar's formidable shadow. Even as an adult, Panikkar had always been comforted by the fact that whenever he went home for a break he would find his uncle there, strong and reassuring. Panikkar, Gouri and the children travelled back to Kavalam for the funeral.

Ramakrishna Panikkar's death left the question of Chalayil up in the air. 'In a matrilineal family set-up, the eldest male member is the inheritor or rather custodian of the joint family—a trust by itself, and the Chalayil family followed this system for two more generations until 1948.' P. Velayudha Panicker explained, 'In that social fabric, these two brothers who were sent to England by the family trust owed (a) certain sense of duty to the family in return.'[7]

That sense of duty defined the Panikkar sons' relationship with Chalayil and Kavalam. It was under the same obligation that, upon Ramakrishna Panikkar's death, Padmanabha resigned his prospering practice in Madras and relocated to Kavalam, to become the karanavar or family head. In his grief, Panikkar leaned heavily on his elder brother. Padmanabha and he remained extremely close, even after their adult lives diverged. There was rarely a moment when Panikkar did not reach out to his brother for solace, for advice or just to chat.

Slimmer and taller than Panikkar, with thick dark hair, a scholarly beard and thick spectacles, Padmanabha was the calmer of the two brothers, with an even temperament and a strong sense of responsibility. There were whispers among the more uncharitable family members about whether a medical man could take on the mantle of a family immersed in agriculture and social reform. Truth be told, there had always been whispers about these two ambitious young brothers, both of whom had gone overseas for their education. The Chalayil homestead was very strongly entrenched in privilege, caste and religion, and upon their return, both brothers had been debarred for two years from praying at or entering their own family temple. The reason: they had committed the ultimate solecism of crossing the seas. Panikkar, who had returned a few years after Padmanabha, had had to repay the expenses his family had incurred for his Oxford education from his earnings.[8]

'It may be weird to the present generation about many customs of the day,' admitted Velayudha Panicker, but that was how things were. Now, with Padmanabha assuming the mantle of the head of the family, though the family elders were pleased at the eldest son taking on the responsibility of running the estate, there were worries about whether Padmanabha would adjust to rural Kuttanad after the bustle of Madras. But Panikkar had no such doubts. He trusted his brother implicitly and knew there was nobody in the family in whose hands he would prefer to see Chalayil. It was time for change.

In this sombre mood, the Panikkars left Kavalam.

He suggested to Gouri that they travel a little before going to Bikaner. He was loath to return to the chaos of reality just yet. It was June 1939, and he knew that the viceroy had not yet given up on his ambitions for federalism. Residents across the states had been directed to apply pressure on non-committal or suitably malleable princes.[9] In the end though, only fifty-one agreed to accede, though plenty offered conditional accession. Despite Linlithgow's best efforts, this wasn't the required number of states needed to move the federation scheme forward under the Government of India Act. The deadline was now extended to the ill-starred date of 1 September 1939.

Meanwhile, Indian politics was going through yet another surge of turbulence. Subhas Chandra Bose had astonished his staunchest critics by getting re-elected as Congress president in 1939. Gandhi was livid and instantly put in motion a campaign of non-cooperation against the usurper, declining coldly to attend the next Congress session in Tripuri in March 1939. Bose was removed from office, his presidency in tatters. He was barred from taking Congress office for three years. Furious, Bose formed a limited party called the Forward Bloc around which he hoped his followers would rally. It met with strong criticism. Nehru described it bluntly as 'evil'.[10]

Domestic politics apart, Panikkar knew that if there was a world war, there would be an inevitable effect on the princely states. But with so many emotions churning in his breast, he refused to think about that just now. Instead, he went to Travancore. What he was doing there is anyone's guess, though the rumour was that he was tipped to be the next Dewan of Travancore.

It was said that the maharaja's formidable mother—and Sir C.P. Ramaswami Aiyar—stood against such an appointment. Ties between Panikkar and Aiyar were considerably strained despite the attempts of many of their colleagues in the chamber (and indeed, Ganga Singh himself) to tell them that friction at this stage could only damage their respective careers. There is no record of Panikkar's conversation with Aiyar during this visit. But in the summer of 1939, the somewhat infamous Dewan of Travancore was at the peak of his powers.

In his autobiography, Jawaharlal Nehru described Aiyar crushingly as 'a full-blooded apologist of British India, especially during the last few years, an admirer of dictatorship in India and elsewhere and himself a shining ornament of autocracy in an Indian state'.[11] He was deeply unpopular with the people, suspected of fostering trouble between the Nairs and the Christians, and known to enjoy repressive crackdowns against popular movements in the state. The British Resident, C.P. Skrine, noted disapprovingly that Aiyar's 'weakness is for power and fame ... a superior person, domineering and contemptuous of the common herd ... his methods are Machiavellian; he rules by dividing, he bribes with office and other favours; he sets traps for his critics and plays on the weakness of his enemies. No wonder the man in the street does not love him'.[12]

Two days in his company were enough for Panikkar to describe him witheringly as 'an egoist who would barter anything, even the country and its freedom, to gratify a moment's vanity'.[13] We don't know quite what else ensued during this meeting, but at the end of it, Panikkar took himself off on a tour of north Malabar. It was, he said later, the 'perfect time' to undertake a field trip to research a novel he was working on. In reality, he was deeply depressed.

His uncle's death and the implosion within the Chamber of Princes had been collectively too much. It was typical of Panikkar that, when he was pushed to the wall, a part of his mind simply detached. He sought refuge, as always, in writing, beginning some of his most well-known works of fiction during this trip. *Daweeduvijayam*, *Hydernaickan* and *Sandhyaragam* were all written during this time—works of Malayalam poetry and prose, ranging over the genres of Kathakali and Champukkal (a mix of medieval Malayalam poetry and prose). He also began work on a historical novel based on the life of Pazhassi Raja, the erstwhile king of a region in North Malabar called Kottayam—not to be confused with the southern Kerala district by the same name.

'Early in life I had come to the conclusion that it is only through work and through the internal discipline which creative activity develops, that a man can find contentment and happiness,' he would write later.[14] 'Nothing has given me that sense of contentment in times of difficulty and crisis as the writing of poetry. There was never a period in my active life when I did not devote at least an hour a day to literary pursuits in Malayalam. I found in translation a discipline of mind which kept away worries and overcame troubles.'

But by the end of summer, it was clear that no amount of writing would keep the outside world away. War was on the horizon yet again. In April 1939, the British Parliament had passed an amendment to the Government of India Act, giving the viceroy full executive powers over the provinces in an emergency. In August that same year, Germany and the Soviet Union signed a pact of non-aggression, much to the consternation of Britain and France. These would be the last weeks of a tense peace that would shatter in September.

Panikkar arrived in Bikaner fighting a sense of bitterness and increasing cynicism. He couldn't stop thinking about 'the folly of the princes' at a time when it was clear that the tide had turned against them. 'With the phenomenal growth of popular forces in British India, it was plain that monarchy was threatened and unless the princes had the intelligence and foresight to choose rightly, they themselves would be swept away.'[15]

He was right.

Gandhi and the Congress had already begun to pay attention to their critics within the party, shifting their policy towards the states. Explaining the change in an interview to the *Times of India,* Gandhi said, 'The policy of non-intervention by the Congress was, in my opinion, a perfect piece of statesmanship when the people of the states were not awakened. That policy would be cowardice when there is all-round awakening among the people of the states and a determination to go through a long course of suffering for the vindication of their just rights ...'[16] It was the culmination of a policy that Nehru had already stated in November 1938—there was no road to freedom, he had said, without the Indian states.[17] In 1939, the AISPC elected Nehru as president during its Ludhiana session. The stage was now set for the fusion of movements between princely and political India.

In Bikaner, Panikkar had no time to worry about the failure of federation or the onset of war. The state had been struck that year by a famine that seriously alarmed British authorities.[18] Historically, Bikaner was no stranger to famines. The living conditions of the peasants were very harsh, both in the khalsa lands, managed directly by the state, and in the areas entrusted in jagirdar to local nobles. The famine of 1939 was the culmination of a food crisis that had been ongoing since 1936.

The court and its ministers swung swiftly into action. Fodder depots were opened across the state. Ganga Singh released nearly Rs 2,00,000 from his privy purse and the maharani arranged for the daily distribution of khichra at the temple of Sri Jagdish in the capital. As the state struggled to regain its balance, the time for federation officially ran out. On the very day of the deadline for Linlithgow's last ultimatum, Hitler's armies invaded Poland. On 3 September 1939, the viceroy brutally reminded India just who was in charge. The United Kingdom had declared war on Nazi Germany, he announced over the radio. India was Britain's largest colony and by virtue of that, it too was at war. As for constitutional change, he said, 'Given the necessity for concentrating on the emergency that confronts us, we have no choice but to hold in suspense the work in connection with preparations for federation.'[19] Zetland went one better, stating pithily that the federal scheme was now in 'cold storage'.[20]

It was a moment of grave setback for India's political history and for many, from Linlithgow to Lothian, a personal defeat. For Panikkar, it was salt in an open wound.

'To serve my country has been another constant ambition ... Instead of serving the country, I have had to serve the princes,' he wrote bitterly.[21]

The Congress was horrified at the viceroy's announcement.

For a long time, the party had resolutely opposed the rise of fascism and Nehru had given innumerable speeches condemning Hitler. Indeed, he had often infuriated New Delhi, simply by being as strong a critic of Chamberlain's policy of appeasement as any of Churchill's peers in the British House of Commons. After considerable internal debate, the Congress ministries finally resigned in eight of the eleven provincial assemblies they controlled. It was an idealistic move and a poorly thought out one. It resigned them to political wilderness, annoyed the British and gave the Muslim League a second wind.

The declaration of war increased surveillance and repression across the country. The Raj was determined not to be distracted by any revolutionary outbreaks that could undermine the war effort. Germans, Austrians and Italians working in India were rounded up in their hundreds. Bengal's fledgling Nazi Party (the Bengali Society for German Culture, set up in 1933) was broken up, and in Europe, surveillance on Indian subjects increased. In the princely states, the Raj began interfering even more than it usually did, usually on the pretext of wartime exigencies. Indian ministers were removed and Englishmen were substituted in Cochin and Kolhapur. In Cambay, Kota and Alar, the powers of the princes were ended or curtailed. Princely expenditure was reduced and personal wealth was inventoried.

Despite the ignominy, the Indian princes, much to Panikkar's disgust, leaped faithfully to the empire's aid. 'Anyone with eyes could see the foundations of British power tottering!'[22] Panikkar wrote crossly. However, the princes felt that aiding the Raj could benefit them. Panikkar was openly scornful of their efforts. 'They were under the impression that this technique of toadying would induce the British to perpetuate their autocratic rule.'[23]

An ironic statement indeed from a man who was running the administration of Bikaner.

Most people spent 1940 assimilating the fact that this was not a momentary geopolitical crisis but a war that threatened life as everyone knew it. The political changes came first. In May 1940, in an extraordinary moment of backchannel politics, Winston Churchill replaced Neville Chamberlain as the prime minister of Britain.

With his hunched shoulders, his gravelly voice, the omnipresent cigar and his florid, bombastic speeches, Churchill has imprinted himself on colonial history, particularly in India, as a racist imperialist of the first water, and for good reason. His policies regarding India would ruin much of the country economically as it moved towards a transfer of power. It was clear that under his prime ministership, a tough India policy would be maintained. Zetland now stepped down, to make way for Leopold Amery.

Amery was an interesting choice. An old schoolfriend of Churchill from Harrow, he had strongly opposed Churchill's line on India. He was pugnacious, intelligent and deaf, with a great personal secret that would only be revealed after the war: he was a Jew.[24] Amery also had no desire to take on the post of secretary of state for India. He had been hoping for a more economic or defence-centric post. Zetland briefed his unenthusiastic successor on the task that lay ahead of him as frankly as possible, though he knew that Amery's views—which were similar to his own—would find little favour with a man as rigidly imperialist as Churchill.

As Germany began its death march across Europe, Gandhi wrote to Linlithgow, offering to speak personally to Herr Hitler, who couldn't possibly be 'as bad as he is portrayed'.[25] Subhas Chandra Bose, on the other hand, was making far more disturbing statements. He was deeply impressed by German victories, and while conceding that Germany *might* be fascist, said that he could not help 'admiring these qualities of hers—how she plans in advance, prepares accordingly, works according to a timetable and strikes with lightning speed'.[26]

So brazen were these statements that by July 1940, he had been clapped into house arrest under the Defence of India Act. The chubby-cheeked Bengali was temporarily out of the way, but the threat for the Congress was Jinnah, who was enjoying a time of rising political market value. His presence on the political scene was encouraged by the viceroy. 'He represents a minority—and a minority that can only effectively hold its own with our assistance,' Linlithgow told Amery smugly.[27] Belatedly, the Congress attempted to patch up its ties with the League by asking it to issue a joint demand for a declaration of British war aims. Jinnah put paid to this attempt by insisting that first, the Congress must stop its 'mass contact' campaign.[28]

To nobody's surprise, Nehru refused.

It was the last straw.

In an article published in January 1940, Jinnah wrote that the British needed to put together a new constitution which recognised that in India, 'there are two nations who both must share the governance of their common motherland'.[29] In March, Jinnah spoke before 60,000 people at Minto Park, Lahore. 'The Musalmans are not a minority,' he told the roaring crowd. 'The Musalmans are a nation by any definition.'[30]

The Lahore Resolution brought into being the idea of separate homelands for Muslims, though at no point did either the League or Jinnah clarify what it meant in granular terms. As a gamble, it seemed to be paying off, with a huge groundswell of popular support for the resolution. The Congress was taken aback, with Nehru dismissing it as 'fantastic', Gandhi calling it 'baffling' and Rajaji condemning it as the product of a 'diseased mentality'. As for the Raj, with its hands full with a war, it seemed wise to have the Muslim League on its side as a bargaining chip. Cold water could be poured on this resolution of Jinnah's, Zetland told Linlithgow, but without 'conclusively rejecting it'.[31] It was the ultimate game of divide and rule, and it would change South Asia forever.

Linlithgow, his dreams of federation ruined, was now obsessed by the war. The German blitzkrieg across Europe brought India sharply into the picture, particularly after Italy's entrance into the war. Once the Suez Canal was closed to the Allies, the route to the eastern parts of the British Empire would be via the Cape of Good Hope. With the empire on the backfoot, nobody in India could look away from the possibility that the Allies could lose the war. The viceroy was also up against a divided Whitehall.

Amery's line in the House of Commons was that Indian constitutional reform could be re-examined at the end of the war. He was in direct opposition to Churchill, who wanted no such thing. The hapless Linlithgow was caught in the crosshairs and in August 1940, he poured oil on troubled waters by putting forth a post-war settlement known (unoriginally) as the August Offer. It was vaguely worded and guaranteed to annoy the Congress, but Linlithgow wasn't looking to do anything beyond succeed in the war effort. India's defence production—Bihari saltpetre was essential for bomb-making, for instance—was crucial to Allied plans. Nor could the viceroy afford to ignore the threat of a possible joint invasion from the Japanese and the Germans. His son found him lying prone on the floor of his study, surrounded by several maps of the ocean, muttering to himself, 'The guns are pointing in the wrong way.'[32]

At a meeting in Wardha in August 1940, the Congress Working Committee recorded its formal rejection of the August Offer, stating that Linlithgow's proposals demonstrated Britain's 'determination to hold India by the sword'.[33] Emergency talks within the party resulted in the setting aside of any personal disagreements over the war. The League's response to the August Offer was less straightforward. Jinnah wanted to use it as a bargaining chip for safeguards, for parity between the League and the Congress, and if possible, for tacit approval of Pakistan. But he was now beginning to overplay his hand. For instance, Jinnah wanted the viceroy to agree that, if the defence portfolio was not awarded to a Muslim, it should not be allocated to any other Indian. The viceroy could hardly agree to that and at the end of September, the League also refused to accept the August Offer. By next month, Nehru was jailed for four years under the Defence of India rules and on charges of sedition.[34] The arrest and conviction of senior Congress leaders such as Azad and Rajaji began on 17 November 1940 and ended on 4 January 1941, by which date nearly 600 satyagrahis had been convicted.

Chapter 32

Bikaner

MEANWHILE IN BIKANER, PANIKKAR WAS HAPPILY FAR FROM THE NATIONAL movement. He and Ganga Singh had got off to a somewhat unusual start. When Panikkar presented his credentials to the maharaja, he handed over a typed sheet of paper. When Ganga Singh inquired what it was, Panikkar answered cheekily, 'It is my dismissal order. The day you do not feel the need for my services please sign it and return it to me.' He produced another sheet of paper. 'This is my resignation letter, which I have signed and the day I feel that I do not want to work for Your Highness, I will put the date on it and hand it to you.'[1]

After that, unsurprisingly, there were no problems with the Maharaja of Bikaner.

When Panikkar's grandson, Parvathy's son Madhavan Nair, heard this story many years later, he was incredulous. But his grandfather was delighted to explain that the first thing he used to do whenever he entered office for the first time was to dictate his resignation letter and keep it in his waistcoat pocket.

'Show me,' Madhavan demanded.

Panikkar promptly fished it out of the waistcoat he was wearing that day.[2]

Bikaner's new foreign minister also did not like to abide by royal customs. Just as Panikkar had made his presence felt to Nehru in the days of his mission in Amritsar, so too did he make it clear to Ganga Singh that he would not kowtow to anyone, regardless of their position. In Bikaner, the custom was to refer to the ruler as annadaata (giver of food). Panikkar flatly refused to do so, intriguing Ganga Singh into asking him why.

'Who is whose annadaata?' Panikkar retorted, delighting the maharaja into quick laughter.[3]

Apart from getting the better of Ganga Singh, Panikkar was also finally not thinking incessantly about constitutional reform or princely intrigues. His days once again found a nice, quiet routine. Every morning, he spent an hour with his works of Malayalam. His novel on Pazhassi Raja, the classic that was to become *Kerala Simham*, was almost complete. He was also working on a spate of other Malayalam poems, which would all be published between 1940 and 1942. In between these endeavours, he also kept an eye on his children.

The eldest daughters—Parvathy and Devaki—were young women, ready to go to university. In those days, the leading colleges were Delhi College (the oldest), located outside the walled city's Ajmeri Gate, St Stephen's College and Hindu College, both at Kashmere Gate at the time. Indraprastha College, then the only college for women, was located on the Delhi ridge some distance away. That was all there was of the University of Delhi in those days, and it was the single-handed creation of the bushy-browed Sir Maurice Gwyer.

Born in London in 1878, Gwyer came to India in 1937 as the first chief justice of the Federal Court of India, but with war on the horizon, Linlithgow gave him the additional portfolio of vice chancellor of Delhi University (DU) in 1938. A fellow of All Souls in Oxford, Gwyer wanted this campus to be akin to his beloved Oxbridge, an all-India university beyond compare. In 1939, he submitted a memorandum asking for a number of professorial chairs, fellowships, scholarships and readerships to be set up. Today's three-year BA and BSc pass and honours degree courses were introduced during Gwyer's time. He invited the richest minds of the time to lecture at DU, from V.K.R.V. Rao to E.M. Forster and Homi Bhabha.

Gwyer was both brilliant and sociable, and on his long list of friends, he counted K.M. Panikkar. With two daughters of college age and a son not far behind, Panikkar suggested chattily that DU must have its own campus, with constituent colleges located at proximity across that campus. Gwyer liked the idea, and with Panikkar's encouragement, the old Viceregal Lodge became the Vice Chancellor's Office of today, and Hindu College and St Stephen's College shifted location to the new campus.

Parvathy was sent to Indraprastha College, which had a hostel on campus. The plan was for Devaki, always the rebel, to follow suit. But she obediently kept her head down, studying for her intermediate degree in Indraprastha College along with her sister. Both were excellent with languages, fluent in Bengali that they'd picked up in Calcutta and Sanskrit that they'd learnt observing from their father. Now that they were growing up, it is easier to see how patterns of sibling closeness developed, born from the circumstances of their schooling. Parvathy and Devaki were and always would be very close, since they had grown up together, far away from home. In a similar vein, Haima and Radha were very close. They too grew up together, away from home. Madhusudan, the keenly intelligent, quiet, bespectacled little boy, grew into his teens alone in Delhi, far from the comforts of home and his siblings. His circumstances led to a curious kind of introverted brilliance. Madhusudan would eventually follow in his father's academic footsteps, but he would always feel overlooked and isolated in comparison to the rest of his family. 'I think he always felt like his father didn't do enough for him,' says a grandniece.[4]

When Parvathy and Devaki arrived in Delhi to continue their education, life for all the siblings brightened a bit. Now, they had a chance to be together during school or university breaks, with the two youngest catching the Kalka Mail to New Delhi. Madhusudan would pick them up at the railway station, and together they would go towards what is North Campus today to spend time with Parvathy and Devaki.[5]

While the children grew accustomed to these changing patterns of life, Gouri was trying to get used to yet another new princely state. To keep her mind busy, she did what came naturally to her: focusing on learning new skills, new languages, new ways of cooking and carpentry. She had plenty of time on her hands now, for all the children were away at university or finishing school.

It was at this time that a young man by the name of Kuttappa Panicker (though no relation of theirs) seems to have come to stay in the Panikkar home. It was hard to find fellow Malayalis so far north, and Kuttappa was affectionately treated as a member of the family. He was a part-time astrologer of some repute, drawing Panikkar's reluctant interest. The older man was not, by nature, superstitious, nor did he believe too much in the ways of the stars and planets. But since his own and Gouri's horoscopes had been cast at their respective times of birth, he continued the tradition for his children and for some of the grandchildren that were yet to come. For those purposes, he relied only on Kuttappa.[6]

The doors of the Panikkar home were also flung open to many guests, most of whom were travelling through India or Asia or transiting through Bikaner. Panikkar was now seen as highly influential: a powerful man with a clever, resourceful mind and a persuasive pen. The ICS officer Maurice Zinkin and his fascinating wife, the journalist Taya Zinkin, often stayed with Gouri and Panikkar, and in the course of time, the two couples became excellent friends. When she arrived in India, Taya came to see Panikkar, intrigued by a common friend's description: 'When you go to India do not miss meeting Mephistopheles; he is the most entertaining and enthralling character in the subcontinent!'[7]

Panikkar was deeply interested in Taya, a feisty polyglot French-Russian émigré. Before she met and married Maurice, she had lived as a refugee across Spain, Haiti, Santo Domingo and finally the United States, where she had studied biochemistry in Wisconsin. When the Panikkars knew her, Taya was rising fast in her chosen career as a foreign correspondent, writing for the *Economist*, *Manchester Guardian* (as the *Guardian* then was), *Le Monde* and *Neue Zuricher Zeitung*. With her keen eye for character and personality, Taya found herself fascinated by the Foreign Minister of Bikaner. 'K.M. Panikkar is indeed the twentieth century version of Goethe's hero,' she declared, '... with his goatee beard, his burning eyes, his scintillating wit, his wonderful flow of anecdotes, his uncontrollable love of pulling the strings, his gaiters and his ethics of the days of Edward the Seventh, when life still went at the leisurely pace of a 1st class Pullman.'[8]

The Zinkins were always curious about understanding changing political trends, particularly in princely India. Panikkar rarely minced his words, telling them frankly, 'The people of Bikaner love their maharaja, but they love India more; they will make him M.P., they will support him against Delhi or another prince, but they will not back him in breaking up the unity of India.'[9]

From him, Taya learned of all the doings in the Chamber of Princes in the decade gone by, of his bitter disappointment in the failure of federation and his hopes for the future. Listening to his arguments, often backed by historical evidence and anecdotes, she saw what others had seen in him: the remarkable ability to compartmentalise his formidable mind. 'Panikkar the historian can, sometimes, dissociate himself from Panikkar the diplomat and then large vistas into the future arc opened to Panikkar the author, and Panikkar the man,' Taya observed.[10]

Bikaner was the right setting for these manifold facets of his personality.

In Panikkar's memoir, he remains stoically anodyne about his years in Bikaner. He prefers to tell a reader that he kept his head down, focusing on social and popular reform in the state. That much was true enough. Ganga Singh was keeping his new minister busy. With his wide remit, Panikkar opened more science classes in the state, set up Masters of Arts classes in colleges and organised funding for private schools. He increased the number of girls' schools and libraries across Bikaner, besides reforming the powers of the state legislative assembly, giving it the same mould as that of Mysore and Travancore. 'During his regime,' recalled Kanwar Jaswant Singh, Panikkar's colleague in the Bikaner government, 'every Bikaneri student who could get admission in a technical college in India either through State efforts or through his own was assured of a substantial scholarship from the Government of Bikaner for higher studies.'[11] Education was one of Panikkar's many great interests, and under his resourceful tenure in Bikaner, he ensured that every idea, no matter how far-fetched it seemed initially, fructified. In achieving this goal, he had the full support of Ganga Singh.

The early days of working with him brought home to Panikkar the fact that, unlike Patiala, Bikaner was a hard worker. 'To see the Maharaja sitting at his office table, surrounded by his numerous stenographers and secretaries and poring over files and correcting drafts is to have a new notion of what an Indian maharaja can be.'[12] Not for nothing had Bikaner reached where he was in the eyes of his brother princes and the Crown. He paid great attention to the duties of his state, beginning his day at eight o'clock sharp by dictating notes and memos to his stenographers. His ministers would meet him through the day, discussing plans, schemes and public works for the betterment of Bikaner, often late into the evening. Ganga Singh was also a bit of a micromanager, keeping a sharp eye on British officers and their agendas within his state. Arthur Lothian, Resident of Rajputana, would disgustedly report that he was hard-pressed to meet Bikaner's ministers alone, without the maharaja being present.[13]

Despite Ganga Singh's reputation, Panikkar was quick to see that he was serving both a practical and a brilliant man, a suave utilitarian who suffered no fools or ditherers. But more than once, Panikkar ran hard into a wall of curious rigidity, a reluctance to venture too far out of his comfort zone. He would describe it tactfully as a 'great strain of caution … which makes him [the maharaja] distrust new ideas and wary of taking up proposals which have not been carefully scrutinised'.[14] Ganga Singh would take a long time to consider some of Panikkar's more radical reforms, though to be fair to the maharaja, once he was on board with an idea, he supported it all the way. After two years in the state, Panikkar's appointment was indefinitely extended. He was now given the title of vice chairman of Bikaner's Council of Ministers.

The statistics show why.

By 1943, despite the exigencies of war, and largely thanks to Panikkar, there were 141 government schools across Bikaner, along with 137 aided schools and 191 private establishments and a degree college with scholarships to study abroad.[15] A Rajasthani Research Institute was set up to study Oriental and Rajasthani lore on a serious basis. It was, for Panikkar, a dream. He believed deeply in the power of education and in the value of preserving India's history and heritage.

For all his unease with the new, Ganga Singh trusted his minister enough to give him carte blanche for how he wanted to transform Bikaner. Much of this remit also depended on how Panikkar pitched his initiatives. This was how the Anup Sanskrit Library had come to be.

Digging about in the basements of the library, Panikkar found a huge, dusty trove of ancient Sanskrit manuscripts. His untrained eye saw that these were priceless and possibly hadn't been seen by anyone for years. Quickly, Panikkar checked his official calendar. The time was coming, he noted shrewdly, for Bikaner's yearly campaign to his people. He knew that the maharaja liked to have events pencilled in for him in advance and added in an initiative to bring in a scholar who could restore Bikaner's ancient Sanskrit heritage.

Bikaner went along with this affably. He knew the value of good public relations as well as Panikkar did, but he was equally aware that his foreign minister was an erudite man, with a keen eye for culture and education. The combination of that, Ganga Singh thought, was excellent. With the maharaja's permission, Panikkar sent for the great Sanskrit scholar C. Kunhiraja to organise the ancient manuscripts of Bikaner and install them as a collection in the library. When Ganga Singh saw how well the initiative had worked, he gave the library to Panikkar to handle personally. Delighted to the core of his academic soul, Panikkar converted it into a public research institution for scholars of Sanskrit and Hindi.

It was just the beginning.

Chapter 33

'Always So Busy!'

PANIKKAR HADN'T HAD THE TIME TO EXPLORE PATIALA DUE TO THE RUSH of federal debates. But he had the time here. He found himself thinking deeply about the geography of Bikaner, an ancient state, much of which was soaked in history and blood. He took to riding out with his assistants, exploring the remotest corners of the state. An area of particular focus was the Saraswati Valley.

In the *Rig Veda*, the Saraswati is both a goddess and a river, the only one deified in Vedic hymns. Always interested in Hinduism and the scriptures, Panikkar seems to have undergone something of a religious immersion—a prolonged period of religious instruction and worship with an unnamed guru—around this time. His grandson recalled that though Gouri was known to always do her puja every day, it was not Panikkar's habit until he was in Bikaner.[1] What prompted him, a man not known to practise Hindu rituals at all, to do such a thing remains a mystery, but Parvathy would recall seeing her father pray every day in Bikaner, particularly to the Goddess Shakti.[2]

Reading more about the Saraswati's trail through the scriptures and ancient Hindu texts made sense then, for Panikkar was deeply influenced by his studies and rituals at this time. His reading taught him that the river mysteriously disappeared in the post-Vedic era, the only major river to do so in northwest India. It reappeared a few centuries later, reported in the Brahamanas and the Mahabharata (whose great war is said to have been fought in Kurukshetra, a region watered by the river) as vanishing in the desert at a point called Vinashana, a revered pilgrimage site. The river went dwindling onwards, eventually retiring into the realm of the mythical at the confluence between the Ganga and the Yamuna as an 'invisible' river. It was one of the fountainheads of India's classical civilisation, though colonial discoveries had pointed to the emergence of the Saraswati as a small stream. It was said to have joined the seasonal Ghaggar River (known as the Hakra), near the present Indo-Pakistan border.

Now that he was here in Bikaner with all kinds of privilege and access at his disposal, it seemed foolhardy to let go of an opportunity to find the real river. As ideas go, it seems remarkable, but one must put it in the context of Panikkar's life. The early 1940s were a rich age of destruction and discovery. Even as war raged across the face of the world, science stood on the cusp of radiocarbon dating which would revolutionise archaeological chronology. A Bedouin shepherd boy tossed a stone into a cave near the Dead Sea, and discovered eight hundred manuscripts in Hebrew, Old Canaanite, Aramaic, Greek, and Latin, dating from Jerusalem's Second Temple period—the Dead Sea Scrolls. In the mid-1940s, Sir Mortimer Wheeler came to India, as the director of the Archaeological Survey of India, triggering a spate of discoveries across the country, from Pondicherry to Taxila to Mysore. These discoveries, of course, continued decades of discovery across the world, right from when Howard Carter discovered the tomb of King Tut in 1922, and archaeologists like John Marshall travelled widely through Central Asia and India. As far as Bikaner itself was concerned, a promising start to find the lost Saraswati River had been made by the quiet, scholarly Italian Indologist, Luigi Pio Tessitori in 1919. A brilliant linguist with a deep interest in Indian vernacular languages, Tessitori had been invited to join the Linguistic Survey of India, with the specific task of leading the Bardic and Historical Survey of Rajputana. His study of ancient Rajputana's literature and grammar laid the foundations of the history of the development of modern Indo-Aryan vernaculars. Delighted by his discoveries, Ganga Singh had encouraged Tessitori to travel across Bikaner, where he was able to identify proto-historic sites in and around the state, including at 'Kali Vanga' (now Kalibangan in Hanumangarh), Baror, Rangmahal and Sardargarh. The seals and pottery he found were the first Harappan seals of the lost Indus Valley Civilisation, and great was his excitement. But in 1919, Tessitori had to rush back to Italy when he heard that his mother was seriously ill. Unfortunately, the dreaded Spanish influenza finished him off before he could ever make his discoveries public. Tessitori died on 22 November 1919 in Bikaner.

Now, twenty years later, when his Prime Minister brought him the question of archaeological exploration, Ganga Singh was pleased. He gave Panikkar carte blanche to pursue promising options. For Panikkar, there was just one choice: Sir Marc Aurel Stein.

In the 1940s, Stein was nearing eighty, but his career was unparalleled. Born in Budapest, he was no stranger to India or the orient. A student of oriental languages and archaeology, Stein had met and befriended the renowned Indologist Rudolf Hoenle in London. He arrived in India on the heels of that meeting in 1885. His heart was set on exploring, like his mentor, but even the greats have to start somewhere. Stein's beginning was as the registrar of the University of Punjab. By the time Panikkar sent for him in 1941, Stein was an established and unscrupulous discoverer, exploring (and looting) widely across Central Asia, the Pamirs and the Silk Road. He was providentially also back in India after a survey of the Roman frontier defence of Iraq and Transjordan. Panikkar had followed Stein's remarkable career and knew he was arrogant and brilliant enough to jump at the chance.

Jump he did.

Stein arrived in Bikaner as a guest of the maharaja in the winter of 1940 and was promptly given a grant of Rs 2,000 to begin work. His task was to examine the large series of ancient moulds along the Ghaggar within Bikaner, and to test two interesting sites by trial excavation. Here, on the dry, dusty riverbeds of the Ghaggar-Hakra, between Hanumangarh in Bikaner and Derawar in Bahawalpur, Aurel Stein found definitive evidence of the lost Indus Valley Civilisation. More than that, he made serious attempts to date the changes in the course of the Saraswati River. His tour ended abruptly in March. It was an incomplete tour, but it was too hot, and Stein was too old and too beleaguered by controversy.[3] Upon his return to Bikaner, Stein told Panikkar that if his work was carried forward, the world would know that the Indus Valley Civilisation had been born in the Ghaggar-Hakra tract. He died shortly thereafter—but before he did so, Stein went one better than Tessitori and published the results of his preliminary survey in Bikaner.

The matter would have ended there, but for Panikkar.

It would be seven years before he had the chance to bring up the subject once again. But in March 1948, less than a month before he took over as India's ambassador to China, Panikkar wrote to Nehru, urging the new prime minister of free India to consider the necessity of a survey in the desert around Bikaner and Jaisalmer. 'With the separation of the Pakistan provinces, the main sites of what was known as the Indus Valley civilisation has *(sic)* gone to Pakistan. It is clearly of the utmost importance that archaeological work in connection with this early period of Indian history must be continued in India. A preliminary examination has shown that the centre of the early civilisation was … the desert area in Bikaner and Jaisalmer, through which the ancient river Saraswati flowed into the Gulf of Kutch at one time.'[4]

Jawaharlal Nehru, a man who understood the value of both Panikkar and history, acted with amazing speed. The next day, a letter from his personal secretary H.V.R. Iyengar enclosed a copy of Panikkar's note to the minister of education. The letter strongly underlined that 'the Prime Minister entirely agrees with the suggestions contained in the note and hopes that the Archaeological Department will undertake the explorations suggested in Jaisalmer and Bikaner'.[5] The proposal was forwarded to the Archaeological Survey of India (ASI), which responded that if a survey had to be carried out, it would require Rs 10,000. Immediately, the request was tangled in red tape from the finance ministry which demanded testily to know why a central department should spend money on a native state, particularly since the PM himself had ordered a curb on expenses. It took a battery of missives for the purse strings to be loosened.

To the quiet Amalananda Ghosh of the ASI has gone the distinction of finding more than a hundred sites of the Harappan civilisation along the Saraswati River in 1950. But this was an expedition that would never have been done without Panikkar's early interest in Bikaner, his insistence on following up on Stein's findings and Nehru's absolute faith in his recommendations.

With typical restraint, Panikkar remains quiet about this extraordinary moment in his life, one which intersected so personally with ancient Indian history. He is silent as well about the larger national movement. Nor does he mention the spate of Malayalam literature that he kept churning out along with his political and administrative work. Between 1942 and 1945, he began to study Sanskrit and Jain classics. In the former, he was trained by the Sanskrit scholar Dr Kunjan Raja, who was in charge of reorganising the Sanskrit Manuscript Library in the state.

A formal study of Sanskrit opened Panikkar's eyes and mind to a whole new perspective on literature and ancient politics. He liked to discuss these views with Devaki and Parvathy, both of whom were Sanskrit scholars themselves. *Chadukthi Mukthavalli*, a collection of 102 individual Sanskrit shlokas, was a product of this period, as was *Mandodari*, a drama along the lines of Sanskrit plays. Panikkar didn't lose sight of history or politics in his novels and dramas. *Hyder Naikken*, for instance, is a drama on the adventures of Hyder Ali. *Kerala Simham* had released in 1941 to wide acclaim. It would become a classic of its time, with a reviewer as late as 1960 finding it justifiably remarkable that 'a man like Panikkar, who had to work so much in other spheres' could find time to 'write a historical novel, pulsating with excitement and vibrant beauty'.[6]

Other dramas and sonnets that Panikkar wrote at this time included *Dhruva Swamini*, a historical drama centred around the Gupta dynasty, and a Kathakali called *Daveedu Vijayam* (Victory of David), a story from the Old Testament. The scale and scope of Panikkar's mind was formidable, even when he was (as he was, when he was writing these plays and poems) relaxing. But in his memoir, he is silent about these attempts at finding joy. He lays emphasis instead on curious political vignettes, such as his work as an emissary for the Maharao of Kutch.

Kutch was a Rajput state in northwestern Gujarat. In 1819, following a short war, a treaty was signed between Kutch and its new overlord, the British Government of Bombay. The treaty included a provision that the British would guarantee the nobles of Kutch (known as the bhayat) full enjoyment of their possessions. The meaning of 'possessions' was left vague, but it was interpreted as including executive, judicial and fiscal powers over the lands of the bhayat. As a result of this treaty, about half the area of Kutch was effectively exempted from the control of the state's ruler, the Maharao. Instead, it was governed by the members of the bhayat. Successive Maharaos of Kutch had sought to curtail the autonomy of the bhayat, but thanks to the treaty of 1819, they made little headway.

Everything changed in 1940 when the Crown changed its policy radically. The Maharao was now allowed to deprive the bhayat of their judicial powers. He could also force them to hand over a large part of their revenues, leaving them with no more than a rubberstamp right to appeal this sudden deprivation. When Khengarji III ascended the throne in 1875, he was all of nine years old. When he was deemed old enough to emerge from the shadows of his regents, he began a long and progressive reign during which he brought his state into the electric, automobile and aviation era (though personally, he liked to live without electricity). Externally at least, he maintained excellent relations with the Crown. He was appointed as an aide-de-camp to Queen Victoria in her twilight years and was one of the few Indian rulers to have attended all three durbars. He renovated temples, built schools, opened ports and expanded railway lines, all with an exchequer that was perpetually short of funds thanks to the treaty of 1819.

Khengarji III's circumstances underwent a dramatic change with the outbreak of the Second World War. Quickly, the Raj put in place administrative reforms to defuse hostility to unpopular princes and merged hundreds of hopelessly small states in Gujarat with larger neighbours.[7] It was, in the Maharao's view, an excellent opportunity to press for more power. The British were happy to consider this request, but they had strong reservations. Khengarji III seemed progressive, but was he really? Their suspicions were based on the touchy issues of customs duties, tariff policies and smuggling.

Kutch had always conducted its tariff policy on a different basis from other maritime states of west India.[8] The state refused to maintain British tariffs at its ports, which meant that all merchandise that crossed the Viramgam Line from Kutch into British India had to pay full duties at the frontier. Unsurprisingly, trade between the two remained low and most of what Kutch imported was consumed locally.[9]

Trouble began when the Maharao opened a new port at Kandla in 1930. Khengarji III hoped that it would be as successful as Nawanagar's port in Bedi and attract a large share of the import trade across northwestern British India. He requested permission from the Government of India to build a railway line to carry goods to markets on the other side of the Viramgam Line.

Delhi knew what this would mean. A railway line and low duties would mean merchants could import goods to Kandla and smuggle them into British India. The Raj refused Khengarji's request unless he agreed to impose British customs duties. The Maharao refused point blank.

Now, this was the middle of 1941. The Allied war effort across North Africa, West Asia and the Pacific was on the backfoot (to put it mildly). New Delhi could really have done without a rebellious ruler whose proximity to crucial ports could hinder supply lines for the entire war. In order to remind the old Maharao who was in charge, the British reasserted control of Kutch, overturning a policy that had been in place for the last century. To Khengarji III's shock, he was informed politely that 'the administration of Cutch is such that under modern conditions, the existing state of affairs cannot longer be permitted to continue'. He was told that either a British political officer would be appointed as dewan, or his administration would be subjected to a commission of enquiry for corruption.[10] 'Everyone knew that the Viceroy's advice, couched in the form of an ultimatum, could be defied only on the pain of a deposition.'[11] Nobody expected that Khengarji III would 'dare to defy it'.

They had not accounted for his feistiness.

He was Ganga Singh's maternal uncle and he now wrote to his nephew, asking for help. Panikkar was dispatched instantly to Bombay, where he found Khengarji III ensconced at the Taj Mahal Hotel, 'quite unperturbed'.[12]

The Maharao told the admiring Panikkar that he had already written to the viceroy, refusing to act in haste. He told Linlithgow airily that 'he needed time till the middle of August to send a considered reply'.[13] Panikkar appreciated this audacity, particularly given the ongoing war efforts, but he advised the Maharao to temper this zinger with a more reasoned response. He drew up a draft response, explaining that the Maharao was ready to introduce all necessary administrative reforms, on the condition that he appoint the dewan himself. They had until 15 August to respond.

On the night of 14 August, Khengarji III agreed to the final draft put together by Panikkar. It was then sent to be typed. Only when it was half done did the typists discover, to their consternation, that they were out of official notepaper. No royal prince would dream of sending official communications on anything less. The typing came to a halt. 'Eventually, some official notepaper was unearthed from the house of a Kutch official.'[14] But by the time the letter was completed and signed, it was already past midnight.

There was no way the letter could be sent.

The Maharao had missed his deadline.

Panikkar had to fire-fight, and fast. He shot off a quick cable to the incensed British Resident E.C. Gibson and telephoned Linlithgow's personal secretary, Sir Gilbert Laithwaite, to explain the delay. Linlithgow, his mind occupied with the war, was in the mood to be somewhat forgiving, especially after he ran his eye down the letter from Kutch and saw that the Maharao had acceded to nearly all British demands.

The crisis was averted and Panikkar went back to Bikaner, politely declining the Rs 25,000 that the grateful Maharao pressed upon him. In the long run though, his intervention came to nothing. In September 1941, Francis Webb was imposed as the new dewan upon the helpless Maharao, which triggered the threatened overhaul of the Kutch administration. Four months later, the Maharao's fifty-year-old son, Vijayaraju, succeeded his father. Infuriatingly, he supported both Webb *and* the new reforms. It was a moment of considerable ignominy for Panikkar and the old Maharao. Despite being checkmated thus, Panikkar enjoyed playing the game of politics. Taya Zinkin remarked that there was, in fact, nothing that her friend loved more, apart from diplomacy and history.

When he wasn't neck-deep in intrigues and politics, Panikkar was preoccupied with matters of home and family. The strain in his marriage seems to have healed over time, but he would always be extra susceptible to the wiles of powerful and intelligent women. Devaki would notice with considerable exasperation that her erudite, scholarly father was often reduced to fits of schoolboy giggles in the presence of, say, Sarojini Naidu or Vijayalakshmi Pandit. But apart from that, there were no other affairs to occupy Panikkar's attention or time. It was just as well, for there was plenty afoot at home.

Parvathy was back from college now, a young woman of marriageable age. Her wedding would take place in Bikaner in the 1940s to the brilliant young mathematician and statistician, Kesavan Raghavan Nair. Today, Nair is remembered as one of India's leading statisticians, having worked across crucial departments (food and forestry being just a few) in the Government of India. When he married Parvathy, however, he was a rising star on the scene: a protégé of the great P.C. Mahalanobis himself, at the Indian Statistical Institute. Nair was from an extremely poor family, but the brightness of his intellectual potential, his natural warmth and his gentle air of dignity was appealing to both Panikkar and Parvathy. The wedding was a simple, elegant one, attended by the maharaja as well. The young couple took up residence in Bikaner for a while, before Nair received his next posting to Dehradun. It was a milestone of sorts for both Gouri and Panikkar to have one child married and out of their nest, so to speak.

These were, once again, years of personal stability. Panikkar maintained his routine of coming home every day for lunch. In the evenings, their khansama would cook them English meals—roast chicken or grilled fish—and Panikkar and Gouri would sit together in quiet conversation after dinner. Between the drudge of daily routine, there were dinners at the palace. Much to Gouri's indignation, Panikkar never took her to the palace for any of these dinners, even though she longed to meet Ganga Singh. But the maharanis of Bikaner themselves never attended, and without their presence, Panikkar felt slightly awkward about bringing Gouri. Only when Ganga Singh once asked him why it was that he never saw 'Madam Panikkar' at these parties did Panikkar retort, 'If your wives couldn't be bothered to come, my wife couldn't either!'[15] The maharaja was so startled that, from then onwards, Gouri was always invited.

In the wider world, much was churning and much had yet to come.

By July 1941, Jinnah's marriage of convenience with the Raj was on the rocks. The clearest example of this was when the viceroy asked the Muslim provincial chief ministers to sit on a National Defence Council but did not invite Jinnah to join them. Furious, Jinnah ordered the chief ministers (who had a nominal attachment to the Muslim League) to boycott the council. They complied, with the exception of Fazlul Huq of Bengal who resigned from the League. He was joined soon by the Nawab of Dacca. The two united in criticising Jinnah—the first warning signs of the movement that would later lead to the creation of Bangladesh.

A keen observer of world events, Panikkar would find much to think about in these developments, but since his time in Bikaner was clearly far from over, he focused on bringing the state into the twentieth century in a big way. Many of his reforms in Bikaner have gone unnoticed and unsung, but he is responsible for the state's heritage and historical preservation. Significantly, he promoted his state's reforms to his friends in the Jewish Agency, Weizmann and David Ben-Gurion. The Jewish Agency supplied quite a bit of the funds—the exact amount remains unknown—for Panikkar's reforms in Bikaner.[16]

He brought in the renowned German art historian, Indologist and staunch Nazi opponent Dr Hermann Goetz to study Hindu and Indo-Muslim art in Bikaner. Goetz was interned by the British in India thanks to the war and his nationality, but while he was around, he was a boon to Panikkar, who loved classical art and who could see that Bikaner's art was in a league of its own. 'To the art lover, it offers a series of masterpieces of Indian Art,' agreed Kanwar Jaswant Singh, '... the Gupta terracottas of the Ghaggar Valley, the Saraswati Statues from Pallu, the early Rajput sets of illustrations, Maharaja Anup Singhji's buildings, the collections of arms and paintings, the private rooms of Maharaja Gaj Singhji and Surat Singhji in the Bikaner Fort and the Rajput miniatures of the beginning of the last century.'[17]

With the assistance of Ganga Singh, Goetz put together a seminal work on Bikaner's art history. His internment interrupted the writing, and it would eventually be published in 1948, under the reign of Sadul Singh. A copy of it still exists in the library of the Indira Gandhi National Council for Arts (IGNCA) in New Delhi.

Panikkar wasn't only interested in history and archaeology. He was also in charge of the state's industrial, agricultural and medical activities, a measure of how much he was trusted by Ganga Singh, and a strong indicator of the fact that, by the mid-1940s, he was virtually running Bikaner. This meant that he was looking after its economic prospects as well, so he was an early participant in the heated discussions over the Bhakra dam. In 1963, Nehru would call the mighty Bhakra dam a 'new temple of resurgent India'.[18] The construction of the Bhakra and Nangal dams, along with their associated canal systems, began in 1948. A concrete gravity dam, Bhakra was 740 feet from its deepest foundation and the second highest in the world, next only to the Hoover Dam on the Colorado River. Harvey Slocum, the American chief engineer of the project, described it as 'probably the most difficult dam ever undertaken'.[19]

The Bhakra dam is rightly upheld as one of independent India's most concrete (pun intended) symbols, but its origin was steeped in colonial politics. The earliest reference to a Bhakra project, or more tamely the idea of a storage reservoir on the Sutlej, dates to 1908. Over the years, the project stopped and started several times, collecting interstate disputes like so much flotsam and jetsam between Punjab (original broacher of the Bhakra project) and Sind; and Punjab and the state of Bahawalpur and the states of Patiala, Nabha, Bilaspur, Faridkot and Bikaner. For Bikaner, the story of the Bhakra dam is woven through its twentieth-century history. Ganga Singh had seen the great famine of 1889–1890 wipe out one-fifth of his state and had no desire to allow that to happen again. With Panikkar's assistance, Ganga Singh pushed to make the nearly 136-kilometre-long concrete canal, built from Ferozepur on the Sutlej, a reality.

Unfortunately, in events presaging the bureaucracy of modern India, the dam was never given much priority until 1948.

There was simply too much to do.

Internally, the Chamber of Princes was going through several upheavals, most notably the new chancellorship of Digvijaysinhji, the young Jam Sahib of Nawanagar. He wasn't a popular choice, given his lack of experience at administration or politics. But the Jam Sahib surprised his critics. He was warm, energetic and practical, and a savvy politician. His first term as chancellor saw him engaging in an administrative overhaul and some public relations to rescue the Chamber of Princes from decrepitude. Once that was done, he put in place two research groups to explore which states would be first in line for talks with politicians to discuss their future in an independent India.[20]

As members of the chamber put their heads together for the umpteenth time, Nazi Germany occupied Poland, Belgium, Holland, Norway and France as well as most of eastern Europe. It attacked the Soviet Union on 22 June 1941. Japan had not yet entered the war, but from India's point of view, the need for new sources of military supplies as well as an independent aircraft industry became urgent. Throughout 1940, Linlithgow worked assiduously to invite political, technical and military delegates to Delhi to discuss how best to coordinate war supplies. At the end of 1940, the Eastern Supply Conference had resulted in the set-up of an Eastern Group Supply Council, staffed by delegates from India, Australia, New Zealand and South Africa. Panikkar recognised these as important moves, presaging a renewed significance of India's place and role in the Second World War. But in many ways, the empire was running out of options. In July 1940, Britain lost eleven destroyers to the German Navy in as many days. Desperate, Churchill asked for help from US President Franklin D. Roosevelt.

Born to wealth, with a cousin in the White House while he himself was at Harvard, Roosevelt was a born politician: attractive, intelligent and witty, with a fine speaking voice and natural charm. His political career was meteoric. He was in the New York Senate at twenty-eight and a decade later, at thirty-eight, he was nominated by the Democratic Party for the vice presidency. A year later, he contracted polio, as a result of which he lost the use of his legs forever. He couldn't hide his disability, but he could and did shield the public and perhaps himself from its severity. He won the presidency in 1932, and was re-elected in 1936, 1940 and 1944. Known popularly as FDR, he was either the saviour of the nation or a socialist tyrant indifferent to personal liberties and an apologist for capitalism. It all depended on who you asked.

Roosevelt had seen the United States through the Great Depression, and as far as the war was concerned, he made it clear that it was not just economic peace that he wanted but international peace. During his presidential election campaign in 1940, he promised voters that he would keep America out of the war. But he couldn't help his belief in the fact that the United States should serve as a 'great arsenal of democracy'.

'Give us the tools,' Churchill pleaded, 'and we'll finish the job.' In March 1941, Roosevelt granted this plea with the Lend-Lease Act, which met both Britain's desperate need for supplies and allowed the United States to prepare for war while remaining officially neutral. But as 1941 wore on, it became clear that Churchill was hard-pressed. Roosevelt dispatched a personal envoy to London to liaise with Churchill. Averell Harriman was a stodgy man with an acute attraction to power. He would soon become known for his role in talks to negotiate the Lend-Lease agreement in Moscow and his torrid affair with Churchill's glamorous daughter-in-law Pamela.[21] In August 1941, Churchill and Roosevelt met on board the *USS Augusta* in Placentia Bay, Newfoundland, to sign the Atlantic Charter. The charter declared American support for Britain and presented both countries as united against Germany. It also underscored the importance of the principles of freedom, self-determination, peace and cooperation. Crucially, it contained a clause supporting 'sovereign rights and self-government'. Roosevelt assumed this applied universally; Churchill that it only referred to countries under occupation by his enemies. There was, he declared tersely in parliament, no reason to assume that it applied anywhere else. This interpretation would lead to considerable friction between Roosevelt and Churchill, particularly in a war that was being fought for liberty. But it bought enough time for the British prime minister to cable his viceroy in October 1941, asking him to stay on until the spring of 1942 at the very least.

It was a prophetic request. On 7 December 1941, Japan attacked Pearl Harbour, crippling the American fleet and making itself master of the Pacific. Hitler stormed into the bloodied vacuum, declaring war on the United States four days later, on 11 December. As the Japanese juggernaut began to engulf Southeast Asia and the Pacific in flame and bloodshed, Britain stood stunned and helpless. There was now no doubt that India would have to hold the line for the empire in Asia.

CHAPTER 34

'To Mark Time Is to Lose India'

IN THE SPRING OF 1942, PANIKKAR RECEIVED A SHOCK.

He had known for some time that the maharaja was ill, but he hadn't known the extent of it. Now, Ganga Singh informed him soberly that he had, for a long time, been living with throat cancer. His doctors had told him that he had mere months to live.

It was a moment Panikkar would never forget. This was the second maharaja he had served with for such a long time. Of Sadul Singh, Bikaner's mercurial son and heir, he knew little, but it was clear that this was yet another turning point in his career.

In fact, turning points were everywhere.

In February 1942, Linlithgow's muttered imprecations about the direction of the guns of Singapore came true. Long held to be an impregnable citadel, the island fell to the Japanese that month. They were here now, at India's door from the south and from the northeast, holding over 62,000 Commonwealth and British troops captive. It was a stunning blow to Britain's prestige in Asia, and it led inevitably to the popular feeling that the British were not, after all, as invincible as they seemed.

The authorities in New Delhi were nervous that Hindus had a 'brotherly feeling' for the Japanese. This wasn't helped by the fact that, just the previous year, in 1940, Subhas Chandra Bose had escaped house arrest in Calcutta. With the help of the Abwehr—German intelligence—he was spirited across Peshawar and Afghanistan to the Soviet Union, where he assumed a new identity as an Italian nobleman, Count Orlando Mazzotta. The 'count' was then taken to Berlin where, once safely inside the Third Reich, Bose began recruiting his fellow Indians to fight against Britain. In 1941, he founded the Free India Centre, set up a transnational radio station broadcasting pro-Axis propaganda to India and formed the Free India Legion, also known as the Tiger Legion, an all-Indian infantry force of volunteers made up of expatriates and prisoners of war, recruited from labour camps like Colditz. Its soldiers swore an oath of allegiance to Subhas Chandra Bose—and Adolf Hitler. By 1942, the Tiger Legion was a thousand men strong.[1]

To British eyes, there were threats everywhere they turned.

In India, for instance, the situation seemed to be spiralling out of control. Constitutionally speaking, the reforms commissioner H.V. Hodson was of the opinion that 'time is not on the side of constitutional sanity'.[2] Indian political leaders were on the same page as Hodson. In December 1941, the Bardoli session of the Congress Working Committee expressed support for the 'peoples who are the subject of aggression and are fighting for their freedom', while contending that 'only a free and independent India can be in a position to undertake the defence of the country on a national basis'.[3]

On 1 January 1942, Sapru appealed to Churchill to break the constitutional deadlock in India by some 'bold stroke' of 'farsighted statesmanship'. What the Congress wanted, he said, was simple: to view India not as a colony but on a constitutional position equal to other dominions of the commonwealth. He called for the Indianisation of the Viceroy's Executive Council to form an interim national government. Churchill, even though his back was to the wall, refused to consider this. He cabled his colleagues at the India Office, warning them of the danger of raising key constitutional questions when the enemy was at its doorstop.[4]

On 24 January 1942, Clement Attlee wrote to Leo Amery, wondering whether it was worth considering if 'someone should not be charged with a mission to try and bring the political leaders together'.[5] In Attlee's opinion, one of the better alternatives favouring Whitehall was to send out an official of high standing to negotiate some kind of settlement. This was what Lord Durham had done in Canada. The only question was: who would this official be? While the Raj and Whitehall debated, it had to contend with the undoubted fact that the United States was a very much interested participant at this time.

In early 1942 then, Churchill was an unhappy man. His government was rapidly becoming unpopular, with constant blackouts, heavy rationing and incessant news of defeats in the Far East. He knew he would have to give way to Roosevelt on something at least, but the US president was being peculiarly adamant about concessions in India. In February 1942, FDR told Harriman to deliver a 'highly sensitive' personal message to Churchill, asking when and what kind of action was being taken.[6] It was a squeeze and Churchill knew it, but he was in no position to revolt. Britain was currently extremely weak. In March, Malaya and Burma had fallen to the Japanese. There was no way that he could push back against Roosevelt, especially not when the United States was itself in the war. As a result, when he had word that Generalissimo Chiang Kai-shek and his wife, the vivacious Madame Soong, intended to visit India that February, he was thrilled. He wrote immediately to the Chinese leader in the fond hope that he would adhere to British policy over India. But this was a gross underestimation of who the generalissimo was and why he was coming to India in the first place.

Chiang Kai-shek was born in a hilly town called Xikou, in the province of Zhejiang near Shanghai in 1887. His father, a small-town salt merchant, had died when he was eight and his widowed mother had struggled to bring up her two children, Chiang and his sister. Chiang was not a particularly prepossessing character, with a penchant for brothels and hard liquor. His neighbours avoided him and his relatives were ashamed of him. Stung by their visible revulsion, Chiang determined to make a success of himself and chose a military career. It was the perfect path to have chosen, for China in the 1920s was a mix of scheming politics and brutish strongarm tactics. By allying himself with Sun Yat-sen, and via Sun's wife, marrying May-ling Soong, one of the most beautiful, independent women in China, he was at the peak of his powers in the 1940s.[7]

Visiting India was not quite as outlandish as it might have seemed. Nationalist China and India had been in touch since the end of the First World War, a relationship driven by cooperation in the anti-imperialist struggle. The British were aware of the dangers of this bonhomie and through the 1920s, bilateral visits were often blocked diplomatically. That hadn't stopped China from closely tracking the course of the Indian nationalist movement over the years. Now, as the war reached new heights, it was hoped that a common strategy could be found, one that would continue in the post-war period.

How this would play out in reality is another story, but when Japan attacked China in the summer of 1937, the Congress had not only expressed public support for the latter but had also sent a medical mission of five doctors post-haste. Nehru himself went to China in August 1939, only to rush back when war was officially declared. But he returned convinced of the need for deeper political cooperation between India and China. In the early years of the 1940s, Chiang and Nehru kept in touch. When Nehru was in jail in 1940, Madame Soong asked Sir Stafford Cripps, then the British ambassador to Moscow, when he would be released from prison.

So this visit by the generalissimo in February 1942 was at least superficially no big surprise. Sir Maurice Hallett, then the governor of the United Provinces, wrote disgustedly that Chiang Kai-shek was here to 'meander through India, with Nehru sticking to him like a burr'.[8] Still, the Raj rolled out the red carpet for him. He was taken to review Indian troops in a Rolls-Royce from which a Union Jack 'fluttered from the radiator cap, like a raccoon tail on a college boy's Ford'.[9] The generalissimo and his wife were given palatial villas for their stay and waited on by liveried servants. He was even made an Honorary Knight of the Bath, Military Division.

While he partook of these delights, Chiang was here because, as he told the viceroy during the formal banquet thrown in his honour,

'To have one look at things is a hundred times more satisfactory than hearsay.'[10] So, he was here to see how the munition factories, from which arms were moving to China across the Burma Road, were functioning and how they were being defended. He was here to talk of the new road being built from Assam into China, and he was here to assess India's general readiness for war. Politically, there was also no harm in taking the temperature of relations between the Congress and the Raj. With the Japanese reaching Malacca, Borneo and the doorstep of Burma (it would fall in a matter of weeks), Chiang was understandably worried.

He was also reporting to Roosevelt. The American involvement in the war, post Pearl Harbour, was considerable, especially in the realms of backchannel diplomacy. Through FDR, the generalissimo's main aim was to put pressure on the empire to accept the Congress Party's demands for Indian self-determination. They were at a quid pro quo: Chiang needed Roosevelt's help for arms and money. FDR, who was in favour of British talks with India, was influenced by Chiang's suggestion that the United States and China could cooperate in putting pressure on Britain to resolve 'the Indian Question'. The US president liked the sound of this, though it must be noted that FDR had never been to the subcontinent. His India policy was at best inconsistent and at worst weak and ineffective. In both cases, it was driven largely by the generalissimo and his own resistance to European colonialism. Still, Roosevelt thought about Chiang's suggestion and wrote to Madame Soong that one possible solution could be the dividing of India into two parts.[11]

While the US president pondered the fate of India, Whitehall was depressed. The recent lethal combination of political and military reversals had forced Churchill to agree despondently to the dispatch of a political mission to India. Here, he found unexpected resistance from his viceroy. His nerves frayed by the fall of Singapore and Burma, Linlithgow insisted that any such visit 'in existing circumstances could be disastrous'.[12] But his pleas fell on deaf ears. On 9 February 1942, Sir Stafford Cripps was announced as the man who would lead Britain's next mission to India.

In the face of this torrent of events, each occurring within days of the other, Panikkar had to think fast. In 1941, he had written a note for the ailing Ganga Singh that compared the policy proposals of the Congress and the Muslim League and concluded that the League posed a far more serious threat to the princely states.[13] This note was written in the aftermath of the Lahore Resolution. In it, Panikkar took the view that, with the League in favour of the creation of Muslim-majority states, the situation was worse than before. It would be possible, for instance, for the North-West Frontier Province (NWFP) to ally itself with Afghanistan to attack Kashmir. This was only a hypothesis, of course, but its consequences would be catastrophic, fracturing the transport and communications system and rendering the rupee valueless.[14] Jinnah might not have fully endorsed Pakistan, Panikkar wrote forthrightly, but the omens were dire. Therefore, he believed the princes had no choice but to embrace the necessity of a central government.

Panikkar's political thoughts in the early 1940s are interesting, if deeply fatalistic. The archival correspondence of the national movement suggests that, in general, nobody was in favour of Partition before 1946. Even then, it was always seen as a decision born from having been left with no choice. Yet, as early as 1941, Panikkar appears to have not only accepted that Pakistan would be a reality but also that it was the only reality worth considering. In a letter to his old friend Syed Mahmud from his Aligarh days, Panikkar wrote, 'I have for a long time now, been a Pakistanist. Without the separation of Pakistan, a central government will not be possible in India. The fear of Hindu majority at the centre, whatever safeguards you may create and wherever pacts you may work out, will drive the Muslims to unreasonable madness.' He continued, 'I have no terrors about even the exchange of population. But the "two eyes theory" and a central government cannot work together. So let us, dear Mahmud, foreswear our past. Consider ourselves failures for having dreamed of a united India.'[15]

This was clearly not a point of view to which he had come easily. Panikkar was by now on the cusp of fifty. He had spent most of his life working for the princes to unite them with provincial India, for a federal cause that was now lost, for a dream of India that to him at least had now shattered. There was no room any more for emotion. From where he stood, joining hands with the Congress was the only practical way forward for the Chamber of Princes. At least the Congress would offer a strong central government along with greater administrative efficiency, strong political institutions and a more modern legal system. Smaller states with no resources for such reforms would have to join with each other or larger states. V.P. Menon and Sardar Patel would call the process 'integration'.

Panikkar called it 'cooperative groups'.[16]

As he watched India move towards a transfer of power, his clear-eyed nationalism was evolving. Tradition was important, but so was the development that could originate from modernising traditions, such as the industrial policy of Mysore or the abolition of untouchability from Travancore. Syed Mahmud, who was then a senior Congress leader, read Panikkar's note and passed it on to Rajaji for his perusal.

Soon Panikkar received a note from Rajaji himself, congratulating him on the depth and foresight of his views, and asking him to take those views to their natural conclusion. Should democratic regimes also be introduced in the states? Wouldn't they guarantee the same rights and duties enjoyed elsewhere across the country?[17] These were the questions with which Panikkar was wrestling when Ganga Singh's health worsened considerably. The cancer was moving fast through his body, and though there was only a dim chance of a full recovery, the maharaja's health was hampered by his love affair with his personal physician, Dr Sivakamu. 'This lady,' Panikkar said spitefully in his memoir, 'was as skilled in surgery as she was in the … intricate art of serving a king.'[18]

To the king's detriment and Panikkar's despair, Bikaner chose to ignore the ministrations of his brilliant German physician Richard Jizchak Weingarten, then the head of the Bikaner State Hospital. This resulted in what Panikkar described as a 'medical crossfire',[19] a messy mix of sorcery, ayurveda, allopathy and priestly incantations. This despite the fact that, as Weingarten himself wrote later, Bikaner led the way when it came to modern medical innovation, favouring Western medical approaches over practices of indigenous medicine.[20]

As Ganga Singh's health declined even further, the Cripps Mission landed in New Delhi.

Stafford Cripps had just returned from an unsuccessful mission to Moscow. A patrician vegetarian with a penchant for nudism and knitting, he was at the time 'a prominent public figure without a public role'.[21] But he was a popular choice as leader of this new mission to India. The viceroy disagreed emphatically, calling him Stafford 'Crapps' behind his back and rather childishly keeping him in Karachi on enforced quarantine before allowing him passage to New Delhi.

Cripps was no fool. He was aware that his political standing hinged on the success of these negotiations. The *Hindustan Times* had already warned ominously, 'Everything depends on how quickly Sir Stafford Cripps gets through his task in this country.'[22]

He already had the reputation of being pro-Congress, but as he told Churchill anxiously, 'The outlook so far as the internal situation goes is exceedingly bad.'

It didn't help matters that he picked a fight with the reforms commissioner straightaway over everything from the communal problem to the princely states. Hodson was wary of Cripps and his agenda from the start, a fact not helped by Cripps's tactless statement that the cabinet was ready to give India whatever it wanted except defence, a fact that neither the British nor the Indians enjoyed hearing. Cripps also wanted to 'redraw' the federal units first. To Hodson's horrified mind, there was 'the germ of the historic conflict' that was to come in 1946–1947.[23] More importantly, a key figure on the scene who was complicating matters still further was FDR's latest emissary—Colonel Louis Johnson. The colonel was an unhappy choice, for there was literally nobody in India who liked him. His own brethren thought he was 'coarse, bombastic and ignorant'.[24] Amery thought he was a 'real mischief maker'[25] and Hodson thought he was an 'indiscreet, ill-informed busybody'.[26]

Despite Johnson's irritating presence, Cripps kept up a public relations barrage. His manner was informal and cheery, a striking contrast to the more aloof viceregal style. He met over forty individuals and delegations, using a mix of consultations, negotiations and midnight meetings. He undoubtedly worked very hard, but he was up against a war that was advancing steadily toward India and communal rifts that were too deep to bridge. Cripps knew that if the Congress was to wait until the war was over, the balance of power might shift in their favour even further than it could already claim. But the Congress was in no mood for conditional promises. They didn't want a 'post-dated cheque on a failing bank'.[27] There had been too many of those in the last two decades. They rejected his offer outright. Nehru, with whom Cripps had been friendly in the 1930s, was coldly suspicious. 'He was a lawyer who stated his case powerfully and expected it to prevail ... He ... left no room for manoeuvre.'[28]

Yet Cripps, to be fair to him, negotiated well beyond his mandate. His final offer to the Congress was one of Indian-staffed administration, with only home affairs and defence remaining in British hands. Such a concession had never been authorised by London.

But fatally, what Cripps *did* promise was the likelihood of Pakistan. At a press conference in Delhi on 29 March 1942, in answer to a question as to whether there was anything to stop two provinces from different parts of India from clubbing together 'to form separate union', Cripps replied, 'That would be impractical. Two contiguous provinces may form a separate union.' In the same breath, he also said that it would not be impossible to have a 'rearrangement of boundaries between the two unions and an exchange of populations to get the larger majority of each'.[29]

It was the first time that the prospect of autonomous provinces *outside* India had been publicly mentioned by the British in an official capacity. Cripps affirmed to the press that, as a dominion, India would be equal in every respect to the United Kingdom and other dominions of the Crown and would be free to remain in or separate itself from the equal partnership of the British Commonwealth.[30] There would be a post-war Constituent Assembly, subject to the right of any province not to accede. This provision entrenched the right of predominantly Muslim provinces to not be coerced into an Indian union. Simply put, it meant that the door to Pakistan was now open.

Hodson was appalled and Linlithgow was furious. 'Having gone so far, why boggle at the word independence with all its appeal to

India?' he snarled at Amery.[31] And so, by the time Cripps left India, his mission had failed on a grand scale, marking a fatal split between the viceroy and the Congress, and between the Congress and the League. 'The less interested we appear now to be in Indian politics the better,' Linlithgow wrote bitterly.[32] It was, as the historian Patrick French has written, a moment of great political and mental alienation.[33]

What of the princely states in this entire imbroglio?

Their position was also left unresolved. They would be free to stand out but encouraged to stay in. But technically, the central question being debated was the issue of sovereignty. The Cripps proposals envisioned several different political successors to the British Raj, including the princely states and some provinces, all of which would continue to exist as relatively autonomous entities. Even though the mission had failed, the princes favoured Cripps's plan precisely *because* Cripps allowed them to stay aloof from any constitutional structure. At a meeting with the Chamber of Princes on 28 March 1942, Cripps told them, 'So far as the paramountcy treaties are concerned, these would remain unaltered unless any state desired to get rid of the paramountcy in order to be able to accommodate itself the better to new conditions ... We should stand by our treaties with the states unless they asked us to revoke them.'[34] He patiently went over his draft, point by point, with the Jam Sahib and with Bikaner, assuring them that they had the right to opt out of the constitution-making body 'if the constitution did not suit them'.[35] It was precisely the kind of assurance that Patel and Menon would be firm in *not* making when the time came.

When the War Cabinet and viceroy heard that Cripps had promised this to the princes, they were collectively furious. The political secretary, Kenneth Fitze, was instructed firmly to inform the chamber that there would be no 'unilateral denunciation of the treaties'.[36] Deeply worried now, the princes decided that it might not harm them to conduct a little public relations at this stage. At Bikaner's behest, Panikkar was deployed for this new mission due to his persuasiveness and his intelligence. His first move was to publish a quick but crucial essay in the influential American journal *Foreign Affairs*.

'The Princes and India's Future' is both smartly written and smartly positioned. It makes no real point beyond the need to protect princely autonomy based on their treaty rights with the British Empire and their independent existence before the empire was established. In modern terms, it would qualify as a puff piece, plugging the importance of princely states in negotiations for a free India. Panikkar's choice of publication was shrewd. It was a good way to reestablish the image of the princes, away from their eccentric, cartoonish portrayals and towards a perception of them as socially progressive, intelligent forces.[37] But what followed from this was an invitation that would keep Panikkar away from India for the rest of that year.

He was asked to participate as a delegate in the eighth annual conference of the Institute of Pacific Relations (IPR) at Mont Tremblant, Canada.

CHAPTER 35

Mont Tremblant

ESTABLISHED IN 1925 AT A HONOLULU CONFERENCE ORIGINALLY organised by the international YMCA, the IPR was by 1942 widely praised as a transnational platform and the 'single best source' for information on the Pacific region.[1] In modern parlance, it did the work of a think tank, with its books and papers being read widely by diplomats, students and servicemen. In the earliest years of the Cold War, the IPR would fall prey to inevitable anti-communist propaganda led by US Senator Joseph McCarthy. It was accused of supporting Mao's forces in China and violating the Internal Security Act in the United States. It was eventually cleared of all charges, but it never really recovered from the McCarthy witch hunt, closing down in 1961.

But when Panikkar arrived in Canada in the winter of 1942, the IPR was at its peak as a critical institutional structure comprising private individuals, scholars, businessmen and journalists. It bridged the Pacific divide at a time of war, performing the crucial task of maintaining dialogue between the East and the West. It was Panikkar's introduction to a new world, one of innovation and reinvention. The IPR's supporters felt that the Second World War, no matter how it ended, presaged a new era of diplomacy based on transparent and consensual decision-making, with an outlook sympathetic to the goals of disarmament, free trade and self-determination. India had a special place on the IPR's agenda. The entry of the United States into the war in 1941 and the resulting expansion of the conflict into the Pacific had given India a central role. More than ever, Indian voices would matter in a post-war world. Edward Carter, the head of the IPR, emphasised that any international gathering would be composed of representative national groups rather than official national delegations.

Carter was a man with connections, particularly with Nehru and Chiang Kai-shek, and he was leading an institution that was debating what a post-war world would look like. In Carter's point of view, an independent India was vital for any new order in post-war Asia.[2] The only problem with this was that any prospective delegation would have to be personally approved by the Viceroy of India.

Linlithgow had no desire to encourage Indian nationalists to travel abroad to take part in an international conference that was deciding on a post-war world. He was also in the middle of launching a vicious smear campaign against the Congress, extending press censorship and intercepting correspondence which would let him know what the future course of political action might be. He procrastinated on Carter's request for a delegation to attend the conference scheduled at Mont Tremblant in Canada that winter. By August 1942, he had other problems on his hands. British intelligence was reporting that a new national movement was imminent. Some reports contained a draft for what would later become the Quit India resolution.[3]

They were right.

On 8 August 1942, the Quit India resolution was accepted by the All India Congress Committee, despite the reservations of Nehru, Azad and Rajaji. In an atmosphere electric with expectation at Golwalia Tank in Bombay, Gandhi proclaimed, '*Karenge ya marenge* … we shall either free India or die in the attempt; we shall not live to see the perpetuation of our slavery!'[4]

Early next morning, the empire struck back. The Congress leadership was slammed behind bars at Ahmednagar Fort. Gandhi himself was whisked off to the Aga Khan's palace in Poona. They would remain imprisoned for the duration of the war.

Following their arrest, the situation across much of north India blew up. Shopkeepers went on strike. Property was vandalised, looted and set on fire, with the police hitting back with equal violence. 'The insurrection was far worse and more dangerous than the public at home in Britain was allowed to know,' recalled Hodson.[5] As the movement grew, arrests took place by the thousands. In Bihar, Linlithgow ordered the aerial machine-gunning of rioting crowds.

Against this backdrop, it seemed hardly likely that the viceroy would allow a motley group of Indians to take their opinions onto an international stage. But in the end, the exhausted Linlithgow simply distanced himself from the entire situation, passing the buck to Ramaswami Mudaliar, then the chairman of the Indian Institute of International Affairs (IIIA), IPR's Indian chapter, set up in 1936.

Mudaliar was delighted.

The delegation he chose consisted of K.M. Panikkar; Zafrullah Khan, a Muslim judge on the Executive Council of the Viceroy of India; Diwan Bahadur S.E. Runganadhan; and Rai Begum Shah Nawaz, a League politician and member of the National Defence Council.

Importantly, as advised by Sir G.S. Bajpai, then the agent general[6] in the United States, the delegates were also to carry out a lecture tour across America to influence American opinion on India.

When their photograph was published in the international press, all sections of the Indian media hooted derisively against a delegation that seemed to be 'packed' in favour of British interests.[7] Delhi's *National Call* giggled, 'They do not represent any group of men in this country and they can all speak very well if they are appropriately briefed on any subjects.'[8] The final delegation was sharply criticised, not just within the nationalist movement but within the Indian Institute itself. Critics pointed out these men had been cherrypicked by Mudaliar rather than by the institute. The delegation included even those who were not official members of the IIIA.

One of the most vociferous opponents of the selection process was Hari Nath Kunzru, a liberal politician and member of the IIIA's governing council. He issued a public statement in which he insisted that these were Mudaliar's 'personal nominees'. Many Indian intellectuals, he said scathingly, preferred to be represented by more independent voices on the global state of affairs. Riven as the IIIA was internally and criticised though it was publicly, it was still one of the first attempts to institutionalise Indian views on international relations, and Panikkar was quite excited at the chance to participate. On 12 November 1942, he set out for Baltimore.

Because of wartime exigencies, the route was a little more circuitous than usual, going via Karachi, Basra and Cairo, and on to Khartoum, Lagos and Bulim in Brazil before finally arriving in Baltimore. It was snowing when he arrived, with thick white drifts piled up in front of doors and windows. The press was notably absent, considering the Chatham House Rules of secrecy applied.[9] Over the next ten days, delegates discussed various possibilities for a post-war order. Only later, once the conference was over, were papers on the agenda released or published.

The India Roundtable at the conference discussed exactly what Linlithgow had feared: the future of a postcolonial India. It touched on a fully Indianised executive council and an exploratory commission that would study questions relating to the constitution and the Constituent Assembly. But on the whole, Mudaliar and his colleagues lived up to the expectations of their critics and delighted the British by urging restraint and moderation regarding Indian independence. 'Ramaswami and his Indian lot were, I think, the prize turn,' gushed the Liberal MP Sir Frederick Whyte to Chatham House staffer Maragret Cleeve. Whyte enjoyed Mudaliar's 'patience and realism', the 'feminine performance' of Begum Shah Nawaz and the 'vigorous' contribution of the ageing Zafrullah Khan.[10]

Carter, who was a vocal proponent of the importance of detaching from British interests, was disappointed with this well-mannered, erudite group's fidelity to British interests. But he knew that his major goal had been achieved: the Mont Tremblant conference put a whole new focus on India and Indian affairs.

It was here that Panikkar began looking at India's regional identity and position in a future postcolonial world. Evidence of this comes from Panikkar's paper, presented at the conference, on 'British India and the Future of Southeast Asia'. He spoke about a proposed post-war regional order akin to a 'Japanese co-prosperity sphere'[11] for the countries of Southeast Asia. The prospects of an economic breakdown were real, he warned, and only the establishment of closer economic and political ties between India and Southeast Asia could help avert such a regional calamity. The paper makes for interesting reading, given the fact that Panikkar was aware of the region's geopolitical importance and India's strategic significance to the empire during the war. He insisted that a free and stable government in India was the prerequisite for security across the region. This was his line of argument in Bierville, and he adapted it to current circumstances by adding that, since Partition was now in the offing, any future diplomacy would require cordial accord between the independent states of Pakistan and India. 'This,' he wrote significantly, 'is the one way in which the Hindu-Muslim problem can finally be settled.'[12]

Before he went to the United States, Panikkar stopped off in London. His paper had been well received and while his mind was still humming with ideas, he wanted to put down more thoughts. Carter had commissioned him to convert the paper into a book, part of IPR's Inquiry Series. This was a prestigious addition to developing views on international relations. Funded by a $90,000 grant from the Rockefeller Foundation, the IPR Inquiry Series attempted to gauge regional solutions for various Southeast Asian countries. Panikkar stayed in London for a few weeks, immersed in writing and research for the book that would become *The Future of Southeast Asia*.

Published in 1943, it became one of the cornerstones of Panikkar's work on foreign policy. It is clear in the book that Panikkar had not moved fully away from his leanings toward 'Greater India'. He presented the same argument in *The Future of Southeast Asia*, though he used the term 'Further India'. The phrase, as Panikkar explained, 'embodies the idea which had been recognized from early days till quite recent times that India and Southeast Asia were connected integrally in their political, social and economic life'.[13] In fact, he argued that this was a connection that had existed since the first century CE. 'From the first century A.D. to the middle of the fifteenth century this entire area, with the possible exception of Burma, was politically within the Indian sphere.'[14]

Panikkar also briefly reminded readers that the future of Southeast Asia, its security and economic development, after being released from Japanese occupation, would in time become related to India. Without a free or stable India, the entire region would remain 'the cockpit of colonial ambitions'.[15] It was in this neat little book that Panikkar first argued that maritime power was paramount. Rule over the seas, he stated, was the key toward stability and economic governance in India.

From London, Panikkar travelled to the United States, where he spent a few days talking to important contacts about the princely states. No matter how tired the princes made him, Panikkar never stopped pushing for their integration into the wider national movement. Nor did he want the world to look away from the states. With the Americans heavily involved in behind-the-scenes diplomacy in India, he knew and understood the value of public relations. In the week that he was there, Panikkar held a series of meetings on the subject of the princely states and the role of the United States once the war was over.[16]

While he was still away, a telegram arrived. It was brief and to the point.

Ganga Singh was sliding downhill and his dewan needed to come home immediately.[17]

Panikkar returned obediently, albeit with dread in his heart.[18] He tendered his resignation as soon as he was back, as was the custom whenever a new maharaja ascended the throne.[19] He had had little contact with Ganga Singh's son, Sadul, and he had 'no idea what shape events would take'.[20]

As he waited for events to fall into place, the tension was relieved by some very happy news on the home front. Parvathy had come home to Bikaner to stay with her mother during the last stages of her first pregnancy. In 1943, the Panikkars were blessed with their first grandson, Madhavan (known affectionately to his family as Kochetan). Parvathy wired her husband the time and date of his birth as soon as she could, so that the data could be sent to the official family astrologer in Parur. Kochetan's arrival was an occasion of huge delight. Parvathy recalled. 'My father went mad. He gave away gifts, donated to charity, distributed alms, organised pujas in various temples, blew up a lot of money.'[21] It was the beginning of Panikkar's innings as a grandparent, and by all accounts, he would be wonderful at it. Those of his grandchildren who are alive today recall an affectionate, humorous man who always had time and patience for them.

In the summer of 1943, Panikkar was summoned by Sadul Singh. To his surprise, the new maharaja greeted him pleasantly, insisting 'that I should not leave him, especially during the early phase of his reign'.[22] Panikkar was happy (and hugely relieved) to agree, but he suspected that Sadul Singh 'needed my services temporarily', the better to dislodge the old ministers of the court, many of whom he heartily disliked.[23]

As it turned out, Sadul Singh would do nothing of the kind. He was as given to dominance and domination as his father had been, but he was not Ganga Singh's son for nothing. He knew quite well that, with the war and the national movement standing as they did, it would be foolish to remove a minister who had been so good for the state. In a rare show of trust, Sadul Singh appointed Panikkar as his prime minister on 31 May 1944.[24]

On the surface of things, all seemed to be going excellently in Bikaner. Sadul Singh threw an official banquet in Panikkar's honour. At dinner, Panikkar made an excellent speech in which he presented a plan for reform in the state.[25] He had done his homework for the speech and he laid out a five-year plan for the development of Bikaner which included a series of 'nation-building activities'.[26] He was as good as his word. When he officially took over, Panikkar put in place core social and economic reforms, many of which set Bikaner on its feet as a modern state.

His first task was administrative reform. Panikkar based this—with considerable and clever foresight—on democratisation. He was working against a backdrop that augured danger for the princely states. In 1943, the British government had approved the Attachment Scheme, which annexed over 400 small states of Kathiawar and central India to neighbouring major states. For the first time, the rule that the British Parliament had no authority to legislate for the states had been broken. The princes were horrified at the possibility that the

Raj could, on a whim, cancel an entire state, as it were. They asked for reassurances, but predictably got none. Given these circumstances, it was clear to Panikkar that the princely states in general were in peril, and as far as Bikaner was concerned, he needed to move fast. Quickly, he lobbied for the enlargement of the powers of the state assembly so that it could enjoy a majority of twenty-nine elected members out of a total of fifty-one, along with greater power to vote on matters of public importance and the state budget.[27] It was a project that began on 10 November 1944 and took up a lot of his attention at the time, for good reason.

Under his aegis, a Development Department (which had already launched welcome initiatives, like sheep farming and wool production) was set up. A City Improvement Committee was established to drive urban planning. Panikkar launched a scientific study of the state's mineral reserves, taking inspiration from Mysore, and began to seriously study the potential benefits of hydroelectric power production for the state. He continued to place a high premium on education, creating a bank of scholarships for local youngsters to travel to other parts of India or abroad. A new Child Welfare and Maternity Department was inaugurated in June 1945. With funds coming in thanks to his contacts in the Jewish Agency, Panikkar pushed through a number of reforms between 1944 and 1945: dispensaries were built, sugar, glass and cement production was begun, new roads were laid.[28]

But while Bikaner, at least to the public eye, continued to thrive, all was not well within the palace. The dewan did not like the new maharaja. Panikkar's portrait of Sadul Singh in his memoir is almost astonishingly mean. He wrote scorchingly that the prince was jealous of his late father's reputation. Not only did Sadul Singh want to surpass that reputation but 'in fact, he could not even tolerate hearing his father's name'.[29] 'Avarice, distrust of his officials, delight in flattery, an overweening vanity and a thirst for fame … all these princely defects were combined in him,' Panikkar wrote. 'It may be wondered how I managed to survive as Dewan for five years under such a prince.'[30]

But survive he did. He had been through the mill a few times now and he had built up an armour of self-preservation. So now it took him all of two weeks to size up Sadul Singh and to audaciously present his acceptance of continuity on certain conditions. The first condition, he said confidently, was that the maharaja would agree to follow his advice on all constitutional and administrative policy. For the rest, he said kindly, Sadul Singh was free to do what he liked.

Panikkar puts down the setting of these conditions to the fact that Bikaner was under the influence of one of his most prominent—and corrupt—noblemen. If this man were to sway Bikaner, there would be trouble. Panikkar told the maharaja in no uncertain terms that if this *did* happen, it was fine by him—'as long as they did not venture to violate the general policy prescribed by me'.[31] This anecdote is astounding, but it is a pattern that was, by now, typical of Panikkar. He was not afraid of being arrogantly confident about his powers, nor was he loath to push back whenever he felt the need to do so. The story—that he was able to now set conditions to a maharaja like Bikaner and even call himself a 'brake' on Bikaner's autocratic tendencies—is telling both of just how far Panikkar had come, and of how defeated the princely order already was.[32]

It also reveals just how much Panikkar loved power and the feeling of being powerful. It is perhaps a natural human tendency, but in Panikkar, the enjoyment was just a little bit *too* ardent. 'Power, to this wise historian, is as intoxicating as the stock exchange to a Marwari,' observed his friend Taya Zinkin.[33]

With the skill that many friends and peers marvelled at, he could, in his mind's eye, zoom out to see the bigger picture. Bikaner's internal reforms must be highlighted in order to show the world that the princely states were not as backward or ridiculous as they were portrayed to be. In fact, if they were managed properly, they could even set an example of the kind of progress that a postcolonial country was capable of. He wrote an essay arguing exactly this point for a 1945 issue of *Commonwealth and Empire Review*.[34] It was the public relations specialist in him, the diplomat who was capable of presenting all sides of the same coin.

Academic and diplomat though he might be, Panikkar was also a harassed father in these days. Devaki was pestering him about going to university. She reminded Panikkar much of himself at her age—eager to learn, eager to explore and hugely ambitious. In her case though, there was a slight hitch in plans. The Panikkars had assumed that, like her sister Parvathy, they would arrange Devaki's marriage after she finished her intermediate degree at Indraprastha College. But Devaki wanted to go to St Stephen's College for an undergraduate degree. The college was, at the time, briefly open to women students. It would be the best place to study politics and philosophy, two subjects that Devaki loved.

For a while, there was deadlock as her parents tried to make the young rebel understand that St Stephen's, though excellent, had no hostel on campus for young women. Finally, caving in to his daughter's demand, Panikkar wrote to his old friend, Sir Maurice Gwyer, asking for help. Promptly, Gwyer sanctioned a bungalow on campus, with a matron to chaperone Devaki and a handful of other hopeful young women who had also gained entrance to the red-bricked portals of St Stephen's College.[35] That bungalow was the beginnings of Miranda House—a hostel for young women scholars at St Stephen's College. It would become a teaching college in 1949, a handful of years in the future (and to which Devaki would return in her later years, as a professor of political science). With Devaki's educational trajectory sorted for now, and with Radha and Haima in their last years of school, Panikkar once again turned his eye to affairs of state and country.

In 1932, Winston Churchill had memorably refused to 'preside over the liquidation of the British Empire'.[36] By 1943, he was on the verge of eating his words. The empire's losses in the east and in Africa had only strengthened the American hand in subcontinental affairs. In India, affairs were not much better. In January 1943, Gandhi embarked on a three-week fast. But for once, he would be the least of the Raj's headaches.

For some time now, Linlithgow had been warning of serious food shortages, particularly in Calcutta and Bombay. In the aftermath of the Japanese occupation of East Asia, the overland roads to India were closed, which had hit the import of foodgrain and rice. The Japanese had arrived so fast and so brutally that no contingency plans were in place. So it was that when Gandhi began his fast, India was staring down the barrel of a famine in Bengal. Across the seas, Churchill throttled the shipping lines that would have brought extra supplies to Britain's largest colony. Instead, supplies were diverted for Operation Torch, an ongoing invasion of French colonies in Africa. Churchill really didn't care whether Gandhi lived or died, but he knew that the empire could do without additional bad optics.

He wrote to Linlithgow to wrathfully ask if there was glucose in Gandhi's drinking water. But the viceroy had had enough. He had seen India through the first years of the war, numerous political crises and the death of his dreams of federation. Now he wanted to go home.

It was appalling timing.

Nobody was ready with an alternative. Names were tossed about from Attlee to Eden. Even the Jam Sahib of Nawanagar was not out of the running.[37] Then Churchill hit upon Field Marshall Archibald Wavell. Stoic (though given to poetry), reserved to the point of rudeness and a brilliant soldier, Wavell would actually prove to be a progressive realist. Possessed of a quiet determination to do something about the crisis in India, where he had served in his very first years in the military, Wavell arrived with no illusions. He took up work immediately, travelling around the country to inspect areas of trouble. He reinstated regular meetings of the eleven provincial governors so that Delhi had coherent reports to send to London. He ordered the army to distribute food to the worst-hit areas of the famine. Privately, Wavell was aghast. Between one and three million people had died over three years of the famine in Bengal. In some areas, entire villages had been wiped out.

Wavell's viceroyalty was a time of confusion for both chamber and viceroy. The domestic political trend within the states in 1939–1945 was more reactionary than progressive. With most states retaining bans on Praja Mandal activity and most rulers obstinately refusing to see the need to change, it was clear that there was a strong chance of a crisis here as well. In 1943, Ganga Singh's death had also marked the end of an era, with a political officer remarking, 'We shall not see his like again.'[38] It did not help that the new viceroy, painfully shy and good-hearted though he was, had such slight knowledge of the princely states that he coined a memory aid for himself ('Hot

Kippers Make Good Breakfasts') to remember the names of the five biggest states.[39]

Certainly, not everything was terrible. Some states had capable young rulers, from Mayurdhwaj of Dhrangadhra to Anand Chand of Bilaspur. But mixed with these good apples were the inevitable bad ones. The Political Department briefed the new viceroy in rather startling terms. Yadavindra Singh of Patiala, for instance, was dismissed as 'magnificent to look at but … conceited and not very intelligent'.[40] Baroda's Pratap Singh was useless, except in matters of women and the turf. Sadul Singh was vain and dictatorial, while Holkar was erratic and sophisticated.

The real change, said the Political Department, was in the calibre of the ministers briefing the princes. Most ministers had changed jobs or had left duties. Panikkar was not actively involved with questions of constitutional reform at the moment. Akbar Rao Hydari had died before Wavell arrived. Mirza Ismail was no longer in Mysore. The chairmanship of the Committee of Ministers was now in the hands of people like the Nawab of Chhatari and Gopalaswamy Ayyengar—possessed of charm and, in Ayyengar's case, integrity, but men who did not possess the same commitment to princely India that had driven ministers like Panikkar and Haksar. Still, with the war reaching its peak, both Whitehall and Delhi decided to wait.

As the Allies swept through Stalingrad and El Alamein, the empire tightened its grip on the princes, particularly in the field of labour laws and wartime contracts. At a time when important decisions were being taken about India's post-war economic development, the durbars found themselves shut out of war rooms on planning and infrastructure, like the Central Roads Board or the post-war mission of Indian industries to Britain and the United States. If they applied for import licences, Delhi fobbed them off with long rambles about supply bottlenecks and low foreign exchange reserves. In 1944, when a plan for the development of air transport in India was released, states like Bhopal—which was not only centrally located but also in possession of airfields—were dismayed to find themselves excluded from the projected networks of trunk passenger routes.[41] This approach suited Wavell. 'We should let time and events work for us, postponing any definite move until the constitutional position becomes clearer with the end of the war.'[42] This was private correspondence between Wavell and Amery, but if Panikkar had seen it, he would have been smug. He had known something like this would happen. That was why he had seen to it that Bikaner was well developed in terms of agriculture and resources. But neither he nor Wavell could have predicted all the potholes in the road to freedom.

In August 1944, Wavell convened a meeting of the provincial governors. The tide was turning for the good in the war. He believed that it was the best time to make fresh moves in India. 'India is quiet now and can be kept quiet until the Japanese war ends, though there is much bitterness among political Indians, who have no confidence in the intentions of HMG to secure political progress.'[43] He suggested an interim government, leading to a gradual transfer of power. When Whitehall dragged its feet, he wrote again, stating seriously that India was 'being treated by HMG with neglect, even sometimes with hostility and contempt'.[44] Churchill's astonishing response to this was that the best time to consider India was at leisure, and with that, he wished the viceroy a happy new year.[45]

As talks continued to fail with dazzling regularity between the Congress and the League, Wavell's reforms commissioner, V.P. Menon, suggested a blueprint for what would eventually become the Simla Conference—'a conference of top leaders of political parties and interests, not exceeding 25 in number, under HE's auspices'.[46]

As preparations began for the ill-starred conference, the leadership of the chamber passed back into the hands of Hamidullah Khan. At a time when the princes were already alarmed and resentful at the ambiguity surrounding their status, the nawab began to vocally espouse the Muslim League's line of unfettered paramountcy. About Bhopal's actions at this point, Panikkar wrote variously and viciously that he was an 'imperialist stooge',[47] 'a Muslim partisan and an enemy of the Hindus',[48] and Liaqat Hayat Khan stormed to the Nawab of Palanpur that Bhopal was an 'out and out Pakistani'.[49]

Panikkar's own relations with a ruler with whom he had truly enjoyed working had plummeted. The last encounters between the two men had been very public fights. It had all started on the night of the chamber's resignation, when Bhopal invited Bikaner, Nawanagar, Patiala and a couple of other princes to his residence for consultations.

Panikkar was not invited.

He heard what happened through the Jam Sahib, who had apparently queried why Panikkar was absent. Bhopal had parried this with the excuse that he had tried to locate Panikkar, but the dewan couldn't be found.

Bikaner, listening to this exchange, scented danger.

He summoned Panikkar first thing next morning, but he was too late.

Nawanagar had got there first.

For a couple of hours that morning, Panikkar was kept busy by the Jam Sahib. While he was occupied, the chamber passed the resolution to resign. When the journalist J.N. Sahni rushed through the halls of the chamber to report the day's proceedings, his reporter who was loitering in the corridors called out to him as Sahni dashed past, 'The puppets have walked out of the show, sir! This spells the end of British rule!'[50]

Bhopal had succeeded in his machinations for now.

Panikkar was appalled. He was even more shocked when the Jam Sahib confessed that he had known of this plot, and that he had agreed to keep Panikkar busy while Bhopal did what he had to do. When Panikkar demanded to know how he could have done such a thing, the Jam Sahib laughed. 'If Hamidullah wants to make a fool of himself, it is not my business to stop him. Nor, for that matter, is it yours.'[51]

The response flabbergasted Panikkar.

It was yet another example of how far princely politics and egos could go. In retrospect though, he was glad he hadn't been part of it. 'I could therefore openly condemn it.'[52]

Condemn it he did, calling it a 'childish stratagem' which would not only leave the Government of India unmoved but would also be detrimental to royal interests.[53] When word reached him that Bhopal now wanted to prevent him from going to London to tell his British connections of his machinations, he was torn between indignation and laughter. 'I never had any such intention,' he would write later.[54]

Yet another fight between the two men had erupted over Bhopal's nomination of the Nawab of Chhatari as the new chancellor of the chamber. Panikkar was critical of the move since Chhatari was seen as a representative of Hyderabad, Bhopal's main ally. 'Some people also suspected this was an attempt to swing the committee to the Muslim camp.'[55] It is a stunning mark of how high desperation was running now that Panikkar was chosen, almost as a wildcard entry of sorts, to stand opposite Chhatari. There was uproar. Panikkar, raged the Bhopal camp, wasn't even royal.

They had a point.

Furious, Bhopal sent Liaqat Hayat Khan and Manubhai Mehta to meet Panikkar and demand on the nawab's behalf why he would be so brazen. 'The Ministers' Committee has to function independently,' Panikkar responded airily. 'My candidature was intended to show the impropriety of the Chancellor's intervention.'[56] So saying, he refused to withdraw his name, sending the nawab into paroxysms of rage.

The matter went to a poll in which Chhatari defeated Panikkar by eight votes to six. It was a close contest, and not surprisingly, Bhopal was infuriated. Bikaner was equally angry because Panikkar, for some reason, had not told him that his name had been thrown into the ring. Sadul Singh had stood by his dewan until now, but he had no love for this kind of public drama and he distanced himself coldly from the ensuing chaos. Bhopal, a close friend of Bikaner's, refused to believe that the maharaja had not known what his dewan was up to and for a time, iciness hung in the air between the two former friends.

To make matters worse, nobody could ignore the fallout of the elections in Britain, which had brought Labour to power and the mousy Clement Attlee onto the political stage, consigning Churchill to near wilderness. Everyone, even the princes, knew what this meant. There was no word for 'decolonisation' in that time, but it was clear that the Raj's days were numbered.

When Wavell visited Swat in the NWFP, he explained to the Wali of Swat that the empire was going to withdraw from India very soon. In the interim, could he do anything for the Badshah Sahib? The Wali's son, present at this meeting, translated this into Pashto for his father, who glared at Wavell. 'A moment ago, he told me that he is the last Viceroy and the British are leaving,' he said irritably. 'Then, how could *he* do anything for *me?'* Aghast, the Wali's son hastily changed this blunt rejoinder to the more polite, 'My father is very thankful and grateful to Your Excellency, but there is no problem for the present.'[57]

Overall, the princes were not thrilled with this change in Britain's government. They now feared the likelihood of this new government allying with the Congress to encourage the formation of an 'exaggerated and unsuitable democracy'.[58] Accordingly, the standing committee drafted a resolution, demanding that the viceroy give the princes a clear answer about where they stood after the war. Wavell pleasantly but firmly retorted that, as yet, there was no change in imperial policy toward the princes. It was better, he implied, that they not ask these questions just yet.

Pushed to the edge, the chamber resigned en masse in December 1944. If they expected the viceroy to feel any amount of panic, they were mistaken. Wavell amiably accepted their resignation.

Horrified, Bhopal wrote to the viceroy immediately. 'We are only asking for fair play and justice.'[59]

There was no response.

The archival papers from this period suggest that the princes had by and large failed to grasp the reality that big constitutional challenges were in the offing. Most princes felt that any devolution of power would be confined to the provinces and that imperial links with the states would continue. Sir C.P. Ramaswami Aiyar, in fact, was of the unkind opinion that most of the rulers were unconvinced that the British would ever leave.[60] But Panikkar was very nearly beside himself with worry. The states were running out of time. Once the real process towards independence began, the princes would be left in the lurch. With crisis following crisis, as 1945 dawned, the Committee of Ministers of the Chamber of Princes made its most forthright statement yet: 'There is no denying that the rulers stand on a perilous precipice.'[61]

Chapter 36

An Unlikely Diplomat

IN FEBRUARY 1945, FRANKLIN D. ROOSEVELT, WINSTON CHURCHILL AND Joseph Stalin arrived in the ruined town of Yalta. The Pacific War was ending. Victory, both in the east and across Europe, was on the horizon. The Japanese onslaught had been halted with the invasion of Iwo Jima. While the Big Three discussed the future, a motley crew of Indian delegates landed in London to attend the third unofficial Conference of the British Commonwealth. They were representing the Institute of International Affairs in India, and were led by Zafrullah Khan, then a judge at the Supreme Court. Panikkar was there too, chosen by Khan because of his intelligent discussions on geopolitics and politics. He was relieved for the respite from the chaos of the Chamber of Princes.

In London, he had the chance to see just where things were going internationally. This conference was attended not just by representatives of Commonwealth countries but of the colonies as well. It took place against several layers of change—in the tide of war, in the empire's view of India and in the perspectives of India's colonial standing. The last was important, given the growing feeling within India that a postcolonial country would need to play an important role in the world after the war. The point to be stressed by Indian delegates at the conference was the need to make political and constitutional moves in India as fast as possible. Hamidullah Khan had sent Mir Maqbool Mohammad to keep an eye on Panikkar's activities in London—a brazen piece of surveillance that didn't escape Panikkar's amused attention.

Though he had other things to do in England. Today it is known as soft power, but Panikkar describes it as 'projection of Hindu culture'. He did not elaborate on what it entailed, but clearly felt it was important enough to have discussions on the subject with Amery, Lionel Curtis and the vice chancellor of Oxford University. What does survive is his intention to publish English translations of books in Sanskrit, Urdu, Bengali and Malayalam, and to plan a cultural exhibition in England to allow Europeans to understand India better. Rather remarkably, he also looked at holding an All India Literary Congress in Jaipur, where British, French and writers of other nationalities could be invited to discuss politics and international affairs. From as far back as his time in Oxford, wherever he went, Panikkar made it a point to speak and write about India—its history, culture, politics and its future. Through this visit, Panikkar's mind was clear. The war was largely over. Now, whatever happened after the British withdrew from India, 'I was certain that the Indian princes would not count for much ...'[1]

By the end of the war, Panikkar's nationalist leanings were plain to see. He was no longer devoted to the idea of princely progress, but to the power of popular politics. He was also sick of the constant machinations in the states, and fed up with petty princely preoccupations like privy purses and gun salutes. His frustration took the form of rudeness. 'It is hardly surprising that, living a dream life in ivory palaces, isolated from their subjects and in ignorance of world conditions, they knew little of the growing might of popular will.'[2]

In truth, though, far from being oblivious, the princes were scared. Their fear had made them overplay their hand, with personal and political intrigues clouding any progress that might have been made. Panikkar was aware of this, and there was a part of him that appreciated this fear, but he was pragmatic enough to know that the time for fear was over. When he returned from England, he went straight to Bikaner to tell him that the atmosphere towards India had changed in England. Something needed to be done and fast.

But again, he hit a wall.

There was always some excuse to prevent Bikaner from discussing matters with his fellow princes. It would be another five months before a general 'crisis' meeting was called to strategise on negotiations with Indian leaders and the British Government of India. In the middle of all this, Parvathy returned to Bikaner, pregnant with her second child. This time, the birth was not a joyful affair. A second son, Krishnan (known to his family as Ani), was born in 1945, but 'when I was born, a pall of gloom descended'.[3] The palace astrologers came running to Panikkar, almost frantic with worry. Baby Krishnan would bring bad luck to the family, they warned. For example, the astrologers said, within a fortnight of his birth, Raghavan Nair would lose his mother. Not only that, but Parvathy would be deserted by her husband who would then leave India altogether.

Horrified, Panikkar forbade Parvathy from sending Raghavan the news of his second son. Two weeks after he failed to get an answer from his wife, Raghavan came tearing up to Bikaner from Dehradun, demanding to know what was happening. After hearing why he hadn't been told, he stared incredulously at all of them. His mother, he said, had indeed died on the fourteenth day after little Krishnan was born. But there was no reason to panic about that—she had already been old and ill. As for deserting his wife and children, he *was* planning to go to England, for he had secured an imperial scholarship to pursue his doctoral degree in London. But, he said crossly, he had no intention of abandoning either Parvathy or his sons.[4]

Reassured by his calm, the Panikkars and Parvathy relaxed. The stay in England would be good for his daughter, Panikkar knew. It would reunite her with her brother who was studying there, and it would keep her and her family safe away from a country that was simmering. Later that year, having seen off his daughter and his grandchildren, Panikkar left for Bombay for yet another meeting with the princes, and as always, he had no idea what to expect.

Two days later, he was more furious than frustrated. The conference, like every other, had been torn apart by internal politics. Panikkar presented his thoughts first, stressing the gravity of the situation and pointing out that 'unless the princes acted wisely, they faced extinction'.[5] Next to speak was the Dewan of Travancore who subjected the chamber to an 'hour long harangue'.[6] It speaks volumes of how desperate the situation was that Panikkar briefly put aside his animosity toward Aiyar, calling his speech 'a model of eloquence and statesmanship'.[7] When the meeting broke for lunch, Aiyar came up to Panikkar and remarked, 'You're quite right, Panikkar. Unless the princes stand together, this will all be over.'[8]

Panikkar nodded but couldn't help asking why Aiyar had chosen this moment to support him. The dewan smiled a little and said frankly that he had spoken out so strongly to forestall any moves by Bhopal to ask for plenipotentiary status as a negotiator. In short, he wasn't prepared to entrust the future of the chamber to Hamidullah Khan. In this he found an instant ally in Panikkar, who plainly didn't like the nawab at this point. But when Aiyar revealed his second line of thought, Panikkar was a little taken aback. What he really wanted, the dewan said, was ten major Hindu states to form one single bloc. The idea had already been mooted to Cochin, Mysore and Baroda. If Bikaner and Jodhpur were on board with it, Aiyar would guarantee the entry of the rest. Panikkar listened to this in growing rage. 'In other words, he wanted all of us to make him our attorney!'[9]

He now decided to take matters into his own hands.

The immediate need as he saw it was to counter Bhopal. So he decided to lie to Aiyar's face, agreeing readily to the idea of a Hindu bloc of states. With lawyerly tact, he avoided allying himself directly to Aiyar's leadership for now, knowing that he didn't really have to promise too much just yet.

After lunch, the princes met again, this time joined by Gwalior and Rampur. After the usual pleasantries, Rampur stood up and exhorted the princes to show unity, eschew jealousies and unite under a single leader. It was a fairly mundane speech—or it would have been had Panikkar not caught Aiyar's eye at that precise moment.

The dewan's lips curved very faintly.

Panikkar sat up a little straighter.

For a time, nothing much happened. Then the Gwalior stood up. Since everyone agreed on unity, he said, there was no need for a committee. Why not, he asked genially, invest Hamidullah Khan with full powers?

There was a deafening pause.

Then Aiyar surged smoothly to his feet. 'The idea is good,' he said, 'but since Travancore is not in the Chamber, it will have to stay out if such plenipotentiary powers are given to the Chancellor.' Pulla Reddi, one of the advisors to the chamber, jumped up to take the dewan's side. Bikaner then spoke up against his own friend, saying that he was not 'agreeable' to the idea of entrusting the fate of the chamber to a single person.[10]

It was over.

The meeting dispersed after passing Panikkar's resolution that the princes and ministers should select a strong negotiating committee to deal with the Indian leaders and the British government. The general view was that in addition to the princes, the committee should include the dewans of all pertinent states from Hyderabad to Baroda and from Kashmir and Patiala to Bikaner. Of all of these, due to the rotations in tenure, only Aiyar, Panikkar and Liaqat Hayat Khan would remain as the original participants of the federalism discussions. Unsurprisingly, Bhopal tried to have Panikkar removed at the last minute from the negotiating committee.

Here he met a wall of defence. The princes of Nawanagar and Patiala insisted that Panikkar stay on the committee, and Bikaner went one better, stating flatly that if Panikkar was excluded, he would resign. Bhopal was shocked speechless. Bikaner's allegiance to Panikkar spelled the end of his friendship with Bhopal.

By the middle of 1945, there was a growing sense that the days of the Raj were numbered. Formulas, plans and drafts were flying about thick and fast. Rajaji had submitted his proposals to Gandhi in which he proposed that the League should endorse independence and cooperate with the Congress in the formation of a provisional interim government for the transitional period. After the war was over, a commission would demarcate contiguous districts in northwestern and northeastern India where Muslims were in a majority. A plebiscite should be held to decide the question of separating from India.

Rajaji's formula was the one that Jinnah would decry as a moth-eaten and mutilated Pakistan. It was just one of the many attempts in the mid-1940s to try and pave the legislative way to independence. Talks between Gandhi and Jinnah, between Whitehall and Wavell, between Liaquat Ali Khan and Bhulabhai Desai continued to founder against political and communal fault lines even as V.P. Menon urged that any impatience that might be felt at this juncture should not 'betray us into any hasty solution'.[11]

The international scenario was hardly reassuring. Hitler's suicide in his underground bunker in Berlin on 30 April 1945, VE Day on 8 May and Labour's victory in Britain's general elections hardened political resolve among India's political leaders. 'We've missed the bus in any case,'[12] Wavell wrote unhappily.

The last hope seemed to be the Simla Conference of 1945, and when even that failed, it made Pakistan an impending reality and not just a hysterical bluff by the Muslim League. In November 1945, Nehru told Wavell that he 'could make no terms whatever with the Muslim League, under its present leadership and policy'. It was, he said angrily, 'a reactionary body with entirely unacceptable ideas'.[13]

The Congress now called for immediate independence under a government of its own choosing. Jinnah announced in retaliation that 'Pakistan is a question of life and death for us'.[14] Small wonder then that Wavell was a worried man. He had to deal with spiralling political events, labour unrest, the sensational trial by court martial of captured officers from Subhas Chandra Bose's Indian National Army, serious food shortages in southern India, a lack of coal, the decimalisation of the Indian rupee and a son who was missing in action in Burma. At the end of his tether, he sent a secret memo to London. 'We are now faced in India, with a situation of great difficulty and danger. Congress leaders everywhere, but particularly Vallabhbhai Patel in Bombay and Nehru and Pant in the United Provinces have been making statements and speeches which can only be intended to provoke or pave the way for mass disorder ...'[15] If there was an uprising, there were alarmingly few troops on the ground to combat it. As one of Commander-in-Chief Claude Auchinleck's military advisors put it, the Raj would be 'extremely lucky to get through till June next without serious trouble'.[16]

As for the princes, they were now staring at a distinctly bleak future. Any paramountcy would not be transferred to a successor government. What Panikkar had been warning all along was now obvious: the princes had no future outside an Indian union.[17] Panikkar noticed as much during the Commonwealth Conference held in London on 9 February 1945. 'One thing was clear to me during this London visit. The World War was drawing to a close. It was beyond question that as soon as it ended, the British would withdraw from India. Whatever then happened, whether Pakistan came about or not and whether India remained in the British Empire or left it, it was certain that the Indian princes would not count for much in an independent India.'[18]

It was a curious dichotomy—India might have been going through all kinds of upheavals domestically, but internationally it was beginning to make its presence felt even though it was still a British colony. Its representatives were included in Allied plans for a post-war world, beginning with the signing of the Declaration of the United Nations in Washington DC in January 1942. At the peace conference in Dumbarton Oaks, backchannel talks between Wavell and Amery centred around India's international importance. Sir G.S. Bajpai represented India at the United Nations Relief and Rehabilitation Administration (UNRRA) meeting in Montreal.[19] At the Commonwealth Conference in San Francisco in 1945, Zafrullah Khan made an enthusiastic speech demanding to know how long Indians would have to wait for independence. 'India will be free and within the Commonwealth, if you will but let her and accord to her the place that is due ...'[20] To Panikkar's eye, it was significant that nobody knew quite how to place India. It was a colony, but a full conference member; a large country, but a poor one, hamstrung by a colonial administration on its last legs.[21]

The confusion and contrast surrounding its international perception made him think harder about India's postcolonial position and policy. It was during this period that he wrote some of his most influential tracts on foreign policy, ones that are considered seminal works even today.

Panikkar had already begun building his position as a scholar of foreign policy and strategic defence during the war years. In 1943, he gave a private lecture at Chatham House on imperial relations and the future of Anglo-Indian linkages. Between 1944 and 1945, he collaborated with the essayist and journalist Guy Wint, an expert on Asian and Middle Eastern affairs, in the activities of a group of scholars and politicians from Britain, India, Australia and Southeast Asia. At the meetings of this group, a wide spectrum of foreign policy issues was discussed, from India's relations with China, Southeast Asia and the Indian Ocean and the need for a treaty between India and England to the promotion of Indian culture abroad. Panikkar wrote several of these memoranda, which were then circulated among members of the group and sent to London.[22] He enjoyed writing these papers. 'It was in one of those discussions, connected with Malaya and Burma, that I put forward one of my favourite themes that it was India's historic role to have prevented the expansion of China to the south of Annam, that it was Indian sea power, which, for a thousand years, had withstood the pressure of Chinese population movement in Southeast Asia.'[23]

At the British Commonwealth Relations Conference, Panikkar wrote a paper on the need for a defensive organisation that would bring together the countries that were part of the empire. Out of this, and another series of lectures and speeches, was born *India and the Indian Ocean*, published in 1945.[24] For those thumbing through it when it came out, Panikkar's thesis was original in the extreme. He used his skills as a historian (and his past work on the Malabar coast and the European powers) to argue that the importance of the sea in Indian history had long and mistakenly been overlooked. 'It may truly be said that India never lost her independence until she lost command of the sea in the first decade of the sixteenth century.'[25] Panikkar pointed to the fact that though India had been invaded via land many times, none of these led to a loss of India's specific identity. This view then allowed Panikkar to present the Mughal period as less significant than it had been considered in the histories of India penned by European scholars. They were important, but they did not define Indian history. 'Few historians have recognized this outstanding fact, for the reason that Indian histories so far have been written not from the point of view of India as a whole, but from the point of view of Delhi and its changing dynasties.'[26]

Peninsular India was different: it was largely maritime and there was an international law of the sea that prevailed in the Indian Ocean with 'complete freedom of trade and navigation'.[27] The real turning point, as Panikkar had noted separately in *Malabar and the Portuguese*, had been the arrival of the Europeans: the Portuguese had been the first to question the principle of freedom of the seas. He took that thesis further in *India and the Indian Ocean*, pointing out that every European force that arrived in India, from the Portuguese to the French, and from the Dutch to the British functioned on the basis of naval dominance. Only the Japanese advance, overland and through the air, across the Pacific, across Southeast Asia and to India's northeastern borders during the Second World War, had temporarily challenged this norm. But in its own way, Panikkar wrote, it reaffirmed the importance of maritime power for Indian defence. 'The era of protected sea communications has ended for India,' he insisted, 'the question of the control of Oceanic seas surrounding India now stares us in the face.'[28] India could best take care of this question by development as a naval power, taking into account its own historical and political role in the region. In the updated edition of *India and the Indian Ocean*, printed in 1951, Panikkar reminded readers that in the post-war world, air power was a definite factor in the control of the seas. 'With mastery of the air, it becomes easier to control the territorially vital sea,'[29] he wrote. He laid out a blueprint based on what he called a 'steel ring' to be created around India, with forward naval bases at Singapore, Mauritius, Yemen (Socatra) and Sri Lanka to defend the Indian Ocean. India could not rest, he argued, in a postcolonial world without shoring up its own defences. He foresaw challenges in the form of threats from the Soviet Union and China, apart from apprehending the emergence of the United States as a key rival in the region, owing to its growing interest in oil shipment from the Persian Gulf. Apart from creating bases, Panikkar argued for the creation of a special international organisation for Indian Ocean security, predicated on a council of regional powers helmed by India, while keeping Great Britain, South Africa, and Australia in important positions.

It was, for its time, a path-breaking framework for postcolonial security, and it is one that keeps Panikkar alive in Indian strategic thought in the twenty-first century as well. He reminded readers forcefully of the fact that he was no pacifist: 'Ahimsa is no doubt a great religious creed, but that is a creed which India rejected when she refused to follow Gautama Buddha.' Turning once again to India's Hindu past, Panikkar added, 'The Hindu theory at all times, especially in the periods of India's historic greatness was one of active assertion of right, if necessary through the force of arms. It is not for Ahimsa and pacificism that Ramchandra stands in Indian religion; it is for an active assertion of what is morally right. Nor does Krishna stand for non-violence … Once we are free from the effects of this idea, and are thus enabled to look facts in the face, it will be clear that Indian freedom can be upheld only by firmly deciding to shoulder our share at all costs in the active defence of the areas necessary for our security …'[30]

In this book, and in other essays he was beginning to work on (all on the subject of naval power), it is interesting to see that Panikkar had finally stepped away from openly espousing a 'Greater India' concept. This is not to say that the heart of his argument had changed, but merely that, given that the world had changed so much, Panikkar also changed his ways of phrasing his arguments. He still stuck by his theory that India's geographical location determined its historical development as much as its political expansion into and beyond the Indian Ocean. As he wrote in *The Strategic Problems of the Indian Ocean*, another monograph he published on the subject, 'The fact that till the end of the thirteenth century A.D. the oceanic area was under the control of Indian naval powers, who conquered and held the islands of the Malayan Archipelago and kept the seas open to trade, obscured the essential importance of the sea to the problem of Indian defence. With the breakdown of Indian naval power in the thirteenth century, the control of oceanic navigation passed, it is true, to the Arabs, but as these merchant adventurers had no political organization behind them, their mastery of the Indian seas for nearly two centuries did not in any way affect the security of India.'[31]

The security of India in its postcolonial future was a subject that he thought about often, though he always instinctively approached his geopolitical ideas with his historian's eye. A couple of years later, for instance, he published a two-part contribution in *The Indian Quarterly* titled 'The Himalayas and Indian Defence'. As always, Panikkar began with history, asserting that the Himalayas' natural role was to isolate India from China and from violent invasions, at least from the northeast.[32] Such invasions as there *had* been in India's history 'were at long intervals and not of a character or size which uprooted the social conditions or modified in any sudden manner the structure and pattern of Indian life'.[33] In one sense, this guaranteed the continuity of Hindu culture and, consequently, of the Indian nation itself.

Read from the perspective of the twenty-first century, this might sound majoritarian to say the least, but it is important to underline that Panikkar's sense of civilisational history was never supremacist. Hinduism, for him, was certainly an Indian identity—even a core identity. But it was not the *only* Indian identity. The idea of India, which he had been working upon since he began his writing career in university, was one that was rooted in cohesion, despite its many plural identities, in which Islam and Christianity, among others, played their own roles.

In this essay, he went on to write that the Himalayas were not always an advantage, especially in this day and age of advancing technologies like air power. But while he advised caution in relying too much on the natural barrier of the mountains, he continued to advocate for maritime power as an innovative and symbolic means of geopolitical independence. Small wonder, then, that Panikkar's stay in London was considered immensely significant and his work was reported to the War Office directly by Claude Auchinleck. 'Panniker *(sic)* is a moderate nationalist with important links with circles in Congress, prepared to work within Commonwealth framework. Series of papers by him on Foreign Policy and Defence which show unusual grasp of realities have attached much notice here. His ideas deserve careful study and cordial relations with him may pay dividends.'[34] The War Office was intrigued enough to put in a rush order for copies of *India and the Indian Ocean*.

Defence wasn't the only subject he was writing on now. As the war drew to a close, he was thinking about India's position as a free country. 'We have to consider that Burma, for example, with her fifteen or seventeen million people with no development and very little army, would not be in a position to defend her frontiers by herself,' he wrote. 'So . . . with the independence of Burma it should be possible to create a commonwealth in which Britain would be given a guarantee of her interests in the East.'[35]

The use of the word 'commonwealth' was a precursor to the body that would eventually form in the 1950s, a Commonwealth in which independent India could participate on the basis of shared strategic and economic interests. This nascent idea of a regional organisation of sorts was based on a convergence of strategic interests rather than an abstract concept of brotherhood or duty. These were still the war years and India was still a British colony, yet Panikkar was now thinking in terms of a solution to *independent* India's defence problems. It was, in his perspective, to be found in two directions: cooperation with Great Britain and in the creation of regional organisations. When Burma and Ceylon (modern Sri Lanka) become independent, for example, they should form a single defence organisation with India. In a broader framework, Indonesia, China, Indochina and the Philippines were also to be included. By pulling all these countries together, a regional postcolonial order would be formed, a bulwark against any ripples of change from the fallout of the war.[36] For the biographer peering into the past, this was a precursor to what would eventually become a distinct push towards Asian regionalism, and for India specifically, this belief would become the foundation of the Look East policy of the 1990s.[37] But was there an adversary against which this order was forming? Panikkar left this suitably vague.

In the 1940s, then, as India continued to wrestle with the process of political reform, Panikkar was looking to a wider, postcolonial future. His experience with the princely states would ensure that he was never far from working for them at a moment's notice, but as the war drew to a close, he was now thinking mostly about Indian defence and foreign policy. Politics was not divorced from his arguments. Freedom was an abstract concept, but in concrete terms, in administrative terms, what did it mean for India? How best could the country exercise its geopolitical independence?

His answer: a strong central government and an abandonment of pacifism.

This argument was yet another path that Panikkar began to explore more thoroughly now. He had been thinking about it for some time. He was no pacifist. He never had been. Long ago, when he had read his paper to the gentlemen of the East India Association as a young man, he had told them, 'I am a nationalist—and a nationalist of what some of you would call an extreme type.'[38] That had never changed for him. Panikkar had always tempered his arguments to suit the stage he spoke on, but in his eyes, pacifism had no place in a nation trying to free itself from the shackles of colonialism. On the contrary, Panikkar fell back now on the ideas of nationalism that he had propagated first as a young student in Oxford University.

He reminded readers forcefully of the fact that he was no pacifist. 'Ahimsa is no doubt a great religious creed, but that is a creed which India rejected when she refused to follow Gautama Buddha,' he wrote. Arguing for a line of defence that continued through the ages of Indian history, Panikkar added, 'The Hindu theory at all times, especially in the periods of India's historic greatness was one of active assertion of right, if necessary through the force of arms. It is not for Ahimsa and pacificism that Ramchandra stands in Indian religion; it is for an active assertion of what is morally right. Nor does Krishna stand for non-violence … Once we are free from the effects of this idea, and are thus enabled to look facts in the face, it will be clear that Indian freedom can be upheld only by firmly deciding to shoulder our share at all costs in the active defence of the areas necessary for our security …'[39]

In this strong statement, he differed rather sharply from Gandhi. When he was asked about it at his lecture in Chatham House in 1943, Panikkar's answer was incisively swift. 'Pacifism is personal to Mr. Gandhi.'[40] He went further in a memo he wrote for the War Office in

1945, encouraging the development of an active military propaganda among the Indian population, youth organisations that promoted discipline and physical drills and aviation clubs in universities.[41]

All this building of strength was to be based on a strong central government, so that India could manage its foreign policy and defences independently. Panikkar was speaking for the creation of Pakistan openly now, as a strategic and geopolitical necessity. It was not, in his opinion, possible to give Muslims sufficient guarantees to feel secure in a democratically elected Hindu state. As he said during his lecture at Chatham House, 'If we are thinking in terms of security and developing India from the viewpoint of industrial possibilities, defences, etc. then a central government will have a greater power than federation can give. If you want a strong central Government in India to reconstruct society in India, what you require would be to reintegrate India on a more equitable basis, and it is necessary that there should be a separation by which the Moslems would find themselves in a position of equality. Then you would get two really strong centralised governments with the possibility of the organization of India into a modern government.'[42]

All his work during this period makes it more than clear that his political experiences over the last decade had made the idea of Pakistan an inevitability. Without Pakistan, India would be a weak federation, condemned to irrelevance or, worse, disintegration.

Panikkar's ideas were read with keen interest by Nehru and by the India Office. Both concluded that, while he was prone to being swept away by his own rhetoric, Panikkar's work was never less than original. 'Those of the staff at the War Office who have read his papers think the same as I do,' wrote General Mosley Mayne, military secretary, India Office. 'Panikkar is certainly a big thinker and a constructive one.'[43]

Chapter 37

'Rajastan'

IN JANUARY 1946, INDIA WENT TO THE POLLS.

Across 296 seats, 26 per cent of the adult population voted to bring in a Constituent Assembly which would oversee independent India's first steps. The mutiny in the Royal Indian Navy, indiscipline in the Royal Indian Air Force and the threatened strikes across the country's postal and transport system did nothing to help matters, beyond exhausting an already fatigued Wavell and beleaguering the short-staffed Home Department and Reforms Office.

The results of the elections saw the Congress winning by a landslide, forming the government in all provinces of British India except Bengal, Sind and Punjab. But it drove home an uncomfortable truth: the League polled nearly three-quarters of the Muslim votes—a stunning improvement from a decade earlier and one that was based entirely on a wave of religious nationalism. Small wonder then that the director of intelligence was reporting to Wavell that India was 'on the edge of a volcano'.[1]

The viceroy was worried, but characteristically, Whitehall dawdled.

Instead, a parliamentary delegation flew out in the first week of January 1946. During their travels from Karachi to Bombay and Madras to Calcutta, the delegation met prominent politicians and princes. They spent much of their time talking about communalism and Pakistan, but they left India with a united opinion. 'Britain is going to get a shock when this parliamentary delegation returns,' noted Muriel Nichols, the only woman in the delegation. 'We must end this summary bureaucracy of ours.'[2] For Reginald Sorenson, a Labour MP and Churchill's enemy on the floor of the House of Commons, 'The states are bound to be drastically affected by the political activity in the provinces contiguous to them, even if unwisely they ignore the red light.'[3] Indian leaders were deeply cynical by this time, with Nehru telling Sorenson acidly 'that it seems a bit of a joke that such a delegation had not come before'.[4] Srinivasa Sastri, then on his deathbed, told Gandhi caustically that nothing would come of the visit. 'Labour or conservative,' he was reported to have said, 'as far as India is concerned, they are all one and the same.'[5]

The delegation returned to England with Jinnah's quiet parting shot ringing in their ears. 'You know the position. Now it is up to you.'[6]

On 22 January 1946, the cabinet agreed that 'a mission of three ministers of cabinet rank should be sent to India, to arrive in the middle of March to conduct the forthcoming negotiations on the constitutional problem'.[7]

The Cabinet Mission consisted of Sir Stafford Cripps, Frederick Pethick Lawrence and A.V. Alexander. Right from the start, it was clear that this was literally and metaphorically Cripps's second coming. He was the man in charge, since he was the only one with any experience of India and its constitutional problems. Pethick Lawrence was technically the leader, but he was considered (rather unkindly) to be a 'foolish old dodderer'[8] with no experience in the art of diplomatic negotiation. Alexander, on the other hand, was baffled by India, preferring to stick to his true loves: whisky and Chelsea's football team.

Within days of their arrival, Cripps, intent on success and ready to pay any price for it, opened personal lines of communication with the Congress and the League. But more importantly for this story, the Cabinet Mission had specific orders from the India Office: to let the princes of India know that their time was up.

In meetings with the mission, several princes assured its members that they were 'ready and willing to cooperate in the new development of India'.[9] This, of course, belied a parallel process that had been set in motion in January 1946. At the end of January, Bhopal called on the chamber's member states to adopt written constitutions providing for popular institutions with elected majorities.[10] A model budget for the smaller states was drawn up and a 'large measure of agreement' was reached on the contents of a uniform civil list.[11] In June, the standing committee fixed a twelve-month time limit to the commencement of this process of 'plumping for democracy'.[12] Collectively, these initiatives promised to transform the political culture of them and turn them into a form of Western constitutional monarchies.

The pace of this was frenetic, though fruitless. In June 1945, Bikaner's legislature was enlarged to provide for an effective majority of elected members. In September 1945, Jaipur's representative assembly held its inaugural session. In July 1946, Kolhapur converted to a dyarchical system and Bikaner and Cochin followed suit one month later. In January 1947, the Maharaja of Mysore ordered his dewan to draw up proposals for a sweeping expansion of franchise and in May 1947, Jawhar and Manipur, states populated mainly by tribals, held their first ever elections.[13] Late in 1945, the rulers of the Eastern Orissa states appointed a special committee to draw up a scheme of federation. In May 1946, ten Deccan states agreed at a meeting in Kolhapur to pool revenues and administrative resources, establish a common legislature and, as far as possible, obliterate their frontiers. In July 1946, the major Kathiawar states, meeting at the instigation of Dhrangadhra, appointed a subcommittee under the chairmanship of the Jam Sahib to draft a constitution for the Kathiawadi Union.

Significantly, most states advertised these changes as interim measures, pending a transition to a full responsible government. In addition, the standing committee now leaned heavily on the concept of regional confederation as a method of strengthening the position of the states at the centre.

But Bhopal was aware that all this meant nothing if the empire did not commit to the survival of the states as constitutional monarchies within the framework of a new India. On 2 April 1946, he met Wavell and the Cabinet Mission to discuss the way forward. 'Naturally,' he said smoothly, 'the Indian states wish to survive and continue their existence, if this is possible, consistently with the progress of India and the world as a whole.'[14] The interview ended somewhat vaguely, since the Cabinet Mission was pressed for time. The nawab was still left with niggling questions, of which a note was attached to the transcript of the interview. Was India to be independent or have a connection with the Crown? Would new treaties be negotiated with the states? What would be the position of the states in a constitution-making body?

At first glance, these seem like strongly obvious questions and ones that should have been asked without preamble. Their existence does nothing to prove the nawab's vitriolic portrayal as a 'peerless Machiavellian' by the likes of Panikkar. At this time, Panikkar explained later, Bhopal was advocating a 'third force' called rather unimaginatively, 'Rajastan', a confederacy of states on par with India and Pakistan. Not only did Hamidullah Khan lay this out at a secret conference at his palace but it was also an idea that had the unsurprising support of Hyderabad and Travancore. The motive behind Rajastan, Panikkar alleged, was to 'curtail the power of the Hindus in independent India'.[15] By forming an alliance with Hyderabad, a Muslim union would be formed in the heart of India, thus undermining Hindu power. The government of Hyderabad, Panikkar mused, would finance this 'devious scheme', aided by Travancore.[16] On the British side, these three were being helped by Sir Conrad Corfield, the head of the Political Department, who was 'anxious to weaken an independent India by any means'.[17]

According to J.N. Sahni, there was not one but two plans for confederation.[18] The first, 'for the consumption of the Congress and the princes', consisted of groups of small and big states pooled together with provinces with a Muslim majority and Hindu minorities, sovereign in their internal affairs, except defence, foreign affairs and communications. To Jinnah, wrote Sahni, Bhopal sold the idea of multiple confederations. The first being a group of states whose rulers could be offered better terms than the Congress would or could offer and who would either by land or sea create a common border to confederate with Pakistan. The rest would confederate with India or remain independent as they liked.[19] The nawab's plan was that 'Hyderabad could be brought into the Pakistan confederation, either by getting an opening to the sea to the harbour of Masulipatnam or, if India remained obdurate, by negotiating with the Portuguese for an opening through Goa, Kashmir . . . could be coerced through local agitation to join Pakistan, rather than India'.[20]

In an interview with the diplomat Uma Shankar Bajpai years later, Sahni argued that this plan would connect Bhopal and the western states of Pakistan (Junagadh, Cambay, Jodhpur and Bikaner) so that better terms could be gained from Jinnah who had already begun to dangle 'blank cheques' in front of the weaker rulers. 'This was also blessed by the Political Department.'[21]

Unsurprisingly, as other princes began to cotton on to a conspiracy, hackles began to rise. Sahni, who was in full possession of the facts, went to Nehru to find out what could be done, only to find his information being 'dismissed . . . as a day dream'.[22] Undeterred, Sahni then arranged a meeting at the Jam Sahib's residence with Sardar Patel, Patiala, Gwalior and Baldev Singh. It was Patel 'the realist' who saw through the plan and asked the Jam Sahib and others to destroy it. 'You manage your friends in the big states,' Patel said. 'Leave the smaller states to me.'[23] As part of this plan, the Sardar asked Sahni to publicise the issue. But before Sahni could do so, the chamber met its Committee of Ministers. At this sitting, Bhopal once again broached the subject of Rajastan and the division of India into three units. The assembled princes cheered, though Bikaner was markedly quiet.

When Bhopal looked confidently around the room, assuming that his case had been won, Panikkar rose. He glanced at the clock. It was half-past twelve, with half an hour before lunch. His speech was pithy, stating bluntly that the Rajastan scheme was dangerous. It would be seen by the Indian public and the subjects of the states as an 'act of betrayal'.[24] Moreover, Panikkar continued, it would 'serve only to strengthen the Muslims and antagonise the Congress'. If Rajastan came to be, what would happen to the princes? What voice would they have in constitutional decisions? Would the people of Mysore or Travancore be allied to their neighbours in British India or to the people of Rajputana? What purpose would this decision serve the states when popular political movements began?

Panikkar looked squarely at a furious Hamidullah Khan.

'This is a plan,' he said firmly, 'to consolidate Muslim power.'

The nawab's expression hardened.

Pushing his advantage, Panikkar continued: out of the princes left in India, everyone was Hindu, except for seven or eight. Even among them, if Bahawalpur, Khairpur and Kalat were excluded, all others were enclaves in Hindustan. Even in the Muslim-ruled states within Hindustan, more than 75 per cent of the people were Hindus. 'The establishment of a new group called "Rajastan" would be a vivisection of Hindu power and if Hindu princes were party to such a vivisection, Hindus would never forgive such a crime.'[25] Panikkar sat down, satisfied that he had, as he had intended, shaken the chamber.

There was silence.

Then Bikaner cleared his throat. 'It would be wrong to decide on such a grave issue without further discussion,' he said pleasantly. 'Since the time is already one o'clock, we cannot do so now. It is best to adjourn until tomorrow.'[26]

Murmuring among themselves, the princes filed out. Panikkar went home, unfazed by the darkling looks being flung at him by Bhopal. He knew the nawab would not easily give up, even though by now most princes were suspicious enough to take their own courses of action. In his study, Panikkar dashed off a quick recap of his afternoon's speech. Armed with it, he left his house and went to the Imperial Hotel where Ramaswami Aiyar was staying.

Panikkar knew that Travancore was a key ally for Bhopal, but he had noticed that during the morning's stormy session, Aiyar had sat quietly, not saying a word.

When he entered the dewan's room at the hotel, he was proved right.

Aiyar smiled at him. 'Excellent speech, Panikkar. I completely agree with it.'

'Thank you. But I don't think the resolution was killed by my speech. I expect it still will be raised again tomorrow.'

'I will take care of that,' Aiyar said grimly.[27]

More than this he would not say.

The next day, before the chamber's session began, Aiyar arose and requested a few moments of the princes' time. 'There was some debate yesterday on a resolution about a Rajastan state,' he said politely. 'I am authorised by the Maharaja, whom I represent, to declare that he will not join any such unit.'

He sat down.

'Only Bhopal, his minister, CP and I knew that CP had throttled his own baby,' Panikkar remarked.[28] This was a strange way to put things, since Travancore had been a long-standing advocate of Indian federalism, not to mention being at the forefront of constitutional reform in India.[29] At this stage, in 1946, Travancore refused to forsake its historic sovereign claims at the altar of a nation state that was *not* envisioned as a unified India. Its relationship with the British was the treaty which it had signed as a sovereign power in its own right. Therefore, once the empire left, Travancore had long argued, it would and could choose its postcolonial future as well as its constitutional form. From this point of view then, Aiyar was far too brilliant to have 'throttled his own baby'. He was simply reasserting his own state's historic and legal rights, as any good lawyer might have done under the circumstances.

With that said, it is important to remember that in the last years before freedom, the machinations behind the scenes were intense and often occurred at the speed of light. The archives of the period lift the lid off what was a veritable pressure cooker. Fingers can and have been pointed at various players by yet other players, but there were very few who were above board.

The stakes were too high and were getting higher every passing day.

Chapter 38

Deadlock

BY MAY 1946, IT WAS TOO HOT TO STAY IN DELHI ANY LONGER.

'The heat made it hard to rationalise, even such problems as whether or not to cross the road, whether to stand up or sit down,' wrote the journalist James Cameron.[1] But the exhaustion was not just due to the heat. 'There were no secrets . . . both attitudes had been argued with a monstrous, monotonous insistence.' So firmly had the lines been drawn and so repetitive were the arguments being made that Nehru was wearied to the point of 'almost achieving the condition of detachment'.[2]

Privately, the Cabinet Mission had decided that there were only two feasible options for India. Scheme A would be a loose federation of the Hindu majority, a Muslim majority and princely states, with communications, defence and foreign affairs being conducted by the central government. At the centre, Hindus and Muslims would have equal representation. There would be a three-tier system of administration: a union government at the top, the undivided provinces at the bottom and in the middle, groupings of princes with a large degree of autonomy and even the possibility of future secession. Scheme B (treated as an emergency fallback) was for the creation of Hindustan and a truncated Pakistan with treaties of alliance between the two countries, but no mutual centre.[3] On 11

April 1946, the British government formally authorised the creation of Pakistan, if only in principle and still very much as a last resort. But in the interim weeks, the sweating Pethick Lawrence decided it was best to decamp to Simla, there to ponder a way forward.

Used to a whirl of gaiety otherwise, Simla was now brought to a halt as politics invaded. On the high hill roads, one might see Nehru riding on his demure piebald mare. If one awoke very early, one might catch a glimpse of the Congress high command assembling on the lawns of Chadwick, the bungalow where Gandhi was staying. 'It was an Old Testament spectacle,'[4] with Gandhi, Patel and Nehru pacing silently up and down the dewy lawns as the sun climbed through the skies behind the sprawling Tudor-style expanse of Peterhoff, one of the old former viceregal residences.

The proceedings of the Cabinet Mission were a 'sterile and difficult affair', with nothing being said to the point and much fruitless groping in the dark. On 12 May 1946, Pethick Lawrence brought this farce to a close. Cameron, who had accompanied the mission, remembered an English official, stony-faced and swaying precariously upright on the back of a rickshaw, clutching his briefcase. He brought word to the press corps staying at the Cecil Hotel that it was over. All that night, nobody slept. The hills were alive with the screams of annoyed monkeys and the shouts of rival columns of Congress volunteers and Muslim youth marching around town, shouting 'Jai Hind' or 'Pakistan zindabad!' In those agonising immediate hours, nobody knew where India was going. When Cameron went to say goodbye to Nehru, he was struck by the sadness in the younger man's face.

'I hope things go in peace.'

'So do I,' Nehru smiled wearily, 'But I know no more than you.'[5]

On 16 May 1946, the Cabinet Mission issued a statement in which they outlined Scheme A and said that their aim was to create a Constituent Assembly of elected representatives from the eleven provinces who would frame a new constitution. As far as the princely states were concerned, any future Indian union should contain both province and princely state, with the states retaining all subjects and powers 'other than those ceded to the Union'.[6] A close reading of the statement showed that neither flattery nor repeated avowals of allegiance to the Crown had worked for the princes. The statement said little about specifics, and instead announced that the 'precise form which their cooperation will take must be a matter for negotiation'.[7] Simply put, the way the princely states would enter the Indian Union would be left to negotiations between the states and the Indian Union. There would be no interference from British authorities.

On 22 May, a memo was released which put it even more baldly: 'When a new, fully self-governing or independent government or governments come into being in British India, the rights of the states which flow from their relationship to the Crown will no longer exist, and all the rights surrendered by the states to the paramount power will return to the states.'[8] The anguished question of paramountcy had finally been laid to rest.

'The void will have to be filled by the states entering into a federal relationship with the successor government in British India or failing this, entering into particular political arrangements with it.'[9] It was a statement calculated to throw any sensible prince into alarm. Philip Mason, then tutor to the Nizam's sons, felt that the memo was a bit 'like telling a rabbit to make its own arrangements with a tiger'. It was worse, he felt, because 'the rabbit had lived so long in so secure a hutch that it did not know it *was* a rabbit'.[10]

But the agony was drawn out by British officials like Pethick Lawrence, who said unnecessarily that there seemed to him 'no reason' why Britain should not continue to have treaty relations with the states.[11] Cripps went even further, saying airily at a press conference that the logical implication of the Cabinet Mission proposals was that the states 'would become wholly independent'.[12]

The princes seized this remark like a lifeline.

Bhopal hopefully interpreted this as the states being free 'inter alia to negotiate the terms of future relations with any foreign power and that foreign power may be England'.[13] In this, he was backed by Aiyar, who argued triumphantly that with the lapse in paramountcy, the Indian states would become independent and then there would be no compulsion on them to accede to the Indian Union.[14]

When Panikkar heard these assumptions, he was torn between being incredulous and furious. 'Any historian will endorse the statement that the Indian princes had never enjoyed full sovereignty,' he wrote crossly.[15] He began a sustained campaign of speaking honestly to whichever prince was in a mind to listen. 'What could be sillier than imagining that they would become independent monarchs, immediately British paramountcy lapsed?' he raged. 'When nationalist feelings were sweeping the country, which state subjects would come forward to fight for these dear monarchs? Since the people of the Indian states had also fought for India's freedom, which wizard could now hold them back from that freedom?'[16]

That is exactly what came to pass. The constitution that was finally promulgated in 1950 retained a core of federalism, but with centralised powers.[17] B.R. Ambedkar put it excellently: 'The use of the term "Union" is deliberate . . . to make it clear that although India was to be a federation, the federation not being the result of an agreement, no state has the right to accede from it.'[18]

Much later, in a memo written for the Union Constitution Committee of the Constituent Assembly in 1947, Panikkar explained, 'Federation is a fair-weather constitution, and in the circumstances of India, it is likely to be a dangerous experiment, leaving the national government with but limited powers, weak and consequently incapable of dealing with national problems.'[19] It was the heart of an argument he had been piecing together since the early 1940s: that once India was past the transfer of power and Partition, its unity was its unassailable achievement, one that had to be protected at all costs. The communal violence and uncertainty that was accompanying the push towards independence rendered any model of federation—like the one he had worked for in the 1930s—untenable.

In this point of view, Panikkar was not alone. Plenty of other political leaders and bureaucrats were thinking along the same lines. Protecting India's unity and presenting it to the world as a stable and cohesive geographical unit was the main consideration driving the likes of Nehru, Patel and V.P. Menon in the high noon of independence.

On 6 June 1946, the Muslim League accepted the Cabinet Mission's statement of 16 May, despite strong reservations. Only the Congress remained ominously silent. Wavell waited ten days for the two parties to join hands to form an interim government. When no such offer was forthcoming, the viceroy tried to force the situation by inviting fourteen political leaders across the spectrum to serve as members in the interim government. This was upended when Gandhi insisted that Azad be included as a nationalist non-League Muslim.

On 24 June, the Congress issued a qualified acceptance in which it left an exit for itself. It refused to recognise an interim government that would be in favour of grouping. Wavell wrote bitterly that this was a 'dishonest acceptance … so cleverly worded that it had to be regarded as an acceptance'.[20] On 29 June 1946, the Cabinet Mission departed, having made sure (they felt) that India's constitution could now proceed to be written.

A bare handful of days after their exit, Wavell's house of cards collapsed. Speaking in his capacity as the new Congress president, Jawaharlal Nehru addressed a meeting of the All India Congress Committee. 'It is not a question of our accepting any plan, long or short,' he announced. 'We will remain in that assembly so long as we think it is good for India, and we will come out when we think it is injuring our cause. We are not bound by a single thing …'[21] Not unnaturally, this created a sensation. At a press conference on 10 July, Nehru was asked to clarify what he had meant.

He did so with alacrity.

'Grouping will not take place in all probability, since everybody outside the Muslim League was already opposed to grouping.'[22]

The statement was enough to provoke the inevitable reaction from Jinnah. One month to the day after the Cabinet Mission had departed, the Muslim League announced the withdrawal of its acceptance of the Cabinet Mission Plan. Jinnah now called for 'Direct Action' to achieve Pakistan and 16 August 1946 would be Direct Action Day. 'This day,' he said, 'we bid goodbye to constitutional methods.'[23]

Nobody was under any illusions that this was the fallout of Nehru's ill-starred press conference. Azad, in a memoir published prudently after he and Nehru were both dead, primly maintained that it was 'not correct'[24] of Nehru to have said what he had. Patel was blunter, calling it an act of 'emotional insanity'.[25]

Meanwhile, the princely states were facing another ordeal.

Their strategy now relied on hammering out an agreement that could ensure the continued existence of multiple sovereignties, even if bound together in a loose alliance. Sovereign functions would be exercised at the state and provincial level, with some powers being ceded to a federal centre. But the durbars still clung to the idea of pursuing independent foreign relations with each other and other countries, believers in the 'mirage of independence', Panikkar huffed scornfully.[26] Nehru felt the same as Panikkar, telling Sir Conrad Corfield that in his opinion, only about a dozen states had inherent survival value.[27]

Worse, what the states needed and did not have now was a united front. They were riven internally by egos, communal divides and local politics. Many were welcoming hosts to the Rashtriya Swayamsevak Sangh (RSS) and the Hindu Mahasabha. Alwar and Bharatpur were known to enjoy fanning communal flames. The work and intensity of the Praja Mandals had expanded, though in many states they were not fully equipped to overthrow princely power just yet. Still, many princes knew it was but a matter of time. Already, their subjects were beginning to buck against their existence. In Dungarpur, the princes were ridiculed as 'dancing like monkeys as the behest of the madari (juggler)'.[28] Elsewhere, states like Travancore refused to even consider the idea of Pakistan. 'Personally, I prefer civil war to Pakistan,' Aiyar wrote to a friend in the United States, '... but to prevent secession, such a civil war may become unfortunately inevitable.'[29]

By his own confession, it wasn't surprising that this was the most gruelling summer of Wavell's life. 'The Mission gave away the weakness of our position and our bluff has been called,' he wrote wearily. 'Our time in India is limited and our power to control events almost gone.' [30] The viceroy's gloom would only increase as the summer passed. Even as he fretted about a serious breakdown of law and order, Whitehall stayed maddeningly quiet until the exasperated Wavell was told by his political secretary George Abell that 'our only course is to get out of India as soon as possible and leave her to her fate ... which will be civil war.'[31]

As Wavell wrung his hands, the Standing Committee of the All India States' People's Conference met to discuss how to proceed.

Nobody was happy that in the states, the voices of the people seemed to be ignored. In this they found support in Nehru who was even more bellicose in his attitude towards the princes, snapping irascibly at the barrister and advisor to the Chamber of Princes Sir Sultan Ahmed that he 'did not care a damn for the princes'.[32] He also pushed for the scrapping of the princes' beloved treaties, referring to anyone speaking of the importance of treaty rights as 'lunatics, knaves or fools'.[33] His statements were calculated to drive terror into the most resilient royal heart. Hamidullah Khan was horrified that after all this, the princely states would be left 'a sort of no man's child, without any effort of the part of the Crown to protect their legal and reasonable demands'.[34]

But the die, for now, was cast. The only question was: how was the Congress supposed to take this bickering, divided royal lot forward into the Constituent Assembly? Who would represent them there? The rulers? The subjects? Congress leaders spoke for the latter, while the rulers naturally were aghast at the thought.

There was deadlock. But it could not hold.

The country was beginning to fall apart.

Chapter 39

The End

IN NOVEMBER 1946, HAMIDULLAH KHAN WAS A BROKEN MAN. 'I AM unhappy about everything in this country,' he moaned to Corfield. 'I am tired of leading a team who have neither the will nor the desire to survive. I am tired of intrigue, calumny and communal feelings of the worst type. The princes, betrayed by the British, are already a lost cause.'[1]

The Nawab of Bhopal lamented against the backdrop of the great Calcutta killings. For three days, blood poured through the streets of Calcutta. Official reports stated that 4,000 people were killed, but today it is accepted that over 6,000 people lost their lives, with over 1,00,000 people left homeless. Partition had not yet happened, but in many ways it was already beginning.

Panikkar read of the killings while he hurried about his business in Bikaner. He was very rarely at home these days, consumed with troubles of a different kind. He had managed to send Madhusudan and Devaki off to England for university, so thankfully, that was two children safely out of the way. He was under no illusions that trouble was heading India's way, starting in Bikaner.

There had been clashes of late between landlords and the peasants. Most of these clashes rapidly assumed a casteist hue, since the jagirdars were usually Rajput, while the cultivators were poor Jats. Resentful speeches by Rajput landlords threatened to destabilise the monarchy. All this unrest was compounded by the activities of the Praja Mandal, which was working behind the scenes to stoke popular protests.[2]

Sensing danger, Sadul Singh acted fast on Panikkar's advice. He asked his astrologer to give him the most auspicious date for a statement to the press. It was duly published on 21 June 1946: 'The object I have in view is the establishment of a form of government which, under the ruler, will be responsible to the people, thus fully associating them with the administration of the state, within a specified time, taking into due consideration the conditions and circumstances existing in the state.'[3]

It was a shrewd move and Panikkar lost no time in sending copies of Bikaner's statement to all the political leaders of new India. 'Coming at this juncture, His Highness has every hope that this historic decision will give a lead to all states of India,' he wrote to Gandhi. 'I hope you will read the statement and also give us your blessing.'[4] But for the first time, he was just a little too late.

Congress leaders replied politely to Panikkar, but nearly all of them asked him to hurry democracy along.[5] Bikaner didn't have the best reputation as far as politics was concerned. Raghalwar Dayal Goel, leader of the local Praja Parishad, ripped the state's reputation to shreds in a letter to the maharaja. 'The present situation in Bikaner is even worse than what it was in British India, where ordinary civil liberties, freedom of press, freedom of association is denied, the municipal board, district boards and legislative assemblies are but a mockery.'[6]

Alongside the difficulty in transitioning to popular government was the unmistakable rise in communal tensions. Muslims were refusing point-blank to participate in the work of the Hindu-dominated Praja Mandals.[7]

These were difficult months to be the Dewan of Bikaner.

On 2 September 1946, the members of the new interim government were sworn into office. Nobody knew what this would mean or achieve, but it was a huge step in the demission of British power. The Congress now began wielding power as though they had already been in possession of it for years. In a clever (if rather rude) move, before each Executive Council meeting, Congress ministers met for tea. To these little gatherings, the viceroy was pointedly not invited. The League, on the other hand, refused to join the interim government. The role of Muslim nominees was disputed.

In this new shadow cabinet, Nehru would hold the portfolio of foreign affairs. Patel took on home and one of his first steps was to ensure that all intelligence reports went directly to the Congress instead of to the viceroy. As Wavell battled to get all parties on board this latest political showboat, he sent yet another secret plan to Whitehall. It was marked 'Breakdown' but privately it was known as Operation Madhouse. Wavell favoured gradual withdrawal northwards and the announcement of a set date of departure.

It was poorly timed.

Attlee, up to his eyes with a burning Palestine, flooding in the south of England, transport strikes, post-war depleted stocks of coal and a housing crunch, had no time to argue with Wavell. The easiest option was to find a new viceroy. Wavell wouldn't know of this until the very last minute. As it was, he spent the dying months of 1946 waiting to hear back from the India Office and on permanent damage control mode in India. In November, for instance, Muslims were savagely killed in Bihar in revenge for the equally horrendous slaughter of Hindus in Noakhali in East Bengal. As riots continued across Bengal, Bombay, the United Provinces and Bihar, Jinnah upped the ante, denigrating the Congress for referring to Nehru as the prime minister. The only solution now, he declared, was 'absolute Pakistan—anything else would be artificial and unnatural'.[8] As London continued to stay obstinately quiet, Wavell wrote again, 'The absence of a definite policy on the part of HMG is a serious matter indeed at a critical time like this.'[9] It was a masterly understatement, but it managed to jog London's conscience enough for a grudging invitation to be issued to Indian leaders for urgent talks.

Nehru, Jinnah, Liaquat and Wavell flew out of Karachi on 1 December 1946, with Baldev Singh representing the Sikhs. Inside the aircraft, the atmosphere was Siberian, with Jinnah incensing his co-passengers by arriving late and then insisting on a glass of beer right after breakfast.

In London, the meeting came to nothing.

On 7 December 1946, Nehru and Baldev flew back to India to attend the first session of the new Constituent Assembly.

It was a poorly attended moment in India's constitutional history. The seventy-five seats of the League were empty and the representatives of the princely states were also absent. When Panikkar discovered this, he was horrified. 'My view was that, irrespective of the (Muslim) League's decision to join or abstain, the Indian states should not keep out.'[10] He sought out Bikaner, who agreed with this representation. Together they sat down for repeated and fruitless meetings with the Nawab of Bhopal.

It was like talking to a wall.

Hamidullah Khan repeated endlessly that though he had approached the Congress on the subject several times, it was Nehru who refused to discuss anything. On the surface, this sounded perfectly plausible, given Nehru's very vocal dislike of the princes. But Panikkar didn't trust Bhopal. After one such meeting, he went to meet his old friend Gopalaswamy Ayyengar. Tall, lean and an excellent lawyer, Ayyengar was then Nehru's principal advisor on matters to do with the princes. 'From our almost daily contacts, the impression I gained was the opposite [of what Bhopal was saying].'[11] But by now, of course, the first session of the Assembly was already underway. There was nothing to do but go home for Christmas and try to relax.

As New Year's Days went, everyone agreed that 1947 began poorly. To begin with, there was the news that during the first session of the Constituent Assembly, Nehru had introduced a resolution asserting that all territories comprising the Raj, including the princely states, would make up an independent union. He maintained carefully that the Government of India had no intention of imposing any form of government on the princely states but insisted that 'no state can have an administration that goes against our fundamental principles'.[12]

What did that mean? Royal fears about that were obliterated by Clement Attlee's announcement on 20 February 1947. It was the intention of His Majesty's Government, he told the House of Commons, 'to take the necessary steps to effect the transference of power into responsible Indian hands, by a date not later than June

1948'. The constitution of free India would be worked out by a fully representative Constituent Assembly in accordance with the framework laid down by the Cabinet Mission.

Lord Louis Mountbatten would be India's last viceroy.

PART VIII

Transfer of Power (1947)

Chapter 40

'Time Is Pressing'

'FROM THE WORD *GO*, THERE WAS TROUBLE,' V.P. MENON RECALLED.[1]

The problem was that there was no elegant, readymade solution for the princely states. In 1946, Gopalaswamy Ayyengar and Rajaji had discussed the possibility of an ambiguously named 'States Secretariat', though at the time, most princes had refused to consider what that would mean for them.

Things had changed in just a handful of months. 'Time is pressing,' wrote V.T. Krishnamachari, Dewan of Baroda, to Bhopal. 'The delay in settling the constitution is strengthening the elements in the country . . . who are determined that there should be disorder. It is high time that the constructive demands . . . came together to fight these forces.'[2]

Bikaner's Sadul Singh felt the same, no doubt helped along by Panikkar. 'States like Travancore and Mysore placed as they are, far from the centre of communal tension, can perhaps afford to go slow . . . with us in Rajputana, the Punjab and central India, the matter is immediate . . . '[3]

Panikkar was in Delhi now, seething with rage. In Madras, over the Christmas holidays, he had met Ayyengar who told him 'without hesitation' that, far from being unwilling, Nehru had, in fact, invited Bhopal several times to at least talk about the question of joining the Constituent Assembly. The nawab had rejected the offer so many times that, finally, Nehru had taken it off the table. Dismayed, Panikkar racked his brains for a way out of this fresh pickle. At yet another meeting with Ayyengar, he suggested a plan in which all other princes could be negotiated with, leaving aside Bhopal. Ayyengar smiled. 'Well, there seems to be no other alternative.'[4] Together, the two friends filled in the fine print of this plan. Once Panikkar was back in Delhi, he sought out Maulana Azad, who he felt would be sympathetic to his problems.

He was right. Azad listened carefully, then suggested starting informal talks between the princes and the Congress leaders. Any dialogue now should be top secret, he advised, with not a word leaking to the press. With the green light successfully obtained, Panikkar dashed back to Bikaner to report to Sadul Singh. The upshot of this was yet another conference, this time with Jaipur, Jodhpur, Rewa and Patiala. These were the five chosen rulers who would meet Congress leaders to begin talks about entering the Constituent Assembly.

Panikkar now departed for Delhi, where he met Ayyengar. A dinner was agreed upon, at Bikaner House on the night of 31 January 1947. Ayyengar agreed to bring Nehru and Patel to the table if Panikkar could guarantee the five princes.

Before this complex piece of backchannel diplomacy could be pulled off, there was one more hurdle to cross. Bhopal had called a conference on 29 January to decide on the royal attitude to the Constituent Assembly. The problem was that it was being held on the same day as a crucial Muslim League meeting in Karachi. Everyone knew that if the League decided not to sit in the assembly, the princes would decide the same. Everyone also knew that both Bhopal and Jinnah were labouring under the illusion that if this came to pass, the Assembly would be reduced to nothing more than a rubber-stamp institution.[5]

At eleven o'clock, the chamber members and their dewans assembled in the hall of Faridkot Palace. Bhopal lost no time in putting forth his resolution, laying out the principles on which he wanted the chamber to operate. These, he said, would be the principles they would demand from Indian political leaders. Panikkar listened in growing horror.

The principles included the immutability of the monarchy, the non-impairment of their sovereign powers and non-interference in internal affairs. It was a resolution guaranteed to create a gridlock.

Panikkar read through a copy of this startling resolution in outrage. He knew that it was seconded by Sir C.P. Ramaswami Aiyar, 'whose arrogance spurred him to challenge the Congress', and by Sir Ramaswami Mudaliar, the Dewan of Mysore, 'whose religion was enmity to the Congress'.

'I was not surprised.'[6]

But before he could say a word, the elderly Dewan of Udaipur, Sir T. Vijayaraghavachari, suddenly cried out, 'If you accept this resolution, it will be your own death warrant!' A shocked murmur rippled around the room.

Vijayaraghavachari stood up. 'What you now contemplate,' he told Bhopal fiercely, 'is like the action of a foolish woman, who tries to dam the Atlantic Ocean with a broom!'[7]

Udaipur's protest was strongly followed by Krishnamachari and by Panikkar himself, but if they thought they had spoken well, they were outdone by Bhopal.

The nawab was inspired that day, giving a speech that surpassed any that he had given during his chancellorship. So passionately did he speak that his resolution, despite Panikkar's best efforts, was carried unanimously.

Panikkar knew that everything now hinged on the dinner that he and Ayyengar had organised at Bikaner House. If he was worried, his memoirs don't show it. 'We had already decided our counter-strategy . . . we did not mind this defeat.'[8]

Panikkar's diplomacy behind the scenes of the Chamber of Princes has gone unsung, but he was very much the main man at this time. From Woodrow Wyatt to Alan Campbell-Johnson and ultimately Lord Mountbatten himself, Panikkar kept channels of communication open with the British Government of India, a vital strategy during a charged historical moment.

Still, the optics were not the best. Newspapers like *Dawn* smirked at the collapse of the Constituent Assembly in the face of royal opposition. Nobody seemed to believe that the princes would eventually enter talks with the Congress. As Panikkar reported to Woodrow Wyatt, 'The reaction in the Congress circles also is that the princes have definitely thrown in their lot with the Muslim League.'[9]

So when the princes assembled in the brightly lit lobby of Bikaner House on the night of 31 January, emotions were running high. Bhopal was also present in his capacity as the Chancellor of the Chamber. Ayyengar, true to his word, brought in Nehru and Patel. Both men were in a mood to be amiable that evening, which was for the best. Bikaner opened parleys as soon as the Congress leaders walked in, stating in a short speech what he hoped the consultations would bring. The princes, he said, were united in desiring freedom and to ensuring that all parties were working in harmony. Now, the ball was in Nehru's court.

Nehru responded suitably, recorded Ayyengar. He was pleasant and cordial, assuring the princes that nothing dangerous was likely to happen, that their fears were all in their heads and that a future central government would not dream of interfering in internal affairs.[10]

Next to speak was V.T. Krishnamachari, making the case that Bhopal's charges that the Congress was averse to the princes joining the Assembly were false. What the chamber really desired to do was to begin laying the grounds for discussions about the way forward.[11] Bhopal tried to cut in, insisting that talks be suspended until his list of conditions was agreed to. Patiala overrode him. Would it help matters, he asked innocently, if Nehru heard of the other positions of the standing committee? Nehru agreed at once, though he added the rider that he knew of Bhopal's list and would not hear of it.

There was a pause.

Then Patiala thumped the table. 'Well, then,' he exclaimed, glaring at Bhopal, 'What more do we want?'

A murmur of agreement was heard.

The nawab changed colour but said nothing.

The moment passed quickly, proceeding to the technicalities of the process of joining the Assembly.[12]

Only later would it come to light that on that fateful evening, Patiala had come with a letter of resignation in case Bhopal tried to force the issue.[13]

Formal discussions between the States Negotiating Committee and the Union Constitution Committee opened on 8 February 1947. On the latter, there were Nehru, Patel, Azad, Ayyengar and Pattabhi Sitaramayya. From the chamber, there were Panikkar, Bhopal, Patiala, Nawanagar, Dungarpur, Bilaspur, Hyderabad and Travancore, with D.K. Sen representing the small states. Talks were crammed with legalese. The princes were deeply worried about their sovereign rights, boundaries, territorial encroachment in terms of grouping and the allocation of seats in the assembly.

The atmosphere was not as pleasant as it had been at Bikaner House. Nehru was no longer quite so cordial and nor was Sardar Patel. A discussion between Nehru and Aiyar became increasingly frosty as it proceeded, ending with an angry exchange in which Nehru insisted that he was free to say that he thought the states were obsolete in modern India. Incensed, Aiyar retorted that by those standards, *he* was free to say that he thought some political parties in India were 'totalitarian'. Another meeting on 24 February came to a crashing halt because Bhopal refused to sit for more than an hour at a time, and that too only with special coffee and a customised paan. Nor would he eat or drink in anyone's presence. The meeting had to adjourn to enable him to partake of his refreshments.[14]

It was during these meetings with the States Negotiating Committee that Sardar Patel emerged as a key player. He rarely spoke, preferring Nehru to lead the discussions. When he *did* open his mouth, it was to issue thinly veiled warnings. India would have no intention of forcing anyone to join it, he said, adding ominously, 'Events may force them.'[15]

To a horrified Bhopal, Patel said calmly, 'To the extent to which you hand over your burdens, there will be no desire to take over your burdens.'

Occasionally, he lost his temper. To Mirza Ismail, who was then serving his short-lived time as dewan to the Nizam of Hyderabad, who asked anxiously if there was any objection to the existence of the monarchy, Patel rapped out, 'No responsible person, no Congressman has said, we don't want you. Don't have any unnecessary suspicion, which creates unnecessary difficulties.'[16]

Confronted by this mix of threat and persuasion, it was not surprising that the chamber was split down the middle. Some of the bigger houses—Bikaner and Patiala, for example—thought it wiser to be safe than sorry and join the assembly. Others continued to push for the states to join only at the last possible minute.[17] The dewans of various states were more or less united, led by Panikkar, in their dislike of Bhopal and his plans.

Bhopal was a lonely man that summer, holding onto his Charter of Rights as a naked man might cling to a fig leaf. In a circular to the Chamber of Princes in April 1947, he repeated, 'The Indian states feel, and feel very strongly, that they have a right to survive and retain their autonomy and independence.'[18]

Statements like this were making Nehru understandably impatient. Towards the end of April, he told a meeting of the AISPC that any state that did not join the assembly would be treated as hostile to India and would bear the consequences of its actions. Pushed by Panikkar and Ayyengar, Patiala went to meet Nehru.

Might he repeat this statement, he asked, as an ultimatum? Nehru, sensing an opening, agreed.

It was exactly the right thing to do.

Most princes agreed to join the assembly immediately, with Aiyar telling everyone, 'There is no reason for us to discuss rights any further. We need only decide on the method of entering the Constituent Assembly.'[19]

This desertion by a major ally gave him temporary pause. While he simmered in silence, Panikkar quickly proposed to the chamber that every state should have one member per million of its population. Ayyengar added that very small states could be clubbed into joint constituencies to whom the same ratio would apply. At least half the members would be elected directly or from legislatures.

Fighting in the last ditch now, Bhopal tried one more time. He called a meeting of his supporters, including Alwar and Nawanagar, in Bombay, where he insisted that the princes must work in unison in the

Assembly. Bikaner, who had arrived to keep an eye on things, walked out. He went quietly to his suite, where he wrote two letters: one to Bhopal, asking that he be excused from future meetings, and the second to the chamber itself, asking its members to act in the larger interests of India.[20] He needn't have wasted paper or ink. Most of the princes knew where they stood by now. As the US consul-general in Bombay told the State Department, 'The princes are fighting a losing battle. Most of them realise it.'[21]

The Bombay conference was a definite end to the reign of the Nawab of Bhopal.[22] He resigned his chancellorship soon after. By the end of March, Bikaner had deputed Panikkar to sit in on the second session of the Constituent Assembly. 'I was the first delegate from any Indian state,' Panikkar would say later, with deserved pride.[23] For years, he had been pushing the states to see that their only way out was to ally themselves with the nationalist movement. Federalism could not save them now, but some shrewdness might help save some shred of dignity. Joining the assembly was just one way to show Indian political leaders that the princes were not just working for the good of their states but for India as a whole.

On 22 March 1947, the Mountbattens arrived in India.

Louis Mountbatten, wrote his official biographer, Philip Zeigler, 'did not merely leap before he looked, but leaped before he even knew whence he was leaping'.[24] Tall, good-looking and known to be reckless, Mountbatten had laid down certain conditions before this particular leap. His first condition, submitted to Attlee on 20 December 1946, was that he would go out to India only 'on the open invitation of all Indian political parties'. This was dropped as impractical, but he was largely given greater liberty in making his own arrangements and writing his own instructions than any other viceroy in the history of modern India.

His second condition was the date for the transfer of power. 'I was the one who said we must have an early date . . . nothing vague about it,' he would tell H.V. Hodson in 1965, blithely ignoring the fact that it had actually been the weary Wavell who had pushed for an early British departure.[25]

The swearing-in ceremony for the new viceroy and vicereine was held in the resplendent Durbar Hall of Viceroy House. As ceremonies went, it was both an indicator of a new era and of the deep divides in India's politics. Nehru and Liaquat Ali Khan were there, grimly ignoring each other. Conspicuously absent, on the other hand, were the Nawab of Bhopal and the Maharaja of Patiala. Both rulers knew the Mountbattens closely, and their absence was more than a breach of protocol; it was a sign that trouble was on the horizon. It wouldn't take long for Mountbatten to discover the political deadlock, but it also didn't mean, as has often been said, that he ignored the problem of the princely states.

The Chamber of Princes was not easily overlooked. Egos and tempers were frayed beyond repair. Mountbatten sent in his deputies to engage with the princes and their advisors first. The diaries of Alan Campbell-Johnson, the viceroy's press secretary, are full of his meetings with the Political Department, with governors and with various rulers. Sir Conrad Corfield was bitter about Bikaner opting to take a place in the assembly, telling Alan Campbell-Johnson that Bikaner's presence there was 'seriously weakening the bargaining power of the princes'.[26] Clearly, Campbell-Johnson noted, Corfield was in Bhopal's camp, seeming to see the princes as a 'potential "Third Force" in the transfer of power'.[27]

His interest piqued, Campbell-Johnson sent for Bikaner's dewan, of whom he had heard much already. Panikkar did not disappoint.

Writing approvingly of his first meeting with Panikkar, Campbell-Johnson described him fulsomely. 'Panikkar sports a small imperial beard. He is a historian, politician and journalist, a man of prodigious learning and profound judgement and no mean practitioner in the dying art of good conversation.'[28]

By the sounds of it, Campbell-Johnson enjoyed himself, asking Panikkar, 'What would you do if you were in Mountbatten's place?'

If he thought this might be a trick question, he was mistaken. Panikkar replied at once that, as a formidable naval strategist himself, Mountbatten must realise that the Raj was best served by the creation of a solid central state based on India's seaboard, on more than three hundred million people, and on geographic and religious unity. 'Hindustan is the elephant and Pakistan the two ears,' Panikkar remarked memorably. 'The elephant can live without the two ears.'[29]

Panikkar's chat with Campbell-Johnson makes fascinating reading simply for the clarity of his thoughts. He made it clear that his interest was a free India and what that would look like. In a four-roomed house, he said, Jinnah 'asks for only one room, but he wants that room to be his own'.[30] His advice was that the empire needn't try harder to give the Indians more than what they wanted. As far as the princes were concerned, he was as clear as he had always been. Once paramountcy lapsed, they would need to seek security within the framework of a dominant political structure. So far, the Congress had refused to outrightly coerce any state to join an Indian Union, but Panikkar made no bones about the fact that he felt that 'the decision facing the princes was . . . to join in or perish'.[31]

Pakistan and the princes weren't the only subjects with which Panikkar was concerning himself now. A day after the Mountbattens arrived in the capital, so too did ninety-three delegates and fifty-one observers from thirty-four different countries. They were there for the Asian Relations Conference (ARC), which would be held between 23 March and 2 April 1947. The conference had been convened by Nehru to bring together different Asian nationalist movements that were all striving for independence. Already evolving a future for free India's foreign policy, Nehru saw the conference as a way to institutionalise emerging links between Asian nationalism and promote solidarity across what would be later known as 'the Third World'.[32] The Asian Relations Conference is usually seen as a precursor (and eventually, a footnote) to the bigger Bandung Conference in 1955, but its convening at the cusp of India's own independence was an undeniably significant moment.

As an idea, it had been born in 1946, the brainchild of the journalist B. Shiva Rao, then closely associated with the Indian Institute of International Relations and afterwards with its rival, the Indian Council of World Affairs (ICWA). Rao had been at the IPR conference in 1945, where he and the Indian delegation's leader, Vijayalakshmi Pandit, had both been annoyed that Western countries were 'not prepared to give up preconceived ideas'. After the conference, Rao had then gone to San Franscisco for the founding conference of the United Nations, where he discovered that Asian ideas and voices continued to be marginalised even here. From this irritation was born the concept of a parallel conference of Asian voices. Rao talked about it first to the ICWA and then, with the council's backing, to Nehru himself.

Nehru was already thinking about his vision for Asia. His Asia was a federation of sorts in which he included New Zealand, Australia, parts of East Africa (Egypt) and select Soviet republics. Colonialism had isolated these vital parts of Asia from one another. A conference like this could bring about new thinking and a new way forward.

Not surprisingly, the conference (and its timing) triggered considerable alarm across both Britain and the United States. In a post-war world, the creation of a unified Asia of sorts was reminiscent of Japanese efforts towards the same in the 1930s. But Nehru was clear that he didn't want an exclusive regional formation. The week of the conference certainly proved that point. That week, as James Cameron reported, 'the city of Delhi was filled with the most intricate variety of people; strange in costume and countenance—brocades from Southeast Asia, bell-bottoms from the Eastern Soviet Republics, braided hair and quilted robes from Tibet . . . dozens of curious languages and poly-syllabic titles. One way or another, as we kept reminding one another, this multitude represented nearly half the population of the world.'[33]

The conference was held in the Purana Qila, the majestic stone structure built by Sher Shah Suri in the sixteenth century. The opening and closing sessions were open to the public and attracted crowds some twenty thousand strong. The official language was English, but interpreters were present for the delegates. A giant map of the continent hung behind the speakers' podium, with the word ASIA written atop it in neon lights. Nehru gave the inaugural address to a standing ovation, in which he declared, 'We have no designs against anybody; ours is the great design of promoting peace and progress all over the world.' In the same breath, he also said firmly that Asians no longer wanted to be 'the playthings of others'.[34]

Nehru's vision for Asia and the Asian Relations Conference has been studied and documented richly[35] and is a story in itself. For this tale, however, two circumstances are important. The first is that the conference was deemed a social and cultural event. As a result, security and defence were purposely taken off the agenda. The final list of subjects was a remarkable first step for Asian geopolitics either way, including as it did migration, racism, women's issues and labour. Security, as it turned out, would become a primary issue for India in its first years of independence.

The second rather prickly cause for concern was India's invitation to Tibet as a separate country despite strong protests from China, and its invitation to a Jewish delegation despite firm objections from the observer Arab delegation. While Chinese concerns over Tibet would play out for India in just a couple of years, Panikkar was most interested in the arrival of the Jewish delegation.

The Jewish Agency had been engaged with India all through the 1930s and 1940s. When the first Indian delegation arrived at the San Francisco conference in 1945, Eliahu Epstein (then the head of the agency's political department in Washington DC) met Sir Firoz Khan Noon, a member of the Indian delegation. Nothing much came of the meeting, but by 1947 it was clear to the agency that India was not a player to be discounted in world politics. An invitation to the ARC was consistent enough with the Congress's traditional policy of supporting Palestinian Arab nationalism while accommodating Jewish religious concerns, and it offered a golden opportunity for the Yishuv to interact with India's nationalist leadership and those from other Asian countries.[36]

The ten-member delegation was led by Hugo Bergmann, a professor of philosophy from the Hebrew University in Jerusalem, and its presence at the ARC was the first major test of India's Palestine policy. With most Arab states absent, the delegation publicly conveyed their case for a Jewish homeland. Bergmann's speech was conciliating: he referred to an aspiration for a Jewish 'old-new homeland' in Palestine while also explaining that their aim was not to dispossess Palestinian Arabs.[37] The speech was hotly contested by the Arab League and Egyptian delegations which certainly did not want

British rule to be replaced by the domination of 'European Zionists'.[38] The Egyptian representative welcomed Jewish settlers, but reasserted that Palestine belonged to the Arabs. Bergmann demanded a right to respond to this statement, but Nehru denied his request. Furious, the Jewish delegation walked out in protest and was only persuaded to return by some Indian delegates who rushed after them. Nehru apologised in his closing speech to Bergmann and his delegation, but reiterated India's policy towards Palestine.[39]

The Jewish delegation had failed this time to obtain explicit public support for the creation of the state of Israel, but that didn't stop it from meeting other points of contact while it was in India—among them, K.M. Panikkar, who was delighted to oblige. During their discussions, Panikkar asked them to bide their time. He strongly felt that following transfer of power and Partition, public opinion in India, especially among the Hindus, would change in favour of the Zionists. He urged the delegation to continue its contacts with important Indian leaders, but was shrewd enough to urge them to avoid those like Gandhi or Nehru who had publicly and forcefully declared their allegiance to Palestine.[40] Congress leaders of their stature, Panikkar told Bergmann, would continue to adopt a pro-Arab stand 'at least as long as they have to appease Muslim opinion'.[41] What should Zionist proponents do then? Panikkar suggested that instead of looking at top leaders like Nehru, Patel or Gandhi, they should reach out to 'leaders of the second rank who are to form and even to voice, their own unbiased opinions'.[42]

And so, as India moved towards the final weeks of its time as a colony, as Panikkar dealt with communalism in Bikaner and his last duties as prime minister of a princely state, he was also working behind the scenes to try and build future ties with an as yet unborn Israeli state. As mentioned before, these were never publicly admitted leanings. India's relationship with Israel would always be controversial, to put it mildly, at least in the early years. Among prominent Indians of his generation, Panikkar was not alone in this duality of private sympathy and public hostility toward the Zionist cause.[43] All through early 1947 though, he was confident enough to tell Zionist leaders that, after Partition, India would be free of Muslim influence and would, as a primarily Hindu nation, be more sympathetic to Zionist aspirations in Palestine. A few years later in his autobiography—which he published in 1955—he sang another song altogether, joining the official chorus against the formation of Israel.

So naturally, *An Autobiography* makes no mention of the secret note he wrote in 1947 as an 'ardent friend'[44] of the Zionist cause on Hindu–Zionist connections post the transfer of power. Dated 8 April 1947, the note is illuminating when it comes to Panikkar's understanding of the Palestine problem, of his evaluation of where Indian politics was heading and what Partition could mean for Jewish political aspirations. He is forthright about where the Jewish Agency failed in garnering support for itself among Indian leaders. 'If there is no widespread expression of sympathy even in orthodox Hindu quarters towards Zionist claims, this is due to a large extent to the neglect of India by the Zionists themselves. No attempt has been made in the past to create such an understanding due no doubt to the "Western" attitude of the Jews in general.'[45]

In this two-page note, Panikkar laid out a blueprint of circumstances as they stood in India at the time. Because 'Islam is a minority in India', he argued, 'the feeling of Muslim solidarity is greater in India than perhaps anywhere else in the Islamic world.'[46] Due to the prevailing political climate on the eve of Partition, the Hindus would unconditionally support 'all matters on which Islam feels strongly'.

Why? For tactical reasons.

In Panikkar's assessment, 'Hindu' support (read: Congress support) to the Arabs would be strategic in forging Hindu–Muslim unity against foreign rule in the dying months of the Raj.

Therefore, as far as Palestine was concerned, 'official Indian opinion will not be different from that of Islamic countries, though it is unlikely that India will do more than follow the lead of the Arab countries in this matter'.[47] But in the same note, he laid in the caveat that, 'it will be wrong to think that Hindu opinion is solidly in favour of Islamic claims in Palestine'. Once Pakistan was established, 'Hindu opinion on the question of Palestine will find its natural and untrammelled expression'.[48]

This is a startling note for many reasons, not least because by now, Panikkar had seen the fallout of not one but two world wars. He had also witnessed the disastrous consequences of the communal trajectory of the freedom movement in India. Still, he predicted that Hindus (the Congress) would appreciate that 'a Zionist Palestine may be an important link in the defence policy of India, that it may, with the support of European nations, be an effective counter-weight to an alliance of Islamic countries in the Middle East … between Hinduism and Judaism there is a great deal in common'.[49]

Therefore, in Panikkar's perception, though free India would not immediately rush to support the Zionist cause, the creation of Hindu-Zionist friendship 'clearly indicated … the interests of both parties'.

For now, he advised the Jewish delegation to wait it out: to have 'representation in Delhi' so that contacts between Hindu leaders and the Zionists could not only be maintained but also deepened in the aftermath of the transfer of power.[50] Until then, the Jewish Agency could, he suggested, initiate programmes of cultural exchange, establish a Hebrew chair in an Indian university and a reciprocal chair for Sanskrit and Indology at the Hebrew University. This wasn't a new idea, since cultural and educational contacts between leading Zionist figures and Indian leaders had been established and had continued since the early 1930s, but what Panikkar was particularly insistent about was that the Jewish Agency focus now on building postcolonial contacts and goodwill in India. He warned the agency that any candidate they depute to India be of 'sufficient intellectual and political calibre as to be in intimate contact with leading personalities'.[51] His memorandum concluded on an optimistic note. 'A limited scheme of this nature will, I feel, produce substantial results which cannot fail to be of advantage both to India and to the Zionists. India has full appreciation of Zionist influence in world politics.'[52]

This is a remarkable prognosis, but Panikkar was, to put it mildly, jumping the gun. For one, he didn't take into account the fact that the Zionists weren't really rating India high on their priority list. For another, he blithely ignored the fact that there was no such thing as a Hindu opinion on Palestine. As the scholar P.R. Kumaraswamy puts it, 'As a gentile, a *kafir* ('unbeliever'), an infidel or a pagan, the Hindu had no sentimental attachment to Palestine, Israel or the holy land; Palestine for him (the Hindu) was as good or as bad as Alaska.'[53] Nor could Panikkar have foreseen that despite Partition, a large number of Muslims would make a deliberate choice to stay in India and emerge as a powerful minority. Their presence would inevitably impact postcolonial India's Israel policy.

Chapter 41

Little Men, Great Causes

THE SECOND SESSION OF THE CONSTITUENT ASSEMBLY OPENED ON 2 April 1947 to galleries crammed with spectators. Sixteen princely states had arrived to sit in the Assembly. Collectively, they were but a fraction of their total number, but as Panikkar said, 'the significance of the event lay in the importance of the states we represented'.[1] Rajendra Prasad welcomed the states, pointing out the 'tremendous task' of nation-building in which they were all involved. B.L. Mitter, the new Dewan of Baroda, spoke next. 'We, the states, are an integral part of India and we shall share the freedom with British India. We, therefore, want to share the responsibility of framing the Constitution.'[2]

He emphasised significantly though that nobody had coerced the princes into joining the Assembly. 'We are here by right of being Indians, not by sufferance.'[3]

Panikkar wasn't expecting to speak during this session, and so was startled when Prasad signalled to him to speak next. Arising from his seat next to Vijayalakshmi Pandit, Panikkar spoke extempore. 'It is a dream which has come true, for at no time in India's history has a representative gathering of people who can speak on behalf of the whole of India met and has taken counsel,'[4] he told the assembly. 'Are we less patriotic in matters connected with India? We are not here as a matter of favour. We have a right to be here for the purpose of cooperating in the great task of organising India's freedom.'[5]

He sat down to thunderous applause. It was a speech very much in Panikkar's forthright, elegant style. It drove home the fact that despite their initial reluctance, the princes would not allow themselves to be sidelined.

If they had known then what was afoot in the viceregal mind, the princes would have been appalled. Mountbatten had drawn up a first draft of a plan to transfer power. Known to history as Plan Balkan, it proposed to divide India into around twelve autonomous provinces. Both provinces and princely states would then be made independent and given the choice to join India or Pakistan.

None of this would come to light until much later, of course, and in blissful ignorance of what was being planned, Bikaner wrote to the viceroy in April 1947, suggesting that Mountbatten meet Panikkar. 'He is one of the most experienced ministers of the states who has been acquainted with all constitutional discussions, ever since the appointment of the Butler Committee in 1927,' Sadul Singh wrote. 'It is no exaggeration to say that there are not many ministers who have got such a grasp of the states' problem or who are in possession of such complete knowledge of the states and their problems. I have complete confidence in him.'[6]

With Campbell-Johnson endorsing this view, Mountbatten sent for Panikkar nearly a month later. On 5 May 1947, at half-past five in the evening, Panikkar was ushered into the warm viceregal study. The interview[7] lasted for an hour. If Mountbatten's minutes after the meeting are anything to go by, Panikkar seems to have 'positively embraced' the idea of Pakistan on the grounds that it would enable a strong centre to be established in Delhi, which the inclusion of Muslim majority provinces would render impossible. He was sure that Jinnah intended to set up an equally strong centre for Pakistan. If that came to pass, India and Pakistan could maintain treaty relations.

A little more problematically, Mountbatten recorded that Panikkar endorsed his (Mountbatten's) original plan for the transfer of power, saying that it was both greatly superior and for the greater good of India in the long run.[8] Now, since this was Plan Balkan—which would cause Nehru to implode with rage and V.P. Menon to threaten to resign in protest—it is quite the assertion to make, and one that is unlikely to be true. Not only was Mountbatten skilled at embroidering his version of the past but Panikkar had also always been a staunch nationalist.

Still, the viceroy reminded Panikkar that any plan that failed to include India within the larger British Commonwealth would be 'no good' for the country. 'You can't have your cake and eat it too,' said Mountbatten. It was a thinly disguised hint, and Panikkar nodded, 'You have put the case more clearly to me than you have before.' He rose. 'I will take the earliest opportunity to speak with Sardar Patel.'

'Well, I hope you will not mention my views to him,' Mountbatten said briskly. 'I'm not prepared to discuss this matter with any member of Congress unless they raise it first.'

'I entirely understand.'[9]

What Panikkar would have done with the substance of this conversation, we shall never know. Because V.P. Menon, on a hot May afternoon in Simla, stepped in to draft a plan (within four hours!) for the transfer of power and Partition, which would irrevocably change the face and fate of South Asia.

On 2 June 1947, the leaders of India's independence movement began arriving in the North Court of Viceroy House to go over a document titled 'Immediate Transfer of Power'.

This was followed by a more theatrical event on 3 June, where the viceroy banged thirty-odd pages of foolscap on the table: a detailed plan, laying out the administrative costs of Partition. The birth of Pakistan would not only be a question of demarcated boundaries and a division of armed forces but it would also be a division of personnel, pens, pins, liabilities and assets and, in one extraordinary case, ducks.[10] It was the first time that the enormity of Partition dawned on Indian political leaders. To the representatives of the states, the viceroy said that demission of the empire's power would proceed along the lines of the Cabinet Mission Plan.

On the evening of 4 June, from the headquarters of All India Radio, Mountbatten spoke to the country. Indians had wanted both independence and Partition. They now had both and it was their duty to make it work.

Nehru spoke next. 'We are little men, serving great causes. But because the cause is great, something of that greatness falls upon us also.'

It was but one of the many unforgettable moments that summer and it was followed by Mountbatten's breezy announcement in front of a battery of national and international media and flashing cameras that transfer of power would take place on 15 August 1947.

This casual way of pronouncing history caused a sensation. Nehru was reported to have exclaimed, 'I can't believe it!' when he heard it himself.[11]

Whether he believed it or not, the deed was done. The Menon Plan delineated the path to India's independence and the birth of Pakistan, but peace hung precariously in the balance. 'There was such little time,' Menon recalled, 'and there was so much to do.'[12] It came down to the fact that the country's administrative machine and law and order had to keep one country running even as it helped another to stand on its own feet, all in a matter of ten weeks.

A chronology of events might give the reader an idea of the scope of questions to be answered in the days remaining, but even then it is but the faintest idea of the kind of pressure that princes and politicians alike were under. No sooner had the plan been accepted than the provincial assemblies met to determine their fates. In a matter of days, arson and murder spread across Punjab, Sind, Baluchistan, East Bengal, West Punjab and the North-West Frontier Province. Efforts to bring over the remaining princely states continued. With many states still not in the Constituent Assembly, Nehru was out of patience, cutting Jaipur dead at an informal dinner. To Manipur, he wrote, 'There is no time left for anyone in India to just wait and see what happens . . . the future of Manipur state obviously lies with the Indian Union.'[13] To Holkar of Indore, he was blunter. 'I really do not care very much whether every state joins the Constituent Assembly or not, because in any event, the states will be affected by the establishment of a strong Indian union. This fact cannot be ignored and thus, the choice for a state is limited.'[14]

Patel, on the other hand, was trying a different tack. The Sardar was no fan of the princes himself, but he had decided coolly that he should start gently. In the first weeks of May, a flurry of royals arrived at Patel's residence at 1 Aurangzeb Road. There was lunch with Jodhpur, and the Jam Sahib arrived a week later with his wife, followed by Patiala. Patel's wooing of the Jam Sahib was a shrewd move to bring the patchwork of Kathiawar princes over to India's side. He knew of the various desperate tactics the princes were still trying. Even as he entertained them at lunches and dinners, draft constitutions were already being penned by the rulers of Bahawalpur and Mandi, while the Raja of Baghat was lobbying his supporters for a Punjab Hill States Union. But now was not the time to act intemperately. Panikkar observed Patel biding his time, but he wasn't possessed of the same calm temperament. For too long had he seen what Bhopal was capable of doing.

'Between Delhi and Pakistan, the vast hinterland between British India and Pakistan was littered with a miscellany of states,' he observed in some alarm. If Bhopal could succeed in uniting these into a single unit, the dangers to Indian unity were myriad. Since he now had access to Mountbatten himself, Panikkar was provoked into an unwise move, telling Mountbatten 'how he (Bhopal) had worked to use the princes as a cat's paw to aid the Muslim cause'.[15]

He erred here, and the viceroy let him know that in no uncertain terms. 'I have known Bhopal for 35 years. He struck me as intelligent and patriotic. It is therefore difficult for me to believe what you say. However, let us see.'

'In six months,' Panikkar wrote later with grim satisfaction, 'he saw.'[16]

This may seem like the last moment in which anyone could or should have been writing a book, but Panikkar was working on yet another manuscript during the early months of 1947. It would be published shortly after transfer of power. *A Survey of Indian History* traces the history of India from antiquity to the end of the British empire. But this is a simplistic and reductive way to put it. The themes in this book are an amalgamation of ideas gleaned from Panikkar's interest in Indian history. The book itself had been born from his desire to correct prevailing historical views. 'The more I read Indian history, the more miserable I felt,' he remembered. 'Anyone could see that the so-called basic documents on which it was based were mostly written by Europeans who had neither knowledge of nor respect for Hindu culture ...'[17]

But time and events kept pushing aside his desire to write a comprehensive work until the energetic young journalist Kusum Nair entered his orbit in 1946. She liked his idea. It was an excellent time to bring out a work of Indian history, with the Congress poised to become India's first independent government. In true bureaucratic style, a committee under the aegis of Jawaharlal Nehru, Jai Prakash Narayan and others had already been formed to examine the feasibility of this and to set up a publishing house. Named National Information and Publications, this press was intended 'to be affiliated to the Congress and to serve the cause of popular education'.[18] Nair was the perfect fit as the editor of this new publishing house. Dynamic and intelligent, she knew Panikkar's proclivities to write sweepingly erudite texts that would likely fly over the heads of layman readers. 'Not more than three hundred pages,' she ordered him briskly. 'No display of learning. I want the manuscript before January (1947).'[19]

To tell a born academic to compress his ideas into a finite number of pages while keeping the language simple and clean is akin to torture. As a result, while Panikkar was very proud of his finished work, *A Survey of Indian History* was the one text with which he really struggled. He wrote every day: in the early hours of the morning before he began his work on the constitutional committees, in between conferences deciding India's future, in office and on trains between states. It consumed him utterly.

In many ways, the finished text is a curious mix of Panikkar's old ideas adapted to a new post-war, postcolonial world. He presented independence as the culmination of a history that spanned millennia. The very ancient, original cultural unity formed around Hinduism remained the element that guaranteed the continuity of this process and at the same time represented the premise for a parallel history that had made it possible on a political level to achieve the unification of the country. He began with the development of a Hindu civilisation born from the fusion of Dravidian and Aryan culture. He followed its spread from Punjab throughout the subcontinent between the sixteenth and seventeenth centuries BCE, to the assimilation of local tribes into the caste system. The common denominator was India's historic and continuous quest for unification, its vibrant cultural expansion and its spiritual unity. Within the pages of this latest book, Panikkar laid out a history of India based on a Hindu culture that united India as a whole and survived attacks from outside. Civilisation in India, he argued, developed from various elements of people on the Indian subcontinent that included the pre-Aryan civilisation, which was discovered in the Indus valley in North India, and the Dravidian civilisation in South India. 'Civilisation did not come to India with the Aryans . . . Not only is Indian civilisation pre-Vedic, but the essential features of the Hindu religion as we know it today were present in Mohenjo-Daro.'[20]

Across its history of numerous invasions, conquests and contacts with foreign civilisations (and here he was repeating points he had been making at various points throughout his career as a historian), India's core remained fundamentally Hindu, and hence, fundamentally Indian. Even in the south of India and on the Deccan plateau, Panikkar argued that it had been the Dravidian civilisation that had brought Hindu culture to the south, besides making the point that 'the Deccan and Peninsular India generally had from the earliest times a civilization independent of the north'.[21] He returned to his ideas of maritime power in Indian history, emphasising that it was the Dravidian civilisation that had developed maritime intercourse in terms of trade and migration with Mesopotamia, Egypt and Palestine, and even lands as far flung as Madagascar. In so doing, it had been the south of India that had spread Hindu civilisation and culture overseas. Panikkar returned, on the eve of independence, to his ideas of 'Greater India'. Once again, the major focus was on the maritime expansion of 'Indian culture and influence both towards Central Asia and to the south-east towards the countries and islands of the Pacific'.[22]

Indian Muslims, according to Panikkar, were part of a broader Islamic culture, which had developed from the interaction of Islam with Hinduism. Had India's encounter with Islam benefited its culture and politics in any way? Panikkar was vague about this. Certainly, Islam had profoundly changed much in society, culture and history, but the great culture of Islam was hardly represented by the Turks and Afghans who entered India in the wake of Muhammad Ghori. A true Islamic force, Panikkar wrote, arose only with the Mughal empire. Yet, Hindus played a key role in this empire, which flourished until Aurangzeb's arrival on the scene. Attempts at unification failed, and India found itself once again fragmented and facing a new challenge: the growth of European powers that based their strength on the sea and from the mid-eighteenth century began to intervene in the wars between the new states that arose from the dissolution of the Mughal empire.

After 1857, it was the Crown that had united India and given birth to a concept of a nation state. Railways, posts and telegraphs, currency, salt administration—these were the main external forms through which this unity was achieved. It was all held together by the doctrine of paramountcy. Panikkar went much further here. He explained that to regain its independence, it was necessary for Indian civilisation to undertake enormous religious and social reform, a great effort at political organisation, a slower economic recovery and a cultural, literary, artistic and scientific renaissance. He argued that by the end of the nineteenth century, Hinduism was fully conscious of its own greatness and powers and ready if necessary to challenge the teachings of rival religions. All these political and religious developments had birthed the national movement, but the Congress had never turned it into a sectarian movement.

This paragraph in *A Survey* deserves to be quoted in full, if only to be appreciated in the light of present day India: 'The period of cooperation with the Muslim League and the interlude of the Khilafat agitation should not blind us to the fact that the strength of the Congress lay primarily in Hindu revival and in an integrated nationalism based on the Hindu masses. The Mahatma himself embodied in his person certain aspects of Hindu spirit. [. . .] Under him, though in a different way, the Congress represented the resistance of Hinduism as a whole to alien domination, though the political purpose of the Congress and its general outlook in regard to the future of India was entirely not sectarian.'[23]

In analysing all of this, the question of sectarianism—of a Hindu bias, to put it simply—has often arisen.

Was Panikkar sectarian?

The answer to that is, quite simply, no.

Panikkar was more keenly interested in the reality of history and in forming a nationalist response to colonialism. He had watched Europeans whitewashing their own colonial pasts for too long to be anything else. History, for him, was not a telephone directory of names and dates but 'human life in action'.[24] As he wrote in *A Survey*, the history of any country could not be seen simply as 'a grand procession of great men or a majestic stream of progress broadening with every age'.[25] Instead, in order to truly understand history, one must see it as 'the conscious effort of a people to achieve a civilisation'.[26] Living up to his reputation for being able to compartmentalise his mind, Panikkar chose to see history being created by people against or because of a definite geographical backdrop, which is why he referenced the Indian Ocean and the Himalayas in separate works.

That said, given the circumstances and times in which he had grown up, Panikkar found the 'Greater India' school of thought to be a reliable answer to a world dominated by empire. As foundational arguments go then, certain facets of Panikkar's views are certainly problematic in retrospect. For instance, his lens viewed India's expansion as peaceful cultural colonisation—yet it was still imperialistic. While he intended to frame Hindu colonialism as different from the Western, he too relied on the same sources, or the interpretations of sources, reached and analysed by Westerners.

A Survey of Indian History contained a separate (though short) chapter on 'Greater India', but as India emerged onto the world stage as a free country, Panikkar dropped the argument altogether. There was no place, he realised, in independent India (or Southeast or South Asia for that matter) for a world view in which Hindu-Indian chauvinism played a central role.

Panikkar wrote the final chapters at the beautiful palace in Kapurthala where he was staying for the maharaja's birthday festivities. He arrived by the overnight train from Bikaner, and while his secretary arranged his papers, he went off to pay his respects to the maharaja. It was a beautiful, sunny day, but he couldn't afford to enjoy it with a deadline hanging over his head. No sooner had he managed to escape to his room to try and write than an ADC came scurrying to call him. He was being summoned to attend a special magic show that Kapurthala had organised for his guests. Irritated, Panikkar went down to the garden, making sure to seat himself in the front row so that his presence wouldn't be missed by royal eyes. After about half an hour, he slipped away quietly to his room, where he bolted the door and sat down to write. He managed to finish one chapter, then hastily changed and rushed down to the ballroom for dinner and drinks. The night was a long one, though it was made bearable by the company of a young, pretty princess from Kapurthala.

The next morning, Panikkar awoke with a thudding headache.

He wanted more than anything to take a day off, but his restless energy pushed him to take a walk in the gardens instead. As he wandered about, gazing listlessly at the gorgeous flowers and trees on the estate, thoughts and paragraphs jumbled about in his tired brain. By the time he returned to his room, he had the core of the chapter down. That evening, after attending yet another ball, Panikkar returned to his room exhausted, his head spinning a little with fine food and fine wine.[27]

He thought briefly about going to bed, but caught sight of his desk, his papers neatly arranged and waiting for him. Exhaustion turned to energy in the blink of an eye. Sitting down without bothering to change out of his formal suit, Panikkar began to write.

It was nearly four in the morning by the time he finished.

It was done.

The book had been written.

As soon as dawn broke, Panikkar sent word to Kapurthala that he wasn't feeling well. He then slept like the dead for the entire day.

A Survey of History missed its deadline of January, but with Kusum Nair's energy and vim behind it, it was published on 15 August 1947. 'It was a load off my shoulders,' Panikkar recalled. 'No other book had given me so much worry.'[28] He recognised its import himself—a new work of Indian history, penned by an Indian historian, to be read by a new generation of readers in a new, free land. More than an honour, it was, for him, 'an unbearable burden'.[29]

He was thrilled, then, when the book became a hit, almost from the moment it reached bookstalls. Editions followed one another and the *Survey* was even adopted as a textbook for the preparation of candidates for the Indian Administrative Service.

Around the same time that he sent the manuscript off to the press, Panikkar also penned his resignation letter as Dewan of Bikaner, requesting that he be allowed to step down as soon as the new constitutional reforms introduced popular government into the state. 'In six months' time from today, Your Highness will be opening a new and, as I fervently believe, more glorious chapter in the history of Bikaner. It is obviously necessary to give the reforms the best possible chance and for this purpose, Your Highness should be able to reconstitute the ministry. With this object in view, I desire most respectfully to vacate the high office to which your Highness has called me and which I have now held for three years. I request that as soon as possible after the new reforms have been brought into force, Your Highness may be pleased to relieve me.'[30]

Chapter 42

Powerplay and Partition

IT WAS AT THIS MOMENT IN INDIAN HISTORY THAT POLITICAL LEADERS across the spectrum stepped aside and allowed their bureaucrats to take over. These were civil servants with less than seventy days to ensure the division of the country and to see to it that infrastructure and personnel were functional enough to take over administration immediately in both India and Pakistan. Panikkar himself had been appointed to all the major committees that would start hammering a constitutional structure into place.

'I sat on the Committee on Fundamental Rights, the Committee on Minorities, the Committee on the Principles of the Constitution and the Committee on the National Flag,' he wrote. 'I served diligently on them.'[1] It is a typical way of brushing aside the work that he *did* do, considering that these were the committees that would begin putting together the nuts and bolts that would hold up the political framework of modern India. As a Central Steering Committee was set up to navigate these choppy waters, Panikkar found himself fighting to keep Bikaner from boiling over.

With Partition only weeks away, the state found itself as border territory overnight. Muslim refugees from the Indian Punjab had already begun walking from Hanumannagar in the north and Rajgarh in the east to try and cross into Pakistan from Bikaner. Travelling about the state on inspection tours, Panikkar was confronted by rage the likes of which he had never seen before.

'Communal opinions in the state have aroused a fury,' he reported to Bikaner after one such tour. 'I was being openly accused of helping the Mussalmans. The concentration of refugees caused fear to the neighbouring villages …'[2]

State authorities were struggling to even control, much less reverse, the flow of early refugees into Bikaner thanks to bloodshed in neighbouring Bahawalpur. Panikkar was close to despair. Partition had not even happened and already there were reports of Sikh mobs barging onto Bhatinda-bound trains, pulling off Muslims and murdering them in broad daylight. In response to these reports, the Muslim-dominated Gang Canal Colony in Bikaner went up in flames of rage. Acting fast, Panikkar sent a small military force to crack down on the violence, but it was rapidly overwhelmed.

In alarm, he wrote to V.P. Menon, who had now been elevated to the position of Secretary, Ministry of States. In the short time that the two men had worked together, they had become excellent friends.

Now, Panikkar needed VP's help.

Could VP come to Bikaner for a quick inspection? VP arrived two days later and was taken on a personal tour of the refugee camps that Panikkar had set up across the state. The situation on the ground was deteriorating rapidly, but Panikkar and VP knew it was prudent to report to Sardar Patel that things were currently under control. The last thing Nehru and Patel needed to know at this time was that Bikaner—a state on the proposed border with Pakistan—was spiralling out of control. 'In Bikaner, the state authorities are fully alive to the dangers of the present situation and are doing their best,' VP reported tactfully to Patel, adding the warning rider, 'But we must help them.'[3]

As VP and Patel began to look for ways in which accession of the states to India could be presented in a tantalising (and ethical) way to the rulers, Panikkar became involved in what would be one of his final acts as Dewan of Bikaner: protecting the state from the slash of Cyril Radcliffe's pen.

In June 1947, the astonished Cyril Radcliffe, one of England's most brilliant lawyers, was told peremptorily that he was to fly out to India to chair a Boundary Commission which would demarcate the country's international borders. Radcliffe had never been to India or anywhere else in South Asia.[4] His knowledge of its geography was weak and his experience with the delineation of international boundaries was non-existent. His mind boggled at the five-week deadline he was given, but he was at heart a stout Englishman, ready to work for British interests.

Despite his misgivings, he accepted the job.[5]

It was a hack job from the start. Radcliffe had no idea of the Indian concerns about the Boundary Commission. Nearly thirty princely states were involved along what would become the Radcliffe Line, and these were apart from the Sikhs. Every ruler was concerned about irrigation and water supply, for which the commission should have had legal and technical experts. But transfer of power was now looming darkly on the horizon. There was no time for technicalities, though there were rubber stamps in place like the Arbitrary Tribunal, which would negotiate with the commission itself. Those negotiations are a separate and riveting story. In later years, Radcliffe shrugged off the retrospective enormity of the task before him. 'Jinnah, Nehru and Patel told me they wanted a line before or on 15 August,' he told the journalist Kuldip Nayyar. 'So I drew them a line.'[6]

But it would never be as simple as that.

From the outset, the commission was hampered by party politics, problematic demographic and cartographic data, a lack of expertise, shortage of time and no preparation for a division that promised to be both religious and political.

By 7 August 1947, a week before independence, Radcliffe was in Delhi, drawing his line alone. The primary factor he was weighing was the separation of 'contiguous majority areas'. Factors like this led him to sever the cities of Lahore and Amritsar, for example. The rest of the line would follow from there, driven by the need to preserve Amritsar's economic and strategic position as far as possible. The same need also dictated the fate of Gurdaspur. He stuck as far as he could to existing British administrative boundaries, though in the Punjab and in Bengal he discussed canals, headworks, roads, railways and ports before turning to the population.[7] 'Water was the key,' Christopher Beaumont, then the secretary to the commission, said later. 'Railways would come second and electricity would run third.'[8]

But Radcliffe was discovering that whatever line he drew, the water supply would inevitably be disrupted for at least one side. The trouble was that the irrigation (and other systems) of Punjab and Bengal had been built to function under a single administration. They were never intended to be divided. Nothing Radcliffe could have done would have allowed either Pakistan or India to operate their infrastructure separately. When he tactfully suggested the obvious—that India and Pakistan operate the irrigation system together—he hit the festering sore between the Congress and the League.

Jinnah said frigidly that he would rather have 'Pakistan a desert, than fertile fields watered by a country of Hindus'.[9] Nehru, on the other hand, testily informed Radcliffe that what India did with India's waters was India's affair.[10]

Realising he had hit a dead end, Radcliffe then metaphorically threw his hands in the air. He decided to leave the matter as an 'award, instead of trying to argue it or elaborate upon it further'.[11]

No sooner had he solved *that* problem than he got anxious queries from Mountbatten who was eager to get the award out and done as soon as possible. 'We shall all be grateful for every extra day earlier that you could manage to get the award announced,' he wrote. 'I wonder if there is any chance of getting it out by the 10th?'[12]

'I do not *think* that I can manage the 10th,' replied the hassled Radcliffe, 'but I think that I can promise the 12th.'[13]

Then, of course, there were the states.

From Lahore, Governor Evan Jenkins was pleading for advance information so he could have security deployed accordingly.[14] Jenkins's urgent cable crossed with one from George Abell, which had the information Radcliffe needed, including a sketched map of the area depicting a 'sharp salient' in Ferozepur for the Zira and Ferozepur districts in Pakistan. The remainder of the area was up in the air, so to speak.

This map would be the cause of much trouble in the weeks before Partition, for the final boundary would differ from the red lines on this sketch. Not only that, information about the map and its contents seems to have leaked almost immediately. As rumours, some of them remarkably accurate, began to fly thick and fast, Kanwar Sain, the chief irrigation engineer of Bikaner, a state that relied heavily on the Ferozepur canal waters, received a secret, urgent letter from the District Commissioner of Ferozepur. Governor Jenkins had ordered the establishment of a new headquarters for Ferozepur outside the current tehsils of Zira, Fezilka and Ferozepur. These three tehsils were likely to be awarded to Pakistan.

Horrified, Sain rushed to the maharaja with this news.

Sadul Singh lost no time in writing to Mountbatten. 'It is strongly rumoured that the Boundary Commission is likely to award Ferozepur tehsil to West Punjab . . . Such an arrangement may gravely prejudice the interests of Bikaner state.'[15]

When there was no response, Sadul Singh sent a special aircraft to Delhi with Panikkar and Sain on board. In the capital, the two men found their way to the viceroy blocked by George Abell. Mountbatten was busy, he insisted, and had no time for random meetings. Panikkar used his influence here to wangle them a meeting on the morning of 11 August.

As it turned out, it wasn't a meeting as much as it was ten minutes of the harried viceroy's time. The interview began poorly.

Panikkar got straight to the point, but he was cut off almost immediately by an angry Mountbatten who shouted, 'The viceroy had nothing to do with the Radcliffe Commission. That commission has been appointed by HMG and it is not to report to me!'[16] For the first time in his life, Panikkar was rendered speechless, both in humiliation and in rage. Seeing the dewan at a genuine loss for words, Sain leaped into the breach, delivering a threat he knew would carry weight at this juncture.

If Ferozepur went to Pakistan, he said, so too would Bikaner.

Whether this was a bluff or not, we will never know, but it had the effect of making Mountbatten go white.

In the pause that ensued, Sain and Panikkar walked out.

It was this interview that changed the future of the Radcliffe Line.[17] Radcliffe's private secretary, Christopher Beaumont, would later speculate that Bikaner used the threat of joining Pakistan as leverage to get the line changed and get the headworks of Ferozepur back into Indian hands.[18] It was also following this disastrous interview that V.P. Menon arrived at Viceroy House at midnight to try and persuade Radcliffe to change the line, only to be blocked by Beaumont. The blockage was temporary.

On 11 August 1947, Jenkins received a message: *Eliminate Salient.*

These were events behind the scenes of India's preparations for freedom. On 3 August, Vijayalakshmi Pandit had departed for Moscow as India's ambassador. By the first week of August, the Indian national flag was being flown to capitals around the world, from Paris to Cairo and from Addis Ababa to Damascus. But nobody remotely associated with Partition wanted to be around on the day itself.

'I station myself firmly on the Delhi airport until an aeroplane from England comes along,' Radcliffe wrote to his friend, Mark Tennant. 'Nobody will love me for my Award about the Punjab and Bengal and there will be roughly 80 million people with a grievance who will begin looking for me. I do not want them to find me.'[19]

Oshar Spate, the Australian geographer who assisted the Muslims on the Boundary Commission, scribbled in his diary, 'I want to have one foot on the running board of the Karachi Mail when the announcement is made.'[20]

For good reason.

'You may well imagine the headaches that have been going on over the states and the race for time and possessions,' Edwina Mountbatten wrote to V.K. Krishna Menon. 'Certainly by 15th August, we shall be transferring power all right, but I really think that the Mountbattens will be transferred to the local asylum!'[21]

Indian political leaders were even more frazzled. The Ministry of States had now put in place a plan for the princes. They would have to let go of defence, communications and foreign affairs. To legally accede, they would need to sign that dreaded document—what the Maharawal of Dungarpur acerbically called the 'Instrument of Execution'.[22] The Instrument of Accession was drawn up by V.P.

Menon, and though Panikkar writes of it as a 'joint effort',[23] this was taking things a bit too far. Any draft sent now to Panikkar would have been more of a polite formality rather than a dual effort, especially from V.P. Menon.

As it was, India had run out of time.

The process of integration and accession would continue long after India stood free and Panikkar wouldn't be involved with that at all. But he did have one last anna to contribute to the transfer of power: the timing of it. The original plan was that the viceroy would arrive on the morning of 15 August and would formally proclaim Indian independence at the Constituent Assembly. Thereafter, the Indian flag would be hoisted.

Panikkar believed that it should be done in precision with what British Parliament had declared: that transfer of power would take place at midnight on 14 August 1947. But this idea was laughed off by Sarojini Naidu and other Indian leaders. Annoyed, Panikkar wrote directly to Nehru, who replied lightly, 'I like the suggestion but two of my colleagues [Patel and Azad] go to bed at precisely 9 o'clock!'

Sensing victory, Panikkar replied in the same vein. 'I'm happy to provide them with beds!'

What Nehru's reaction was to this remains unknown, but the hour of the transfer of power was changed to midnight.

India was free and with her freedom, Panikkar's twenty-year service to the Indian states had finally come to an end. He already knew his next assignment. Vijayalakshmi Pandit had insisted that he accompany India's second delegation to the United Nations General Assembly (UNGA) in New York in September 1947. His papers were in order and he was scheduled to leave by 11 September 1947.

Before he could leave, Panikkar would witness first-hand the price India had paid for its freedom, one of 'bloodshed and bestiality'.[24]

As Punjab went up in flames and riots began in Old Delhi, Panikkar lived each day in terror. His sixteen-year-old daughter Radha was then reading for her BA in Indraprastha College, close to where the violence was occurring. He cabled V.P. Menon immediately, asking that a car be sent to collect her and if she could stay with VP and his family in Curzon Road (now Kasturba Gandhi Marg).

VP acted immediately, and Radha came to stay at the Menon home in Delhi for a week, while she waited for her father to arrive from Bikaner.

But his arrival was delayed.

Refugees from Bahawalpur were flooding into Bikaner by the thousands, bringing news that the Hindus were being 'hunted like animals'.[25]

In Bikaner, the Hindus wanted revenge.

Panikkar refused to permit such a thing, ordering the state army to put down riots. Pulling together a heavy police convoy, he managed to get some 4.5 lakh Muslims over the newly drawn border into Pakistan.

It was like staunching a haemorrhage with a Band-Aid. On the northern and eastern borders of Bikaner, over 1,00,000 Muslims gathered with their families, household goods and cattle. On no account could they be permitted to enter Bikaner. Panikkar knew that if they did, Hindus would murder them without a second thought. Their only alternative was a dangerous trek to Pakistan, over 300 kilometres long.

What should he do?

He needed to get to Delhi, to get to his daughter and to ask VP how to handle the situation in Bikaner.

But no trains were running.

Panikkar went to Sadul Singh in despair.

The closest station to Delhi was Rewari, on the borders of Bikaner. The maharaja granted Panikkar a police escort and ordered a special train to be deployed for his dewan. The only real order Sadul Singh gave Panikkar was to shave his goatee immediately. There were troubling reports that 'RSS workers were entering trains and killing everyone who looked like a Muslim'.[26]

Panikkar reached Delhi without mishap, but it was not the city he had left only a few weeks ago. The skies burned a dull orange-grey, blurred with ash and smoke from the fires burning across the river. Word was that over 10,000 Muslims had been slaughtered. With dread in his heart, Panikkar finished his meeting with VP as quickly as possible and got out of the city with Radha. They reached Rewari on time, at nine o'clock that night, but the station was eerily deserted. The guard travelling with them suggested nervously that they halt there for the night.

Early the next morning, Panikkar heard raised voices. When he went to check, he found a group of well-dressed, pleasant-faced young men arguing with the inspector assigned to his saloon. There seemed nothing untoward about them except, as he drew closer, for the glint of swords. Suppressing a sudden thrill of fear, Panikkar asked what was happening. The inspector explained that these young men were asking that Panikkar's saloon be shifted towards the end of the train. Violence was expected ahead, and nobody wanted the Dewan of Bikaner and his daughter to be hurt.

The leader of the armed men now came up to Panikkar, and once again, he was struck by how pleasantly innocuous these young men were. 'Please forgive the inconvenience, sir,' the man said, in reasonably good English. 'But if your saloon stays in the middle, the mob may damage it.'

'I have no objection, but what is happening?' Panikkar demanded, adding rather foolishly, 'I hope you are not doing anything against the law?'

'Oh no, nothing illegal,' the young man said cheerfully. 'I merely planned to sell 1,500 tickets to Pakistan.'

This sounded bizarre but hardly murderous.

Panikkar agreed to let them on board the train.

He was to regret that decision for the rest of his life.

When the train pulled into Mahendragarh in Patiala, the platform was clogged with people, mostly Muslim. There were women with crying babies. Fearful old men clutching what little they possessed. Young men, their eyes flat with fear. Children confused and scared. The Patiala army had barricaded the station to prevent them from leaving.

It didn't take much to know what would happen next.

Nor did it take much to realise that the young man with the pleasant face had lied.

The army now began to move, herding the terrified crowd toward the train.

The train whistle blew.

It was leaving the station.

As it began to move slowly, the army prodded the crowd faster. 'Why are you hesitating?' the soldiers sneered. 'You're going to Pakistan.'

As the overcrowded train pulled out of the station, gangs began to run behind it, shouting and mocking.

Panikkar pulled the curtains of his windows closed.

There was nothing to do now but wait.

In an hour, the train arrived at Jaipur Pali, a tiny one-horse station in a mountain cleft. On both sides, the Aravallis loomed menacingly. Looking out of the window, Panikkar saw people lining the foothills at intervals. They stood in silence, like watchful sentries.

Cold fear churned in Panikkar's stomach as the train juddered to a stop. It was scheduled to stop there only for a minute, but the engines cut off.

In the eerie silence that followed, the screams began.

A mob had arrived, seemingly out of nowhere, armed with knives and scythes.

Later, Panikkar would remember that on the faces of this mob, there was no anger or hatred, just a curiously determined expression.

They were here to kill.

The sentries at the foothills never moved as cries of 'Bharat Mata ki Jai' and 'Hindu dharma ki jai' rent the air. People, many bleeding or maimed, began to limp past the windows, trying to run for their lives. Some stumbled towards the hills, blind with terror. It was then that Panikkar realised what the sentries were there for.

'There was no escape—even in flight.'[27]

There was no escape for him and Radha either.

All Panikkar could do was sit frozen in fear and pray that nobody came towards his carriage. He had no desire to attract attention towards either himself or his daughter. But as the young man had promised, nobody came that way. Panikkar could see him coming and going, his clothes spattered with blood, shouting to his men to move faster, and reporting quietly to the inspector outside Panikkar's carriage.

Outside, the cries changed. 'Mahatma Gandhi ki jai!'

Humans often crack under the oddest kinds of pressure.

Panikkar snapped now.

Getting up, he went to the door.

The young man grinned at him. 'It's all over, sir. There are no more children of Satan left here.'

'I am unable to stop you,' Panikkar said, his voice shaking. 'But why do you call Gandhi's name during this atrocity. Stop that at least.'

'Certainly, sir,' said the young man courteously. He leaned out and shouted at his men to stop calling Gandhi's name during the carnage.[28] It was another hour before the killings ended—and the looting and raping began.

It would be nightfall before the train reached Bikaner.

These, then, were Panikkar's first real images of free India.

He would never forget them.

CHAPTER 43

Success

AFTER THE HORRORS OF BIKANER, THE AUTUMN COLOURS OF LAKE Success were almost cleansing in their beauty. 'It was as if nature was clothed in fresh garments every day,'[1] Panikkar would write in wonder later. He didn't have much time on his hands to absorb the natural beauty, though. India was making its first representation at the UNGA as a free country, but it was doing so against the backdrop of Partition, Pakistan, communal violence and a war in Kashmir. It was also doing so at a time when decolonisation was overlapping with the Cold War, when Britain was still seeing the fallout of Kashmir as its own unfinished business and when the United States, under Harry Truman's presidency, was preoccupied by events in the Middle East.

India made a strong showing, standing for peace, upholding the UN Charter and abhorring Franco's fascism in Spain. Much of this came from Nehru's ideas on foreign policy, which had been developing since the 1920s. But in practical terms, Nehru had no desire for India to be caught in the crosshairs of another war. As he forthrightly put it, 'India has not yet recovered from the effects of the last war. India, therefore, does not want to get entangled in another war, if it comes.'[2]

His view was shared by many senior officials. 'Some stray spark may ignite the gunpowder that is lying about at any time,' felt Sir G.S. Bajpai.[3] If war broke out then, 'all our schemes of progress would have to be pushed aside for many, many years', especially since India could not afford to stay aloof. Inevitably, by virtue of its independence and emergence on the world stage, it would either be involved or affected by any war.[4]

Non-alignment, at least in the first months of India's independence, was necessary to counter power dynamics and court bigger ideals like disarmament, decolonisation and conflict resolution.[5] This would change as the months passed and more crucial security factors crept into the practice of foreign policy.

Behind the scenes of this idealism, the rancorous politics made it next to impossible to have any dialogue. You wouldn't think it if you looked at the schedule of the delegates. Pandit's calendar was so crammed with dinners, parties and meetings that she was forced to turn down a tea reception by US First Lady Bess Truman.[6] Panikkar himself was quite busy socially, with dinner with Mrs Eleanor Roosevelt figuring high on his list of engagements.

Politically, there was much to do. After briefing him on the day he arrived, Pandit took him with her to speak to Andrei Manuelsky, leader of the Ukrainian delegation in the General Assembly. India and the Soviet Union had established diplomatic relations in April that year, but their relationship in these first weeks of India's independence could at best be described as correct, despite Pandit's appointment to Moscow. Panikkar got an eyeful of that over lunch at Manuelsky's palatial residence a few kilometres from Lake Success. Pandit inquired about 'the reason for the less cordial attitude of the Soviet Union to the Indian delegation this year'.[7] Manuelsky's answer was frank. 'What is your interest in Korea and (the ongoing civil war in) Greece? To us, these are vital areas for our defence. Why should India interest herself against our interest in these matters?'[8] For Panikkar, it was the clearest example that at least for now the Soviet Union was generally suspicious of India's approach to international relations.

He was in the United States only for a couple of months but it was enough time to see that the world was dividing itself now into two blocs: the United States versus the Soviet Union. India would have to navigate the creation of its own foreign policy against this backdrop.[9]

Of personal interest to Panikkar at this time was the formation of the eleven-member UN Special Committee on Palestine (UNSCOP).

By now, he had had enough time to see that his prognosis to Hugo Bergmann's delegation, made only a few months earlier, did not fit the current geopolitical situation. British resolve to remain in the Middle East was collapsing. The Second World War had left Britain victorious, but financially depleted. It now lacked both the funds and the desire to maintain control of colonial possessions that were agitating, with increasing violence, for independence. Meanwhile, Zionist pressure in Palestine was intensifying, aided by the unauthorised immigration of Jewish refugees on an unprecedented scale, propelled by the horrors of the Holocaust and the post-war chaos in Europe. The Arabs, on the other hand, were determined that no more Jews should arrive, and that Palestine should achieve independence as an Arab state. Since Britain's primary goal now was simply to keep its strategic and oil interests in the Middle East and Asia safe, it needed Arab states to cooperate. As a result, Whitehall threw its support behind Arab opposition both to Jewish immigration as well as the creation of Israel, and escalated the problem to the United Nations. The US State Department was on board with this, though Truman was casting a spanner in the works by insisting that Jews be allowed to enter Palestine.

On 31 August 1947, a majority report of the UNSCOP recommended that the region be partitioned into an Arab and a Jewish state. Despite the partition of communities, the region would retain the character of an economic union. Jerusalem and its environs were to be international.

India had to draft its own Palestine policy in the face of this reigning chaos. When Palestine came up before the United Nations for discussion, India was preparing for independence. It was also in the unique position of being a founding member of the UN *despite* being a dominion of the British Empire. The report of the UNSCOP was submitted two weeks after transfer of power in India. Unsurprisingly, the developments in the subcontinent influenced how India looked at Palestine. Now Congress leaders were aware that any solution to the problem should not ignore Jewish interests—but how would that be achieved without diluting the Arab character of Palestine? It was a dilemma that caused much friction between Nehru and the two different envoys to the UNGA on Palestine: Asaf Ali and Sir Abdur Rehman.[10]

The prime minister was clear: 'How to reconcile the two [Arab and Jewish] claims is the problem before us. I do not venture to express an opinion, except vaguely to say that perhaps an autonomous Jewish area within an independent Palestine might lead to a solution ... The general attitude of India must necessarily be friendly to both parties, but clearly indicating that an agreement must have Arab approval.'[11]

As early as 23 April 1947, then, when the First Special Session of the UN General Assembly was in progress, New Delhi felt that any solution to the Palestine problem 'must lie on the lines of the Arab state with the inclusion of an autonomous Jewish area'.[12] This was in tune with the Congress Party's traditional position vis-à-vis Palestine, especially since 1939.

The UNSCOP submitted its report on 1 September 1947. Most of its recommendations were unanimous or near unanimous. On issues such as the termination of the mandate, the granting of independence to Palestine, transitional arrangements under the United Nations, the safeguarding of holy places and the protection of minorities, the committee members were united. Guatemala and Uruguay refused to endorse the majority opinion that 'any solution for Palestine cannot be considered a solution for the Jewish problem in general'.

But on the core issue of the future political status of Palestine, the UNSCOP stood divided. A seven-member majority consisting of Canada, Czechoslovakia, Guatemala, the Netherlands, Sweden and Uruguay opted for the partition of Palestine. India, Iran and Yugoslavia put forth a federal plan. Australia refused to endorse either plan.[13]

Viewing the problem in Palestine as 'a clash between two intense nationalisms', the majority plan rejected the demands of both the Arabs and the Jews. Any worthwhile, viable and realistic solution would have to be one of compromise.

The main features of India's federal plan, on the other hand, were that Palestine would be a federal and independent state. Delivered despite Abdur Rehman's strong reservations against it, the federal plan dismissed the partition plan as being unworkable. The mandate adopted by the League of Nations in 1922 that granted administrative power over Palestine to the British would soon be terminated.[14] In its place, according to the federal plan, there should be a transition administration whose tenure would not exceed three years; federal Palestine would consist of Arab and Jewish states; each state would enjoy internal autonomy, excluding 'national defence, foreign relations, immigration, currency, taxation for federal purposes, foreign and inter-state waterways, transport and communication, copyrights and patent';[15] the federal state would have a bicameral legislature; and the constitution would safeguard, among other things, the equality of all citizens with regard to the political, civil and religious rights of the individual and the linguistic, religious, ethnic and cultural rights of the people as a whole.[16]

Panikkar watched as Vijayalakshmi Pandit publicly explained India's stand on Palestine on 11 October 1947. She argued that peace in Palestine was vital because of its geographical proximity with India and repeated that Palestine was predominantly an Arab country. In an independent Palestine, Pandit suggested, the Jews should be given strong autonomy in the areas where they had a clear majority, but she refused to link the questions of displaced Jews in Europe and of Palestine.[17]

The Indian plan was, in the end, a massive failure, disappointing both Arabs and Jews equally. It offered only civic and religious rights to the Jews when they were aspiring for political sovereignty. As the scholar P.R. Kumaraswamy has explained, the Indian plan 'placed *aliya* under joint federal control and thus restricted its scope. Irrespective of their ideological orientation, everyone in the *yishuv*, from the revisionists to the bi-nationalists, was unanimous on unrestricted Jewish immigration. *Aliya*[18] was the cardinal principle, indeed the *raison d'être* of Zionism. It was therefore unrealistic to expect the Zionists to subject this core issue to an Arab veto.'[19]

The Arabs, on the other hand, demanded complete independence. The suggestion of Jewish autonomy as a precondition for that independence was rejected outright. Again, simply put, the Arabs saw the federal plan as India giving far too much leeway to the Jewish cause.

That the Zionists were unhappy with India's attempt to strike a middle path was plain to see for Panikkar, who met his old friend Chaim Weizmann again after years. 'He was of course very patient with me but, like all great men, adamant when it came to what he considered to be a cause of absolute justice.'[20] Weizmann wasn't the only member of the agency who met Panikkar during his time in the United States. There were repeated attempts by the Jewish Agency to convince the Indian delegation at the UNGA, through Panikkar, to modify its policy.

In New York, Panikkar met Weizmann, Moshe Sharrett and Eliahu Epstein several times from September to October to discuss the pros and cons of the partition plan.[21] He had talked enough with the Indian delegation to know that its hands were tied. They would not defy Nehru's specific instructions to vote against the partition plan, though Panikkar was also aware that there were, as there had been before, disagreements within the delegation over Nehru's position. Pandit, for instance, had definite reservations herself about the viability of the federal plan, warning the Ministry of External Affairs in a letter on 8 October 1947 that the plan had little support and legitimacy because both contending parties, including the Arabs, rejected it. She suggested that India abstain from voting on the partition plan to leave a door open for itself, but like Rahman and Ali before her, she was unable to defy Nehru.[22]

In the end, the partition plan was carried through by the UNGA, recognised by leading Zionists to be the best possible outcome on a tormented issue. It was, in their eyes, at least a sign of international recognition of Jewish claims to Palestine.[23]

In his book *Two Chinas*, Panikkar sings a very different song from the memorandum he wrote secretly in the fevered summer of 1947. 'On the question of a Jewish State in Palestine, however, my sympathies were not all with the Zionists,' he writes sanctimoniously. 'While sympathising with the claim of the Jews for a national home in Palestine, I thought that their demand for a State based on religious exclusivism was in the first instance likely to revive Islamic fanaticism, and secondly was unjust to the Palestine Arabs. We, on the Indian delegation, were … in favour of a cantonal federation in which the Jews and Arabs would live together as neighbours.'[24]

This is not true at all obviously, but it is clear that, by the time *Two Chinas* was written and published in 1955, Panikkar had decided the best course of action was to stay as politically correct as possible. He was also writing in retrospect as a member of independent India's diplomatic corps, not to mention coming off a controversial diplomatic appointment to China. It would not have done to expose political leanings that, even in 1955, would have caused any kind of further furore.

'It was of course useless to argue … about the rights of the Arabs and the wisdom of the Indian solution,' he wrote. 'In this case, the excuse was in itself something which tried to explore a path of peace.'[25]

But Panikkar was present when Weizmann personally appeared to testify before the Political Commission of the UNSCOP. The room was packed when Weizmann, 'looking very much like an Old Testament prophet',[26] appeared and slowly made his way to the dais, supported on both sides by younger men. Weizmann struggled to speak that day. He was ill, his sight was failing and he wasn't the best speaker of the English language, but Panikkar couldn't help admiring his clear passion for the cause of Israel. 'Everyone there … realised that the old man who was addressing them stood for something which to him was more than all the riches of the world.'[27]

The Indian delegation stood by the federal plan even though most of its members knew it was a doomed cause. On 29 November 1947, the UNGA rejected the Indian federal plan to adopt the majority group's amended partition plan in Palestine. Known in its final form as Resolution 181, its passing saw all the Islamic Asian countries voting against partition, while the Arabs made a narrowly defeated proposal to query the resolution at the International Court of Justice. As they had done in 1937, the Arabs fiercely opposed partition both in principle and because nearly half of the population of the new Jewish state would be Arab. A majority of thirty-three states supported the partition plan, while India was one of the thirteen delegations (and one of the seven non-Arab countries) to vote against the partition solution.

A few months after the partition of the subcontinent, India also refused the two-nation theory in Palestine. Speaking before the Constituent Assembly of India on 4 December 1947, just days after the UN General Assembly had voted for the partition of Palestine, Nehru declared, 'After a great deal of thought we decided that this (the federal plan) was not only a fair and equitable solution of the problem, but the only real solution of the problem. Any other solution would have meant fighting and conflict.'[28] Be that as it may, India's plan was quietly buried by the international community.

After watching this debacle playing out, Panikkar focused on his last assignment at the UNGA as a member of the Third Committee (Economic and Social) of the General Assembly. He advocated for international assistance for the solution of socio-economic problems in economically backward countries. To abandon them would be a danger to all the peoples of the world, he argued. This should not be left wholly to the initiative of the governments concerned, for in many cases, they had no technical knowledge or organisational experience. This would be a recurring theme for Panikkar and would form the main subject of his lectures at the Institute d'Etude de Development, Economique et Social of the Sorbonne in 1959. A slightly summarised version of these lectures would eventually be published some years later under the title *The Afro-Asian States and their Problems*.

His work done, Panikkar was now free to return to India. On his way, he stopped in London to meet Krishna Menon, whom he liked very much. In the Savoy where he was staying, Panikkar bumped into Muazzim Jah, the Nizam's youngest son. Something about his presence—and Hyderabad's current febrile political situation—raised Panikkar's hackles immediately. He sought out his old friend Colonel Waghre, Muazzim's physician, and invited him casually for dinner. Over a convivial meal that evening, the colonel let slip that Muazzim was in London to organise a contingent of arms that would be run into Hyderabad by an Australian pilot named Sidney Cotton. Pakistan was supporting this venture.

Aghast, Panikkar hastened back to India where he immediately sought out Sardar Patel to let him know that this was happening. The Sardar heard him in silence. Then he nodded curtly. 'We will see to it.'

It was all he said, but the next day's papers had a terse statement from the Government of India. All planes incoming from Pakistan were to land in Bombay or Delhi for inspection. Planes refusing to adhere to these regulations would be shot down.

PART IX

Our Man in Peking (1948–1955)

CHAPTER 44

To China

SHORTLY AFTER HIS RETURN FROM THE UNITED STATES AT THE END OF 1947, Nehru asked Panikkar casually if he would like to go for a drive. Delighted, Panikkar agreed. Ten minutes of silence later, Nehru abruptly asked, 'Are you free to go abroad on an ambassador's posting?'

Not unnaturally, Panikkar was thrilled, though he kept his expression neutral. 'My work in Bikaner is coming to an end,' he replied politely. 'As soon as I free myself from my commitments there, I should be at your disposal.'

'When do you think you should get free?'

'Say, by 1st of April?'

'Why not earlier?' Nehru asked in some confusion. 'Isn't the Maharaja introducing popular government?'

Panikkar explained that he still had work to do with the various subcommittees of the Constituent Assembly. With some hesitation, he ventured to add that, rather than going to China, he would like to stay on in India and work instead on the Constitution.

Nehru laughed. 'That will take more time than you can imagine,' he said cheerfully. 'I should have liked you to be free earlier, but we can wait until April.'[1]

It should have been a matter of some honour to have been asked by India's prime minister to go to China as ambassador, but

Panikkar was far from feeling chipper about everything else. Records from Mountbatten's official archives show that in January 1948, Panikkar was deeply anxious. He wanted to leave the country as fast as he could—he could foresee trouble ahead for the princely states. Integration had not gone as smoothly as Indian officials had anticipated, and for at least a couple of years, Panikkar wanted to ensure that he wasn't in the country.[2] That Nehru wanted to send Panikkar to China was no secret, clearly, but the lawyer in Panikkar enjoyed the complexities of constitutional wrangling.

'Sardar Panikkar said that he was prepared to offer his services to India in whatever capacity the government might choose,' reads a transcript of an interview between Panikkar and India's last viceroy. 'His Excellency said that he would consider suggesting to the Prime Minister that Sardar Panikkar should be appointed some sort of constitutional adviser, rather than ambassador to China.'[3]

Panikkar was quite pleased at this suggestion, for in the first year of Indian independence, he was closely involved with working out the semantics of a postcolonial India taking its place in the Commonwealth for the first time. Work on the new constitution would involve semantic acrobatics again—the removal of the word 'dominion'; the potential in the word 'republic' and the potential linkage of India with the Crown. But that story is beyond the scope of this one, for the bulk of it would be carried out by others, like Sir B.N. Rau, in Panikkar's absence.

There were those in Mountbatten's office who insisted that Panikkar would be 'wasted' in China, and that India would benefit from having him as a constitutional advisor rather than an ambassador.[4] Still others tried to dissuade the viceroy from sending him anywhere—either as an ambassador or a constitutional advisor. 'I suggest that Y[our] E[xcellency] should proceed with caution in this matter,' wrote one official snidely. 'Panikkar is not, according to the best of my belief, altogether persona grata with Nehru. He is inevitably looked upon with a certain amount of suspicion (he is very clever and has a reputation for personal ambition). He is one of a category of men whom I am sure that it is Nehru's intention to appoint to representative posts outside the country, rather than to retain in Delhi.'[5]

This assessment, however, was an erroneous one. Panikkar was, at the time, perfectly simpatico with Nehru.

The choice of K.M. Panikkar as India's ambassador to China in 1947 has in retrospect been the cause of both controversy and debate. But it was a decision based on many factors. The first was trust and long-standing friendship. Nehru had known Panikkar since his days in Amritsar and at the *Hindustan Times* in the 1920s. He had never lost track of Panikkar's career, following his arguments for federalism and for getting the princes on board with the Indian Union. The Indian prime minister had also read Panikkar's works on foreign policy and history, especially during the war years, with keen interest. His sister Vijayalakshmi Pandit's endorsement of Panikkar's intelligence counted with Nehru too. He had always been thinking about how to present India to the wider world, and from his reading of Panikkar's work, he knew this ambition was a shared one. Now that India was looking to consolidate its position as a postcolonial power, particularly in South Asia, that presentation became even more important.

India was already in the unique position of being an international presence by 1945, from Dumbarton Oaks to San Franscisco. But with independence, new eyes and ears were needed. Nehru insisted that it could not be those who had worked previously for the British as 'that would in effect be a British approach with the background of British foreign policy',[6] and would lead to India being looked upon as a satellite of the empire. 'I am anxious to have public men as our ambassadors,' he mused to Bajpai, '… more especially with regard to some of our first appointments.'[7] Panikkar, by 1948, was very much a public man, and what was more invaluably, he had shown himself to be more than capable of wearing multiple hats.

India did not as yet have trained career diplomats. Even as Krishna Menon reported a keen interest from European capitals to establish relations with the newly independent India, there was a severe manpower crisis, one that was accentuated with the transfer of power and Partition.

To put things in perspective, independent India needed about three hundred diplomats to start with. There were only about fifty people actually available who commanded enough experience to qualify. Small wonder that Girija Shankar Bajpai was forced to reply to Menon that 'the possibility of opening new missions abroad is scant in the extreme'.[8]

With personnel in short supply and India dealing with successive internal crises in the wake of transfer of power and partition, Nehru simply couldn't afford to send people he didn't know to important postings. This often resulted in 'strange choices',[9] like Asaf Ali's appointment as India's ambassador to Washington DC in January 1947,[10] and some controversial ones, like his sister's appointment as India's ambassador to Moscow, all of which resulted in the creation of policies that were not always in line with those of the Ministry of External Affairs (MEA). Panikkar's appointment, given this backdrop, was very much in accordance with Nehru's thinking about how to choose ambassadors in the first hectic days of Indian independence.

Then there was the fast-changing foreign policy situation regarding Tibet and China. Nehru had a vision for what he wanted to achieve in Asia. In 1946, he wrote for the *New York Times*, 'A free India will link together the Middle East with China. India is so situated as to form the centre of a group of Asian nations for defence as well as trade and commerce.'[11] He wrote this essay against the backdrop of the excellent relations between India and Nationalist China in the inter-war years.

But the Asian Relations Conference should have been the first indicator that, while idealism was all very well, realpolitik and pragmatism should have been the first principles of the hour.

Nehru envisioned the ARC as a harbinger of solidarity when it was actually a mirror to how far that solidarity would go. Nationalist China was furious that India had invited Tibet as an independent country, suspecting Nehru of wanting to 'promote his personal prestige'.[12] In addition, China was also outraged over the map hanging in the main conference hall, which showed Tibet outside China and its mention as India's neighbour. Nehru mollified the Chinese representatives by welcoming China as 'that great country to which Asia owes so much and from which so much is expected'.[13]

In May 1947, Chiang Kai-shek's Kuomintang (KMT) government, also known as the Nationalists, sent Luo Jialun as its ambassador to India as a gesture of support from one Asian country to the other.

Luo's appointment, short and ill-starred though it was, is little studied in India. According to his diary, he was summoned early in 1947 by the generalissimo and told that he would be going to India as the Republic of China's ambassador. The bespectacled serious-faced Luo was more of an academic than a diplomat and he was considerably startled at this request. But Chiang was persuasive. China was looking, he said, for a man with academic credentials and excellent knowledge of the Tibet issue. Cultural, civilisational and academic ties were to be the cornerstones of bilateral relations between independent India and China.

Luo fit this bill despite his own misgivings on the subject. He had always been an industrious, brilliant student, and he had trained in history at Princeton, Columbia, London, Paris and Berlin. In 1919, he had been a prominent leader of the May Fourth Movement, the cultural and anti-imperialist political movement which grew out of student protests in Peking and marked a move towards populist politics in China.[14] At the time of his appointment as ambassador to India, Luo had taught history at universities across China and was a respected scholar in his own right. Chiang Kai-shek was aware of his political leanings and his academic accomplishments, and to his mind, the professor would be an asset in India.

Luo would live up to Chiang's hopes during his time in India, authoring a poem to celebrate Indian independence and a paper on Chinese sources for Indian history while he was in India. He also used his knowledge of frontier issues like Xinjiang and Tibet—knowledge that China could use to reinforce its own ideas of sovereignty over Tibet. Before leaving for India, Luo was personally briefed by Chiang Kai-shek. He was told to tell Nehru that, 'except for China's own interests, India's interest is the most important one to China'.[15] He was also asked to keep an eye on the workings of the Muslim League and to see to it that the Chinese embassy in India functioned as a kind of research centre for Tibetan affairs.

Luo's arrival in India on 3 May 1947 was symbolic for many reasons. It coincided with China's victory in the Second World War and India's navigation of its final days of being a colony. It also coincided with the turning of the tide of civil war in China, with the victory of the Chinese Communist Party (CCP) under the chairmanship of savvy, brutish Mao Tse-tung seeming ever more likely, and the winding down of the Raj's policies in Tibet.

By April 1947, the Foreign and Political Department was telling Hugh Richardson, its political officer in Gangtok, that if, in the light of the participation of a Tibetan delegation in the most recent Chinese National Assembly, China and Tibet should work out some kind of modus vivendi between them, India should neither object nor interfere.[16] On 23 July 1947, in a message approved by His Majesty's Government, Tibet was informed that, after transfer of power, Lhasa would deal exclusively with New Delhi, 'upon whom alone the rights and obligations arising from existing treaty provisions will thereafter devolve'.[17] Tibet agreed to abide by the Simla Convention (1914) and reserved its right to discuss the question of trade and boundaries in the future which, much to Richardson's irritation, it did not do.[18]

As these niggles continued, in October 1947, India and China found themselves at odds over the question of the grant of an Indian visa to the newly appointed Chinese Amban or high official who would be proceeding to Lhasa via India. India insisted that the visa be granted subject to a no-objection certificate from Lhasa as per past precedent. China, on the other hand, said that the visa should be granted without consulting Lhasa at all.

These irritants were the backdrop against which Panikkar was dispatched to China. He would be taking over from K.P.S. Menon, India's agent-general in Chongqing since 1943. Menon was fully aware that he was in China at a time when it stood at the crossroads between the old and the new. He had reported from across Nationalist China now for five years: during the ongoing civil war and the slow unravelling of Kuomintang power and during the changing role and influence of the United States. From Menon's detailed, eloquent and brisk reports, Nehru understood just a little more than Chiang Kai-shek would have liked. By 1947, Menon was writing directly to Nehru, much as Panikkar would do. His last report, filed on 15 December 1947, still did not foresee the communists taking control entirely. He felt that they could hold Manchuria and some northern provinces, while the Kuomintang would cling to the rest.[19]

Between December 1947 and April 1948 much would change. The communists were definitely on the way to victory and India was no longer quite as timorous as it had been in 1947. The Raj may have left, but New Delhi now had Washington DC and a full-blown Cold War to contend with. From 1949 to 1956—basically the length of Panikkar's tenure as ambassador to China—American and Indian policymakers differed over the nature of the China threat, its urgency and how to deal with it. The nature and nuance of those differences have formed the subject of several books, but in simple terms, American officials saw China as hostile and sought to contain it. India, on the other hand, was convinced that China did not pose an external threat in the foreseeable future. With an ongoing Cold War, Delhi felt that there was no need for India to get involved in conflict. Non-alignment hadn't been defined or institutionalised as a movement as yet, but in those days, it was an active choice to counter the power dynamics of the Cold War. It was an excellent platform on which to support disarmament, to mediate conflict and to continue to decolonise. Against this backdrop then, men like Nehru and Panikkar were of the belief that India and China shared a civilisational history that could be used to bilateral advantage.

It wasn't a particularly new belief. Since the early twentieth century and especially in an age defined by two world wars, Asia was a major focus of interest. Rabindranath Tagore's trip to China in 1924 had contributed to making Sino–Indian unity a fundamental element of Asian regional identity. The importance of this bilateral relationship had increased through the 1930s and 1940s when the Congress organised a boycott of Japanese goods in the face of Japan's aggressive militarism, when Nehru visited China in 1939 to establish contacts with the Kuomintang and when Chiang Kai-shek reciprocated the visit in 1942.

In postcolonial times then, it made sense to Indian foreign policy mandarins and to the prime minister himself that the threads of pan-Asian solidarity should be taken up and carried forward. As a result, at least for now, India was seeking to engage with China. Panikkar, with his vast experience of history and his keen eye for postcolonial foreign policy, was an easy choice to send to a country which was important, and for which the policy trajectory was fairly set—at least for the time being. His brief was simple: to report on the changing trajectory of the war and to report to Nehru on the feasibility of allying with the communists should they come to power.

On 2 March 1948, Delhi cabled London, with a request to the king: 'My government propose to appoint Sardar K.M. Panikkar, now Prime Minister of Bikaner, as Ambassador to China in succession to K.P.S. Menon who will be reverting to India,' Mountbatten wrote. 'Grateful if His Majesty's approval could be obtained to proposal.'[20]

The request was swiftly granted.

'The King approves appointment of Panikkar.'[21]

When he first got the news, in the spring of 1948, of his new posting, Panikkar went to see Sarojini Naidu in Lucknow. For him, she had become a kind of maternal figure. Every time he passed through Delhi, he made it a point to go to her home on Curzon Road to have a meal with her and give her all his news. During the convening of the Constituent Assembly, Naidu hadn't been keeping well, and Panikkar had fallen into the routine of picking her up at nine in the morning every day and driving her to Parliament House. Naidu was old now and ailing, but her mind was as clear and undimmed as it had always been. He spent three happy days with her, chatting about stories and people that had passed long ago. When he went to say goodbye to her, she smiled at him. 'I do not think, Panikkar, that I shall live to hear from you the stories of Cathay.'[22]

She was right, for she died in 1949 while he was still away in China. But he carried her words with him as he boarded the PanAm flight with Gouri, Radha and Haima on the night of 13 April 1948.

His emotions were mixed. In January 1948, as he was finishing his time in Bikaner and as he closed his discussions on India's future with

Mountbatten, Panikkar had received word from Padmanabha. Their mother was ill. Panikkar needed to come back home immediately.

Shaken, he dropped everything and returned to Kavalam. His mother was all of seventy-three years old, and she was in fine physical health. Mentally speaking, however, it was another story. 'Mother no longer cared for life,'[23] he remembered. With his new job due to start in April, he wasn't sure how long it would be before he could—or, indeed, if he would—see her again. So he spent the last months of his time in India at home with her in Kavalam.

Kochu Kunjiamma had surrendered the reins of the household long ago to her capable elder son, but she still kept an eye on her two sons, seeing to it that they ate their meals on time and went dutifully to the temple. Her only desire, as she told Panikkar when he arrived, was to see her eldest granddaughter—Padmanabha's daughter—married in her lifetime. Swiftly, the two brothers arranged a quiet wedding that Kunjiamma was able to attend.

She died soon after.

Panikkar was devastated. Radha recalled that the entire family would take long trips to Kavalam every other year, but Panikkar went every year by himself.[24] He loved his home, and he had always adored his quiet, kind and strong mother. He'd watched her grow old, immersing herself in religious texts and scriptures. As long as she could read with her spectacles and the light of a traditional oil lamp, she had done so. When her eyesight failed completely, novels and poems were read to her. She was more religious than Panikkar had ever been or ever would be. In her old age, her morning prayers lengthened until nearly noon, when she would break her fast. Evenings were similarly engaged. 'Constantly immersed in thoughts of God, death presented no terrors for her.'[25]

It was while he was grieving in Kavalam that Gandhi was assassinated by a fanatic's bullet. 'Rarely in human history has such an event evoked so universal a lament,' Panikkar wrote later.[26] His own shock and grief ran deep. Gandhi's stature as a national leader would never be equalled, and in a time when India had barely recovered from intense communal carnage, this was the worst thing that could have happened.

To pick up the reins of daily life then, when such grievous blows had been dealt one after another, required almost stupendous effort.

As he settled now on the plane that would carry him across the Himalayas to China, Panikkar's mind flitted between nerves and anticipation.

On the one hand, there was a buzz of elation at the thought of representing his newly independent country on foreign soil. On the other, there was the sharp prick of anxiety. His conversations with Luo had told him much he needed to know about China, but he still had to find out for himself how much those conversations differed from reality.

Shanghai was a shock to the senses, even for the worldly Panikkar. This was the peak of Sir Victor Sassoon's opulent, opium-fuelled grip on the city. A Baghdadi Jew, Sassoon had inherited the banking dynasty that originated in Iraq and then spread to London, Bombay and China. He came to cosmopolitan Shanghai as a serious investor in real estate, with an accumulated capital of $85 million. Sassoon lived in the magnificent Cathay Hotel on the Bund, where the Panikkars were temporarily staying. His money had peppered the city with architectural wonders—the Embankment Building on Suzhou Creek, the Metropole Hotel and Cathay Mansions, all of which still stand today. He liked beautiful women, racehorses and artisanal cocktails, and he recreated the Shanghai skyline with neon modernity.

Panikkar would soon discover that underneath the art deco opulence lay a darkly seamy side to the city. For one, inflation was soaring through the roof. Radha recalled that when the family went shopping they carried an entire suitcase of money.[27]

'The Consul-General was a gentleman named Krishnamurthy,' she remembered. 'They had a daughter named Girija, who was our age. When my father went on his official engagements, we spent time with them.'[28]

Communities have a way of gravitating to each other and given the number of Indians who were settled in China at the time, the Panikkars were never really alone. For this, Panikkar was relieved. He was travelling with three women and he had no desire to leave them alone in a strange country. Gouri, in particular, wasn't acclimatising well. She missed her own country and her own home, and was taking time to adjust to Chinese food. So when a Punjabi family whom we only know by the name of Kapoor took Radha and Haima to shop for bolts of crepe de chine, he was more than happy to let them go.[29]

In *Two Chinas*, Panikkar writes of another Shanghai—of the sinister Tu Yen-shen, a notorious gangster and dope king who emerged after the war as a philanthropist and a highly respected dignitary in the city. Born in the slums of the French concession, Tu was a jack of all trades—an orange seller, dope trafficker and bouncer by turns—until he took over Shanghai's underworld. More importantly, he was Chiang Kai-shek's main financier and tough man. It was he who kept the French concession calm when Chiang's armies reached the outskirts of Shanghai and it was through Tu's influence that the secret societies of Shanghai united against the communists.[30]

Small wonder that, after the excitement of Shanghai, the Panikkars found Nanking rather tame. The capital was a sleepy, walled city, set amidst tea houses, lakes and purple-hazed mountains. Outside the city walls was the Xuanwu Lake, full of fat lotus flowers in the summer, with five islands interconnected by arched bridges. 'On some evenings when my father was free, we would go boating, like the *shikaras* on Dal Lake,'[31] Radha remembered. On other days, the family went for walks to the Sun Yat-sen memorial, or exploring further to the Xiao Mausoleum, the resting place of the Hongwu Emperor, the founder of the Ming dynasty.

Unlike Hong Kong and Shanghai, where there had been bustling Indian communities, in Nanking, the Panikkars, along with the other officials of the Indian embassy and the Sikh contingent posted there to guard it, were practically the only Indians. As a result, they were objects of considerable fascination for the local community. 'I remember on one occasion, we went shopping with Mother and another lady from the embassy. No sooner had we entered the shop than a crowd gathered outside, all curious to see us.'[32] The Indian women were dressed in saris, with Gouri and the other older lady wearing red kumkum in the middle parting of their hair. 'They [the people] must have thought we were from another planet!'[33]

The Indian embassy was situated in Peking Lu, and though the house was small and unsuitable for an embassy, it was in a good locality with other diplomatic residences near it. Opposite the Panikkar home, for instance, was the Egyptian Legation, and the Portuguese, Burmese, Afghans, Australians and Americans were a few doors down. But what really held Panikkar's attention was the Indian flag flying atop the embassy building. 'My heart quickened at the sight,' he would write in his memoir. 'It was the symbol of a free India in a foreign capital and it was my responsibility to guard the dignity of that flag.'[34]

His ability to guard it would, in later years, be subject to fierce question.

It would only take eight months after Panikkar's arrival in China for the Kuomintang regime to collapse on top of itself like a badly built house of cards. During the first few weeks though, the civil war had not yet reached the gates of Nanking and so the semblance of a functional democracy continued.

Radha and Haima were enrolled at the prestigious Ginling College for Women, where they stayed as boarders. Funded by American missionaries and established in 1913, it was one of the few universities in China where the medium of instruction was English. With the girls safely taken care of, Panikkar could focus on the political side of life in Nanking.

A National Assembly had at last been convened. Tibet was present, but again, Lhasa made a mistake. On being persuaded by the Chinese Amban to join the assembly, Tibet did so on the promise that it would be able to finally clarify its position vis-à-vis China. But to the Tibetans' disappointment, they were given no such chance. Under the new Chinese constitution, Tibet was treated as a 'province' albeit of 'special character'.

Panikkar noticed this. To his mind, it was the first indicator (of many) that trouble was now definitely in the offing. More worryingly, the Kuomintang were not quite as gung-ho about India as he had thought. If anything, he noted, it was patronising. 'Independence of

India was welcome, but of course it was understood that China as the recognized Great Power in the East after the war expected India to know her place.'[35]

When Chiang Kai-shek was re-elected president, Panikkar observed that there was a considerable body of opinion in favour of his resignation. In fact the assembly's choice of Li Tsung-jen as vice president, he remarked, was 'the first political defeat' for Chiang.[36] But he did notice that although 'everyone felt happy, and the Americans, and to a lesser extent the British, felt that China was now well set on a road to democratic evolution ... no one seemed in the least worried about the People's Liberation Army (PLA) or the regime that Mao Tse-tung had established in inaccessible regions'.[37]

He was thinking fast about this developing situation.

By May 1948, almost all of northern China, with the exception of the Peking-Tientsin corridor and some areas in Manchuria, had fallen under communist control. Tibet featured high on Panikkar's list of priorities at this point, given the previous year's friction between India and China on the subject at the ARC. He had done his homework on Tibet, and he knew that the Kuomintang government wanted to re-discuss the consequences of the Simla Convention of 1914, which had defined British India's relations with Tibet and China and which Chiang's regime did not recognise.[38] In delicate geographical terms—ones which would have a direct impact on Panikkar's career and reputation as India's ambassador to China—the Simla Convention had drawn an eastern border along the so-called McMahon Line, but this had not been ratified by China.[39] In the western sector, Indian maps indicated an 'undefined' border, which from 1945 began to be represented with a coloured band that included the extensive but uninhabited Aksai Chin plateau in Indian territory.[40]

In the summer of 1948, a few weeks after he had arrived, Panikkar wrote to Sir Ralph Stevenson, the British ambassador in Nanking. 'India recognises Tibet to be under the suzerainty of China; equally she recognises the autonomy of Tibet and claims the right to conduct direct negotiations and to maintain a diplomatic mission in Lhasa. She has also special trade and commercial rights by agreement and generally Tibet is treated as a semi-independent state. In fact it was the official policy of the British Government that the recognition of the suzerainty of China was conditional on China's acceptance of Tibet's autonomy in which India claimed to have a special interest … The collapse of the Chinese authority was utilised by the Indian Government to consolidate its position. The present relationship with India may be said to be based on agreements concluded between 1914 and 1919, the period of China's extreme weakness. But even in 1914, China never resiled from her thesis that Tibet was a part of Chinese territory, no doubt autonomous, but all the same, from the international point of view, Chinese.'[41]

But, as he made clear to Stevenson, the changing balance of the civil war could potentially damage India's standing with China. 'If by peaceful means China could bring Tibet within her framework, India may not perhaps object. If China tries to reduce Tibet by a military campaign, India cannot sit back for two reasons: in the first place, there are certain obligations which have come to her as a successor Government. Though India may not interpret those obligations in the same manner as Britain did, she cannot without dishonour withdraw from commitments to Tibet: to support her diplomatically in the maintenance of her autonomy; to supply her with arms and equipment; to train her officers … It has also to be remembered that an effective Chinese Government or even influence in Lhasa will mean the immediate revival of claims against Nepal, Bhutan and Sikkim and also the denunciation of the McMahon Line.'[42]

This stand was supported in the Government of India's request to Hareshwar Dayal, the political officer in Sikkim in July 1948, to inform Lhasa that 'the Government of India who had succeeded to the rights and obligations of the British Government of India would continue to abide by the existing treaties until either party should wish to enter into fresh arrangements'. In the meantime, Tibet was assured that India would be ready for an adjustment of the Indo–Tibetan frontier, particularly in the Tawang area.[43]

These were all stands that India would, in the very near future, either conveniently dismiss or renege on, much to Tibet's dismay. But in 1948, the Chinese weren't too pleased that India was even considering upholding its 'rights' in Tibet, much less agreeing to adjust the frontier.

In October 1948, Stevenson cabled London that Panikkar had reportedly received a note from the Chinese Foreign Office which stated that 'the Chinese government wish to regulate their relations with India by a treaty of commerce and amity, which as drafted by the Chinese government, would contain a provision for redefinition of the boundaries of China and India'.[44] Panikkar held his ground, replying that any trade arrangements previously concluded by the British Indian government with Tibet could not be arbitrarily abrogated without consulting the Tibetans themselves. As he put it, 'the Indian government having accepted the obligation of H.M.G. towards Tibet continued to recognize Tibetan autonomy and only the suzerainty as opposed to the sovereignty of China'.[45]

As Panikkar waited on the tide of war to tell him which way India's policy needed to go, Chiang Kai-shek and Madame Chiang returned from their summer vacation. It was now the end of August.

Two days after their return to Nanking, the Panikkars were invited for a quiet, informal dinner. It was during the lengthy chat post a delicious meal that Panikkar 'realised that Chiang had an abiding interest in India's freedom and secured progress'.[46] The two men discussed Pakistan, Kashmir, the British and the communists, and Panikkar noted with interest that at no time did Madame Chiang leave the room. In fact she spoke too, on the need for India and China to continue working together to maintain harmony on the Asian continent. Panikkar agreed with that largely, but the problem to his mind, which he didn't naturally say out loud, was *which* China did India want to work with?

He could already see the Kuomintang beginning to rupture from within, not to mention the fact that it was now losing ground rapidly to the communists. He also knew that Nehru was as aware of what was about to happen as anyone in the Ministry of External Affairs. In a note dated 12 September 1948, Nehru wrote, 'In regard to China and the Far East, nothing much can be done except to maintain friendly relations. China is in a state of utmost turmoil. We should not attach ourselves too closely to any party in China so as to make the other party hostile to us. Naturally, as a government, we incline towards the present government of China.'[47]

Knowing all this, and especially Nehru's position, Panikkar tactfully suggested that the best way forward for India and China's bilateral relations was to establish internal order in both countries first. Chiang nodded coolly. 'That is precisely what I think,' he said. 'I can wipe out these Communists in a matter of six months. By that time, I expect your country would have also tided over its initial difficulties.'[48]

Panikkar was severely taken aback at this sudden and unexpected condescension, but it was clear that Chiang was now finished with the subject of politics. He moved on to other subjects of conversation, leaving the Indian ambassador shaken.[49]

After the dinner was over, the generalissimo offered Panikkar the use of his private aircraft so that the Indian ambassador could visit the northern capital of Peking. When the plane landed in the city, Panikkar knew immediately that all was not well. The word on the street was that Tsinan, one of the great provincial capitals, had fallen to the communists. It was the first of China's great cities to be taken by them. It was all anyone could talk about. The general feeling had been that the communists did not have the strength to capture or hold big cities.

Panikkar stayed in Peking for ten days, walking around as much as he could. It had obviously been in its day a great imperial city of equally great beauty. Since the Manchus descended from their homeland in the northeast to defeat the Ming in 1644 (and establish their own Qing Dynasty, 1644–1911), Peking had consisted of four distinct walled cities—the Tartar City, the Chinese City, the Imperial City and, lying not just at the heart of Peking but of the whole Chinese empire, the Forbidden City. Here, in the 'Great Within', lived the emperor (until the last, Puyi, was expelled in 1924), protected and hidden from prying eyes by rust-coloured walls above which could be seen the glittering yellow tiles of the roofs. Deep in this complex stood the emperor's dragon throne—the ultimate symbol of imperial power.[50] The Forbidden City shone like lacquer and gold under the sun, with pleasure gardens and artificial hills, low-roofed houses with endless courtyards, pools and rock gardens.

But despite the beauty, Peking was a dilapidated, unhappy city now, dirty and crammed with refugees from the civil war. The foreign community, the diplomats and missionaries who had formed the beating heart of the city's legation quarter, were leaving Peking en masse. Only a few were left behind—mostly academics teaching at the university and Russian émigrés too poor to leave. Theirs was a gilded world of parties, plays and gaiety, despite the hyper inflation that made everyday life a misery. Indeed, Panikkar's fastidious aesthetic sense was pained at what he saw on the streets of Peking. 'In the Temple of Heaven, universally recognized to be one of the most beautiful buildings in the world, more than a thousand students were living just as they liked, more than fifty of them sleeping in the robing room of the Son of Heaven. The filth which covered the sacred grounds was indescribable … It was altogether a painful sight.'[51]

While he was in Peking, he had dinner with General Fu Tso-yi, the most important Kuomintang commander in the north, to whom the Americans were supplying arms and who would later defect to the communists. Word was that General Lin Biao had taken over the surrounding countryside and Chiang Kai-shek himself was soon arriving in Peking. Panikkar hastened back to Nanking before actual fighting broke out.

The city had changed radically in the ten days that he had been absent. The National Day celebrations had been called off, those who could afford to leave were leaving the city in droves and the trains and roads alike were clogged with the exodus. Despite the ominous tension though, there was a curious matter-of-factness. Even as gunfire began to sound beyond the western gates of the city, Peking's citizens were out in the parks and streets, practising tai chi, skating, browsing through bookstalls or airing their pet birds.[52]

The fall of the Nationalist government in China was a historic moment. *Life* magazine flew in the photographer Henri Cartier Bresson to document the dying gasps of the old order. On 4 December 1948, *Life* published its first reports from Bresson, describing how 'ice was decking the lakes which mirror the gold roofs of the old Ming palaces and Communist armies were driving Peiping's (Peking's) defenders behind the city's high grey walls'.[53] North China had fallen.

Shortly after his return from Peking, Panikkar wrote the memorandum for which he is now famous (or infamous depending where you stand): *China Goes Communist*. He predicted that 'if the Kuomintang Government falls, Tibet will make a public declaration of her independence and request recognition from India, Britain and the United States. The British position has always been in favour of recognising the independence of Tibet and in the changed circumstances, America may not also hesitate. If Outer Tibet's claim to independence is recognised by Britain, America and India, there may be some hope of keeping the new Chinese Communist State away from the Indian border'.[54]

In addition, he argued that a communist victory could decisively change things in another area that he saw as a potential conflict zone: Southeast Asia. Panikkar argued that the Kuomintang had lost credibility by refusing to support national movements in these countries and that this had benefited the communists. Their victory in China would certainly strengthen this trend. 'The communist flood will therefore overflow and submerge the countries of South-East Asia, unless there is outside guarantee. If a line is drawn on the Siam border and the area to the South of it including Burma and Malaya brought under effective organization, it may be possible to stem the tide. The importance of South-East Asia not only to the security but also to the economic life of India need not to be emphasised. What India's policy should be in relation to these countries is a matter for the most careful consideration.'[55]

In December 1948, Nehru wrote to Panikkar, asking him to stay in informal contact with the communists without conveying recognition or commitment.[56] Sardar Patel and G.S. Bajpai were more concerned about the security aspects of a communist victory. But Nehru was of the opinion that Delhi would have to deal with facts as they existed. Rather than isolating communist China, it was important to integrate it with the international community.[57] That same month, the Indian prime minister wrote to Stafford Cripps, saying that 'what was likely to happen' to the Kuomintang had been 'evident' for over a year now. In general, he said, he felt that the

'Communists had some able men at the top, and they had, with some success, adapted the Communist theory to Chinese circumstances'.[58]

The general (rather smug) feeling in New Delhi was that, with the fall of the Kuomintang, China would naturally take some time to recover. In the interim, it was only natural that India would be at Asia's centre, just as Nehru had envisioned. Loy Henderson, then the ambassador in New Delhi, reported as much to Washington DC, which was keeping a sharp eye on the situation. 'There is apparently a feeling that China is destined to disappear for some time, as a world force, leaving India as the foremost Asiatic power, courted on one side by capitalistic powers of the West and on the other by Communist powers of eastern Europe and Asia.'[59]

Much of this attitude was shown directly to poor Luo Jialun, stuck in Delhi as Nationalist China's ambassador. Luo's diary entries of late 1948 show an increasingly angry, bitter man, suddenly shut out of the Indian government's good books.

In February 1949, the Nationalist government moved from Nanking to Guangzhou. It asked foreign embassies to do the same.

India refused.

Its reasoning was pragmatic: the situation was too risky on the mainland to risk an outright move. Nor was it the only foreign embassy that did not make the move. But under this situation of high bilateral pressure, it was indicator enough of the fact that India was already shifting alliance from the Nationalists to the communists. Luo was furious. 'Internationally, there is no emotion, no morality and no justice. Only snobbishness and realism exist. Why not go to hell!'[60]

In Shanghai, where he had been touring to examine the situation on the ground, Panikkar watched as, under the communists, China and its people began to make one last push against the corrupt Nationalists and foreign colonialism. He was beginning to realise that Mao and his men might be unknown quantities in the eyes of the world, but they were not looking to passively take national power. They were keen on taking what they believed was their rightful place in the ranks of world powers.

In January 1949, Chiang's government made a desperate final bid for help, asking that the four major powers—the United States, the

Soviet Union, the United Kingdom and France—mediate in the civil war. The request was rejected within ten days.

With the complete cut-off of foreign assistance and any chance of mediation along with the losses in north China and the defeat in the battle over the River Huai, Chiang knew that his time was up. He resigned his presidency on 21 January 1949. Li Tsung-jen succeeded him as acting president, but he too knew that the days of the Nationalists were numbered. Still he tried his best, seeking help from both the United States and the Soviet Union.[61]

In January 1949, the Tibetan mission in Nanking, where the Dalai Lama's brother was staying, sought Panikkar's advice. They too were seeing communist advances and they feared the worst. Apprehensively, they insisted that 'Tibet's independence should receive international recognition and that Tibet looks to India's support for its claim with Britain and America.'[62]

Panikkar wrote to Delhi, asking for instructions. Delhi advised him that if he was approached again, he was to assure them of Indian sympathy and mention that the revision of the Tibetan policy was now unlikely in the event of the change of government in Nanking. Raking up the issue of Tibetan independence would do the new dispensation more harm than good. He was also to tell them that Tibetan apprehensions were exaggerated.

Rather dangerously for future policy, Delhi also added, 'We, on our part, will adhere steadfastly to our present policy of seeking to uphold Tibetan independence, subject to the suzerainty of China.'[63] This was a foolish faux pas, which Delhi tried to correct by hastily sending a follow-up cable. 'The last sentence in the (above) telegram is not to be taken to mean that GOI have changed their views in regard to the status of Tibet and recognised Chinese suzerainty over Tibet unconditionally. Government of India's willingness to recognise Chinese suzerainty is dependent on Chinese government's willingness to give formal recognition to Tibetan autonomy and to agree to the frontier between Tibet and China.'[64]

In yet another telegram, sent on 13 March 1949, Delhi advised Panikkar to inform the Kuomintang that India's relations with Tibet were governed by the Simla Convention of 1914. He was also to tell

Nanking that the Government of India 'cannot enter into discussions about (their) relations with Tibet or the status of Tibet without Tibetan participation'.[65]

Panikkar returned to Nanking on 20 April 1949 on the last train that the Kuomintang would ever run, amidst a forest of rumours that the communists would cross the Yangtse River in a matter of days. The day after he arrived, the rumours were proved right: communist forces led by Marshall Ch'en I crossed the Yangtse River and four days later, entered the gates of Nanking, forcing Li's government to scramble to Canton. In the aftermath of their departure, law and order broke down. Schools and colleges were closed across Nanking. Radha and Haima had come home weeks ago and passed their days studying quietly at home.

The morning after Li's government had fled, Panikkar ventured to walk about the quiet town. He was ignored for the large part. The mob knew what they wanted: they systematically looted the houses of Kuomintang leaders and officers. 'From my chancery, I could see the official residence of the mayor being plundered by the inhabitants of the locality,' he would recall. 'It was done in a civilized and orderly manner, old women being helped by younger people to carry what they had collected!'[66] To Panikkar's surprise, there was no rioting or damage. The looters broke only such things as they needed to—a door frame, a glass window pane—'which they carried away, quietly as if they were withdrawing a deposit from a bank'.[67]

In the afternoon, Panikkar went to meet Dr Leighton Stuart, the American ambassador. A New Testament scholar and a missionary who had served nearly his whole life in China, Stuart was an unlikely diplomat, much like Panikkar. Like Panikkar, he was caught on the horns of a political and ideological dilemma. For years, his support had been toward Chiang's Kuomintang, but the aftermath of 1948 had shown him that the decline of the Nationalists was inevitable and the possibility of Soviet intervention in the war was high. He had spent much of 1948 pleading fruitlessly for assistance from Washington, or at least support for a coalition government. By 1949, though, Stuart's mind had changed.

He believed that to accommodate the communists was the only way in which American influence in China could be preserved, and he asked the State Department for informal but direct contact to be authorised. He wasn't too hopeful about a response, but Dean Acheson, the secretary of state, thought there was merit in this proposal, though he warned that if the communists did anything to harm American interests, the entire policy would have to be re-examined.[68] On the April afternoon when Panikkar met him, Stuart's home was guarded by communist guards. The ambassador was lying down with a fever, though Panikkar was allowed entry as a fellow diplomat. In *Two Chinas*, Panikkar writes that Stuart 'assured me that there was no immediate danger of the communists crossing the Yangtse and that if they attempted to do so they would lose a million men and many costly attempts would be necessary before a foothold could be established on the southern side'.[69]

This does not seem likely at all, given the archival correspondence between Stuart and the State Department. If anything, Stuart was, until the very end of the Nationalist government, alive to the dangers of the communists. Panikkar did not stay at the embassy for long, going to the British embassy to meet Sir Ralph Stevenson who also struck a note of caution as far as the communist takeover was concerned.

If Panikkar professed to be confused by what he was hearing, the facts on the ground belied it all. More people were following the advancing communist forces. By the afternoon, the streets were clogged with people who wanted to see what was happening. 'We drove about everywhere, watching the endless procession of the P.L.A. (People's Liberation Army) marching through the famous Ching Shan Street. Except ourselves and the Burmese (and of course the Soviets) the other diplomats remained indoors, apprehensive lest their presence might lead to some untoward incidents. By the evening the crossing was completed and the Kuomintang capital effectively occupied.'[70]

By April 1949, word had spread that India was intending to de facto recognise the communists. Desperate, Luo met the foreign secretary in Delhi again. He managed to secure a promise that India would not recognise the communists. The problem was that he no longer trusted India's word. He wrote home to Guangzhou, warning Chiang of India's desire for power, its arrogance and the fact that New Delhi had no intentions of keeping its promises. He was right.

As the communist armies forced the Kuomintang into retreat in the spring of 1949, Nehru was sure that 'the Communist Government is the real government of China … it is in our interest to seek early opening to establish whatever relations are possible with that government'.[71] Nehru now asked K.P.S. Menon to keep a close watch on developments in Tibet. 'We shall think of the policy we should pursue there, in case anything happens,'[72] he told the foreign secretary.

It was the first sign that with the rise of communist China, India was wavering already in its stand on Tibet.

In this fast-changing scenario, Hugh Richardson, on 15 June 1949, underlined the importance of Tibet's new status with the communists now clearly taking charge. It was a position with which Menon agreed.[73] The foreign secretary believed that Tibetan officials would resist the communists if they insisted on major changes. He underlined the need for reforms in Tibet, as well as the supply of arms and ammunition and the strengthening of the northeastern frontier.[74] This was a line that Panikkar himself had taken in his letter to the British ambassador just a year before. However, Sir Girija Shankar Bajpai struck a note of caution. He insisted that if aid was being given to Tibet, it shouldn't be seen as undue provocation by the communists. He also argued for the necessity of taking precautionary military measures for the defence of the Indian frontier.[75]

Nehru disagreed with both men.

'I do not think there is any necessity at present for our Defence Ministry or any part of it to consider possible military repercussions on the Indo-Tibetan frontier. The event is remote and may not arise at all. Any present thought being given to it will affect the balance we are trying to create in India.'[76]

But this assessment didn't factor in the Tibetans, who played with fire that year by expelling the Chinese Amban (even though he was an appointee of the Nationalist government) with his entourage and escort, just before the communists took Peking. It was enough for the Chinese to fly into a collective rage and pin the blame on India. Pro-communist newspapers in China began to run editorials slamming India and Nehru. Peking Radio insisted that India was part of a plot to remove the Chinese mission in Lhasa; the *People's Daily* ran an editorial which said, 'Nehru and Company are openly engineering a cleavage between the different peoples in China, undermining their unity, and interfering in their internal affairs by declaring in the name of foreign country that Tibet has now recognised Chinese suzerainty.'[77]

Reading the papers in some alarm, Panikkar wrote to Nehru immediately. 'Communist leaders have had some kind of misunderstanding about your personal attitude towards them.' Nehru was considerably startled, professing the allegations to be 'fantastic'.[78]

The prime minister would have done well to pay attention to the memo that his ambassador in Nanking had written in November 1948, in which Panikkar had warned clearly that 'it is possible to expect that the new China will do its utmost to regain control over all the territories of the old empire, in continuity with the policy already initiated by Chiang Kai-shek and that it will seek to extend its influence and reassert its prestige. It can be assumed with practical certainty that the policy of a Communist China will be intensely nationalist. As the Soviet policy is the inheritor of the dreams of Peter the Great, the ambitions of Catherine and the conquest of the later Czars, the policy of Mao Tze Tung will combine the claims of all previous dynasties from the Hans to the Manchus and will not voluntarily accept any diminution of territory, claims or interests which China has inherited'.[79]

While Delhi hammered out a new policy direction, Panikkar was living through an agonising period of limbo during which the diplomats of the embassies in Nanking were virtually under house arrest. There was no question of a shortage of food, but foreign embassies struggled to pay their employees, since the communists had banned the exchange of money. Anticipating that this would happen, Panikkar had stored a quantity of silver dollars, hoping to tide over the crisis with this in reserve. Two weeks in, the supply ran out and the Indian embassy, running low on food supplies, was forced to borrow from the communists for their needs.[80]

All diplomats were then told 'politely but firmly' that they had no diplomatic privileges and would be treated as 'distinguished foreigners'. They were to be alluded to as 'ex-ambassadors'. There was at the time no foreign office as such, just a Foreign Personnel Bureau where diplomatic secretaries had to present themselves with an interpreter since all business was conducted only in Chinese. No communication in any other language was permitted and surveillance and censorship alike increased. Every conversation was in the presence of shorthand stenographers who took down every word that was uttered. No cyphers were allowed, nor were couriers. If anyone wanted to go for a walk, they had to do so with a heavy security escort and within the city boundaries. The number of cars allotted to each embassy was cut down. As Panikkar recalled rather sardonically, 'Our movements were restricted; our diplomatic activities were made impossible; but otherwise we were left to ourselves with no interference of any kind.'[81]

As the days passed, the diplomatic community trapped in Peking Lu became ever more jittery. Nobody knew when they would be allowed to leave or indeed *if* they would be allowed to leave. To break the tension, the Canadian and Portuguese ambassadors began a bridge club for beginners. 'The Peking-Lu Bridge Club became the standby of the more nervous among my colleagues.'[82]

Panikkar went occasionally, but for him as always, the true refuge lay in writing. With almost military discipline, he divided his day into three parts: the mornings to be used to study Chinese literature and history, the late afternoons for a book on the Indian freedom movement and the evenings for a translation of Kalidasa's epic *Kumara Sambhava* into Malayalam. The world of Chinese history, language, philosophy and politics was a new one for Panikkar, and despite his physical constraints at the time, he enjoyed the intellectual exercise of letting his mind run free through uncharted waters.

It is at this point that he began compiling what would eventually become a formidable English anthology of twelve short stories by modern Chinese authors. 'Only Chinese writers themselves can tell adequately of the problems confronting their people and of how they have been solved,' he would write. In his preface, Panikkar explains the criteria of selection in detail. He emphasises both the texts' 'intrinsic interest' and their ability to 'give a true picture of the development of China since the Revolution of 1911'. The Chinese scholar Yan Jia believed that this anthology, the first of its kind by a sitting diplomat, was more than a literary collection—it was a historical archive of voices from within China (albeit voices that Panikkar handpicked himself).[83]

But given where he was posted, security and geopolitics were never far from his mind. Based on what he was seeing in China at this moment, Panikkar proposed the creation of a consultative mechanism uniting Asia and Western countries. This proposal would take years to culminate, but it would lead to the negotiation of the Colombo Plan and the Commonwealth Development Aid Mechanism.[84]

By now three weeks had passed with no hope or idea of how to get out of Nanking. The diplomatic community was alarmed to hear that the American vice-consul had been summarily imprisoned on charges of 'not obeying the orders of the military authorities'.[85] Leighton Stuart himself was under house arrest, a stalemate that would continue until the closure of the US embassy in March 1950. A tank was parked in front of the American Embassy Club. In the shade of the trees in the compound, members of the diplomatic corps met to mutter anxiously about whether it was right to stay or necessary to leave.

The problem was, how did they get out of there?

There were no ships calling in Shanghai which would or could stop in Nanking. Any foreigner bent on leaving China had to apply for what was known as a 'shop guarantee', which meant that Chinese businessmen had to vouch and take responsibility for any departing foreigner. The Dutch ambassador, the resident expert in international law, told everyone loudly and repeatedly that this demand was irregular to say the least.

But everyone knew that that was meaningless.

On 1 July 1949, Mao Tse-tung made the speech for which he is famous today, declaring that new China leaned to one side and one side only: towards the Soviet Union. When the speech was broadcast, Panikkar was at lunch at the Canadian embassy. As they listened, the diplomats began to murmur amongst themselves. Leighton Stuart went pale.

It was over for many of these ambassadors. One way or another they would have to leave.

Panikkar's own instructions were to stay on until the end, but these were not easy instructions to abide by when the conversation every day centred around how best to get out of Nanking. And conditions continued to get worse. Though supplies had been plentiful in the beginning, as time passed, Kuomintang ships blockaded the coast in a last-ditch attempt to fight the communists, and the flow of goods dried up. The British and the Americans refused to run the blockade, and so the diplomats in Nanking had to ration food. There was no butter or milk. Communications were cut off eventually. For six months, the community lived in a virtual bubble, with no access to radio, letters or newspapers. The Kuomintang was also bombing Nanking, and in one air raid, the local power station was hit.

Nanking was now without water or power.

The French ambassador finally left on board a ship sent from Indochina. The Americans sent the *USS Gordon Castle* to fetch Leighton Stuart shortly thereafter. Britain was currently involved in a diplomatic incident involving its warship the *Amethyst*, which had been ordered to sail up the Yangtse River from Shanghai to Nanking to supply and, if required, evacuate the British embassy in case the communists crossed into Nanking. In the taking of Nanking, the *Amethyst* had been disabled. The British were horrified that there was now no naval cover in case the communists decided to attack Hong Kong. Surprisingly, the *Amethyst* triggered a reassessment of India's strategic importance for the British Empire.

Orders were given by the British cabinet to reinforce the military garrison in Hong Kong, but it was felt that to seek diplomatic support from the Commonwealth countries of Asia was equally vital.[86] India's response at this moment was considered to be of great value, with P.J. Noel-Baker, then the secretary of state for the Commonwealth, arguing that a statement from Nehru would be 'the most valuable moral support'.[87]

India's sudden arrival on the regional geopolitical landscape was unprecedented. In the summer of 1949, Nehru was still very much inclined to wait and watch. The communists had only just taken over. They would take time to settle down and indicate how they intended to act towards India.[88] In the aftermath of the takeover, the prime minister was thinking about what impact a communist regime might have in Tibet or Xinjiang. He was still unsure about recognising the communists. In a letter to his chief ministers in May 1949, Nehru insisted that India's guiding principle and desire 'has always been and is to retain the friendship' of China.[89] As he wrote to his sister, then the Indian ambassador in Washington, India would be in no hurry to recognise the new regime, 'but we are just not going to stand up as crusaders against it'.[90]

So when his opinion was asked during the *Amethyst* crisis in the summer of 1949, he realised that geopolitics was changing far faster than he had anticipated.

'Pandit Nehru while admitting that aggression must, of course, be resisted, suggests that "our policies may be so framed as to avoid the possibility of such a situation arising",' Noel-Baker reported in June. 'He personally doubts whether the Chinese communists would wish to take action that would mean war with a great power.'[91] Even more forthright was Nehru to his sister, then posted in Washington. In July 1949, he wrote to Pandit, instructing her to decline an invitation to join a 'Pacific Pact' with anti-Communists in Asia: 'As a realist, one has to recognize that Communists control the greater part of China and may, before long, control the whole of that country. In broader interest of international peace, it is not desirable that we should do anything that would make cultivation of normal friendly relations with the new China difficult, if not impossible.'[92]

As it was, the *Amethyst* eventually slipped safely out of communist waters by the end of July 1949. But the incident served to underscore how important India was becoming in the Asian theatre of the Cold War. During the summer of 1949, Britain was wondering whether recognising the communists was really the only way forward. So too was the United States. Their interests, though, were divergent. Britain was wondering about China with an eye on its own commercial interests in the country and its colonial possessions, including Hong Kong. The United States, on the other hand, was looking at China more strategically against the backdrop of the Cold War.

India's role in all of this was crucial.

The British were not unduly concerned, since Nehru's tendency so far was to 'write off the menace from that direction [the communists]'.[93] The Americans, however, had no clue about Indian thinking. Washington had so far not made any real efforts to consult India on China, but that would change in May 1949, when Stuart told the State Department (presumably based on information from Panikkar) that the rumour in Nanking was that the Indian government was intending to recognise the communist government 'after a decent interval'.[94] The United States now pivoted to understanding the benefits of India in this situation, with President Truman noting that India was 'key to the whole Asian situation'.[95] Reports from the Central Intelligence Agency (CIA) and the State Department were, by September 1949, highlighting India's significance as China's only potential rival in Southeast Asia.[96] In this fluid situation, India was 'the most solid element with which the United States can associate itself'.[97]

With this realisation, the Americans tasked Loy Henderson with the job of telling New Delhi that it should consult the Americans before recognising the communists. Sir Girija Shankar Bajpai, to whom Henderson spoke, assured him that India would speak with both the United States and Britain before doing anything of the kind. The conversation between Henderson and Bajpai was sent to Stuart in Nanking, and he in turn told Panikkar that Washington had secured a 'promise' of full cooperation from New Delhi on this issue.[98]

Panikkar was upset.

From where he was standing, the United States was clearly angling to pressure the communists to secure its own trade and commercial interests. This tactic would likely also put pressure on other governments to undermine the role and influence of the British.

He now advised New Delhi that any agreement with the Americans on this 'cannot fail to give the impression to the new government in China that we are allowing ourselves to be used for furtherance of American interests'.[99]

Panikkar's telegram was read out in full to Loy Henderson by K.P.S. Menon. Following Panikkar's lead, Menon said that, though India didn't exactly want to barge in, it did wish to retain a 'free hand'.[100] Unsurprisingly, this wasn't to American liking. Henderson was told to go back and have another conversation. Again, Henderson sought out Bajpai, who repeated that if there were any important decisions taken on this subject, they would be taken in Delhi. He didn't say outright what was clearly implied: Delhi would do the talking, not Panikkar.[101]

Chapter 45

The People's Republic of China

ON 1 OCTOBER 1949, THE PEOPLE'S REPUBLIC OF CHINA CAME INTO BEING. 'The question of withdrawal thus became an immediate one,' Panikkar wrote later. The only problem was that New Delhi was anxious that he stay on. This would put him in an untenable position, since he would have no official position and could hardly work until India declared its official recognition of the communist regime. That recognition was bound to take its own sweet time, considering the Kuomintang was still in possession of Canton and wide swathes in the southeast of China. In many provinces, fighting still continued.

Panikkar sent a hasty letter to Nehru explaining the case and asking that he be withdrawn along with the other diplomats.

The withdrawal of the diplomats was not elegant or honourable. 'Most diplomats regretted that they had stayed behind at all,'[1] Panikkar observed. 'The Chinese communists were not standing any patronage from the West; and it was as sadder and wiser men that most of them embarked on British ships, which evacuated the last survival of imperialist domination from the mainland of China.'[2]

As far as India was concerned, Panikkar was worried. Since February 1949, he had been warning the powers that be that the communists did not fully trust Nehru or India, and by August that mistrust had found its way into Chinese newspapers, with reports against Indian policy in general and specifically against Nehru for 'alleged complicity in American policy in Asia'.[3] By September, that vocal mistrust had muted into what Panikkar described as 'cautious watchfulness'. If New Delhi was watching Peking, so was Peking watching New Delhi. Under the circumstances, Panikkar advised New Delhi to take a policy of patience and caution based on 'mutual toleration and non-interference in each other's internal affairs'.[4]

The Indian ambassador said not a word about Tibet at this point.

By the time he arrived in New Delhi, it was mid-October 1949 and trouble was in the offing. For one, he arrived to find an atmosphere of distinct hostility directed against him from his colleagues in the Ministry of External Affairs. It was a known fact that, pending the formalities, Nehru fully intended to send him back to China. Plenty in the MEA saw this as a violation of protocol, especially since Panikkar had already served as ambassador to the previous Chinese regime.

There was also dissension within the Congress itself as far as the timing of the recognition of the new government went. Leaders like Rajaji and Sardar Patel were advocating that India not rush into things. In June 1949, the Sardar had written to Nehru, telling him that it was best if India stayed away from the communists for now. The main concern for India was Sikkim and Tibet. 'I anticipate that, as soon as the Communists have established themselves in the rest of China, they will try to destroy Tibet's autonomous existence. You have to consider carefully your policy towards Tibet in such circumstances and prepare from now for that eventuality.'[5]

Nehru ignored that advice as well.

Six months later, Patel and Nehru would lock horns again on the timing of India's recognition of the communist government. 'My own feeling is that we do not stand to gain anything by being in the lead [by recognising China ahead of most other countries],' the Sardar warned. 'In case you feel we must recognise China ahead of others, I feel we must have a discussion in the Cabinet.' Nehru's reply to this was, 'If we follow others, it would mean that we have no policy of our own.'[6]

In October, Nehru departed on a state visit to the United States. The visit was a marker of the fact that India was now an active player in at least the American strategic framework. The optics around it were excellent for India. *TIME* put Nehru on its cover and declared India was the 'anchor for Asia'. Nehru was hailed as 'the strongest figure in a troubled continent'. Where American policymakers had previously dismissed the idea of materially assisting India, now in October 1949, Henderson proposed a $500 million economic package as incentive.[7] Nehru was pleased about this. India could use the aid. He was still clear that the country could not afford to be involved in another war, but the communist victory was making him take another look at China. He knew he couldn't continue his support of the Kuomintang just because of his friendship with the generalissimo. As he wrote pragmatically to his sister, 'We have to take facts as they are.'[8]

If the communists were in power, Nehru felt, then no good would come from isolating them. In what has been termed 'mirror imaging', the Indian prime minister's perception of communist China was that it would act and react much like India had done after independence: focus on internal issues in a pragmatic, rather than ideological, way. Simply put, Nehru believed that China would not seek war.[9]

This was in direct contradiction of what Panikkar was writing from China: that ideology mattered to the communists and that the party leadership was 'fanatically imbued with a sense of mission to refashion society'.[10]

The prime minister wanted to look at China with an attitude of 'friendly expectation'[11] rather than consider what might happen if China took over Tibet. Where Panikkar was suggesting consultative mechanisms for regional cooperation, Nehru saw pacts of any kind as provocative. Alliances limited autonomy and the greatest example of that, he believed, had been the two world wars. He didn't want to include India in any pacts that stood against communism. The door must be left ajar for friendly relations with the communists in China. Panikkar, who had been warning Delhi to show that it was not, as Peking suspected, allied to the United States, was relieved at this stand. But there were still choppy waters to be navigated.

Chiang Kai-shek and his coterie were not exactly thrilled that Nehru was in Washington. 'The Chinese Ambassador here and the delegation at Lake Success are very angry with India,' Pandit wrote to her brother from the United Nations in New York. 'They are extremely bitter ... about the reception that you are expected to receive.'[12]

The fury of the Chiang Kai-sheks aside, there was also the fact that Nehru was still looking at Asia much as he had done in early 1947. A united, oppressed Asia was pushing back against the domination of the West, he felt, and that was an excellent thing, irrespective of whichever party held power. In simple words, new China represented a new nationalism, and nationalism, in Nehru's experience, was always an evolving concept. In this case, he felt that it was a response to the failures of the nationalist government. If anything, this only strengthened his resolve to not let a similar situation develop in India. For this, economic and foreign assistance was key, and both Patel and Nehru agreed that Washington's help was vital.[13]

What did Panikkar think of this?

Nehru was keen to find out. He cabled K.P.S. Menon in Delhi and asked for a summary of Panikkar's views and recommendations.[14]

Menon cabled back the same evening.

Panikkar's views were simple, if pithy. He said that the new government in China was here to stay; that this moment in history was much more than a revolution, but an 'Asian upheaval'; that the United States would hold off recognising China for as long as possible, thanks to the latter's association with Soviet expansionism; and that Britain was willing to accord early recognition. In the light of these circumstances, Panikkar advised Delhi that since its primary considerations were peace and friendly relations, it would do well to accord recognition 'at the proper time, without waiting for recognition by European powers'.[15]

This line was hard to disagree with since it was rooted in precisely the kind of foreign policy that Nehru was looking to espouse. Menon took Panikkar's argument a little further and warned the Indian prime minister that, 'To display a hostile attitude towards the new Government in China, or to delay recognition unduly after that Government has announced itself as the legal Government of China will be merely to throw the Chinese Government into the hands of Russia and to destroy whatever slender hope there may be of the emergence of what may be called a Nationalist-Communist Government of China.'[16]

Even Bajpai, that cautious hawk, was on board with this view. The American refusal to recognise the new government, he said, was 'anti-communist hysteria ... China is too big to be bullied or ignored; either attitude would only drive its communist masters deeper into the arms of the USSR.'[17]

But this did not mean, for Bajpai, that India was to rush in where fools feared to tread. Premature recognition could generate negative repercussions for India just as the United Nations Security Council was due to discuss Kashmir. 'If we recognise before even the U.K. and Canada have decided to do so, we run the risk, and it is a real risk, of an unfriendly approach to our point of view on Kashmir, not only by the permanent Delegate of China but by all others who consider our recognition of the new regime to be premature,' he mused. 'The countervailing advantage of recognition is, I confess, not clear to me.'[18] But Bajpai and Patel's voices were lost in the buzz of those who supported early recognition, like Panikkar.

And so it was that, buffered by the views of his officials in Delhi and in Nanking, Nehru gave US Secretary of State Dean Acheson the distinct impression that India was 'leaning toward early recognition', with heavy emphasis on India's own proximity to China.[19] According to the scholar Tanvi Madan, the United States might have assigned India a role in its strategic script, but that didn't mean that India was willing to play ball.[20]

Indeed, in his memoirs, Acheson recalled that he had found the Indian prime minister to be both 'prickly and arrogant ... and too ready to pick on the faults of others ... without recognizing any of his own'.[21] Altogether, he found Nehru 'one of the most difficult men with whom I have ever had to deal'. As the *New York Times* said sadly, Nehru 'declined to encourage the slightest hope' that Washington would or could have an ally in India.[22]

Nehru's refusal to play ball in the United States was against the ironic backdrop of a furious onslaught by the Chinese press, which unanimously slammed him as 'a thoroughly loyal servant of the US imperialists', and a 'leader of the anti-Communist and anti-national liberation movement in Asia'.[23]

Meanwhile in Delhi, Sardar Patel was in meetings with the American charge d'affaires, Howard Donovan. Over lunch, he told Donovan categorically that though foreign affairs was usually Nehru's domain, he was particularly interested in the communist regime in China and its recognition. In his opinion, there was no need to hurry in recognising Mao's regime. Towards the end of lunch, the Sardar asked Donovan to stay in touch on the subject. More than this he would not say, but Donovan reported to Washington that Patel 'will weigh very carefully … the effect recognition would have on the Communist problem in India … Patel can be a powerful factor in opposing the faction which decries prompt recognition of China.'[24]

Following up on these conversations, Panikkar, who was also still in Delhi, invited Donovan to lunch as well. After lunch, when the two men sat down to talk, Panikkar told Donovan bluntly that he thoroughly disliked communism and that he did not want India to immediately recognise communist China.[25] However, he said in an echo of Nehru, facts had to be faced. India's thousand-mile frontier with China was more pressing than any economic interests that Great Britain and the United States might have.

Communism, in Panikkar's opinion, was greatly overrated as a menace. He expected no particular friendship from the communist government through the fact of recognition. But, as he explained to the rapt Donovan, 'If diplomatic relations were established, countries so doing would be in a better position to protect their interests and might exert some modifying influence on Communist governments, whereas without recognition, nothing could be achieved.'[26]

It is fascinating to know that, like Nehru, Panikkar didn't seem to expect war or violence even *after* the memorandum he had written in 1948. As ambassador to China, he has often been accused of sending misleading information about events on the ground. But the archives of the period suggest that, at least in his first stint as ambassador to China, Panikkar followed where Nehru led. As the communists came to power, Nehru had already clearly stated that the last thing he wanted was to antagonise Mao and his men. India could not have peace in Asia with a restive China at its border. So Panikkar told Donovan that he expected relations with China to be characterised by 'sound unfriendliness, such as now exist between Britain and Russia, where both recognise each other, but both know that there is no danger of war ... The Communist government in China might attack the Government of India on the radio and indulge in pin-pricks, but both India and China know there is no danger of war and nothing could be achieved.'[27]

Where did Tibet stand in all this?

In September 1949, Bajpai told the British high commissioner in Delhi that he had discussed the question of Tibet with Nehru. The present Government of India was as anxious as any past government to retain Tibet as a buffer between India and China, he said firmly, and they certainly did not want to see any increase in Chinese, and still less, Chinese communist influence there.[28]

However, Bajpai also felt that if the Chinese pressured Tibet enough, Lhasa would not be able to withstand the strain. India wouldn't be of help there since it did not yet have the military resources to 'effectively defend' Tibet. The only option for India, said Bajpai, would be to defend its own borders against Chinese aggression.[29]

India's political officer in Gangtok, Hareshwar Dayal, agreed with this view. Only recently Qinghai, on the borders of Tibet, had fallen to the communists. The communists had also occupied Xinjiang. Dayal suggested an urgent reconsideration of Indian policy. 'The occupation or the domination of Tibet by a potentially hostile and possibly aggressive Communist power would be a threat to the security of India,' he wrote to Delhi forthrightly. 'Apart from the opportunity that such proximity would afford communist infiltration into India, it would encourage the Chinese communists to press their country's long-standing claim to large parts of the Assam tribal areas and also perhaps revive pretensions to suzerainty over Ladakh, Sikkim, Bhutan and Nepal.'[30]

Dayal urged that military supplies be made to Tibet if only to buy time and prove India's respect to her obligations. He knew that Delhi's recognition of the communist regime was inevitable, and so it would be 'prudent to seek an early opportunity of explaining the GOI's views and commitments in regard to Tibet to the new Government of China'.[31]

But it was Panikkar who actually penned the beginnings of a postcolonial policy towards Tibet given the changed circumstances in China. Technology and time had both advanced, in his opinion. The long-standing idea that Tibet was a geographically difficult country to invade was a myth. It had been crossed and invaded in fact a total of six times—by the British, the Chinese, the Dogras and thrice by the Gurkhas. He dismissed Bajpai's views of maintaining Tibet as a buffer state. 'A solution of the Tibetan issue must … be sought through diplomatic negotiations and the sooner we abandon such ideas as maintaining Tibet as a buffer state or political or military intervention or of thinking wishfully about effective resistance by the Tibetans, the better we shall be to deal with the issue on diplomatic levels.'[32]

India had upheld the theory of 'Chinese suzerainty', Panikkar wrote, despite the attempts of 'Anglo-Indian diplomatists to make the acceptance of Chinese suzerainty conditional on the assurance that the autonomy of Tibet will be guaranteed to us … [this] was never accepted by China even in the days of her extreme weakness'.[33] It was the Chinese position, consistently maintained, that Tibet enjoyed autonomy thanks to its internal relationship with China. Beyond 'trade rights and recognized boundary', India's interests in Tibet were but 'shadowy', Panikkar argued. Any military intervention in Tibet to safeguard the Tibetans was out of the question. His recommendation to the prime minister was that the wisest policy would be to give such assistance 'as we can' to the Tibetans. If a 'situation develops' India was to remain 'strictly neutral' on the grounds that Tibet was China's internal affair.

This was a turnaround from what he had written to Sir Ralph Stevenson from Nanking in 1948. Now, over a year later, Panikkar refused to consider the possibility of safeguarding Tibetan interests through the United Nations. In his opinion, the Soviet Union would veto any moves to help Tibet on an international platform. Besides, India had enough problems in the United Nations, with Hyderabad still on the UN agenda.

K.P.S. Menon was inclined to agree with Panikkar that, given the arrival of the communists, there was nothing India could do to save Tibet. But he disagreed fiercely with the sudden premise that India had never regarded Tibet 'as an independent country'. He argued that, on the contrary, India had inherited the commitments of the British government, specifically quoting from the Eden Memorandum of 1943 that Chinese suzerainty in Tibet could only be accepted on the understanding that Tibet was regarded as autonomous. According to Menon, to treat Tibet as an 'internal affair' of China was out of the question.[34] 'It is true that we are *not* now in a position to uphold, by force or by diplomacy, Tibetan independence or even Tibetan autonomy, but it is no use blinking at the fact that if we proceed to treat a Chinese invasion of Tibet as an "internal affair" of China, we shall be executing a volte-face and lending ourselves to the reproach that we have backed out of solemn engagements. Tibet will accuse us of a breach of faith and the unkind critics in the United Kingdom itself will not hesitate to say that we have let Tibet down.'[35]

Bajpai scribbled a stern footnote to this. 'We cannot and therefore should not expect to help the Tibetan government in order to pick a quarrel with and wage a war against the communists. We cannot, however, without the most careful consideration give up the special relationship that we have with Tibet. My provisional view is that this is one of the matters to be taken into account when we take up with the communist regime the question of recognition.'[36]

A couple of months later, confusion about where India stood with regard to Tibet and China still prevailed. This confusion deepened when the Panchen Lama congratulated both Mao and Chu Teh (the vice president of the People's Republic of China and commander-in-chief of the People's Liberation Army) and wished for an early liberation of Tibet. In their reply, the Chinese leaders assured him 'the People's Government and the liberation army will satisfy the wish of the Tibetan people'.[37]

Shortly thereafter, K.P.S. Menon spoke to the British high commissioner about India's concerns on retaining its mission in Tibet. Menon mused that the mission 'had in fact no right to be at Lhasa since the 1914 Treaty [the Simla Convention] which had not been accepted by China only provided for occasional visits'.[38]

To Loy Henderson, in January 1950, Menon was even more confusing. India would give diplomatic support to Tibet to enable it to retain its autonomous status if the Chinese refused to recognise such autonomy, he said. In the same breath, Menon also repeated that 'India wished to leave the matter alone and would not initiate any conversations with the Chinese regarding Tibet unless compelled to do so by Chinese actions.'[39]

On 16 November 1949, Nehru went on record in a press conference in New Delhi. It was a month before India's formal recognition of the People's Republic of China, though everyone in Delhi knew it would happen any day. Asked about India's views on Tibet, the prime minister answered in fluent Hindi that, for the last forty years, during British rule in India, 'a certain autonomy of Tibet' had been recognised. At the same time, regarding China's position in Tibet, 'a vague kind of suzerainty was recognized'. These matters had never been clearly defined, Nehru said. 'The matter remained vague …'[40]

If the matter was vague, Nehru was even more ambivalent. 'In a vague sense we have accepted the fact of Chinese suzerainty,' he said. 'How far it goes, one does not know.'[41]

This was a sensational remark, highlighting the fact that India's official position on Tibet on the eve of recognising the People's Republic of China was quite simply: No Comment.

For this ambiguity and for the fact that New Delhi now seemed to have doubts about Tibet, Panikkar was blamed—at least by the British to start with. It was to the British that Panikkar spoke, for instance, while he was in Delhi, saying that 'the present Lama regime was out of date and weak to resist any real pressure from the Chinese Communists. He said that even a small expedition could dispose of the present regime (in Lhasa)'.[42]

Just why this should have been a source of irritation when Bajpai was saying much the same thing is anyone's guess. The only point where Panikkar seemed to differ from Bajpai was that it was in India's interests to strengthen ties with China's new government so that India's own hand in Tibet would remain strong. Yet even Menon joined the British to say that Panikkar's views were 'perhaps too realistic' since they were 'roughly to the effect that there was nothing India could do to prevent the Chinese from taking over Tibet'.[43] Again, this was an already existing position, so there is no real basis for why the British blamed Panikkar here.

The correspondence on the matter from that period illuminates just how deep the fissures of uncertainty ran on the subject of China—between New Delhi and its man in China, between Nehru and the MEA, and between Nehru and Sardar Patel.

Nehru had not listened to either Bajpai or Dayal, both of whom made strong cases for shoring up India's defence and military capabilities, particularly on the northeastern frontier. Then there was Sumul Sinha, the new political officer in Lhasa, who told Delhi that the Foreign Bureau of the Tibetans in Lhasa was anxious to negotiate a new treaty with India. This was based on a desire to gain an assurance from Delhi that it regarded 'Tibet as an independent country and NOT (repeat NOT) merely an autonomous region'.[44]

The Tibetans were seeking modern arms and ammunition with machinery for the manufacture of ammunition, and training of troops, Sinha said. According to him, diplomatic negotiations on Tibet after recognition of the new government in China 'would be our best line'.[45]

Nehru didn't pay attention to that either.

Over and over, the prime minister reposed faith in the inhospitable terrain and climate of Tibet as well as the mountains that separated Tibet from India, despite Panikkar's strong warnings that geography could no longer be a factor for inaction. 'Our policy has been vague about Tibet. It has been inherited from the British days. We have recognised the autonomy of Tibet under some kind of vague suzerainty of China. Strictly speaking, in law, we cannot deny that suzerainty,' Nehru wrote to his chief ministers in December 1949.[46]

This dithering continued, finding utterance in the most alarming statements. On 17 December 1949, Nehru told the Standing Committee of the Indian Legislature on Foreign Affairs that 'if the Chinese wished to enter Tibet, there was no one to hold them back, except perhaps the climate'.[47] In a meeting with Menon, Dayal and Panikkar, Nehru acknowledged that Tibet's independence lacked international acceptance, but China's refusal to recognise the terms of the Simla Convention (1914) made it difficult for India to take up the cudgels in Tibet's support. The prime minister was more annoyed about the fact that China felt that Delhi was acting as a 'Trojan Horse' for Britain and the United States. He insisted that this feeling should be discouraged emphatically, ending the meeting with the strong statement that 'a threat to Nepal, Sikkim, Bhutan, Ladakh and the MacMahon Line areas will be resisted with all our force'.[48]

Just how India was going to do that given its limited defence capacities was left unaddressed. Nehru's focus, it seems, was entirely on the fact that India had to demonstrate its own autonomy in the ongoing Cold War. Returning from the United States, he sent a memo to the MEA concluding that 'Both Panikkar and Stevenson are anxious that recognition should be given as early as possible. They think that delay might be injurious. Panikkar further thinks that our recognition should not follow the Commonwealth Foreign Ministers' Conference but should precede it. He has laid stress in China, as I have done in public and private, that our decision will be our own, though of course we shall consult others. For us to take any action in the wake of the Foreign Ministers' Conference, apart from the delay involved, would also mean that we could not act independently. This might well affect our position in China.'[49]

On 21 November 1949, India instructed its mission at the United Nations that it should 'avoid any speech or action that may be inconsistent with the unavoidable recognition of the new Chinese regime'.

Meanwhile, highlighting how deeply divergent the views within the MEA were at this time, Girija Shankar Bajpai was humming a very different tune. He told Loy Henderson that in recognising China, the Government of India was not undertaking to 'flirt' with Chinese communists, Soviet communists or indeed any other communists. India was alive to the dangers of communism and had no illusions about existing links between Soviet Russia and communist China. But Bajpai explained that India would be in an invidiously embarrassing position if countries like Burma and others in South Asia recognised communist China while India held back. On the other hand, if India waited for Britain to recognise China, 'it would be charged internally with following in the United Kingdom's footsteps rather than having a foreign policy of its own'.[50]

As far as Tibet was concerned, a telegram sent that same month to the embassy in Peking from New Delhi shrugged at its possible takeover. Delhi was clearly following what Nehru saw as Panikkar's line of thought. If the Chinese regime decided to 'liberate' Tibet, nothing would stop them, barring 'miracles or serious international complication'.[51] The idea of maintaining Tibet as a buffer state was completely unrealistic. A buffer state could exist only if such a state were independent. 'It has never been our point of view that Tibet is an independent country,' the telegram read, taking a view that was perpendicular to Menon's. 'We have in fact upheld the theory of Chinese suzerainty.'[52] More tellingly, the telegram included the line, 'If China decides to make her suzerainty effective, we have hardly any right to intervene so long as our Treaty interests are safeguarded.'[53]

With Tibet neatly out of the way (or so Delhi thought), on 19 December 1949, Menon told Henderson that Nehru had requested him to express the hope that the United States would not take amiss India's recognition of the People's Republic of China in view of its geographical position. All things told, Menon said politely, 'Government of India felt it could not wait longer to establish relations with the regime controlling so close a neighbour.'[54] He added placatingly that India hoped to use its relations to prevent the communists from passing completely into Moscow's hands.

Not everyone was delighted with this decision. Sardar Patel tried once again to get Nehru to stall the issue. 'It seems your intention is to recognise China soon after the UNO session ends, even if it means that others are not ready by then or are prepared to do so,' he wrote to the prime minister. 'My own feeling is that we do not stand to gain anything substantial by giving a lead in the matter and that, while recognition must come sooner or later, if we are somewhat late in the company of others, it would be worthwhile delaying a bit.'[55]

It was too late for Patel's advice.

On 30 December 1949, India became the first non-communist Asian country to recognise the new regime in China.

Chapter 46

Return to Peking

cCHINA'S RESPONSE TO INDIA'S DECISION TO RECOGNISE IT WAS QUICK and decisive.

At Peking's request, Delhi asked its charge d'affaires, A.K. Sen, to conduct preliminary negotiations for the establishment of diplomatic relations.[1] China was ready with its preconditions: that the new regime would take on all properties and assets in India, that Delhi would no longer recognise the Kuomintang or its members and that it would support the expulsion of Nationalist China from the United Nations and support communist China's entry.[2]

Having made its decision, these were but formalities for New Delhi, but the paperwork would take its own time, as it often does. In the meantime, Panikkar, who knew he would be going back to China again, was forced to kick his heels in New Delhi. To keep him busy, Nehru nominated him temporarily to the Public Service Commission, primarily to represent the MEA. He would be selecting the new batch of civil servants, the first fleet of its career diplomats. The commission interviewed candidates in Delhi, Allahabad, Patna, Calcutta, Nagpur and Bombay.

It was a novel experience for Panikkar. 'For many years, I had been out of touch with the younger generation and this all-India tour, extending over four months, gave me an exceptional opportunity of judging both the quality of our university education and the intellectual capacities of the new generation.'[3] He was fascinated by how narrow the scope of education had been for young Indian students. What little they knew was from the colonial point of view, with little or no understanding of their own Asian context.

Meanwhile, Panikkar found himself quite caught up in other things too. When Devaki was studying in England, communism was at its peak there. Small wonder then that she had returned an ardent communist. Upon her return to India, she had gone off to Trivandrum. It was a fiery time to have been there, considering rural politics was taking an increasingly violent turn and the communists, led by the likes of K. Damodaran and E.M.S. Namboodiripad, were on the rise. Among the communists was a brisk, intelligent and bespectacled young man by the name of M.N. Govindan Nair.

Known to his friends simply as 'MN', Nair was born in 1910 in Pandalam, a village in the heart of southern Kerala. Studying at the school run by the Nair Service Society, he had involved himself from an early age in working for the upliftment of lower castes. Spurred by his rage at the deep caste cleavages in Malabar society, MN studied law in college in Trivandrum. It was while he was at university that he heard of Gandhi. He went off immediately to Wardha, where he was trained in Gandhian ways and introduced to prominent Congress leaders. Socialism was, in the mid-1920s and early 1930s, very much on the rise in India, and MN was immediately attracted to the ideology.

He never looked back. Poring through book after book at the ashram in Wardha, MN realised that the best way he could contribute to alleviating caste suffering and inequality was by involving himself in politics. He would go on to become the general secretary of the Communist Party of India (CPI), and it was under his secretaryship that the CPI would eventually come to power in the general elections in Kerala in 1957.

But in 1949, deeply immersed in his politics and his ideals, he wasn't looking for love until he saw a sweet-faced, sari-clad young woman with long dark hair and a charming smile inaugurating the college union of University College, Trivandrum.

It was love at first sight for both Devaki and MN. They wanted to be married immediately. Panikkar, caught in the crosshairs of what he knew was an uncomfortable geopolitical moment, told the young couple to wait for a year. It would hardly have been helpful for optics that his daughter was in love with a rising young communist leader in the heart of India.

Devaki, for whom MN represented everything she had been searching for—principled, upright and committed to his cause—agreed reluctantly. The blow of waiting was sweetened somewhat when her father told her to come along with them to China if a new posting came about. He had by now had also been offered the post of high commissioner to Islamabad. Pakistan would have been a tricky country to choose, but before he could decide either way, Peking agreed to have Panikkar back as India's ambassador.

'When I came to Peking, I had imagined my mission to be nothing more than that of witnessing the development of a revolution and of working for a better understanding between China and India,' Panikkar would write later, somewhat disingenuously. This could hardly have been his actual belief, given the frantic discussions over recognition and Tibet just a few weeks ago. Indeed, with regard to Lhasa, Panikkar stated outright that he knew that the policy of looking upon Tibet as an 'area in which we had special political interests could not be maintained'.[4]

Did he though? His reports from China were to prove otherwise, but for now, his main focus was to find his footing in a regime he knew next to nothing about. The Panikkars stayed for two days in Hong Kong. They were travelling with only Radha now. Though Devaki and Haima often visited them in China, as the youngest daughter, Radha spent a lot of time with her parents. In the days of the revolution and Gouri's constant illness, her presence was a great comfort to her father and mother.

After meeting some friends in Hong Kong, the Panikkars embarked for Tientsin aboard the *Poyang*. This was a light little ship that rolled and pitched most uncomfortably, causing both Gouri and Panikkar to become embarrassingly seasick.

After some days, the *Poyang* entered Taku Bar, as the port of Tanggu was colloquially known. If Panikkar had been nervous about his first assignment in Nationalist China, he was sincerely agitated now. 'I knew that my previous experience, either in the West or in Kuomintang China, would be of no great help to me.'[5] His memoir takes the distinctly Nehruvian position of sympathy to an Asian people standing up 'against nations which had oppressed them for a hundred years',[6] but Panikkar was always a little more pragmatic than that.

Peking had changed almost beyond recognition. There was now a sense of brisk officialdom, even in the most European of hotels and legation quarters. From the start, Panikkar refused to stay within the designated quarters for the foreign embassies in the city. 'I had no desire to be associated with the Quarter, which stood so much for European domination in the East.'[7] The house which A.K. Sen had found him, on the other hand, was perfect. A beautiful residence with 'numerous courtyards and reception rooms in the Chinese style', it was just outside the legation area of the Forbidden City. Panikkar's favourite part was the pavilion attached to the garden, which had scenes from the great Chinese novel, *The Dream of the Red Chamber*, painted on its sides. In a flight of fancy, he named it 'The Courtyard of Domestic Felicity'.

Three days after his arrival in Peking, he was received by Zhou En-lai. Panikkar's description of him is extraordinary: 'He is a well-set-up, handsome man, youthful in appearance, with a mass of black hair and a face which is pleasant and at the same time completely composed.' Zhou was dressed impeccably and had an air of calm dignity, but what really struck Panikkar were his hands: 'Not only were they carefully tended, but the fingers were like tender onion shoots … and he gesticulated with them with great effect.'[8] Both Nehru and Zhou held extremely difficult jobs, but Panikkar was quick to note that while Nehru was often betrayed into looking worried, except when he smiled or laughed, Zhou 'smiles only faintly and he generally maintains an attitude of impenetrability'.[9] From a meeting that lasted over an hour, Panikkar came away with the impression that Zhou was 'no doctrinaire, but a practical statesman' who, despite being a staunch communist, had his feet 'firmly planted on mother earth'.[10]

The next step, of course, was to meet Chairman Mao himself, to present his credentials. The tendency of the new regime was to receive its envoys late at night. During the day, Mao had no time. Panikkar was not unnaturally excited at 'the idea of a talk with one who had changed the course of history so violently in Asia'.[11] Was Mao, he wondered, 'a new Chingiz, an emperor thinking in terms of altering the map of a continent, or the chosen leader of a resurgent people?'[12]

Panikkar's description of Mao is almost lyrical, detailing a heavily built, tall man, with broad shoulders and a short but thick neck. His forehead was broad and his hair thick, though his encroaching baldness, to Panikkar, made him seem even more impressive. The Indian ambassador marvelled at the fact that there was no cruelty in this man's eyes or around his mouth. Here, he wrote admiringly, was a man who had risen from the dirt of poverty, 'leading his flock like a new Moses to the promised land'.[13]

His descriptions of Zhou and Mao leave a reader in no doubt of his admiration for the communist leaders and his tendency to romanticise the brutal wresting of power from the nationalists.

The presentation of credentials took place on 20 May 1950 in a suitably grand environment: the Palace of the Fragrant Concubine, a relic from the Manchu days, following which Mao officially met Panikkar. Panikkar thought Mao an impressive but not intimidating man, a man of philosophy and history, 'a little dreamy, but absolutely sure of himself'. Even more startlingly, Mao reminded Panikkar of Nehru. 'Both are men of action with dreamy, idealistic temperaments,' he recalled in *Two Chinas*, '… both may be considered humanists in the broadest sense of the term.'[14]

Given that *Two Chinas* was published in 1955, this description is almost laughably removed from reality. Even at the time, Panikkar's lyrical descriptions of China's new leaders did nothing to disprove what foreign policy mandarins from New Delhi to London were already beginning to mutter.

Reports on India's ambassador to Peking were not encouraging. Word had got around that Panikkar had remarkable ease of access to China's top leadership. He had already—before any other ambassador—been on a round of visits to the new leadership's top political personalities during his first weeks as India's envoy. Not only that but Mao and his top officials also threw a succession of banquets and dinners for the Panikkars.

Panikkar reciprocated as far as hospitality was concerned, but importantly, he proved himself remarkably adept at balancing the peculiar blend of Cold War and communist diplomacy that characterised China now. There were Soviets, there were the countries that had recognised China, those who had recognised China but were still negotiating diplomatic representation, and those who had not recognised China but kept on an official in the country anyway.

There were also the Americans, with the CIA keeping a sharp eye on the Indian ambassador and his communist daughter. In June 1950, the CIA grimly noted that Panikkar had said that his main mission in Peking was to 'convince the leaders of the CCP that China's identity lies with the other Asiatic countries, rather than with the Soviet Union'.[15]

With this motley crew, Panikkar had to engage artfully, especially since the Chinese thought nothing of cutting anyone dead who did not conform to what they wanted them to do. India, with its declared policy of non-alignment, had to maintain friendly relations with everyone, and that involved an intricate diplomatic pirouette that Panikkar pulled off with such success that, before long, resentment began to bubble. The Chinese leadership's obvious attention to Panikkar generated both gossip and rumour.

TIME published a photograph of the Indian ambassador presenting his credentials to Mao with the unflattering description: 'Contact Man between Peking and New Delhi is Sardar K.M. Panikkar, bowing low to Mao Tse-Tung whom he greatly admires. Oxford-educated Panikkar loves to parade his nodding acquaintance with European history. He served under several maharajas, calls himself a "reformed landlord," cultivates his resemblance to Lenin by wearing a Leninesque beard.'[16]

London was also keeping an eye on Panikkar. A note by the British Commonwealth Office described Panikkar as having 'a strong belief in Asia's destiny'. This was not incorrect—Panikkar *did* believe in the concept of a rising Asia, much as Nehru did. But what is significant here is the British holding the view 'that India should hold the "Ring Fence" against invasion from the North and that the Indian Navy should be built up as the police force for the whole Indian Ocean area'.[17]

It was a mark of how fast times were changing that *India and the Indian Ocean*, a security document for which Panikkar had been hailed during the war, was now seen as a threat.

This particular brief on India's ambassador outlines Panikkar as a man with singularly strong communist leanings, 'believing the communist seizure of power to have been inevitable and in the circumstances the only solution to China's immediate problems'.[18] The Commonwealth Office suggested contemptuously that 'with a scholar's ability, Sardar Panikkar possesses also the defect to which the academic mind is liable, the formation of theories based on abstract speculation insufficiently related to practical reality, and it is significant that there is a school of thought in the Government of India which holds that he went to Peking with set ideas and is not reporting objectively but fitting the facts to his theories'.[19]

Nor did his colleagues in the MEA seem to stand by him. One of his greatest critics was Sir Girija Shankar Bajpai who wrote to Vijayalakshmi Pandit that he regarded Panikkar as being 'a little too responsive to the atmosphere, whether for our conviction or as a safe guide to our policy. His eulogy of the men who now rule China, their great reforms and their friendship for us, leaves me somewhat sceptical, especially the last ...'[20] In yet another letter to Pandit, Bajpai sniped, 'Panikkar's enthusiasm, genuine or feigned, causes me personally a good deal of difficulty at times. The P.M. is impressed with his reports and I have to work hard to control his enthusiasm when, in my own rather conservative judgement, caution seems to be necessary.'[21]

During the days of the empire, Panikkar had been seen as a scholar of considerable repute, with ideas guaranteed to provide a perspective worth studying and considering. During these new, fevered days of decolonisation, that perspective had flipped on its head. Panikkar was now seen as a 'high pressure gentleman who plugs a line'.[22]

This, of course, suggests that there was a line to be plugged. It stands to reason that ambassadors who are sent out on foreign postings have a brief to fulfil. Nehru had made no secret of the fact that it was in India's interests to keep friendly relations with the People's Republic of China. But this discounts the possibility that Panikkar had definite ideas of his own about what he saw and experienced in China which, judging by the reports he was sending to Nehru at this time, he certainly did.

Well settled in by now, Panikkar had made the discovery that the CCP leadership, fresh to politics from the world of guerilla warfare, was eager to learn about India. Their thirst for knowledge led Panikkar to shrewdly engage with them on matters of Indian foreign policy. Before long, he was giving official lectures to the foreign office in China and to its Institute of International Relations. To everyone, he spoke of Indian geopolitics and what India expected from China. His reports to Delhi reflected what he was seeing on the ground. The question here is, of course, *what* he was actually seeing. Panikkar makes no bones about his admiration for the CCP leadership or how it clawed its way to power. His delight in what he saw shone through in his reports to Delhi. 'The spirit here is something magnificent,' he wrote to Nehru, 'and it will be of the greatest benefit to us, if some of our younger politicians could come and see what is happening in China.'[23]

Nor did he make any bones about the apparent sincerity of the party leadership to forge an alliance with India. His reports to Nehru in the first months of 1950 border on the effusive—and slightly delusional. To begin with, Panikkar insisted that the new government was a coalition in which, certainly, the communists were prevalent, but which implemented a common programme worked out together with other national forces.[24] To his mind, China's latest agrarian reforms were an excellent example of how this worked. Far from the collectivisation of the land, they had allowed the formation of a class of smallholders who would most likely be opposed to any such action in the future.[25]

In yet another report, Panikkar explained the 'problems' confronting New China. 'With a mixed economy as its immediate objective and a Coalition Government as its present machinery, New China resents being labelled Communist. It claims to be a new democratic state preparing itself for socialism ... The revolution that has taken place in China can only be considered as a national democratic revolution.'[26]

His constant meetings with China's new leaders also gave him the impression that it would be possible to build friendly relations between the two countries, given that Mao himself incessantly talked about the history of good relations across Asia and about the more recent common goal of getting rid of imperialism.[27] Panikkar's most open confession of his belief in the CCP's intentions towards India are in a letter dated 17 June 1950, in which he wrote, 'I am fully satisfied that the desire which the Chinese leaders (including Mao Tse-tung and Chu Teh ...) express is not merely a formal expression of goodwill. They are really sincere, for they have in the first place a deeper feeling of Asian solidarity than the Kuomintang and secondly, they realise the similarity of the problems facing Asian countries as a result of the withdrawal of European influence. The communist leaders are anxious to develop good relations with India if they can do so, without compromising their special relationship with the Soviets.'[28]

That feeling of 'Asian solidarity', he felt, extended to all the countries of Southeast Asia. 'I do not think that it will be right to say that China has aggressive intentions in regard to the countries in that region,' he mused in a report to the MEA.[29]

In yet another letter, Panikkar explained that from where he stood, even the communist alliance with the Soviet Union was one that was born from compulsion rather than common interests. 'I am inclined to think that what led the People's Government to make a firm alliance with Moscow was the fact that the Kuomintang had, during the civil war, the active sympathy and support of U.S.A. In fact the Peking authorities look upon the support now being extended to Taiwan as a form of aggressive intervention by the Americans. The ill-concealed designs of American strategists on the Asian coast of the Pacific, including the support to the South Korea regime and the discussion of bases in Japan and assistance to Bao Dai, also left the Peking regime with no option but to tie itself up definitely with Moscow.'[30]

It was music to Nehru's ears.

More importantly, it was proof that sending Panikkar to China had been the right choice. 'Only today I received a letter from Panikkar together with a report on present-day China … Here also you will see an entirely different world with its own way of thinking on problems. What a vast difference there is between this and the U. S. view of China as a stooge of Moscow!' he told his sister triumphantly. '[It] is a complete misunderstanding of the China situation to imagine that they function like a satellite State of Russia. Only one thing will push them in that direction to some extent. And even then this cannot go far. That one thing is isolation from the rest of the world. The U.S. policy is the one policy which will make China do what the U.S. least want.'[31]

Nehru's jubilation unfortunately was short-lived.

The year 1950 marked the intertwining of two simultaneous international dynamics. The wars in Korea and Tibet would change India's China policy forever and, at a personal level, change Panikkar's career and status permanently.

When Panikkar arrived in Peking in the summer of 1950, Tibet was in free fall. To go into the legal and political history of Tibet would to be to write several other books, but suffice it to say that, in 1950, a clear determination of its status—its independence, its sovereignty—remained elusive. The devil was in the details, literally and metaphorically speaking as far as India was concerned.[32]

After the establishment of the People's Republic of China, Zhou En-lai informed a delighted Panikkar that the establishment of friendly relations among Asian countries in general—and India, Nepal, Burma and Indonesia in particular—would lead to a better understanding of the Chinese position in Southeast Asia. Nehru, on the other hand, felt that before they went to other South Asian countries, they had better settle matters between themselves over the question of Tibet.[33] The Indian prime minister was still looking at China as a civilisational power with which India had a shared history stretching back to ancient times. Whether it was ruled by the Kuomintang or the communists, according to the scholar Avtar Singh Bhasin, didn't really matter to him. So he began campaigning for the entry of New China into the UN Security Council. In this aim he met formidable opposition, not least from the United States, but he stuck to his guns. In 1955, Nehru would turn down a permanent seat on the UNSC for India in favour of China taking 'her rightful place'.[34] This has been a particularly contentious claim in Indian geopolitical history and heated debates still persist on the subject. There were, in fact, two offers made to India to join the UNSC: one, which has been publicly discussed by the constitutional scholar A.G. Noorani,[35] made by the Soviets in 1955, and an earlier one, made by the United States in 1950. This latter offer lies buried in Vijayalakshmi Pandit's papers at the Prime Ministers' Museum & Library (PMML) in New Delhi, with her brother grimly refuting any American attempt to unseat China at the UNSC in favour of India. Nehru was at his plainest in this letter to his sister, 'So far as we are concerned, we are not going to countenance it. That would be bad from every point of view. It would be a clear affront to China and it would mean some kind of a break between us and China … We shall go on pressing for China's admission in the UN and the Security Council. … India because of many factors, is certainly entitled to a permanent seat in the security council. But we are not going in at the cost of China.'[36] Cold War dynamics aside, Nehru was being determinedly principled. He wanted to ensure that the United Nations remained a viable venue for the resolution of international conflict on the basis of sustained dialogue and attempts at internationalism; to keep this effort up was to forestall war.

Mao, on the other hand, was grimly realistic. The 'liberation' of Tibet was the first on the communist agenda. 'Although Tibet's population is small, its international position is extremely important and we must occupy it.'[37]

The CCP was acutely aware of Tibet's strategic location, abutting Xinjiang, Qinghai, Sichuan and Yunnan. Communist China's first policy statement on Tibet was an outright warning. 'The fact that Tibet is Chinese territory is known to all the world and has never been denied by anybody. Lhasa authorities have no right to send any mission and to express its so-called "independence".'[38]

Small wonder then that Menon had hastily told Donovan that Delhi had no desire to make an issue out of this. Even less did Delhi desire to be the main venue for talks between Tibetans and foreign powers as the 'communist government would probably charge Delhi with becoming the centre of conspiracy to affect the separation of Tibet from China ...'[39] Menon was repeating Nehru's line, since he had already told Dayal, on 9 January 1950, 'Nothing should be done which creates complications and which cannot be followed up later. Insistence on recognition to Tibetan independence is likely to affect Tibetan interests adversely and bring Tibet into direct collusion with the Communist government of China. GOI do not propose to act as instruments of any anti-communist bloc in Tibet or elsewhere.'[40]

Meanwhile, and quite contrarily, Nehru asked the political officer in Lhasa to tell Tibet that 'the GOI intend to continue their relations with Tibet as an autonomous state on the basis of the 1914 convention. It is clear that the new Chinese government will raise the Tibetan question sooner or later and when they do, GOI will help Tibet diplomatically ...'[41]

Tibet didn't believe a word of that.

It was right not to.

Still, Lhasa made one last desperate appeal for help to New Delhi, asking for arms and ammunition. Dayal assured Delhi that there was no risk in helping Tibet out. After all, it had done so earlier, even going to the extent of training the Tibetan army in Gyantse. But events were moving far fast now.

Dayal's suggestion was ignored.[42]

On May Day 1950, Peking Radio reiterated that one of the tasks of the People's Liberation Army was to liberate Tibet along with Taiwan. On 9 May, Sherab Gyatso, the vice chairman of the Chinghai People's Government, in a message from Radio Sian addressed to the Dalai Lama, warned that the PLA would soon set out to liberate

Tibet. He invited the Dalai Lama to send a delegation to Peking for the peaceful liberation of Tibet.[43]

On 13 May, just a week before Panikkar was due to present his credentials to Mao, China accused the Indian government of being part of a reactionary clique along with the US government and 'conspiring an imperialist expansion into a territory under the authority of the Chinese government, namely Province of Tibet'.[44]

CHAPTER 47

An Interlocutor in Korea

WOULD CHINA TAKE TIBET PEACEFULLY OR BY FORCE?

There was no longer a question of 'if' in the summer of 1950. It was considered inevitable, particularly against the backdrop of the communist invasion of Korea. Given the way the foreign policy establishment in New Delhi was already thinking at this time, the betrayal that is evident in later documentation is rather baffling.

On 25 June 1950, eight army divisions of the Democratic People's Republic of Korea, comprising 9,000 men, supported by 150 Soviet medium tanks, mobile artillery and supporting aircraft, crossed the 38th parallel in three columns and moved rapidly through the Uijongbu Gap to invade the Republic of Korea.

For the United States, this was a shock. These were the years of the 'Red Scare'. Catastrophe had narrowly been averted in Greece and Italy as communist partisans had very nearly prevailed, and few could forget that Eastern Europe was firmly a part of the Soviet bloc. President Truman lost no time in announcing the intensification of American support to South Korea in the form of naval and air reinforcements. Alongside, he strengthened the US forces in the Philippines, increased military assistance to French forces in Indochina and ordered the US Seventh Fleet to prevent an attack on Formosa (Taiwan).

Korea was now at the epicentre of a broader Cold War against communist forces.

For China, it was a bolt from the blue. It had no desire to have the Americans at its doorstep so soon after the communist takeover and with Tibet on the boil with India. To add to Peking's concern, Chiang Kai-shek offered 25,000 troops to fight in Korea. Nobody took this seriously and the offer was ultimately declined politely by the United States on the grounds that these troops could be used to defend Formosa. But it did nothing to allay communist nerves.[1]

For India, the invasion of Korea was a bigger shock. It had major implications for a stable Asia and was a hard test of India's policy of non-alignment. At the time of the invasion, India was presiding over the UN Security Council. With no time to report to Delhi, its representative, B.N. Rau, voted in favour of the resolution condemning Pyongyang.[2] Delhi, however, presented a case for impartial arbitration, assuming the role of what the historian Vineet Thakur has called 'diplomatic entrepreneurship'.[3]

Nehru now qualified India's support as 'only moral'. India did not have the military or financial capability to entangle itself in a war of this kind.[4] Importantly, as far as China was concerned, Nehru wrote to both Britain and the United States that the broader Western approach to communism was misguided. Asia was transitioning towards independence still and communism appealed to the continent's largely agrarian, colonised people. In trying to root out communism, the West was only going back in time towards its colonial precedents. The Indian prime minister appealed to the West to understand the 'mind' of Asia. Extraordinarily, he used this precise moment to lobby to include communist China on the United Nations Security Council, so that the West could 'signal to the newly independent people of Asia that it had overcome the colonial mindset'.[5] What was more, as Nehru told the British foreign secretary, Ernest Bevin, 'If treated as equals [at the UN], Mao Tse Tung and his colleagues might make an independent and constructive contribution to the solution of world problems.'[6]

Watching this, Panikkar sent a tempered assessment of the situation in Tibet to New Delhi shortly after he arrived, saying that he was inclined to think that the Chinese were working in the first instance for peaceful liberation with a show of military force.

'If this policy fails, they will certainly attack.'[7]

His assessment of the developments in Korea, on the other hand, seemed almost tailor-made to Nehru's own ideas about China and its position in Asia. 'I feel satisfied that, if there was a conspiracy against peace, Peking was not a party to it,' Panikkar wrote to Bajpai in a separate memo on Korea. He presented China not as a Soviet satellite but an independent country afraid of Western control. 'In fact the Chinese government seems to have been taken totally unaware by the sudden and extraordinary developments in the Pacific. What has come to them as a great shock is the American decision about [asking the Seventh Fleet to prevent an invasion of] Taiwan. Whether the Korean issue is localised or not, it is certain that American action in the Pacific has made any approach between China and the Western powers absolutely impossible. The worsening of the relationship with Britain is certain to affect, at least in some measure, the Chinese relations with us and they are likely to keep us at arm's length.'[8] Panikkar insisted that China would never permit a resurgence of Western influence. His report on Korea tied in with Nehru's own thinking on Asia and, given his status and position as ambassador in Peking, would form the basis of the prime minister's arguments against American policy in Korea.

On 12 June 1950, the Ministry of Defence warned the MEA of the early possibility of a Chinese invasion of Tibet. Over 3,00,000 PLA men had amassed in Khota under the leadership of Chu Teh. The report predicted that the invasion would begin from Chamdo or Jyekundo as it was a shorter route, close enough to Lhasa. China kept the pressure up, steadily moving its troops closer and closer to Tibet even as it dangled a carrot of negotiation before Lhasa's envoy, Tsepon Shakabpa.

The drama with Shakabpa would be a running and an angry subplot in the heightening of tensions between India and China that summer.

That same month, Panikkar repeated to Delhi that the Peking government would first opt for peaceful methods to assert its authority and 'only if Lhasa authorities are recalcitrant will take military action'.[9] He also warned that in the meantime, the 'Governor of Sinning (Xining) in Inner Tibet has now made a definite offer of autonomy to Tibet with warning of military action in case Tibet does not agree … [this] indicates completion of military preparations'.[10]

These were two critical messages sent by Panikkar that summer as PLA troops converged on Tibet. They should have been enough warning to Delhi of the possibility of Chinese invasion in case Lhasa failed to negotiate. But Delhi was also dealing with its new role as a diplomatic envoy in a regional conflict. Since the People's Republic of China was not represented at the United Nations and since it did not have diplomatic relations with the Western powers, India became the interlocutor between China and the West. Dean Acheson, in a letter to Nehru on 26 July, requested him to ask China to refrain from intervention in Korea or Formosa.[11]

For India, these were tricky waters to navigate. New Delhi knew that Washington wasn't thrilled with India's support for Moscow in getting Peking a seat on the Security Council. Why, US officials demanded, did India link the aggression in Korea with concerns over a UN seat for China? On the other hand, India couldn't understand why Truman's administration had linked festering issues in Taiwan and Indochina with Korea, given that the region was already unstable. Nehru repeated that if there was war in any part of Asia, 'it has some close effect on India'.[12]

Indian officials believed American actions such as the dispatch of the Seventh Fleet to the Taiwan Straits in June would provoke China. Panikkar reported that, for China, the two regions were different. In Korea, Peking didn't want to be involved, and in Taiwan, it would not back down. In addition, Panikkar warned, the Chinese were wary of the American defence ties with Thailand, its involvement with Indochina and the visit of General MacArthur, the supreme allied commander, to Taiwan. Any doubling down from Washington would push Peking towards Moscow.

'During the last two and a half months I have been noticing a very considerable change for the worse in China's attitude to external problems. There has been a mounting feeling in favour of war with America, which in terms of current propaganda is called "strengthening the will to resist" American aggression. Every method open to a very powerful organised propaganda machine has been turned on to create the feeling in China that America is determined to force a conflict on China.'[13]

This view was shared by policy hawks in Washington, like George Kennan. Even Bajpai, who differed often and strongly from Panikkar on key security issues, was inclined to believe that the US approach was counterproductive, and based on Panikkar's own advice, suggested ways that the United States could cool Chinese suspicions about its geopolitical intentions.[14]

New Delhi got no joy from US officials on these counts. MacArthur dismissed Nehru's stance as 'appeasement', while Acheson warned London and Delhi it was Peking, not Washington, that needed to reassure others, especially if the perception of China was to change.[15]

Wrapped up as it was in Korea, Delhi seemed to be unaware of Tibet's own games playing out under its nose. Through the month of July 1950, Tibet gained a strategically central role in American foreign policy, thanks to Korea and the need to contain communist expansion. Tsepon Shakabpa, the Tibetan envoy, was the key player in this.

His brief was impossible—to gain an assurance of Tibet's territorial integrity from China, along with conditions of non-interference in the succession arrangement with the Dalai Lama—an acknowledgement of Tibet's desire to remain independent—and no military deployment in Tibet.[16]

Shakabpa knew Peking wouldn't hear of this. Playing for time, he requested Peking for a change in the venue of talks to either Delhi or Hong Kong, a request he knew would be denied. In Delhi, Shakabpa quietly met British and American officials. From Washington, he expected some support, since it was not only staunchly anti-communist, but had already expressed its desire to aid Tibet. But as Shakabpa was to find out, this support was conditional on Indian cooperation. This was disappointing for the Tibetan envoy, who told US officials desperately that 'India seems prepared to hand Tibet over to the Chinese'.[17]

That tactic failed.

Washington insisted that Tibet ask India for additional aid, or at the very least, to permit passage of aid from abroad. Shakabpa knew that no such aid would be forthcoming from Delhi and he offered to prepare landing fields in Gartok, Lhasa or Chamdo. The offer was rejected by Washington, which wanted India to be involved at any cost.

Despairing, Shakabpa promised to get back to US officials—and did not.

Puzzled, Washington contacted the MEA to find out what had happened to Shakabpa. That was the first Delhi had heard of any such negotiation. Alarmed and angry, K.P.S. Menon categorically denied the making of any such request by Tibet. But even with this knowledge, Delhi did nothing about Shakabpa's presence, continuing to stick to its official position that an amicable solution to the problem of Tibet lay in establishing 'friendship and understanding' between Delhi and Peking. This was a position endorsed by Panikkar who was continuing to insist that that China wanted to maintain 'the friendliest of relations with India'.[18] As long as the reports from Peking were optimistic, Delhi seemed reassured.

The scholar Avtar Singh Bhasin has argued that, at this time, China was pursuing a two-pronged policy of keeping Panikkar happy, and through him, keeping Delhi assured of its friendship, even as it continued being indifferent to India's concerns about Tibet. Bhasin maintains that Panikkar could not have known what was happening in Tibet since the Indian Mission in Lhasa was not answerable to him but to the political officer in Gangtok—so he would need to be specifically informed by Delhi to know what was happening in Lhasa.[19]

The political officer in Gangtok had radically different reports on Tibet. Dayal warned Delhi constantly that the loss of Tibetan autonomy would only hurt Indian interests. 'Communist domination of Tibet would cause nervousness and unrest among the border people along the whole of India's northern frontier from Ladakh to Assam and policing of that frontier which has hitherto required negligible military effort and expenditure would assume immediate practical importance.'[20]

Dayal was blunt, asserting that China's claims of liberating Tibet from Anglo-American influence were false. He pointed to the steady accumulation of PLA troops on the Tibetan borders and pleaded with Delhi to acknowledge that 'India's interest in Tibetan autonomy is, essentially, for its own security.'[21]

While Dayal was advising caution and self-defence, Panikkar was telling Chinese Vice Foreign Minister Zhang Hanfu that the Government of India 'never had nor do they have now any political or territorial ambition in Tibet' and they only wished to stabilise the Chinese-Indian border.[22] This statement was welcomed by the Chinese government, though Peking was now growing impatient.

It had long been expecting Shakabpa to come to Peking, but he was dragging his feet in New Delhi instead. Peking had had enough reassurance from New Delhi to know that it would neither interfere nor discuss the issue. The war in Korea was throttling Chinese space for manoeuvre, particularly with the American involvement and the arrival of the US Seventh Fleet in the Taiwan Straits.

Zhou once again told Panikkar that Tibet was its internal problem and it did not even have a semi-independent status.[23] If this was meant to be reassurance, it failed to find its mark with the Indian prime minister. Nehru cautioned Panikkar that an invasion of Tibet would upset the already unstable equilibrium in the Himalayas. Matters were already on a knife-edge with security concerns in the wake of the Korean war and the American bombing of Manchuria. Since Tibet was already keen to negotiate, China should desist from invading outright since it could also destabilise already nervous border states in India.[24]

It speaks volumes about the prime minister's contrary moods that, at the same time that he told Panikkar this, he was also irritable with his political officers in Sikkim and Lhasa, who were warning that the communist arrival would unnerve people in Indian border states. The prime minister felt these messages expressed an unnecessary nervousness, since he did not believe 'any such attempt at pressure tactics is likely to succeed because, ultimately, we have no effective sanctions'.[25] India could do little more than give diplomatic support to Tibet in so far as it was feasible.

Nehru left it to Panikkar to take these views, however best he could, to the Chinese government. This Panikkar obediently did, only to receive the blunt retort that 'China did not recognise that Tibet enjoys anything like a semi-autonomous status'.

When he reported the outcome of this meeting to Nehru, Panikkar proceeded to annoy the prime minister exceedingly by likening what was happening in Tibet to 'our own attitude towards Hyderabad'. Perhaps he knew this would incense Nehru, for he added soothingly, 'They [the Chinese] will not now proceed to attack Tibet unless all efforts at peaceful settlement have been exhausted and secondly, they realise that India will not tolerate any kind of interference with her established boundaries.'[26]

But this wasn't an official stand from China. It was Panikkar's perception, one he was relaying to comfort the worried prime minister. It was also very wide of the mark, considering Zhou's blunt rejection of any Indian rights or influence in Tibet.[27]

To Delhi, China continued being superbly vague, even though India via Panikkar kept insisting that it wanted nothing in Tibet but the continuance of its own historic and legal rights and the recognition of the boundary.[28] It is at this exact juncture and in its latest assurance to Peking on 24 August 1950 that New Delhi proceeded to make a faux pas for the ages. Within the pages of this document was the line: 'the forthcoming negotiations (between Lhasa and Peking) will result in a harmonious adjustment of legitimate Tibetan claim to autonomy with the framework of *Chinese sovereignty* [emphasis mine]'.[29]

The use of the word 'sovereignty' was disastrous. It negated every assurance India had made to Tibet that Delhi intended to respect Lhasa's autonomy under Chinese suzerainty. China now naturally believed that India had finally recognised Tibet as part of China.

The devil sat in the details.

Later, Panikkar would be accused of being the man who switched the words *suzerainty* with *sovereignty*. So much credence did this gossip attain that M.O. Matthai, Nehru's wily, catty private secretary, would write about it in his memoirs: 'A telegram was sent to Panikkar authorising him to formally communicate to the Chinese Government India's recognition of Chinese suzerainty over

Tibet. Panikkar changed the world into "sovereignty." Later, when questioned, Panikkar took shelter behind the familiar excuse of corruption in transmission of the cypher telegram.'[30]

This is almost certainly untrue. However, the former foreign secretary Nirupama Rao says, 'Suzerainty itself, it must be acknowledged, has had little legal significance or operability in the post-1945 world. Sovereignty is the key word,' Rao writes in her book, *Fractured Himalaya*. 'But could Panikkar have been more elliptical in his communication with the Chinese, leaving the whole issue of Chinese sovereignty over Tibet an open question, not requiring such immediate endorsement by an official representative of New Delhi? Perhaps he could have.'[31] She argues that Panikkar was a seasoned geopolitician, a man who was not careless with words and who knew the weight of semantics.

Avtar Singh Bhasin strongly disagrees that the choice would have been his to make: 'In any communication coming from headquarters for delivery to the host government, ambassadors are not allowed to make any change.'[32]

Importantly, Panikkar was operating on the basis of not just instructions from New Delhi, but with a degree of consistent ambiguity about the position of Tibet. New Delhi had never gone firm on a policy towards Tibet until the communist regime came to power, and even then, it scrambled to find its footing in a rapidly evolving situation. Records indicate that Delhi was to blame here; two months and twenty-four days later, Delhi would tell Panikkar that 'the use of *sovereignty* in the 24 August note had been an oversight'.[33] Nehru wrote separately to Panikkar, lightly saying that the question of 'sovereignty' versus 'suzerainty' was rather academic.[34]

Thus, while Panikkar certainly didn't help matters by sending very mixed signals from China as he obediently tried to follow Nehru's brief, Delhi was to blame as well for its laxity and confusion with regard to Tibet.

In any event, China was annoyed. It charged India with attempting to influence and 'obstruct the exercise of its sovereign rights in Tibet' after saying that it recognised the question of Chinese sovereignty over Tibet. Panikkar was in such a pickle, caught between what he was seeing in reality and the line from New Delhi that he had to follow. He wondered morosely if any further clarification was even necessary, since the damage was already done.[35]

Chapter 48

Tibet

TOWARDS THE END OF 1950, THE REPORTS PILING UP ABOUT INDIA'S MAN in Peking were too snide and vicious to ignore. It was not just his superiors in New Delhi who didn't like Panikkar or the hold he seemed to have over the Indian prime minister. Subimal Dutt, India's future foreign secretary, would savagely describe Panikkar as 'a man without moral compass'. [1] Inevitably, gossip would carry to Panikkar's ears.

The lonely, beleaguered Indian ambassador in Peking kept himself busy, immersing himself in travelling around China or writing. But the developing diplomatic imbroglio weighed heavy on his mind. He distracted himself in September by writing to Zionist leader Emannuel Olsvanger. Israel had just been recognised as an independent nation by India, and Panikkar felt it was the right time to make contact with Zionist leaders and welcome the creation of Israel. He then added, 'This is one of the few occasions when the Government of India may be said to have been behind its own public opinion, for you know very well, as a result of your wide travels in India, that public opinion was almost wholeheartedly in favour of an early recognition of your government. There was also never any doubt of the friendliest feelings that both the government and the people of India had towards the State of Israel.'[2] This was a personal telegram, but it is remarkable nonetheless, especially given Panikkar's current position as Indian ambassador in China and his prior position on the Indian delegation to the UNGA and indeed, his own country's official position on Palestine.

Shortly towards the end of September, succour was provided to Panikkar in the shape and form of Triloki Nath Kaul, who would serve as his deputy in Peking.

Short and stocky, with a receding hairline, piercing hazel eyes and bushy eyebrows, Kaul arrived in Peking with considerable apprehension. New Delhi had heard just a little too much about K.M. Panikkar and the trouble he was causing over Tibet. Kaul had no idea what to expect, though he admitted freely that he had been asked by Bajpai to 'keep an eye on the ambassador in Peking, who allegedly had a tendency to be excessively pro-Chinese'.[3] But as he wrote in his memoirs later, his first meeting with Panikkar cleared his mind of its doubts.

The initial impression was a striking one: a short man, with 'Lenin's big head and a short Ho Chi-Minh beard',[4] with sharp penetrating eyes and the capability of being a captivating, always entertaining raconteur. 'I found him not only interesting to talk to but also stimulating, deliberately provocative, dramatic at times, but with a sense of history which enabled him to see far ahead and adjust his mind accordingly.'[5]

As the days passed and Kaul fell into the rhythm of life in Peking, he began to understand Panikkar better. Nehru had warned him that the older man was capable of being a little too dramatic, but Kaul, watching Panikkar at work, now understood why he was quite so popular in China, first with the nationalists and now clearly with the communists. This was an intellectual of the first water with a brilliant mind, a fine sense of dry humour and the rare capacity to negotiate skilfully under pressure. Panikkar, unlike everything Kaul had heard, was not arrogant about the vast scope of his knowledge. He adjusted to every conversation, with a skill Kaul wished he possessed too.

'He did not put you off by a show of his superior mind but won your confidence and admiration by his skilful probing, encouraging you to express your opinions and keeping his options open. He was not dogmatic but pragmatic.'[6]

Kaul had heard from Bajpai and Nehru and indeed, from American foreign policy mandarins, that Panikkar had been swept off his feet by the communists, but on the contrary, 'he seemed to have a prejudice against the USSR, which he balanced by his admiration for new China so as not to appear anti-communist'.[7]

As New Delhi and Peking wrestled over Tibet, characteristically, Panikkar threw himself into writing his next book. The result of those labours, *Asia and Western Dominance*, would be published in 1953.

September edged into winter in Peking and Kaul noticed that the stress was beginning to tell on Panikkar. Gouri fell seriously ill that winter. Doctors diagnosed her with rheumatic fever, but her health remained tenuous at best throughout the end of 1950 and early 1951. She couldn't breathe if she lay down, which meant she had to sleep sitting up. Rest eluded her and she was constantly plagued by fever. 'Once or twice, we feared for her life,' Panikkar remembered.[8]

Caught between looking after Gouri and the constant tension that his work entailed, Panikkar was rarely in office. Kaul tried to persuade him to spend a little more time in the office, even going to the extent of changing the décor in the hopes of attracting the aesthete in the ambassador. But Panikkar stuck to his habit of coming in for not more than an hour a day. He told Kaul bluntly that he found most of the diplomatic representatives 'rather dull'. His main points of contact among foreign legations were the British and the Swiss, while Kaul ran around networking with the Soviets, the Burmese and the others. Having a deputy in Peking was some relief for Panikkar, who took to calling Kaul over every evening for a cup of tea or a drink. Over drinks and snacks, the two men would chat about home, the Cold War, America, the Soviets and China. 'He would tell me, with a twinkle in his eye, about how he had hoodwinked some of the Western representatives,' Kaul remembered. 'They used to flock to him every time he met Chou En-lai or other Chinese leaders to get some crumbs of information to send to their Foreign Offices. Panikkar took an almost mischievous delight in sending them off the trail.'[9]

This was being a little too honest for Kaul, who was slightly alarmed. He remonstrated with Panikkar, suggesting that perhaps he should not mislead his colleagues. But to his consternation, Panikkar merely laughed, waving them away as a 'bunch of fools', and adding that 'he had utter contempt for them'.[10]

Dismayed as he was by this sort of behaviour, Kaul couldn't help admitting that working with a man so intelligent was a delight. 'He and I worked as a team, and kept no secrets from each other.'[11] If they differed in their theoretical and academic analyses, Panikkar would goad Kaul into reciting the different manifestos to find out where exactly they differed. Kaul didn't mind in the least. Working with Panikkar, he found, was a bit like working with a rather eccentric but brilliant professor.

In between work, Panikkar would take Kaul around Peking, sometimes by themselves and sometimes with Devaki and her best friend from England, a Chinese girl named Christine. The two girls were often away, travelling across China themselves. For Devaki, being in communist China was a delight. To her own travels, she brought her unique sense of history and politics and the fluent Russian she had learned in England. She also seriously alarmed China-watchers in Delhi, the United Kingdom and the United States by indulging in a little pro-communist journalism of her own. In an article she published in the *Indian Daily Mail* in March 1951, Devaki defended the PRC's alliance with the Soviet Union. 'Naturally China prefers help from a country which treats her as an equal and is a friend rather than from countries which will take every opportunity to disrupt the new regime.'[12] She railed against the devious methods of the United States and the propaganda spread by 'a capitalist press, including our own'.

Unsurprisingly, this article was enough to have Devaki put immediately under surveillance by an aghast CIA. A daughter so openly communist could hardly have been beneficial to a beleaguered Panikkar, but he refused to see how his daughter's ideologies were anyone else's business but her own.

A historian himself, Panikkar was acutely aware of the depthless history that China possessed. The Old City of Peking remained his favourite. Kaul would remember it as the centre that held the balance between north and south China, just a few hours away from the Great Wall and the famous Ming Tombs. Panikkar showed him around the Temple of Heaven, the Nine Dragon Pagoda, the Forbidden City and Tiananmen Square. On long holidays, they would go off to Peita Ho near the sea, where a cottage could be rented. Panikkar, who loved his food, introduced his deputy to Peking's narrowest and most winding streets, most of which ironically housed the city's best restaurants, where Kaul was revolted by the ambassador's delight in frog's legs, monkey's brain and python's heart. On weekends, Panikkar took Kaul to discover Peking's many beautiful museums, or shopping for Ming porcelain, silks or the famous Tang dynasty horses. The Indian ambassador, his deputy discovered, was a great connoisseur of the arts. He enjoyed the opera both for its dramatic opulence and for its effectiveness in conveying propagandist messages.[13]

The two men talked wistfully of India sometimes, and Panikkar remembered the old days and how things had changed with partition. 'He delighted in running down people whom he called "Somnathists" or revivalists, who wanted to rebuild old temples desecrated by some of the Muslim invaders,' Kaul remembered. 'He was vehemently secular in his outlook and non-religious with a vengeance.'[14] Neither Panikkar nor Kaul had the time to travel out of Peking in 1950, since geopolitics dominated much of their time. But in the capital alone, it was clear that there was a new energy, 'an evangelical atmosphere everywhere and complete faith in Mao's leadership'.[15]

But there were differences that both Indians noticed. There was, for instance, no individual privacy. Everyone was a member of a group and led a group life. Nationwide movements against corruption were launched with merciless efficiency and no compassion was shown to anyone considered to be an enemy. Foreigners were suspect. Contact with them was forbidden, a fact that made it hard to build a network among people who were not authorised government officials.

On 3 September 1950, Panikkar had Zhou over for dinner. The Chinese premier, in a gesture of friendly attention (which the Chinese had become remarkably adept at) brought his wife with him. The main subjects for discussion were China's apprehensions regarding Formosa and the bombing of Manchuria. Reporting on his conversation with Zhou over dinner, Panikkar told Delhi what China was worried about was actually Xinjiang. Peking had no intentions of 'taking immediate military action against Tibet itself'.[16]

Whether Nehru believed this or not at this juncture is something we will never know, but three days later, on 6 September, the prime minister met the defeated Shakabpa and warned him that 'Indian diplomatic support was available only for autonomy. The alternative was Chinese invasion. Tibetans must make a choice between war and peaceful settlement.'[17]

Neither man was truly transparent in this conversation.

Nehru didn't tell Shakabpa that he wasn't sure if Tibet would really enjoy the same 'autonomy' as before. Shakabpa on his part didn't tell Nehru that he was continuing talks with the Americans or that he had been promised aid to resist Chinese occupation.

Across the Himalayas, China was running out of patience as the months edged towards winter. There was now a growing belief that UN forces would cross the 38th parallel into the north. Peking was worried about the Yalu River being crossed in the aftermath of the Battle of Inchon. On 21 September, Zhou met Panikkar and told him bluntly that since 'the UN claimed to have no obligations towards China, she also had none to the UN'.[18]

Panikkar was severely taken aback at this outspoken statement of Chinese policy. This meant that, if the US-led UN forces were to cross the 38th parallel, China would fight. He confirmed this suspicion a few days later in a chat with the Chinese acting chief of staff Nie Rongzhen, who frankly said that China was bent on a more aggressive policy. It no longer cared about consequences. These points formed the basis for Panikkar's report to Delhi in which he said that India was no longer in a position to offer counsel to China without being misconstrued. China was unlikely to directly involve itself in Korea unless a world war broke out with the UN forces crossing the 38th parallel. Horrified at Panikkar's report, Nehru wrote immediately to Zhou, praising Chinese restraint under the circumstances.[19]

Zhou did not deign to reply.

Instead, in his official report to the National Committee, the Chinese premier explicitly stated what China intended to do: 'The Chinese people absolutely will not tolerate foreign aggressor nor will they SPINELY tolerate seeing their neighbour being SAVAGELY invaded by imperialists ... There is no doubt that China views international situation as menacing her security and independence and will fight if American forces try to occupy Korean territory.'[20]

On 3 October 1950, Panikkar was awakened at midnight, and his steward nervously told him that Chen Jiakang, the director general of Asian Affairs in the PRC foreign ministry, wished to speak with him downstairs. Bundling himself hastily into his dressing gown, Panikkar hurried downstairs to the drawing room. Chen told him courteously that Zhou En-lai wanted to see him immediately.[21] At Zhou's residence half an hour later, the table was set for tea for two. Zhou, Panikkar recalled later, was 'as courteous and charming as ever', and while he apologised for awakening the Indian ambassador at this mean hour of the night, he simply stated that 'if the Americans cross the 38th parallel, China will be forced to intervene in Korea'.[22] His demeanour gave no sign of worry, nerves or agitation, and he smiled as he offered Panikkar a second cup of tea.

Panikkar rushed back to the embassy and cabled New Delhi at half past one in the morning. The next day, Nehru lost no time in letting Truman and Attlee know what was happening.

With the second largest contingent in Korea, Britain was alarmed. Provoking China in Korea could also lead to an attack on Hong Kong. The stakes were high for London. The British Joint Chiefs of Staff were led by the commander of the British forces in India and Burma during the Second World War, Field Marshal Sir William Slim, who knew a great deal about China. Slim had been worried since July that moving north of the 38th parallel would provoke Chinese intervention. When Panikkar's message arrived in London, it reinforced his fears. But the British intelligence community, led by the Joint Intelligence Committee (JIC), which prepared synthesised estimates for the British prime minister, was more cautious. It dismissed Zhou's warning as not being specific enough.

For his part, Truman was not convinced. Even though the head of the China desk at the state department emphasised that this was unlikely to be a bluff, the US president didn't trust the Indian ambassador at all. 'The problem that arose in connection with these reports was that Mr. Panikkar had in the past played the game of the Chinese Communists fairly regularly, so that his statement could not be taken as that of an impartial observer,' he would write in his memoirs. 'It might very well be no more than a relay of Communist propaganda.'[23]

It speaks volumes about how deep the distrust of Panikkar was already running that an American president felt this way and was unafraid to say so. Indeed, the American establishment at this time, whether it was diplomatic or CIA, unanimously suspected Panikkar of communist tendencies and of being singularly untrustworthy.[24] Dean Acheson, for instance, cuttingly dismissed Panikkar's warning as the 'mere vapourings of a Panicky Panikkar'.[25] Walter McConaughy, the former US consul general in Shanghai, was asked for his opinion of the situation on the ground. He replied that not only was Panikkar a 'man without integrity of character and without deep moral convictions', but that McConaughy was convinced—though on what basis remains unclear—that Panikkar was so consumed with anti-colonial sentiment that he had developed an aversion to the Western world. As a result, he was heavily leaning towards China and any dispatch he sent from Peking must be 'taken with a large grain of salt'. As he rather nastily put it, 'Panikkar's Mephistophelian quality is not limited to his spade beard.'[26]

When he heard that the United States had refused to take his reports seriously, Panikkar was deeply upset. In his diary, he wrote, 'America has knowingly elected for war, with Britain following. The Chinese armies now concentrated on the Yalu will intervene decisively in the fight. Probably some of the Americans want that. They probably feel that this is an opportunity to have a show down with China. In any case MacArthur's dream has come true. I only hope it does not turn into a nightmare.'[27]

It is a sad, frustrated entry, which is how Panikkar felt those days. The divisions in opinion about him were not a secret. In a telegram, the Indian prime minister had tried to comfort him. 'All this, of course, does not affect our policy in the slightest. It only confirms it, and shows the immaturity of American judgement ... I'm supposed to have "sold out" to Mao through your bad influence. Panikkar is referred to as "Panicky". It really is amazing how great nations are governed by very small people.'[28]

But Panikkar was beyond comfort at this point. He was never a very expressive man, nor was he given to public displays of emotion, but for his loyalty to his country to be thus called into question was too much for him. His refuge now was to wrap himself in a cloak of cold hauteur. It did nothing to endear him to colleagues who were already suspicious of him—and the events of that winter only proved to Panikkar's critics that the Indian prime minister was being guided by an ambassador who was telling him what he wanted to hear, and more damagingly, seemingly did not know how to read the events on the ground.

On 7 October, 9,000 seasoned PLA troops crossed the Yangtse River into Tibet. They were met by a terrified, poorly trained force of 4,000 Tibetan soldiers who were rapidly overwhelmed. By 11 October, the People's Liberation Army was nearing Chamdo, a large town in eastern Tibet, on the way to Lhasa. The regional governor tried frantically to contact his capital to let them know what was coming but there was no response. Four days later, in the midst of chaos, Lhasa finally replied.

'Right now it is the period of the Kashags' picnic and they are all participating in this,' the horrified governor was airily told. 'Your telegrams are being decoded and then we'll send you a reply.'

Incensed, the governor hung up on the call, but not before he had been betrayed into shrieking, 'Shit the picnic!'

On 15 October 1950, Chamdo would have his last communication with Lhasa.[29] It was also the beginning of the end for Tibet. The PLA entered Lhasa on 26 October, carrying portraits of Mao. The battle had been quick and savage. Nearly 5,700 Tibetans had been killed in a matter of days.[30] The Dalai Lama, then just about fifteen years old, would write mournfully later that he was now 'faced with the prospect of leading my country to war'.[31]

Five days after China invaded Tibet, Mao sent a terse memo to his ambassador in India, to deliver to Nehru personally. In this message, he repeated what Zhou had been telling Panikkar all these days: that 'Tibet is Chinese territory' and so, as a 'domestic problem', the PLA 'must enter Tibet'. He also made clear his intentions in Korea: 'China cannot tolerate seeing its neighbour being invaded and do nothing. The responsibilities for spreading the war are for the invading countries to bear. The people of China love peace. However, in order to protect peace, they are never afraid of wars against invasion.'[32]

Nehru was in despair.

'Zhou En-lai and his colleagues should be aware of our friendly feelings towards China,' he wrote unhappily to Panikkar. '[I]n adopting this attitude, we have often displeased many of the western powers, but we have followed our own independent line because we considered it right. Even as regards Tibet, we have sought no special or economic advantages for ourselves; we have merely asked for the continuation of such relations that have been built up between Tibet and us owing to geographical contiguity and cultural and economic links. All that we have suggested for Tibet is autonomy within the framework of Chinese sovereignty to be attained by peaceful negotiations.'[33]

If the prime minister was unhappy now, his biographer Sarvepalli Gopal pointed out later that it was largely because his view of China and its intentions had been naïve.[34] His idealistic vision of Asia, with India and China as the two largest powers and partners on the map, lay in smithereens.

There was simply too much happening too fast. For instance, as Avtar Singh Bhasin points out, once again, the word 'sovereignty' had been repeated in Nehru's last letter to Panikkar. It may have been a letter meant for Panikkar's eyes alone, but the use of the word itself—and by the prime minister no less—pushed it into common usage.

Nearly sixty years later, and even with access to far more documents on the subject than there were before, the fissures within the MEA itself and Panikkar's own decidedly shaky reportage make it hard to pin down a single scapegoat or blame a single culprit. The archives spill over with correspondence on the subject. The documents show clearly that signs of a Chinese invasion of Tibet were entirely visible, and had been for some time, as well as the fact that, over time, India had continued to fail to understand China's motivations regarding Tibet.

Ever since the People's Republic of China had come into being in 1949, Peking had been clear that Tibet was part of the five races, and that it belonged to China. But India's assumption that British rights in Tibet would carry over to independent India was also where the trouble lay. K.P.S. Menon, for instance, observed, 'I doubt whether anything will be gained by seeking clarification whether the new Government would be prepared to honour its international obligations vis-a-vis India, flowing from treaties between India and China. These treaties between China and India were originally treaties between China and Great Britain; we have inherited them as the successor Government in India. The Chinese Government may be inclined to take the view, as the Kuomintang Government themselves took of many treaties in the nineteenth century, that they were "unequal treaties." The treaties which really concern us are those relating to Tibet. The provisions of many old treaties with China regarding Tibet have been superseded by the events since 1910 and by the tripartite convention of 1914, which India and Tibet have ratified but not China. Any attempt to have the position clarified will lead to endless controversy.'[35]

Therefore, the notion that a margin of ambiguity could favour India was not just Panikkar's idea. But Panikkar's memoir suggests that the Chinese hadn't said a word about any such thing. Mere 'rumours' of an invasion, he avers, were circulating.

This is an odd claim to make. In August 1950, Liu Po-Cheng, head of the Southern Command of the PLA, issued a proclamation to Tibetans stating that the People's Liberation Army would 'soon march towards Tibet with object of driving out the British and American aggressive forces so as to make Tibetans return to the Great Family of the People's Republic of China'.[36] Panikkar repeated this message verbatim in a cable to New Delhi. His cable was responded to by New Delhi, which expressed 'grave concern'[37] about this decision of the Chinese government. In the same breath, New Delhi repeated that it had no designs on Tibet. It was merely 'animated solely by desire to see Sino-Tibetan relations adjusted by peaceful means on basis of enduring friendship among three countries, China, Tibet and India'. An invasion of Tibet 'may NOT only be described as aggression but may threaten world-peace'.[38] In closing, Panikkar was asked to relay this message to Zhou. New Delhi anticipated that it would be rebuffed, but that the 'risk must be taken in the larger interests of world peace'.[39] All of this archival correspondence makes it clear that Panikkar was fully aware that an invasion was indeed about to take place.

As the Indian Mission in Lhasa began to report the clashes in Chamdo and its consequences, Loy Henderson met Bajpai in Delhi to seek confirmation of what was happening on the ground. He was told that a strong message had been sent to Panikkar, asking him for immediate confirmation of the invasion. In addition, Bajpai said, he had sent a heated telegram to Nehru in which he had stated clearly that if the news of the invasion was correct, then it should be regarded as a sign of indifference to Indian considerations and a lack of China's appreciation for India's efforts on its behalf. 'After it [India] had conveyed to the world that China would intervene in Korea in case US forces should enter North Korea, it would be ironical if China, instead of intervening in Korea, should now invade Tibet.'[40] Henderson was annoyed, believing that Tibet had 'lost heart' because of Delhi's flip-flopping, but neither he nor Acheson wanted to pressure India too hard.[41]

Walter McConaughy of the State Department had a different view of things. He reported to the assistant secretary for Far Eastern Affairs that 'Panikkar showed great reluctance to carry out his instructions to counsel the Chinese Communists against an armed invasion of Tibet … Even when the Communist Chinese military leaders were openly voicing threats against Tibet, he was discounting the possibility of any military action there.'[42]

In their book, *Tibet: An Unfinished Story*, Lezlee and Stefan Halper unearthed new declassified documents from the archives of the Chinese Ministry of Foreign Affairs that not only tell a different story but add a bizarre dimension of outright deception. According to these documents, Panikkar had been told by Vice Foreign Minister Zhang Hanfu as early as 12 August 1950 that 'military operations toward Tibet have begun, or will begin shortly'. Halper and Halper state, on the basis of the documents they accessed, that the Indian ambassador chose not to inform his prime minister that the People's Liberation Army were amassing on Tibet's borders in preparation for an invasion.[43] As Sarvepalli Gopal would write later, 'Because of the shortcomings of Indian diplomacy in Peking, the Chinese reacted to India's protest with a surprise which was not wholly feigned.'[44] Gopal added damningly, to cover his own discrepancies in reportage, Panikkar 'explained to his own Government what he described as sudden change of Chinese policy in Tibet, by their expectations of a general war'.[45]

Why would Panikkar have refrained from reporting such a crucial piece of information to a prime minster to whom he was undoubtedly deeply loyal? Halper and Halper certainly don't offer any explanation of this. On the whole, this seems bizarre. Why would he have committed a major breach of protocol that would definitely come with damaging consequences?

A few days later, following up on India's expressed alarm at the invasion, Zhou wrote frostily to Nehru, 'On 31 August 1950, the Chinese Ministry of Foreign Affairs informed the Indian Government through Ambassador Panikkar that the Chinese People's Liberation Army was going to take action soon in west Sikang, according to set plans, and expressed the hope that the Indian Government would assist the delegation of the local authorities of Tibet, so that it might arrive in Peking in mid-September.'[46]

Zhou was backed by the director general of the Ministry of Foreign Affairs, Chen Jiakang, who stated that he had specifically informed Panikkar on 30 August 1950 that the PLA would be going into Sikang. 'This is not a new plan. This is a determined plan,' he said at a meeting of senior Chinese officials. 'I remember informing Ambassador Panikkar of the point on August 30th, while visiting the Ambassador with Director General Qiao Guanhua.'[47]

A declassified foreign ministry memo of the discussion between Panikkar and Zhang Hanfu on 21 October 1950, a day after PLA troops crossed the Yalu river, drives the point home: 'Any person who obstructs the liberation of Tibet and opposes our peaceful liberation must bear all responsibilities.'[48] It was not only Panikkar who was told of Chinese intentions in Tibet. The gist of it was repeated in separate conversations with Chinese officials in a battery of meetings between 10 and 26 October 1950.

On 26 October, Menon called on the Chinese counsellor, Shen Chien, and referred him to the reports of China's invasion of Tibet. Icily, Menon said that India had expected China to show the basic courtesy of informing India of its decision and that this would set back China's entry to the UNSC. This line of argument had no impact on Shen, who responded only to say that Tibet was a part of China, so to call it an invasion was erroneous.[49]

Meanwhile, Panikkar persisted with his line that China's decision to launch an attack on Tibet was prompted by the bombing in Manchuria by the United States, by the ongoing war in Korea and its extension toward the northeastern borders of China. As he wrote to the MEA at the time, 'PRECIPITANCY of action in Tibet is linked ... with the possibility they foresee of a general war in which they fear that unfriendly countries may stir up trouble in that area.'[50] Whether anyone paid heed to this or not at this juncture is unknown.

Astonishingly, Nehru addressed a press conference on 27 October in which he maintained that China's real intentions were not clear. There were reports directly to the contrary, with the addition of news from Lhasa that the internal situation was dire and that Tibet wanted to appeal to the United Nations. Lhasa was horrified to hear broadcasts on All India Radio denying reports of a Chinese invasion even as Peking Radio was loudly blaring the exact opposite.[51] On 30 October, Zhang Hanfu told Panikkar, 'The People's Republic of China would like to make it clear that Tibet is an integral part of Chinese territory and the problem of Tibet is entirely a domestic problem of China. The Chinese PLA must enter Tibet, liberate the Tibetan people and defend the frontiers of China. This is the resolved policy of the Central People's Government.'[52] To make sure this time that the message reached its intended destination, Ambassador Yuan, the Chinese ambassador in Delhi called upon K.P.S. Menon and repeated verbatim what Peking had told Panikkar.[53]

Declassified documents from the Chinese foreign ministry show that both Mao and Nehru were fully aware that these conversations were happening. Mao approved the issues to be discussed by Yuan, and Menon came armed with personal notes from Nehru, specifically telling the Chinese that, for Nehru, Tibet was a part of China.[54] More to the point, the MEA and the prime minister himself had long been expecting an invasion. Nehru himself had predicted an invasion in 1949, and his MEA officials agreed that it was inevitable that matters would, at some point, come to a head in Tibet.[55]

Against this backdrop, the frantic cables from New Delhi to Peking asking Panikkar to let China's political leadership know that invasion would have 'serious consequences' assume the appearance of rubber-stamp protests. It was clear by now that China cared not a jot about consequences.[56]

It wanted Tibet and Tibet it would have.

CHAPTER 49

Aftermath

THE INDIAN MEDIA WAS UP IN ARMS.

Every newspaper was dominated by front-page headlines of the invasion of Tibet. In a public speech in the capital, Sardar Patel said angrily, 'A peaceful country like Tibet has been invaded and it may not survive. We did not think this would happen. We were maintaining friendly relations with China.'[1] He accused China of not accepting India's advice against military action in Tibet: 'We do not know what will be the outcome of this. Tibet is a religious-minded country. There has been no aggression from its side. But when one is intoxicated with power, one does not realize what one is doing.'[2]

Patel was as angry behind the scenes as he was in public. On 7 November 1950, weeks before he died, he wrote to Nehru, laying out his fears and proposed strategy under the changed circumstances. The Sardar took a bleak view of both Panikkar's and China's actions. 'I regret to say that neither of them comes out well as a result,' he wrote. 'The Chinese Government has tried to delude us by professions of peaceful intention. My own feeling is that at a crucial period they managed to instil into our Ambassador a false sense of confidence in their so-called desire to settle the Tibetan problem by peaceful means.'[3]

For Patel, the invasion showed that China represented both an internal and external threat to India. It did not see India as a friend despite Delhi's attempts to convince it of friendship and trust. Patel slammed the Government of India's response to the invasion, believing that Peking would see accommodation as a sign of weakness. He called for a threat assessment; analysis of India's existing and required defence capabilities; reconsideration of Delhi's support for Peking at the UN; strengthening of India's northeast and of Bhutan, Nepal and Sikkim; internal security measures in India's border states; improvement of transport and communication lines to the border; manning of key border posts; reassessment of India's Tibet presence and its position on the McMahon Line; and, finally, the re-examination of India's external relations—including with the United States.[4]

In this entire screed, Panikkar comes off poorly. 'Our Ambassador has been at great pains to find an explanation or justification for Chinese policy and actions.' Patel said grimly. 'As the External Affairs Ministry remarked in one of their telegrams, there was a lack of firmness and unnecessary apology in one or two representations that he made to the Chinese Government on our behalf.'[5]

Patel was not the only one critical of Panikkar at this point. The ambassador came in for strident criticism from the Ministry of External Affairs in New Delhi about his 'half-hearted' representations to Peking about Tibet. K.P.S Menon raged, 'While we have been expressing our grave concern on a Chinese invasion, the Ambassador does not appear to have conveyed our sentiments with anything like the force with which we expected him to do so. He does not appear to have realised that not merely India's honour, but her interests are involved in the satisfactory settlement of the Tibetan problem. The McMahon Line, our trade marts in Gyantse and Yatung and our representation in Lhasa, all these will now be in jeopardy and more than these the interests of world peace will be retarded.'[6]

Scenting blood in the water, G.S. Bajpai attacked as well. 'The Ambassador, for some inexplicable reason, seems to persist in his erroneous conceptacle of Chinese claims and Chinese maps. Even in his note, he expresses the earnest hope that further military action will not be necessary, conceding by implication that such military action as may have been taken already was necessary.'[7]

Bajpai's criticism found a kindred spirit in Sardar Patel. The two men discussed the implications of the Chinese advance regularly. On 3 November 1950, Bajpai laid out a note on a prospective way forward. He suggested that India's mission in Lhasa and offices in Gyantse and Yadong be withdrawn as a measure of protest. 'The alternative would be war,' he felt, '... for which we are not prepared.'[8] As a matter of strategic importance, Bajpai felt India needed to declare that the McMahon Line was 'our frontier'.[9]

Patel read Bajpai's note with keen interest. He wrote personally to Bajpai when he was finished. His letter was short and blunt. Chinese moves here had upset all of India's security calculations. Now India would have to keep in mind a number of factors—its northeastern frontier, China's political ambitions, the likelihood of a boundary dispute. In his view, China was a 'thoroughly unscrupulous, unreliable and determined power practically at our doors'. Any friendly or appeasing approaches to China could 'either be mistaken for weakness or would be exploited in furtherance of their ultimate aim'.[10]

The prime minister was shattered.

It was the beginning of a long downward spiral in his attempt to cling on to a vision of a friendly China that would cooperate with him in his visions for a postcolonial Asia. How could the Tibetan border have been threatened thus, he demanded. Whatever the situation and reasons for attack, Nehru insisted that they were 'without foundation'. When Panikkar tried to explain again that China's actions were driven by its larger fears about regional security in which it felt that India was playing a Machiavellian role, Nehru cast it aside bitterly. If that was what the Chinese thought, he wrote back, 'they are less intelligent than I thought them to be'.[11]

No, he insisted, China's actions were 'incomprehensible' to him.[12]

Again, how Peking's actions, of which it had not only been repeatedly warning but which Nehru himself had foreseen just a year ago, were incomprehensible under the circumstances is baffling.

But for now, matters were deadlocked. Delhi continued to pressure Panikkar to remind the Chinese of their promises and relationship with India. On his part, Panikkar continued to remind Delhi that these were no longer important considerations for the Chinese.

But his word had ceased to matter in Delhi.

On 30 October, Bajpai told the US ambassador that he had drafted a strongly worded note to the Chinese foreign office. He read it out to Henderson. The note accused China of acting with a 'certain amount of deceit'. It dismissed Chinese fears that an 'unliberated Tibet presented danger to Communist Chinese security, in view of the ambitions of the great powers in that region'.[13]

Discussing the note with Nehru, Henderson asked the Indian prime minister how Washington could help. Emphatically, Nehru responded, 'The US can be most helpful—by doing nothing.' His words proved what Henderson had been suspecting for a while: India was going to stay the course, despite this bitter setback. Nehru stressed the long-term advantages of a working relationship with a regime that was clearly here to stay. He was clearly still inspired by Panikkar's earlier reports in which Mao had told him that 'India and China cannot afford to have war.'[14] Panikkar had also reported that Mao saw many similarities between India and China, and that would have only buffered Nehru's idea that the two countries could cooperate.

Now, Nehru set aside Patel's warnings. For him, it was clear that India currently lacked the military capacity to prevent the takeover of Tibet. Nor was it possible to undertake the kind of muscular military build-up that Patel envisioned in his letter. If India did that, Nehru believed that it would only serve as a provocation rather than a deterrent. Meanwhile, any attempt at stopping the Chinese advance would likely fail and lead to Chinese hostility towards India and constant insecurity at India's borders. Nor did Nehru think there would be any real Chinese military invasion of India in the 'foreseeable future'. But he did concede that 'gradual infiltration' across the border and Chinese occupation of disputed territory was possible—and indeed a risk. This required improving connectivity to India's tribal areas in the northeast, which were not well integrated with the country, and preparation to prevent any Chinese infiltration. In short, the Indian prime minister continued to believe that the best approach was reaching 'some kind of understanding' with China, as long as Peking desired the same.[15] Listening to this, Henderson reported back to the state department that India's Tibet policy had finally changed for good.

But even as Nehru tried to adjust his Tibet and China policy, he could not put aside his irrational rage towards Panikkar. 'We cannot help thinking that your representation to the Chinese government was weak and apologetic,' he wrote in cold fury in one letter. 'In fairness to the Chinese government as well as to ourselves, our views regarding the threatened invasion of Tibet and its probable repercussions should have been communicated to them clearly and unequivocally. This has evidently not been done ... the Chinese government's action has jeopardised our interests in Tibet and our commitments to Tibet and our persistent efforts to secure the recognition of China and the interests of world peace have suffered a serious setback.'[16]

Bajpai seized the moment to add in a swipe of his own. 'What interest the Ambassador thinks he may be serving by showing so much solicitude for the Chinese Government's policy of false excuses and wanton high-handedness towards Tibet passes my understanding,' he stormed. 'I feel it my duty to observe that, in handling the Tibetan issue with the Chinese government, our ambassador has allowed himself to be influenced more by the Chinese point of view, by Chinese claims, by Chinese maps and by regard for Chinese susceptibilities than by his instructions.'[17]

Panikkar was deeply hurt by this attack.

He tried to exonerate himself in a lengthy letter, but the prime minister was not impressed. It was the beginning of the decline of Panikkar's diplomatic career. Nehru would never forgive him for China. In hindsight and given the heaviness and ambiguity of the odds stacked against him, this is unfair to Panikkar. He had his flaws, but he was not the only one to blame for an equally flawed policy toward China and Tibet.

Nor was Tibet the only problem that Panikkar and India faced at the moment.

Truman and his men refused to take India's warnings—coming as they did from Panikkar—seriously. Consequently, on 7 October 1950, on American insistence, the UN General Assembly passed the

'Uniting for Peace' resolution empowering the UN command to enter North Korea. In truth of course, American troops were already on the ground and had been there since 1 October. As they advanced across the jungles of North Korea, the Chinese appeared, for the first few days, to buckle under the onslaught. It was enough time for Nehru and Panikkar to be jointly panned in the Western media and among Western diplomats for being fooled by the Chinese.

Dean Acheson's mocking sobriquet—Panicky Panikkar—now found its way into international headlines. For Panikkar, it was a time of immense embarrassment and humiliation. Not only had he been hauled over the coals for the Chinese invasion of Tibet, but he was now being publicly mocked for passing on—to his credit—very reliable intelligence, which could have prevented a war.

By early November 1950, it became clear that the soldiers the Chinese had sent in were only civilian volunteers. These boys had managed to enter North Korea via Manchuria and they were inflicting damaging blows on South Korean and US-led troops. As a result, on 8 November, the UN Security Council accepted a British resolution allowing China to appeal to the Council. The appeal, which was both bitter and acrimonious, resulted in a deadlock.[18] Britain sent John Hutchison, its ambassador in China, a message for Zhou to try and resolve the situation. 'It was a strange communication,' Panikkar would recall, 'an elucidation of the objectives of the United Nations in Korea, an assurance from Britain that Chinese boundaries would be respected.'[19]

Nehru cabled from Delhi instructing him to give full support to this, but Panikkar disagreed with the sense of the message. When Hutchison came to speak with him about it, Panikkar didn't mince words. 'I frankly told him that I doubted whether the Chinese would look at any proposal which did not include an offer of direct negotiations of the whole issue with them; and that I considered that the idea of Britain assuring China of the inviolability of her boundaries was patronizing, to say the least.'[20]

Still, he told Zhang Hanfu of the offer and told him that he would be well advised to use it as an opening for further talks. 'Though I put the arguments strongly, I could not have sounded very convincing,' he mused ruefully, 'for the simple reason that I was not convinced myself.'[21]

The silver lining to all this was that relations between India and China were slowly improving. By 8 November 1950, having read and digested Sardar Patel's note on foreign policy, and having received a conciliatory note from Peking, Nehru had absolved China of any 'studied deception', and charged China only with 'extreme discourtesy'.[22] Writing to Panikkar at the end of November, he insisted that the main goal was to avoid war and to maintain peace with China. 'These relations inevitably will depend on to some extent upon Chinese policy in Tibet.'[23]

Seizing gratefully at this lifeline, Panikkar set about restoring his good image in Peking and with Nehru. At the end of November, he hosted a dinner at which he persuaded A.K. Sen, a talented sarod artiste, to give a private performance at the Panikkar household. The guest list was small but exclusive, including most members of the Chinese foreign ministry, along with some Chinese intellectuals, writers and painters. It was a happy, relaxed evening after a long time, and as he smiled and talked with his guests, Panikkar 'couldn't help feeling that it was strange that such a peace should reign in Peking, when the whole world seemed to be frightened of developments in Korea'.

But peace, in those days, seemed to be an illusion.

A brief moment of happiness for the Panikkar family had come in November 1950, when Haima was married. But now, back in Peking, Gouri, whose health had been improving by inches, suffered a setback as the cold of that winter dug its claws into the city. So ill did she become that there were several points through December and January when she was at death's door. But Panikkar had no time to pay full attention to her or his family at this juncture.

On 1 December 1950, Truman announced that the United States was considering the feasibility of nuclear use in Korea. Not unnaturally, this caused a sensation, though Panikkar observed wryly that the Chinese were unmoved. Quickly, Nehru urged Atlee, who was going to Washington to meet Truman, to impress upon the US president the 'absolute necessity of avoiding use of the atom bomb' and to limit the authority of General MacArthur who was fuelling the war.[24]

It is interesting to see that, though Nehru might doubt Panikkar on Tibet, on the issue of Korea, he leaned heavily on the pragmatism of the ambassador. Indeed, Korea would become Panikkar's saving grace. His steering of India's diplomacy at this point would restore his credibility in Nehru's eyes and do much to restore his image as a diplomat and negotiator.

On 8 December, Nehru, through Panikkar, proposed to China to agree to a ceasefire to be followed by Great Power talks, demilitarisation and withdrawal of the forces to the 38th parallel. Both Nehru and Panikkar felt that the Chinese proposal for a complete withdrawal of UN forces from Korea as a precondition for ceasefire or negotiations, as demanded by the PRC representative to the United Nations Security Council, Wu Xiuquan, was impracticable.[25] Meanwhile, Nehru instructed B.N. Rau, who was chairing the UNGA that year, to insist on immediate negotiations to end hostilities and on assuring China that, following the cessation of hostilities, talks on Korea and Formosa would be held on an equal footing.[26]

On 11 December, Zhou sent for Panikkar. The two men had an hour-long conversation in which the premier, according to Panikkar, kept repeating, 'What do the Americans want? Do they want peace as we do? Are they going to persist in aggression? This Attlee-Truman communique clearly shows that they want war, not peace.'[27]

Panikkar replied soothingly that government policies should not be judged from communiques, but Zhou was impatient with this mollification, replying tersely, 'So far as the 38th parallel is concerned, it is we, China and India, who wanted to uphold it. But MacArthur has demolished it and it exists no longer.'[28] He demanded US withdrawal from Formosa, China's admission into the UN and the withdrawal of all foreign troops from Korea, following which the Korean problem would be solved by Koreans themselves.

It was enough to worry Panikkar intensely. He could see that 'the Chinese would not stop at the 38th parallel and the allies of America would be forced to trail behind in any action the U.S. proposed'.[29] His anxiety increased with the news that Truman had declared a national emergency in the United States. As an air of hysteria took hold, the only talk was of mobilisation and military preparedness. Watching the Chinese closely, Panikkar noted that the more agitated the Americans got, the calmer the Chinese became. 'They seemed to enjoy the reactions they were making on the Americans. The secrecy of the communist world gives you an uncanny feeling. This lack of reaction is even more frightening than if they had blustered and threatened.'[30]

India was working overtime at the United Nations to prevent another military conflict in the region. In January 1951, India sponsored a UN resolution, backed by Britain, which called for a ceasefire and negotiations. The United States supported it in the full knowledge that Peking would reject it. Peking did exactly that, triggering a wide wave of criticism against the Indian government. But Nehru still clung stubbornly to hope, publicly insisting that the Chinese response was not an 'outright rejection'.[31]

When Nehru's appeal for peace to Stalin and Acheson fell flat, Bajpai warned that India should avoid getting involved in efforts that did not have the support of the permanent members of the United Nations Security Council. In particular, he warned, there was a likelihood that the Soviet Union would not support this and that, at best, the United Kingdom and the United States would only be neutral. If that happened, India would be seen as having failed yet again.[32]

Nehru wasn't having it.

Still holding on to his fast-fading dreams of Asian solidarity, he insisted that 'all the troubles in the Far East arise from the failure of the rest of the world to adjust itself to the changes which have taken place in Asia'. By that yardstick, it was the United States that had erred in crossing the 38th parallel, despite Chinese (and Indian) warnings to the contrary. By refusing to come to the table for talks, the United States was, in Nehru's view, only compounding its mistakes.[33]

American commentators and policymakers alike were united in their collective frustration with Nehru. Many believed that he was playing into Peking's hands.[34] Henderson warned Bajpai that collective failure to check aggression would only lead to more bellicosity from

China.[35] Acheson couldn't understand 'what means India would propose to use to check aggression'.[36]As tensions between the United States and India built,Vijayalakshmi Pandit wrote anxiously to Bajpai, explaining her concerns over the 'considerable hostility' towards India as a result of various China-related disagreements.[37] Bajpai sighed mournfully in agreement. 'For the time being at any rate, we are isolated and that, over Kashmir and other issues, Pakistan and our enemies will exploit our isolation to the full.'[38]

The first inkling of how bad things were getting was when Delhi asked for food aid in the winter of 1950 and was told frankly by the US State Department that aid was dependent on India's approach to Kashmir and to Korea.

This was a mistake.

Nehru's hackles were instantly raised. 'We are a sensitive people and we react strongly to being cursed at and run down,' he said indignantly. 'Our general reaction, whenever any pressure is sought to be applied upon us by any country, is to resent it and maybe to go against it.'[39] Finally, India stated coldly that it would prefer a loan to a grant, but the entire fracas did nothing to ease tensions between the two countries.

The next steps were the legalities. In a resolution adopted by the UN General Assembly on 14 December, an appeal was made to China and the United States to declare a ceasefire, followed by steps for a Pacific settlement. A three-member ceasefire group, consisting of Nesrollah Entzam from Iran, B.N. Rau from India and Lester Pearson from Canada, was constituted to make recommendations on the 'basis on which a satisfactory ceasefire in Korea can be arranged'.[40] Rau reported to Nehru that an initiative from the Asian countries under the leadership of India had become inevitable to block the six-power American-sponsored resolution that sought to label China as aggressor. He added significantly that this was the best middle path open to the United Nations, based on Panikkar's assessment that a ceasefire would be acceptable to China if a preliminary understanding was reached on withdrawal of the UN forces and accepting China's claims to Formosa.[41]

These proposals were cabled to Panikkar in January 1951. The Indian ambassador stared at them in astonishment. 'My difficulty, which Mr. Nehru fully understood but Rau sitting in New York did not realize, was that I had no answer to the first question the Chinese were bound to ask: Have the proposals been approved by the American Government?'[42]

In fact, while encouraging Rau and others to put forward proposals intended to draw out the Chinese, the Americans had so far refused to commit themselves. In the proposals wired to Panikkar, there was no mention of Taiwan or of the Korean settlement. Nervously, Panikkar went to Zhang Hanfu and presented the proposals. He asked for nothing but their reaction. Zhang's response was equally simple: did these proposals also represent the Government of India's view?

Panikkar hadn't been expecting that question, but he managed to parry it deftly by saying that India didn't want to put out a view without considering Chinese reactions. The situation was only temporarily defused. But a real opportunity for some kind of progress came about within the first few weeks of January. On the evening of 12 January 1951, Panikkar received a telegram from Nehru, who was in London attending the Commonwealth Summit. He suggested a new conference on Korea 'without anything tacked to it'.[43]

At the moment, Panikkar was dining at T.N. Kaul's home with Chiao Kan-hua, the vice chairman of the Policy Committee of the foreign office, and Chen Jiakang, the director general of Asian Affairs. Their reaction seemed favourable to Nehru's suggestion, but this burst of enthusiasm received a sharp check the very next morning, when Radio Peking announced that the original Commonwealth proposals had been modified by the inclusion of a provision for a ceasefire prior to the negotiations, followed by a four-nation conference for the achievement of a settlement.

Panikkar was a little worried by the ceasefire clause and he was right to be, for the Chinese refused to consider it. On 15 January, Panikkar presented Zhang Hanfu with a tabular analysis of the Commonwealth Summit declaration. He had made a table showing how the present proposals differed from the previous ones, with the objective of showing the Chinese that they had nothing to be worried about. He was taking another considerable risk here, since Delhi had not authorised him to interpret the text on his own and offer elucidations in his personal capacity. But he told the Chinese that his views were 'in conformity' with the Indian prime minister's views. Since the matter was urgent and Nehru was away at Chequers for the weekend, Panikkar appeared to have no other choice.

Luckily, this gamble worked.

Next morning, there was word from the Chinese foreign office: Zhou En-lai would see Panikkar at nine o'clock that night. 'I cannot remember any occasion in my whole life when I was so excited,' Panikkar recalled later. He knew that on this meeting hinged everything Nehru had been working for to establish India in a position of power in the Cold War. A rejection now meant a defeat for Nehru. Panikkar was acutely aware of that and of the fact that this was a potential chance to compensate in some way for the disaster of Tibet. If he could manage to pull this off, perhaps bridges could be mended between himself and Nehru.

Hardly able to sit in one place, Panikkar could barely wait until the evening. He and Kaul arrived at the foreign office punctually. Zhou was not there as yet, so the Indians were received courteously by Chen Jiakang. Panikkar was bursting to ask him what the final decision was, but that would have been a breach of protocol. An agonising ten minutes passed, filled with pleasantries and niceties, before Zhou arrived, accompanied by his interpreter and Chiao Kan-hua.

From the first moment, it was clear to Panikkar that this was not going to be a rejection. The meeting lasted half an hour, during which Zhou fulsomely complimented Nehru and Panikkar as well for his exhaustive notes and memoranda. On 17 January, Panikkar cabled Zhou's reply.

The Chinese premier maintained that a ceasefire before negotiations would only give the United States 'a breathing space'. He indicated that the existing international obligations were not as clearly specified as the Cairo and Potsdam agreements. But he *did* give a set of counter proposals. For one, Zhou suggested a seven-power conference in China, comprising the PRC, the US, the USSR, the UK, France, Egypt and India, based on an agreement of withdrawal of non-Korean troops from Korea and self-determination by the Koreans of their own affairs. He added that the topics of negotiation should include the withdrawal of US forces from Formosa and China's status at the United Nations.[44] Significantly, Zhou told Panikkar that these were merely suggestions, not ultimatums.

Nehru was thrilled. Here at last was a clear sign that the Chinese were willing to negotiate. Quickly, he followed up this lead by dashing off a letter to Zhou in which he requested the premier to overlook 'forms of words' and assess the reality.[45] Nehru wrote to Panikkar as well, asking him to impress upon Zhou that, apart from the United States, other powers in the West had accepted nearly all of China's demands.

Panikkar and Nehru's efforts had paid off.

In a specific reply to Canadian Prime Minister Louis St Laurent's query on the Chinese proposals routed through Panikkar, China suggested that a ceasefire for a limited period could be agreed upon at the first meeting of the proposed conference by China. The Chinese further clarified that withdrawal of all foreign forces would mean that the Chinese 'volunteers' in Korea would also be advised to return.[46]

Panikkar would later say that this was only a 'qualified acceptance', and as things went, the United States would cut short these attempts at conciliation. Washington insisted on a UN resolution that qualified China as an aggressor country and which made negotiations conditional to a ceasefire. India would grow increasingly frustrated as matters dragged on. After China backtracked in July 1952 on its in principle acceptance of an India-UK prisoner repatriation formula that could have led to a settlement, an exasperated Nehru threw his hands in the air, exclaiming that both sides 'express their desire for settlement, but neither is prepared to give in … and wants the other to do so'. He was unhappy that Peking had not been 'straight' with India. But he found the American military approach—and continued bombing in the midst of peace efforts that only made Peking more intransigent—to be 'outrageous'.[47]

In the background of this tense, frenetic atmosphere was the spectre of Gouri's plummeting health. Doctors had warned Panikkar that she would not survive another winter in China. 'During all the difficult days of November, December and January, when I had to carry on the most delicate negotiations, I had this heavy load on my mind.'[48]

Then there was the fact that the MEA in Delhi was still deeply suspicious of Panikkar. The question of whether China was continuing to feed the Indian Embassy in Peking with exaggerated or fake information to pressure the United States into negotiations on its own terms persisted. In London, Britain's new foreign minister, Anthony Eden, doubted Chinese sincerity. Panikkar's reputation had preceded him at Whitehall, and Eden was openly sceptical of Panikkar's reliability.[49] It would take yet another round at the United Nations for matters to be resolved, but as first steps went, there was no doubt that Panikkar had played a pivotal role in bringing both parties to the negotiating table.

It was a milestone moment in a professional relationship that had become intensely complex with Panikkar's posting to China. On the one hand, Nehru was hugely relieved. Panikkar's presence on the spot had proved immensely useful and the Indian prime minister would continue to keep him on as a constant point of reference for India's Korean policy. Even when Panikkar was posted to Egypt as ambassador, Nehru would seek his advice on complex tactical issues of the armistice negotiations that were technically outside the purview of an ambassador accredited in Cairo.[50]

But while matters in Cairo and Korea were one story, Tibet would always be a far more difficult layer in their relationship. Nehru sent Panikkar words of comfort when the ambassador was being publicly vilified over China, but in reality the Indian prime minister was doing his best to assure the watchful Americans that he had nothing in common with Panikkar. In November 1951, at dinner with Chester Bowles, then the US ambassador to India, Nehru made haste to let Bowles know that, as far as China was concerned, Panikkar and he didn't at all agree. In fact, the prime minister averred, a great pointer as to Panikkar's character was the fact that he had represented 'some of the most reactionary princes' in the fight for Indian independence.

'He stated Panikkar usually succumbed to whatever situation he was in,' noted Bowles. 'Today, he tends to dangerously idealise the

Chinese scene.'[51] Nehru explained that he had sent Panikkar to China not as a Leftist ambassador to a new communist regime, but as a man whom India believed would get along with Chiang Kai-shek. Now that the communists were in power, he spread his hands helplessly, 'Panikkar's views, as in the past, had changed abruptly.'[52]

Panikkar, of course, had no idea that Nehru was working to hedge his own bets with the Americans, and he continued in the happy belief that 'the Prime Minister alone stood by me'.[53]

It was a good thing that he had that illusion to bolster him, for the days ahead were about to get rapidly worse.

Chapter 50

Last Chance in China

ON 26 JANUARY 1951, THE INDIAN EMBASSY IN PEKING HELD A RECEPTION to celebrate the first anniversary of the founding of the Indian Republic. Panikkar had invited Mao himself. Nobody knew whether the chairman would attend. For days, rumours of his illness had been circulating in Peking. So when Mao arrived at the Peking Hotel for dinner, it was the social and political coup of the season.

A tall, loose-limbed figure, he entered the hall clothed in a peaked cap and a long, brown woollen overcoat that draped loosely over his shoulders and reached almost to his ankles. The guests fell silent as security guards removed the coat from the chairman's shoulders and he walked into the great hall, smiling affably. As the Chinese and Indian national anthems played, Mao took his seat at the head of the table, to the right of Panikkar. The Indian Embassy's Chinese-language expert, and Mao's Columbia-educated English interpreter, stood behind his chair. Kaul remembered that all eyes were glued to Mao's broad, smiling face. 'This was a signal honour shown to India in view of our improving relations.'[1]

Before the meal, Mao stood to say a few words. He looked around the room, a slight smile on his moon-shaped face, before he began speaking in short, simple sentences. 'It is a great day. The Indian people are a fine people. There have been thousands of years of friendship between the people of India and China.'[2] He hoped, too, that Nehru would visit the People's Republic of China soon.

Mao's speech was translated into English by his interpreter and once it was done, Panikkar rose to his feet, 'beaming like a beaver'.[3] The Indian ambassador responded much in the style of the chairman, speaking also in short, simple sentences. His speech was translated into excellent Chinese, while Kaul, who could speak fluent, if ungrammatical Russian, was persuaded by Panikkar to translate for the Soviets. It was a relaxed, convivial evening, with toasts being proposed and drunk gambe—empty the cup—style. For a moment it seemed as though the clouds of tension and suspicion that had darkened bilateral ties in 1950 were dissipating.

But that was just for a moment.

In January 1951, Bajpai told Henderson that Tibet was likely beyond saving. Besides, there was so much going on internationally that India was 'giving little thought to Tibet'.[4] The US ambassador was considerably annoyed, finding India's assessments of Chinese intentions to be 'wishfully warped'.[5] But the combined effects of the disastrous earthquake in Assam in August 1950 and the Chinese occupation of Tibet inevitably did push India towards a more assertive policy in the Himalayan border areas.

In February 1951, Indian troops entered Tawang and an administrative reorganisation took place with the creation of the North-East Frontier Agency (NEFA). The aim was to consolidate the presence of the Indian state's civil administration in areas that until then had enjoyed little political visibility at the national level. This state-building exercise was supposed to prevent, through the development of local populations, the infiltration of Chinese influence and strengthen Indian control south of the watershed.[6] The fact that it took place without any opposition from the Chinese was regarded by the Government of India as 'indicating that the People's Republic of China was psychologically prepared to accept the McMahon Line as the de facto boundary'.[7]

In his memoir about his time in China, Panikkar writes that, during the spring of 1951, he was out of the city, touring the countryside to inspect and report back on educational and health infrastructure. He was also dealing with the slight furore caused by Devaki's marriage to MN, a fact that had been remarked upon with a kind of grim satisfaction in internal CIA reports.[8] This was the kind of controversy that the media everywhere loves to make much of. Panikkar dealt with it in a quiet letter to the prime minister. He would stand by his daughter, even if her marriage was (given the circumstances) remarkably poor timing.

On the political front, Panikkar's memoir makes no mention of the fact that the friendliness that Mao had shown in January was already beginning to drift. In March 1951, Zhou brought up the subject of Tibet with Panikkar once again. He repeated that Nehru was welcome to visit China, but Peking had given certain assurances to Lhasa, including the 'recognition of the Dalai Lama as the temporal and spiritual leader … and autonomy for Tibet, subject to central government control of frontiers and foreign policy etc'.[9] The premier also added that Tibet had agreed to send a delegation to China to negotiate a peaceful settlement.

Panikkar assured Zhou that India's interest in the matter was peaceful, with no desire to 'carry on political intrigues'. Zhou nodded and said that China 'recognised India's friendly interest in Tibet and that their decision not to advance on Lhasa or undertake military operations within Tibet, but to carry on peaceful negotiations, was in conformity with India's views'. Zhou also expected India to 'recognise the moderation of Chinese policy' in this context.[10] He warned Panikkar though that should the Dalai Lama be persuaded to take asylum in India, it 'would bring a dark cloud between our good relations of friendship'. He ended this meeting with a peculiarly ominous warning, which Panikkar reported to Delhi. 'As India's interests were that the peace of her frontier should not be disturbed … he hoped that the Indian government will not encourage the Dalai Lama to leave the country.'[11]

Panikkar initially told Zhou that if the Dalai Lama did come to India, it would not be possible to refuse him entry.[12] He assured Zhou that it would be only spiritual and not political. But the premier's warning was enough for Delhi to quickly scramble to assure Peking (and tell Lhasa) that 'we feel the flight of the Dalai Lama to India will leave Tibet leaderless and will serve no useful purpose'.[13] Nehru eventually assured Tibet of India's diplomatic support. 'We would naturally like to continue direct relations between India and Tibet.'[14]

As negotiations between Peking and Lhasa continued, a goodwill delegation arrived in Peking at the end of April 1951. It was an unofficial mission, with many of its members 'connected with front organisations', but it was actively encouraged by Panikkar. It was led by Pandit Sunderlal and contained mostly intellectuals, writers and academics, like the economist and educator V.K.R.V. Rao, the editor of *Blitz* magazine, Russi Karanjia, and the author Mulk Raj Anand, 'none of whom could be accused of pro-communist politics'.[15] The mission toured China and were generally treated with great friendliness by the political leadership, but Panikkar was slightly disgusted by the fact that they 'appeared to be more Sinophile than the Chinese themselves'.[16]

On 1 May, Panikkar attended the May Day celebrations in Peking, which he had been greatly looking forward to. It was as fabulous as he had expected, with cloudless blue skies and golden sunlight. The diplomatic corps was present in full in the galleries that had been especially constructed for them. At ten o'clock precisely, Mao presented himself on the balcony. It was a signal for the marchpast to begin and Panikkar watched in awe as an immense procession, 'armed with banners, portraits of leaders of the proletariat of all countries and cartoons of American action',[17] began to stride past in perfect synchronisation. It was a massive rally with 7,00,000 men, women and children marching past ceaselessly for six hours. For Panikkar, it was yet another symbol of communist China's undoubted strength and the faith that the people reposed in this new leadership.

Tibet would have felt differently.

Negotiations[18] between Peking and Lhasa resulted in the signing of the 17 Point Agreement on 23 May 1951. It was the beginning of the end of Indian influence in China—if there had been any at all to begin with. The Dalai Lama heard the announcement on the radio and was appalled, though by October 1951, he was forced to conclude that this was the only way forward for his people. As for India, in the end, it had little to offer Tibet in its hour of need. And warning signs of further trouble existed even then. In September 1951, shortly before Panikkar left China, Zhou told him politely that the question of the stabilisation of the Tibetan frontier—a matter of common interest to India, Nepal and China—could be settled by discussion between the three countries. Attaching importance to the word *stabilisation*, Panikkar assumed that Zhou meant there was no territorial dispute between India and China.

He was to regret that assumption.

As 1951 drew to a close, Panikkar, Gouri and Devaki left Peking to tour Sian, Lanchow, Yenan and travel through the Gobi Desert to the famous Dunhuang caves on the borders of Xinjiang. The differences between the provinces he saw, the developments in the villages, the stories of Sir Aurel Stein systematically looting the beautiful caves at Tung Huan and the beauty of the regions interested Panikkar deeply. His memoir of the China stint, however, provide an insight into the methodical way in which the new regime was eliminating those it perceived to be enemies of the state, including religious sects that had large followings and also Christian missionaries and nuns. Foreigners were not spared either, and the result was long incarceration since exit visas to leave China were next to impossible to attain. Panikkar's own tour was chaperoned, but he still wrote glowingly of how land reform had 'broken the chains, made the village'.

Another point of interest was his visit to the interiors of northwest China to the ancient site of Dunhuang on the Silk Route, where he was witness to the ravages inflicted on this place of world heritage by Western archaeologists like Aurel Stein, who had taken 9,000 ancient manuscripts (Buddhist sutras and scrolls) and paintings for a paltry sum of Rs 500 from the caves. The French scholar Pelliot followed to complete the ransacking systematically so that 'no manuscript of value was left there for anyone to acquire'.

But observations aside, the Indian ambassador was already thinking of leaving China. The dangers to Gouri's health were too high, and he was, quite frankly, tired by the stresses of this posting, which gave him no time to rest or spend much time with his family.

Nehru gladly gave him permission to relinquish his post by October 1951, but the order changed: Panikkar was instructed to return to China in February 1952 for a few more months. The prime minister wanted him there to negotiate the final stages of the ceasefire in Korea. In October 1951, after his last diplomatic tour was over, the Panikkars departed China.

No matter where one stands on the spectrum of assessing K.M. Panikkar and his ambassadorship in China, it is interesting that, while events in Tibet and Korea were playing out, he was putting together a manuscript which would be published in 1951 under the somewhat arrogant pseudonym of Chanakya. *The Indian Revolution* is the first of his many comparisons between India and China and what he saw as 'the two Asian revolutions'.

As he put it, 'Asia has been witnessing the simultaneous consummation of two revolutions. Her most ancient communities, India and China, have during the last three years transformed themselves through revolutionary processes … More important are the possibilities of reactions of these two revolutions on each other, and their influence on the other peoples of South-East Asia.'[19]

China had an edge over India, Panikkar argued. After all, they had an organised and vast army, a centralised and strong ruling party. But their core disadvantage was that their economy was in shambles: there were few industries and agriculture, thanks to the war, was stunted. Nor, he argued, was there any real administrative or scientific expertise, such as India possessed. This was a view that he also put down in his reports to the prime minister.[20] The real revolution, he felt, would be in society, one for which India—through its revival of Hinduism—was ready. 'No stronger weapon could have been put in the hands of those who desired to reshape Indian society and give it purpose and vitality.'[21]

The reformation of the Hindu religion was thus an essential prerequisite of social legislation. Hindu communal organisations such as the Hindu Mahasabha were, for Panikkar, merely a reaction to the opposite organisation by Muslims who, from the very beginning, aimed at the independence of the religious minority. In this context, he attached great importance to the ability of the Congress to maintain its secular beliefs in the twentieth century.

Contact with Europe also made direct contributions to the new India, bringing in ideas of democracy, gender equality and secularism. From this contact with the West, Hinduism had only emerged stronger, and as a result, Indian identity was more international and cosmopolitan. It was now up to the Indians themselves to rewrite and reinterpret their own history and identity, as Nehru had done in his *Discovery of India*. In a sense, that process had already begun with independence and all that had come with it: territorial integrity, a written constitution, secularism and democracy.[22] In China, seismic changes like these had had to be imposed by force. Panikkar would never stop comparing China with India, and as time passed, he would begin dreaming of a time when their interests and futures could converge: a true Nehruvian image of Asian solidarity.

After dropping their daughter in New Delhi, Panikkar and Gouri left for Europe, where he would be the deputy head of India's UNGA delegation. His talks with leaders and diplomats across Paris and London were informative enough for him to return and report to Nehru that he had noticed two trends. One, during the Cold War, Europe would not be able to challenge or influence American action in the Far East. Consequently, Panikkar argued that tensions in the East would continue.

Panikkar had also developed his first tenuous links with Vietnam via Ambassador Hoang in Peking and based on his conversations with Hoang and with other Vietnamese leaders he met in Paris, he was convinced that France was anxious to quit Indochina, but would not be permitted to do so by the Americans. He recommended that, under the circumstances of the Cold War, any policy other than non-alignment would be 'suicidal' for India.[23] Pleased with this report, Nehru asked Panikkar to stop in Rangoon on his way to China to meet Thakin Nu, the Burmese prime minister.

In Panikkar's geopolitical worldview, especially regarding Indian security, Burma was vital. As early in 1946, he had written that the defence of Burma was essentially the defence of India. 'No responsibility should be considered too heavy for India, when it comes to the question of defending Burma.'[24] Soon after its independence though, Burma was plunged into a civil war. Indian concern over this sudden disarray naturally sharpened with the emergence of the People's Republic of China in 1949, which shared common borders with India and Burma. Nehru persuaded Commonwealth countries to provide military and economic aid to Burma, while Indian assistance encompassed both military and economic assistance and the bolstering of the U Nu regime. Nehru's primary aim was maintaining a friendly, non-aligned and non-communist buffer between India and China. This strategy catered also to preventing the destabilisation of northeast India, where the Nagas, Mizos, and Meities straddle the India-Burma border.

But Burma in the early 1950s was concerned about China. The concern was mutual, and when Panikkar visited Rangoon, the relations between Peking and Rangoon were testier than ever publicly acknowledged. The fallout of the Korean War had seen 2,000 Kuomintang troops flee into the jungles of northeast Burma after being routed by the PLA. In 1951, several offensives were launched by these KMT troops into the neighbouring province of Yunnan. It was to discuss how to deal with this problem that Panikkar was in Rangoon. Based on his conversations with Zhou and Nehru, Panikkar was able to assure the worried Burmese government that Peking would make no move that would create trouble in Burma.

'What the Burmese Government wanted to hear from me was a general appreciation of the situation in China in relation to South-East Asia, and more specifically whether in my judgement the Chinese would raise the question of the undefined boundary as the Kuomintang by various irregular acts had tried to do before its expulsion.'[25] Panikkar promised to discuss the boundary issue with the Chinese personally, if he was authorised to do so by Nehru. Pleased, the Burmese threw him an elaborate and very long dinner that stretched until two in the morning. Panikkar was exhausted by eleven o'clock, but the Burmese laughed and said that the party had only really begun once the Chinese ambassador (who had been present as well) departed at half past eleven.

We do not know whether or not he discussed Burma in China, for Panikkar's last stint in China, which lasted some six or seven months, was overshadowed by even more controversy than before.

In retrospect, one can only wonder why the negotiations for the boundaries with Tibet were left to Panikkar, given that he had already severely let down Nehru in this respect once before. Still, until now, China's strategy had been 'to avoid making or retracting any explicit border claims', though on the basis of internal military reports, Mao and Zhou knew India had consolidated its presence in Tawang and other areas south of the McMahon Line.[26] The Chinese scholar Dai Chaowu has used Chinese foreign ministry archives to highlight the fact that Zhang Jingwu (Peking's representative in Lhasa) and Yang Gongsu (director of the Tibet Bureau of Foreign Affairs) had studied the documents relating to the Simla Convention and the map showing the McMahon Line, signed by the Tibetan and British Indian representatives in 1914. Based on their study, Chaowu argues, Zhang and Yang concluded that 'the Simla Convention and the legality of the McMahon Line were the basis for India's extraterritorial claims in Tibet'.[27]

They advised Peking to proclaim the old treaties as invalid and ask the Indian side to withdraw from the 'recently occupied areas'. But Peking decided that the time was not yet ripe to push forward with border talks, a stand that was repeated in April 1952 to the Indian Mission in Lhasa.[28] This was despite the fact that India had explained its position on the McMahon Line publicly, beginning with Nehru himself, on a number of occasions. Even the foreign ministry in Peking had been told by T.N. Kaul in March 1951 that, unless the McMahon Line was accepted as the boundary, there would be problems in the bilateral relationship.[29]

China bided its time.

In the spring of 1952, Panikkar was pleased to see several gestures of goodwill between India and China. The India-China Friendship Association was formed, with Tripurari Chakravarty, professor of Chinese history at Calcutta university, as secretary of the organising committee. In April, Dr Mohanlal Atal became the first unofficial Indian leader to visit China, going as the Indian delegate to the World Peace Council. That same month, at the invitation of the Chinese government, the Government of India sent a cultural delegation on a six-week visit to China. It comprised fourteen members, of whom twelve were non-officials, and was led by Vijayalakshmi Pandit.[30] The delegation had been carefully chosen and briefed at length by Nehru. The prime minister told them that Pakistan and China were the most important countries for India, and while there was peace along the long border between India and China, 'we must not let China have the upper hand'. The journalist Frank Moraes noticed that Nehru 'deprecated' references to Tibet on which he said 'the Chinese were sensitive'.[31]

The members of the Indian delegation arrived in Canton on 28 April 1952 on a four-engine Bharat Airways plane—the first foreign aircraft (with the exception of Soviet ones) to be allowed into communist China. On 30 April, Premier Zhou En-lai hosted a banquet for the mission. Pandit was impressed by the limited scope of what she was shown. 'Nowhere else in the world can one be so proud of being Asian, as in China,' she declared.[32] In her letter to her brother, Pandit struck the same note as Panikkar had done in his descriptions of Mao and Zhou. The chairman's appearance in public, she said, called Gandhi to mind. As with the Mahatma, 'the public doesn't just applaud him, they worship him. There is both love and adoration in the glances of those who look at him. It is moving to see.' As for Zhou En-lai, he 'is a great statesman and possesses abundant vitality and charm. He is polished and has a sense of humour which is terribly infectious. One has to join in his laughter—and he laughs often. He makes one feel at home in a moment and his conversation loses nothing in translation.'[33]

Privately, however, T.N. Kaul observed dryly that Nehru's sister wasn't too thrilled with her experience in Peking. 'Mrs Pandit had perhaps expected wild fanfare and frontline publicity, at least a meeting with Mao,' he wrote later. 'The Chinese were busy with their own struggle and still gave a lot of attention to the delegation, but she was not happy. She expressed her dissatisfaction to me and Prof. Jha and we both tried to pacify her but she still sulked.'

It wouldn't do, naturally, to have Nehru's sister upset. Kaul hastily asked Panikkar to help, and was relieved when the ambassador swept in with immense charm. 'He called her "*Madamissima*," and told her many stories and anecdotes,' Kaul recalled. Indeed, Panikkar pulled out all the stops, using his influence and contacts within Chinese political circles of power to show the goodwill mission an excellent time in China. He didn't forget geopolitical advantage either, organising an intimate little dinner with Zhou En-lai, Chen Jiakang for Pandit, Kaul and himself to discuss the armistice negotiations ongoing at the United Nations. Though he would himself write that the success of this mission was due to Pandit's 'personality and charm', it was also due to Panikkar himself and the undoubted power he wielded in Chinese society and politics.

On 14 June 1952, Zhou sat down with Panikkar and told him that China presumed India would be prepared to negotiate for fresh arrangements. After all, Zhou said persuasively, surely India did not wish to claim 'special rights' based on unequal treaties of the past.

Panikkar was willing to 'negotiate a settlement on all points'.

Pleased, Zhou suggested that while they negotiated the stickier issues, India could perhaps convert its mission into Lhasa into a consulate general. In return, China would set up a consulate general in Bombay.[34] Panikkar sent on this request to Delhi, adding that Zhou hadn't touched the boundary question and so neither had he.

Nehru was instantly suspicious. Why had Zhou not referred to the frontier at all? He didn't like the premier's silence and told Panikkar so in his reply. 'We think it is rather odd that, in discussing Tibet with you, Zhou En-lai did not refer at all to our frontier. For our part, we attach more importance to this than to other matters.' There was a lot at stake now, considering Nehru had told parliament that the direct frontier with Tibet, as well as the frontiers with Nepal, Bhutan and Sikkim, should remain unchanged.[35]

'In our instructions to you dated 25th January, you were asked to specify our interests including those on the frontier. We presume you have done so,' Nehru continued. 'If so, we can presume that Zhou En-lai's silence means some kind of acquiescence. It is not for us to suggest any reconsideration. At the same time, I should like to be assured on this point. I leave it to you to exercise your discretion in this matter.'[36]

Panikkar replied that the Chinese were aware of India's interest in the integrity of Nepal and had not raised any questions about it.

Nor had they objected to the prime minister's public statements on the matter. The ambassador now said that he didn't want to make this an issue. India, he said, should stick to the position that the frontier had been defined 'and there is nothing for us to discuss'. According to Panikkar, it would be legitimate to 'presume that Chou En Lai's silence on this point and his NOT having even once alluded to Sikkim or Bhutan at any time even indirectly during our conversation would mean acquiescence in, if NOT acceptance of our position'.[37]

This was an alarming level of presumption from a sitting ambassador, but it is a telling indicator that Nehru did not protest further. What he *did* do was tell Panikkar that he was okaying Zhou's suggestions only on the caveat that this proposal should be part of a comprehensive agreement.[38] Panikkar promptly conveyed this to the Chinese—making no mention of the caveat.[39] Thrilled, the Chinese pressed their advantage, suggesting that the new incumbent to Lhasa should now be designated a consul general.[40]

India agreed to that as well.

It was a massive and permanent tactical error—India had now accepted Chinese sovereignty over Tibet and the fact that any further Chinese actions in Tibet were part of China's internal affairs.

As Panikkar went ahead with changing India's relationship with Tibet and China forever, his old critics resurfaced. On 11 April 1952, K.P.S. Menon wrote furiously that a child could see through China's games. The attitude of the PRC, he wrote, was far from straightforward, and could, in fact, be termed 'cunning'.[41] If this was what Peking had done in Tibet, he demanded, how long before Sikkim, Bhutan or even Darjeeling and Kalimpong stood 'liberated'? 'The Chinese have long memories; irredentism has always played a part in the policy of the Chinese government whether imperial, Guomindang or Communist.'[42] For Menon, India was clearly inviting trouble when it decided that the border issue would not figure in the negotiations on Tibet.

Girija Shankar Bajpai, now Governor of Bombay, added his voice to the chorus of criticism on Panikkar's decision. Writing scathingly to Menon, he slammed Panikkar's tactics in Peking. 'This business of

Sino-Indian relations over Tibet, would, in my judgement, be best handled comprehensively and not piecemeal.'[43]

With Bajpai and Menon coming down so heavily on Panikkar, Nehru felt some slight doubts at having told the ambassador that he could go ahead. In Delhi, he had already given a press conference on the subject, in which he said, 'You cannot treat Tibet as an independent country with an independent representative from us … it has to be negotiated with China and Tibet both.'[44] Now, he wrote worriedly to Menon, wondering if 'our attempt at being clever might overreach itself' and whether it was just best to be straight with the Chinese.[45]

It was too late.

At the end of June 1952, Panikkar's diplomatic tenure in communist China came to an end. His role in the boundary negotiations with Tibet was not over, but he would be leaving for the warmer shores of Egypt. Upon his departure, Zhou hosted a small farewell dinner. His wife was present, as were Zhang Hanfu and Chen Jiakang. Kaul, also present, noted that the atmosphere, despite ongoing discussions with India over Tibet, was relaxed and friendly. Zhou was at his best that evening, mixing courtesy and diplomatic polish with humour. The meal was elaborate, eight courses in all, ranging from bird's nest soup, to fish, chicken and vegetables. At the beginning and end of each course, toasts were drunk with that potent liquor mao-tai. Seeing Kaul wrinkling his nose at the bitter odour of the drink, Zhou laughed and explained that the liquor was distilled from sorghum and water from a special spring in Kweichow. 'It had twice the strength of vodka,' recalled Kaul. 'You could light it with a matchstick.'

Panikkar dodged the mao-tai, asking his younger deputy to drink it for him. Kaul could hardly refuse, especially since Zhou smiled, 'If I, fifteen years older, can drink it, why can't you?' Kaul downed six glasses and thanked his stars that the evening was finally over. That's when the exuberant Zhang Hanfu said that, since Panikkar was leaving, it called for Kaul to drink six more glasses. The poor deputy protested feebly, but to no avail. Panikkar merely laughed and clapped his shoulder.

Six more mao-tais went down, and Kaul finished the evening with a hazy view of Panikkar laughing merrily and a burning sensation in his gut.[46]

On a warm summer day in June, Kaul went to see off the Panikkars at Tientsin. Panikkar 'seemed already in the Court of King Farouk and Queen Nariman', his deputy would remember later. He had bought an old diamond watch fixed to a fan of ostrich feathers to present to the Queen, for which he had paid about two million JMP (or Rs 1,000 at the then rate of exchange). It was typical of Panikkar, already looking ahead, and looking to charm his way to the top of the political ladder in yet another posting.

China had changed his life in more ways than Panikkar would care to admit, either publicly or privately. As he stood on the decks of the boat that would take them to Hong Kong, he looked out at the bustling harbour below. In the space of four years, he had witnessed a revolution and the emergence of a new regime, 'the end of an epoch and the beginning of another', as he would put it. It had been a time of chaos and confusion, but he couldn't help feeling that communist China signalled the dawn of a new era, one which the world had yet to understand.

'In general I may summarize my impression of New China as a tremendous upheaval which has transformed what was a highly civilized but unorganized mass of people into a great modern State. It has released great energies, given the Chinese people a new hope, and a new vision of things,' he wrote years later, adding presciently, 'compared with the State, the individual has lost all value, and this is the strange thing in China which adds a tinge of sorrow even when one appreciates and admires what the revolution has done for China and Asia generally.'[47]

In his mind, though he 'was happy to feel that there was no outstanding issue between us and the Chinese'. In this assessment, Panikkar was to be proven tragically wrong—yet again.

Chapter 51

To Cairo

ON 2 SEPTEMBER 1952, THE GOVERNMENT OF INDIA ANNOUNCED THE appointment of K.M. Panikkar as India's ambassador to Egypt.

Egypt had long dominated Indian thinking. As early as 1949, New Delhi declared that 'the preeminent position of Egypt in the Arab world makes our relations with that country of particular importance'.[1] At a time when several Arab countries were being persuaded to enter into enticing military alliances by the West, it was not so much Israel that was important now, but Egypt.[2]

The Panikkars were arriving in a country in crisis. The trouble reached back to the mid-1930s, when Italian aggression in Ethiopia had set the conditions for the return of the Egyptian monarchy to constitutional rule—and for an agreement with Britain. The Anglo-Egyptian treaty of 26 August 1936 was essentially a military pact that guaranteed London's strategic interests, but it also accepted the prospect of full Egyptian sovereignty. With this compromise in effect, Egypt could finally apply for membership in the League of Nations, thus resuming an autonomous foreign policy for the first time since 1882.

But after the end of the Second World War, Egypt's unsuccessful attempts to renegotiate the 1936 treaty with London to free itself from British encumbrances, coupled with serious internal problems, fuelled a crisis that ended in the Free Officers' coup of July 1952. Led by the likes of Mohamed Naguib and Gamal Abdel Nasser, the revolution ushered in a wave of profound political, economic and social change and contributed to the escalation of decolonisation and the development of Third World solidarity during the Cold War.

Initially, the movement focused on grievances against the corrupt, flashy King Farouk I, but it had more wide-ranging political ambitions. In the first three years of the revolution, for instance, the Free Officers moved to abolish the constitutional monarchy and aristocracy of Egypt and Sudan, establish a republic, end the British occupation of the country and secure the independence of Sudan. Its agenda was staunchly nationalist and anti-imperialist, expressed chiefly through rising Arab nationalism.[3]

For India, which had very little influence in the area, the main aim was to create a bridge to Muslim countries, thus bypassing Pakistan. Panikkar's remit was not just Egypt, but Syria, Lebanon, Jordan and Libya. This was the area designated as West Asia in those days.

India's ties to this region were historically complex. On the one hand, there was the legacy of the British Raj, on the other, the dense network of relations between the different national movements—Arab, Turkish, Jewish and Indian—especially in the inter-war period, which profoundly influenced the formulation of Indian policy.

Panikkar, therefore, was accredited as the ambassador to Farouk I, King of Egypt and Sudan. That was the expectation of the Egyptian government of all diplomatic representatives in Cario, though Nehru made it clear that this was not in any way a stance in the dispute. On New Delhi's part, it supported Egyptian sovereignty over the Canal Zone, though it had no intentions of sacrificing the Sudanese people's right to self-determination. In his memoir, Panikkar explained it succinctly, 'Nehru accepted my argument that, as Egyptian sovereignty over Sudan was unquestioned, the formal acknowledgement of this in the Letter of Accreditation to the King would not result in any abridgement of British authority.'[4] This was a position designed to be in complete harmony with Great Britain and would prove to be advantageous in the year that Panikkar was ambassador in Cairo.

In this first decade of the Cold War, India's primary concern in the Middle East was Pakistan. As the number of Arab states grew over the years, the scholar P.R. Kumaraswamy writes, 'it soon became a simple function of the math: one Israel versus many Arab states'.[5] With Pakistan's efforts to forge an Islamic bloc, India was deeply concerned. Since 1948, Pakistan had hosted and organised official and semi-official meetings and conferences with Islamic leaders. The Mufti of Jerusalem visited Pakistan frequently. Islamabad's ideological opposition to Nasser's brand of secular nationalism had led to the forging of closer ties with conservative regimes in the Middle East, such as Iran and Saudi Arabia, while its support for the pro-West Hashemite kingdom had seen the cementing of strong military ties with Amman.[6] Unsurprisingly then, India's foreign policy in the Middle East was almost obsessed with Pakistan. When 'Panikkar was appointed to Cairo,' his friend Eliahu Elath, then serving as the Israeli ambassador to the Court of St. James, noted later, 'Nehru told him to do his utmost to prevent the Arab countries from identifying themselves with Pakistan.'[7]

But even without Pakistan, it was clear that Islam was playing a significant role in Indian strategic calculations. In the words of the scholar G.H. Jansen, 'Without Islam the Afro-Asian movement would probably have aborted. And without the Afro-Asian movement there would have been no "non-aligned" group of nations, and without that group there would not have been the economic Group of Seventy-Seven, the underdeveloped South in the current North-South dialogue.'[8]

It was a world of immense diplomatic potential for Panikkar, given his links with the Zionist movement and with the creation of Israel in 1948. But he was, for the moment, more concerned about his wife. On their way to Cairo, the Panikkars stopped first in Delhi, where Panikkar was debriefed by the Ministry of External Affairs for six weeks (breezily dismissed in his memoir as a period of 'doing nothing!'[9]). He gave some lectures at the Delhi School of Economics as well, before Gouri felt well enough to travel again. Panikkar had taken her to numerous doctors, but nobody had been able to discover just what was wrong with Gouri. Long journeys exhausted her easily, and she fell sick far more often than she ever had before she had moved to China.

Still, he hoped that the weather and climate of Egypt—warm and humid as it was—would suit her better than the frozen winters of Peking.

The Panikkars (Radha was still with them) landed in Cairo at one in the morning in the middle of 1952, and moved into a palatial, colonnaded bungalow on the banks of the Nile. Gouri seemed a little better at this change in temperature, and after reassuring himself that he could leave her alone in the care of their daughter, Panikkar got to work.

True to form, he had prepared exhaustively for the posting. As is often the case with diplomacy, he had to hit the ground running. After presenting his credentials to the Regency Council, his first priority was to establish contact with other ambassadors and leading public figures in Egyptian politics and society and to begin practicing Indian policy in the region as soon as possible. In this aim, he was ably assisted by his friend and former colleague in China, Sir Ralph Stevenson, then posted to Cairo (1950–1955) as the British ambassador. Stevenson was happy to introduce Panikkar to important people, like the ambassadors of the United States and France and several Arab League ministers. Between themselves, the two men discussed Indian policy towards the region, especially focusing on the Pakistan factor.

'Essentially the Indo-Pakistan troubles in international matters is the quarrel of co-wives about the alleged neglect of the husband,' Panikkar told Stevenson, probably startling him. 'There is no difference in their foreign policy. Pakistan made a half-hearted attempt to align herself with Islamic countries. But she discovered that while Islam is still a force to be reckoned with, as a positive policy an Islamic alliance is not a possibility ... So if we can get our "domestic" problems settled—and I do not despair of a settlement—there will be working cooperation between India and Pakistan in foreign policy, for India realises that her external defence is bound up with Pakistan and Pakistan realises that her support in any crisis must come from India. It will take another two or three years before these ideas seep into the minds of the ordinary politicians.'[10]

Apart from being touchingly optimistic, this was a largely overconfident reading of regional dynamics. Pakistan would soon turn towards the United States, bringing the Cold War ever closer to the subcontinent, and its ties with India would never be the same again. For now though, Nehru's brief to Panikkar was to bridge the gulf between India and the Arab countries, especially Egypt. This was likely to be a little tricky, since Egypt at the time was locked in a political showdown with Britain over two main issues: the Anglo-Egyptian condominium over Sudan and the question of the Suez Canal Zone.

Before he could begin building his network of contacts in the city, Panikkar was thrown a slight curveball.

Dr Radhakrishnan, then the vice president of India, announced his intention to come and stay with the Panikkars in Cairo. Panikkar was glad to receive a good friend from the old days in Oxford, but the timing was poor to say the least. He was new to Cairo and the family was not fully settled in just yet. Nor could he afford to show the vice president that he knew nobody in Cairo. Who would attend any reception that he threw? Desperate, Panikkar sought out Stevenson and begged him for help in persuading other members of the diplomatic corps to attend a dinner reception for the vice president.

His next worry was how Naguib and Nasser would receive Radhakrishnan. India and Egypt were, under the prevailing political circumstances, still trying to navigate a fresh relationship. Nehru and Nasser would develop a close relationship between 1953 and 1955. But Panikkar had not been long enough in Cairo to know which way the winds were blowing. 'Any failure to honour him would be a discourtesy to India and a personal rebuff to me.'[11]

Hastily, Panikkar called on Mohammad Fawzi, the new foreign secretary. Fawzi agreed to meet Radhakrishnan and opened further diplomatic doors for a relieved Panikkar. Egyptian officials agreed to meet Radhakrishnan's flight with full protocol.

Panikkar heaved a sigh of relief—which stuck in his throat the night the vice president landed.

Radhakrishnan didn't have an inoculation certificate. Without it, he was trapped on the tarmac. Frazzled, Panikkar had to awaken a sleeping General Naguib to get the vice president out of the airport. Radhakrishnan stayed for three days during which, apart from the usual rounds of talks and dinners, he persisted in quoting ceaselessly from scripture.

Panikkar saw him off with great relief. He could now turn his attention to travelling around the region, meeting the leaders of Jordan, Palestine, Syria and Lebanon.

During his first diplomatic tour, Panikkar was accompanied by Gouri and Radha, along with his secretary, a Palestinian youth named Sayed. Sayed was a refugee of the Arab-Israel war, working with the Indian embassy as an interpreter at the time. Panikkar liked Sayed's cheerful intelligence, but there was one factor that made him even more appealing.

He was the Grand Mufti's nephew.

Thrilled, Panikkar lost no time in persuading Sayed into organising a meeting with the Mufti himself, which opened another door to building friendly relations with the Arabs of Palestine. It catered to official policy, though it must be noted that Panikkar continued his contacts with Israeli ambassadors and the Yishuv, yet another facet of Indo-Israeli ties in the early 1950s.

The autumn of 1952 was both perfect and peaceful, filled with Panikkar's favourite things: history, culture, good food, pretty women and geopolitics. They went from Damascus to Jordan, Panikkar dwelling with equal delight on the historic architecture of the Old City of Jerusalem and the beauty of Lebanese women. He kept an eye, as always, on the global geopolitical scene, particularly at the United Nations, where Krishna Menon had taken over his role in the mediation between the United States and China in October 1952. By 25 October 1952, Menon had prepared a draft resolution on the thorniest issue at the time: the treatment of the prisoners of the Korean war.

The core of Menon's solution was straightforward—that the United Nations would, after the armistice, set up an independent commission to take custody of all prisoners who did not want to be repatriated to their respective countries and thereafter decide upon their final status. The plan was backed by Britain, Canada and even China (which was not then a member of the UN). Again, it was scuppered by the United States. Acheson, then in his last days as secretary of state, rejected it on the grounds that it did not settle the fate of the non-repatriate prisoners permanently. It gave, he believed, 'the Communists a ready-made pretext for breaching the Armistice'.

The United States' constant nitpicking would have daunted a stronger man. Instead, Krishna Menon patiently reworked his proposals. Still, Acheson was unmoved—until the rug was ripped out from under his feet. Suddenly, what had till then been only under informal discussion became a formal resolution, with India going ahead and tabling it on 19 November 1952. The Americans were furious at this forcing of their hand, spreading the rumour that Menon was a Trojan Horse for the communists. Four days later, it was the turn of the Soviet Union to tear into the hapless Menon, with the Soviet foreign minister, Andrei Vyshinsky, accusing him of being an American agent. With Vyshinsky's attack, Acheson immediately and predictably changed his stance, now praising Menon's statesmanship and getting the ball rolling on having the resolution suitably amended for the Americans.

Poor Menon was shattered by Vyshinsky's unexpected attack. Panikkar knew exactly how it felt to be attacked thus and lost no time in sending him a sympathetic and encouraging letter from the Middle East. 'I have been following with the greatest admiration your valiant efforts to get an agreed formula on the Korean peace talks,' he wrote. 'Though the proposals are on the same lines as we discussed when you came to Delhi, only your personal influence could have secured for them the support, which has automatically changed the whole posture of affairs ... From the meagre news one gets from the papers, it is not possible to judge what the prospects are of the resolution getting through the political committee. But whether it succeeds or not, you have done something which is of lasting value, because you have really organized world opinion in favour of a constructive proposal.'[12]

By the beginning of winter, the Panikkars had to hurry back to Cairo from Beirut, where they had spent the last weeks of autumn. The military coup was turning into a political revolution. Soon, Gamal Abdul Nasser would take direct political charge. The main concern here was that several of the new incumbents were members of the fanatical and orthodox Muslim Brotherhood. The risks of this new Egypt siding with Pakistan were too great to ignore. 'It seemed to me that the best method was to build up closer contacts with members of the revolutionary council.'[13] The only problem was that he didn't really know these new takers of power.

Panikkar bided his time.

The waiting yielded new perspectives on the leader who had just taken power. Gamal Abdul Nasser would later become the symbol of Arab nationalism, not to mention the recognised leader of the Arab world. But in 1952, he was thirty-five years old, still insecure politically and still searching for the right path to follow in world affairs. His was a generation that had grown up during the years of decolonisation but was also deeply influenced by the revolutionary political culture of the 1930s and 1940s, especially by organisations such as the Muslim Brotherhood and Young Egypt.

Nasser and his peers did not subscribe to a common ideology, but most of them were from the same socioeconomic background, harbouring similar aspirations and frustrations—and vague plans for overthrowing the existing political order. They were fully aware of the advantages of allying and cooperating with the West, but they were reluctant to fully commit to it. Nasser's Egypt in its early years was characterised by ambiguity, adapted to his country's interests and circumstances, and not afraid of cooperating when and where it had to. This would become a useful strategy for playing the West off against the East, thus enhancing Egypt's position in Arab, African and Muslim circles.[14] Panikkar, assessing Egypt's new leader, sensed an opportunity. The questions of Sudan and the Suez Canal Zone became the greatest drivers of modern Egyptian nationalism, and would be the most useful factors that the Indian ambassador could leverage to strengthen India's position.

Concerns over Sudan dated back to 1899, when the British Empire discovered that, having conquered it, it now had to govern the country. But administration of this vast and inhospitable land was complicated by the legal and diplomatic knots that accompanied its conquest. The Sudanese campaigns had been fought to protect not just imperial positions but also the waters of the mighty River Nile. The Egyptian treasury had borne the greater part of that expense, and equally, Egyptian troops outnumbered the English troops in the Anglo-Egyptian army. Still, the empire didn't want to just hand Sudan over to Egyptian rule. The Anglo-Egyptian Condominium (1899) was the result of this compromise. Sudan was given separate political status under which sovereignty was jointly shared by the Khedive and the British Crown, and Egyptian and British flags were flown side by side.

In reality of course, there was no equal partnership between the two. The empire dominated from the start, and though modernisation did come to Sudan, resentment came faster. Scorned by the English, cut adrift from their own tribal and religious affiliations, the Sudanese turned to the Egyptians for comfort and guidance. Sudanese nationalism was born in the twentieth century, but it would only be after the Second World War that it came to a head. The Free Officers' Revolution had brought men with more understanding of Sudanese aspirations to power, but when the Egyptians tried to renegotiate the 1936 Treaty with London, Sudan proved to be an insoluble obstacle.

The principle of Sudanese self-government was accepted. For the British, it was a step towards independence, but for the Egyptians, it was a temporary measure, pending the full unification of the Nile Valley. The non-resolution of the Sudanese issue led to a radicalisation of anti-colonial and anti-Western sentiment among Egypt's political parties. Faced with London's refusal to recognise Egypt's sovereign rights over Sudan as a precondition for negotiating British withdrawal and the future of the Suez Canal base, in 1951, the Egyptian government unilaterally abrogated the 1936 treaty and began encouraging anti-British boycotts in the Canal Zone.[15]

With this serving as his historical and political context, Panikkar established friendly contact with Salah Selim, Minister of State for Sudan Affairs at the Command Council of the Revolution.

To Selim, he suggested, 'Tackle the easiest first; and until you win there, do not let on that you are bothered about the others.'

'Which of them do *you* think is the easiest?' Selim inquired curiously.

Pleased at the ease with which he had got his chance, Panikkar instantly said, 'Sudan, without a doubt.'

'How do you make that out? Such a large territory with so much investment? Surely they won't give up all this.'

'They won't cede it to you, perhaps. But they will certainly give it up.'

Bewildered, Selim pressed him for an explanation.

'The British will not concede Sudan as part of Egypt,' Panikkar explained helpfully. 'But they may agree to make it independent of both you and themselves.'[16]

This was a tantalising prospect for Selim, but he cavilled at the fact that the British were encouraging local nationalism in Sudan. Panikkar pressed his advantage, laying out a new alternative: new Egypt could present itself as a supporter of complete Sudanese independence. This would prevent the British from encouraging local nationalists and force the empire to quit the region entirely.[17] As he put it, 'If you want to send the British out of Sudan, you should join hands with the Sudanese nationalists. When you two come together, the British will have no leg to stand on.'[18]

A few days after this little chat, Naguib summoned Panikkar for a meeting. In the course of their conversation, he remarked, 'The Revolutionary Council has endorsed your suggestion regarding Sudan. We are sending Saleh Selim for direct negotiations with the Sudanese leaders.'[19]

By bypassing London entirely, Cairo reached a direct agreement with the main Sudanese political forces, in which they recognised the right to self-determination though a plebiscite. This meant the Sudanese would have to choose between full independence and association with Egypt. Presented with a fait accompli, London could hardly refuse to sign a similar agreement on 12 February 1953. It was a major success for the new Egyptian government which, in line with

Nehru's ideas, avoided the use of force and presented a new political alternative while taking Sudanese aspirations into account.[20]

The fact that Panikkar had involved himself quite so deeply with internal politics was not lost on Ralph Stevenson, who knew his friend's ways of old. One day, Stevenson invited Panikkar over for tea. Almost as soon as the Indian ambassador had sat down, Stevenson said shortly, 'Why are you doing this when both our countries are members of the Commonwealth?'

Panikkar blinked. 'What is it that I'm supposed to be doing?' he inquired innocently.

'My information is that you are advising them in these discussions regarding the Sudan.' Stevenson looked squarely at him. 'Is it proper for you to work against Britain?'

'What advice am I giving them?'

The British ambassador laughed. 'During the last three weeks, Saleh Selim has called on you four times and Sultan Hamid (the thirty-fourth sultan of the Ottoman Empire) has called on you three times. I know this for certain. Are you suggesting that they came to see you just for a cup of tea?'

Panikkar sat back in his chair. 'Certainly, they came to see me. But how do you assume that my advice to them was prejudicial to Britian? My only desire is to see that your negotiations result in a settlement that is satisfactory to the Sudanese. Do you imagine that I would do anything to damage Sudanese interests?'

'I know the whole story, Panikkar,' Stevenson sighed. 'The claims of Sudan were our trump card. By making [it] the Egyptians' argument, you have completely disarmed us.' He looked at Panikkar. 'Never mind all that. Does Nehru know about this sleight of hand of yours?'

'I don't think you have any right to ask that question,' Panikkar said coolly. 'Supposing I ask you—does Eden know that *you* are asking *me* these questions?'

Stevenson wisely didn't push further, but before his friend left, he brought Sudan back into the conversation. 'The treaty … is nearly ready. As you wished, it grants full independence to the Sudan.'

There was a caveat here. Stevenson explained that the provisions of the treaty would only come into effect after a general election, which had to be free and fair.

'We should like a Committee to supervise the election,' he continued. 'Its Chairman should be a neutral person … preferably an Indian. Can this be arranged?'[21]

Panikkar knew just the man.

In the beginning of 1952, India had held its own first general elections as an independent country. It had been a massive exercise, involving 4,500 seats across an electorate spread over nearly a million square miles, the creation of electoral infrastructure from scratch and a terrifying lack of staff, among other serious social, demographic and geographic issues.[22] It had been managed by a single man: a quiet mathematician and judge from West Bengal named Sukumar Sen.

Panikkar had, like every other Indian, watched in awe as elections of a staggering scope and capacity were successfully held. He couldn't think of anyone better to recommend to the vast land of Sudan. Based on Panikkar's strong recommendations, Sen would chair the International Commission in charge of free elections in Sudan. Sen would spend fourteen months organising the country's polls, drawing heavily from Indian election laws and making suitable amendments to suit Sudan's specific needs.[23]

In the long run, Stevenson adjudged Panikkar's advice to the Egyptians to be both sound and sensible. In a report to the foreign office, the British ambassador confirmed: 'Although Panikkar talks a great deal and although his ebullience and rather impish sense of humour are liable to cause him to be misunderstood and misquoted, I am sure myself (though I may be starry-eyed about him) that the advice which he gives to the Egyptians is on the whole pretty sound, particularly when he is talking about their relations with Great Britain.'[24]

From Stevenson's correspondence, it is clear that Panikkar's actions in Egypt were not limited to simple mediation or machinations against Pakistan. His conversations with the nationalist regime in Cairo became a new delineation of non-alignment for India in the 1950s. The negotiating skills that Kaul had noticed in China came in handy now and they worked well. On the day of the signing, a delegation from the Command Council of the Revolution visited Panikkar to thank him for his help.[25]

Initially, the British were resigned at the effects of Panikkar's machinations.

'For all that he is so unreliable, Panikkar is a likeable rogue,' William Strang, permanent undersecretary at the foreign office, commented. 'Though I have no doubt that the net result of his passion for "helping both sides" is anything but helpful to us.'[26]

But the foreign office's wry resignation faded fast over the stickier issue of the Suez Canal Zone. Here, the unilateral abrogation of the 1936 Treaty presented the potential for a dangerous crisis. Nasser's rise to power meant that, for the Egyptians, Britain was an unnecessary presence. The Cold War was assuming wider proportions and on this new canvas, oil from the Middle East was important for the defence of Western Europe. With British bases in Palestine no longer a matter of choice, the Canal Zone was a bastion of security for the wider region.

Visiting military installations in the Suez Canal Zone in February 1953, Panikkar realised just how strategically crucial it was to reach an agreement on this subject. The area was, however, certainly Egyptian territory. In his view, the country should, under ideal circumstances, be able to exercise its sovereignty here. This would naturally mean a complete evacuation by Britain—but that didn't seem to fit the bill either, given the strategic location, size and importance of the base. One of the largest airfields in the world was present here, as also elaborate facilities for the repair of trucks, tanks and aircraft. 'It was an ever present demonstration of Britain's military power and in its shadow, Egyptian independence could never flourish.'[27] Musing over the possibilities, Panikkar came to the conclusion that cooperation between Egypt and Britain in the Zone was necessary.[28]

In these ponderings, he was pre-empted by Stevenson, who had no desire to be hijacked. He called on Panikkar shortly after negotiations between Egypt and Britain began in the spring of 1953.

'You've heard that we're now discussing the question of our military base. What are your views on this?'

'I've had no instructions from our government on this matter,' Panikkar said truthfully.

Stevenson wasn't convinced. 'Still, Panikkar, what are *your* personal views?'

'How can I express any views without knowing all the facts?' Panikkar parried, though he couldn't resist adding, 'One thing, however. If the proposals that emerge are not acceptable to the Egyptians, the Government of India will certainly not think they are fair. Having objected to British troops on our soil, how can we argue that they should be quartered in Egypt, against the will of the Egyptians?'

'Oh really?' Stevenson retorted, annoyed. 'Well, remember one thing. The presence of a strong British contingent here will help the security of India. The Suez Canal is vital to you too.'

'Your assumption is that India's security depends on British troops. I reject that suggestion. There is no need for you to keep a base in Egypt for our protection. As for the Canal, what is the harm to us if the Egyptians run it?'

The answer wasn't exactly to Stevenson's liking, but he replied good-humouredly enough, 'I expected you to be favourable to the Egyptians. Now I am sure.'

'Let me ask you one question. If, instead of quitting India, Britain had insisted on retaining a military base there, do you imagine our countries would have remained friends?'

'One can say no.'

'Then, why not wind up this base, which they consider prejudicial to their independence, and win their friendship too?'

'I can follow your argument,' Stevenson said readily. 'But there are many factors involved. When we left India, our position in the area was weakened. If we leave Suez, it won't just be Suez that goes. The whole question needs thorough analysis. No decision is possible otherwise.'[29]

In the negotiations that dragged on for the better part of a year against a tense backdrop of unrest in Egypt, friction between London and Washington over the management of the negotiations and internal frissons within the British government (especially between Churchill and Anthony Eden), Panikkar played no further part. But he did intervene in one other matter. When negotiations opened, Britain had demanded that the United States also be a party. The reasoning was simple: the defence of the Middle East was principally an American responsibility. Any military change here would strategically affect Washington. When news of this reached Panikkar, he knew it was a tactic to secure American support for the British point of view. If both Washington and London pressured the Egyptians, the latter stood to lose.

Panikkar dashed off to see General Naguib and explained the wider geopolitics at stake.

'I quite appreciate what you say, Ambassador, but what can I do?' Naguib asked. 'We have already agreed.'

The same day, Panikkar arranged to meet with Nasser to tell him the same thing.

The younger man's response was different. 'We have to somehow get out of this commitment to let the Americans in on the talks. A way must be found.'

Nasser suggested asking Naguib to announce that it was the decision of the full Revolutionary Council that Washington remove itself from the talks.

'That's quite good, but it is not enough,' Panikkar said. 'The Americans will be affronted if they are first invited and then shut out.'

'True. I shall meet Cauffrey [the US ambassador] now and set things right.'

Panikkar agreed that this was the right thing to do and added that Nasser should let Cauffrey tactfully know that it was not because Egypt had no faith in America that it was taking this attitude but because they preferred to keep the US in reserve as a possible mediator for the future.[30]

Eventually, an agreement was reached in the summer of 1954.[31] India made efforts to tone things down, but Panikkar's involvement was limited, though he did write to the British MP Woodrow Wyatt, insisting that the British would have to be content with what they were getting, since the Egyptians were not in a position to make further concessions.[32]

'Actually the feeling is that they have gone very much beyond what they had originally planned and they feel that, after having agreed to maintain the base, to keep a large body of British technicians and to make the base available in case of an attack on Arab countries is really asking them too much to go further … Egyptian leaders are not men who take hasty decisions. But after all they represent a revolutionary sentiment, which must show itself in the claim to complete independence of their country. I wonder what is possible at this stage.'[33]

Considering that negotiations at the time were deadlocked over niggles like whether British personnel left on the base would wear military uniform or civilian clothes, Panikkar's assessment was as realistic and pragmatic as possible. The impression of British diplomacy though was that in the end, Panikkar's (and therefore India's) support had been with the Egyptians.[34] It was the right impression and it would be solidified by Nehru's arrival in Cairo in June 1953 in a visit that was strategically timed with Krishna Menon already beginning to market the idea of a Non-Aligned Movement (NAM) at the United Nations.

The visit was propelled by Panikkar, who hinted to the prime minister that a stop in Cairo to meet the young leader of Egypt would serve several geopolitical goals. Nehru agreed to stop over on his way back from the Commonwealth Conference in London. It was a three-day visit, but it was the beginning of a much greater movement. The Non-Aligned Movement would come to fruition and definition in 1956, but this first visit laid much of the groundwork for India's policy in the Middle East and bringing a powerful Arab voice on board the NAM bandwagon. The prime minister held a number of important conversations at the ambassador's residence, and towards the end of his time in Cairo, there was a four-hour drift down the Nile during which Nasser, Naguib and Nehru discussed the future of India-Egypt ties. When the cruise came to an end, Panikkar escorted Nasser off the boat.

'Well, Colonel? What do you think of Panditji's ideas?'

'The significance of what he has told us will become clear only in time. But one thing is plain. We cannot hope to achieve much as a military government. Only a popular approach can bring results. From today, I am with the people.'[35]

In the middle of Panikkar's time in Cairo, he became involved with Tibet yet again. It had been over a year since he had left China, but he had continued to be in touch with Nehru on the subject of the border with China. The prime minister was undeniably and very visibly skittish on the subject, despite writing firmly on 29 July 1952 to both Menon and Panikkar, 'On reconsideration I accept Shri Panikkar's advice that we should not make specific mention about the frontiers.'[36] Now, in 1953, border talks were coming up between India and China. Despite everything that had passed between the two men, Panikkar's views on Tibet in 1953 were illuminative of Nehru's trust in him. These views were also to be the former Indian ambassador's enduring imprint on India's China and Tibet policy.

By 1953, India's approach to the frontier was already fairly well set. Nehru's biographer, Sarvepalli Gopal, would write that as far as the prime minister was concerned, India's borders with China were 'firm, well-known and beyond dispute'.[37] Nehru had also made several equally firm statements, leaving no room for further controversy over the McMahon Line: 'Our maps show that the McMahon Line is our boundary and that is our boundary—map or no map … We stand by that boundary, and we will not allow anybody to come across that boundary.'[38]

As Nirupama Rao writes, the problem lay in the fact that, except for Sikkim, the border had not been demarcated jointly with China on the ground; the boundary in the western and middle sectors had not been defined in detail by treaty and only, as Nehru would say, by custom, usage and tradition.[39] The bigger trouble lay in the fact that Panikkar, while he had been India's ambassador to China, had not pushed for the definition of the border. On his part, the Indian prime minister chose to overlook the officials within the MEA who insisted, contrary to the ambassador in Peking, that there should be a border settlement in any negotiations between India and China.[40] Panikkar himself had responded to the copy of the furious letter Bajpai had written to K.P.S. Menon, saying that India had unequivocally stated its own position, and if the Chinese had 'anything to say about it, it was for them to raise it'.[41]

Not surprisingly, Bajpai was even more livid at this insouciant letter. Answering Panikkar two days later, he tore into the former ambassador, saying bluntly that he was not convinced by Panikkar's argument about why China had not raised the question of the frontier. The Chinese had never accepted the McMahon Line and there was no way that India could consider this question as settled. 'The practical difficulty of telling them that we regard the McMahon Line as our frontier and shall treat it as such, without requesting them to answer or commit upon this point, is not quite apparent to me. If they are friendly and accept the present position, they need not say anything about it. If they should do so now, but a dispute arises sometime in the future, we can quote this silence as acquiescence in support of our case. If they are not as friendly to us as we are to them and do not wish silence to be construed as acquiescence, they will have to come out into the open now and we shall know where we really stand: that may possibly leave us sadder men but also wiser.'[42]

Bajpai's anger rings down through the ages. Had Panikkar insisted on a clear definition of the border by the Chinese, had he passed on Nehru's specific instructions about a caveat, matters would have developed very differently. In the end, it had been Panikkar's views—that India's maps were clear enough and that the Indian prime minister had been public enough with his views on the border—that carried the day. Nehru remained uncomfortable about how matters stood, though in 1953, he added that, 'if occasion offers itself and especially if any challenge to the frontier is made, then we shall have to make this particularly clear'.[43] And so it came to pass that in December 1953, on the eve of fresh talks with the Chinese, New Delhi was struggling with whether to raise the question of the frontier with Tibet at all.

Panikkar was asked for his advice as the last man on the ground in Peking. His response, mentioned in the MEA briefing note, is slightly staggering. If at all the Chinese raised the frontier, the Indians speculated, they should be told that there was 'nothing' to discuss as the frontier was 'clearly defined'. If the Chinese were to raise the 'illegality' of the Simla Convention of 1914, they could be told that 'convention or no convention, our frontier is well defined and well recognized by long custom and usage'. And if they suggested that talks on the frontier be postponed, one option would be to walk out of the talks 'as suggested by Sardar Panikkar', although this would defeat the very object for which the conference had been called and could lead to border incidents with China. Another option, the less extreme one, would be 'maintain our stand about the frontier and refuse to accept the Chinese stand or discuss it, and proceed to other items'. And if the Chinese refused to do so, then the negotiations should be broken off.[44]

Sarvepalli Gopal would define Panikkar's diplomacy in Peking as 'remiss'. But more than that, it was a compartmentalised policy. In his first years in communist China, Panikkar followed a Nehruvian line of Asian solidarity, a line that was idealistic, based on what he (and Nehru) saw as a shared civilisational history, and a policy that evolved from one event to the next. In his last few months in Peking though, the omission of a discussion on the frontier was a dangerous loophole that would be cleverly exploited by the Chinese in the years to come. In the years following 1953, India's relations with China would become increasingly flawed and brittle.

The blame for that would eternally be pinned on Panikkar.

Shortly after Nehru left Cairo, Panikkar applied for six weeks' leave.

Gouri was increasingly fragile. While she was well enough to travel with him occasionally, doctors were still, after all these months, unable to find out what ailed her. Armed with a recommendation to see a specialist at the Hospital for Tropical Diseases in London, the Panikkars and Radha departed for England.

Gouri was checked into hospital for a week so that doctors could run tests. We don't know if the outcome of the tests were successful or not, but Panikkar reports in his memoir that after this stint, 'we spent the rest of our stay going around and meeting friends'.[45]

Gouri had never been to Europe or England, and despite her fatigue, she perked up considerably at the prospect of seeing London. Panikkar had a number of friends in the city, including the young Maharaja of Kutch, with whose grandfather (the old Maharao

Khemgarji) Panikkar had worked in the 1940s. The Panikkars stayed with the maharaja for some days, before the journalist (and Panikkar's very good friend) Guy Wint arrived to take them sightseeing—and to furtively tell Panikkar that Eliahu Elath, the current Israeli ambassador to the Court of St James and an old friend, wanted to meet him. Since Panikkar was going on to Cairo, and his remit included nearly the whole of the Middle East, it would be difficult to meet Elath (or other Zionist leaders) later.

Panikkar agreed, and Wint set up the meeting.

To Gouri and Radha, he said not a word, focusing on showing them the delights of Hyde Park, Covent Gardens and St Paul's Cathedral.

'I almost recaptured my first raptures at seeing London,' Panikkar recalled, though his real joy was at being able to show his wife and daughter the England that he loved. Ten days into the visit, the Panikkars went down to Cambridge and Oxford, where he met his friend, the military historian Captain Basil Liddell-Hart.

It was here, in the sunny English countryside, that Panikkar was 'able to do something else', as he put it, during his stay. Liddell-Hart, who loved his intrigues as much as he loved his history, made the necessary arrangements for a meeting between Panikkar and Elath. According to Panikkar, he wanted 'to avoid any news leaking to the press, and accordingly, we [he and Liddell-Hart] arranged for Elath to meet me as if by accident, on a Sunday while I was visiting Liddell-Hart at his country house.'[46]

Not surprisingly, Panikkar skims over this meeting in his memoir, saying only, 'As our discussions affect many matters of current controversy, it would be improper to describe them here. In brief, it seemed to me that there was a slight chance of successful mediation [of the Arab-Israeli conflict].'[47]

And so, on 6 September 1953, the Panikkars met for lunch at Liddell-Hart's country home in Marlow, Buckinghamshire, a picturesque village in the Thames Valley. The Elaths arrived close to half-past twelve and after a pleasant meal, talking about China and the old days, 'the ladies went out into the garden and we opened our own discussions'.[48]

Panikkar might have been coy about revealing the substance of this meeting, but Elath suffered no such qualms. He submitted a twelve-page report in which he analysed the conversation with Panikkar as a leading indicator of India's views on the establishment of diplomatic ties with Israel.

'Panikkar has been a friend of mine for good many years,' he wrote. 'I first met him in London during the 1937 coronation celebrations, and he then put me in touch with a number of Indian leaders attending the coronation. We have since met fairly frequently … We were both at the UN General Assembly in 1948, and I saw him again more briefly last year (i.e. 1952) in London. I had heard from several mutual friends that he had been asking after me, and looking for a chance of meeting me again privately, since his official position as Indian Ambassador to Egypt and other Arab countries … now makes it impossible for him to meet me in public.'[49]

Elath reported that the overall tenor of the meeting was negative. 'Panikkar said he was doubtful whether any progress would be made in this direction [i.e. recognition of diplomatic ties with Israel] in the near future. Though Nehru was quite determined not to move from the stand he had taken on full recognition of Israel … he would not be able to do more than maintain the status quo as long as India needed the support of the Arabs within the "Asian bloc" in the United Nations—and anyhow, at least this neutrality on the question of Kashmir, when this came up for further discussions at the UN … According to Panikkar, therefore, the question of exchange of diplomatic missions between our two countries is hardly practical politics at the moment.'[50]

Clearly, for Elath, this was an important conversation, and one that revolved entirely around the Arab-Israeli conflict. As India's ambassador to all the four states bordering Israel—Jordan, Syria, Lebanon and Egypt—Panikkar's access and position was enviable. He was able to give Elath a clear-eyed assessment of the affairs of the Middle East and leave him with a promise that he would 'speak to Naguib and Nasser about this'.[51]

The Panikkars spent the summer travelling over the continent, from France to Belgium and thence to Holland and Switzerland.

When they finally returned to Cairo, the elections in Sudan were over, and Britain and Egypt were deadlocked on the matter of the now free Sudan. There was nothing more that Panikkar could do here, beyond awaiting the arrival of Vijayalakshmi Pandit who was due to visit on her way back to New Delhi.

The visit passed off innocuously enough and it was followed some months later by a visit from the British Labour Party leader, Aneurin Bevan. Bevan and his wife Jennie Lee were stopping in Cairo on their way to Israel. They would be in Cairo for five days after which, since they were old friends, the Panikkars had planned to take them on a tour of Luxor.

'We welcome in him an enemy in the clothing of a friend,' said a Cairo newspaper sardonically on the day the Bevans landed.

That was certainly one way to put it.

Aneurin Bevan was then a power to reckon with in British politics (though he would resign in April 1954, after accusing Clement Attlee of surrendering to American pressure over a proposed multinational defence organisation in Asia and the Pacific). Known for his oratory and his intense commitment to socialism, Bevan had definite views on Nasser and the Suez crisis. For him, it was a situation that was seeing the old order of power politics colliding with revolutionary demands for independence. As he put it, the 'moral sense of the world was outraged by the very brutality of the attempt by great powers to impose their will by armed force on a weaker nation'.[52]

In his eyes, the crisis in the Suez was a clear case for a new attitude to national independence and sovereignty. Nasser's actions were not the precursor for a social revolution. In fact, Bevan argued that if anything, Nasser derived his powers from 'resentment against Western imperialism', rather than a focus on improving socioeconomic conditions in Egypt.[53] Instead of trying to redistribute property, for example, Bevan argued, Nasser and his colleagues only focused on nationalist sentiment and on building up the nation-state. Unfortunately for Nasser, Bevan continued, he had 'not realised that to keep on stirring the pot of nationalist passions is not conducive to the creation of conditions favourable to long term economic projects'.[54]

All told this made for a stormy visit.

The Bevans were greeted at the airport with a bouquet of fresh pink roses for Jennie, a busy MP herself. They would be staying, reported *TIME* magazine snidely, with their old friend, 'the diplomat who did so much to persuade India's Nehru not to be beastly to the Communist Government in Peking'.[55] The *TIME* reporter smirked, 'Currently, Panikkar is working with might and main to persuade Egypt to abandon the West and take up neutralism. So, everybody concerned was quick to appreciate the official mischief that could result when such practiced twisters of the British lion's tail as Bevan, Panikkar and the Egyptians got together.'[56]

Later, the Bevans were photographed chatting to President Naguib who, in pajamas and dressing gown, was recovering from a bad attack of flu. They rounded off their Cairo trip with a dinner with Nasser and the Revolutionary Council, where the discussions went on until midnight. The next day, Bevan was asked about it at a press conference, where he diplomatically said, 'I merely listened.'

Panikkar, who was present at the meeting, would have disagreed. The dinner went well, until the conversation veered into political channels. From then onwards, it became decidedly stormy. Nasser, despite his eloquence, was unable to shake Bevan of the view that his dictatorship was not a valid political necessity. At the end of dinner, Bevan stood up. 'How long do you intend to retain such unrestrained power in your own hands?' he demanded.

'Until the corruption and inequity in Egypt are ended,' replied Nasser.

Bevan laughed, 'Which not even God has so far achieved!'[57]

He said as much at yet another press conference where he was asked his views on Egypt's revolution. 'There's no revolution. What happened was a coup d'état with a revolutionary façade. The revolution has still to come.'[58]

Panikkar would not be in Egypt for much longer, but one of the highlights for him was the publication of the book on which he had been working while he had been in Peking. *Asia and Western Dominance* was published to wide acclaim and controversy in November 1953. It was quite possibly one of Panikkar's most ambitious books, threading together his belief in an Asian sense of unity and common history. He was writing both as a historian and a serving member of India's diplomatic corps, and it is not entirely surprisingly that, despite its ambitious scope, the arguments he put forward now tended to align with modern India's politics. Equally unsurprising then is his theoretical shift *away* from a 'Greater India' discourse.

The book critically considered European imperialism, beginning with the Portuguese, in Asia. The fundamental thesis on which the text was built was the unity of the period between Vasco da Gama's arrival in Calicut in 1498 on the one hand and Indian independence and the Chinese revolution on the other: a historical epoch defined by common features. The first of these was the domination of maritime power over the Asian continental mass. The Indian Ocean also returned as a protagonist in this text. By controlling the seas, Europeans would impose a commercial economy on Asia from the establishment of the Portuguese spice monopoly to modern large-scale capital exports. Politically, the consequence was the domination of the West which brought with it the doctrine of racial superiority, attempts at conversion and the solidarity of European peoples against Asians.

The European challenge marked a discontinuity in Asian history as it put into question at different levels the social and religious organisations of Asia, the ideologies and the political and economic systems.

Panikkar emphasised four phases in which political conditions became too oppressive: a two-and-a-half-century period of European expansion in which contact remained rather limited (1498–1750), followed by a period of conquest (1750–1858). Then there was a phase of domination (1858–1914) and finally, one of retreat and Asian revival (1918–1939).

In his estimate, it was the internal conditions of the Asian countries that determined the degree of penetration of foreign influence. In China, for example, the transition from the Ming dynasty to the Manchu empire strengthened the country at a crucial moment, allowing it to regain control over peripheral areas such as Xinjiang and Tibet, and indirectly over kingdoms such as Korea and Cambodia.

In succession, the Portuguese, the Spanish, the Dutch and the British had tried to establish relations with China, but if they had succeeded in establishing trade, diplomatic and political relations had been much more difficult.[59] Until the mid-eighteenth century therefore, all the European nations that had succeeded one another in Asia had been unable to establish themselves as territorial powers.

From the middle of the eighteenth century however, things began to change. Starting in India, the Europeans were able to gain territorial and political dominance. To explain this shift, Panikkar took into account the internal situation in Asian countries. In India, the conquest was thus attributed to the divisions and wars that had shattered the Mughal Empire and given the French and the British trading companies the opportunity to insert themselves into local conflicts. For the British, the conquest of India during a century of wars was the starting point for expansion into Asia. Starting from the status of a 'possession' and a colony, British India, by slow stages, developed into an 'empire', no doubt subordinate to the authorities in London, but claiming to be heard in its own right and often forcing the home government into policies with which it was not in entire agreement. The civil service bureaucracy had been, according to Panikkar, the first and most important factor responsible for India's transformation from 'possession' to 'empire'.

The two great Asian civilisations thus faced the same challenge, namely Western imperialism, but their experiences were very different. The government in India, at the centre of an imperial political system that extended from Afghanistan to Persia, Burma and Tibet, began to behave according to its own judgements and interests despite the British government's reassertion of its authority over the country. In China meanwhile, the indirect influence of foreigners and the humiliation of the country grew through various means: control over river routes, European settlements and concessions, extraterritoriality rights, the right of protection towards Christians and attacks on tributary states. Even in China however, during the very heyday of imperialism, a reaction was felt. The defeat in the Sino-Japanese war and the scramble for concessions was followed by the Boxer Revolt and then the more modern and Westernised revolt that led to the establishment of the republic.

But the real turning point in relations between Asia and Europe was, according to Panikkar, the First World War, which he described as the 'European civil war'. This process of change continued across the interwar years and finally came to fruition in India, China and Japan after the Second World War.

Panikkar reminded his international audience of the Indian ships that had once navigated around the Indian Ocean, 'including the entire coast of Africa,' long before Vasco da Gama had even arrived. He continued with his argument that Indian dominance was not a new circumstance in the region, nor was India unknown to the wider western world, from Egypt to Rome, from China to Champa. Although Panikkar briefly mentioned the existence of 'Indian colonies' in Southeast Asia in terms of Indian emigration across the empire during the early twentieth century, he renounced any hint of the discourse of 'Greater India'.[60]

All of this was innocent enough. But two specific chapters caused the greatest controversy and brought down a hail of angry criticism on Panikkar's head. The chapters in question dealt with, respectively, the Christian missions and relations between Russia and Asia.

In the first, Christian proselytism was described as a particularly odious aspect of Western culture. Missionaries were presented, except in the first short period, as arrogant people, incapable of a true understanding of local cultures and willing to resort to all sorts of compromises and dishonesty to gain the favour of those with political power and thus be able to spread Christianity. Moreover, they were an instrument of imperialism, favoured by the growth of the political clout of the European powers.[61] For this view, Panikkar was slammed as an 'extreme nationalist ... suspicious of the supra-national loyalties that foreign missionaries may evoke and who is resentful of their claim to a higher apprehension of spiritual truth than his own countrymen have achieved'.[62]

But in truth, Panikkar had never wavered from this outlook since 1916. It was not a sudden aversion to proselytisation, but one that had for him always been intimately linked to not just his idea of a Hindu nation, but to Indian identity. Panikkar had always believed that as long as Hinduism beat in the heart of India, the country could absorb the most diverse influences. But Christianity to him represented a real danger. It was too exclusive to allow for adaptation. The acceptance of Christianity, Panikkar believed, would lead to a clean break in India's cultural identity.

The other chapter that gained negative attention was to do with Russian imperialism. The subject is a separate topic in *Asia and Western Dominance* because, in Panikkar's eyes, it was qualitatively different from the others. Firstly, it was a land expansion and not a maritime one. Secondly, the worst and most humiliating features of European expansion were absent: the Russians had refrained from intervening in wars with China for the opening of its markets, from the opium trade, from the forced export of Chinese labour on plantations, from religious proselytising, from acts of vandalism. This was a slightly questionable reconstruction of events, though it enabled Panikkar to explain the origin of the influence of the Bolshevik revolution in Asia. Communist ideas had come to Asian countries, but in each the effect was different, depending on its individual society and polity. But on the whole, Panikkar felt that it wasn't so surprising that a suppressed peoples embraced communism as a potential path to liberation.

He was promptly accused of reflecting Mao's visions in his own words. One reviewer put it bitingly, 'Clearly this is an account of the relation of Western nations to China seen, not merely through Ambassador Panikkar's Asian eyes, but also through Chairman Mao's Communist Chinese eyes.'[63] Another reviewer tore into Panikkar's 'opportunism' in presenting this theory, presenting an image of communism—based on Chinese propaganda—that would appeal to Asian public opinion.[64]

To take that chapter out of the context of the rest of the book is unfair since it is in the whole picture that Panikkar's vision for Asia emerges. In different ways, India and China were responsible for an Asian rebirth in the twentieth century. Now, going forward, he hoped for their paths to converge. It was an undoubtedly Nehruvian vision, founded in the civilisational history the two countries shared. The only trouble was that, by the time it was published, Panikkar had been unfairly branded as a communist.

A more balanced review was provided by the historian Percival Spear, who wrote, 'Another of Mr Panikkar's favourite ideas is Asianism. Some mysterious force is sweeping Asia giving a sense of unity as against Europe and America. That there is a common sentiment against non-Asian intervention and control which till recently has meant European control is certain and very natural. For the suggestion that it is anything more, no evidence has been produced. A common *positive* sentiment requires a community of ideas and values such as exists in Europe and India. But there is no such community of ideas in Asia. There are three separate civilizations in Asia which have, on the whole, kept remarkably distinct. The one big contribution which India has made to China (Buddhism) is an element of Chinese culture about which the new China is far from enthusiastic.'[65]

Yet another reviewer wrote that Panikkar's vision was too idealistic, based merely on the hope that a common historical experience might lend an ideological basis to Nehru's dreams of non-alignment in Asia.[66]

This is not to say that the reviews were all bad. Panikkar got excellent reviews of his ideas in *The Times* (London), and Woodrow Wyatt and E.M. Forster gave it glowing reviews. He sent a copy to Nehru who wrote back, after carefully reading it, with a note of warm congratulations. He had spent nearly twenty-five years dwelling on these ideas, and to the end of his days, Panikkar was very proud of *Asia and Western Dominance*. He was prouder still when Nehru, having read it, suggested that Panikkar return early to India to help the prime minister with a problem that was giving him a hard time: the reorganisation of the states.

PART X

A Curtain Falls (1955–1963)

CHAPTER 52

'The Real Task Has Just Begun'

PANIKKAR RETURNED TO A COUNTRY THAT HAD CHANGED IRREVOCABLY in the years since transfer of power. Nor was the process of change final or finished.

By Partition, India had lost an area of 3,64,737 square miles and a population of 81.5 million. By integrating the states, an area of nearly 5,00,000 square miles had been brought in, with a population of 86.5 million (not including Jammu and Kashmir).[1] The artificial barriers between the states and the provinces might have been removed, but as Sardar Patel dryly put it, 'the real task has just begun ... We have to weave new fabrics into old materials; we have to make sure that simultaneously the old and the new are integrated into a pleasing whole—a design which would fit well into the pattern of all India.'[2]

The states would now have to fit into a common administrative mould. This was always going to be hard, with a varying range of readiness and efficiency across the states. States like Hyderabad and Mysore, for instance, were easy enough to integrate, administratively speaking. In the case of states merged with provinces, the Government of India assumed control of all central subjects, leaving the provincial subjects to be administered by the provincial governments concerned.

Where isolated small states were merged into bigger provinces like Madras or the United Provinces, the difficulties were easy to surmount. But in the case of Orissa, where the mergers doubled the province in size, and the Central Provinces and Bombay, where larger areas had to be merged, it was a nightmare for officials. The provincial governments had to absorb some states into old districts and constitute others into new districts. Administrative, judicial and revenue systems had to be streamlined and synchronised and new electoral rolls had to be prepared. In these unions, administration had to be built from scratch: from the division of the union into taluks and tehsils, to the creation of a properly staffed secretariat, to its representation with a new legislature. Everything had to be tacked into place before the Constitution of India was promulgated in 1950 and before India went to the polls in its first general elections in 1951–1952.

Working at lightning speed, the Ministry of States had managed to pull together all the states into the same constitutional relations with the Centre as the provinces. There was a scheme of financial integration in place and the Indian States Forces were to be absorbed into the Indian Army. But both Sardar Patel and V.P. Menon underlined that 'real integration had to take place in the minds of the people'. As Patel said in the months before he passed away, 'Almost overnight, we have introduced in these states the superstructure of a modern system of government. The inspiration and stimulus has come from above, rather than below, and unless the transplanted growth takes a healthy root in the soil, there will be a danger of collapse and chaos.'[3]

As always, he was prescient.

The question of language had always been a simmering one; its history stretched back to the years predating independence and integration. The Congress was fully alive to the importance of language in a country as diverse as India. Since the end of the First World War and throughout the 1920s, the Congress had committed itself to a programme for linguistic reorganisation of the states. Regional language committees had been formed to foster political participation at the local level. An official acceptance of the principle came in 1928 with the Nehru Report, which advocated the inclusion of linguistic states as part of the official agenda. For the elections held in 1946, one of the planks of the Congress manifesto was that insofar as they were able, states ought to be formed on a linguistic and cultural basis.[4]

But it was never a comfortably adopted principle.

As India edged closer to freedom, the Indian prime minister was a worried man. The trajectory of the freedom movement, with its deeply communal polarities and a plan for partition, had been enough to warn him of the potential dangers that lay ahead. It had been one thing to insist on the princely states entering the union of India, but now that they were being brought on board, the technicalities of organisation and reform were migraine-inducing. In addition, Partition had led to an influx of terrified refugees and their rehabilitation alone had changed the cities of Delhi, Bombay and Calcutta almost beyond recognition. In 1947, India was looking at the prospect of being divided on the basis of religion. Did it really need to be divided further on the basis of language?

Nehru now began to wonder if multicultural and multilingual states could instead provide a template for harmony.

The prime minister said as much to the Constituent Assembly in December 1947. The Congress *had* promised linguistic provinces, he said, but with the country still staggering from the aftereffects of partition, 'The first essential … is for India as a whole to be strong and firmly established, confident in her capacity to meet all possible dangers and face and meet all problems.'[5]

In itself it was a pragmatic view to take and it was shared by Patel and V.P. Menon, the officials in charge of integration. It was better to defer the creation of linguistic provinces at least until such time as India was surer of itself and its internal security. The prime minister talked this over with Gandhi and managed to persuade him to agree with this. Gandhi was willing to wait—'the reluctance to enforce linguistic redistribution is perhaps justifiable in the present depressing atmosphere'—but he clung to the principle of it. In a prayer meeting held on 25 January 1948, Gandhi returned to the subject of linguistic states and declared, 'there should be as many provinces in the country as there are major languages … if linguistic provinces are formed, it will also give a fillip to the regional languages'.[6]

A week later, Gandhi was dead. He left behind a country battling problems of rehabilitating refugees and providing them with gainful employment, a war in Kashmir and military action in Hyderabad, framing a new Constitution and new economic development plans.

In 1950, India became a republic. The newly prepared Constitution recognised three categories of states and a separate identity for the centrally administered units.[7] Shortly thereafter, the parliament passed the Representation of the People Act, which set the voting age at twenty-one and gave the right to vote to every Indian who had resided continuously in a constituency for 180 days or more.

In the spring of 1951, India went to the polls for the first time in its independent history. The country's first general elections were held against an ongoing war in Vietnam and Korea; the disenfranchisement of the Cape Coloureds by South Africa's Afrikaner National Party; the testing of the first hydrogen bomb; and the assassinations, in quick succession, of the king of Jordan and the prime ministers of Iran and Pakistan. Amidst all this, the creation of linguistic provinces was not priority. As the best way of postponing decisions on this subject, Nehru favoured the appointment by the Constituent Assembly of a committee to investigate and report on the feasibility of linguistic provinces. If this committee obtained a large measure of agreement, then one or more specific boundary commissions could be appointed.[8]

And so, the Linguistic Provinces Commission (known popularly as the Dhar Commission), a committee of jurists and civil servants, came into being. Its report recognised the popularity of the support for linguistic divisions but concluded firmly that this was not the time to wade into unknown waters.[9]

Unsurprisingly, this cool practicality was met with outrage. So loud was the clamour that a weary Nehru appointed a fresh committee. He put himself and Patel on it along with party historian and 'faithful South Indian non-entity'[10] Pattabhi Sitaramayya. This committee was unoriginally known as the 'JVP Committee', named for the first names of its members. It went further than the Dhar Commission had done and presented the argument that language was not just a 'binding force, but a separating one', repeating that, under the current circumstances, 'every separatist and disruptive tendency should be rigorously discouraged'.[11]

Still, the JVP Committee left a loophole in its report, stating that the problem could be 're-examined' in the light of public demand. It would prove to be quite the tipping point in modern Indian history.

In 1948 and 1949, there was a renewed push across India for linguistic autonomy. There was for instance, the campaign for Samyukta (Greater) Karnataka, aiming to unite Kannada speakers across Madras, Mysore, Bombay and Hyderabad. Running parallel to this was the struggle for Samyukta Maharashtra, which sought to bring together Marathi speakers in a single political unit. The Malayalis were not to be outdone. They had been clamouring for a state of their own based on the merger of the princely states of Cochin and Travancore with Malabar, a demand that had been made to V.P. Menon himself and that he had hastily dodged. There was even a Mahagujarat movement. These were but a few of the movements that had come to life in the years before the first elections.

But without question, the fieriest and most vigorous movement was among the Telugu speakers of the Andhra country. Telugu was spoken by more people in India than any other language besides Hindi. It had a rich literary history and was associated with symbols of Andhra glory like the Vijayanagara empire. While India was still under British rule, the Andhra Mahasabha had worked hard to cultivate a sense of identity among the Telugu-speaking peoples of the Madras Presidency who, they argued, had been discriminated against by the Tamils. After transfer of power, Telugu speakers demanded via petitions, marches and fasts that the Congress implement its old resolutions in favour of linguistic states. So heated did this movement grow that, in 1950, former Madras chief minister T. Prakasam resigned from the party on the issue of statehood.

Cutting across party lines, Telugu-speaking legislators in the Madras Assembly urged the immediate creation of a state to be named Andhra Pradesh. As the Central government looked the other way, in the monsoon of 1951, a Congress politician-turned-godman named Sitaram went on a hunger strike in support of the cause of Andhra

Pradesh. He gave up the fast in five weeks after the Gandhian leader Vinoba Bhave intervened, but it was the first indicator that matters were spiralling out of control. With the general elections around the corner, the atmosphere in Andhra was tense. During his campaign tour in the Telugu-speaking districts, Nehru was met at several places by protesters waving black flags and shouting, 'We want Andhra!'[12]

At this point, both the prime minister and the chief minister of Madras, then Rajaji, had gone on record, saying that they did not believe that the creation of Andhra was a good idea. They stated that if Andhra came into being, Madras would not be part of it. Statements like these did nothing to calm the atmosphere, especially since most Telugu-speakers had a strong demographic presence in Madras and believed they had a strong claim to it. In all, the signs were ominous and despite its successes elsewhere, the Congress would poll poorly in these districts, winning a mere 43 of the 145 seats from the region in the Madras Legislative Assembly. The bulk of the other seats were won by parties supporting the Andhra movement. These included the communists, who returned an impressive forty-one members.

The results of the election encouraged the revival of the Andhra movement. Towards the end of February 1952, Swami Sitaram resurfaced, marching through the Telugu-speaking districts to lobby for support. He had upped the rhetorical ante as well, using slogans like 'Andhras are ready to pay the price to achieve the same'.[13] Furiously, Nehru told parliament on 22 May 1952, 'For some years now, our foremost efforts have been directed to the consolidation of India. Personally, I would look upon anything that did not help this process of consolidation as undesirable. Even though the formation of linguistic provinces may be desirable in some cases, this would obviously be the wrong time. When the right time comes, let us have them by all means.'[14]

The problem with this declaration was that nobody knew what the right time was or when it would come. Fed up with waiting, the Andhras intensified their protest. On 19 October 1952, a man named Potti Sriramulu would create history by going on a hunger strike in Madras.[15]

Sriramulu was not unknown to Gandhi. An engineer and a satyagrahi, he was a firm Gandhian, but he had a tendency to go on fasts much like Gandhi himself to achieve his political goals. 'I know he is a solid worker,' Gandhi would say of him. 'Though he is a little eccentric.'[16] Usually, Gandhi could keep a check on Sriramulu's more rebellious moods, but in 1952, Gandhi was dead and Andhra meant more to Sriramulu than anything else ever had.

He would stick to this fast until the bitter end.

On 3 December 1952, Nehru wrote a harassed letter to Rajaji. 'Some kind of fast is going on for the Andhra Province and I get frantic telegrams. I am totally unmoved by this and I propose to ignore it completely.'[17]

By this time, Sriramulu had not eaten for six weeks.

The support for his cause grew as each day passed, with hartals in many towns.

A week after his defiant letter to Rajaji, Nehru was forced to climb down from his position. The time had clearly come to accept the Andhra demand, 'otherwise complete frustration will grow among the Andhras, and we will not be able to catch up with it'.[18]

It was too late.

On 15 December, fifty-eight days into his fast, Potti Sriramulu died.

The hell that Nehru had been warning against, the hell he had been trying to prevent, now broke loose. Government offices were attacked, trains were halted and defaced. The damage to state property ran into millions of rupees. Several protesters were killed in police firings.[19] Faced with the prospect of widespread and possibly uncontrollable protests and violence, the beleaguered prime minister caved. Two days after Sriramulu's death, Nehru released a statement: Andhra Pradesh would come into being. Sriramulu had become the catalyst to redrawing the map of India.

Over the course of the next few months, Telugu districts of the Madras province were identified for separation. Rajaji was helpless but enraged as he grimly attended the inauguration of the new state of Andhra at Kurnool on 1 October 1953.

Nehru was no less livid and not a little afraid.

'We have disturbed the hornet's nest,' he wrote grimly to a colleague. 'I believe most of us are likely to be badly stung.'[20]

This was the context that greeted Panikkar upon his return to India in February 1954. He met Nehru some days later, and was taken aback at how haggard and worried the prime minister looked. The demand for language had not died down in the aftermath of the creation of Andhra Pradesh. Always a man with an eye fixed on the heights of democratic idealism, issues like language seemed to Nehru to be a red herring and bound to end in administrative chaos. 'If the country and its policies are going to be influenced and controlled in this manner,' he wrote wearily to his chief ministers in the summer of 1953, 'then indeed, we may say goodbye to any kind of progress or unity … I am sorry for this because it denotes an outlook with which I have no sympathy whatsoever and which, I am sure, if given free play, would bring utter chaos in a great part of India.'[21]

Whatever he said privately to his ministers, in public, Nehru had to maintain that the reorganisation of the states was an inevitability. 'That process has begun,' he said during a speech in October 1953. 'Let us not be afraid of it or be sorry about it.'[22]

The prime minister announced the appointment of the States Reorganisation Commission (SRC) in parliament on 22 December 1953, laying great emphasis on the need to preserve and strengthen the unity and security of India, as well as on the financial, economic and administrative considerations.[23] The political and public response to this announcement was thankfully encouraging, but Nehru wasn't entirely sure.

Could the SRC be counted on to prevent disintegration?

Nehru gave Panikkar the impression that he was 'leaning heavily' on it to do so.[24] He told his former ambassador that the commission would have complete independence and its members would have the rank of Union ministers. On it, Panikkar would be joined by Syed Fazl Ali, a former supreme court judge and sitting governor of Orissa, and Hriday Nath Kunzru, a parliamentarian and public worker. It would have eighteen months to turn in its report.

The commission's brief from the prime minister staggered Panikkar slightly. Apart from deciding on the advantages of linguistic grouping, the SRC was to consider the unique administrative problems of the provinces. After integration, the provinces had been divided into three classes according to their degrees of autonomy. Part A states were the traditional British provinces of Madras, Bombay and the rest. Part B states were either former Indian states like Hyderabad and Mysore or groups of states like Travancore-Cochin, Madhya Bharat and Saurashtra. The Union government had certain special powers regarding the Part B states and was also empowered to appoint some of their officials, including advisors, to improve their administration. Part C states included territories like Ajmer, Tripura and Coorg, which had legislative bodies with nominal powers. Without uniformity in the provincial administration, the federal structure of the Constitution could not function efficiently. This was another task confronting the SRC. The last consideration was to suggest suitable administrative changes to strengthen national unity (always a prime consideration for Nehru) after the reorganisation of the states.

Clearly, the SRC had an unenviable time ahead of it.

Now, as early as 1951, Panikkar had already written (under the pseudonym of 'Chanakya') his views on why the Congress—and Nehru—were dawdling over the prospect of linguistic reorganisation. 'The provinces organised on an ethnical and linguistic basis will inevitably develop regional patriotism and undermine the hard-won unity of India ... Create provinces on the basis of linguistic groups will be to consolidate and give political expression to that feeling of local patriotism, helping to obscure the wider patriotism, which India wants to develop.'[25] So he was, at least in this, on the same page as the prime minister. By the time the report was presented to parliament in 1955, however, Panikkar's views towards the reorganisation of the states would have undergone a radical change.

The three men of the SRC spent the first three months in Delhi, studying the individual states, their administrative and financial positions at the time of integration and the challenges they presented to the Union of India. Even sitting in their office in Delhi, they could see that the tasks ahead of them were gargantuan in size and scope. To go into the details of each state and province is obviously beyond the purview of any single manuscript. But from a bird's eye view, it was clear to the SRC that any reorganisation would not much affect the north Indian provinces. Bengal, Bihar, Uttar Pradesh, Rajasthan and Orissa were already constituted on a linguistic basis. The most they needed was a little tweaking of the boundaries among them. Only Punjab in the north would be a problem.

The clamour for a Sikh state in Punjab united both linguistic and religious claims. The Sikhs had lost much of their land to Pakistan. They did not want to share space with the Hindus. In 1950, the Hindus comprised roughly 62 per cent of the population of the Indian Punjab, with Sikhs being about 35 per cent. But there was a regional divide here as well: the eastern half of the state spoke Hindi, with Hindus comprising about 88 per cent of the population.[26] The western half was a Punjabi-speaking region, with Sikhs constituting a little over half the population. The glitch was that if all Sikhs had Punjabi as their first language, so did many Hindus. But the Hindus were prone to view Punjabi as a local dialect of Hindi, whereas the Sikhs insisted it was not just a language in its own right, but also a holy one, spoken by Guru Nanak himself. This demand, as Panikkar well knew, had found its way into the politics of the state. Over the years, that demand had solidified into an ambiguous hint at secession. Within that, there were fissures too: the Jat peasants wanted a Sikh province within India, not a sovereign nation, and the low-caste Sikhs, who feared the Jats, were opposed to the Akali Dal.

Panikkar foresaw that problems would abound 'in the territory south of the Vindhyas'.[27] The Bombay Presidency alone comprised what would become the states of Gujarat, Maharashtra and Karnataka, each with its own problems. In Karnataka, for instance, the Kannadigas were spread over five regions: the southern districts of Bombay, the Bidar region of Hyderabad, Mysore, Coorg and South Kanara in Madras. Spread out thus, the Kannada-speaking peoples then just had one state which was wholly theirs: Mysore. If a new state of Karnataka was organised, it would affect all five existing regions.

As far as Kerala was concerned, there was the question of clubbing Malabar and Malayalam-speaking Kasaragod with Kerala, while ceding Tamil-speaking Nanjanad and Shenkottah to the Tamil state.

Hyderabad was another problem, since it comprised three language groups, the biggest of which spoke Telugu. Politically and administratively, its unity was only really centred on the Nizam. Without separating Hyderabad's three language groups, the reorganisation of the southern states was, in Panikkar's opinion, impossible. But how did one partition Hyderabad? How would its dismemberment impact the Muslims in the state?

These were just a handful of the administrative problems confronting the harassed members of the SRC that summer.[28]

The idealistic problems were even greater. Nehru had charged the SRC with recommending solutions to strengthen national unity within the framework of the Constitution. That left the three men facing a fundamental question: which type of state is most cohesive in a federal union? A state in which there is one predominant language group or a multilingual state? Could such a question be answered?

In May 1954, with summer in full bloom, the commission set off on a tour of the country to try and see if their questions could be answered in any practical way. In total, they would travel to 104 places, a feat involving over 38,000 miles of travel and the interviewing of over 9,000 persons. They travelled from Assam to the Cape, visiting remote areas like Nagaland and the North-East Frontier Agency. Panikkar travelled alone with the SRC's deputy secretary, A.K. Roy, to the Laccadives. They travelled via naval frigate, disembarking at several islets between Minicoy and the Amindivu Islands. Over and above this, the SRC received and examined 1,52,250 documents from organisations and individuals interested in its work. Its tour showed Panikkar what actually lay beneath the outward veneer of a stable rising power with an erudite, liberal prime minister at the helm of affairs.

On the international stage, India was a recognised diplomatic envoy of peace in key geopolitical flashpoints. But within its own borders, there were clearly choppy waters to be navigated. To the east, there was trouble in Jharkhand, the Naga Hills and Assam, with each state wanting to secede from the Indian union. In 1955, by the time the commission put together its report, a little-reported war for secession was raging across the Naga Hills. In Jharkhand too, an

Adivasi movement was pushing for its own freedom. So strong was this secessionist strain that when Kunzru, Panikkar and Ali arrived, they were met by black flags and deafening shouts of '*Jharkhand alag praant hai* (Jharkhand is a separate area)!'[29]

Secession, rights and language were heated issues this summer. 'I am deeply distressed at the turn the linguistic states controversy is taking,' Nehru wrote unhappily in June 1954. 'The most fantastic claims are sometimes made … We cannot uproot all our history just because some abstract logic requires it. Necessary changes should certainly be made, but the fewer changes the better.'[30]

If Panikkar had read this letter, there is little doubt that he would have agreed. As he travelled about the country, all his previous political, professional and personal experiences were coming to the fore. The failure of federation, partition and its aftermath, his own abiding interest in history and geopolitics were all factors that drove him to emphasise the need for unity and cohesion. Regional nationalism within an overarching national framework was only going to be disruptive.

Emotions were running high. Every region felt it had special rights and privileges that the commission should take notice of. In Malabar, Panikkar was seriously embarrassed by several pressure groups trying to influence him on the subject of division. 'For many years, prominent Malayalis were pleading for the establishment of a united Kerala incorporating all of them,' he wrote later. The Tamils and the Andhras were quite happy to let go of the Malabar district from their states. Panikkar didn't see any roadblocks to the creation of a separate Malayalam-speaking state. But there were those who vociferously disagreed. Some of the disagreements were political: the Travancoreans of Nanjanad were bitterly opposed to ceding the region to the Tamils, since the Travancorean royal family came from there. 'Fazl Ali and Kunzru were at first generally inclined to let the entire area west of the Ghats remain in Kerala. But after observing the geographical features of the area, the village environment and the dress and habits of the people, they were also convinced that it was a Tamil area.'[31]

Other disagreements were ideological (or just plain odd, depending on where one stood). Krishna Menon, for instance, had written a long lament to Nehru, arguing passionately against the creation of a new state of Kerala on the grounds that it could well end up becoming a communist citadel. 'There is no emotional fervour for linguism in the Malayalam speaking area as there was in Andhra,' he wrote crossly. 'It is a recent and artificial agitation of which the main exponents are a few fanatical people. The best and greatest support comes almost entirely from the elements that are against the Congress and the Government, namely the Socialists, Communists and such others. The reason for their support has nothing to do with the merits of the issue, but are solely determined by the hope of conquest of power.'[32]

Nor did Krishna Menon want a separate Tamil state. In the same letter, he raged, 'In the Tamil country ... there will develop an indigenous type of fascist orientation which is the racial Tamil outlook. A separate Tamil province will be very anti-Indian, anti-national ... Therefore the only hope and right procedure in my view is to create a Southern State, a Dakshin Pradesh, as a corollary to Uttar Pradesh, which could include the present Tamil Nad, Travancore, Cochin, Malabar and possibly Kanara up to Kasargode ... We will Balkanise India if we further dismember the States instead of creating larger units.'[33]

Panikkar was justifiably annoyed when he heard of this. But yet again, he was facing loud and angry calls against his involvement in dividing the land he called home. Many in the newborn state of Kerala were opposed to ceding Kanyakumari, Nagercoil or Shenkottah to a separate Tamil state, and in the commission's report, they would see Panikkar's hand in this. The blame heaped upon his head bewildered Panikkar.

'A good many people in Travancore thought that my conceding this point [Kanyakumari] was a betrayal of Kerala,' Panikkar would write in bewilderment later. 'I thought of myself only as a Keraleeya.'[34]

In Maharashtra, the SRC was given a pile of documents quarrelling over the position of the city of Bombay. There was the Bombay Citizens' Committee which was clear that 'on the grounds of geography, history, language and population or the system of law, Bombay and North Konkan cannot be considered as a part of the Mahratta region as claimed by the protagonists of Samyukta

Maharashtra'.[35] Opposing this was the Samyukta Maharashtra Parishad. Within its ranks were Maharashtrians of all political persuasions, Left and Right, secular and communal, Brahmin, Maratha and Harijan. The parishad sought a state that would unite Marathi speakers dispersed across many different political units. In their minds however, there was no doubt that such a state could have only one capital: Bombay. The history of the dispute was bitter and long-running, reaching back to colonial times and it would become a particularly hot political potato for the SRC.

Hyderabad (where Panikkar flew into a rage with the Nizam for inviting them for talks via an ADC rather than personally) was their last port of call, where a month-long stay was enough to convince them that south India would have to be divided into four states: Kerala, Karnataka, Tamil Nadu and Andhra Pradesh. Kunzru and Fazl Ali were satisfied. In their minds, this was the most major readjustment to India's political map. The northern states needed no microscopic adjustments. Panikkar dissented here, arguing for the bifurcation of Uttar Pradesh, much to Kunzru and Ali's consternation.

Attempts to persuade him to change his mind proved fruitless, and with matters standing deadlocked over the question of the bifurcation of Uttar Pradesh, the commission broke up for the summer and a much-needed rest. Kunzru had an assignment in Japan and Panikkar had to fly to Paris, there to submit his chapters on a UNESCO history project.

The final report of the States Reorganisation Commission stands at 267 pages. It was submitted in October 1955, four months over its June deadline. The report first carefully outlined the arguments for and against linguistic states. It urged a 'balanced approach' that recognised 'linguistic homogeneity as an important factor conducive to administrative convenience and efficiency' yet not 'as an exclusive and binding principle, over-riding all other considerations'. Among these other considerations were of course the unity and security of India as a whole.

Ali, Kunzru and Panikkar envisaged the abolition of any distinction, even formal, between the states born from British provinces and those derived from former princely states, and the reduction of the number of units from twenty-seven to thirteen, with three territories administered by the central government (Delhi, Manipur, and the Andaman and Nicobar Islands). The SRC proposed the creation of three new language-based states (Malayalam-speaking Kerala, Vidarbha with part of the Marathi-speaking population and Kannada-speaking Karnataka) and two bilingual states (Bombay with two languages, Marathi and Gujarati—enlarged to include areas of the neighbouring provinces where these two languages were spoken, and Punjab where the two languages were to be Hindi and Punjabi, in turn enlarged to include the former princely states of Patiala and the East Punjab States' Union and Himachal Pradesh, the latter Hindi-speaking). Hyderabad was to continue as a separate state, albeit with a considerable territorial reduction, until 1961 when the state assembly could vote to annex it to Andhra Pradesh.

In nineteen chapters, the report outlined specific proposals for reorganisation. With respect to the southern states, it seemed easy enough to redistribute areas according to the major language zones: Telugu, Kannada, Tamil and Malayalam. Districts and taluks (subdistricts) were reallocated with regard to which linguistic group was in a majority. Four compact states would replace the melange of territories deriving from the British period. With regard to north India, the SRC sought to divide the huge Hindi-speaking belt into four states: Bihar, Uttar Pradesh, Madhya Pradesh and Rajasthan. In the east, the existing provinces would stay as they were, with minor adjustments. The commission rejected the demand for tribal states to be carved out of Bihar and Assam, nor did it agree to the creation of a Sikh state or the allocation of Madras to Andhra Pradesh. However, its most contentious recommendation was not to permit the creation of a united Maharashtra. They respected the arguments of the Samyukta Maharashtra movement, they said, but they could 'not lightly brush aside the fears of the other communities'.

Panikkar hadn't bothered to hide his opinions on Uttar Pradesh. It was attached in a ten-page appendix to the main report. Looking to the future and drawing on precedents laid down by the United States, the Bismarckian Reich and the Soviet Union, Panikkar proposed the division of Nehru's home state of Uttar Pradesh. He pointed to the population of the state, which stood at a whopping 604 lakh at the time. 'My point was that if the U.P. were bifurcated, there would be greater uniformity in the sizes of the states, failing which the excessive size and weightage of the U.P. would prove detrimental to the unity and integrity of the country.'[36]

It was essential for the smooth functioning of a federal state that all units should be evenly balanced, in Panikkar's opinion. Forthrightly, he wrote that 'it would be easy to see that this preponderant influence which would accrue to a very large unit could be abused, and would in any case be resented by all the other constituent units'.[37] Modern governments he observed, 'are controlled, to a greater or lesser extent, by party machines, within which the voting power of a numerically strong group goes a very long way'.[38] Given this, was it desirable to 'place any unit in a position to exercise an unduly large measure of political influence?'[39]

As he pointed out, the political dominance of Uttar Pradesh had already begun 'to create feelings of distrust and resentment' in the other states of the Union. It was resented, for instance, not only in the south of India but also in Punjab and Bengal. He said that it was imperative to divide Uttar Pradesh into two. The northwestern districts of the state could be carved out and combined with parts of Madhya Pradesh to create a new 'Agra State' with an estimated population of twenty-four million. The residual state of Uttar Pradesh would have forty-one million people. This division would rectify what in Panikkar's view was 'the major and basic weakness of the Indian Constitution—the extraordinary disparity between one unit and the rest'.[40]

If Ali and Kunzru were aghast by this suggestion, Govind Ballabh Pant, then the sitting chief minister of Uttar Pradesh, was incandescent with rage. Pant, whose ferocity on the subject of a united Uttar Pradesh belied his physical resemblance to a sad-eyed walrus, held strong sway in the Congress at the time. 'The Congress executive and the Government of India were expected to bow to his wishes,' Panikkar recalled. 'In this situation, my friends advised me that my arguing for a division of Uttar Pradesh would be unpalatable to the

Congress High Command and the Union Cabinet and it might even prejudice my career. Perhaps they were right.'[41]

Nobody had expected the release of the report of the States Reorganisation Commission to be carried through peacefully. Nehru himself, though he had been insisting that everyone should accept the proposals that would be made, was terribly anxious. 'Life is becoming very complicated here,' he wrote gloomily to his sister. 'The report of the States' Reorganization Commission is going to be the last straw.'[42]

But even he could not have imagined 'what a commotion the report produced'.[43] In Punjab for example, the Sikh discontent at being denied a state of their own and being merged with Himachal Pradesh found vocal expression. Opposed to them were the Rashtriya Swayamsevak Sangh, the Jan Sangh and the Hindu Mahasabha. A compromise was sought that would accommodate the Sikhs, but it denied the validity, in principle, of claims that were religiously and not linguistically motivated. Himachal Pradesh was not integrated into the state of Punjab but placed under the administration of the Central government. Both Hindi and Punjabi were declared official languages.

The most serious trouble though, came from Maharashtra. The subject of Bombay as the capital of a bilingual state was discussed in parliament on 15 November 1955. S.K. Patil, the MP for Bombay, insisted that the SRC could have and should have gone further than it had. Speaking after him, the Congress MP from Pune, N.V. Gadgil, said vehemently, 'There is a limit. That limit is, nobody can compromise one's self-respect, no woman can compromise her chastity and no country its freedom!' The report of the commission had caused great pain throughout the Marathi-speaking world, Gadgil warned. If these sentiments were not heeded, then the future of Bombay would be decided on the streets of Bombay. The reports of protest meetings should make it clear 'that anything short of Samyukta Maharashtra with the city of Bombay as capital will not be acceptable'.

The SRC urged Maharashtrians to accept the loss of Bombay in the name of national unity. Incensed, politicians from both the Right and the Left seized this opportunity to stoke the flames. Within days, as Gadgil had warned, the matter spilled out onto the streets. On the morning of 16 January 1955, mobs rampaged through the streets of Bombay. Nearly 400 protests were made and the city was brought to a standstill as 15,000 policemen were called out to battle the rioters. Shops and factories were closed and buses and trains didn't run. Effigies of Nehru were burned. When Taya Zinkin, while reporting on the story, stopped to take a photograph of Nehru's portrait, lying smashed and trampled on the ground, 'tremendous cheers' rose from the crowds watching on the balconies and roofs above her head. 'Take it, take it and show the world what we think of Nehru,' they shouted.[44]

The prime minister was horrified. The question of linguistic reorganisation was 'more serious than even the situation created by the Partition', he told a colleague a little dramatically. 'We have to give a positive lead.'[45] But how was that to happen? Nehru was fully aware, and had been since the creation of Andhra Pradesh, that having conceded one state, it was inevitable that the rest would follow. Like all major movements of change, when it first began, the movement for linguistic states created near terror among India's political leaders. All of them had not only lived through Partition but had steered the country through that nightmare. Nobody wanted to relive it. 'Any attempt at redrawing the map of India on the linguistic basis,' wrote the *Times of India* in early February 1952, 'would only give the long awaited opportunity to the reactionary forces to come into the open and assert themselves. That will lay an axe at the very root of India's integrity.'[46]

Gauging public reaction, especially G.B. Pant's fury at Panikkar's proposal to bifurcate Uttar Pradesh, the Chief Minister of Bengal, B.C. Roy, leapt into the fray. He suggested the alternative of combining adjoining states into larger units based on economic factors and offered the example of bringing Bengal, Bihar and Assam together in one such group. For some reason this appealed to Nehru, who had been thoroughly upset by the commission's proposals.

All through the weeks after the report had been tabled in parliament he had been lamenting its recommendations. 'I think it will be true to say that this whole question of the reorganisation of the States has created a most difficult problem and critical situation for all of us,'[47] he wrote angrily. Roy's alternative seemed to offer him some kind of relief and he grasped at it blindly, wondering about the division of India into similar zones. Nehru's approval of Roy's suggestion raised hopes for Krishna Menon and his model of a Dakshina Pradesh. Angry and humiliated, Panikkar spoke publicly against this at Delhi, stating unequivocally that the combination of the states into zonal 'super-states' was fraught with danger, that the arguments brought up to support such a thesis were 'fallacious' and that the states *should* be reorganised on the basis of language.

When Nehru was asked about Panikkar's speech at the Amritsar session of the Congress, he was livid. Taya Zinkin, there to report on the proceedings, had never seen him so angry. She cabled Panikkar, who had gone to Nepal on holiday. 'What have you done? Nehru is furious with you.'[48] Several of Panikkar's friends rang to tell him that this time the fat was truly in the fire. In his memoir, he writes that he 'never had the least apprehension'[49] that the prime minister would turn his back on him over an honest difference in opinion, but Panikkar was clearly worried enough to immediately sit down and write out a long memo justifying his views and send it to Delhi.

Four days later when he was back in Delhi, he went to meet Nehru who was 'extremely friendly'[50] about it. The heat of his temper had cooled, as it usually did, and he was now set on making the best of matters. In fact, to Krishna Menon who had seized the chance to push for his idea of Dakshina Pradesh once more, the prime minister was categorical. 'When you wrote to me previously and sent me a long note on Kerala and so forth, I circulated your note to a number of my colleagues in the Cabinet and in the Congress Working Committee. Many of them agreed with you. But I am afraid you do not quite appreciate the kind of forces we have to contend with in India at the present moment,' he wrote firmly. 'When you suggest that States should become merely administrative divisions and far greater power should be concentrated in the Centre, you say something which is utterly beyond anyone's capacity to do at the present moment ... We have tried our best and failed. We have decided, therefore, not to bewail our lot but to face the situation as best as we can.'[51]

Nehru rarely lost a chance to express thinly veiled displeasure over the findings of the report. At a speech in Kumool in 1955, he said, 'When we asked a Commission to do a job, I left them to do it as best as they could. And when it came out, some parts of it came to me as a surprise. That does not mean that I disagreed or agreed with them. They merely were novel ideas to me.'[52] But, regardless of where he was speaking, he insisted that the government of India would work with the SRC's recommendations.

The SRC's report would be the final word on the subject—at least for the moment.

Nothing more was said about either the 'super-states' or of Dakshina Pradesh. It would take another year and a half for the states to be reorganised according to the recommendations of the SRC. In that time, a new idea of India had been born, with a revitalised sense of its identity.

By then too, Panikkar had had enough time to really reflect on what he had seen during the commission's tour. 'Every State had its own claims which it put forward with an almost imperialistic desire for additional territory,' he mused. 'It was strange to see national leaders, even those who had suffered and sacrificed for the freedom of India, quarrelling among themselves about a village here and an *ilaqa* there and prepared to go to the extent of offering civil disobedience to enforce their claims. The lesson that I drew from it was that with the generality of people in times of peace, narrow parochial interests count for much more than broad national interests.'[53]

This was a new India, but a fragile one underneath its armour of strength and stability. Transfer of power and Partition had not provided the answers that colonial India had sought. There were, if possible, even more questions now: what did it mean to be Indian? Where did local identities fit in with a broader national identity? What did the growth of regional nationalisms mean for the country as a whole? Panikkar brought to these questions his perspectives of having served India abroad. He knew that the international stage was fluid. How would external threats affect Indian nationalism? Everything that he had seen—war, freedom, decolonisation, a communist revolution, the reorganisation of the states and the redrawing of the map of South

Asia—over the last two decades stirred an urge to revisit his old work, to revise it and update it according to the times he had lived through.

Panikkar's first instincts were always those of a historian and an academic. To the end of his days, he never stopped thinking, or allowing his ideas to evolve and adapt to the changing times. His sixtieth birthday was celebrated and feted in his home town. A young man by the name of B.J. Chacko had pulled together a compilation of memories and tributes from those who had known and had worked with Panikkar for the last three decades. The contents page alone reads like a historical *Who's Who*—from Sir C.P. Ramaswami Aiyar to Sir G.S. Bajpai to Taya Zinkin. Panikkar was proud and pleased when the volume came out, spending much time leafing through its pages in wonder and noting, in some delight, that even men like Bajpai and Aiyar had unbent enough to write a few lines of appreciation. It was typical of Panikkar's appeal to those who knew him or followed his work: he could be provocative, even infuriating, depending on who you were in his life. Those who knew him well knew that in his attempts to provoke lay a puckish enjoyment in knowing he had managed to slip under his opponent's skin. Through even Panikkar's most embarrassing public moments, it was difficult not to appreciate the brilliance of his mind, and the undoubted services he had rendered his country in the years gone by.

It was also typical that his brain was already ticking over to what came next. He had been thinking a lot about India, about where it stood in the world and in South Asia, and much of that thought would colour his writing in the years to come. Of this, there was an almost stunning quantity, even by his standards. In Malayalam, he wrote a long introduction, surveying the entire field of Vedic literature, to the poet (and by now his very good friend) Vallathol's translation of the Rig Veda. It was a difficult task, since Panikkar was, at the time, travelling across the country with the SRC, and also dividing his time between Gouri (who had never really recovered from her ill health in China) and his children and grandchildren. 'However, I did manage it,' he noted proudly, 'and am gratified to think that the work met with the poet's approval.'[54]

He also worked, rather startlingly, on a translation of the Greek tragedy, *Electra*. The inspiration had come from Panikkar's version of light reading: an English verse translation of the play. When the poet Sankara Kurup reached out to him asking for a new manuscript to be published by his new press at the Sahitya Parishad, Panikkar promptly dashed off a Malayalam translation. Aside from this, he wrote the short poem, *Amba Pali*, and a novel in Malayalam on the life of the Rani of Jhansi. Apart from this, he continued writing prodigiously in English. These were new ideas that he was putting forth now, influenced by India's independence, its new place on the international stage and his own observations during his travels with the SRC. Most of these ideas found voice in several speeches that Panikkar was giving across the country, and some of them, it must be said, were decidedly startling to those who were listening.

In a speech on 'The New Dynamism'[55] given in 1955, for instance, Panikkar argued that while Indian regional languages and literatures had their own value, they could not be allowed to hijack the body politic. The only language that could play a national role was Hindi. English could be given up. Indians owed it neither loyalty nor attachment, despite its merits of having once been a language of colonial administration.[56] The same applied to regional identities and aspirations. Each of these identities were not separate from the larger Indian identity—they were part of an intrinsic whole.

In ideas like these, he found an opponent in Nehru. The prime minister disagreed with quite a few of Panikkar's new views, but the disagreement was always erudite and civilised. At the bottom of it all lay a complex and old friendship, which neither Panikkar nor Nehru ever forgot. But undoubtedly, in these last years of both their lives, Panikkar made it difficult for Nehru to remember that friendship.

In response to Panikkar's ideas about Hindi, for example, Nehru put his own views on record at a speech at the Kerala Kalamandalam in 1955. 'Nothing surprises me so much as any controversy as to the relative merits of our languages ... The fact is that we have to develop all these languages ... Each language will no doubt take its own identity as it should and there is no question of submerging it.'[57]

In addition to language, Panikkar continued to write and talk about India's directions of progress in this new world. He credited the SRC with holding firm to the principle of unity and safeguarding the cohesion of the nation, even as it made space for regional identities and aspirations. India needed to renew itself, make strong scientific and technological progress, if it had to stand shoulder to shoulder with global powers.[58] It also needed to keep a check on disruptive forces in all fields, while making space for voices that demanded to be heard.

Geopolitics was a crucial factor that India needed to take into account, and his experiences in China had taught him as much. In *Geographical Factors in Indian History* and *Hindu Society at a Crossroads* (both published in 1955), Panikkar referred yet again to Hindu 'empires' in Java, Sumatra, Siam, Indo-China and the 'colonization' of the Pacific islands by the Hindus.[59] But this was still a point made in the context of India's historical record of cultural expansionism, particularly in South India. The Cholas and Pallavas had interests in what Panikkar called 'Further India': Malaya, Siam, Indochina and Indonesia. His references to Indian influence in Southeast Asia was to provide a clue for the international relationships that existed in the remote past. Importantly, given his experience in China, he now included a chapter on the Himalayas in *Geographical Factors in Indian History*.

The geographic conditions around India had changed, he wrote. Tibet was no longer a de facto demilitarised area, drawing land threats away from India. 'The fact that the Chinese were unable in the past to organise a strong military area in Tibet should not blind us to such possibilities in the future. It may not be a danger in the immediate future, but there is no doubt that an organised modern state in Tibet will alter the character of the Himalayan problem ... The Himalayan boundary will no longer be the dead boundary that it has been since the beginning of Indian history.'[60]

Even more significantly from the light of the present day, he also wrote in this book about the need to balance the north of India with the south. Panikkar referred to history again to remind readers that the south of India had always developed independently of the north. Now that India was politically and administratively united, it needed to learn both the lessons of history and geography. 'Any attempt to impose a unification by the more populous North over the people of the South will be disastrous, for it will awaken the latent racial feelings of difference and geography will again tend to assert itself.'[61]

From the vantage of 2025, it is a prescient warning.

The historian in Panikkar was never far below the surface. For him, the process of the formation of a nation-state lay in its history. In his speech 'On Historical Studies' delivered for the Indian History Congress in 1955, Panikkar acknowledged that 'the unity of India as a nation is a recent concept and the attempt to read back into Indian history a permanent motivation which was not only absent, but which would have seemed to most people unnatural, is at the root of our failure in the historical field'.[62]

India, he argued, must be seen not in terms of a succession of conquering rulers or dynasties, but in terms of its people. Its people were the real driving forces behind the creation of India's history. They always had been and always would be. For those reasons, India needed to keep its society united. This required, in his view, 'a strong central government having full control of the resources of the nation, a very high level of industrialisation, a political and economic integration of the country, which would overcome the internal contradictions present in our society, an advancement in scientific research and technical application of such research as would rise us to the level of a powerful state.'[63]

The internal cohesion Panikkar spoke of could not be achieved without a more solid social structure. As always, this meant, for him, a strong Hindu core. In these fresh days of independence, it was a shrinking of his colonial idea of a 'Greater India,' based on a Hindu-Indian civilisational identity. He dealt with this issue in *Hindu Society at Cross Roads*, which took up many chapters from his *Hinduism and the Modern World* (1938). In this new edition, Panikkar reiterated his historical analysis of a defensive Hinduism.

Independence had remedied the absence of a national authority with powers to legislate for the vast majority of the Hindus. 'For the first time in history, there is now in India an authority created by the people themselves, which has not only affirmed its right to legislate for the Hindus but is able to exact obedience ... The Constitution of India ... not only has assumed but has proclaimed in the clearest terms its right and duty to legislate for social needs ... What the legislature is unconsciously seeking to do is to convert the unorganised masses of Hindus into a single community.'[64]

While Panikkar never strayed down the path of militant Hindutva supremacism, statements like these were undoubtedly problematic, moving away from a Nehruvian secularism.

In a speech during the convocation address at Tagore's Visva Bharati, Panikkar 'decided to attack the escapism of those who would retreat from the temptations and responsibilities of life, in an attempt to nourish the spirit'. Whatever the foundations of Hinduism taught, he said bluntly, Hindu culture did not flourish in the forests or ashrams. Lord Ram and Lord Krishna did not renounce their world or their wealth. There was no need to embrace or worship poverty as a prerequisite to spiritual progress. Tagore might prescribe a retreat to nature, he felt, but 'little did they realise that all was not austerity in Shantiniketan'.[65]

For Panikkar then, Hinduism was now becoming a central argument, the crux around which a nation like India could consolidate. In endorsing this view, he seemed to be in agreement with the historian R.C. Majumdar in postulating that postcolonial India could survive only as a tolerant Hindu nation. Nehru was both astonished and troubled at these arguments, continuing to believe that, for India's future, the religious factor would be irrelevant to cohesion. He was also annoyed at the fact that speeches like these laid him personally open to international questioning at a time when India could well have done without it. Citing Panikkar's speech at Visva Bharati, the French journalist Tibor Mende asked the prime minister directly if Hindu customs were capable of adapting to the secular ideals of the Constitution. 'Naturally there are all kinds of people in India, more specially among the intellectuals,' Nehru parried. 'But I think the conception of Hindu society as a very conservative society—a society opposed to change is incorrect.'[66] Without mentioning Panikkar's name, the prime minister insisted that the constitutional legislation of modern times was not a barrier or an inhibition to change.

From sometime in 1955, there was a noticeable change in Panikkar. A baptism by diplomatic fire had taught him much. Now, he would not say only what the prime minister wanted to hear. Even though he knew Nehru was furious with him over his assessments on the reorganisation of the states, he stuck to his guns publicly and privately. He also was unafraid to speak publicly about his changing views on Hinduism and India's political progress. To a packed hall at the University of Baroda in 1956, Panikkar spoke of multidirectional flows of culture across Southeast Asia and the international network of scholars, pilgrims and monks at the North Indian Buddhist hub of Nalanda.

Panikkar was still sticking to a Greater India landscape: the torch of the Indian civilisation, he averred, had blazed across Central Asia, to China, Korea, Japan and across the Pacific. The Indian heroes of this historical saga were figures such as the translator Kumarajiva who had played, around the fourth century CE, a prominent role in the introduction of the Buddhist Mahayana doctrine in China. 'His was a name that everyone in India should cherish,' Panikkar told the students at Baroda, 'because he had been a pioneer of the diffusion of Indian civilization and left his mark on the history of the Far East.'[67]

There were problems with persisting with these views in a postcolonial world. To be sure, a Greater India narrative was a vivid window into India's ancient past. As a storytelling paradigm, it was an excellent way to locate India's Golden Age in the pre-Islamic era and to remind younger generations of the country's cultural, commercial and spiritual influence over not just Central and Southeast Asia, but Europe and England as well. But sticking to a Greater India view in the 1950s meant a marginalisation of other connected histories. Just one example is the overlooking of the ocean-spanning networks of (non-Hindu) trading communities operating from the subcontinent's northwest maritime fringes or even the history of indenture across the empire. Scholars like Panikkar were still seeking to define India's past, but the extent to which this involved erasing or excluding other histories is questionable. As a response to colonialism, particularly from a young student at Oxford, it had been an apt, nationalist response in the early years of the twentieth century. As a diplomat speaking in a post-war, postcolonial world, shaped by an ongoing Cold War, views like these were both single-minded and chauvinistic.

CHAPTER 53

Summers in Paris

'WHERE WOULD YOU LIKE TO GO NEXT?' NEHRU ASKED.

Panikkar thought about it and said quite frankly that he would like very much to go to Paris. 'But first, I should like a six month vacation!'[1]

He wasn't to know it yet, but it was the beginning of a rapidly falling dusk.

Panikkar's first stop was Paris, in the first week of April 1956. He was one of the three to whom the UNESCO project on writing the history of the scientific and cultural development of mankind had been assigned. As the subject indicated, it was one of the organisation's most ambitious undertakings. The project had run into trouble from its inception. It had originally been thought of by the British biochemist Joseph Needham who had concluded that the most important catalyst driving historical change was cultural interchange. Based on his studies on the history of science in China, Needham believed that studying the history of cultural interchange could lend a new perspective to understanding humanity and produce an intellectual and civilisational history of the world.

UNESCO liked the abstractness of this idea, but in true bureaucratic style, it formed a commission to delineate the way forward. Ralph Turner, the American historian who was brought on board this commission, suggested a chronological way forward and the need to delegate work to experts.[2] A hitch occurred in 1954, when UNESCO decided that it wasn't possible to produce an unbiased study of the twentieth century from *one* scholar. The volume would be assigned to an American, a European *and* an Indian scholar. The historian and New Deal activist Caroline Ware was chosen as the author-editor of this volume and the Dutch historian, Marxist and literary scholar Jan Romein was co-author-editor. For the Indian author, the initial man chosen was the historical advisor to the Indian high commission in London, Kuruvila Zachariah. When he died a year after his nomination, a frantic search for a substitute ensued. Only then, at the end of 1955, was Panikkar's name given to the commission.

The trio were perfect for the job. Ware had just edited a volume in which she highlighted the importance of culture to lend added depth to the study of social and political institutions. Romein had just finished a teaching stint in newly independent Indonesia.[3] Panikkar was going on to an ambassadorship in France and had a long and rich history in academia. Their combined experience was considered suitable to write a study of nationalism in Asia. As the commission put it to Panikkar, 'It is felt by all members of the Commission that with your knowledge of the East as well as the West, your experience in current affairs, and your view on the present course of mankind, your active collaboration in this project would allow [it to present] an original and balanced view of the course of human thought and culture in the twentieth century.'[4]

Later there would be controversy around Soviet participation in the project, which led to demands to revise the text by scholars beyond the Iron Curtain. It was, after all, the height of the Cold War, and with the Soviets involved, European and American academia darkly suspected a communist bias.[5]

Romein, Ware and Panikkar met in Amsterdam, which was freezing in April. The canals had not yet thawed and an icy wind blew through the mornings. Their work was regimented and suited the academic in Panikkar to the ground. He and Ware stayed in a hotel in central Amsterdam. Panikkar would come down for breakfast at eight in the morning and have about one hour after coffee for his own work. At the time, apart from working on this vast project, Panikkar was working on a translation of Sophocles's *Oedipus* into Malayalam as well as writing a preface for *The State and the Citizen*. The ability to switch between genres and languages had only sharpened over the years and he was able to get a considerable amount of work done before he and Ware left at nine in the morning for the University of Amsterdam where Romein was currently head of the history department. Until lunch time, the three would work quietly without a break. Over meals, they read out their work to each other and debated each other's arguments. In a month, the volume's shape and content was more or less ready.

Panikkar would study the beginning of history chronologically, organising his study around a refutation of Eurocentrism and returning to his pet themes of conquest, the successful revival of Hinduism from a 'national' perspective, and the renewed edge of dynamism that Asian resurgence had received from its encounter with the West.[6] He would argue as he often had in the recent past that it was the inherent resilience and strength of the Indian civilisation that had permitted the assimilation of Western ideas. The book stood completed in April 1960, but it would run into trouble then as well. Soviet and Eastern European scholars presented counterarguments to their central thesis and on more than one occasion the three authors had to fight further changes until UNESCO finally agreed to represent Soviet alternatives in a second volume.[7]

There was criticism as well from scholars who argued against the failure to use definitions of 'totalitarianism', which Soviet communism could be defined as, as well as opposition from religious scholars who were infuriated at the definition of religion as a transient element in the process of social and political change. Much of this back and forth was also due to the contentious timing of the project, written as it was during the harsh ideological climate of the Cold War. All this delayed the publication of the book and eventually it would only be published in 1966 to extremely negative reviews, by which time Panikkar had passed away.

Still, his time in Europe were years when Panikkar threw himself with almost monk-like fervour into studies and academia. On his way to France in August 1956, he stopped over in England for a week as Vijayalakshmi Pandit's guest for a catch up on all things personal and political. She was, as always, delighted to see him. He had dropped by at a particularly sensitive moment in Indian geopolitics.

Two weeks earlier, President Gamal Abdel Nasser of Egypt had stunned the world by announcing the nationalisation of the Suez Canal. Now, the world was only weeks away from the tripartite invasion by Israel, Britain and France of Egypt in October 1956, and India was deeply anxious about this brewing crisis. Nehru had, in fact, been blindsided by Nasser's decision to nationalise the canal. He had met the Egyptian president along with Marshal Tito in Yugoslavia only a few weeks earlier and had had no inkling that this was coming. As Nehru put it in a letter to John Foster Dulles, the US secretary of state after Acheson, 'the whole future of the relations between Europe and Asia' hung in the balance.

The Indian government anticipated an enormous fallout of the crisis on India both economically and politically, as any 'restriction of traffic through the canal or blockade or imposition of higher tolls would have harmful results and might even prejudice the progress of the Second Five Year Plan'.[8]A delegation was being put together, led by Krishna Menon, to broker some kind of compromise between Egypt and Britain, while 'adopting a line opposed to the UK attitude'.[9]

Mrs Pandit (also on the delegation) sent her brother a quiet cable: would he consider Panikkar's presence on the delegation?

Nehru's reply was swift and curt: 'I have consulted [N.R.] Pillai and [Subimal] Dutt. Both of them feel, and I agree with them, that Panikkar's association with our delegation may lead to difficulties and complications. He is a person of strong views which he expresses in an uninhibited manner ... He has not been in touch with us for some months and is therefore not fully acquainted with our approach.'[10]

As it turned out, the Suez crisis was not exactly a shining moment for Indian diplomacy, but Nehru's observation on Panikkar was a telling one: the former ambassador to Egypt's recent outspokenness (not to mention the SRC report) had annoyed his prime minister into refusing to consider him altogether for diplomatic assignments.

However, he continued in happy ignorance of these quiet asides on his behaviour. After staying with Pandit in London, he travelled down to Oxford, where he stayed at his alma mater for some time, wrapped in peaceful study, occasionally stepping out to meet old friends for meals or drinks. Before he left, he went one last time for a dinner in the main hall. Harry Truman was there that night, having been awarded an honorary doctorate in civil law. The former US president sat next to Panikkar at dinner that night and several times Panikkar caught him eyeing him strangely. After dinner, Truman came up to him. 'You were in China during the Korean War, weren't you?'

'Yes, sir.'

'Yes, I remember now. I was a little hard on you in my book, wasn't I?' Truman laughed.

'Think nothing of it. One doesn't always have the facts in these matters.'

From England, Panikkar travelled to Warsaw, where he delivered some lectures at the university before visiting Auschwitz. The relics of the horrors that the Nazis had left behind struck Panikkar like a blow. He had known many of the men and women who had died in the gas chambers. As he wandered through the macabre halls, he felt a sense of devastating loss and sorrow at what the world had seen and what his friends had died for.

By the end of 1956, he was in Paris and had taken over his duties as ambassador. 'At that time, France had practically no ties with India,' Panikkar would recall. 'My main duty was to arrange for purchase of arms and military aircraft, which was done by specialists and needed only my formal supervision. In the field of commerce also, there was a specialist to attend to details. All told my impression was that notwithstanding its prestige, the Paris embassy was a comparatively easy post.'[11]

But in truth, if Paris was easy, it was not due to prevailing political and geopolitical conditions. Excluding technical matters such as the purchase of fighter planes from Dassault, Panikkar's political brief in Paris was simple enough: to identify in advance the terminal nature of the crisis of the Fourth Republic caused by the Algerian war and to assess the possibility of the return of the venerable Charles De Gaulle to power.

France's internal politics at the time was in severe crisis. The socialist-led administration of Guy Mollet was fracturing under the weight of internal dissent on how it was handling the war in Algeria. Indeed, by January 1957, torture was an eerily acceptable form of combat in the French army. Word of its doings in Algeria was beginning to spread and that same month, Panikkar was reporting to Nehru that a 'grave crisis of conscience' was developing in France as a result of the evidence of 'Nazi methods' of dealing with the civilian population in Algeria.[12] 'The note you have sent gives a more connected idea, not only of what is happening in Algeria, but of reactions in France,' Nehru noted approvingly. 'I am glad you have sent this.'[13]

By August that year, some 24,000 Muslims had been interned. This number alone was more than four times the population of the National Liberation Front of Algeria (FLN), which was fighting against French forces, and nearly 10 per cent of the entire Muslim population of Algeria. The French army continued to hold the upper hand with the FLN suffering a death toll of almost 2,600 from direct action alone. But as time passed and censorship failed, news of French atrocities in Algeria began to spread across the world, eroding public support for the war at home and alienating heads of state internationally from John F. Kennedy (then a rising young senator) to Jawaharlal Nehru.

Worryingly for Nehru, the Chinese were involved in Algeria as well. The FLN and Chinese leaders had first met at Bandung in 1955, when the participants including China had endorsed the Algerians' demand for independence. Following that conference, the Chinese began establishing more formal relations with states in Africa and the Middle East, with an embassy in Cairo by May 1956 and trade relations developing with Tunisia, Libya, Nigeria, Ghana, and Ethiopia.[14] By 1957, China was reassessing its strategy in the region, finding much value in non-state actors where it could engage with anti-colonial campaigns. This reassessment coincided with a time when state actors were losing their appeal. For example, Egypt under Nasser had begun suppressing communists and was hostile to the revolutionary regime established in Iraq in July 1958.[15] Beijing's whole-hearted embrace of radical non-state actors like the FLN underscored a growing sense of community that India couldn't keep up with. When Nehru explained that he felt unable to pressure France at the United Nations in Algeria's favour in September 1958, the Chinese were quick to recognise the newly declared Provisional Government of the Republic of Algeria.

All this coincided rather unfortunately with the beginning of the real downslide in bilateral ties between India and China. Zhou En-lai had visited India in the winter of 1956, but from 1957 onwards, matters between the two countries would move steadily beyond the point of no return. The spectre of Tibet (and Panikkar's failures therein) appeared on the horizon once again. As Nehru grew ever more irritated and tense about China, those irritations reflected in his correspondence with Panikkar. It was in France then that Panikkar's friendship with Nehru began finally to openly crack under the strain of a corresponding crisis that was developing over the Himalayas with China.

In February 1957, Panikkar tried to report on what he was noticing domestically in France—that Guy Mollet was bent on European economic integration. He wrote that he had studied 'the major changes that France is planning, in association with others, to re-establish a balance in the affairs of the world'. In his opinion, 'the three basic proposals which are about to take shape [are]—the European economic union, known as the Common Market, Eurafrica and Euratom, the three together constituting a solid base for a new European structure'. At the end of his letter, Panikkar added prophetically, 'Whether it takes 5 years or 10 years, it is now fairly obvious that the three major European countries—France, Germany and Italy—together with the Benelux area will come together for economic and industrial development and naturally their political orientation will also undergo a radical change … It will undoubtedly mean a shift in the balance of power', with Europe achieving 'in a short time under Franco-German leadership … a position at least equal with the other two Great Powers.'

Responding to his ambassador, Nehru was dismissive. 'This makes very interesting reading. The tendencies you mention are obviously there, and I have little doubt that the pressure of events will add to them ... Nevertheless, I rather doubt if the process will be as rapid as you have indicated.'[16] On the same day, Nehru suggested to Subimal Dutt, the foreign secretary, that Panikkar's note should be printed for circulation to members of the Cabinet and to the major missions. However, the prime minister added the curt rider, 'Shri Panikkar is a keen observer, but he tends rather to go ahead of facts and difficulties and slightly to dramatize events. What he says is, I think, true in essence, but I rather doubt if his timetable is at all correct.'[17]

In March 1957, a month after Panikkar had reported to Nehru, Guy Mollet signed the Treaty of Rome, establishing the European Economic Community (France, Belgium, Luxembourg, the Netherlands and West Germany). It would come into full effect on 1 January 1958. The treaty proposed the progressive reduction of customs duties, the establishment of a customs union and the creation of a single market for goods, labour, services and capital across member states. It also proposed the creation of a Common Agriculture Policy, a Common Transport Policy, a European Social Fund and established the European Commission. In his memoir, Panikkar mentions nothing of this, and the archives make it fairly clear that between 1957 and 1958, the ambassador had not much to do in France.

That didn't stop him from keeping his fingers in the pies that interested him. For instance, Panikkar was still pushing for contacts between India and Israel. With the rise of Pakistan as a factor in India's Israel policy, the relationship was decidedly complex. Speaking to his biographer Michael Brecher a year after the Bandung Conference in 1955, Nehru admitted, 'Conditions were and still are that the Arab nations and Israel don't sit together. They do sit at the United Nations, but apart from that, they just don't sit. And one is offered this choice of having one or the other. It is not logical, my answer—but there it is.'[18] As the scholar P.K. Kumaraswamy writes, 'It was the Pakistani factor that precluded Nehru from normalizing ties with Israel. Despite all his commitments to dialogue, independence, and the moral high ground, when it came to the Arab-Israeli conflict, Nehru often fought with Pakistan and succumbed to its political pressures.'[19]

Israel, on the other hand, stayed away from India during those first years of its creation. Only on the eve of the Suez Crisis in 1956 did Nehru receive an informal message from David Ben-Gurion, then the prime minister of Israel, 'to the effect that Israel had made a mistake in leaning on the Western Powers and the Israelis now realized more than ever that they were of Asia and must look to Asia'.[20] Clearly, the relationship needed to be renegotiated.

In 1957, Ben-Gurion sent a copy of the *Jerusalem Post Reporter* to Panikkar in France, highlighting a report in which he urged Israeli students to take up the study of Asian philosophy which, according to the Israeli prime minister, was important in Israel's future ties with Asia. Panikkar sent this on to N.R. Pillai, then the foreign secretary, with an accompanying note, 'I think it shows an attitude of mind on the part of Israel which we should encourage, even if we are not proceeding now with any proposal for exchanging diplomatic representatives.'[21] There is no evidence about whether his hints were followed up with in New Delhi.

Panikkar's account of his years in Paris are almost bland, speaking mostly of the people who came to stay with him. The guest list reads like a who's who of Indian politics and culture at the time, from Acharya Kripalani to Kamaladevi Chattopadhyaya; from H.V.R. Iyengar to Zakir Hussain and Morarji Desai. He speaks very little about his travels across the French African colonies and the long motoring trip through Europe, touching Germany, Czechoslovakia, Austria, Yugoslavia and Italy. Even less does he speak about his brief holiday with Marshal Tito, who invited the Panikkars to stay at on his country estate in Brioni.

Foreign policy, through Panikkar's last year in France (1958 to 1959), assumed something of a backseat, though in his memoir he does write that he met Charles de Gaulle. His conversations with de Gaulle and France's general precariousness at the time told Panikkar that not only would there be a political crisis in the near future, but that de Gaulle would return in its aftermath to power. Panikkar reported the same to Delhi in April 1958.[22]

That is, in fact, what happened. On 1 June 1958, de Gaulle came to power as the last prime minister of the Fourth Republic of France. He made a trip to Algeria on 4 June, promising economic, political and social reforms. Upon his return to Paris, de Gaulle appointed a committee to draft a constitution for the Fifth Republic and to reframe the French-Algerian relationship. It was envisaged that under the new arrangement, Algeria would be associated with, but not be an integral part of France. The referendum on the new constitution took place in September 1958. Despite intimidation by the FLN, 80 per cent of the Muslim voters in Algeria turned up to vote, of which 96 per cent approved the new constitution. Following the mandate, Charles de Gaulle conceded the possibility of self-determination for Algeria.

Panikkar's two main briefs in France were over. Around this time, Vijayalakshmi Pandit wrote to her brother. She had met Panikkar in London in the autumn of 1958, where he was waiting for Gouri to undergo an operation for her cataracts. The ambassador told her that on 6 December 1958, he would be leaving Paris upon completion of two years in the post. He was now looking forward to being nominated to the Rajya Sabha as a member of parliament. The prime minister was considerably annoyed. He was also under intense stress at this time. India's ties with China had achieved their zenith in 1956, even though, as Nirupama Rao puts it, 'subterranean undercurrents of wariness and sub-optimal levels of mutual trust lingered below the surface'.[23] From 1957 onwards, the relationship began to slowly unravel.

On the surface, goodwill and cultural exchanges continued. A thirty-eight-member troupe of the Peking Variety Theatre gave performances in various Indian cities and a military goodwill delegation led by Marshal Peng Dehuai visited military centres in various parts of India from 23 January to 2 March 1958. Delegations from India visiting China included those from the Young Men's Christian Association of India, the All India Trade Union Congress, film delegations, the All India Federation of Educational

Associations, medical and teaching professions, the India-China Friendship Association and the Indian Youth Congress. The leading economist and statistician P.C. Mahalanobis and the prominent Buddhist scholar Rahul Sankrityayan were also guests of the Chinese government. Scholarly exchanges during this period covered many development-related fields of work, including statistics (Zhou was very impressed with the work of the Indian Statistical Institute), water and power, state planning, agrarian cooperatives, irrigation, steel production and small-scale industries.

But the frontier's shadow was long and dark.

Throughout the mid-1950s, accusations of border intrusions continued to be traded between both countries. Nehru wasn't unduly worried though what *did* perturb him was how Indian territory was shown to be Chinese in China's maps. He raised his concerns with Zhou En-lai during his visit to China in 1954, but he was politely told that the maps in question were based on the old Kuomintang maps which had not yet been revised by the People's Government. The old fears of whether he had made a mistake in allowing Panikkar to not press the frontier issue revived.

Then in December 1956 and January 1957, the question of the McMahon Line came up again. The Chinese premier touched upon Tibet—the exiles in Kalimpong, their influence on the Dalai Lama and Tibetan resistance to China. But significantly, Zhou claimed to have known 'nothing about the McMahon Line until recently, when we came to study the border problem after liberation of China'.[24]

Nehru was puzzled. He explained the history of the Simla Conference that had decided the McMahon Line, to which the Chinese government had not raised any objection.

'Surely, the Chinese Government always knew about it [the McMahon Line]?' he asked Zhou in bewilderment.[25]

They had not apparently.

Pushed into a corner, the Indian prime minister then suggested that the two sides talk things over again and possibly agree on 'some principle'.[26] Zhou agreed, albeit ambivalently. In retrospect, it was a policy of deliberate acquiescence. For years, Beijing played along with the cartographic misunderstanding, not questioning Indian claims.

The Chinese premier maintained politely that the border between the two countries had never been formally defined and the temporary maintenance of the status quo was intended to avoid incidents.

Border transgressions continued throughout 1957 and 1958. In September 1957, news broke of a new highway constructed by China linking Xinjiang and Tibet through the Aksai Chin plateau in northeast Ladakh, claimed by India as a part of Jammu and Kashmir and falling within its territory in the definition of the frontier with China. The Government of India was both baffled and horrified. Technically, it had no right to be. The construction of the road had been widely reported and B.N. Mullick, then the director of the Intelligence Bureau, and his men had been collecting intelligence on the ground since the early 1950s. R.K. Nehru, then in the Ministry of External Affairs, corroborates the fact that reports about the construction of the road were available to India from at least 1955. He adds, however, that the Indian ambassador in Beijing was never informed of the fact and that even the prime minister was not aware of it.[27]

In 1958, revolt was brewing in Tibet and the bilateral relationship between India and China was rapidly freezing over. In a letter to Krishna Menon, Nehru lamented, 'The general Chinese attitude to us in many small matters has not been at all friendly or even sometimes courteous . . . '[28]

Things were about to get a lot worse, and the news that Panikkar was talking openly of leaving his post to return to India and that he was expecting a Rajya Sabha seat was infuriating to an already stressed prime minister. 'He has not written to us officially about his leaving his post in December,' he snapped at his sister. 'I am told that he has been talking about it to odd people. I did not know anything about it.'[29]

Whether the prime minister did anything about this information or not, we shall never know. At any rate, events were rather tragically precipitated. In April 1959, Panikkar went to Munich, where he was scheduled to deliver keynote speeches across two days. On his way back, he spent an evening with Badruddin Tyabji, then the Indian ambassador to Germany. At the end of the evening, Tyabji shook hands heartily. 'I've never seen you in such excellent health! Congratulations!'

That same night, Panikkar suffered a stroke.

He was rushed to hospital with his entire left side paralysed. Doctors moved fast, and within a week, some mobility had returned. 'But even I had doubts if the person who got up from the hospital bed was the same man,' Panikkar wrote.[30]

Life as he knew it was over.

CHAPTER 54

Full Circle

I spread my shawl on the lawn for a little rest in the evening, feeling so restful.
There are no glorious flowers in this wonderful garden,
Only one or two useless country plants stand there.
The bitter gourd creeps over the hedgerow and the children are playing on the other side, with gusto.
And here and there, on the branches of these huge trees, birds on their way stop to sprinkle their songs.
Let the world and its business go on unhindered,
Let the ambitious ones put in more effort.
For me, today, weary of life's long journey, just a little rest for a little while is all I want.
Here on this grass, let me lazily stretch my legs and lie down for a quiet repose.[1]

PANIKKAR WROTE THESE RATHER SAD LINES NOT LONG AFTER HIS STROKE. For a year, he was bidden to stay in France. Air travel had been forbidden, with doctors fearing the return of a possibly fatal clot. He was warned not to work, not to concentrate on anything for more than hour. He was to live a severely restricted life.

Weighed down by grief, Panikkar resigned the post of ambassador and booked the next voyage home to India.

He was never fully well again. The voyage left him weak and shaken and for six months, he was an invalid. 'Once reading and writing are ruled out, what is left for a man like me?'[2] His memoir makes for sad but prosaic reading. 'I consider the rest of my time only as the evening of my life ... I am conscious that I may not have the strength to turn out any considerable work in future. However, I have not lost the hope that I may regain something like normal health and still lead a useful life.'[3]

As it turned out, he would live for another four years in indifferent health. Nehru, taking pity on his old friend, put aside his frustrations and nominated Panikkar to the Rajya Sabha in July 1959. The Panikkars were given a house on 14, Akbar Road in the heart of New Delhi, where their children and grandchildren came often to visit. Madhavan, Parvathy's eldest son, would remember his grandfather encouraging him to play chess with him. 'It was to strengthen his mind after his stroke,' he remembered.

Gouri was also not keeping well, though she kept up a show of fierce independence. Ambika, her granddaughter, remembered family trips to conservative Trivandrum, where Gouri would smoke with great flair, disregarding the horrified looks she was receiving from passers-by. She kept herself busy with her carpentry and her gardening, though reading was limited for a time after her cataract surgery. But where it should have been a time of rest and recuperation for a couple in their early sixties, it was one of immense strain.

In August 1958, the Indian government decided to take up the frontier issue formally with China. The decision was prompted by the publication of a map in the *China Pictorial* (July 1958), which showed large areas of Indian territory, including four out of five divisions in India's then North-East Frontier Agency (now Arunachal Pradesh) and a considerable stretch of many thousand square miles in north and eastern Ladakh, within the territorial confines of China. A note from the foreign office in Delhi to the Chinese Embassy on 21 August 1958 asked that necessary corrections be made in these maps. China responded pleasantly that a survey had not yet been done, nor had China consulted its neighbouring countries about a new way to draw the boundary.[4] Nehru wrote personally to Zhou, expressing his incredulity that China was now talking of new surveys where there was no dispute over the areas concerned. These boundaries were well-known and fixed, he said. Zhou replied on 23 January 1959 in a letter in which he rejected Nehru's view that the McMahon Line represented the boundary with China in the northeast, adding that a friendly settlement could be reached for this section of the boundary. As far as the western section (Ladakh) was concerned, Zhou felt that India and China should maintain the status quo (keeping to the border areas under their jurisdiction).[5]

There was worse to come.

The events of March 1959—the uprising in Tibet and the flight of the Dalai Lama across the Himalayas into India—have been richly and severally documented.[6] But it marked a point of no return for India's ties with China. A demonstration outside the Chinese consulate in Mumbai protesting the events in Tibet saw a portrait of Mao Tse-tung being pasted on the consulate walls following which the crowd hurled 'tomatoes and rotten eggs' at it. The Chinese were livid, summoning Ambassador G. Parathasarathy to complain of this 'huge insult' and to hand him a note which he would tell Delhi was 'offensive in tone and unreasonable in demand'. In the Rajya Sabha, the entire policy that had been pursued until that point in history came under vicious attack, forcing the prime minister on the defensive. Panikkar, a new Rajya Sabha MP, was in parliament during these debates. It made for hard hearing, considering his fellow members of parliament were in a thorough rage at what was happening at India's borders. Clinging to his health, he rose on 8 December 1959, to publicly defend his motives.

It was a short speech, since he could not speak or stand for long.

Action, Panikkar said, had been taken on the basis of what had been plausibly foreseen. 'The eastern boundaries were dead boundaries. The Himalayas were more than a dead boundary, because they constituted a rampart which nobody could pass,' he said on the floor of the house. 'All that situation suddenly changed, changed not because of anything that we did, but changed because of historical evolution and because of the great revolutionary changes that had come over Asia.... All that could have been foreseen, all that could have been done, was done in order to make that boundary a live boundary for us also … We have also to think of the future. It is for the first time a great power has come to our border … A power which is increasing its strength and is being organized as a power-conscious State coming near our border. We also for the first time after many hundreds of years have become united, have become a power State in a small way organising our own economic life, organizing the strength that is in us. So what we see here is the juxtaposition of two States, both great, both capable of putting forward considerable strength … We cannot get away from that, these two countries living together, one with 600 million people and the other with 400 million, both contemporaries in history from very early days, and the idea that they can be permanently hostile to each other is something which we cannot for one moment imagine.'[7]

On 9 December 1959 Nehru himself had to speak, to support the choices he had made and to support his man in China. The subject of China was allotted seven hours to be discussed, and tempers ran very high that day. Of necessity, the prime minister was forced to speak in alignment with his former ambassador. 'There was a brief but very important reference … in Mr Panikkar's short speech yesterday. We are facing one of the major historical changes of the world, of Asia and of India … it is not a minor matter … For the first time, two major powers of Asia face each other on an armed border. For the first time, a world power … sits near our borders and frontiers … That itself changes the whole context, the whole picture … So we face each other there and we face other in anger at the present moment, and we are going to face each other, not today or tomorrow, but for hundreds and hundreds of years … I am glad that Mr. Panikkar, with his great experience of both these countries drew attention this major historical fact: that is, we are sitting … looking at these problems at a turn of history's wheel, a major turn which has never taken place in the past.'[8]

Nehru denied that this was a new problem. 'In those early years of this present day republic, the Chinese Republic, Mr. Panikkar was our ambassador there, and I read through his notes on the subject and our notes to him and our decisions. From the very first day … the question was whether we should raise it in an acute form at that stage. We decided—whether it was right or wrong, you can judge now; it is easy to be wise after the event … we decided not to, and still, we do not see how we could have decided otherwise.'[9]

Nehru insisted, as Panikkar had done in 1950 and now, that the question of the frontier had always been a certainty. 'Why should we go about asking China to raise this question, when we felt sure about it? Why invite discussion about a thing on which we had no doubt? … Mr. Panikkar himself advised us at that time, "Yes, you need not raise it; but declare it openly." We declared it in Parliament, we declared it before the Chinese government and all that … But at no time during this entire period did they challenge our map.'[10]

Matters with China would never be the same again, and for Panikkar it was a troubling end to a public career. For the first time, he could see how deviously the Chinese had played their game, and for first time too, he saw how deeply the frontier had impacted Indian politics and geopolitics—and his friendship with a prime minister he deeply respected.

'The Indian Embassy in Peking had betrayed the best interests of India in Tibet … It is a pity and a shame that today that gentleman has been appointed by the President as the representative of the Indian people [in the Rajya Sabha]'.[11] Comments like these from his colleagues in the Rajya Sabha cut him to the quick. For as long as he could remember, he had devoted his mind to thinking about India, its place in the empire and in the world. He had spent his life working for its cause, to understanding its history and its politics.

Only for it all to have come to this.

He retired from public life in 1960, devoting much of his time to writing and reading as much as he could. He held quiet positions in academia, as vice chancellor first of the University of Kashmir (1961–1962) and then finally at the University of Mysore (1963). His health continued to fluctuate, but Panikkar continued to keep his mind active. In *Problems of Indian Defence* (1960), for instance, he explained the new problems that confronted an independent India in the Cold War: the withdrawal of British naval power from the Indian Ocean, the difficulties of finding regional cooperation with

Pakistan and the importance of recognising that the Himalayas were not the dead boundaries that he had dismissed them as, but a live frontier.[12] He continued to insist on internal cohesion, maintaining links with historical heritage and unity in a democracy. Political unity, laws, democratic structures and citizens' rights were the new cohesive elements of contemporary India as a secular state, though Panikkar remained obstinately fixated on the idea that the heart of Indian culture and of the nation itself remained Hinduism. Integrity, for Panikkar, had to come from within, without seeking shortcuts of bureaucratic forms of cohesion.

Unsurprisingly, perhaps, in that view to which he had always stuck Panikkar created something of a scandal when he refused to cooperate with Dr Sampurnanand's Committee on Emotional Integration in 1962. The committee was an initiative aimed at finding ways through which education could make Indians' sense of national belonging more emotionally homogenous in the face of communal, casteist and other fissiparous tendencies.[13]

Panikkar was the only vice chancellor in the country who did not want to be involved. In hindsight, he was only standing by a principle he had always believed in. Since his younger days in the 1920s, Panikkar had been solidly against what he scornfully called 'the standardisation of intelligence'.[14] This was precisely what he believed Sampurnanand's Committee called for, particularly with its recommendations on nationalising textbooks, emphasis on unity and rituals such as singing the national anthem. To Panikkar's mind, this rigidity would do nothing beyond lending an ideological backing to the concept of what a nation was. To a mind that had been allowed to freely rove across and engage with myriad subjects and ideas, this was appalling. Nationalism, Panikkar felt, could neither be an act nor a performance. Small wonder then that he wanted nothing to do with Sampurnanand's ideas.

'He spoke very disparagingly of the Committee ... bluntly asking why an effort should be made for integration in India, when there were countries in Europe like France, Germany, Spain etc, all independent, living separate lives and making no effort to come together,' Sampurnanand wrote in shock to Nehru. 'The whole talk of integration, in his opinion, was silly and bound to fail.'[15] Panikkar alleged that not only had he met Nehru, but that Nehru knew nothing about the committee or its work. When the members of the committee remonstrated with him, Panikkar became so outrightly angry that Bakshi Ghulam Mohammad had to intervene. 'The way that his mind functions on the very important question of national integration cannot in my opinion be ignored,' felt Sampurnanand.[16]

Nehru was resting at the time in Kashmir. He was exhausted at the time, fretting over building tensions with China and still distraught over the death of Edwina Mountbatten in 1960. In ordinary circumstances and had Panikkar gone about expressing himself a little more tactfully, the prime minister may well have agreed with him. But Panikkar had, in recent times, done enough and more to try Nehru's nerves. For some time now, he had found himself disagreeing with a mind whose intelligence and scope he had once enjoyed. In 1957, when he had been asked for an opinion on an essay by Panikkar, he had coldly dismissed it. 'There are some things which he has said with which I do not agree, and there are many with which I do agree. We allow free expression of opinion.'[17] Now, to Sampurnanand, he was even more blunt. 'He is a man with considerable ability, but also a good deal of conceit. His saying that I did not know anything about your committee was, of course, absurd.'[18]

Panikkar knew nothing of this, and by this time, it is doubtful whether he would have paid much attention. He had lived long beyond what the doctors in France had predicted, but he knew he was coming towards the end of his days.

He continued to write as he had always done. For him, it was much more than an academic pursuit. It was, as it had always been, a need, a necessity to channel not only his thoughts and emotions, but in these twilight years, the work that he produced collectively speak of a man deeply immersed in the discovery of his own nation and in constructing a modern Indian 'identity' that would never deny its past. These last works reflect a hardening stand around the central theme of Hinduism as India's cohesive core, and also highlight another recurring theme for Panikkar: he was always profoundly influenced by the fact that he came from what he saw as a 'peripheral' area,

Kerala, and from an upper caste, the Nairs. He was equally influenced by the fact that the Nairs were, when he was growing up, going through a time of great changes, economic, social and cultural, all of which was stemming from forceful contact with Western modernity. While Panikkar would always remain strongly attached to his own region and language, he also acknowledged his own family's need to appropriate the new 'English' culture to maintain the privileged status it enjoyed in society.

Had he known that he had been passed over to become vice chancellor of Kerala University at this point, 'because it is rather doubtful if he is very popular in his own homeland',[19] he would have been deeply hurt. In all his works of fiction and poetry, his love for his homeland shines brightly, as does his respect for its customs and traditions. These tensions drove the development of his own ideas of India, a nation caught between tradition and modernity. Hinduism, the heart of Indian identity, had to be defended against the dangers it faced; social structures preserved; the English language rejected. In his constant oscillation between the values of unity and diversity, modernity and tradition, Hinduism remained his one lodestar, as did India's inherent resilience in the face of constant change.

These were not typically religious or supremacist ideas, but rather philosophical principles and intellectual traditions, all of which were concerned with his principal question: *What does it mean to be Indian?* It had been a question that had driven Panikkar all his life. He had been born in a time of too much change to ignore its call and it would become one of the central themes of his life. In his search for answers, he would annoy and exasperate colleagues, friends and family alike with his arrogance, his pomposity and his smug self-belief. Over his commitment to certain views—like those over China and Tibet—he had lost friends and created rifts in modern Indian geopolitics that would endure long after he had passed.

But in equal measure, Panikkar's was a mind that fascinated and compelled with the intricacy and depth of its erudition. His had been a restless life, from Travancore to England, from Bhopal to Patiala to Bikaner, from China to Egypt and from Syria to Paris. He had been at the frontline of several political and geopolitical events that had been landmarks in modern Indian history and foreign policy. He had served India in capacities he had never thought of when he first boarded the steamer to England all those years ago. He had worked as an editor, an emissary, an academic, a diplomat, a journalist, a constitutional lawyer and a politician. He had lived life well: he had met the important men of his age, he had dined with kings and he had loved a good woman and was surrounded by children and grandchildren who adored him.

Now, in his late sixties, he was tired: physically, emotionally and mentally.

To his family, Panikkar talked often of death. 'He didn't fear death,' his grandson Krishnan would recall. 'As he used to say, he was at "peace with his Maker".'[20]

In those days, it was the practice for people to send black-bordered white postcards announcing the death of a loved one. The sight of one of these in the mail would irritate Panikkar no end. 'When I pop off, don't send these stupid things,' he would harrumph. Intrigued, one day, Krishnan asked what else he wanted or didn't want when he finally died. 'I want to go like Rafi did,' Panikkar said, referring to a former Union minister who had collapsed and died while speaking at a public meeting. 'I do not want any rituals followed. If you were to fling me by the roadside, it would make no difference. I would not know it. However, I would like to imagine that you fellows would give me a good burn.'

This energetic conversation, marked by his grandfather's recent tired crotchetiness, led Krishnan to wonder later if Panikkar had had some kind of premonition that the end was near. Certainly his behaviour in the months that followed seem to prove this idea. Panikkar spent October and November travelling across the country, visiting all his children. He even went home to Chalayil 'on what was quite obviously a farewell visit'. In the winter of 1963, he sent for his daughter Radha, then married happily to an engineer, K.C. Mohan. She brought her family to visit him in Mysore, where he was finishing his term as vice chancellor. It was the last time she would see her father again.

On 10 December 1963, the day Panikkar died, he fixed an appointment with his physician to come and see him before he went to a meeting.

He had invited the great Bengali poet Amiya Chakravarty to Mysore University for a lecture. Panikkar was in good spirits that day. He was looking forward to the seminar, enjoying the idea of learning something new. In case the doctor found anything disturbing, he rescheduled his appointment for the next day. If Gouri got wind of anything wrong, she would forbid him from going to the lecture altogether.

At the meeting, it was a packed hall. Panikkar was pleased, though he was beginning to be uncomfortably aware of a tightening around his chest. He introduced Chakravarty and watched—almost as though he were detached from his body—the audience in his vision blur. As Chakravarty began to deliver his lecture, Panikkar stepped off the stage and quietly requested a professor who was in the audience to preside in his stead. He said nothing about anything being wrong. 'Those who saw him that day could not make out from his face that he was ill or in pain,' Krishnan recalled. 'All that they commented on was the way he had clutched his hat over his heart.'

Panikkar managed to make it to his car, ordering his driver to rush him home. By the time they had covered the short distance home, he couldn't move. The sudden greyness of his face was enough to alarm the driver, who rushed inside, calling urgently for Gouri.

She ran out, around the car to the backseat, where Panikkar was half-lying, half-sitting, slumped over. 'Grandmother held his head in her lap,' Krishnan said. 'He made as if to speak—and died in her lap.'

He was rushed to hospital. But Gouri knew it was all over.

The news of K.M. Panikkar's death spread like wildfire all over the country. The first aid to arrive were some Malayali students from Mysore University. Gouri was all alone in a strange city. Her children hadn't arrived yet. Panikkar's students helped to keep the house clean and quiet as the first mourners began to arrive.

Soon, a man called Gopalan Nair arrived. 'Grandmother had not met him previously but knew of him as he was married to their dear friend Kuttappa Panikkar's niece. He took charge and informed the family.'

The first familiar face she saw was a peon from Trivandrum who had as a young boy worked for the Panikkars and who had rushed to Mysore as soon as he heard the news. Chief Minister S. Nijalingappa, on whose insistence Panikkar had taken over at Mysore University, also arrived, folding his hands in condolence.

Parvathy, Krishnan and Madhusudan arrived the next day, via the morning flight from Delhi. Shortly thereafter, Padmanabha and the rest of the family at Chalayil arrived, along with the other Panikkar daughters. Panikkar's body was taken out of his house with a guard of honour by a contingent of the National Cadet Corps (NCC) before it was taken around the city on a flower-bedecked truck. Throngs lined the route the cortege took to the cremation ground near Chamundi Hill, outside Mysore.

'My uncle and I sat next to his body in the truck and the two of us performed his last rites,' Krishnan remembered. Before the pyre was lit and the last rites commenced, a detachment of the NCC present at the cremation grounds fired three salvoes in the air.

Across India, his family, young and old, mourned the loss of a man who had adored all of them in equal measure. Panikkar had not been an easy husband, but he had loved Gouri deeply and she had loved him too. Their marriage had seen its share of lively fights, as does any long-lived union, but with him, she had seen not just all of India, but most of the world. She had been by his side during the mercurial highs of his career, as well as its most despondent lows. She had stood by him when public storms broke over his head in China. Above all, she had been tremendously proud of the man she had married. With him, she had grown from a shy, uneducated girl who could hardly speak English to a fine woman, strong and fiery with a mind and voice distinctively her own. Now she would carry his memory with her for as long as she lived, until her death in 1988. His children and grandchildren remembered a humorous man, full of stories, jokes and history. No matter how busy he had been, Panikkar had always had time for the younger generation, sitting with them for hours, equally at ease with simple stories and Sanskrit classics.

Schools and law colleges across Mysore and Bangalore held condolence meetings that December. Despite his stature, Panikkar had always been accessible to his students; his jovial sense of humour and easy erudition both awed and inspired. In the last years of his working life, he had pushed himself to stay mentally active and alert, refusing to bow to illness. He had always been proud of his mind, of its curiosity, its keenness and its joy in being alive to new views and perspectives on everything under the sun. In the end, he had died as he would have wanted to: organising a lecture by one of the great poets of the day, so that those attending might learn something new.

As the rituals that he had disdained were performed, the 'stupid' cards that he had scorned went out to friends, family and colleagues across the world. Personal messages of condolence poured in for Gouri from Panikkar's numerous friends in Southeast Asia and the princely states, from Britain to America, from the governor of Mysore to the prime minister of India. In Delhi, Nehru was bereft at the loss of a man who had succeeded in rousing his annoyance and admiration in equal measure. 'His death,' he wrote, 'is a loss to the nation.'[21]

He meant every word. More than a colleague, Panikkar had been a friend, an intelligent voice of reason and a mind Nehru had enjoyed testing as the two men worked in their different capacities to shape modern India.

On the cold, grey morning of 11 December 1963, both houses of parliament rose to their feet in New Delhi, standing in silence for some time to pay their respects to a man who had been a giant of their time—and in whose shadow generations would walk for years to come.

Notes

CHAPTER 1

1. Ayyappa Panicker, 'Kavalam', from *Pathumanippookkal* (*Poetry at Midnight*), translated by P. Ravindran Nayar, Folio Books, 2010. Available at: https://www.boloji.com/poem-articles/29/from-kavalam-to-kavalam.
2. K.M. Panikkar, 'Some Aspects of Nayar Life', *The Journal of the Royal Anthropological Institute of Great Britain and Ireland*, Vol. 48, 1918, pp. 254–293.
3. P. Velayudha Panicker, *A Sardar from Kavalam*, unpublished and undated, p. 5.
4. Velu Ramon Pillai and Puthenveetil Govinda Kerala Panikkar, *Land Reclamation in Kerala*, Asia Publishing House, 1965, pp. 16–17.
5. This was the family home to which the women of the Panikkar family were sent for their confinements during the last stages of their pregnancies.
6. K.M. Panikkar, *An Autobiography*, translated from the Malayalam by K. Krishnamurthy, Oxford University Press, 1954, p. 2.
7. Kavalam was not quite the boondocks that Panikkar painted it to be. It was home, for instance, to a rich literary pantheon from the Niranam poets (pioneers of Malayalam bhakti literature and authors of the Bhagavad Gita, Ramayana and Mahabharata in Malayalam) to the Kannassan poets to Kunchan Nambiar, master of Malayalam satirist poetry.
8. P. Velayudha Panicker, *A Sardar from Kavalam*, p. 13.
9. K.M. Panikkar, *An Autobiography*, p. 3.
10. Ibid.

11. Samuel Mateer, *Native Life in Travancore*, W.H. Allen & Co., 1883, p. 210.
12. Ibid., p. 353.
13. K.M. Panikkar, *An Autobiography*, p. 3.
14. P. Velayudha Panicker, *A Sardar from Kavalam*, p. 14; K.M. Panikkar, *An Autobiography*, p. 3.
15. This cheerful decade of progress met with a sadly bitter end as resentments between Ayilyam Thirunal and Rao began to crack their working relationship. At the end of the decade, the king was publicly accusing his government's best minister of colluding with the British without his consent. By 1872, Rao had departed the state with no small amount of bitterness between the two men.
16. K.M. Panikkar, 'Some Aspects of Nayar Life', pp. 259–260.
17. The joint family under the matrilineal system is known as tharavad, kudumbakkar or veedu. It formed the nucleus of the society. The eldest male was considered the head of the family, known as the 'karanavar', and he controlled all the family assets. However, his sons did not inherit the properties; instead, inheritance went to the children of his sisters. Through this system, descent and the inheritance of property were passed from the maternal uncle to nephews or nieces. The right of the child was with the maternal uncle or the mother's family rather than the father or the father's family. Through this bloodline, surnames, titles, properties are inherited from the child's uncle or mother. In a word, this system was known as marumakkathayam. For a fuller understanding, see Robin Jeffrey, *The Decline of Nair Dominance: Society and Politics in Travancore, 1847-1908*, Vikas Publishing House, 1976, pp. 135–136.
18. K.M. Panikkar, *An Autobiography*, p. 26.
19. P. Velayudha Panicker, *A Sardar from Kavalam*, p. 8.
20. Ibid., p. 4.

CHAPTER 2

1. K.M. Panikkar, *An Autobiography*, p. 6.
2. Konniyoor R. Narendranath, *Sardar Panikkar: His Life and Times*, Builders of Modern India Series, Publication Division, Government of India, 1998, p. 4.
3. K.M. Panikkar, *An Autobiography*, p. 6.
4. Ibid.

5. Ibid.
6. Ibid.
7. Bipan Chandra, *India's Struggle for Independence: 1857-1947*, Penguin Books, 1988, p. 121.
8. The takeover of the estates and the arrangement of family affairs was a new portfolio for the harassed Ramakrishna who had until then only managed the agricultural side of things. But as the younger members of the family left home to pursue more lucrative careers, there was no one to supervise the paddy fields. Ramakrishna had had no choice but to farm out the land to tenants.
9. K.M. Panikkar, *An Autobiography*, p. 10.

CHAPTER 3

1. Ottoline Morrell, *Early Memoirs*, Faber & Faber, 1963, p. 45.
2. Stephen McKenna, *While I Remember*, George H. Doran & Company, 1921, p. 79.
3. D. Nichols Pigache, *Café Royal Days*, Hutchinson Books, 1934, pp. 187–188.
4. He wasn't the only one who arrived in England that month. The Indian political leader Lala Lajpat Rai was also present. Rai would spend the next six months mingling with the likes of Sidney and Beatrice Webb and George Bernard Shaw, besides taking an avid interest in the British trade union movement.
5. Norman Mackenzie & Jean Mackenzie, *The Diaries of Beatrice Potter Webb*, Northeastern University Press, 2001, diary entry of 23 Apil 1914, p. 101.
6. David Lloyd George, *War Memoirs*, Vol. II, Odhams Press, 1938, pp. 1141–1142.
7. K.M. Panikkar, *An Autobiography*, p. 16.
8. Richard Symonds, *Oxford and Empire: The Last Lost Cause*, St. Martin's Press, 1983, p. 13.
9. It had in fact been Churchill who had first warned of a war after a trip to Germany in 1912. At the time, he had been contemptuously dismissed as a sabre-rattler.
10. Barbara Tuchman, *The Guns of August*, MacMillan Books, 1962, p. 25.
11. Anne de Courcy, *Margot At War*, Weidenfeld & Nicolson, 2015, p. 137.

12. Roderick MacLean, *Royalty and Diplomacy in Europe, 1890-1914*, Cambridge University Press, 2001, p. 67.
13. Miranda Carter, *The Three Emperors: Three Cousins, Three Empires & The Road to War*, Penguin Books, 2009, p. 418.
14. K.M. Panikkar, *An Autobiography*, p. 17.

CHAPTER 4

1. K.M. Panikkar, *An Autobiography*, p. 17.
2. Ibid.
3. Ibid.
4. Ibid., p. 18.
5. Ibid.
6. K.P.S. Menon, *Many Worlds: An Autobiography*, Oxford University Press, 1965, p. 20.
7. Farzana Shaikh, *Community and Consensus in Islam: Muslim Representation in Colonial India, 1860-1947*, Imprint One, 2012, p. 167.
8. Ibid. Also see Gail Minault, *The Khilafat Movement: Religious Symbolism and Political Mobilization in India*, Columbia University Press, 1982, pp. 46–48.
9. 'Publication of the Report of the Lee-Warner Committee, Appointed in 1907, to Enquire into the Indian Students' Problem in the United Kingdom', F.No. 92-93, Part B, Education Department, 1922, National Archives of India (hereafter NAI). Also see Rehana Ahmed & Sumita Mukherjee, *South Asian Resistances in Britain, 1858-1947*, Bloomsbury Books, 2011.
10. Ibid.
11. Nehru and Gandhi, for instance, engaged with the Congress Political Agency, founded by Dadabhai Naoroji.
12. It all happened smoothly and in the most banal fashion. A mixer was being held at the Imperial Institute in South Kensington. Sir William Curzon-Wylie, the India Office representative, smiled and made pleasant small talk before stopping on his way out to speak to a young student. That student was Madan Lal Dhingra who, in the middle of the conversation, calmly pulled out a gun and fired four rounds, point blank.
13. Richard Popplewell, *Intelligence and Imperial Defence: British Intelligence and the Defence of the Indian Empire, 1904-1924*, Routledge Books, 1995.

14. Nigel West, 'Sir John A. Wallinger', Oxford Dictionary of National Biography, https://www.oxforddnb.com/display/10.1093/ref:odnb/9780198614128.001.0001/odnb-9780198614128-e-67772.
15. Richard Popplewell, *Intelligence and Imperial Defence: British Intelligence and the Defence of the Indian Empire*, p. 139.
16. Note on K.M. Panikkar, R/1/1/1714, India Office Records (hereafter IOR).
17. 'Antecedents of Mr. Panikkar', R/1/1/1714, IOR; 'Extract from the Madras Classified List of Political Suspects &c., 1923', L/PJ/12/264, IOR; 'Indian students and societies at Oxford and Cambridge: Scotland Yard. Reports on individuals and conferences. Feb. 1936-Apr. 1946. Earlier files destroyed', L/PJ/12/4, IOR.
18. K.P.S. Menon, *Many Worlds: An Autobiography*, p. 20.
19. Judith Brown, *Modern India: The Origins of an Asian Democracy*, Oxford University Press, 1985, p. 191.
20. 'Extract from the Madras Classified List of Political Suspects &c., 1923', L/PJ/12/264, IOR; 'Indian students and societies at Oxford and Cambridge: Scotland Yard. Reports on individuals and conferences. Feb. 1936-Apr. 1946. Earlier files destroyed', L/PJ/12/4, IOR.
21. 'Antecedents of Mr. Panikar', R/1/1/1714, IOR; 'Extract from the Madras Classified List of Political Suspects &c., 1923', L/PJ/12/264, IOR. Also see Paramasiva Subbarayan, 'A Tribute to Panikkar', in B.J. Chacko (ed.), Sardar K.M. Panikkar: *Shashtyabdapoorthy Souvenir*, Mathrubhumi Press, 1954, pp. 92–95.

CHAPTER 5

1. *The Eagle*, St. John's College, University of Cambridge, 1915, pp. 329–332.
2. Ibid.
3. Saul Dubow, 'Colonial Nationalism, the Milner Kindergarten and the rise of South Africanism, 1902-1910', *History Workshop Journal*, Vol. 43, 1997, pp. 53–85. Also see Deborah Lavin, *From Empire to International Commonwealth: A Biography of Lionel Curtis*, Clarendon Books, 1995.
4. J. Lee Thompson, *A Wider Patriotism: Alfred Milner and the British Empire*, Pickering & Chatto, 2008, p. 152. Also see Deborah Lavin, *From Empire to International Commonwealth: A Biography of Lionel Curtis*.
5. Ibid.

6. K.M. Panikkar, 'India and the Imperial Cabinet', *The Commonweal*, Vol. 6, 13 August 1915.
7. Ibid.
8. Ibid.
9. Natesan didn't quite know what to expect of Gandhi, either the man or the myth that was being built around him even then. When Gandhi arrived in Madras one morning in 1915, Natesan went down to the station to meet the barrister who had taken the nation by storm. Expecting him to be travelling first class, he waited accordingly at the platform, even as a mob some 2,000 strong began to gather near the third-class compartments. In time, Gandhi stepped off the train from the third-class compartments, making Natesan shifting uneasily even years later.
10. K.M. Panikkar, 'Louis Kossuth and the Hungarian Revival', *Indian Review*, Vol. 16, No. 5, 1915, pp. 387–389.
11. Author's interview with R.M. Nair, April 2022.
12. R.L. Mehta, 'Sardar K.M. Panikkar: An Appreciation', in B.J. Chacko (ed.), *Sardar K.M. Panikkar: Shashtyabdapoorthy Souvenir*, pp. 88–89.
13. Paramasiva Subbarayan, 'A Tribute to Panikkar', in B.J. Chacko (ed.), *Sardar K.M. Panikkar: Shashtyabdapoorthy Souvenir*, p. 92.
14. K.M. Panikkar, 'Europe and Nationality', *The Commonweal*, Vol. 4, 27 August 1915.
15. Ibid.
16. Ibid.
17. K.M. Panikkar, 'Some Economic Illusions', *The Commonweal*, Vol. 5, October 1915.
18. Ibid.
19. K.M. Panikkar, 'The London Money-Market and the War', *Commonweal*, Vol. 5, October 1915.
20. K.M. Panikkar, *An Autobiography*, p. 21.
21. C. Kunhan Raja, 'Modern Currents in Malayalam Poetry', *Triveni Journal*, Vol. 6, No. 7, Jan–Feb, 1929.
22. K.M. Panikkar, 'What Life Has Taught Me,' *Bhawan's Journal*, 5 January 1964, Bharàtiya Vidya Bhawan, pp. 46–50.

CHAPTER 6

1. K.M. Panikkar, 'The Claim of Imperial Citizenship', *Commonweal*, Vol. 6, 15 September 1916.

2. The historian Sukanya Banerjee (*Becoming Imperial Citizens: Indians in the Late Victorian Empire*, Duke University Press, 2010) locates what she calls 'narrative registers', formed at common but different sites of power and thought: law, politics, women and bureaucracy.
3. Foreign and Political Department, Secret, General Branch, August 1917, NAI, pp. 10–99.
4. According to BNSA, any person born within His Majesty's Dominions was a natural British subject. The Act also allowed for the issuing of imperial certificates of naturalisation which would recognise such a person as a British subject in the eyes of the empire.
5. K.M. Panikkar, 'Citizenship and Identity', *The Commonweal*, Vol. 7, October 1916. Also see K.M. Panikkar, 'India and Imperial Reconstruction', *The Commonweal*, 10 November 1916, Vol. 6, July–December 1916, and K.M. Panikkar, 'India's Place in the Empire', *The Commonweal*, 12 January 1917, Vol. 7, January–June 1917.
6. Ibid.
7. For more, read Jolita Zabarskaitė, *Greater India and the Indian Expansionist Imagination, c. 1885-1965: The Rise and Decline of the Idea of a Lost Hindu Empire*, DeGruyter Oldenbourg, Heidelburg, 2023, and Yorim Spoelder, *Visions of Greater India: Transimperial Knowledge and Anti-Colonial Nationalism, c. 1800-1960*, Cambridge University, 2024.
8. K.M. Panikkar, 'Citizenship and Identity', *The Commonweal*, Vol. 7, October 1916.
9. See James Foreman Peck, *A History of the World Economy: International Economic Relations since 1850*, Harvester Wheatsheaf, 1995.
10. K.M. Panikkar, *An Autobiography*, p. 35.
11. K.M. Panikkar, *An Introduction to the Study of the Problems of Greater India*, T.K. Swaminathan, 1916, p. 15.
12. Ibid., pp. 55–56.
13. Ibid., pp. 84–86.
14. Ibid. Also see K.M. Panikkar, 'The Problem of Education in the Colonies', *The Modern Review*, Vol. 21, 1917. pp. 58–61; K.M. Panikkar, 'The Educational Problem of Indian Nationalism', *The Modern Review*, Vol. 23, 1918, pp. 7–17; K.M. Panikkar, 'The Illusions of Anglo-India, Pt. IV: Social Myths', *The Commonweal*, 1917, Vol. 7, 1917, pp. 127–128.
15. Ibid., pp. 55–56.

16. Feriel Nissa Kissoon, 'The Creole Indian: The Emergence of East Indian Civil Society in Trinidad and Tobago, c.1897-1945', Ph.D. Dissertation, King's College, London, June 2014, p. 84.
17. K.M. Panikkar, 'The Illusions of Anglo-India, Pt. I: The Cult of Efficiency', *The Commonweal*, Vol. 7, January 1917.
18. K.M. Panikkar, 'The Illusions of Anglo-India, Pt. II: Historical and Geographical Myths', *The Commonweal*, Vol. 7, February 1917.
19. Ibid.
20. C.P. Ramaswami Aiyar, 'Introduction', in K.M. Panikkar, *An Introduction to the Study of the Problems of Greater India, i-vi, here ii.*
21. Ibid., p. 128.
22. Ibid.
23. K.M. Panikkar, 'The Illusions of Anglo-India, Pt. III: Hypnotism by Hypothesis', *The Commonweal*, Vol. 7, March 1917.
24. Margery Sabin, 'Ramananda Reviewed', *Economic and Political Weekly*, Vol. 51, No. 42, 2016, pp. 38–43.
25. K.M. Panikkar, 'The Educational Problem of Indian Nationalism', *The Modern Review*, Vol. 23, 1918, pp. 7–17.
26. Ibid.
27. Minutes of the Meeting of the East India Association, undated, part of the Panikkar estate's private collection.
28. K.M. Panikkar, 'The Problem of Education in the Colonies', *The Modern Review*, Vol. 21, 1917. p. 58-61; K.M. Panikkar, 'The Educational Problem of Indian Nationalism', *The Modern Review*, Vol. 23, 1918, pp. 7–17; See also 'Discussion on Foregoing Paper', *The Asiatic Review*, Vol. 13-14: 39, 1918, pp. 307–317, here p. 310.
29. Ibid., p. 316.
30. Minutes of the Meeting of the East India Association, undated, part of the Panikkar estate's private collection.
31. K.M. Panikkar, 'Some Aspects of Nayar Life', *Journal of the Royal Anthropological Institute*, Vol. XLVIII, 1918, pp. 254–293.
32. K.M. Panikkar, 'What Life has Taught Me'.
33. Dr Thomas Strong to K.M. Panikkar, 6 July 1917, Christ Church, Oxford University. Quoted in Panikkar, *An Autobiography*, pp. 22–23.
34. K.M. Panikkar, *An Autobiography*, p. 34.

CHAPTER 7

1. Ibid., p. 28.
2. Ibid.

3. Diary of the Rev. George Woodford, Entry for 16 September 1918, http://agiusww1.com/wp-content/uploads/2018/04/The-sinking-of-the-SS-Tasman.pdf.
4. Ibid.
5. Ibid.
6. K.M. Panikkar, *An Autobiography*, p. 26.
7. Diary of the Rev. George Woodford, Entry for 18 September 1918, http://agiusww1.com/wp-content/uploads/2018/04/The-sinking-of-the-SS-Tasman.pdf.
8. Ibid.
9. Ibid.
10. Ibid.

CHAPTER 8

1. K.M. Panikkar, *An Autobiography*, p. 27.
2. 'Rice for Travancore', *The Hindu*, 19 December 1918. Available at: https://www.thehindu.com/archives/from-the-archives-dec-19-1918-rice-for-travancore-the-new-arrangements/article25775131.ece. Also, P.S. Govinda Pillai's 'Great famine goddess' is arguably the first cartoon that was ever published in the state. The drawing depicting the hapless subjects being crushed by the 'famine goddess' under British rule appeared in the fifth edition of a Kollam-based magazine called *Vidushakan*.
3. The First World War ended the purely colonial status of the dominions. Their military contribution to the Allied war effort ensured them an equal say in the formulation of imperial policy. Although there was no formal definition of dominion status, a pronouncement by the Imperial Conference of 1926 described the dominions as 'autonomous communities within the British Empire, equal in status, in no way subordinate one to another in any aspect of their domestic or external affairs, though united by a common allegiance to the Crown and freely associated as members of the British Commonwealth of Nations.' For more, see F.R. Scott, 'The End of Dominion Status', *American Journal of International Law*, Vol. 38, No. 1, January 1944, pp. 34–39.
4. Satyendra Sinha, 'Proceedings of the Imperial War Cabinet', TNA/CAB 23/40, Records of the Cabinet Office, National Archives, United Kingdom (hereafter NAUK).

5. For an overview of this issue, see S.H. Patil, *The Congress Party and Princely States*, Himalaya Publishing House, 1981, pp. 17–89.
6. K.M. Panikkar, *An Autobiography*, p. 27.
7. Ibid.
8. Ibid., p. 28.
9. Elizabeth Cooper, *The Harim and the Purdah: Studies of Oriental Women*, Century Books, 1915, pp. 154–155.
10. *Aligarh Institute Gazette*, Aligarh, 5 August 1992.
11. Hamilton Gibb, *Mohammedanism*, Oxford University Press, 1996, p. 81.
12. Masood's personal life continued to run on an opposite track to his professional one. He divorced his first wife soon after marrying her and he lost heavily in the stock exchange crash of 1929.
13. Sarojini Nadu to Syed Mahmud, 17 August 1916, quoted from Makarand Paranjpe (ed.), *Sarojini Naidu: Selected Letters, 1890s to 1940s*, Kali For Women, 1996, p. 117.
14. K.M. Panikkar, *An Autobiography*, p. 28.
15. Ibid.
16. In 1921 Banerjea was knighted and accepted office as minister of local self-government in Bengal. Attacked by extreme nationalists as a turncoat, he was defeated in the 1924 dyarchy elections by a Swarajist candidate. It was the end of his political career. He would die a year later, in 1925.
17. Ibid., p. 29.
18. A. Raghu, *Duty, Destiny and Glory: The Life of Sir CP Ramaswami Aiyar*, Orient Blackswan, 2014, p. 55.
19. K.M. Panikkar, *The Working of Dyarchy in India*, D.B. Taraporevala & Sons, 1928, p. 32.
20. Gandhi to O.S. Ghate, 30 January 1919, *Collected Works of Mahatma Gandhi (CWMG)*, Vol. 15, Navjivan Trust, 1972, p. 81.

CHAPTER 9

1. K.M. Panikkar, *The Working of Dyarchy in India*, p. 32.
2. Margaret MacMillan, *Paris 1919: Six Months that Changed the World*, Random House, 2003, p. 464.
3. K.M. Panikkar, *The Working of Dyarchy in India*, p. 28.
4. K.G. Saidiyan, 'Panikkar: A Fragmentary Appreciation', in B.J. Chacko (ed.), *Sardar K.M. Panikkar: Shashtyabdapoorthy Souvenir*, p. 62.

5. Ibid.
6. Ibid.
7. Author's interview with Radha Mohan, 2022.
8. K.M. Panikkar, *An Autobiography*, pp. 27–28.
9. David Lelyveld, 'Three Aligarh Students: Aftab Ahmad Khan, Ziauddin Ahmad and Muhammad Ali', *Modern Asian Studies*, Vol. 9, No. 2, 1975, pp. 227–240.
10. K.G. Saidiyan, 'Panikkar: A Fragmentary Appreciation', in B.J. Chacko (ed.), *Sardar K.M. Panikkar: Shashtyabdapoorthy Souvenir*, p. 63.
11. K.M. Panikkar, *An Autobiography*, p. 29.
12. Ibid., p. 334.
13. Ibid.
14. Ibid.
15. Ibid., p. 30.
16. Shrabani Basu, *For King and Another Country: Indian Soldiers on the Western Front, 1914-1918*, Bloomsbury Books, 2015, p. 211.
17. Following the defeat of Germany and Ottoman Turkey in World War I, their Asian and African possessions, which were adjudged not yet ready to govern themselves, were distributed among the victorious Allied powers under the authority of Article 22 of the Covenant of the League of Nations. The mandate system that resulted from this distribution was essentially a compromise between the Allies' desire to keep the colonies and their grand assertation that territorial annexation was not their aim. The mandates were divided into three groups on the basis of their location and their level of political and economic significance, and were then assigned to individual Allied victors known, unsurprisingly, as the mandatory powers. Theoretically speaking, the exercise of these mandatory powers was supervised by the League's Permanent Mandates Commission, though there was no real way to enforce its powers. The mandate system was replaced by the UN Trusteeship system in 1946. For more, see C. Stahn, *The Law and Practice of International Territorial Administration: Versailles to Iraq and Beyond*, Cambridge University Press, 2008, pp. 73–91.
18. K.M. Panikkar, 'The Native States and Indian Nationalism', *Modern Review*, Vol. 25: 1, 1919, pp. 37–44.
19. Ibid.
20. For more, see Manu Pillai, *False Allies: India's Maharajahs in the Age of Ravi Varma*, Juggernaut Books, 2021.

21. Rosita Forbes, *India of the Princes*, E.P. Dutton & Company, 1941, p. 126.
22. Yvonne Fitzroy, *Courts & Camps in India: Viceregal Tours, 1921-1926*, Methuen & Co Ltd, 1926, pp. 154–165.
23. Ibid.
24. Livia Manera Sambuy, translated by Todd Portnowitz, *In Search of Amrit Kaur*, Chatto & Windus, 2023, p. 86.

CHAPTER 10

1. K. Ishwara Dutt, 'Sardar K.M. Panikkar: A Personal Tribute', in B.J. Chacko (ed.), *Sardar K.M. Panikkar: Shashtyabdapoorthy Souvenir*, pp. 171–172.
2. Konniyoor R. Narendranath, *Sardar Panikkar: His Life and Times*, p. 32.
3. K.M. Panikkar, *An Autobiography*, p. 342.
4. A.L. Basham, 'Modern Historians on Ancient India', in C.H. Philips (ed.), *Historians of India, Pakistan and Ceylon*, Oxford University Press, 1961, p. 272.
5. Ibid., p. 6.
6. K.M. Panikkar, 'The Native States and Indian Nationalism', p. 11.
7. Ibid., p. 14.
8. Ibid., pp. 69–70.
9. Vanya Vaidehi Bhargav, *Being Hindu, Being Indian: Lala Lajpat Rai's Ideas of Nationhood*, Viking Books, 2024, p. 306.
10. K.M. Panikkar, *Sri Harsha of Kanauj: A Monograph on the History of India in the First Half of the 7th Century AD*, D.B. Taraporevala and Sons, 1922, pp. 34–35.
11. For more, see Michael Fisher, *Indirect Rule in India: Residents and the Residency System, 1764-1858*, Oxford University Press, 1998.
12. 'Royal Conference in Simla', *The Tribune*, 14 July 1916.
13. K.M. Panikkar, *Essays on Educational Reconstruction*, Ganesh & Co, 1920, p. 7.
14. Ibid., p. 15
15. Ibid., p. 26.
16. Bipan Chandra, *India's Struggle for Independence: 1857-1947*, p. 171.
17. Reported in *Bombay Chronicle*, 9 November 1921, as part of 'Report on Native Papers for the Week Ending November 19, 1921', IOR. Available at: https://jstor.org/stable/saoa.crl.25637247.

18. John Last, 'The Prince of Wales' Trip to India in November 1921 was a Royal Disaster', JSTOR, 2 February 2022. Available at: https://daily.jstor.org/the-prince-of-wales-1921-trip-to-india-was-a-royal-disaster/.
19. Ibid.
20. Reported in *Nusrat*, 10 November 1921, as part of 'Report on Native Papers for the Week Ending November 19, 1921', IOR. Available: https://jstor.org/stable/saoa.crl.25637247.
21. K.M. Panikkar, *An Autobiography*, p. 33.
22. Ibid., p. 31.
23. K.M. Panikkar, *Sri Harsha of Kanauj: A Monograph on the History of India in the First Half of the 7th Century AD*, pp. 29–30.
24. K.M. Panikkar, 'The Interpretation of History', *The Hindustan Review*, Vol. XLV, No. 271, April 1922, pp. 316–323. Republished in a summarised version: 'What Indian History Means' in 'Indian Periodicals', *The Modern Review*, May 1922, pp. 633–634.
25. K.M. Panikkar, *Imperialism: In Practice & Theory*, India Printing Press, 1922, p. 37.
26. Ibid., p. 11.
27. Ibid., p. 79.
28. K.M. Panikkar, *An Autobiography*, p. 33.

CHAPTER 11

1. K.M. Panikkar, *An Autobiography*, p. 33.
2. Ibid.
3. P. Rajaraman, *The Justice Party: A Historical Perspective (1916-1937)*, Poompozhil Publishers, 1988, pp. 212–220.
4. K.M. Panikkar, *An Autobiography*, p. 34.
5. Konniyoor R. Narendranath, *Sardar Panikkar: His Life and Times*, p. 38.
6. Anecdote in 'Go Betweens', *The Hindu*, 27 April 2004.
7. K.M. Panikkar, *An Autobiography*, p. 35.
8. Ibid.
9. Ibid.
10. A. Aiyappan, *Social Revolution in a Kerala Village: A Study in Culture Change*, Asia Publishing House, 1966, p. 135.
11. Ibid.

12. Mary Elizabeth King, *Gandhian Nonviolent Struggle and Untouchability in South India: The 1924-1925 Vykom Satyagraha and Mechanisms of Change*, Oxford University Press, 2020, p. 77.
13. Ibid.
14. K.M. Panikkar, 'Europe and Asia', *Modern Review*, Vol. 34, No. 4, 1923, pp. 423–427.
15. K.M. Panikkar, *History of Kerala, 1498-1801*, Annamalai University, 1959, p. 12.
16. K.M. Panikkar, *An Autobiography*, p. 38.
17. Dilip Menon, *Caste, Nationalism and Communism in south India: Malabar 1900-1948*, Cambridge University Press, 1994, pp. 81–82. Also see Louise Ouwerkerk, *No Elephants for the Maharaja. Social and Political Change in the Princely State of Travancore (1921–1947)*, Manohar Publishers, 1994
18. Margaret Cousins, *The Awakening of Asian Womanhood*, Ganesh & Co, 1922, pp. 121–122.

CHAPTER 12

1. 'Answers to Drew Pearson's Questions, After 5 February 1924', *CWMG*, Vol. 27, pp. 7–10.
2. Ibid.
3. Bipan Chandra, *India's Struggle for Independence: 1857-1947*, p. 215.
4. J.S. Grewal, *Master Tara Singh in Indian History: Colonialism, Nationalism and the Politics of Sikh Identity*, Oxford University Press, 2017, p. 130.
5. K.M. Panikkar, *An Autobiography*, pp. 39–40.
6. Narsingha Rao to G.F. Ogilvie, 21 April 1923; A.B. Minchin to Political Department, 5 May 1923; Nabha to Lord Reading, 5 May 1923. All these letters are in F.No. 401, Home & Political Department, NAI.
7. Report of Special Commissions, 7 July 1923, F.No. 148, Part II, Home and Political Department, NAI.
8. Barbara Ramusack, 'An Incident at Nabha: Interaction between Indian States and British Indian Politics', *The Journal of Asian Studies*, Vol. 28, No. 3, 1969, pp. 563–577.
9. K.M. Panikkar, *An Autobiography*, p. 39.
10. Jawaharlal Nehru, *Toward Freedom: An Autobiography*, Beacon Press, 1941, p. 97.
11. K.M. Panikkar, *An Autobiography*, p. 39. Gidwani was not so lucky, interned for the better part of a year until his health was broken.

The fallout of the arrest of Congress leaders, particularly one as influential as young Jawaharlal, alienated the Congress from the SGPC for a while. It also highlighted fissures within Sikh politics, with conservative Sikhs feeling the SGPC had no business entering the political arena. Other major Sikh states like Jind and Faridkot moved from sitting on the fence to siding with the government in their attitude towards the Akalis.

12. Jawaharlal Nehru, *Toward Freedom: An Autobiography*, p. 100; Barbara Ramusack, 'An Incident at Nabha: Interaction between Indian States and British Indian Politics', *The Journal of Asian Studies*, Vol. 28, No. 3, 1969, pp. 563–577
13. Panikkar's instructions were laid out in writing by Nehru in 'Nehru to Panikkar', 27 March 1924, F.No. 4(1)/1924, AICC, Prime Ministers' Museum and Library (hereafter PMML).
14. Statement on Nabha, 4 March 1924, *CWMG*, Vol. 27, pp. 29–31.
15. K.M. Panikkar, *An Autobiography*, pp. 40–41.
16. Nehru to Sampurnanand, 12 March 1924, *Selected Works of Jawaharlal Nehru* (*SWJN*), Vol. 2, Jawaharlal Nehru Memorial Fund, 1972–2020, p. 143.
17. Nehru to Gandhi, 13 March 1924, *CWMG*, Vol. 27, p. 65.
18. Ibid.
19. Gandhi to Nehru, 15 March 1924, *CWMG*, Vol. 27, p. 66.
20. Author's interview with R.K. Nair, April 2022.
21. Gandhi to Nehru, 16 March 1924, *CWMG*, Vol. 27, pp. 73–74.
22. Nehru to Panikkar, 27 March 1924, *SWJN*, Vol. 2, p. 149.
23. See F.No. 4(1) (KW) (1)/1924, AICC Papers, PMML. Also see Nehru to Panikkar, *SWJN*, Vol. 1, pp. 384–385.
24. Ibid.
25. Note by a Correspondent of the CID, Punjab, 18 April 1924, IOR/R/1/1/1518.
26. Panikkar to Gandhi, 11 April 1924, *CWMG*, Vol. 27, p. 77.
27. Nehru to Panikkar, 2 April 1924, *SWJN*, Vol. 2, pp. 150–151.
28. Ibid.
29. Ibid.
30. Nehru to Kitchlew, 27 April 1924, *SWJN*, Vol. 2, p. 152.
31. Gandhi to Mangal Singh and Raja Singh, 5 April 1924, *CWMG*, Vol. 27, pp. 177–178.
32. Gandhi to Panikkar, 5 April 1924, *CWMG*, Vol. 27, p. 178.

33. K.M. Panikkar, *An Autobiography*, p. 41.
34. Panikkar to Gandhi, 11 April 1924, Gandhi Ashram, Sabarmati, Ahmedabad. Quoted from Rita Paolini and Marco Elli, *Indian National Identity and Foreign Policy: Reevaluating the Career of K.M. Panikkar, 1894-1963*, Palgrave MacMillan, 2023, pp. 49–50.
35. Ibid.
36. Nehru to Panikkar, 2 April 1924, F.No. 4(1)/1924, AICC, PMML.
37. See Mohinder Singh, *The Akali Struggle: A Retrospect*, Atlantic Books, 1988.

CHAPTER 13

1. Panikkar to Gandhi, 18 April 1924, intercepted by the British, IOR/R/1/1/1518.
2. Panikkar to Gandhi, undated, Gandhi Ashram, Sabarmati, Ahmedabad. Quoted from Rita Paolini and Marco Elli, *Indian National Identity and Foreign Policy: Reevaluating the Career of K.M. Panikkar, 1894-1963.*
3. Gandhi to Panikkar, 9 April 1924, *CWMG*, Vol. 27, p. 202.
4. As a site of protest, Vaikom could not have been better placed. It was easily accessible via boat and road to the neighbouring princely state of Cochin and with the Shertallai peninsula across the backwaters, an Ezhava working class had grown up around the coir industry.
5. For more, see Robin Jeffrey, 'Temple-Entry Movement in Travancore, 1860-1940', *Social Scientist*, Vol. 4, No. 8, 1976, pp. 3–27. Available at: https://www.jstor.org/stable/3516377.
6. Panikkar to Gandhi, 21 April 1924, *CWMG*, Vol. 27, p. 281.
7. Gandhi to Panikkar, 10 April 1924, *CWMG*, Vol. 27, p. 215.
8. Dilip Menon, *Caste, Nationalism and Communism in south India: Malabar, 1900-1948*, pp. 81–82.
9. Gandhi to Kesava Menon, 3 April 1924, *CWMG*, Vol. 23, pp. 272–273 and Kesava Menon to Gandhi, 19 March 1924, *CWMG*, pp. 560–561.
10. Gandhi's Interview to *The Hindu*, 15 April 1924.
11. Panikkar to Gandhi, 16 May 1924, Gandhi Ashram, Sabarmati, Ahmedabad. Quoted from Rita Paolini and Marco Elli, *Indian National Identity and Foreign Policy: Reevaluating the Career of K.M. Panikkar, 1894-1963.*
12. Ibid.
13. K.M. Panikkar, *An Autobiography*, pp. 42–43.

14. Ibid.
15. Ibid.
16. Nehru to A.M. Khwaja, 6 June 1923, *SWJN*, Vol. 1, p. 359.
17. K.M. Panikkar, *An Autobiography*, p. 44.
18. Ibid.
19. The story did not end too happily for Nabha, whose position was now much weaker than before. He was taken to Kodaikanal as a prisoner in February 1928. Here, he lived out the rest of his lonely years, dying in 1942, alone and unsung.
20. K.M. Panikkar, *An Autobiography*, p. 46.
21. Ibid.
22. Nehru to Panikkar, 30 April 1924, *SWJN*, Vol. 2, pp. 153–154.
23. Panikkar to Gandhi, 31 July 1924, Gandhi Ashram, Sabarmati.
24. Notes by C. Kaye, 21 July 1924, F.No. 255/I/25, Political Branch, NAI.
25. Nehru to Panikkar, 13 June 1924, *SWJN*, Vol. 2, p. 159.
26. Ibid.

CHAPTER 14

1. K.M. Panikkar, *An Autobiography*, p. 48.
2. Nehru to Mohammad Ali, AICC I.No. 4(1) (KW) (ii), 1924, p. 431, PMML.
3. Nehru to Panikkar, 25 July 1924, *SWJN*, Vol. 2, p. 160.
4. Nehru to Panikkar, 30 July 1924, *SWJN*, Vol. 2, p. 161.
5. Konniyoor R. Narendranath, *Sardar Panikkar: His Life and Times*, p. 45.
6. Ibid.
7. Mohammad Ali to Gandhi, 12 July 1924, Mohammad Ali Papers, NMML.
8. Gandhi, as reported in *The Hindu*, 17 September 1924.
9. Editorial, *Hindustan Times*, 27 September 1924.
10. *Hindustan Times*, 14 April 1925.
11. *Hindustan Times*, 17 October 1924.
12. K.M. Panikkar, 'The Past and the Present', *The Modern Review*, Vol. 36, No. 4, 1924, p. 387.
13. Ibid.
14. *Hindustan Times*, issues of 7, 8, 20 and 23 November 1924.
15. *Hindustan Times*, issues of 19, 26 and 27 February 1925.
16. *Hindustan Times*, issues of 14 and 15 October 1924.

17. K.M. Panikkar, *An Autobiography*, p. 52.
18. Parayath E. Raman Menon, 'Sardar K.M. Panikkar: A Running Pen Picture', in B.J. Chacko (ed.), *Sardar K.M. Panikkar: Shashtyabdapoorthy Souvenir*, p. 98.
19. Ibid.
20. Rabindranath Tagore, *Greater India*, S. Ganesan, 1921, p. 31.
21. Ibid., p. 53.
22. Konniyoor R. Narendranath, *Sardar Panikkar: His Life and Times*, p. 52.
23. K.M. Panikkar, *An Autobiography*, p. 54.
24. Ibid.
25. Ibid.
26. *Hindustan Times*, 18 March 1925.
27. Konniyoor R. Narendranath, *Sardar Panikkar: His Life and Times*, p. 54.

CHAPTER 15

1. The final judgements were pronounced on April 6, 1927. Three (later four) men were sentenced to death, and one was given life imprisonment. Azad remained unapprehended and was killed in an encounter with the police in February 1931. The severity of the sentences—particularly of capital punishment—provoked a considerable outcry among the general Indian populace. Several attempts were made to save the four who were sentenced to die, including the passage of a motion in the legislative council of the United Provinces (the colonial precursor to Uttar Pradesh) and a petition to the British viceroy, but they were rejected. The four men were executed in December 1927.
2. R.L. Mehta, 'Sardar K.M. Panikkar: An Appreciation', in B.J. Chacko (ed.), *Sardar K.M. Panikkar: Shashtyabdapoorthy Souvenir*, p. 87.
3. K.M. Panikkar, *An Autobiography*, p. 56.
4. Ian Copland, *The Princes of India in the Endgame of Empire, 1917-1947*, Cambridge University Press, 2009, pp. 33–41.
5. K.M. Panikkar, *An Autobiography*, p. 57.

CHAPTER 16

1. K.M. Panikkar, *An Autobiography*, pp. 60–61.
2. Parayath E. Raman Menon, 'Sardar K.M. Panikkar: A Running Pen Picture', in B.J. Chacko (ed.), *Sardar K.M. Panikkar: Shashtyabdapoorthy Souvenir*, p. 97.

3. Roger Nash Baldwin, 'The Capital of the Men Without a Country', *The Survey*, 1 August 1927, pp. 460–467.
4. Kalidas Nag, *Memoirs*, Vol. II, Writer's Workshop, 1991, pp. 102–103.
5. K.M. Panikkar, *An Autobiography*, p. 61.
6. Kalidas Nag, *Memoirs*, Vol. II, pp. 15 and 150.
7. Ibid., pp. 102–103.
8. Michael Goebel, 'The Capital of the Men Without a Country: Migrants and Anticolonialism in Interwar Paris', *The American Historical Review*, Vol. 121, No. 5, 2016, pp. 1444–1467.
9. R. Nalenan, *Arnold Mononutu*, Gunung Agung, 1981, pp. 16–17, 31, 62.
10. Klaas Stutje, *Behind the Banner of Unity: Nationalism and Anti-colonialism among Indonesian Students in Europe, 1917-1931*, Ph.D Thesis, University of Amsterdam, 2016. Available at UvA-DARE, at https://pure.uva.nl/ws/files/2806111/174460StutjeThesiscomplete.pdf.
11. A list of its members shows the breadth and expanse of the AECO's influence. Apart from the two Chinese members, national representatives included Georges Margouliès (Russia), Alimardan Bey Topchubachev (Azerbaijan), Nimbousheff Darja (Kalmyks), Hakopian (Persia), Henri Abel Kouchakji (Syria), Prabodh Chandra Bagchi, Kavalam Madhava Panikkar, Mukerjee, Chatterjee (British India), Ting Chao Tsing, Tung Meau (China), Li Tsing Sie (Korea), Narita Shigeo (Japan), Prince Areno Yukanthor (French Indochina), Duong Van Giao (French Indochina), Bui Quang-Chiêu (Cochin China) and Arnold Mononutu (Dutch Indies).
12. For more, read S.R. Ashton, 'Imperialism and Nationalism in South-East Asia', in Judith Brown (ed.), *The Oxford History of the British Empire, Vol. 4: The Twentieth Century*, Oxford University Press, 1999, p. 466. The first sign of this change had come in 1921, when Britain reviewed its treaty with Japan. In the wake of the First World War, when Japan had been making designs upon China, Britain had allowed the treaty to lapse, forcing the construction of a costly naval base in Singapore in case of a future crisis.
13. 'Een verblijdende Phase uit onze nationale beweging', Indonesia Merdeka, Vol. 3, 1925, p. 85.
14. Report, Prefet de Police, Direction de la Sûreté, 1925, quoted in Klaas Stutje, *Behind the Banner of Unity: Nationalism and Anti-colonialism among Indonesian Students in Europe, 1917-1931*, Ph.D thesis, University of Amsterdam, 2016.

15. Ibid.
16. NL-HaNA, Koloniën / Kabinet-Geheim Archief, 1901-1940, 2.10. 36.51, inv. nr. 283, 13 September 1926, H14. Quoted from Klaas Stutje, *Behind the Banner of Unity: Nationalism and Anti-colonialism among Indonesian Students in Europe, 1917-1931.*
17. K.M. Panikkar, *An Autobiography*, p. 60.
18. 'Extract van de lezing van KM Panikkar getiteld "the necessity of Asiatic Unity" gehouden op de Alg. Vergadering te Den Haag', Indonesia Merdeka, 4.3-4, June–July 1926: 59.
19. Nalenan, Arnold Mononutu, 16-17, 31, 62; NL-HaNA, Commissariaat Indische Zaken, 2.10.49, inv. nr. 2692, report 1927, appendix A, 75, p. 218. Quoted from Klaas Stutje, *Behind the Banner of Unity: Nationalism and Anti-colonialism among Indonesian Students in Europe, 1917-1931.*
20. See for instance, K.M. Panikkar, 'La tache de Lord Irwin nouveau vice-roi des Indes', *Europe Nouvelle*, Vol. 9, No. 434, 1926, pp. 828–830.
21. K.M. Panikkar, 'The Psychology of the Hindu-Muslim Riots', *Contemporary Review*, Vol. 131, No. 738, 1927, pp. 230–236.
22. K.M. Panikkar, 'The Colour Problem in the British Empire', *Revue des Nations*, Vol. 1, No. 2, 1927, pp. 102–110.
23. K.M. Panikkar, 'Militarism and Empire', *Modern Review*, 39: 3, 1926, 266-8, and 'The Reflex Action of Colonialism on Europe', *Revue des Nations*, 1:5, 1927, pp. 126–30.
24. K.M. Panikkar, *An Autobiography*, p. 61.
25. *La Jeune Republique*, 10 December 1926. Also see Juliette Veillier-Duray with Leonie Burunel, *Mahatma Gandhi*, Ganesh Publishers, 1928, p. 60.
26. Ibid.
27. Author's interview with Ambika Nair, December 2023.
28. George Claretie, *La Figaro*, 8 June 1927.
29. A. Moin Zaidi & Shaheda Gufran Zaidi (eds), *Encyclopaedia of the Indian National Congress*, S. Chand & Co, 1976, Vol. 8, p. 542.
30. For more see Jehuda Reinharz, 'Chaim Weizmann: Statesman Without a State', *Modern Judaism*, Vol. 12, No. 3, 1992, pp. 225–242. Also see William M. Matthew, 'India, Palestine and the Balfour Declaration', *The Balfour Project*, available at: https://balfourproject.org/india-palestine/.
31. K.M. Panikkar, *In Two Chinas: Memoirs of a Diplomat*, Hyperion Press, 1981, pp. 13–14.
32. K.M. Panikkar, 'The Necessity of Asiatic Unity', *Indonesia Merdeka*, Vol. 4., Nos. 3–4, June–July 1926, pp. 56–58.

CHAPTER 17

1. For more, read Gearoid Barry, *The Disarmament of Hatred: Marc Sangnier, French Catholicism and the Legacy of the First World War, 1914-1945*, Palgrave MacMillan, 2012.
2. His career before that balanced on the knife edge between death and liberation. He was arrested for his dissidence by the Dutch in 1934 and sent to the infamous concentration camp of Boven Digul in West New Guinea. He remained a political exile until the eve of the Japanese invasion in the Second World War. Hatta and Sukarno—Indonesia's first president—would collaborate with the Japanese in order to reach independence, but the Japanese were always false allies. Only when Hatta and Sukarno were kidnapped by members of the students' union in Indonesia did the two of them declare independence. As prime minister, Hatta repressed the communist revolution in Java, a measure that gained struggling Indonesia much-needed Western support. He led the Indonesian delegation to the United Nations–sponsored Hague Conference in 1949, which culminated in the Dutch recognition of independent Indonesia.
3. Like most political exiles in Paris at this time, Topchubachev had been ousted by the Bolsheviks, though he didn't identify with them ideologically.
4. Mohammad Hatta, *Mohammad Hatta, Indonesian Patriot: Memoirs*, Gunung Agung, 1981, pp. 200–201.
5. K.M. Panikkar, *An Autobiography*, p. 64.
6. Gearoid Barry, *The Disarmament of Hatred: Marc Sangnier, French Catholicism and the Legacy of the First World War, 1914-1945*, p. 129.
7. Ibid.
8. Mohammad Hatta, *Mohammad Hatta, Indonesian Patriot: Memoirs*, pp. 200–201.
9. Ibid.
10. K.M. Panikkar, Documents, 'Asia and Peace', *Indian Quarterly*, Vol. 2, No. 2, 1946, pp. 192–195, first published 22 August 1926 and reprinted by Panikkar himself in 1946.
11. Mohammad Hatta, 'Manifest of the Asiatic Delegation at the Bierville Congress for Peace', in Verspreide Geschriften, ed. Mononutu et al., pp. 154–157; 'Where there is no justice, there is no peace', *Mohammad Hatta, Indonesian Patriot: Memoirs*, pp. 201–202.

12. K.M. Panikkar, Documents, 'Asia and Peace', *Indian Quarterly*, first published 22 August 1926.
13. Mohammed Hatta, 'Manifest of the Asiatic Delegation at the Bierville Congress for Peace', in *Verspreide Geschriften*, ed. Mononutu et al., pp. 154–157; 'Where there is no justice, there is no peace', *Mohammad Hatta, Indonesian Patriot: Memoirs*, pp. 201–202.
14. K.M. Panikkar, 'The National Movement in India', *Indonesia Merdeka* 4.1, February 1926, pp. 3–5.
15. Ibid.
16. K.M. Panikkar, ibid; See also Mohammad Hatta, 'Non-cooperation', *Indonesia Merdeka* 8.4, July 1930, pp. 61–64.
17. Cicely Hamilton, *Modern Germanies as Seen by an Englishwoman*, Dent & Sons, 1931, pp. 140–145.
18. K.M. Panikkar, *An Autobiography*, p. 66.
19. Ideologically, Chatto clashed wildly with M.N. Roy, the Comintern's chosen representative for Indian affairs since 1920. Their rivalry split their supporters down the middle across Moscow and Berlin. Chatto sought to work with the nationalist movement, while Roy argued that the Comintern needed to build its own Indian Communist Party. Between the two, the more persuasive Roy was the winner.
20. For more on Munzenberg, see Sean McMeekin, *The Red Millionaire: A Political Biography of Willi Munzenberg, Moscow's Secret Propaganda Tsar in the West*, Yale University Press, 2005.
21. Nehru would just as quickly earn Chatto's ire when he hastily disowned any association with the League after it became a front for the Comintern's functions in India.
22. Jawaharlal Nehru, *Toward Freedom: An Autobiography*, p. 155.
23. Nehru, Press Statement in Brussels, 9 February 1927, *SWJN*, Vol. 2, p. 270.
24. Nehru, Speech at Brussels Congress, 10 February 1927, *SWJN*, Vol. 2, p. 275.

CHAPTER 18

1. Reading to Nizam of Hyderabad, 27 March 1926, F.No. 13-Political (Secret), Foreign & Political Department, Nos. 1-49, 1924–1926, Government of India, NAI.
2. E.P. Thompson's Note, 17 July 1926, F.No. 302-Political, Foreign & Political Department, NAI.

3. For more, see Ian Copland, *The Princes of India in the Endgame of Empire, 1917-1947.*
4. Jai Singh of Alwar, Speech to the Chamber of Princes, 27 February 1930, F.No. 19-IV (1926), PSO, Royal State Archives (hereafter RSA) of Alwar.
5. K.K. Pillai to Manubhai Mehta, 12 July 1928, Nos. 286-311, RSA of Bikaner.
6. Panna to Patiala, 28 March 1927, F.No. 48/1, Bhopal Regional Office (BRO), NAI (Bhopal).
7. John Allsebrook Simon, *Retrospect: The Memoirs of the Rt. Honourable Viscount Simon*, Hutchinson Books, 1952, p. 45.
8. K.M. Panikkar, *An Introduction to the Princely States*, Gyan Publishing House, reprinted in 2023, p. 141.
9. K.M. Panikkar, *An Autobiography*, p. 69.
10. Ibid., p. 70.
11. Gearoid Barry, *The Disarmament of Hatred: Marc Sangnier, French Catholicism and the Legacy of the First World War, 1914-1945*, pp. 154–155.
12. K.M. Panikkar, *An Autobiography*, p. 74.
13. Jawaharlal Nehru, *An Autobiography with Musings on Recent Events in India*, Bodley Head, 1989, p. 156.
14. Kerala Putra, (pseudonym assumed by K.M. Panikkar), *The Working of Dyarchy in India, 1919-1928*, D.B. Taraporevala & Sons, 1928, p. 44.
15. Ibid., p. 122.
16. Ibid., p. 116.
17. Ibid.
18. Ibid., p. 155.

CHAPTER 19

1. K.M. Panikkar, *An Autobiography*, p. 72.
2. Author's interview via email with Radha Mohan, October 2020.
3. K.M. Panikkar, *An Autobiography*, pp. 70–72.
4. Author's interview with Ambika Nair, 23 November 2021.
5. In the late nineteenth century, British imperial policy towards Jammu and Kashmir was guided primarily by the fear of a Russian advance towards India through the Pamirs, as well as by the turmoil north of the Hindukush and the Himalayas, then under the nominal rule of China. In this volatile mix was also the independent Emir of Afghanistan, whose lands extended as far as the northwestern

frontier of the subcontinent. Small wonder then that the British kept the hands of Kashmir's maharajas firmly tied.

6. Note by Sir Bertrand Glancy, undated, Crown Representative, Political Department, Indian States Records (1880-1947), R/1/1/1714, IOR.
7. Chaudhri Muhammad Ali, *Emergence of Pakistan*, Columbia University Press, 1967, pp. 218–219.
8. It wasn't the first such strike. In 1847, 4,000 workers set out for Lahore in an astonishing 'migration march', certainly the first such class struggle in India. More struggles followed through the late nineteenth century.
9. G.M.D. Sufi, *Kashir: Being a History of Kashmir from the Earliest Times to Our Own*, Vol. I, Light & Life Publishers, 1974, p. 809.
10. Cabled by Norman Cliff, foreign editor, *News Chronicle*, 21 June 1946, quoted from Ghulam Mohammad Bakshi, *Kashmir Today*, Bombay Provincial Congress Committee, 1946, p. 44.
11. K.M. Panikkar, *An Autobiography*, p. 76.
12. Karan Singh, *Heir Apparent: An Autobiography*, Oxford University Press, 1984, pp. 5–7.
13. K.M. Panikkar, *An Autobiography*, p. 77.
14. Wakefield's own memoir doesn't mention why he was removed from what seems to have been a warmly successful time in Kashmir, and the secret appears to have died with him in Rawalpindi in 1948.
15. K.M. Panikkar, *An Autobiography*, p. 77.
16. Karan Singh, *Heir Apparent: An Autobiography*, pp. 12–13.
17. Ibid.
18. See *Manual of Instructions to Officers of the Political Department of the Government of India* (1909), iii–v, IOR/ R/ 2/ 18/ 117. Reforms, Butler said piously, should 'emanate from the Durbar … since the methods sanctioned by tradition in States are generally well adapted to the needs and relations of the ruler and people.'
19. Ibid.
20. Stephen Legg, *Round Table Geographies: Constituting Colonial India*, Cambridge University Press, 2023, p. 38.
21. Ibid., pp. 43–44.
22. K.M. Panikkar, *An Autobiography*, p. 78.
23. A family of Croatian descent, the Nedous eventually married into the local community. Begum Akbar Jahan, the granddaughter of

Michael Adam Nedou, the original proprietor of Nedou's Hotel, married Sheikh Abdullah in 1933.

24. Author's interview with Ambika Nair, 15 July 2023.
25. Ibid.
26. Syed Sharifuddin Pirzada, *The Collected Works of Quaid-e-Azam Mohammad Ali Jinnah*, East and West Publishing Company, 1986, Vol. II, p. 127.
27. A copy of the questionnaire issued by the committee can be found in Appendix I, *Report of the Indian States Committee*, (n 76). Replies to the questionnaire are collected in a single volume, *Replies Received to the Questionnaire Issued by the Committee*, IOR/ V/ 26/ 272/ 3.
28. Ian Copland, *The Princes of India in the Endgame of Empire, 1917-1947*, pp. 67–69.
29. K.M. Panikkar, *An Autobiography*, p. 79
30. Irwin to Geoffrey Dawson, 21 July 1928, Irwin Collection, Box 8, University of York.
31. K.M. Panikkar, *An Autobiography*, p. 80. For a copy of the tract itself, see *British Crown and the Indian States*, IOR/L/P&S/20/248.
32. K. Iswara Dutt, 'Sardar K.M. Panikkar: A Personal Tribute', in B.J. Chacko (ed.), *Sardar K.M. Panikkar: Shashtyabdapoorthy Souvenir*, p. 173.
33. Balfour Declaration, Imperial Conference, Inter-Imperial Relations Committee, File E-129 (Secret), C.No. 142, 1926. For more on this subject, see Stephen Legg's excellent study, *Round Table Geographies: Constituting Colonial India*.
34. W.D. McIntyre, 'The Strange Death of Dominion Status', *The Journal of Imperial and Commonwealth History*, Vol. 27, No. 2, 1999, pp. 193–212.
35. Barbara Ramusack, *The Princes of India in the Twilight of Empire: Dissolution of a Patron-Client System, 1914-1939*, pp. 190–191.
36. Patrick French, *Liberty or Death: India's Journey to Independence and Division*, HarperCollins, 1997, p. 85.
37. For more, read Stephen Legg, *Round Table Geographies: Constituting Colonial India*.
38. See 'Speech Delivered by the Maharaja of Patiala on the Occasion of the Visit of the Indian States Committee to Patiala, February 1928', in Bhupinder Singh, *Public Pronouncements by His Highness the Maharaja Dhiraj of Patiala in Connection with the Indian States Committee*, Spottiswoode, Ballantyne and Co., 1928, pp. 12–13.
39. Priyasha Saksena, *Sovereignty, International Law, and the Princely States of Colonial South Asia*, Oxford University Press, 2023, p. 109.

40. *The British Crown and the Indian States: An Outline Sketch Presented to the Indian States Committee on Behalf of the Standing Committee of the Chamber of Princes*, 1928, IOR/ L/ PS/ 20/ 248, p. 98. Scott issued a joint opinion along with several other highly qualified jurists. See Joint Opinion of the Right Honourable Leslie F. Scott, KC, MP; Mr Stuart Bevan, KC, MP; Mr Wilfrid A. Greene, KC; Mr Valentine Holmes and Mr Donald Somervell, in Appendix III, *Report of the Indian States Committee*, (n76). An earlier version of the opinion was published as 'The Crown and Indian States: English Counsels' Opinion', *Indian States Review*, 27 October 1928, IOR/ R/ 1/ 1/ 4673(2).
41. See 'Speech Delivered by the Maharaja of Patiala on the Occasion of the Visit of the Indian States Committee to Patiala, February 1928', in Bhupinder Singh, *Public Pronouncements by His Highness the Maharaja Dhiraj of Patiala in Connection with the Indian States Committee*, p. 15.
42. Minutes of a discussion at Government House, Mysore, between the Indian States Committee and the Mysore Government, 19 March 1928, 51-54, IOR/V/26/272/3. Also see Letter from Political Secretary to the Nizam of Hyderabad to the Secretary of the Indian States Committee, 24 April 1928, F.No. 12-R, Reforms Branch and Foreign and Political Department, NAI.
43. Minutes of evidence given before the Indian States Committee at Montagu House, Whitehall, 26 November 1928, 648, 650, *Oral Evidence Recorded Before the Committee*, IOR/ V/ 26// 272/ 3.
44. See Joint Opinion of the Right Honourable Leslie F. Scott, KC, MP; Mr Stuart Bevan, KC, MP; Mr Wilfrid A. Greene, KC; Mr Valentine Holmes and Mr Donald Somervell, Appendix III, *Report of the Indian States Committee*, (n76). An earlier version of the opinion was published as 'The Crown and Indian States: English Counsels' Opinion', *Indian States Review*, 27 October 1928, IOR/ R/ 1/ 1/ 4673(2).
45. It is important to keep in mind that this was not a pathbreaking suggestion. The idea of a round table conference that would include all of India's various political constituents had been floating about since the early 1920s. In April 1921, Bikaner had suggested an RTC to Reading. In the same year, Tej Bahadur Sapru had suggested an RTC between Reading, Gandhi and leading nationalists. In 1924, the Swaraj Party had called for an RTC to devise a new constitution. In 1925, Congress leaders called for an RTC that would be similar

to a constituent assembly. Irwin's proposal, if anything, watered the meaning of the RTC down to an advisory mechanism.

CHAPTER 20

1. P. Velayudha Panicker, *A Sardar from Kavalam*, p. 25.
2. K.M. Panikkar, *An Autobiography*, p. 80.
3. Ibid.
4. Quoted in the Report of the All India States' People's Conference, Bombay, 1939, pp. 6–7.
5. Priyasha Saksena, *Sovereignty, International Law, and the Princely States of Colonial South Asia*, p. 112.
6. K.M. Panikkar, *His Highness the Maharaja of Bikaner: A Biography*, Oxford University Press, 1937, p. 322.
7. For chronology and context, see Note to Viceroy by Standing Committee of the Chamber of Princes, 28 June 1929, Bundle 7, File 2, NAI (Bhopal), Chamber Section; Circular Letter from Maharaja of Patiala, 29 April 1929, Bundle 7, File 2, NAI (Bhopal), Chamber Section.
8. Note dated 2 July 1930, AP 47/10/42 (33A).
9. Undated memo, COP, PSA, F.No. 37(21) of 1931.
10. Hamidullah Khan, quoted in *Times of India*, 15 January 1931, p. 14.
11. Joseph McQuade, 'Beyond an Imperial Foreign Policy?: India at the League of Nations, 1919-1946', *The Journal of Imperial and Commonwealth History*, Vol. 48, No. 2, 2020, p. 284.
12. See G.R. Abhyankar, *Problem of Indian States*, Aryabhushan Press, 1928; and P.L. Chudgar, *Indian Princes under British Protection: A Study of their Personal Rule, their Constitutional Position and their Future*, Williams & Norgate Ltd, 1929.
13. Balraj Krishna, *Sardar Vallabhbhai Patel: India's Iron Man*, Rupa Publications, 2005, pp. 296–297.
14. This may have taken some doing, because not every princely state agreed with the entirety of the report.
15. Quoted from John Zubrzycki, *Dethroned: Patel, Menon and the Integration of Princely India*, Juggernaut Books, 2023, pp. 24–25.
16. For more, see Manu S. Pillai, *False Allies: India's Maharajahs in the Age of Ravi Verma*, Juggernaut Books, 2021.

17. K. Iswara Dutt, 'Sardar K.M. Panikkar: A Personal Tribute', in B.J. Chacko (ed.), *Sardar K.M. Panikkar: Shashtyabdapoorthy Souvenir*, p. 173.
18. Jadunath Sarkar, 'Review: Malabar and the Portuguese', *Modern Review*, Vol. 47, No. 1, 1930, p. 72.
19. Ibid.
20. Ibid.
21. K.M. Panikkar, *Gulab Singh, 1792-1858, Founder of Kashmir*, Hopkinson, 1930.
22. Ibid., p. 37.
23. Bipan Chandra, *India's Struggle for Independence, 1857-1947*, p. 257.

CHAPTER 21

1. K.M. Panikkar, *The Evolution of British Policy Towards Indian States, 1774-1858*, Calcutta University Readership Lectures, 1930, p. ix.
2. Prem Nath Bazaz, *The History of Struggle for Freedom in Kashmir*, Kashmir Publishing House, 1954, p. 141.
3. 'Autocracy to Govern India', *Daily Telegraph*, 14 November 1930.
4. Judith Brown, *Gandhi's Rise to Power: Indian Politics 1915-1922*, Cambridge University Press, 1972, p. 108.
5. K.M. Panikkar, *An Autobiography*, p. 82.
6. 'Gandhi's Peace Terms: Dominion Status at Conference', *Daily Telegraph*, 19 August 1930.
7. Patrick French, *Liberty or Death: India's Journey to Independence and Division*, p. 102.
8. Ibid.
9. Haksar to Sapru, November 1929, Sapru Papers, G2142, F.No. 6/7, quoted in Ian Copland, *The Princes of India in the Endgame of Empire, 1917-1947*, p. 76.
10. Ian Copland, *The Princes of India in the Endgame of Empire, 1917-1947*, p. 76.
11. K.M. Panikkar, *An Autobiography*, p. 83.
12. Note on Meeting between Alwar and the AGG, Rajputana, Col. Ogilvie, 12 February 19928, RSA Alwar, PSO, F.No. 121-I of 1928.
13. Minutes of Conference at Viceregal Lodge, Simla, 14-15 July 1930, IOR/L/R85/13/557.
14. Ibid.
15. Natwar Singh, *The Magnificent Maharaja: The Life and Times of Maharaja Bhupinder Singh, 1891-1938*, Rupa Publications, 2012, p. 172

16. Note by Irwin, 5 August 1930, IOR R/1/1/2024.
17. Ian Copland, *The Princes of India in the Endgame of Empire, 1917-1947*, p. 82.
18. Note by Patiala, Undated, June 1930, Patiala State Archives (PSA), Chamber of Princes Section, F.No. 36(10) of 1929.
19. Note by Bikaner, 2 July 1930, encl. in Bikaner to Hydari, 6 July 1930, AP R/1/47/10/42 (33A).
20. Nicholas Owen, *The British Left and India: Metropolitan Anti-Imperialism, 1885-1947*, Oxford University Press, 2007, p. 180.
21. Robin Moore, *The Crisis of Indian Unity, 1917-1950*, Oxford University Press, 1974, p. 155.
22. K.M. Panikkar, *An Autobiography*, p. 97.

CHAPTER 22

1. Note by Keyes, enclosed in Letter to Irwin, 2 July 1930, Keyes Collection, Box 30.
2. For more on this see Priyasha Saksena, *Sovereignty, International Law, and the Princely States of Colonial South Asia*.
3. Nizam of Hyderabad to Maharaja of Patiala, 10 October 1930, Gwynne Collection, Box 8.
4. Natwar Singh, *The Magnificent Maharaja: The Life and Times of Maharaja Bhupinder Singh, 1891-1938*, p. 200.
5. Robin Moore, *The Crisis of Indian Unity, 1917-1950*, p. 155.
6. V. Hardas, 'A Brief Life-Sketch', in N. Dixit (ed.), *Dharmaveer Dr. B.S. Moonje*, Commemorative Volume, Centenary Commemorative Committee, Nagpur, 1972, p. 5.
7. Diaries of B.S. Moonje, 29 October 1930, Moonje Papers, NMML.
8. Ibid.
9. Maharaja of Alwar, 'The Princes and Dominion Status', *Asiatic Review*, Vol. 26, January 1930.
10. Activities of the Various Indian States' People's Conference, relating to the Problems of the Future of the Native States in India, F.No. PP_000000010098, Private Papers of M.R. Jayakar, NAI.
11. Jinnah to Robert Stopford, 4 November 1930, in BL/IOR/Eur. Mss./E.346/9.
12. UKNA/PRO/30/69/578ii.
13. William Wedgwood Benn to Irwin, 14 November 1930, in BL/IOR/Eur.Mss./C.152/6.

14. Ellis Ashmead-Bartlett, 'Round Table Conference: Prospect of an Agreed Report Almost Impossible', *The Daily Telegraph*, 27 October 1930.
15. G. Mueeinuddin, 'Colour Prejudice and Mixed Marriages', *United India*, June 1929.
16. Benn to Irwin, 27 June 1930, Eur MSS C152/6/IOR/BL.
17. 'Purdah in the Heart of London', *Daily Telegraph*, 29 October 1930.
18. B.S. Moonje, 5 November 1930, Diaries of B.S. Moonje, Moonje Papers, NMML.
19. Harry Haig, Secretary of State to Viceroy, 7 November 1930, Irwin Collection, Box 5.
20. Minutes of the 5th Meeting of the Indian States Department, 10 November 1930, Patiala State Archives, Chamber of Princes, F.No. 37(20) of 1931.
21. Stephen Legg, *Round Table Geographies: Constituting Colonial India*, p. 50.
22. Tej Bahadur Sapru, India Office, 1931a, p. 25.
23. Hari Singh, Speech by Kashmir at the Round Table Conference, 12 November 1930, Indian Annual Register, 1930, Pt. II, p. 280.
24. Maharaja of Alwar, India Office, 1931(a), p. 43.
25. See Diaries of B.S. Moonje, 17 November 1930 and 28 November 1930, Private Papers of B.S. Moonje, NMML.
26. Lord Reading, India Office 1931(a), p. 114.
27. Benn to Lord Irwin, Briefing Paper, 25 November 1930, UKNA/PRO/30/69/578ii.
28. Irwin to Lord Halifax, 23 November 1930, Halifax Collection, Box 27.
29. Benn to Lord Irwin, Briefing Paper, 25 November 1930, UKNA/PRO/30/69/578ii.
30. Note of Conversation with Mr. Panikkar, 25 November 1930, Stopford Papers, MSS Eur E346/9/IOR.
31. K.M. Panikkar, *His Highness, the Maharaja of Bikaner: A Biography*, p. 338. Also see Ian Copland, *The Princes of India in the Endgame of Empire, 1917-1947*, pp. 80–91.
32. Memo by Scott, enclosed in Letter to Haksar, 18 November 1930, PSA, COP, F.No. 37(21) of 1931.
33. Ibid.
34. Natwar Singh, *The Magnificent Maharaja: The Life and Times of Maharaja Bhupinder Singh, 1891-1938*, p. 205.

35. Panikkar to Bhopal, 4 June 1931, BRO, Bhopal, Chamber Section. F.No. 22, C-4/9 od 1932-33.
36. Rima Hooja, *Crusader for Self-Rule: Tej Bahadur Sapru & the Indian National Movement*, Rawat Books, 1999, p. 154.
37. Oriental and India Office Collections (hereafter OIOC), Mss Eur. 220/34.
38. Harry Haig to Lord Irwin, F.No. 147/130-R, Reforms Branch (1930), NAI.
39. Lord Sankey to the Viceroy of India, 15 December 1930, IOR/Eur. MSS G52/6.
40. Memorandum by Sir Reginald Glancy, on 'Attitude of the Indian States' Delegation towards Federation', September 1, 1931. Also see Robin Moore, 'The Making of India's Paper Federation, 1927-1935', in C.J. Phillips & Mary Wainwright (eds), *The Partition of India, Policies and Perspectives*, Allen & Unwin, 1970.
41. 'A Maharaja's Anniversary Banquet', *The Graphic*, 27 December 1930. Also see Malcom Hailey, 18 December 1930, BL/IOR/Eur.MSS/ E220/3.
42. Note of Conversation with Mr. Panikkar, 25 November 1930, Stopford Papers, MSS Eur E346/9, IOR.

CHAPTER 23

1. Hawthorne Lewis, 24 April 1933, F.No. 55/33-R, Reforms Branch (1933), NAI.
2. Interview with Bikaner, *Times of India*, 23 June 1931.
3. K.M. Panikkar, *An Autobiography*, p. 85.
4. Anees Jung, *Night of the New Moon*, Penguin Books, 1993, p. 41.
5. Wavell, *Viceroy's Journal*, p. 34, quoted in Stephen Legg, *Round Table Geographies: Constituting Colonial India*, p. 51.
6. Abidaa Sultan, *Memoirs of a Rebel Princess*, Oxford University Press, 2004, p. 93.
7. L. Rushbrook-Williams, 'India Between the Conferences', *Foreign Affairs*, Vol. 9, No. 4, July 1931, pp. 624–637.
8. Haksar, 'Policy pursued by Indian States Delegation at the Round Table Conference', Confidential Memo, No. 2, undated, RSA, Sirohi, Sadar Office, F.No. 127/1931.
9. K.M. Panikkar, *An Autobiography*, p. 89.
10. Ibid.

11. L. Rushbrook-Williams, 'India Between the Conferences', *Foreign Affairs*, Vol. 9, No. 4, July 1931, pp. 624–637.
12. OIOC, MSS Eur F237/11.
13. Patiala's Note on Federation and the Indian States, 15 June 1931, F.No. 44, 1053/1931, Coll. 11, PIC (1931-1950).
14. Barbara Ramusack, *The Princes of India in the Twilight of Empire: Dissolution of a Patron-Client System, 1914-1939*, p. 209.
15. Interview with Bikaner, *Times of India*, 23 June 1931.
16. Bhulabhai Desai to Patiala, 28 August 1931, Bhulabhai Desai Papers, NAI.
17. Maharaja of Patiala, Statement Explanatory of Memorandum on Federation and the Indian States, undated, IOR/L/PS/13/603.
18. Note on Federation and the Indian States, 13 June 1931, F.No. 31-S (Special), Foreign & Political Department, NAI.
19. Haksar to Sapru, 22 July 1931, Sapru Papers, 1st Reel, IOR Neg 4,987.
20. Haksar to Sapru, 12 June 1931 and 13 July 1931, Sapru Papers, 1st Reel, IOR Neg 4,987.
21. Ian Copland, *The Princes of India in the Endgame of Empire, 1917-1947*, pp. 96–97.
22. Nehru to Patiala, 16 September 1931, *SWJN*, Vol. 5, pp. 37–40.
23. Sir Prabhashankar Pattani, 'The Indian States: A Letter on their Relations with British India', September 1930, Templewood Collection, No. 532(2A).
24. 'Note on the Implications of Federation', Circular Letter from Bhopal, 12 May 1932, IOR/L/PS/13/547.
25. Note by P.J. Patrick, 21 May 1932, IOR/L/PS/13/603.
26. Author's interview with Ambika Nair, November 2021.
27. Ibid.
28. 'Note on the Implications of Federation', Circular Letter from Bhopal, 12 May 1932, IOR/L/PS/13/547.
29. Panikkar to Patiala, 22 July 1931, file 28, basta 31, PSAP.
30. Maharaja of Patiala to Willingdon, 17 August 1931, F.No. 31-S, Foreign & Political Department (Special), NAI.
31. OIOC, MSS Eur 237/11
32. Patrick French, *Liberty or Death: India's Journey to Independence and Division*, p. 84.
33. Ibid.
34. William Wedgwood Benn, April 1931, BL/IOR/D714/11.

35. Nehru to Patiala, 16 September 1931, Vol. 5, *SWJN*, pp. 37–40.
36. Speech by Liaqat Hayat Khan at the Second Indian Round Table Conference, 30 November 1931, from Adrian Sever (ed.), *Documents and Speeches on the Indian Princely States*, Vol. 2, pp. 494–497.
37. Ibid.
38. Working Committee instructions to Gandhi, 11 September 1931, sent by Nehru to Gandhi in London, quoted from Stephen Ashton, *British Policy Towards the Indian States, 1905-1939*, Curzon Press, 1982, p. 239.
39. Stopford to Lord Peel, 16 October 1931, Stopford Papers, Collection 7.
40. Ian Copland, *The Princes of India in the Endgame of Empire, 1917-1947*, pp. 105–106.
41. K.M. Panikkar, *An Autobiography*, p. 88.
42. Ibid.

CHAPTER 24

1. That same year, Winston Churchill resigned from the Conservative Party. His ideas of empire were deeply racist and he had zero interest in understanding that a dismissal of Indian nationalism and sentiments might be an outdated policy. To tactful suggestions that he might want to rethink how he felt about India, he snarled, 'I'm quite satisfied with my views of India. I don't want to be disturbed by any bloody Indian!' See Ben Pimlott (ed.), *The Second World War Diary of Hugh Dalton, 1940-1945*, Cape Books, 1986, p. 126.
2. Hoare to Lothian, 3 March 1932, Templewood Collection, Box No. 14.
3. Revised Proposals for a Confederation Scheme, 8 February 1932, File 2, Basta 29, Punjab State Archives.
4. For the full report, see 'Report to His Highness the Chancellor', undated, File 7, Basta 29, Punjab State Archives.
5. Information conveyed by Mir Maqbool Mahmood on the telephone from Delhi, 16 March 1932, File 2, Basta 29, Punjab State Archives. Also see K.M. Panikkar, *The Indian Princes in Council: A Record of the Chancellorship of His Highness the Maharaja of Patiala*, Oxford University Press, 1936, p. 105, and 'Resolution Passed by the Chamber of Princes', 1 April 1932, *Indian Annual Register*, Vol. 1, 1932, p. 380.
6. Willingdon to his son, 5 April 1932, Willingdon Collection.
7. Richard Glancy to Sir Findlater Stewart, 29 February 1932, Findlater Stewart Collection, Box 11.
8. K.M. Panikkar, *An Autobiography*, p. 90.

9. Rushbrook-Williams to Hoare, 3 March 1932 and 1 April 1932, Private Office Papers, 1/PO/58.
10. John Davidson to Bikaner, 30 March 1932, enclosed with Davidson to Hoare, 31 March 1932, Templewood Collection, Box No. 14.
11. Rushbrook-Williams to Mehdi Yar Jung, 8 and 22 July 1932, AP R/1/47/10/105.
12. Quoted from Willingdon to Hoare, 10 July 1932, Templewood Collections, Box 5.
13. Willingdon to Hoare, 12 September 1932, Templewood Collection, Box 6.
14. Ibid.
15. K.M. Panikkar, *An Autobiography*, p. 89. Also see Haksar to Sapru, 4 September 1932, Sapru Papers, 6/7, G2142.
16. Roland Wild, *Ranji: The Biography of Colonel His Highness Shri Ranjitsinhji*, Rich & Cowan, 1934, p. 293. Also see K.M. Panikkar, *An Autobiography*, p. 89.
17. For more of this, read K.M. Panikkar, *Caste and Democracy*, Hogarth Press, 1933.
18. A.K. Damodaran, Seminar on K.M. Panikkar, Vol. I, Sahitya Akademi, 1994. Audio-tape recording SAK-226_1-AC, dated 21 June 1994. Available at: https://archive.org/details/dni.ncaa.SAK-226_1-AC.
19. Ibid.
20. Ibid.

CHAPTER 25

1. Report by K.M. Panikkar on the conference between the viceroy and the princes in September 1932, 24 October 1932, Chamber Section, Bundle No. 20, File No. 17 (Old F.No. P/115), NAI (Bhopal).
2. Minutes of a meeting held at Viceregal Lodge, Simla, 20 September 1932, IOR/R/1/1/4688(1).
3. Sir Philip Chetwode to Irwin, 11 September 1932, quoted in F.W.F. Smith, *Halifax: The Life of Lord Halifax*, Hamilton House Publishers, 1965, pp. 327–328.
4. Ibid.
5. Ian Copland, *The Princes of India in the Endgame of Empire, 1917-1947*, p. 121.

6. Report by K.M. Panikkar, 24 October 1932, F.No. 17, Chamber Section, NAI (Bhopal). Also see Haksar to Sapru, 5 October 1932, Sapru Papers, 6/7, G2142.
7. Liaqat Hayat Khan to Patiala, 9 December 1932, COP, PSAP, F.No. 38(47) of 1932.
8. Scott was reluctantly allowed to attend on the condition that the Jam Sahib pay his bills. Since Nawanagar was already owed a hefty sum from the chamber for previous legal advances, he was not best pleased with this arrangement.
9. Memo by Scott and Rushbrook-Williams for Nawanagar, 8 December 1932, IOR L/P&S/13/668.
10. K.M. Panikkar, *An Autobiography*, p. 92.
11. Note by Nawanagar, 20 March 1933, PSA, COP, F.No. 37(39) of 1933.
12. K.M. Panikkar, *An Autobiography*, p. 96.
13. Haksar to Sapru, 28 March 1932, Rima Hooja, *Crusader for Self-Rule: Tej Bahadur Sapru & the Indian National Movement*, p. 203.
14. Ibid.
15. Ibid.
16. K.M. Panikkar, *An Autobiography*, p. 88.
17. Nawanagar, Speech of 24 March 1933, *Indian Annual Register*, Vol. 1, 1933, pp. 478–479.
18. Willingdon to Harcourt Butler, 28 March 1933, Butler Collection, Box 54.
19. Roland Wild, *Ranji: The Biography of Colonel His Highness Shri Ranjitsinhji*, pp. 308–311.
20. Ian Copland, *The Princes of India in the Endgame of Empire, 1917-1947*, p. 125.
21. *The Indian States Gazette*, Vol. 3, No. 4, April 1933, p. 7.
22. K.M. Panikkar, *An Autobiography*, p. 91.
23. Ibid.
24. Ibid.
25. Ibid.

CHAPTER 26

1. Baron Jean Pellanc, *Diamonds and Dust*, translated by Stuart Gilbert, John Murray, 1936, p. 166.
2. K.M. Panikkar, *An Autobiography*, p. 85.

3. Natwar Singh, *The Magnificent Maharaja: The Life and Times of Maharaja Bhupinder Singh, 1891-1938*, p. 2.
4. Lucy Moore, *Maharanis: The Lives and Times of Three Generations of Indian Princesses*, Viking Books, 2004, p. 170.
5. K.M. Panikkar, *An Autobiography*, p. 99.
6. Nadir Khan, as it turned out, would indeed be assassinated in the winter of 1933. His son Zahir Khan would peacefully ascend the throne, ushering the longest reign by a single ruler since the foundation of the Durrani Empire in the eighteenth century.
7. K.M. Panikkar, 'A Further Note on Safeguards', Undated, F.No. 26, Basta 31, PSAP. Also see Note of Discussions at the India Office, 24 January 1934; Viceroy to Secretary of State, 26 January 1934, IOR/L/P&S/13/651.
8. K.M. Panikkar, *An Autobiography*, p. 94.
9. Papen would narrowly escape with his life during Hitler's purge of the SA. He would go on to work for Austria's annexation by Germany and be tried as a war criminal during the Nuremberg trials.
10. K.M. Panikkar, *An Autobiography*, pp. 94–95.
11. A good source for this is Natwar Singh's biography of Bhupinder Singh, *The Magnificent Maharaja: The Life and Times of Maharaja Bhupinder Singh, 1891-1938*.
12. Jawaharlal Nehru, *Toward Freedom: An Autobiography*, p. 399.
13. N.C. Kelkar to Gandhi, 22 June 1934, quoted in Stephen Ashton, *British Policy Towards the Indian States, 1905-1939*, pp. 238–239.
14. K.K. Aziz, *Rahmat Ali: A Biography*, Sang-e-Meel Publications, 2008, p. 92.
15. For a detailed understanding of the chain of events, see Ian Copland, *The Princes of India in the Endgame of Empire, 1917-1947.*
16. Hydari to Bertrand Glancy, 23 December 1934, AP R/1/47/10/299.
17. Bikaner to Srinvasa Sastri, 7 January 1935, Sastri Papers, F.No. G-4, NMML.
18. Haksar to Sapru, 27 March 1935, Sapru Papers, Reel 8, IOR Neg 5004.
19. Hydari to Glancy, 21 February 1935, IOR/L/PS/13/607.
20. Ian Copland, *The Princes of India in the Endgame of Empire, 1917-1947*, p. 138.
21. Letter to Willingdon, 27 February 1935, IOR/L/PS/13/607.

CHAPTER 27

1. Dr Rajendra Prasad, *Indian Annual Register*, July-December 1934, Vol. 11, pp. 237–256.
2. Patiala, Chamber of Princes, January 1935. Quoted in Ian Copland, *The Princes of India in the Endgame of Empire, 1917-1947*, pp. 134–135.
3. Patiala, 22 January 1935, quoted in K.M. Panikkar, *Indian Princes in Council*, pp. 118–120.
4. K.M. Panikkar, *An Autobiography*, p. 95.
5. Verbatim Record of Speeches at the Conference in Bombay, 25 February 1935, IOR L/P&S/13/682.
6. Ibid.
7. Patiala, Bhopal and Bikaner to the Political Secretary, 27 February 1935, from Adrian Sever (ed.), *Documents and Speeches on the Princely States*, Vol. II, B.R. Publishing, 1985, pp. 504–507.
8. For a thorough, detailed and more legal analysis, see Priyasha Saksena, *Sovereignty, International Law, and the Princely States of Colonial South Asia*.
9. Secretary of State to Viceroy, 7 March 1935, IOR/L/PO/92.
10. The Government of India Bill: Views of Indian States. Available at: https://www.legislation.gov.uk/ukpga/1935/2/pdfs/ukpga_19350002_en.pdf.
11. Patrick French, *Liberty or Death: India's Journey to Independence and Division*, p. 119.
12. Churchill to Clementine Churchill, 2 March 1935, quoted from Martin Gilbert, *The Churchill Collection*, Hillsdale College Press, 2013, Vol. V, p. 1097.
13. Hydari to Coward & Chance, 11 March 1935, IOR/L/PO/92.
14. Jayakar to Sapru, 12 April 1935, Jayakar Papers, NAI.
15. William Croft to Clive Wigram, 7 March 1935, IOR/L/PO/92.
16. Willingdon to his son, 12 April 1935, Willingdon Private Papers.
17. Hoare to Willingdon, 9 May 1935, Templewood Collection, Box 4.
18. Baron Jean Pellanc, *Diamonds and Dust*, p. 163.
19. Ibid.
20. Ibid., p. 170.
21. Author's interview via email with Radha Mohan, October 2021.
22. K.M. Panikkar, *An Autobiography*, p. 98.
23. For more on this, see Anne D'Courcy, *Diana Mosley: Mitford Beauty, British Fascist, Hitler's Angel*, HarperCollins, 2004, pp. 196–200.

24. Natwar Singh, *The Magnificent Maharaja: The Life and Times of Maharaja Bhupinder Singh, 1891-1938*, p. 215.
25. Jarmani Das, *Maharaja*, Hind Pocket Books, 2008, p. 54.
26. Ibid., p. 56.
27. Ibid.
28. K.M. Panikkar, *An Autobiography*, p. 99.
29. Ibid.
30. Ibid., p. 104.
31. Ibid., p. 100.
32. Bipan Chandra, *India's Struggle for Independence: 1857-1947*, pp. 312–313.
33. Monckton to Zetland, undated, October 1935, Monckton Papers, Balliol College, F.No. 86, Collection 11.

CHAPTER 28

1. Quoted from a letter from Patiala to W.G. Neal, 2 August 1935, in Natwar Singh, *The Magnificent Maharaja: The Life and Times of Maharaja Bhupinder Singh, 1891-1938*, p. 220.
2. Sharada Dwivedi, *The Automobiles of the Maharajahs*, Om Books, 2003, p. 135.
3. Patiala to Hitler, 27 September 1935, quoted from Jarmani Das, *Maharaja*, p. 58.
4. K.M. Panikkar, *An Autobiography*, p. 100.
5. Ibid.
6. Zetland to Linlithgow, 30 May 1937, IOR/L/P&S/13/613.
7. Brunyate to Hydari, 1 February 1935, AP R/1/47/10/411.
8. Wylie to Glancy, 4 January 1937, Zetland Collection, NAI.
9. Panikkar to Desmond Young, 8 February 1934, Home (Political) Department, F.No. 33/4/35, NAI.
10. Ibid.
11. Draft Summary of the Proceedings of the Conference at Moti Bagh Palace, Patiala, at 3 PM on 27 January 1936, F.No. 29, Basta 31, PSAP. Also see Report of Committee appointed by HH Patiala to examine the Government of India Act (1935), F.No. 29, Basta 31, PSAP.
12. Patiala to standing committee, 26 February 1935, enclosed in Dholpur to Gwynne, 6 May 1936, Gwynne Collections, Box 1.

CHAPTER 29

1. H.V. Hodson, *Autobiography* (unpublished), p. 184.
2. John Glendevon, *Viceroy at Bay: Linlithgow in India, 1936-1943*, Collins, 1971, p. 22.
3. OIOC MSS Eur F125/22, No. 19.
4. S.A. Gowher Rizvi, *Linlithgow in India: A Study of British Policy and the Political Impasse in India, 1936-1943*, Royal Historical Society, 1970, p. 36.
5. Jawaharlal Nehru, 'On the Indian Situation', *Bombay Chronicle*, 19 November 1935, *SWJN*, Vol. 7, p. 35.
6. Bipan Chandra, *India's Struggle for Independence: 1857-1947*, p. 295.
7. Ibid.
8. Sir Arthur Cunningham Lothian, *Kingdoms of Yesterday*, John Murray, 1951, p. 144.
9. 'India: Partnership and Cooperation', *TIME* Magazine, 12 October 1936.
10. Patiala State, Memo on Instrument of Accession and Connected Matters, Vol. I, Pt. I, F.No. 36, basta 32, PSAP; Panikkar to Prime Minister, 24 August 1936, Memo on Instrument of Accession and Connected Matters, Vol. I, Pt. I, F.No. 36, basta 32, PSAP; Panikkar to Patiala, 15 December 1936 and Secret Note for Personal Information and Consideration of His Royal Highness, F.No. 35, Basta 32, PSAP.
11. Fortnightly reports from Local Governments and Administrations on the Political Situation in India, for the month of February 1937, F.No. 18/2/37, Home Department, Government of India, NAI. For more on this, see Harrison Akins, *Conquering the Maharajas: India's Princely States and the End of Empire, 1930-1950*, Manchester University Press, 2023.
12. Papers relating to the Accession of Mayurbhanj State to the Federation and notes of discussions held with that State, F.No. 18/12/37, Foreign & Political Department, NAI.
13. Gwyer to Patrick, 4 April 1936, IOR/L/P&S/13/608.
14. Wadhams to Patiala, 10 August 1936, COP, F.No. 35(76) of 1935-1938, PSAP.
15. Report by Panikkar and Wadhams, COP, F.No. 31, basta 29 of 1936, PSAP; Also see Panikkar, 'Notes on the Government of India Act 1935', February 1937, Federal Papers, Vol. II, NMML.
16. Ian Copland, *The Princes of India in the Endgame of Empire, 1917-1947*, p. 153.

17. Opinion of J.H. Morgan, 17 February 1937, Federal Papers, Vol. II, NMML.
18. Ibid.
19. Kamaladevi Chattopadhyay, 'Avoiding Reality', *Servant of India*, 16 May 1935, p. 257.
20. Sir Arthur Cunningham Lothian, *Kingdoms of Yesterday*, p. 145.
21. Ian Copland, *The Princes of India in the Endgame of Empire, 1917-1947*, p. 154.
22. K.M. Panikkar, 'The Next Step', Federal Papers, Vol. II, NMML.
23. Haksar to Panikkar, 23 March 1937, Federal Papers, Vol. II, NMML.
24. Opinion of Tej Bahadur Sapru, 22 February 1937, Federal Papers, Vol. II, NMML.
25. Report of the Constitutional Committee of the Chamber of Princes, Federal Papers, Vol. II, NMML.
26. Brown to Panikkar, 19 March 1937, Federal Papers, Vol. II, NMML.
27. Wadhams to Panikkar, 28 November 1936, File 31, basta 32, PSAP.

CHAPTER 30

1. K.M. Panikkar, *An Autobiography*, p. 103.
2. Ibid., p. 90.
3. Ibid., p. 121.
4. Ibid., p. 90.
5. Ibid., p. 105.
6. OIOC, P&J (S), 553/1937.
7. Patrick French, *Liberty or Death: India's Journey to Independence and Division*, p. 134.
8. Sunil Purushotham, *Sovereignty, Federation and Constituent Power in Interwar India, 1917-39*, Duke University Press, 2020, p. 428.
9. Jawaharlal Nehru, *Dawn*, 4 May 1937.
10. Report by K.M. Panikkar, 17 July 1937, F.No. 110/1937, COP Section, PSAP.
11. K.M. Panikkar, *An Autobiography*, p. 104.
12. Patrick French, *Liberty or Death: India's Journey to Independence and Division*, p. 137. Also see Syed Sharifuddin Pirzada, *The Collected Works of Quaid-e-Azam Mohammad Ali Jinnah*, Vol. II, p. 374.
13. Ibid.
14. Stanley Wolpert, *Shameful Flight: The Last Years of the British Empire in India*, Oxford University Press, 2006, pp. 147-148.

15. Resolution of the Indian National Congress, 21 February 1938, *Indian Annual Register*, i(1938), pp. 299–300.
16. Narendra Sarila, *Once a Prince of Sarila: Of Palaces and Tiger Hunts, of Nehrus and Mountbattens*, I.B. Tauris, 2008, p. 138.
17. M.R. Jayakar's Correspondence re: Indian States and the Question of Indian Federation, Private Papers of M.R. Jayakar, PP_000000010682, NAI.
18. Ibid.
19. Panikkar to Bikaner, 10 November 1938, F.No. 2044, MGSTA.
20. K.M. Panikkar, *An Autobiography*, p. 119.
21. Syed Sharifuddin Pirzada, *The Collected Works of Quaid-e-Azam Mohammad Ali Jinnah*, Vol. II, pp. 305–306.
22. Julia Boyd, *Travellers in the Third Reich: The Rise of Fascism, 1919-1945*, Pegasus Books, 2018, p. 281.
23. Note by Paul Patrick, 3 March 1939, IOR/L/PS/13/618.
24. Notes on States' Rights, undated, IOR/L/PS/13/618.
25. John Glendevon, *Viceroy at Bay: Linlithgow in India, 1936-1943*, p. 118.
26. Ian Copland, *The Princes of India in the Endgame of Empire, 1917-1947*, p. 173.
27. Report of the Proceedings, Committee of the States' Ministers, Bombay, 12-14 April 1939, Vol. V, Pt. B, F.No. 36, Basta 32, PSAP.
28. Francis Wylie, *Federal Negotiations in India, 1935-1939 and After*, in C. Phillips and Mary Wainwright (eds), *The Partition of India, Policies and Perspectives*, p. 521.
29. Bikaner to Linlithgow, 17 June 1939, IOR/L/P&S/13/621.
30. Appreciation of the Position resulting from the Princes' Decision with Regard to Federation, Reforms Office, Federal Branch, F.No. 18/39, NAI. Also see V.P. Menon, *The Story of the Integration of the Indian States*, Orient Blackswan, 1957, pp. 40–41.
31. K.M. Panikkar, *An Autobiography*, p. 119. Also see Ganpat Rai to M.R. Jayakar, 16 June 1939, Ganpat Rai Papers, NMML.

CHAPTER 31

1. K.M. Panikkar, *An Autobiography*, p. 120.
2. Ibid.
3. Author's interview via email with R.M. Nair, 19 April 2022.
4. Ibid.
5. David Lloyd George, *War Memoirs*, Vol. II, Odhams Press, 1938, p. 345.

6. Notification Regarding the Appointment of Mr Kavalam Madhava Panikkar, 2 May 1939, F.No. XX/1929, MGSTA. Also see Order of the Maharaja of Bikaner, Re: Appointment of Mr. Panikkar, 2 May 1939, F.N. 7204/1939, GSTAB.
7. P. Velayudha Panicker, *A Sardar from Kavalam*, p. 7.
8. Ibid.
9. Ian Copland, *The Princes of India in the Endgame of Empire, 1917-1947*, pp. 179 and 279.
10. Leonard A. Gordon, *Brothers Against the Raj: A Biography of Indian Nationalists Sarat and Subhas Chandra Bose,* Viking Books, 1990, p. 392.
11. Jawaharlal Nehru, *Toward Freedom: An Autobiography*, p. 140.
12. C.P. Skrine, 'Impressions of Travancore', October 1938, F.No. 739-P (Secret), Political Department, NAI.
13. K.M. Panikkar, *An Autobiography*, p. 116.
14. K.M. Panikkar, 'What Life Has Taught Me', p. 49.
15. Ibid.
16. Gandhi, Interview with the *Times of India*, 24 January 1939.
17. Jawaharlal Nehru, Message to States' People, *Journal of the All India States' Peoples' Conference*, published from Bombay in *National Herald*, 30 November 1938, *SWJN*, Vol. 7, p. 408.
18. Fortnightly Report to the India Office on the Political Situation in Indian States in 1940, First Half of January 1940, undated, F.No. 71(Secret), Political Department, 1940, CRR, NAI.
19. V.P. Menon, *The Story of the Integration of the Indian States*, p. 45.
20. Ian Copland, *The Princes of India in the Endgame of Empire, 1917-1947*, p. 181.
21. K.M. Panikkar, *An Autobiography*, p. 109.
22. Ibid.
23. Ibid.
24. Amery's son, John, on the other hand, was hanged as a Nazi after the war. For more, see William D. Rubenstein, 'The Secret of Leopold Amery', *Historical Research*, Vol. 73, No. 181, June 2000.
25. Gandhi to Linlithgow, 26 May 1940, *CWMG*, Vol. 72, No. 128.
26. Sisir Kumar Bose & Saugata Bose (eds), *Subhas Chandra Bose: The Alternative Leadership, Speeches, Articles, Statements and Letters, June 1939-1941*, Permanent Black, 1998, Vol. 10, 13 March 1940, p. 82.
27. Linlithgow to Amery, 10 June 1943, Nicholas Mansergh and E.W.R. Lumby (eds), *Transfer of Power* (hereafter TOP), Vol. III, p. 1052.

28. Patrick French, *Liberty or Death: India's Journey to Independence and Division*, p. 149.
29. S.A. Gowher Rizvi, *Linlithgow in India: A Study of British Policy and the Political Impasse in India, 1936-1943*, p. 116.
30. Stanley Wolpert, *Shameful Flight: The Last Years of the British Empire in India*, p. 181.
31. Zetland to Linlithgow, 4 April 1940, OIOC, MSS Eur F125/19.
32. John Glendevon, *Viceroy at Bay: Linlithgow in India, 1936-1943*, p. 315.
33. V.P. Menon, *The Transfer of Power in India*, Orient Blackswan, 1957, p. 94.
34. Sarvepalli Gopal, *Jawaharlal Nehru: A Biography*, Vol. I, Oxford University Press, 1979, pp. 268–270.

CHAPTER 32

1. Author's interview with R.M. Nair, 19 April 2022.
2. Ibid.
3. Ibid.
4. Author's interview with Ambika Nair, 29 September 2024.
5. Author's interview with R.M. Nair, 19 April 2022, and with Radha Mohan, 10 October 2021.
6. Author's interview via email with Vijay Nair, 20 April 2022.
7. Taya Zinkin, 'Sardar Panikkar as I Know Him', in B.J. Chacko (ed.), *Sardar K.M. Panikkar: Shashtyabdapoorthy Souvenir*, p. 117.
8. Ibid.
9. K.M. Panikkar, quoted in Maurice and Taya Zinkin, *Britain and India: Requiem for Empire*, Chatto & Windus, 1964, p. 113.
10. Taya Zinkin, 'Sardar Panikkar as I Know Him', in B.J. Chacko (ed.), *Sardar K.M. Panikkar: Shashtyabdapoorthy Souvenir*, pp. 118–120.
11. Kanwar Jaswant Singh, 'Sardar K.M. Panikkar', in B.J. Chacko (ed.), *Sardar K.M. Panikkar: Shashtyabdapoorthy Souvenir*, p. 152.
12. K.M. Panikkar, *His Highness the Maharaja of Bikaner: A Biography*, Oxford University Press, 1937, pp. 364–365.
13. Lothian to Glancy, 1 December 1939, file 210(17), p(s)/39, acc. n. 153, CRR, NAI.
14. Ibid.
15. P. Velayudha Panicker, *A Sardar from Kavalam*, pp. 103–105.

CHAPTER 33

1. Written statement from R.K. Nair, dated 25 August 2012, from the private papers of the Panikkar family.
2. Ibid.
3. Nationalist China had already issued its first shrill accusations of theft against Stein for looting the ancient Buddhist monasteries along the Silk Road.
4. Nayanjyot Lahiri, 'What Lies Beneath', *Hindustan Times*, 16 February 2008.
5. Ibid.
6. Konniyoor R. Narendranath, *Sardar Panikkar: His Life and Times*, p. 118.
7. For more on this, see John McLeod, *Sovereignty, Power, Control: Politics in the States of Western India 1916-1947*, Brill, 1999.
8. Ibid., p. 222.
9. Ibid.
10. Telegram to E.C. Gibson, Resident of Kutch, 12 June 1941, IOC R/2/599/3.
11. K.M. Panikkar, *An Autobiography*, p. 122.
12. Ibid.
13. Ibid.
14. Ibid.
15. Author's interview via email with R.M. Nair, 20 April 2022.
16. It wasn't only Panikkar who encouraged Jewish financing in his state. The Jewish Agency was considerably interested in the princely states, an interest that was deeply reciprocated. Among them Shanmukham Chetty, the dewan of the princely state of Cochin expressed an interest in establishing 'trade connections between Cochin and the Jewish Agency for Palestine'.
17. Kanwar Jaswant Singh, 'Sardar K.M. Panikkar', in B.J. Chacko (ed.), *Sardar K.M. Panikkar: Shashtyabdapoorthy Souvenir*, p. 155.
18. Nehru, Speech on the Inauguration of the Bhakra-Nangal Dam, 22 October 1963, quoted from Dinesh C. Sharma, 'Towering Temple of Resurgent India', *The Tribune*, 20 October 2023. Available at: https://www.tribuneindia.com/news/comment/towering-temple-of-resurgent-india-warts-and-all-554842.
19. Ibid.
20. Minutes of Constitutional Study Circle, Delhi, 5 December 1941, BRO, Bhopal, Political Department, Chamber Section, F.No. 1/6/1/1941.

21. Nobody in Britain particularly minded this scandalous alliance. Lord Beaverbrook, who accompanied Harriman to Moscow as the British representative, chortled, 'To have FDR's personal representative, the man charged with keeping Britain safe, sleeping with the Prime Minister's daughter in law *(sic)* was a wonderful stroke of luck.'

CHAPTER 34

1. For more on this, see Ben MacIntyre, *Colditz: Prisoners of the Castle*, Penguin Random House, 2023.
2. Hodson, Note on the Tour of the Reforms Commissioner, from 8 November to 7 December 1941, to Madras, Assam, Bengal and Bihar, L/P&J/8/509, TOP, Vol. 1, pp. 8–15.
3. Bardoli Resolution, 30 December 1941, TOP, Vol. I, pp. 881–884.
4. See TOP, Vol. I, p. 13.
5. Attlee to Amery, 24 January 1942, TOP, Vol. I, No. 35.
6. This was a fraught meeting for Harriman who had to summon every ounce of tact to the fore. Later, he would describe it as one of the most difficult assignments he had handled for Roosevelt, knowing that Churchill was a heartfelt imperialist who would never back down on the issue of India.
7. An excellent account of Chiang's career and life and that of Madame Soong may be found in Jung Chang, *Big Sister, Little Sister, Red Sister*, Jonathan Cape, 2019.
8. Hallett to Linlithgow, 21 February 1942, TOP, Vol. I, pp. 348–350.
9. Ibid.
10. Theodore White, 'Chiang Kai-shek', *LIFE* magazine, 2 March 1942. Available at: http://www.cbi-theater.com/life030242/life030242.html.
11. Madame Chiang Kai-shek to Nehru, 13 March 1942 and 26 June 1942 in Jawaharlal Nehru (ed.), *A Bunch of Old Letters*, Penguin, 2005, pp. 476–478 and pp. 494–496.
12. Linlithgow to Amery, 7 February 1942, TOP, Vol. I.
13. K.M. Panikkar, 'The Political Outlook for the States', undated, F.No. 7204/1939, MGSTA.
14. Ibid.
15. Panikkar to Syed Mahmud, 13 July 1941, Mahmud Papers, NMML.
16. K.M. Panikkar, *An Introduction to the Study of Relations of Indian States with the Government of India*, Martin Hopkinson, 1927.

17. Rajaji to Panikkar, 21 August 1942, F. 7204/1939, MGSTA.
18. K.M. Panikkar, *An Autobiography*, p. 130.
19. Ibid.
20. Dr R.J. Weingarten, Paper 190, 161/7208/1938, MGS Trust.
21. Peter Clarke, *The Cripps Version: The Life of Sir Stafford Cripps, 1889-1952*, Allen Lane, 2002, p. 257.
22. Leader, *Hindustan Times*, 21 March 1942.
23. H.V. Hodson, unpublished autobiography, p. 168.
24. Patrick French, *Liberty or Death: India's Journey to Independence and Division*, p. 168.
25. Ibid.
26. H.V. Hodson, unpublished autobiography, p. 168.
27. Patrick French, *Liberty or Death: India's Journey to Independence and Division*, p. 173.
28. Sarvepalli Gopal, *Jawaharlal Nehru: A Biography*, p. 286.
29. Stafford Cripps, Text of press conference, 29 March 1942, TOP, Vol. I, pp. 539–540.
30. Text of Draft Declaration, 28 February 1942, TOP, Vol. I, p. 226.
31. Linlithgow to Amery, 2 March 1942, TOP, Vol. I, p. 332.
32. Linlithgow to Amery, 7 March 1942, TOP, Vol. II, p. 50.
33. Patrick French, *Liberty or Death: India's Journey to Independence and Division*, p. 173.
34. Note by Cripps on Interview with the Delegation of the Chamber of Princes, 28 March 1942, TOP, Vol. I, pp. 510–511.
35. Stafford Cripps, Interview with the Jam Sahib and Bikaner, 29 March 1932, TOP, Vol. I, p. 487.
36. Linlithgow to Amery, 13 September 1943, TOP, Vol. IV, p. 244.
37. Correspondence between Panikkar and Bikaner, 7 and 11 July 1942, MGSTA.

CHAPTER 35

1. John Willitt's phone conversation with Jacob Viner, 18 September 1950 at Rockefeller Foundation, F.No. RG 1.1, Series 200, Box 353, Folder 4198.
2. It was Carter, in fact, who would encourage the creation of the Indian Council of World Affairs (ICWA), which would spearhead the Asian Relations Conference in 1947 and go on to become independent India's primary think tank.

3. Patrick French, *Liberty or Death: India's Journey to Independence and Division*, p. 179.
4. Bipan Chandra, *India's Struggle for Freedom, 1857-1947*, pp. 459–460.
5. Hodson, unpublished autobiography, p. 175.
6. An agent general was the colonial equivalent to an ambassador for India in the years before independence.
7. George Morrell, a State Department officer travelling with Louis Johnson, cabled this to Cordell Hull, 10 November 1942, in RG 50, Central Decimal Files, 811.43/IPR/185, NAKA.
8. 'Pacific Delegation', *National Call*, 8 November 1942.
9. Known more formally as the Royal Institute of International Affairs, Chatham House is a British think tank based in London. In its time, it was the first of its kind, founded by Lionel Curtis. Its discussion rules are today known as 'Chatham House Rules', which state that a participant in a meeting can discuss the content of the meeting with the outside world but cannot discuss who attended or identify a specific individual.
10. Michael Anderson, *Pacific Dreams: The Institute of Pacific Relations and the Struggle for the Mind of Asia*, PhD dissertation, University of Texas, 2009. Available at: https://repositories.lib.utexas.edu/server/api/core/bitstreams/1c1c5959-cdce-4dcc-b9a6-043c5ae3bc4c/content, p. 78.
11. Japan's military expansion into Southeast Asia and the Pacific during the war had led to their declaration of their goal to create a Greater East Asia Co-Prosperity Sphere after the war. This would, in their eyes, be a region freed from European suppression and a realm where all the countries and peoples within would co-exist in co-prosperity under the aegis of Japan.
12. K.M. Panikkar, *The Future of South-East Asia: An Indian View*, MacMillan & Co, 1943 p. 32.
13. Ibid., p. 7.
14. Ibid.
15. Ibid., p. 17.
16. Craik to Bikaner, 2 September 1942; Note by Panikkar to Bikaner, September 1942; Panikkar to Bikaner, 1 December 1942, file 7204/1939, MGSTA.
17. Mandhata Singh to K.M. Panikkar, 3 January 1943, F.No. 7204/1939, MGSTA.
18. 'Impressions of Bikaner', 7–9 March 1943, by George Gillan, Resident for Rajputana, F.No. 5(5); F.No. 5(5), CRR, NAI.

19. Panikkar to Sadul Singh, 30 March 1943, F.No. 7204/1939, MGSTA; Panikkar to Sadul Singh, 22 April 1943, F.No. 7204/1939.
20. K.M. Panikkar, *An Autobiography*, p. 130.
21. Parvathy Panikkar, quoted by her son on email in April 2022.
22. K.M. Panikkar, *An Autobiography*, p. 130.
23. Ibid.
24. Order by HH the Maharaja, 31 May 1944; Sadul Singh to Panikkar, 27 June 1944, F.No. 7204/1939, MGSTA.
25. Speech by HH Maharaja of Bikaner, at the Dinner at Lalgarh, in honour of Panikkar, Prime Minister of Bikaner, 24 July 1944. Also see K.M. Panikkar's speech, F.No. 7204/1939, MGSTA.
26. Panikkar to Sadul Singh, 30 April 1943, PM Diaries, F.No. 4182, MGSTA.
27. 'More Intimate and Active Association of the People with the Administration of the State. Text of the Proclamation by His Highness the Maharaja', *Bikaner Bulletin*, November 1944, pp. 3–4.
28. Meeting on Five Years Development Scheme, 17 March 1945, file 55–58, basta 48, Prime Minister Office (hereafter PMO), Rajasthan State Archive (hereafter RSAB), Bikaner. 'Reconstruction, Development and Welfare. Prime Minister's Survey of Government Activities in Legislative Assembly', *Bikaner Bulletin*, November 1945, pp. 9–12. Also see 'Panikkar to Sadul Singh', 1 June 1945, P.M. diaries, file 4182, MGSTA and The Private Secretary to H.H. the Maharaja of Bikaner to Panikkar, 7 December 1944; Panikkar to the Private Secretary, 13 December 1944, file 7204/1939, MGSTA, Panikkar to Sadul Singh, 8 June 1945, P.M. diaries, file 4182, MGSTA.
29. Ibid.
30. K.M. Panikkar, *An Autobiography*, p. 131.
31. Ibid.
32. Ibid.
33. Taya Zinkin, 'Sardar Panikkar as I Know Him', in B.J. Chacko (ed.), *Sardar K.M. Panikkar: Shashtyabdapoorthy Souvenir*, p. 117.
34. K.M. Panikkar, 'The Indian States, Adjusting to Changing Times', *The Commonwealth and Empire Review*, Vol. 79, No. 80, 1945, pp. 3 and 135.
35. Author's interview with R.M. Nair, April 2022.
36. John Charmley, *Churchill: The End of Glory: A Political Biography*, Harcourt, 1992, p. 514.

37. Leo Amery, *The Empire at Bay: The Leo Amery Diaries, 1929-1945*, Hutchinson, 1988, p. 840.
38. Charles Herbert to Lothian, 12 February 1943, Lothian Collection, Box 9.
39. Penderel Moon (ed.), *Wavell: The Viceroy's Journal*, Oxford University Press, 1973, p. 463.
40. Note by Francis Wylie, 9 August 1944, IOR/R/1/1/4152.
41. Recommendations of Aviation Sub-Committee of COMs, 16 April 1944, BRO, Bhopal, Political Department, Chamber Section, F.No. 7/1/7 of 1944.
42. Wavell to Amery, 20 April 1944, TOP, Vol. IV, p. 901 and TOP, Vol. V, 28 November 1944, pp. 241–245.
43. PRO Premier, 4/46/12/811.
44. Note by Wavell, 24 October 1944, TOP, Vol. V, pp. 127–129.
45. Patrick French, *Liberty or Death: India's Journey to Independence and Division*, p. 221.
46. V.P. Menon to Evan Jenkins, 13 October 1944, TOP, Vol. 5, pp. 111–112.
47. K.M. Panikkar, *An Autobiography*, p. 138.
48. Ibid.
49. BRO Bhopal, Political Department, Chamber Section, 94, 10/1, 1943.
50. J.N. Sahni, *The Lid Off: 50 Years of Indian Politics*, Deep Publications, 1971, p. 210.
51. K.M. Panikkar, *An Autobiography*, p. 140.
52. Ibid.
53. Ibid.
54. Ibid.
55. Ibid.
56. Ibid.
57. Fredrik Barth, *The Last Wali of Swat: An Autobiography*, Orchid Press Publishing Limited, 1995 p. 101.
58. Fortnightly Report from The Residents, July-December 1945, F.No. 18/6, Home Department, NAI.
59. Bhopal to Wavell, 26 February 1945, TOP, Vol. V, pp. 618–619.
60. US Consul General, Bombay, to Secretary of State, Washington DC, 8 November 1946, State Department, decimal file 845.00/11-846.4.
61. Interim Report of the Ad Hoc COMs, 1 February 1938, BRO, Bhopal, Political Department, Chamber of Princes, F.No. 58/4/36, 1944.

CHAPTER 36

1. Ibid.
2. Ibid.
3. Email from R.K. Nair to his brothers R.M. Nair and R.D. Nair, 6 September 2012. Forwarded to the author in April 2022.
4. Ibid.
5. K.M. Panikkar, *An Autobiography*, p. 145.
6. Ian Copland, *The Princes of India in the Endgame of Empire, 1917-1947*, p. 212.
7. K.M. Panikkar, *An Autobiography*, p. 145.
8. Ibid.
9. Ibid. In his memoir, Panikkar wrote magnanimously, if entirely untruthfully, 'I would not have objected, if the proposal had come from a minister less egoistic or authoritarian.' But what *was* true was that at this point, Sir CP had not gained any goodwill from his peers, so there was not really anyone who would have supported him.
10. Ibid.
11. V.P. Menon to Wavell, L/P&J/8/519, 17 August 1944, TOP, Vol. IV.
12. Penderel Moon (ed.), *Wavell: The Viceroy's Journal*, entry of 29 April 1945.
13. Penderel Moon, *Divide and Quit: An Eyewitness Account of the Partition of India*, Vol. 2, Oxford University Press, 1988, pp. 169–170.
14. Patrick French, *Liberty or Death: India's Journey to Independence and Division*, p. 248.
15. Wavell to Amery, 20 November 1945, TOP, Vol. VI, pp. 451–455.
16. Patrick French, *Liberty or Death: India's Journey to Independence and Division*, p. 249.
17. Pethick Lawrence to Wavell, 25 September 1945, TOP, Vol. 6, p. 78.
18. K.M. Panikkar, *An Autobiography*, p. 142.
19. This was an administrative body, providing social welfare to nations ravaged by the war.
20. Zafrullah Khan, 1 April 1945, *India Quarterly*, Vol. 1, No. 2, pp. 178–179.
21. K.P.S. Menon, *Many Worlds: An Autobiography*, p. 216.
22. K.M. Panikkar, 'Biographical Sketches', undated, F.No. 1293, Panikkar Private Papers, NAI.
23. Ibid.
24. K.M. Panikkar, *India and the Indian Ocean: An Essay on the Influence of Sea Power on Indian History*, MacMillan Company, 1945.

25. Ibid., p. 7.
26. Ibid., pp. 82–83.
27. Ibid.
28. Ibid., p. 81.
29. Ibid., p. 15.
30. Ibid., pp.16–17.
31. K.M. Panikkar, *The Strategic Problems of the Indian Ocean*, Kitabistan, 1944, pp. 5–7.
32. K.M. Panikkar, 'The Himalayas and Indian Defence', *Indian Quarterly*, Vol. 3, No. 2, 1947 and 'The Himalayas and Indian Defence, Part II', *Indian Quarterly*, Vol. 3, No. 3, 1947.
33. Ibid.
34. C. in. C. in India to War Office, 15 February 1945, L/WS/1/1343, IOR.
35. K.M. Panikkar, 'A New Approach to Indian Problems', Private Discussion Meeting, 25 January 1943, F.No. 8/907, Royal Institute of International Affairs (RIIA).
36. For more, see Rita Paolini & Mauro Elli, *Indian National Identity and Foreign Policy: Reevaluating the Career of K.M. Panikkar, 1894-1963*. According to Paolini and Elli, this structure was reminiscent of the ideas of nationalists who identified this area as 'Greater India'.
37. For more, see Amitav Acharya, 'India's Look East Policy', in David Malone, C. Raja Mohan and Srinath Raghavan (ed.), *The Oxford Handbook of Indian Foreign Policy, 2015*, pp. 556–572.
38. Author's interview via email with R.K. Nair, April 2022.
39. Ibid., pp. 16–17.
40. K.M. Panikkar, 'A New Approach to Indian Problems', Private Discussion Meeting, 25 January 1943, F.No. 8/907, Royal Institute of International Affairs (RIIA).
41. K.M. Panikkar, 'Memorandum on Defence and National Efficiency', L/WS/1/1343, 1945, IOR.
42. K.M. Panikkar, 'A New Approach to Indian Problems', Private Discussion Meeting, 25 January 1943, F.No. 8/907, Royal Institute of International Affairs (RIIA).
43. General Mosley Mayne to Walter Cawthorn, 22 February, L/WS/1/1343, IOR.

CHAPTER 37

1. Penderel Moon, *Divide and Quit: An Eyewitness Account of the Partition of India*, Vol. 2, p. 225.
2. Raj Kumar, *Women and the Indian Freedom Struggle*, Vol. 6, Pointer Publishers, 1998, p. 19.
3. Reginald Sorenson, *My Impressions of India*, Meridian Books, 1947, p. 164.
4. Ibid., p. 106.
5. B.R. Nanda, *Mahatma Gandhi: A Biography*, Oxford University Press, 1958, pp. 170–175.
6. Sorenson, *My Impressions of India*, p. 112.
7. TOP, Vol. 6, p. 833.
8. Woodrow Wyatt, *Confessions of an Optimist*, HarperCollins Publishers, 1985, p. 139.
9. Ian Copland, *The Princes of India in the Endgame of Empire, 1917-1947*, p. 222.
10. Speech to Chamber of Princes, 18 January 1946, *Indian Annual Register*, Vol. I, p. 349.
11. Ian Copland, *The Princes of India in the Endgame of Empire, 1917-1947*, p. 213.
12. Press Statement by the Standing Committee, 11 June 1946, enclosed in Bhopal to Wavell, 19 June 1946, TOP, Vol. 7, pp. 980–981. Also see *Bombay Chronicle*, 11 June 1946.
13. *Times of India*, 11 April 1947, 6 July 1946; *Bombay Sentinel*, 21 August 1946.
14. Note of Interview between the Cabinet Mission, Wavell and the Nawab of Bhopal, 2 April 1946, TOP, Vol. 7, pp. 84–87.
15. K.M. Panikkar, *An Autobiography*, pp. 147–149.
16. Ibid.
17. Ibid. In his own memoir, Corfield rejects this allegation out of hand.
18. J.N. Sahni, *Truth About the Indian Press*, Bombay Allied, 1974, pp. 215–216.
19. Ibid.
20. Ibid.
21. J.N. Sahni, Oral History, NMML.
22. Ibid.
23. Ibid.
24. Ibid.

25. K.M. Panikkar, *An Autobiography*, p. 151.
26. Ibid.
27. Ibid.
28. Ibid.
29. Politics in Travancore had developed along distinct but connected lines to the Indian freedom movement. It had a legislative council from 1888, and a consultative assembly from 1946, though both institutions enjoyed little substantive power. Flagship parties like the Congress or the Communist Party came to the state only after they had established themselves across the rest of the country. By the 1930s, influenced by mass nationalism in British India, political activity began to concern itself with self-government. Much of this was led by Aiyar. In 1928, he made a masterful speech in Mysore in which he drove home the simple point that a federal constitution suited India. The speech was honest in its appreciation of the American system and its dissatisfaction with the British system. Aiyar would take these ideas to their natural culmination with his US-modelled constitution in Travancore in January 1946.

CHAPTER 38

1. James Cameron, *An Indian Summer: A Personal Experience of India*, Penguin India, 2000, p. 94.
2. Ibid.
3. Attlee was horrified by this, insisting that it should be an option only if the alternative was 'complete failure' to reach any other kind of agreement. But if this *was* the outcome, he warned, 'India will be confronted by grave dangers.' See TOP, Vol. 8, p. 261
4. James Cameron, *An Indian Summer: A Personal Experience of India*, p. 95.
5. Ibid.
6. British Declaration on India, F.No. 48, Home Department (1946), NAI.
7. Ibid.
8. V.P. Menon, *The Story of the Integration of the Indian States*, pp. 495–496.
9. Ibid.
10. Philip Mason, *A Shaft of Sunlight: Memories of a Varied Life*, Vikas Publishing House, 1978, p. 212.

11. Notes of a Meeting of Cabinet Delegates and Wavell, with Representatives of the Standing Committee of the Chamber of Princes, 2 April 1946, TOP, Vol. 7, p. 98.
12. Stafford Cripps, Text of Press Conference, 16 May 1946, TOP, Vol. 7, p. 597.
13. Bhopal to Wavell, 29 July 1946, TOP, Vol. 8, p. 183.
14. K.M. Panikkar, *An Autobiography*, p. 151.
15. Ibid.
16. Ibid.
17. For more, see Madhav Khosla, *India's Founding Moment: The Constitution of a Most Surprising Democracy*, Harvard University Press, 2020; Ornit Shani, 'The People and the Making of India's Constitution', *The Historical Journal*, Vol. 65, No. 4, 2022, pp. 1102–1103; and Rohit De, *A People's Constitution: The Everyday Life of Law in the Indian Republic*, Princeton University Press, 2018.
18. B.R. Ambedkar, quoted in Amarjit Narang, 'India: Ethnicity and Federalism', in Bhagwan Dass Dua & Mahendra Prasad Singh (eds), *Indian Federalism in the New Millennium*, Manohar Books, 2003, p. 73.
19. K.M. Panikkar, 'A Note on Some General Principles of the Union Constitution, May 1947' in B. Shiva Rao (ed.), *The Framing of India's Constitution: Select Documents*, Indian Institute of Public Administration, 1968, Vol. II, p. 534.
20. Wavell, Viceroy's Journal, p. 305.
21. Nehru, 7 July 1946, in Sir Maurice Gwyer & A. Appadorai (ed.), *Speeches and Documents on the Indian Constitution, 1921-1947*, Oxford University Press, 1957, Vol. II, pp. 612–615.
22. Ibid.
23. Ian Stephens, *Pakistan*, Ernest Benn, 1967, p. 103.
24. Maulana Abul Kalam Azad, *India Wins Freedom*, Orient Blackswan, 1968, p. 61.
25. Patel to D.P. Mishra, 24 July 1946, in Durga Das (ed.), *Selected Correspondence of Sardar Patel, 1946-1950*, Navjivan Press, 1971, Vol. III, pp. 153–154.
26. K.M. Panikkar, *An Autobiography*, p. 151.
27. Nehru to Corfield, 27 April 1947, TOP, Vol. 10, p. 463.
28. Fortnightly Report, July–December 1945, F.No. 18-16, Home Department, NAI.

29. Sir C.P. Ramaswami Aiyar to Mrs Marley, enclosed in Consul General Bombay to Secretary of State, Washington DC, 20 January 1946, US State Department, decimal File 845.00/1-2046.
30. Penderel Moon, *Divide and Quit: An Eyewitness Account of the Partition of India*, Vol. 2, p. 368.
31. Ibid., p. 336.
32. Ian Copland, *The Princes of India in the Endgame of Empire, 1917-1947*, p. 241.
33. V.P. Menon, *The Story of the Integration of the Indian States*, p. 42.
34. Bhopal to Wavell, 2 June 1946, TOP, Vol. 7, p. 780.

CHAPTER 39

1. Bhopal to Corfield, 23 November 1946, TOP, Vol. 9, pp. 156–157.
2. Rajputana, Fortnightly Reports, 1–15 January 1944, F.No. 6(6), Political (Secret)/44, acc. No. 68, NAI.
3. Statement by HH Maharaja of Bikaner, 17 June 1946, F.No. 162, MGSTA.
4. Panikkar to Gandhi, 17 June 1946, MGSTA.
5. See, for example, Sardar Patel to K.M. Panikkar, 20 June 1946, Sardar Patel Correspondence, Vol. 3.
6. Goel to Bikaner, 17 June 1946, F.No. 24, AISPC Papers, NMML.
7. Copy of Representation by Bikaner State Muslims, addressed to Nawabzada Liaquat Ali Khan, 16 July 1946, F.No. 248-P (Secret)/46, acc.no. 68, NAI.
8. TOP, Vol. 9, pp. 74–75.
9. Ibid., p. 119.
10. K.M. Panikkar, *An Autobiography*, p. 152.
11. Ibid.
12. Jawaharlal Nehru, Constituent Assembly Debates, Vol. I, Parliament Digital Library. Available at: https://eparlib.nic.in/handle/123456789/4.

CHAPTER 40

1. V.P. Menon, Interview with H.V. Hodson, undated, 1965, SOAS Archives.
2. Krishnamchari to Bhopal, 14 April 1947, TOP, Vol. 10, p. 241.
3. Sadul Singh to Mountbatten, 3 April 1947, TOP, Vol. 10, p. 110.

4. K.M. Panikkar, *An Autobiography*, p. 153.
5. Ibid.
6. Ibid.
7. Ibid.
8. Ibid.
9. Panikkar to Wyatt, 15 February 1947, TOP, Vol. 9, p. 406.
10. Conversation at Bikaner House, 31 January 1947, Ayyengar Papers, File 4, NMML.
11. K.M. Panikkar, *An Autobiography*, p. 156; and B.L. Mitter, quoted in *Times of India*, 15 February 1947.
12. K.M. Panikkar, *An Autobiography*, p. 157; Also see Panikkar to Wyatt, 15 February 1947, TOP, Vol. 9, pp. 725–726.
13. Ibid.
14. H.V.R. Iyengar, Oral History Transcript, NMML, pp. 139–140.
15. Proceedings of the States Negotiating Committee, 8 February 1947, File 5, Ayyengar Papers, NMML.
16. Proceedings of the States Negotiating Committee, 9 February 1947 and 6 March 1947, File 5, Ayyengar Papers, NMML.
17. Bikaner to Mountbatten, 3 April 1947, TOP, Vol. 10, pp. 110–111.
18. 'Princes Not Sitting on the Fence: Bhopal Ruler', *The Statesman*, 27 April 1947.
19. K.M. Panikkar, *An Autobiography*, p. 157.
20. Minutes, 1 April 1947, BRO Bhopal, Political Department, Special Branch, 106, 61/58/47, TOP, Vol. 8, p. 107.
21. Consul General, Bombay to Secretary of State, Washington DC, 11 February 1945, US State Department, decimal file 845.00/2-1145.
22. Conversation with K.M. Munshi, as reported to the Consul General, Bombay, encl. in Consul General Bombay to Secretary of State, Washington DC, 14 April 1947, US State Department, decimal file 845.00/4-1447.
23. K.M. Panikkar, *An Autobiography*, p. 158.
24. Philip Zeigler, *Mountbatten: An Official Biography*, Weidenfeld & Nicolson, 2001, p. 116.
25. Mountbatten, Interview with H.V. Hodson, SOAS Archives.
26. Alan Campbell-Johnson, *Mission with Mountbatten*, Jaico Publishing House, 1951, p. 49.
27. Ibid.
28. Ibid.

29. Ibid.
30. Ibid.
31. Ibid.
32. The term seems to have been used, if the British High Commissioner's reports are to be believed, at the conference itself though Alfred Sauvy would officially define the 'third world' later in 1952. Also see Leslie Wolf-Phillips, 'Why "Third World"?: Origin, Definition and Usage', *Third World Quarterly*, Vol. 9, 1987, pp. 1311–1327.
33. James Cameron, *Point of Departure: An Experiment in Autobiography*, Grafton Books, 1969, p. 247.
34. *Asian Relations: Being a Report of the Proceedings and Documentation of the First Asian Relations Conference*, Asian Relations Organisation (ARO), 1948, pp. 24–25.
35. Some excellent places to start are Vineet Thakur, 'An Asian Drama: The Asian Relations Conference, 1947', *The International History Review*, Vol. 41, No. 3, 2019, pp. 673–695, and Carolien Stolte, 'The Asiatic Hour: New Perspectives on the Asian Relations Conference, New Delhi, 1947', in N. Miskovic, H. Fischer-Tine, N. Boskovska (eds), *The Non-Aligned Movement and Cold War: Delhi-Bandung-Belgrade*, Routledge, 2015, pp. 57–75.
36. There was a near total absence of Arabs at the Conference. The Arab League was represented by an observer, but six Arab countries (Iraq, Lebanon, Saudi Arabia, Syria, Transjordan and Yemen) did not accept individual invitations. The Egyptian delegation linked Arab non-attendance to the participation of the Jewish delegation. For more, see P.R. Kumaraswamy, *India's Israel Policy*, Columbia University Press, 2010.
37. For the complete text of Bergmann's speech, see *Asian Relations: Report of the Proceedings and Documents of the First Asian Relations Conference, New Delhi, March-April, 1947*, Indian Council of World Affairs, 1947.
38. Godfrey H. Jansen, *Zionism, Israel and Asian Nationalism*, Institute for Palestine Studies, 1971, pp. 191–192.
39. For more, see P.R. Kumaraswamy, *India's Israel Policy*, and Nicolas Blarel, *The Evolution of India's Israel Policy: Continuity, Change and Compromise Since 1922*, Oxford University Press, 2014.
40. K.M. Panikkar, 'A Memorandum on Hindu-Zionist Relations', 8 April 1947, S25/7485, Central Zionist Archives (hereafter CZA), Jerusalem.
41. Ibid.

42. Report on the Inter-Asian Conference, 6 April and 17 April 1947, CZA, S25/7485.
43. This duality must be seen and contextualised against the backdrop of not just the Indian national movement and the princely states, but the changing geopolitics of the time. The Zionists didn't just reach out to Hindu nationalists, but several significant attempts were made with Muslim leaders, princely states and Indian institutions and academics. An excellent understanding may be gained from P.R. Kumaraswamy, *India's Israel Policy*.
44. Bergmann and Shimoni, 'Report on the Inter-Asian Conference', CZA, S25/7485.
45. K.M. Panikkar, 'A Memorandum on Hindu-Zionist Relations', CZA, S25/7485. This was a view that many Zionist leaders themselves agreed with, with many internal documents and letters lamenting the lack of sufficient outreach to prominent Indian leaders, like Nehru.
46. Ibid.
47. Ibid.
48. Ibid.
49. Ibid.
50. Ibid.
51. Ibid.
52. Ibid.
53. P.R. Kumaraswamy, 'K.M. Panikkar and Indo-Israeli Relations', *International Studies*, Vol. 3, No. 2, 1995, pp. 327–337, here at p. 336.

CHAPTER 41

1. K.M. Panikkar, *An Autobiography*, p. 159.
2. Constituent Assembly Debates, April 1947, Vol. II. Available online at: https://www.constitutionofindia.net/constitution-assembly-debates/.
3. Ibid.
4. Ibid.
5. Ibid.
6. Bikaner to Mountbatten, 3 April 1947, TOP, Vol. 10, p. 68.
7. Viceroy's Interview with Sardar K.M. Panikkar, 5 May 1947, No. 130, Mountbatten Papers, University of Southampton.
8. Ibid.
9. Ibid.

10. Sometime in 1946, the department of agriculture under the Bengal government ordered sixty ducks from England. Bengal's Muslim League cabinet led by H.S. Suhrawardy sanctioned this order and a poultry farm in London was asked to deliver the birds. The ducks arrived in Calcutta in July 1947, along with a neat bill of £250. With transfer of power and partition only weeks away, this was the worst timed invoice in modern history. Amidst reigning chaos, the finance secretary refused to pay for the hapless ducks. After all, he irately demanded, who would get the ducks: the government of West Bengal or that of East Bengal? Would the ducks be divided between the two, with both paying for their respective portions? Nobody knew. 'While protracted departmental inquiries continue, the neglected ducks await the result in a city warehouse,' sniggered *The Statesman*. Anecdote from Anwesha Sengupta, 'Breaking Up: Dividing Assets between India and Pakistan in Times of Partition', *The Indian Economic and Social History Review*, Vol. 51, No. 4 (2014), pp. 529–548.
11. Philip Zeigler, *Mountbatten: An Official Biography*, p. 570.
12. V.P. Menon, Interview with Hodson, SOAS Archives.
13. Nehru to Manipur, 22 May 1947, Krishna Menon Papers, NMML.
14. Nehru to Holkar, 22 June 1947, Krishna Menon Papers, NMML.
15. K.M. Panikkar, *An Autobiography*, p. 160.
16. Ibid.
17. Ibid., p. 184.
18. Ibid.
19. Ibid.
20. K.M. Panikkar, *A Survey of Indian History*, National Information and Publications Ltd, 1947, pp. 3–6.
21. Ibid., p. 75.
22. Ibid., pp. 79–85.
23. Ibid., p. 120.
24. Tarasankar Banerjee, 'Sardar K.M. Panikkar' in R.C. Majumdar (ed.), *Historians and Historiography in Modern India*, Institute of Historical Studies, 1973, p. 78.
25. K.M. Panikkar, *A Survey of Indian History*, p. 235.
26. Ibid.
27. K.M. Panikkar, *An Autobiography*, pp. 186–187.
28. Ibid.
29. Ibid.

30. Panikkar to Sadul Singh, 1 June 1947, F.No. 7405/1947, MGSTA.

CHAPTER 42

1. K.M. Panikkar, *An Autobiography*, p. 159.
2. Panikkar to Sadul Singh, 8 May 1947 and 16 June 1947, F.No. 4182, MGSTA.
3. V.P. Menon to Sardar Patel, undated, Sardar Patel Papers, NMML.
4. His practice in London was so prosperous that his long-time clerk drove a Rolls-Royce and owned a flat in the south of France.
5. For more, read Lucy Chester, *Borders and Conflict in South Asia: The Radcliffe Boundary Commission and the Partition of Punjab*, Palgrave MacMillan, 2009.
6. Nisid Hajari, *Midnight's Furies: The Deadly Legacy of India's Partition*, Penguin Random House India, 2016, p. 123.
7. TOP, Vol. XII, pp. 75–79.
8. Christopher Beaumont, interview to Lucy Chester, quoted in Lucy Chester, *Borders and Conflict in South Asia: The Radcliffe Boundary Commission and the Partition of Punjab*, p. 80.
9. Leonard Mosley, *The Last Days of the British Raj*, Weidenfeld & Nicolson, 1961, p. 199.
10. Ibid.
11. Radcliffe, Letter to Michel, 28 March 1965, quoted in Aloys Michel, *The Indus Rivers: A Study of the Effects of Partition*, Yale University Press, 1967, p. 194.
12. Mountbatten to Radcliffe, 8 August 1947, TOP, Vol. XII, p. 291.
13. Ibid.
14. TOP, Vol. XII, p. 584.
15. TOP, Vol. XII, p. 638.
16. Kanwar Sain, *Reminiscences of an Engineer*, Young Asia Publications, 1978, p. 121.
17. To be clear, this wasn't the only interview that was putting pressure on Mountbatten. Patiala wrote to the viceroy on 12 August 1947, asking him bluntly to re-engineer the boundary in Punjab. Liaquat Ali Khan was furious about Gurdaspur. All of it accumulated into intense pressure on the viceroy.
18. Christopher Beaumont, interview to Lucy Chester, quoted in Lucy Chester, *Borders and Conflict in South Asia: The Radcliffe Boundary Commission and the Partition of Punjab*, p. 123.

19. Radcliffe to Mark Tennant, 13 August 1947, quoted in Edmund Heward, *The Great and the Good: A Life of Lord Radcliffe*, Barry Rose Publishers, 1994, p. 42.
20. Oshar Spate, 19 July 1947, in Lucy Chester, *Borders and Conflict in South Asia: The Radcliffe Boundary Commission and the Partition of Punjab*, p. 145.
21. Edwina Mountbatten to V.K. Krishna Menon, 10 August 1947, Krishna Menon Papers, NMML.
22. Narayani Basu, *VP Menon: The Unsung Architect of Modern India*, Simon & Schuster India, 2020, p. 350.
23. K.M. Panikkar, *An Autobiography*, p. 163.
24. Ibid., p. 166.
25. Ibid.
26. Ibid.
27. Ibid.
28. Ibid.

CHAPTER 43

1. K.M. Panikkar, *An Autobiography*, p. 174.
2. Nehru, Speech in Sambalpur, 12 April 1948, *SWJN*, Vol. 6, p. 3.
3. Bajpai to Vijayalakshmi Pandit, 4 June 1948, Vijayalakshmi Pandit Papers, Vol. I, SF. No. 56, NMML.
4. Nehru to Premiers of Provinces, 3 November 1947, *SWJN*, Vol. 4, p. 446; Nehru to Vijayalakshmi Pandit, 23 January 1948, Vijayalakshmi Pandit Papers, Vol. I, SF No. 54, NMML; Nehru, Reply to Debate on Foreign Policy in Constituent Assembly, 4 December 1947, *SWJN*, Vol. 4, p. 596, and Nehru, Address at Public Meeting, Kanpur, 28 August 1949, *SWJN*, Vol. 13, p. 5.
5. Swapna Kyona Nayudu, *The Nehru Years: Indian Non-Alignment as the Critique, Discourse and Practice of Security, 1947-1964*, PhD Dissertation, King's College, London, 2016; Manu Bhagavan, *India and the Cold War*, Penguin Books, 2014; Paul McGarr, *The Cold War in South Asia: Britain, the United States and the Indian Subcontinent, 1945-1964*, Cambridge University Press, 2013.
6. Manu Bhagavan, *Vijaya Lakshmi Pandit*, Penguin Random House India, 2023, p. 400.
7. K.M. Panikkar, *An Autobiography*, p. 176.
8. Ibid.

9. Panikkar explains more of this in *In Two Chinas: Memoirs of a Diplomat*, pp. 9–15.
10. Asaf Ali, in fact, was so vehemently pro-Arab in his endeavours that he succeeded in infuriating both Nehru and the Jewish Agency in equal measure.
11. Nehru to Abdur Rahman, 2 May 1947, *SWJN*, Vol. II, pp. 474–475.
12. Ministry of External Affairs telegram to Asaf Ali (April 23, 1947), F.2(16)- UNO- I/47, NAI, New Delhi.
13. P.R. Kumaraswamy, *India's Israel Policy*, pp. 98–100.
14. The British were given a 'dual mandate', that is, on behalf of Palestine's inhabitants on the one hand, and on behalf of 'international society' on the other. The Balfour Declaration was incorporated into the preamble and second article of the Mandate for Palestine. Britain thus also had a 'dual obligation' towards both Arabs and Jews. While the mandate included the main parts of the Balfour Declaration, such as the proclamation of support for a Jewish national home, under the mandate's terms Britain had an obligation to conduct its policy in Palestine in accordance with the needs of both Jews and Arabs. This included creating political, administrative and economic conditions that would facilitate the independent rule of the communities under British control. These objectives were an integral contradiction in the mandate. For more, see Statement on the Termination of the Mandate on Palestine, 15 May 1948, available at: https://ismi.emory.edu/resources/primary-source-docs/1948%20-%20PALESTINE-HMG%20termination%20of%20Mandate%201948.pdf.
15. UNSCOP Report, 2:38. For a detailed deconstruction of the history of India in the UNSCOP, see P.R. Kumaraswamy, *India's Israel Policy*, pp. 85–107.
16. Asaf Ali and Abdur Rehman's individual equations, vis-à-vis Palestine and the United Nations, are laid out in superb detail in P.R. Kumaraswamy, *India's Israel Policy*.
17. UN [UNSCOP] 1947: Vol. II, A/364, Add. 1, 9 September 1947, pp. 47–58
18. Aliya is the immigration of Jews from the diaspora to, historically speaking, the geographical land of Israel or the Palestine region. Traditionally described as 'the act of going up' towards Jerusalem, moving to Israel or 'making aliya' is one of the most basic tenets of Zionism.

19. P.R. Kumaraswamy, *India's Israel Policy*, p. 101.
20. K.M. Panikkar, *In Two Chinas: Memoirs of a Diplomat*, p. 12.
21. Ibid., p. 13. Also see Yitzshak Gerberg, *The Changing Nature of Israeli-Indian Relations, 1948-2005*, PhD Dissertation, 2008, p. 74. Available at: https://uir.unisa.ac.za/handle/10500/2936. See also Nicolas Blarel, *The Evolution of India's Israel Policy: Continuity, Change and Compromise Since 1922*, and Chaim Weizmann, *Trial and Error: The Autobiography of Chaim Weizmann*, Harper & Brothers, 1949, p. 570.
22. Nicolas Blarel, *The Evolution of India's Israel Policy: Continuity, Change and Compromise Since 1922*, p. 200.
23. Ibid.
24. K.M. Panikkar, *In Two Chinas: Memoirs of a Diplomat*, p. 13.
25. Ibid.
26. Ibid.
27. Ibid.
28. Nehru, Constituent Assembly Debates, December 1947, Vol. II. Nehru gave B.R. Rau (B.N. Rau's brother) the responsibility of finding a new solution which would conciliate both the Arabs and the Jews. Rau suggested an intermediary new solution between partition and federation which seems to have gained Weizmann's interest. But the plan was never considered. Instead, a day before British withdrawal from Palestine, the state of Israel was proclaimed on 14 May 1948.

CHAPTER 44

1. K.M. Panikkar, *An Autobiography*, p. 180, and *In Two Chinas: Memoirs of a Diplomat*, p. 10.
2. Typescript memorandum from Captain Ronald Vernon Brockman, CIE, CBE, RN, Private Secretary to the Governor General of India, to Louis Mountbatten, Earl Mountbatten of Burma, Governor General of India, 17 January 1948, MS62/MB/1/D/132/10, Mountbatten Papers, University of Southampton.
3. Carbon copy of the typescript record of an interview held on 16 January 1948 between Louis Mountbatten, Earl Mountbatten of Burma, Governor General of India, and Kavalam Madhava Panikkar, Prime Minister of Bikaner, 16 January 1948, MS62/MB/1/D/132/14, Mountbatten Papers, University of Southampton.

4. Typescript memorandum from Captain Ronald Vernon Brockman, CIE, CBE, RN, Private Secretary to the Governor General of India, to Louis Mountbatten, Earl Mountbatten of Burma, Governor General of India, 17 January 1948, MS62/MB/1/D/132/10, Mountbatten Papers, University of Southampton.
5. Typescript memorandum from Lieutenant Colonel Vernon Forbes Erskine Crum, MC, Conference Secretary to the Governor General of India, to Louis Mountbatten, Earl Mountbatten of Burma, Governor General of India, 17 January 1948, MS62/MB/1/D/132/9, Mountbatten Papers, University of Southampton.
6. Note by Nehru, 2 September 1946, *SWJN*, Vol. 1, pp. 489–491.
7. Nehru to Bajpai, 5 December 1946, *SWJN*, Vol. 1, pp. 549–550.
8. Bajpai to Krishna Menon, Telegram 7331, 3 September 1947, 19-Eur/47, MEA, NAI.
9. Rakesh Ankit, 'America, India and Kashmir, 1945-1949: "If Ignorance about India in this Country is Deep, Ignorance about the [Princely] States is Abysmal!"', *Diplomacy and Statecraft*, Vol. 27, No. 1, 2016, pp. 22–44.
10. Ali's wife, Aruna, was a committed and fierce socialist, a factor that caused considerable consternation in American circles.
11. Tansen Sen, *India, China and the World: A Connected History*, Rowman & Littlefield, 2017, p. 339.
12. Avtar Singh Bhasin, *Nehru, Tibet and China*, Penguin Random House, 2021, p. 22.
13. Tansen Sen, *India, China and the World: A Connected History*, p. 339.
14. Students had gathered on 4 May 1919 in Tiananmen Square to protest the Chinese government's weak response to the Treaty of Versailles, under which Japan was allowed to retain territories in Shandong that had been surrendered by the German Empire.
15. Quoted in Fang Tien-Tze, 'An Assessment of Ambassador Luo Jialun's Mission to India, 1947-1949', *China Report*, Vol. 50, No. 3, 2014, pp. 1–13. Luo would establish quiet contact with Pakistani leaders as well, reporting to Nanking that Pakistan was not a country to be ignored. He was also in touch with Liaquat Ali Khan to let him know that the Republic of China would recognise Pakistan—once the United States did so.
16. Foreign Department to Political Officer (hereafter PO), 8 April 1947, TOP, Vol. X, p. 156.

17. PO to Ministry of External Affairs, 23 July 1947, Foreign Department, F.No. 12(4)-NEF/47, NAI. Tibet's response to this was to thank Britain but continue to ask for the return of its territories—Darjeeling, Bhutan, Sikkim, Ladakh, Tawang and others. See, for instance, 16 October 1947, F.No. 12(4)-NEF/47 (Secret), MEA, NAI, and 24 March 1948, F.No. 7/2/NEF/48 (Secret), Foreign Department, NAI.
18. Governor General to Secretary of State, 29 August 1947, Foreign Department, F.No. 12(4)-NEF/47 (Secret), NAI, and Richardson to PO, 14 January 1948, Foreign Department, F.No. 12(4)-NEF/47 (Secret), NAI.
19. K.P.S. Menon, *Many Worlds: An Autobiography*, pp. 234–235.
20. Copy of a typescript telegram from Louis Mountbatten, Earl Mountbatten of Burma, Governor General of India [via the Foreign Ministry, New Delhi], to Sir Alan Frederick Lascelles, Private Secretary to the King, Buckingham Palace, London, 2 March 1948, MS62/MB/1/D/226/71, Mountbatten Papers, University of Southampton.
21. Copy of a typescript telegram from Sir Alan Frederick Lascelles, Private Secretary to the King, Buckingham Palace [London, United Kingdom], to Louis Mountbatten, Earl Mountbatten of Burma, Governor General of India, New Delhi, 3 March 1948, MS62/MB/1/D/226/72, Mountbatten Papers, University of Southampton.
22. K.M. Panikkar, *In Two Chinas: Memoirs of a Diplomat*, p. 18.
23. K.M Panikkar, *An Autobiography*, pp. 180–181.
24. Author's interview with Radha Mohan, 16 October 2021.
25. K.M. Panikkar, *An Autobiography*, pp. 180–181.
26. Ibid.
27. Author's Interview with Radha Mohan, 11 December 2021.
28. Ibid., 6 October 2020.
29. Ibid.
30. K.M. Panikkar, *In Two Chinas: Memoirs of a Diplomat*, p. 30.
31. Author's Interview with Radha Mohan, 6 October 2020.
32. Ibid.
33. Ibid.
34. K.M. Panikkar, *An Autobiography*, p. 198.
35. K.M. Panikkar, *In Two Chinas: Memoirs of a Diplomat*, pp. 26–27.
36. Ibid., p. 22.
37. Ibid.

38. In 1914, Henry McMahon had proposed the division of Tibet into one part that was under Chinese control and an independent part under the Dalai Lama. Peking had refused to ratify this treaty. Following the failure of the conference in Simla, Britain reserved the right to deal with Tibet directly, recognising it as autonomous but under Chinese suzerainty. In this way, extraterritorial rights were obtained directly from the Tibetan government, a position which independent India had inherited.
39. The issue had been settled directly between the representatives of Tibet and British India by imposing a demarcation line along the Himalayan watershed, that is the McMahon Line. By the 1930s though, British Indian official maps had begun showing the McMahon Line as a definite boundary. Indeed, the 1938 edition of volume XIV of the Aitchinson's Treaties (a collection of documents of British India's government) conveyed the impression that China, not having ratified the Simla Convention, had lost its rights on Tibet.
40. By 1954 official maps by the Survey of India stopped showing the caption 'undefined' on the western sector of the boundary, thus including almost the whole of Aksai Chin—which was strategically crucial for Chinese control on Tibet—in Indian territory.
41. Panikkar to Stevenson, 21 May 1948, L/PS/12/1340, IOR.
42. Ibid.
43. MEA to PO Sikkim, 4 September 1949, Foreign Department, F.No. 7/13/NEF/49-Secret, NAI. Also see Avtar Singh Bhasin, *Nehru, Tibet and China*, pp. 27–28.
44. Telegram, London to Foreign Office, 13 October 1948, FO 371/69739, NAUK.
45. Nirupama Rao, *The Fractured Himalaya: India, Tibet, China, 1949-1962*, Penguin Random House India, 2022, p. 81.
46. K.M. Panikkar, *In Two Chinas: Memoirs of a Diplomat*, p. 31.
47. Jawaharlal Nehru, 12 September 1948, *SWJN*, Vol. 7, p. 610.
48. K.M. Panikkar, *An Autobiography*, p. 200.
49. Michael Sheng has also noted that Chiang Kai-shek 'barely concealed his disdain for India … that smacked of xenophobia and national self-grandiosity'. See Michael M. Sheng, 'Mao, Tibet and the Korean War', *Journal of Cold War Studies*, Vol. 8, No. 3, 2006, p. 24.
50. Julia Boyd, *A Dance with the Dragon: The Vanished World of Peking's Foreign Colony*, I.B. Tauris Books, 2012, p. 10.

51. K.M. Panikkar, *In Two Chinas: Memoirs of a Diplomat*, p. 37.
52. Julia Boyd, *A Dance with the Dragon: The Vanished World of Peking's Foreign Colony*, p. 287.
53. Ibid.
54. K.M. Panikkar, 'When China Goes Communist', 22 November 1948, FO 371-75798, NAUK.
55. Ibid.
56. Nehru to K.P.S. Menon, The Situation in China, 5 December 1948, *SWJN*, Series 2, Vol. 8, p. 416.
57. K.M. Panikkar, *India and the Indian Ocean: An Essay on the Influence of Sea Power in Indian History*, and K.M. Panikkar, *The Future of Southeast Asia: An Indian View*. See also Nehru to PoPs, 1 July 1949, *SWJN*, Series 2, Vol. 12, p. 293; Nehru, Note to Foreign Secretary, 5 December 1948, in Avtar Singh Bhasin, *Nehru, Tibet and China*, p. 87; K.M. Panikkar to K.P.S. Menon, 7 September 1949, in Avtar Singh Bhasin, *Nehru, Tibet and China*, p. 138.
58. Nehru to Cripps, 17 December 1948, *SWJN*, Vol. 8, p. 335.
59. *Foreign Relations of the United States* (hereafter FRUS), Near East, South Asia and Africa, Vol. V, Pt I, Telegram 1108, dated 22 December 1948.
60. Luo's diaries (untitled), p. 288, quoted in Fang Tien-Tze, 'An Assessment of Ambassador Luo Jialun's Mission to India, 1947-1949'.
61. For more see Yu Ming-Shaw, *An American Missionary in China: John Leighton Stuart and Chinese-American Relations*, Harvard University Press, 1992. When the United States heard that Li was seeking help from Washington even as he agreed with the Russians to help eliminate American influence from China, they called his request for a statement of support 'incredible'. The Russians, in the end, refused to even acknowledge Li.
62. Indian Embassy, Nanking to MEA, 12 January 1949, Foreign Department, F.No. 7/2/NEF/48-Secret, NAI.
63. MEA to Indian Embassy, Nanking, 15 January 1949, Foreign Department, F.No. 7/2/NEF/48-Secret, NAI.
64. Ibid.
65. MEA to Indian Embassy, 13 March 1949, Foreign Department, F.No. 7/2/NEF/48-Secret, NAI.
66. K.M. Panikkar, *In Two Chinas: Memoirs of a Diplomat*, p. 75.
67. Ibid.
68. Secretary of State to Stuart, 30 March 1949, FRUS Vol XI, p. 750.

69. K.M. Panikkar, *In Two Chinas: Memoirs of a Diplomat*, pp. 75–78.
70. Ibid.
71. Note by Nehru, 3 June 1949, F.No. 611-CA/49 (Secret), MEA, NAI.
72. Warren Smith, *Tibetan Nation: A History of Tibetan Nationalism and Sino-Tibetan Relations*, Westview Press, 1997, p. 247.
73. F.No. 611-CA/49 (Secret), MEA, NAI.
74. Ibid.
75. Ibid.
76. Ibid.
77. Avtar Singh Bhasin, *Nehru, Tibet and China*, pp. 46–47. Also see Extract from the Monthly Report of Mission Lhasa, 15 September 1949, Document 0101, in Avtar Singh Bhasin (ed.), *India-China Relations, 1947-2000*, Vol. II, Geetika Publishers, 2018, and Article by a Chinese Jurist in *People's Daily*, 13 September 1949, Document 0098, in Avtar Singh Bhasin (ed.), *India-China Relations, 1947-2000*, Vol. II.
78. MEA to PO Sikkim, 4 September 1949, Foreign Department, F.No. 7/13/NEF/49-Secret, MEA, NAI; MEA to Indian Embassy, Nanking, 16 August 1949, F.No. 611-CA/49 (Secret), MEA, NAI. Also see Panikkar to Nehru, 12 February 1949, F.No. 825/CJK/49, MEA, NAI.
79. K.M. Panikkar, 'When China Goes Communist', 22 November 1948, FO 371-75798, NAUK.
80. K.M. Panikkar, *An Autobiography*, pp. 227–228.
81. K.M. Panikkar, *In Two Chinas: Memoirs of a Diplomat*, p. 85.
82. Ibid., p. 55.
83. Yan Jia, 'Subterranean Translation: The Absent Presence of Shen Congwen in K.M. Panikkar's Modern Chinese Stories', *World Literature Studies*, Vol. 1, No. 12, 2020, pp. 5–18.
84. K.M. Panikkar, *In Two Chinas: Memoirs of a Diplomat*, pp. 55–56. Also see Daniel Oakman, *Facing Asia: A History of the Colombo Plan*, ANU Press, 2010.
85. Ibid.
86. No. 70, Extract from Conclusions of the Meeting of the Cabinet, 9 May 1949, in S.R. Ashton, G. Bennett & K. Hamilton (eds), *Documents on British Policy Overseas*, Series I, Vol. VIII, Chapter 5, *Britain and China, 1945-1950*, Routledge Books, 2002, p. 268.
87. Ibid. Also see No. 72, Memorandum by P.J. Noel-Baker on Hong Kong, 18 May 1949, in S.R. Ashton, G. Bennett & K. Hamilton (eds), *Documents on British Policy Overseas*, Series I, Vol. VIII, Chapter 5, *Britain and China, 1945-1950*, p. 268.

88. Nehru, Letter to Chief Ministers, 14 May 1949, G. Parthasarathi (ed.), *Letters to Chief Ministers, 1947-1949*, Vol. I, Oxford University Press, 1998, pp. 343–344.
89. Ibid.
90. Nehru to Vijayalakshmi Pandit, 1 July 1949, Doc 80, in Avtar Singh Bhasin (ed.), *India-China Relations, 1947-2000*, Vol. II, p. 117.
91. No. 82, Memorandum by P.J. Noel-Baker on Hong Kong: Attitude of Other Countries, 18 May 1949, in S.R. Ashton, G. Bennett & K. Hamilton (eds), *Documents on British Policy Overseas*, Series I, Vol. VIII, Chapter 5, *Britain and China, 1945-1950*, p. 268.
92. Cable to Vijaya Lakshmi Pandit, New Delhi, 19 July 1949, in *Selected Works of Jawaharlal Nehru*, Series 2, Vol. 12, p. 389.
93. No. 72, Memorandum by P.J. Noel-Baker on Hong Kong: Attitude of Other Countries, 18 May 1949, in S.R. Ashton, G. Bennett & K. Hamilton (eds), *Documents on British Policy Overseas*, Series I, Vol. VIII, Chapter 5, *Britain and China, 1945-1950*, p. 268.
94. Telegram from US Ambassador (Stuart) to Secretary of State, 17 May 1949, FRUS, Vol. IX.
95. Tanvi Madan, *Fateful Triangle: How China Shaped U.S.-India Relations During the Cold War*, Brookings Institution Press, 2020, p. 19.
96. Robert McMahon, *Cold War on the Periphery: The United States, India and Pakistan*, Columbia University Press, 1996, pp. 50–51.
97. Tanvi Madan, *Fateful Triangle: How China Shaped U.S.-India Relations During the Cold War*, pp. 19–20.
98. Vijay Gokhale, *Crosswinds: Nehru, Zhou and the Anglo-American Competition over China*, Vintage Books, 2024, p. 43.
99. Doc. 0078, Telegram from Panikkar to K.P.S. Menon, 10 June 1949, in Avtar Singh Bhasin (ed.), *India-China Relations, 1947-2000*, Vol. II, pp. 114–116.
100. Telegram from Loy Henderson to Secretary of State, 17 June 1949, FRUS, Vol. IX.
101. Ibid., 21 June 1949.

CHAPTER 45

1. Panikkar, *In Two Chinas: Memoirs of a Diplomat*, p. 63.
2. Ibid.
3. Panikkar to Nehru, 10 August 1949, F.No. 611-CA/49 (Secret), MEA, NAI.

4. Panikkar to K.P.S. Menon, 7 September 1949, F.No. 611-CA/49 (Secret), MEA, NAI.
5. Patel to Nehru, 4 June 1949, from Durga Das (ed.) *Selected Correspondence of Sardar Patel, 1945-1950*, Vol. 8, Navjivan Press, 1971, p. 136.
6. Ibid., p. 509.
7. Not everyone was thrilled about this sudden belief in India's abilities. The deputy assistant secretary of state for the Near East and South Asia, Raymond Hare, was just one among a crowd of sceptics.
8. Nehru to Vijayalakshmi Pandit, 1 July 1949, *SWJN*, Vol. 12, pp. 408–409.
9. Tanvi Madan, *Fateful Triangle: How China Shaped U.S.-India Relations During the Cold War*, p. 21.
10. Panikkar to K.P.S. Menon, 7 September 1949, F.No. 611-CA/49 (Secret), MEA, NAI.
11. Note by Nehru on India and Indonesia, 28 June 1949, *SWJN*, Vol. 12, p. 371.
12. Vijayalakshmi Pandit to Nehru, 23 September 1949, Vijayalakshmi Pandit Papers, Vol. II, NMML.
13. Patel to Nehru, 6 May 1948, and Nehru to Patel, 21 May 1948, Durga Das (ed.) *Selected Correspondence of Sardar Patel, 1945-1950*, Vol. 6, pp. 371–372. Also see Nehru to Pandit, 8 June 1948, Vijayalakshmi Pandit Papers, Vol. I, SF No. 54, NMML. At the time, Nehru was critical of Russia's 'apparent lack of any sense of ethics in international affairs', a feeling which naturally ruled out any avenues of cooperation with the Soviet Union, at least temporarily.
14. Nehru to K.P.S. Menon, 11 October 1949, F.No. 710/CJK/49, MEA, NAI.
15. K.P.S. Menon to Nehru, 12 October 1949, in F.No. 710/CJK/49, MEA, NAI.
16. Note by K.P.S. Menon, 25 August 1949, in F.No. 710/CJK/49, MEA, NAI.
17. Note by G.S. Bajpai, 25 August 1949, in F.No. 710/CJK/49, MEA, NAI.
18. Note by G.S. Bajpai, 18 November 1949, in. F.No. 710/CJK/49, MEA, NAI. Also see Rakesh Ankit, *The Kashmir Conflict: From Empire to the Cold War, 1945-1966*, Routledge Books, 2016.

19. MemCon of Meeting between Truman, Nehru, Acheson and Bajpai, 13 October 1949, FRUS, *The Near East, South Asia and Africa*, Vol. VI, p. 1752.
20. Tanvi Madan, *Fateful Triangle: How China Shaped U.S.-India Relations During the Cold War*, p. 22.
21. Dean Acheson, *Present at the Creation: My Years in the State Department*, W.W. Norton & Company, 1988, pp. 334–336.
22. Arthur Krock, 'Mr. Acheson's Troubles Now Cover the Globe', *New York Times,* 4 December 1949. p. E3.
23. Indian Embassy, Nanking to MEA, 4 November 1949, Jawaharlal Nehru Papers (1st Part), File 30, NMML.
24. FRUS, 4 November 1949, *The Far East*, Vol. 1, Doc. 182.
25. FRUS, Doc. 190, Telegram 1,375, 7 November 1949, *The Far East*, Vol. 9. Also see Avtar Singh Bhasin, *Nehru, Tibet and China*, p. 38.
26. Ibid.
27. Ibid.
28. Telegram, UK High Commissioner in Delhi to Commonwealth Relations Office London, rptd Nanking, 18 September 1949, FO 371/76314, NAUK.
29. Ibid.
30. PO to MEA, 20 October 1949, Foreign Department, F.No. 7/13/NEF/49-Pt II, Secret, NAI.
31. Ibid.
32. K.M. Panikkar, Note on Tibetan Policy, 4 November 1949, F.No. 7/13/NEF/49-Secret, MEA, NAI.
33. Ibid.
34. K.P.S. Menon, Note on Panikkar's Tibetan Policy of 4 November 1949, written on 12 November 1949, in F.No.7/13/NEF/49-Secret, MEA, NAI.
35. Ibid.
36. Note by G.S. Bajpai, 21 November 1949, in F.No. 7/13/NEF/49-Secret, MEA, NAI.
37. Indian Embassy, Nanking to MEA, 29 November 1949, F.No. 7/13/NEF-49-Part II, Secret, MEA, NAI.
38. Telegram, UK High Commissioner in Delhi to Commonwealth Relations Office London, rptd Nanking, 17 November 1949, FO 371/76314, NAUK

39. Loy Henderson to Secretary of State, 10 January 1950, Telegram 793B 00/1-1050, FRUS, *East Asia and the Pacific*, Vol. VI.
40. Proceedings of a Press Conference addressed by Prime Minister Nehru, 16 November 1949, Nehru Papers, F.No. 31 (Part I), First Part, NMML.
41. Ibid.
42. Telegram from the UK High Commissioner to the Commonwealth Relations Office London, 6 November 1949, FO 371/76314, NAUK.
43. Nirupama Rao, *The Fractured Himalaya: India, Tibet, China, 1949-1962*, p. 96.
44. Telegram from PO Lhasa to MEA, 4 November 1949, Nehru Papers, F.No. 31 (Part I), First Part, NMML.
45. Ibid.
46. Nehru to Premiers of Provinces, 1 December 1949, *SWJN*, Vol. 14, Part I, p. 367.
47. PM's Meeting with Senior Officials, 30 December 1949, F.No. 7/13/NEF/49-Part II, Secret, MEA, NAI.
48. Ibid.
49. Note by Nehru, 17 November 1949, F.No. 170/CJK/NEF/49, MEA, NAI.
50. FRUS, 6 December 1949, Telegram 1,518, *The Far East*, Vol. IX.
51. MEA to PO Sikkim and Lhasa, 11 November 1949, Nehru Papers, F.No. 31-Part I, First Part, NMML.
52. Ibid.
53. Ibid.
54. FRUS, 19 December 1949, Doc. 253, *The Far East*, Vol. IX.
55. Patel to Nehru, 6 December 1949, in Durga Das (ed.) *Selected Correspondence of Sardar Patel, 1945-1950*, Vol. 8, pp. 86–87.

CHAPTER 46

1. MEA to Indian Embassy, Nanking, 6 January 1950, Nehru Papers, Vol. 34, p. 84, NMML.
2. Indian Embassy, Peking, to MEA, 15 March 1950, quoted from Avtar Singh Bhasin, *Nehru, Tibet and China*, p. 68.
3. K.M. Panikkar, *An Autobiography*, p. 233.
4. K.M. Panikkar, *In Two Chinas: Memoirs of a Diplomat*, p. 102.
5. K.M. Panikkar, *An Autobiography*, p. 233.
6. Ibid.

7. K.M. Panikkar, *In Two Chinas: Memoirs of a Diplomat*, p. 77.
8. Ibid.
9. Ibid.
10. Ibid.
11. Ibid., p. 79.
12. Ibid.
13. Ibid.
14. Ibid.
15. CIA, 'Aims of the Indian Ambassador, K.M. Panikkar', Report No. 364, 1 June 1950, Approved for Release in 1999, https://www.cia.gov/readingroom/.
16. Pandit to Nehru, 5 February 1951, Vijayalakshmi Pandit Papers, 1st Instalment (1951-1963), NMML.
17. FO371/83558, NAUK.
18. Ibid.
19. FO371/83558, NAUK.
20. Bajpai to Pandit, 21 August 1950, Vijayalakshmi Pandit Papers, Vol. I, SF-62, NMML.
21. Bajpai to Pandit, 10 September 1950, Vijayalakshmi Pandit Papers, Vol. I, SF-62, NMML.
22. FO 371/99378, NAUK.
23. Panikkar to Nehru, 17 June 1950, F.No.770(3)/CJK/50, MEA, NAI.
24. Ibid.
25. Panikkar, Report of talk with General Roshin, USSR Envoy to People's Republic of China, 17 June 1950, F.No. 770(3)/CJK/50, MEA, NAI.
26. Panikkar, A Preliminary Analysis of the Problems of New China, Note to Nehru, 1 July 1950, F.No. 771/CJK/50, MEA, NAI.
27. Indian Embassy, Beijing, to MEA, undated, F.No. 170/CJK/49, MEA, NAI.
28. Panikkar to Nehru, 17 June 1950, F.No. 770(3)/CJK/50, MEA, NAI. See also Panikkar to K.P.S. Menon, 15 June 1950, F.No. 770/CJK/50, MEA, NAI.
29. Panikkar, A Preliminary Analysis of the Problems of New China, Note to Nehru, 1 July 1950, F.No. 771/CJK/50, MEA, NAI.
30. Ibid.
31. Nehru to Vijayalakshmi Pandit, 30 August 1950, *SWJN*, Vol. 15, Part I, pp. 380–383.

32. For more, see Nirupama Rao, *Fractured Himalaya: India, Tibet, China, 1949-1962* and Avtar Singh Bhasin, *Nehru, Tibet and China.*
33. Nehru to Panikkar, 2 October 1951; Zhou's Conversation with Panikkar, 28 September 1951 and Panikkar's Conversation with Zhou at dinner, 2 October 1951. Quoted from Avtar Singh Bhasin, *Nehru, Tibet and China*, pp. 76–77.
34. Mervyn Goldstein, *A History of Modern Tibet, 1913-1951*, Vol. 2, University of California Press, 1989, p. 21 and 58. Also see Jawaharlal Nehru to Vijaya Lakshmi Pandit, 30 August, 1950, in Vijaya Lakshmi Pandit Papers I, Subject File No. 60, Subject: 1949, 1950-51, Letters received by V.L. Pandit as Ambassador to Washington from Jawaharlal Nehru concerning India's relations with US, Pakistan and other countries and developments at home, p. 137, NMML.
35. A.G. Noorani, "The Nehruvian Approach," in H. Y. Sharada Prasad and A. K. Damodaran (ed), Review of *Selected Works of Jawaharlal Nehru*, second series, vol. 29, *Frontline* 19, no. 2 (January-February 2002). Available at: http://www.frontlineonnet.com/fl1902/19020810.htm.
36. Jawaharlal Nehru to Vijaya Lakshmi Pandit, 30 August, 1950, in Vijaya Lakshmi Pandit Papers I, Subject File No. 60, Subject: 1949, 1950-51, Letters received by V.L. Pandit as Ambassador to Washington from Jawaharlal Nehru concerning India's relations with US, Pakistan and other countries and developments at home, p. 137, PMML. .
37. Ibid.
38. Statement by Spokesman, China's Foreign Office, 20 January 1950, quoted from Avtar Singh Bhasin, *Nehru, Tibet and China*, p. 67.
39. FRUS, 20 January 1950, Telegram 793B.02/1-2050, Vol. VI.
40. MEA to Mission Lhasa, 9 January 1950, MEA, F.No. 7/13/NEF/49-Part II, Secret, MEA, NAI.
41. Ibid.
42. PO to MEA, 18 April 1950, MEA, F.No. 7/13/NEF/49-Part II, Secret, MEA, NAI.
43. Warren Smith, *Tibetan Nation: A History of Tibetan Nationalism and Sino-Tibetan Relations*, p. 272.
44. Peking Radio Broadcast, 13 May 1950, quoted in Avtar Singh Bhasin, *Nehru, Tibet and China*, p. 75.

CHAPTER 47

1. K.M. Panikkar, *In Two Chinas: Memoirs of a Diplomat*, p. 105.

2. The MEA was furious, insisting that a 'Yes' vote would have committed India to a position that might have been difficult to retract later. The MEA's disagreement with Rau—known as the 'saint of the United Nations'—would become startlingly bitter. Finally Delhi was forced to take his side, though he was asked not to commit to anything further without specific instructions from Delhi.
3. Vineet Thakur, 'India's Diplomatic Entrepreneurism: Revisiting India's Role in the Korean Crisis, 1950-1952', *China Report*, Vol. 49, Issue 3, 2013.
4. Nehru, *SWJN*, Vol.14, Part II, p. 312.
5. Ibid.
6. *SWJN*, Vol. 14, Part II, p. 372.
7. Indian Embassy, Beijing, to MEA, 26 May 1950, F.No. 7/13/NEF/49-Part II, Secret, MEA, NAI.
8. Panikkar to Bajpai, 29 June 1950, F.No. 761/CJK/50, MEA, NAI.
9. Indian Embassy, Beijing, to MEA, 6 June 1950, Nehru Paper, F.No.46, Part I, First Part, pp. 64, 64a and 65.
10. Ibid.
11. Dean Acheson to Nehru, 26 July 1950, *SWJN*, Vol. II, Vol. 14, Part II, p. 358-359.
12. Nehru, Speech, National Press Club, Washington DC, 14 October 1949, *SWJN*, Second Series, Vol. 13, p. 307.
13. Panikkar to Nehru, 'War Psychosis in China', 1 November 1950, F.No. 770/CJK/50, MEA, NAI.
14. Henderson to Acheson, regarding meeting with Bajpai, 5 July 1950, FRUS, Vol. VI, p. 368; Bajpai to Pandit, 21 August 1950, Vijayalakshmi Pandit Papers, Vol. I, SF No. 56, NMML; and Henderson to Acheson, 4 September 1950, FRUS, Vol. VI, p. 482.
15. Henderson to Acheson, 9 July 1950, FRUS, Vol. VI, p. 372; Henderson to Acheson, on conversation with Bajpai, 24 August 1950, FRUS, Vol. VI., pp. 446–448; Acheson to AmEmb UK, 13 August 1950, FRUS, Vol. VI, pp. 432–433, and Acheson to AmEmb India, 1 September 1950, FRUS, Vol. VI, pp. 478–480.
16. Warren Smith, *Tibetan Nation: A History of Tibetan Nationalism and Sino-Tibetan Relations*, p. 277.
17. See FRUS, Vol. VI, p. 377 and US Foreign Policy Doc, 9 June 1950, FRUS, Vol. VI, p. 361. Also see Tsering Shakya, *The Dragon in the Land of Snow*, Columbia University Press, 1999.

18. Panikkar to Nehru, 2 August 1950, Nehru Papers, F.No. 53 (Part II), pp. 185–186 and Indian Embassy, Nanking, to MEA, 10 August 1950, F.No. 729-CJK/49 (Secret), MEA, NAI.
19. Avtar Singh Bhasin, *Nehru, Tibet and China*, p. 84.
20. PO to MEA, 17 August 1950, Nehru Papers, F.No. 52 (Part I), First Part, p. 181, NMML.
21. Ibid.
22. Note handed by the Foreign Minister of China to the Indian Ambassador, 21 August 1950, in *Treaties Signed and Memoranda Exchanged between the Governments of India and China, 1949-1959*, Ministry of External Affairs, Government of India. Quoted in Nirupama Rao, *The Fractured Himalaya: India, Tibet, China, 1949-1962*, p. 102.
23. Zhou En-lai to Panikkar, 22 August 1950, Nehru Papers, F.No. 52 (Part II), First Part, pp. 314–316, NMML.
24. See PO to MEA, 19 August 1950, Nehru Papers, F.No. 52 (Part I), First Part, pp. 123–124, NMML. Also see Nehru to Panikkar, 19 August 1950, Nehru Papers, F.No. 52 (Part I), First Part, p. 120, NMML.
25. Nehru to Panikkar, 17 August 1950, Nehru Papers, F.No. 52- Part I, First Part, pp. 125–126, NMML.
26. Panikkar to Nehru, 22 August 1950, Nehru Papers, F.No. 52 (Part II), pp. 314–316, NMML.
27. Ibid.
28. MEA to Indian Embassy, Beijing, 24 August 1950, Nehru Papers, F.No. 52 (Part II), First Part, p. 275, NMML.
29. Ibid.
30. M.O. Matthai, *Reminiscences of the Nehru Age*, Vikas Publishing, 1978, p. 168.
31. Nirupama Rao, *Fractured Himalaya: India, Tibet, China, 1949-1962*, p. 103.
32. Avtar Singh Bhasin, *Nehru, Tibet and China,* p. 89.
33. Chinese Note to MEA, 17 November 1950, *SWJN*, Vol. 15, Part II, p. 343. Also see Nehru to Panikkar, 20 November 1950, *SWJN*, Vol. 15, Part II, p. 350.
34. Ibid. Delhi had an unfortunate history of doing this. In January 1949, the Ministry of External Affairs, in a telegram to Nanking, stated, 'We on our part will adhere steadfastly to our present policy of seeking to uphold Tibetan independence, subject to the suzerainty of China.' See MEA to Indian Embassy, Nanking, 15 January 1949,

F.No. 7/2/NEF-48 (Secret), NAI. It was only in March, two months later, that India clarified that the last telegram should 'not be taken to mean that GOI have changed their views in regard to the status of Tibet and recognised Chinese suzerainty over Tibet unconditionally'. See MEA to Indian Embassy in Nanking, 21 March 1949, Telegram D1445-NEF/49 in F.No. 7/2/NEF/49 (Secret), MEA, NAI.

35. Panikkar to MEA, 26 August 1950, *SWJN*, Vol. 15, Part II, p. 350.

CHAPTER 48

1. Amit Das Gupta, *Serving India: A Political Biography of Subimal Dutt, 1903-1992, India's Longest Serving Foreign Secretary*, Manohar Books, 2017, p. 234.
2. K.M. Panikkar to Emmanuel Olsvanger, 19 September 1950, Foreign Office F.No. 71/14b, Israel State Archives, Jerusalem, in P.R. Kumaraswamy, 'K.M. Panikkar and Indo-Israeli Relations', *International Studies*, Vol. 32, No. 3, 1995.
3. T.N. Kaul, *Diplomacy in Peace and War: Recollections and Reflections*, Vikas Publishing. 1979, pp. 23–24.
4. Ibid., p. 35.
5. Ibid.
6. Ibid.
7. Ibid.
8. K.M. Panikkar, *An Autobiography*, p. 237.
9. T.N. Kaul, *Diplomacy in Peace and War: Recollections and Reflections*, p. 35.
10. Ibid.
11. Ibid.
12. Devaki Panikkar, 'The Modern China', *Indian Daily Mail,* 18 March 1951. Available at the National Digital Library of Singapore at https://eresources.nlb.gov.sg/newspapers/digitised/article/indiandailymail19510318-1.2.28.
13. K.M. Panikkar, *In Two Chinas: Memoirs of a Diplomat*, p. 136.
14. Ibid.
15. Ibid.
16. Panikkar to MEA, 3 September 1950, Nehru Papers, F.No. 54, Part I, First Part, pp. 125–126, NMML.

17. Conversation of Prime Minister with Tibetan Delegation, 6 September 1950, in Avtar Singh Bhasin (ed.), *India-China Relations, 1947-2000*, Vol. III, p. 351.
18. Vineet Thakur, 'India's Diplomatic Entrepreneurism: Revisiting India's Role in the Korean War, 1950-1952', pp. 273–298.
19. *SWJN*, Vol. 15, Part I, p. 397-399. He warned Ernest Bevin of this too, but the British Foreign Secretary blew it off as a Chinese bluff.
20. Zhou's Report to the National Committee, 2 October 1950, Nehru Papers, F.No. 58 (Part I), p. 65, NMML.
21. K.M. Panikkar, *In Two Chinas: Memoirs of a Diplomat*, p. 109.
22. Ibid.
23. Harry S. Truman, *Years of Trial and Hope: Memoirs*, Doubleday & Company, 1956, p. 383.
24. The Central Intelligence Agency did prepare a National Intelligence Estimate on November 6, 1950, titled 'Chinese Communist Intervention in Korea'. But in this report, it assessed that there were only 30,000 Chinese troops south of the Yalu. The problem with the CIA at this time was its assumption that the communist world was a monolith in which Stalin dictated all the moves. The agency had missed out on the fact that Stalin had encouraged the Chinese to fight, without promising troops on the ground to assist. Mao, furious at this betrayal, had struck anyway. Korea would be the festering heart of the rivalry that would soon emerge between China and the Soviet Union, but that was still to come.
25. David Halberstam, *The Coldest Winter: America and the Korean War*, Hachette, 2008, p. 415.
26. Memorandum by Walter McConaughy, 12 October 1950, Records of the Office of Chinese Affairs, 1945-1955, Collection in the *Gale Archives Unbound*.
27. K.M. Panikkar, *In Two Chinas: Memoirs of a Diplomat*, p. 150.
28. Nehru to Panikkar, 25 October 1950, *SWJN*, Vol. 15, Part II, p. 443.
29. Mervyn Goldstein, *A History of Modern Tibet, 1913-1951*, p. 692; Tsering Shakya, *The Dragon in the Land of Snow*, p. 44, and Lezlee Brown Halper and Stefan Halper, *Tibet: An Unfinished Story*, Hurst Publishers: 2013, pp. 98–99.
30. Michael M. Sheng, '*Mao, Tibet and the Korean War*', pp. 22–23.
31. Dalai Lama, *Freedom in Exile: The Autobiography of the Dalai Lama*, HarperCollins, 1991, pp. 53–54.

32. Instruction from Chairman Mao on Discussion between Menon and Ambassador Yuan, 12 October 1950, Archive No. 105-00011-01(1), Memo 169, Ministry of Foreign Affairs, People's Republic of China. Quoted in Lezlee Brown Halper and Stefan Halper, *Tibet: An Unfinished Story*, pp. 98–99.
33. Nehru to Panikkar, 2 October and 12 October 1950, F.No. 58 (Part I), p. 65 and F.No. 59 (Part I), p. 204, Nehru Papers, First Part, NMML.
34. Sarvepalli Gopal, *Jawaharlal Nehru: A Biography*, Vol. II, pp. 106–107.
35. Memorandum by K.P.S. Menon, 17 October 1949, F.No. 170/CJK/49, MEA, NAI. See also Note by K. Zachariah, 24 October 1949, F.No. 170/CJK/49, MEA, NAI.
36. Telegram, Indian Embassy in Beijing to MEA, 3 August 1950, Nehru Papers, F.No. 50 (Part I), First Part, p. 31, NMML.
37. Top Secret Telegram, MEA to Indian Embassy in Beijing, 5 August 1950, Nehru Papers, F.No. 50 (Part I), First Part, pp. 29–30, NMML.
38. Ibid.
39. Ibid.
40. FRUS, *East Asia and the Pacific*, Vol. VI, Telegram 918, dated 13 October 1950. Also see MEA to Panikkar, 17 October 1950, Nehru Papers, F.No. 60 (Part I), pp. 102–103, First Part, NMML.
41. Henderson to Acheson, 27 October 1950, FRUS, Vol. VI, p. 540.
42. Memorandum for Mr. Jessup and Mr. Rusk, 'Credibility of KM Panikkar, Indian Ambassador to Communist China', 12 October 1950, p. 4, Secret Memorandum, US Intelligence and China: Collection, Analysis and Covert Action, CI00515, Digital National Security Archive.
43. Report to Shen Jian in India: Contents of Panikkar's Discussion on Tibetan Trade Problems with Vice Minister Zhang, 12 August 1950, Document No. 105-00011-01 (1), Chinese Foreign Ministry Archives. Quoted in Lezlee Brown Halper and Stefan Halper, *Tibet: An Unfinished Story*, pp. 106–107.
44. See Letter from Zhou En-lai to Prime Minister Nehru in 'An Incoming Note on India's Interference of our Liberation of Tibet and our Reply Note', Document No. 105-00010-03, Chinese Foreign Ministry Archives. Quoted in Lezlee Brown Halper and Stefan Halper, *Tibet: An Unfinished Story*, pp. 106–107. Also see Sarvepalli Gopal, *Jawaharlal Nehru: A Biography*, Vol. II, pp. 106–107, and B.N. Mullick, *My Years with Nehru: The Chinese Betrayal*, Allied Publishers, 1971, p. 66.
45. Sarvepalli Gopal, *Jawaharlal Nehru: A Biography*, Vol II, pp. 106–107.

46. Letter from Zhou En-lai to Prime Minister Nehru in 'An Incoming Note on India's Interference of our Liberation of Tibet and our Reply Note', Document No. 105-00010-03, Chinese Foreign Ministry Archives. Quoted in Lezlee Brown Halper and Stefan Halper, *Tibet: An Unfinished Story*, pp. 106–107.
47. Discussion at the Ministry of Foreign Affairs of the Central People's Government in "A Memorandum of India's Interference of our Liberation of Tibet and our Reply', 16 October 1950, 2 PM at the Foreign Ministry Headquarters, Document no. 10500010-02. Quoted in Lezlee Brown Halper and Stefan Halper, *Tibet: An Unfinished Story*, pp. 106–107.
48. Discussion Record with Indian Ambassador in Memorandum on India's Interference of our Liberation of Tibet and our Reply, 21 October 1950, Document No. 105-00010-02 (1), Chinese Foreign Ministry Archives. Quoted in Lezlee Brown Halper and Stefan Halper, *Tibet: An Unfinished Story*, pp. 106–107.
49. Menon to Shen, 26 October 1950, Nehru Papers, F.No. 61 (Part I), First Part, pp. 114–115, NMML.
50. Panikkar to MEA, 27 October 1950, Nehru Papers, F.No. 61 (Part I), First Part, p. 224, NMML.
51. Avtar Singh Bhasin, *Nehru, Tibet and China*, p. 100.
52. 28. and 30 October 1950, Nehru Papers, F.No. 61 (Part II), First Part, pp. 130–133, NMML.
53. Note by Foreign Secretary on his Meeting with the Chinese Ambassador, 2 November 1950, Nehru Papers, F.No. 62 (Part I), First Part, p. 81, NMML.
54. Exchanges between PRC Foreign Ministry and the Chinese Embassy in India, regarding India's Interference of our Liberation of Tibet, Archive no. 105-00011-01(1). Also see Discussion between Shen Jian and Menon, 26 October 1950, Chinese Foreign Ministry Archives. Quoted in Lezlee Brown Halper and Stefan Halper, *Tibet: An Unfinished Story*, pp. 106–107.
55. See Nehru to Matthai, 10 September 1949, *SWJN*, Second Series, Vol. 13, p. 260. Also see Panikkar to Nehru, 17 June 1950, F.No. 770(3)-CJK/50, MEA, NAI, and K.P.S. Menon to Vijayalakshmi Pandit, 26 July 1950, Vijayalakshmi Pandit Papers, Vol. II, SF No. 14, NMML.

56. MEA to Panikkar, 17 October 1950, Nehru Papers, F.No. 60 (Part I), First Part, pp. 102–103, NMML, and Nehru to Panikkar, 19 October 1950, Nehru Papers, F.No. 60 (Part I), First Part, pp. 103–106, NMML.

CHAPTER 49

1. Tribute to Swami Dayanand, Speech at the Rishi Dayanand Nirvan Utsav, 9 November 1950, in *For A United India: Speeches of Sardar Patel 1947-1950*, Publications Division, Ministry of Information and Broadcasting, Government of India, 1967.
2. Ibid.
3. Patel to Nehru, 7 November 1950, Durga Das (ed.), *Selected Correspondence of Sardar Patel, 1945-1950*, Vol. X, pp. 335–341.
4. Ibid.
5. Ibid.
6. Notes by Menon, Bajpai and Nehru, 25 October 1950, Nehru Papers, F.No. 61 (Part II), p. 76, and Note by Bajpai, Nehru Papers, F.No. 61 (Part II), pp. 11–12, First Part, NMML.
7. Note by Indian Embassy, Beijing to MEA, 24 October 1950, Nehru Papers, F.No. 61 (Part II), First Part, p. 77, NMML and Note by Bajpai, Nehru Papers, F.No. 61 (Part II), First Part, p. 78, NMML.
8. Nehru, Patel and China, in NMML Digital Archive.
9. Ibid.
10. Patel to Bajpai, 4 November 1950, Nehru Papers, F.No. 62 (Part II), First Part, NMML.
11. Nehru to Panikkar, 25 October 1950, Nehru Papers, F.No. 61 (Part I), First Part, pp. 54–57, NMML.
12. Ibid.
13. Avtar Singh Bhasin, *Nehru, Tibet and China*, p. 98.
14. Panikkar to Nehru, 20 May 1950, quoted in Avtar Singh Bhasin, *Nehru, Tibet and China*, p. 280.
15. Note by Nehru on China and Tibet, 18 November 1950, in Durga Das (ed.), *Sardar Patel Correspondence, 1945-1950*, Vol. X, pp. 342–347.
16. Nehru to Panikkar, 27 October 1950, Nehru Papers, F.No. 61 (Part II), First Part, p. 22, NMML.
17. Bajpai to Nehru, 31 October 1950, *SWJN*, Series 2, Vol. 2, p. 107.
18. Harry S. Truman, *Years of Trial and Hope: Memoirs*, p. 419.
19. K.M. Panikkar, *In Two Chinas: Memoirs of a Diplomat*, p. 115.
20. Ibid.

21. Ibid.
22. PM's Note on Policy Towards South and Southeast Asia, 8 November 1950, quoted in Avtar Singh Bhasin, *Nehru, Tibet and China*, p. 102.
23. Nehru to Panikkar, 27 November 1950, quoted in Avtar Singh Bhasin, p. 104. Nehru still, amazingly, was not clear about the differences between suzerainty and sovereignty. In a speech to parliament on 7 December 1950, he even produced an equation for it: 'autonomy plus sovereignty leads to suzerainty'.
24. *SWJN*, Vol. 15, Series II, p. 418.
25. *SWJN*, Vol. 15, Series II, p. 450.
26. *SWJN*, Vol. 15, Series II, p. 452.
27. K.M. Panikkar, *In Two Chinas: Memoirs of a Diplomat*, p. 118. For further information on these meetings, see Harry S. Truman, *The Memoirs of Harry S. Truman*, volume ii, *Years of Trial and Hope, 1946-1952*, pp. 394–413, and Dean Acheson, *Present at the Creation: My Years in the State Department*, pp. 478–485. Also see FRUS, Vol. III, *Western Europe*, 1950: United States Minutes: Truman-Attlee Conversations, First Meeting, the White House, Washington DC, 4 December 1950.
28. K.M. Panikkar, *In Two Chinas: Memoirs of a Diplomat*, p. 119.
29. Ibid.
30. Ibid.
31. John Lewis Gaddis, *Strategies of Containment: A Critical Appraisal of American National Security Policy during the Cold War*, Oxford University Press, 2005, p. 110. Also Robert Trumbull, 'Peiping Rejection Disappoints India', *New York Times*, 19 January 1951, p. 3.
32. *SWJN*, Vol. 15, Part I, pp. 371–372.
33. 'Nehru asks West to Keep Peace Aim', *New York Times*, 18 January 1951, p. 3; 'Indian Gives View', *New York Times*, 25 January 1951; and 'Text of Indian Delegate's Speech', *New York Times*, 21 January 1951, p. 4.
34. James Reston, 'Split between US & West on Asia held at Critical Point', *New York Times*, 24 January 1951, p. 6.
35. Henderson to Acheson, January 27, 1951, FRUS, 1951 Vol. VII-1, p. 138.
36. Acheson to AmEmb India, January 30, 1951, FRUS 1951 Vol. VII-1, p. 148.
37. Tanvi Madan, *Fateful Triangle: How China Shaped U.S.-India Relations During the Cold War*, p. 41.

38. Pandit to Bajpai, October 16 and December 11, 1950, and Bajpai to Pandit, October 29, 1950, Vijayalakshmi Pandit Papers (I), SF No. 56, NMML.
39. Nehru to Krishna Menon, June 26, 1948, *SWJN*, SS, Vol. 6, pp. 463–465.
40. UNGA A/C.1/643, 1951. Interestingly, this was the meeting that was a precursor to Asian-African united front at the United Nations that resulted in the non-aligned movement later.
41. K.M. Panikkar, *In Two Chinas: Memoirs of a Diplomat*, pp. 120–125. Also see BN Rau Papers, 24 December 1950, NMML.
42. Ibid.
43. Ibid.
44. *SWJN*, Vol. 15, Series II, Part II, p. 478.
45. *SWJN*, Vol. 15, Series II, Part II, pp. 491–493.
46. *SWJN*, Vol. 15, Part II, p. 494.
47. Tanvi Madan, *Fateful Triangle: How China Shaped U.S.-India Relations During the Cold War*, pp. 45–50.
48. K.M. Panikkar, *In Two Chinas: Memoirs of a Diplomat*, p. 126.
49. Vineet Thakur, 'India's Diplomatic Entrepreneurism: Revisiting India's Role in the Korean Crisis, 1950-1952', pp. 273–298 and Tanvi Madan, *Fateful Triangle: How China Shaped U.S.-India Relations During the Cold War.*
50. Vijayalakshmi Pandit to Nehru, 4 December 1952, Vijayalakshmi Pandit Papers, NMML; See also Nehru to N. Raghavan, 23 August 1953, *SWJN*, Vol. 23, Series 2, p. 522.
51. Chester Bowles to Secretary of State, Telegram. 611.91/11–751, 7 November 1951, FRUS, 1951, *Asia and the Pacific*, Vol. 6, Part 2.
52. Ibid.
53. K.M. Panikkar, *In Two Chinas: Memoirs of a Diplomat*, p. 114.

CHAPTER 50

1. T.N. Kaul, *Diplomacy in Peace and War: Recollections and Reflections*, pp. 50–54.
2. K.M. Panikkar, *In Two Chinas: Memoirs of a Diplomat*, p. 136.
3. T.N. Kaul, *Diplomacy in Peace and War: Recollections and Reflections*, p. 55.
4. Henderson to Acheson, January 25, 1951, FRUS, *1951, Vol. VII: Korea and China, Part 2*, Washington DC: GPO, 1983, p. 1529.

5. Henderson to Acheson, January 12, 1951, FRUS 1951, Vol. VII-2, pp. 1506–1508.
6. See B.N. Mullick, *My Years with Nehru: The Chinese Betrayal;* Madhav Khosla (ed.), *Letters for a Nation: From Jawaharlal Nehru to his Chief Ministers, 1947-1964*, Penguin Allen Lane, 2014, and Berenice Guyot-Rechard, *Shadow States: India, China and the Himalayas, 1910-1962*, Cambridge University Press, 2017, pp. 95–126.
7. Karunakar Gupta, 'Hidden History of the Sino-Indian Frontier, 1947-1954', *Economic and Political Weekly*, Vol. 9, No. 18, 4 May 1974, pp. 721–726.
8. CIA Report, 5 March 1952, OCI. No. 3886.
9. Indian Embassy, Beijing to MEA, 22 March 1951, Nehru Papers, F.No. 78 (Part I), First Part, pp. 6–7, NMML.
10. Ibid.
11. Ibid.
12. Ibid. Also see Avtar Singh Bhasin, *Nehru, Tibet and China*, p. 120.
13. MEA to PO, Sikkim, 24 March 1951, Nehru Papers, F.No. 78 (Part I), First Part, p. 99, NMML
14. MEA to Embassy in Peking, 31 March 1951, Nehru Papers, F.No. 78 (Part I), First Part, p. 115, NMML.
15. K.M. Panikkar, *In Two Chinas: Memoirs of a Diplomat*, p. 140.
16. K.M. Panikkar, *An Autobiography*, p. 285.
17. K.M. Panikkar, *In Two Chinas: Memoirs of a Diplomat*, p. 139.
18. The Chinese had their own five-point agenda, which stated that the Dalai Lama should not 'go to a foreign country', and that once 'national regional autonomy' was granted to Tibet, 'the Dalai Lama's traditional position will continue'. They claimed that they did not 'harbour vindictive desires'. Quoted in Nirupama Rao, *The Fractured Himalaya: India, Tibet, China, 1949-62*, p. 133.
19. K.M. Panikkar (pseud. Chanakya), *The Indian Revolution,* National Information & Publications Ltd, 1951, p. 86.
20. Panikkar to Nehru, 17 June 1950, F.No. 770(3)/CJK/50, MEA, NAI, and Panikkar, 'A Preliminary Analysis of the Problems of New China', 1 July 1950, F.No. 771/CJK/50, MEA, NAI.
21. K.M. Panikkar, *The Indian Revolution*, p. 31.
22. Ibid., pp. 125–126.
23. K.M. Panikkar, *In Two Chinas: Memoirs of a Diplomat*, p. 135.
24. K.M. Panikkar, *The Future of Southeast Asia: An Indian View.*
25. K.M. Panikkar, *In Two Chinas: Memoirs of a Diplomat*, p. 136.

26. Dai Chaowu, quoting from the Archive of Ministry of Foreign Affairs of the People's Republic of China, 'Conditions of the Current Military, Political and Economic Conditions in Tibet', 12 April 1952, in 'From Hindi-Chini Bhai-Bhai to International Class Struggle against Nehru: China's India Policy and the Frontier Dispute, 1950-1962', in Amit Das Gupta & Lorenz Luthi (eds), *The Sino-Indian War of 1962: New Perspectives*, Routledge, 2017, pp. 51–52.
27. Ibid.
28. Mission Lhasa to MEA, 24 April 1952, Nehru Papers, F.No. 125 (Part II), First Part, p. 387, NMML.
29. Foreign Ministry Archives of the People's Republic of China, Document 105-00119-02 (1), 'Summary of the Conversation between Director Chen Jiakang and Counsellor Kaul', 26 March 1951, quoted in Dai Chaowu, 'From Hindi-Chini Bhai-Bhai to International Class Struggle against Nehru: China's India Policy and the Frontier Dispute, 1950-1962', in Amit Das Gupta & Lorenz Luthi (eds), *The Sino-Indian War of 1962: New Perspectives*, pp. 51–52.
30. For more, see Manu Bhagavan, *Vijaya Lakshmi Pandit*.
31. Nirupama Rao, *The Fractured Himalaya: India, Tibet, China, 1949-1962*, p. 145.
32. Ibid.
33. Vijayalakshmi Pandit to Nehru, 16 May 1952, F.No. 123, C. Rajagopalachari Papers, Fifth Installment, NMML.
34. Indian Embassy, Beijing to MEA, 15 June 1952, Nehru Papers, F.No. 134 (Part I), First Part, pp. 148–149, NMML.
35. Telegram, Nehru to Panikkar, 16 June 1952, Nehru Papers, F.No. 134 (Part II), First Part, p. 136, NMML.
36. Ibid.
37. Panikkar to Nehru, 17 June 1952, Nehru Papers, F.No. 134 (Part II), First Part, p. 137, NMML.
38. Nehru to Panikkar, 16 June 1952, Nehru Papers, F.No. 134 (Part II), First Part, p. 202, NMML.
39. Panikkar to Nehru, 23 June 1952, Nehru Papers, F.No. 136 (Part I), First Part, p. 11, NMML.
40. Indian Embassy Beijing to MEA, 18 July 1952, Nehru Papers, F.No. 139 (Part I), First Part, p. 113, NMML, and MEA to Indian Embassy, Beijing, 31 July 1952, Nehru Papers, F.No. 140 (Part II), First Part, pp. 328–329, NMML.

41. Note by K.P.S. Menon, 11 April 1952, Vijayalakshmi Papers (Second Installment), SF No. 19, NMML.
42. Ibid.
43. Bajpai to N.R. Pillai, Foreign Secretary, 14 July 1952, Nehru Papers, F.No. 138 (Part II), First Part, NMML.
44. PM's Press Conference, 21 June 1952, Nehru Papers, F.No. 138 (Part II), First Part, NMML.
45. Nehru to N.R. Pillai, Foreign Secretary, 14 July 1952, Nehru Papers, F.No. 138 (Part II), First Part, NMML
46. T.N. Kaul, *Diplomacy in Peace and War: Recollections and Reflections*, pp. 50–53.
47. K.M. Panikkar, *In Two Chinas: Memoirs of a Diplomat*, p. 179.

CHAPTER 51

1. India, *MEA Report, 1948-1949*, p. 4, quoted in P.R. Kumaraswamy, *India's Israel Policy*, p. 169.
2. Onkar Marwah, 'India's Relations with West Asian, North African Countries', *Middle East Information Series*, No. 22, February 1973, pp. 21–27.
3. Selma Botman, 'The Liberal Age, 1923-1952', in Martin Daly (ed.), *The Cambridge History of Egypt*, Vol. II: Modern Egypt from 1517 to the End of the Twentieth Century, Cambridge University Press, 1998, pp. 285–308.
4. K.M Panikkar, *An Autobiography*, p. 243.
5. P.R. Kumaraswamy, *India's Israel Policy*, p. 168.
6. Mehtab Ali Shah, *The Foreign Policy of Pakistan: Ethnic Impacts on Diplomacy, 1971-1994*, I.B. Tauris Books, 1997, p. 27.
7. Eliahu Elath to Walter Eytan, 8 September 1953, F.No. 2413/29, Israel State Archives. Quoted in P.R. Kumaraswamy, *India's Israel Policy*, p. 169.
8. Godfrey H. Jansen, *Militant Islam*, Harper & Row, 1979, p. 96.
9. K.M. Panikkar, *An Autobiography*, p. 247.
10. Panikkar to Stevenson, 5 May 1950, FO 371/83021, NAUK.
11. K.M. Panikkar, *An Autobiography*, p. 257.
12. Panikkar to Krishna Menon, quoted in Jairam Ramesh, *A Chequered Brilliance: The Many Lives of V.K. Krishna Menon*, Penguin Random House India, 2020, p. 314.
13. K.M. Panikkar, *An Autobiography*, p. 280.

14. Elie Podeh, 'The Drift Towards Neutrality: Egyptian Foreign Policy During the Early Nasserist Years, 1952-1955', *Middle Eastern Studies*, Vol. 32, No. 1, 1996, pp. 159–178.
15. For more, read Rimi Ginat, *Egypt and the Struggle for Power in Sudan: From World War II to Nasserism*, Cambridge University Press, 2017, and Eve Troutt Powell, *A Different Shade of Colonialism: Egypt, Great Britain and the Mastery of the Sudan*, Berkeley, 2003.
16. K.M. Panikkar, *An Autobiography*, p. 280.
17. Ibid., p. 270.
18. Ibid.
19. Ibid.
20. Joel Gordon, *Nasser's Blessed Movement: Egypt's Free Officers and the July Revolution*, Oxford University Press, 1992, pp. 159–172, and Rimi Ginat, *Egypt and the Struggle for Power in Sudan: From World War II to Nasserism*, pp. 195–199.
21. K.M. Panikkar, *An Autobiography*, pp. 285–286.
22. Ramachandra Guha, 'Democracy's Biggest Gamble: India's First Free Elections in 1952', *World Policy Journal*, Vol. 19, No. 1, 2002, pp. 95–103.
23. For more, see S.Y. Qureishi, *An Undocumented Wonder: The Great Indian Election*, Penguin, 2019.
24. Stevenson to James Bowker, 29 January 1953, FO 371/102743, NAUK.
25. Lionel Lamb to William Strang, 14 April 1953, FO 371/102757, NAUK.
26. William Strang to Lionel Lamb, 8 May 1953, FO 371/102757, NAUK.
27. K.M. Panikkar, *An Autobiography*, p. 284.
28. Stevenson to Foreign Office, 28 February 1953, FO 371/102796, NAUK.
29. K.M. Panikkar, *An Autobiography*, pp. 284–285.
30. K.M. Panikkar, *An Autobiography*, pp. 285–286.
31. William Louis, 'Prelude to Suez: Churchill and Egypt', in Roger Louis (ed.), *Ends of British Imperialism: The Scramble for Empire, Suez and Decolonisation*, I.B. Tauris, 2006, pp. 609–626.
32. Panikkar to B.G. Kher, 5 July 1953, *SWJN*, Series 2, Vol. 23, pp. 531–532 and Panikkar to Wyatt, 7 November 1953, FO 371/102820, NAUK.

33. Ibid.
34. Michael Creswell to Foreign Office, 5 November 1953, FO 371/102820, NAUK.
35. K.M. Panikkar, *An Autobiography*, p. 287.
36. Nehru to K.P.S. Menon and K.M. Panikkar, 29 July 1952, *SWJN*, Series 2, Vol. 19, p. 651.
37. Sarvepalli Gopal, *Jawaharlal Nehru: A Biography*, Vol. II, p. 176.
38. Parliamentary Debates, 20 November 1950, Vol. V, Part I, pp. 155–156. Available online at: https://sansad.in/ls/debates/historical.
39. Nirupama Rao, *The Fractured Himalaya: India, Tibet, China, 1949-1962*, p. 165.
40. B.N. Mullick, *My Years with Nehru: The Chinese Betrayal*, pp. 157–156.
41. Panikkar to Bajpai, 4 August 1952, Nehru Papers, F.No. 142 (Part II), First Part, pp. 106–107, NMML.
42. Bajpai to Panikkar, 7 August 1952, F.No. 134 (Part II), Nehru Papers, First Part, pp. 222–223, NMML.
43. Nehru to Secretary General, MEA, 'Situation on the Northeast Frontier', *SWJN*, Vol. 21, pp. 555–558. The prime minister continued to cling obstinately to the geographical factors that put India in a position of advantage with regard to Tibet.
44. Note by the MEA on 'Main Points which may arise during discussions at the Peking Conference', 3 December 1953, Nehru Papers, F 2187, pp. 200–208, NMML.
45. K.M. Panikkar, *An Autobiography*. p. 278.
46. Ibid.
47. Ibid.
48. Ibid.
49. Eliahu Elath to Walter Eytan, 8 September 1953, F.No. 2413/29, Israel State Archives. Quoted in P.R. Kumaraswamy, *K.M. Panikkar and Indo-Israeli Relations*, p. 335.
50. Ibid.
51. K.M. Panikkar, *An Autobiography*, p. 280.
52. Aneurin Bevan, 'How Ike can take the Lead', *Tribune*, 21 December 1956, pp. 1 and 12.
53. Aneurin Bevan, 'It must be World Control for all the Commercial Waterways', *Tribute*, 3 August 1956, p. 5.
54. Aneurin Bevan, 'Suez: Now What?', *Tribune*, 7 May 1957, p. 7.

55. *TIME*, 'The Middle East: Technically Friendly Enemy', 11 January 1954. Available at: https://content.time.com/time/subscriber/article/0,33009,819322,00.html.
56. Ibid.
57. K.M. Panikkar, *An Autobiography*, p. 293.
58. *TIME*, 'The Middle East: Technically Friendly Enemy', 11 January 1954. Available at: https://content.time.com/time/subscriber/article/0,33009,819322,00.html.
59. Panikkar noted the same for Japan: a strengthening of central authority with the assertion of the shogunate over feudal anarchy was matched by a rising xenophobia towards foreigners.
60. K.M. Panikkar, *Asia and Western Dominance: A Survey of the Vasco Da Gama Epoch of Asian History, 1498-1945*, Allen & Unwin, 1953, p. 165.
61. Ibid., pp. 375–376.
62. Kenneth Ballhatchet, 'Asian Nationalism and Christian Missions', *The International Review of Missions*, Vol. 46, No. 182, 1957, p. 202.
63. Filmer Northrop, 'Asia and Western Dominance by K.M. Panikkar', *The Far Eastern Quarterly*, Vol. 14, No. 2, 1955, pp. 262–263.
64. Guy Pauker, 'Panikkarism: The Highest Stage of Opportunism', *World Politics*, Vol. 7, No. 1, 1954.
65. Percival Spear, 'Asia and Western Dominance by K.M. Panikkar', *Asian Review*, Vol. 50, No. 182, 1954, p. 166.
66. Hugh Seton-Watson, 'Asian Nationalism', *Encounter*, Vol. 1, 1956, p. 73.

CHAPTER 52

1. V.P, Menon, *The Story of the Integration of the Indian States*, p. 564.
2. Ibid.
3. Ibid.
4. Report of the States Reorganisation Commission, p. 14. Available at https://www.mha.gov.in/sites/default/files/State%20Reorganisation%20Commisison%20Report%20of%201955_270614.pdf.
5. Robert D. King, *Nehru and the Language Politics of India*, Oxford University Press, 1997, p. 102.
6. *CWMG*, Vol. 90, p. 86.
7. Article 1, Constitution of India (1951).

8. Nehru to Rajendra Prasad, 16 and 17 February 1948. Quoted in Sarvepalli Gopal, *Jawaharlal Nehru: A Biography*, Vol. II, pp. 256–257.
9. Report of the Linguistic Provinces Commission (Constituent Assembly of India, 1948), paras. 146 and 147. Available at https://archive.org/details/dli.ministry.21082.
10. Patrick French, *Liberty or Death: India's Journey to Independence and Division*, p. 257.
11. Ramachandra Guha, *India After Gandhi: The History of the World's Largest Democracy*, Picador India, 2017, p. 214.
12. Selig Harrison, *India: The Most Dangerous Decades*, Princeton University Press, 1960, pp. 234–235.
13. *Times of India*, 24 February 1952.
14. Ramachandra Guha, *India After Gandhi: The History of the World's Largest Democracy*, p. 224.
15. For more, see K.V. Narayana Rao, *The Emergence of Andhra Pradesh*, Emescobooks, 2017.
16. Gandhi to T. Prakasam, 4 January 1947, in G.V. Subba Rao (ed.), *History of Andhra Movement*, The Committee of History of Andhra Movement, 1982, pp. 496–497. Also see *CWMG*, Vol. 86, p. 242.
17. Ramachandra Guha, *India After Gandhi: The History of the World's Largest Democracy*, p. 224.
18. Ibid.
19. P.R. Rao, *History of Modern Andhra*, Sterling Publishers, 1984, p. 130.
20. Sarvepalli Gopal, *Jawaharlal Nehru: A Biography*, Vol. 2, p. 259.
21. Jawaharlal Nehru, 2 July 1953, quoted from Madhav Khosla (ed.), *Letters For a Nation: From Jawaharlal Nehru to his Chief Ministers, 1947-1963*, p. 60.
22. *The Hindu*, 3 October 1953, p. 7.
23. Parliamentary Debates, 1953, Part II, Vol. 10, cols. 2,842-2,843. Available at: https://eparlib.nic.in/bitstream/123456789/893468/1/01_III_10-04-1953_p27_p52_PII.pdf.
24. K.M. Panikkar, *An Autobiography*, p. 297.
25. K.M. Panikkar (pseud. Chanakya), *The Indian Revolution*, pp. 155–156.
26. Ramachandra Guha, *India After Gandhi: The History of the World's Largest Democracy*, p. 221.
27. K.M. Panikkar, *An Autobiography*, p. 299.

28. For more, read B.V.R. Rao (ed.), *The Constitution and Language Politics of India*, B.R. Publishing Corporation, 2003, and Mahadev Apte, 'Multilingualism in India and its Sociopolitical Implications: An Overview', in William Jane O'Barr (ed.), *Language and Politics*, The Hague, 1976, pp. 141–164.
29. Ramachandra Guha, *India After Gandhi: The History of the World's Largest Democracy*, p. 220.
30. Nehru to Chief Ministers, 15 June 1954, in Madhav Khosla (ed.), *Letters For a Nation: From Jawaharlal Nehru to his Chief Ministers, 1947-1963*, p. 72.
31. K.M. Panikkar, *An Autobiography*, pp. 291–293.
32. Krishna Menon to Nehru, 28 September 1955, Krishna Menon Papers, NMML. Quoted in Jairam Ramesh, *A Chequered Brilliance: The Many Lives of V.K. Krishna Menon*, p. 352.
33. Ibid.
34. K.M. Panikkar, *An Autobiography*, p. 303.
35. Memorandum Submitted to the States Reorganisation Commission, quoted in Ramachandra Guha, *India After Gandhi: The History of the World's Largest Democracy*, p. 215.
36. K.M. Panikkar, *An Autobiography*, p. 307.
37. Report of the States Reorganisation Commission, pp. 244–252.
38. Ibid.
39. Ibid.
40. K.M. Panikkar, Appendix, Uttar Pradesh, Report of the States Reorganisation Commission, pp. 244–252.
41. Ibid.
42. Nehru to Vijayalakshmi Pandit, 13 September 1955, quoted from Sarvepalli Gopal, *Jawaharlal Nehru: A Biography*, Vol. II, p. 261.
43. Ibid.
44. Taya Zinkin, *Reporting India*, Chatto & Windus, 1962, p. 108.
45. Nehru, 23 January 1956, SF. No. 68, C.D. Deshmukh Papers, NMML.
46. *Times of India*, 26 February 1952.
47. Nehru to Chief Ministers, 16 January 1956, in Madhav Khosla (ed.), *Letters For a Nation: From Jawaharlal Nehru to his Chief Ministers, 1947-1963*, p. 76.
48. K.M. Panikkar, *An Autobiography*, p. 310.
49. Ibid.

50. Ibid.
51. Nehru to Krishna Menon, 9 November 1955, quoted in Jairam Ramesh, *A Chequered Brilliance: The Many Lives of V.K. Krishna Menon*, p. 354.
52. Nehru, Speech in Kumool, 9 December 1955, *SWJN*, Vol. 31, Series 2, pp. 26–27.
53. K.M. Panikkar, 'What Life Has Taught Me', p. 3.
54. K.M. Panikkar, *An Autobiography*, p. 304.
55. K.M. Panikkar, 'The New Dynamism', and 'Sanskrit in Modern India', in K.M. Panikkar, *The State and the Citizen*, Asia Publishing House, 1956, pp. 37–50 and pp. 124–135.
56. Ibid.
57. Nehru, Speech at the Kerala Kalamandalam, 26 December 1955, *SWJN*, Series 2, Vol. 31, p. 112.
58. Nehru to Panikkar, 2 November 1957, *SWJN*, Series 2, Vol. 40, pp. 301–303, and K.M. Panikkar, 'Technology and the Modern State', *The State and the Citizen*, pp. 63–71.
59. K.M. Panikkar, *Hindu Society at a Crossroads*, Asia Publishing House, 1955, and *Geographical Factors in Indian History*, Bharatiya Vidya Bhavan, 1955.
60. K.M. Panikkar, *Geographical Factors in Indian History*, p. 71.
61. Ibid., p. 90.
62. K.M. Panikkar, 'On National History', 1955, *The State and the Citizen*, pp. 94–95.
63. Ibid., pp. 97–98.
64. K.M. Panikkar, *Hindu Society at a Crossroads*, p. 57.
65. K.M. Panikkar, *An Autobiography*, p. 311.
66. Nehru in conversation with Tibor Mende, Fourth Session, 9 January 1956, *SWJN*, Series 2, Vol. 31, pp. 495–497.
67. Yorim Spoelder, *Visions of Greater India: Transimperial Knowledge and Anti-Colonial Nationalism, c. 1800-1960*, p. 313.

CHAPTER 53

1. Ibid., p. 315.
2. For more read Poul Duedahl, 'Selling Mankind: UNESCO and the Invention of Global History, 1945-1976', *Journal of World History*, Vol. 22, No. 1, 2011, pp. 101–133.

3. Romein's wife had been given Anne Frank's unpublished diary by Frank's father, Otto, who was unable to find a publisher for it. When Romein read the diary, he was struck by its poignant simplicity and wrote an enthusiastic article about it in a local Dutch paper. It was his article that triggered global interest in Anne Frank's diary and resulted in its subsequent publication.
4. Carl Burckhardt to K.M. Panikkar, 15 November 1954, AG 8-SEC-SCHM1-2-83.24, UNESCO. Quoted in Rita Paolini and Marco Elli, *Indian National Identity and Foreign Policy: Reevaluating the Career of K.M. Panikkar, 1894-1963*, p. 214.
5. Louis Porter, *Cold War Internationalism: The USSR in UNESCO, 1945-1967*, PhD Dissertation, University of North Carolina, 2018, pp. 363–380.
6. See Panikkar to Metraux, 22 February 1955, 13 June 1955 and 19 April 1961, and Panikkar to Carneiro, 3 June 1957. Both in AG 8-SEC-SCHM1-2-83.24, UNESCO. Both quoted in Rita Paolini and Marco Elli, *Indian National Identity and Foreign Policy: Reevaluating the Career of K.M. Panikkar, 1894-1963*, p. 214. Also see Ware, Panikkar & Romein, *History of Mankind: Cultural and Scientific Development*, Vol. VI: The Twentieth Century, Harper & Row, 1966.
7. 'Ware to Métraux', 2 August 1965, AG 8-SEC-SCHM1-2-83.23, UNESCO. 'Panikkar to Métraux', 16 August 1960, AG 8-SEC-SCHM1-2-83.24, UNESCO. 'Romein to Carneiro', 20 July 1960, AG 8-SEC-SCHM1-2-83.25, UNESCO. Quoted in Rita Paolini and Marco Elli, *Indian National Identity and Foreign Policy: Reevaluating the Career of K.M. Panikkar, 1894-1963*, p. 216.
8. Swapna Kyona Nayudu, 'India's Moment in the Suez Canal Crisis', 15 January 2018, *Hindu BusinessLine*. Available at: https://www.thehindubusinessline.com/todays-paper/tp-opinion/indias-moment-in-the-suez-canal-crisis/article9321343.ece.
9. Nehru to Vijayalakshmi Pandit, 9 August 1956, *SWJN*, Series 2, Vol. 34, pp. 402–403.
10. Ibid.
11. K.M. Panikkar, *An Autobiography*, p. 314.
12. Nehru to Panikkar, 30 March 1957, *SWJN*, Vol. 37, Series 2, p. 584.
13. Ibid.
14. See D. Chau, 'The French-Algeria War, 1954-1964: Communist China's Support for Algerian Independence', in D. Stoker (ed.),

Military Advising and Assistance: From Mercenaries to Privatisation, 1815-2007, Routledge, 2008, pp. 111–115.

15. Gregg A. Brazinsky, *Winning the Third World: Sino-American Rivalry during the Cold War*, University of North Carolina Press, 2017, pp. 178–180. It has been argued that American intervention in Lebanon provided an opportunity for Beijing to foster Arab-Chinese resistance against American imperialism, but the key shift was Beijing's dissatisfaction with moderate nationalists like Nasser. For more, see Jeffrey James Byrne, *Mecca of Revolution: Algeria, Decolonization and the Third World Order*, Oxford University Press, 2016.
16. Nehru to Panikkar, 4 February 1957, *SWJN*, Series 2, Vol. 36, p. 467.
17. Ibid.
18. Michael Brecher, *The New States of Asia*, Oxford University Press, 1963, pp. 210–211.
19. P.R. Kumaraswamy, *India's Israel Policy*, p. 195.
20. Sarvepalli Gopal, *Jawaharlal Nehru: A Biography*, Vol. 2, p. 277.
21. Panikkar, Note to N.R. Pillai, 21 July 1957, *SWJN*, Series 2, Vol. 38, p. 752.
22. K.M. Panikkar, *An Autobiography*, p. 330.
23. Nirupama Rao, *The Fractured Himalaya: India, Tibet, China, 1949-1962*, pp. 232–233.
24. Ibid., pp. 314–315. For more, see Alastair Lamb, 'The McMahon Line', in Alex McKay (ed.), *The History of Tibet*, Vol. 3*: The Tibetan Encounter with Modernity*, Curzon Press, 2003, pp. 101–126.
25. Ibid.
26. *SWJN*, Series 2, Vol. 36, pp. 594–601.
27. In his oral history transcript, R.K. Nehru says that the Chinese were "thinking in terms of a quiet exchange, in the sense that 'you occupy NEFA [now Arunachal Pradesh], we will keep on making our claims on our maps etc. We will occupy Aksai Chin, then some time later, we will settle it.'" R.K. Nehru, Oral History, Acc.No. 324, NMML. Also see Nirupama Rao, *The Fractured Himalaya: India, Tibet, China, 1949-1962*.
28. Nehru to Krishna Menon, 14 October 1958, quoted in Sarvepalli Gopal, *Jawaharlal Nehru: A Biography*, Vol. 3, p. 83.
29. Nehru to Vijayalakshmi Pandit, 5 July 1958, *SWJN*, Series 2, Vol. 43, p. 432.
30. K.M. Panikkar, *An Autobiography*, p. 334.

CHAPTER 54

1. English translation provided by the poet Ayappa Panicker at the Sahitya Akademi seminar on K.M. Panikkar, in 1994.
2. K.M. Panikkar, *An Autobiography*, p. 334.
3. Ibid.
4. Nirupama Rao, *The Fractured Himalaya: India, Tibet, China, 1949-1962*, p. 332.
5. Ibid.
6. Nirupama Rao, *The Fractured Himalaya: India, Tibet, China, 1949-1962*; Srinath Raghavan, *War and Peace in Modern India*, Permanent Black, 2009; Jeremy Friedman, *Shadow Cold War: The Sino-Soviet Competition for the Third World*, University of North Carolina Press, 2015; Avtar Singh Bhasin, *Nehru, Tibet and China*.
7. Rajya Sabha Debates, India and China, 8 December 1959, cols. 1813-7. Available at: https://eparlib.nic.in/handle/123456789/7.
8. Nehru, In the Rajya Sabha: India-China Relations, 9 December 1959, *SWJN*, Second Series, Vol. 55, pp. 303–318.
9. Ibid.
10. Ibid.
11. Lok Sabha Debates, 2nd series, vol. XI, col. 6312. Available at: https://eparlib.nic.in/handle/123456789/7.
12. K.M. Panikkar, *The Problems of Indian Defence*, Asia Publishing House, 1960.
13. Report of the Committee on Emotional Integration, Ministry of Education, Government of India, 1962. Available at: https://archive.org/details/dli.csl.2029/mode/2up.
14. K.M. Panikkar, *Essays on Educational Reconstruction in India*, Ganesh & Co, 1920, p. 128
15. Sampuranand to Nehru, 13 June 1962, *SWJN*, Series 2, Vol. 77, p. 870
16. Ibid.
17. Nehru to Algurai Shastri, 18 July 1957, *SWJN*, Series 2, Vol. 38, p. 819.
18. Nehru to Sampuranand, 26 June 1962, *SWJN*, Series 2, Vol.77, p. 250.
19. Nehru to B. Ramakrishna Rao, 20 October 1959, *SWJN*, Series 2, Vol. 53, pp. 368–369.

20. This anecdote and all that follows are from an email sent by R. Krishnan Nair, in April 2012 and shared with the author in April 2022.
21. Nehru, 'On the Death of Shri K.M. Panikkar', 11 December 1963, *SWJN*, Series 2, Vol. 84, p. 684.

Bibliography

List of Archives

British Library, London
United Kingdom National Archives, Kew Garden (NAUK)
National Archives of India, New Delhi (NAI)
Prime Minister's Memorial Museum and Library Society, New Delhi (PMML) *or*
  Nehru Memorial Museum and Library (NMML)
Punjab State Archive, Patiala (PSA)
Maharaja Ganga Singhji Trust Archive, Bikaner (MGSTA)
Rajasthan State Archive, Bikaner (RSAB)
Central Intelligence Agency (CIA)

Private & Public Papers

K.M. Panikkar Private Papers, NAI
Panikkar Estate (family-owned)
M.R. Jayakar, NAI
B.N. Rau Papers, NMML
C.D. Deshmukh Papers, NMML
C. Rajagopalachari Papers, NMML
H.V.R. Iyengar Oral History, NMML
Ganpat Rai Papers, NMML
V. Srinivasa Sastri Papers, NMML
Jawaharlal Nehru Papers, NMML
AICC Papers, NMML
AISPC Papers, NMML
Gopalaswami Ayyengar Papers, NMML
Federal Papers, NMML
Vijayalakshmi Pandit Papers, NMML
V.K. Krishna Menon Papers, NMML
Mohammad Ali Jauhar Papers, NMML

Mirza Ismail Papers, NMML
B.S. Moonje Papers, NMML
Irwin Collection, University of York
Mountbatten Papers, University of Southampton
Templewood Collection, University of Cambridge
Howell Arthur Gwynne Collection, Bodleian Archives
Willingdon Private Collections, British Library
Findlater-Stewart Collection, British Library
Robert J. Stopford Papers, British Library

Newspaper/Magazine Archives

The Hindu
The Daily Telegraph
The New York Times
Dawn
TIME Magazine
LIFE Magazine

Selected Bibliography

G.R. Abhyankar, *Problem of Indian States* (Aryabhushan Press, 1928)

Dean Acheson, *Present at the Creation: My Years in the State Department* (W.W. Norton & Company, 1988)

Rehana Ahmed & Sumita Mukherjee, *South Asian Resistances in Britain, 1858–1947* (Bloomsbury Books, 2011)

Harrison Akins, *Conquering the Maharajas: India's Princely States and the End of Empire, 1930–1950* (Manchester University Press, 2023)

A. Aiyappan, *Social Revolution in a Kerala Village: A Study in Culture Change* (Asia Publishing House, 1966)

Leo Amery, *The Empire at Bay: The Leo Amery Diaries 1929–1945* (Hutchinson, 1988)

Rakesh Ankit, *The Kashmir Conflict: From Empire to the Cold War 1945–1966* (Routledge 2016)

Michael Anderson, *Pacific Dreams: The Institute of Pacific Relations and the Struggle for the Mind of Asia*, PhD dissertation (University of Texas, 2009)

Richard Ashton, *British Policy towards Indian States* (Curzon, 1982)

Maulana Abul Kalam Azad, *India Wins Freedom* (Orient Blackswan, 1968)

Sukanya Banerjee, *Becoming Imperial Citizens: Indians in the Late Victorian Empire* (Duke University Press, 2010)

Tarasankar Banerjee, *Sardar K. M. Panikkar, the Profile of a Historian. A Study in Modern Indian Historiography* (Ratna Prakashan, 1977)

Robert Barnes, *The US, the UN and the Korean War* (I.B. Tauris, 2014)

Fredrik Barth, *The Last Wali of Swat: An Autobiography* (Orchid Press Publishing Limited, 1995)

Gearoid Barry, *The Disarmament of Hatred: Marc Sangnier, French Catholicism and the Legacy of the First World War, 1914–1945* (Palgrave MacMillan, 2012)

Narayani Basu, *VP Menon: The Unsung Architect of Modern India* (Simon & Schuster India, 2020)

Shrabani Basu, *For King and Another Country: Indian Soldiers on the Western Front 1914–1918*, (Bloomsbury Books, 2015)

Manu Bhagavan,

-(ed.), *India and the Cold War* (The University of North Carolina Press, 2019)

- *Vijayalakshmi Pandit* (Penguin Randomhouse India, 2023)

Avtar Singh Bhasin, *Nehru, Tibet and China* (Penguin, 2021)

Shyam Krishn Bhatnagar, *History of the M.A.O. College, Aligarh* (Asia Publishing House, 1969)

Nicolas Blarel, *The Evolution of India's Israel Policy: Continuity, Change and Compromise since 1922* (Oxford University Press, 2014)

Christopher Bayly, *The New Cambridge History of India, Vol. 21: Indian Society and the Making of British Empire* (Cambridge University Press, 1988).

Sisir Kumar Bose & Saugata Bose (eds), *Subhas Chandra Bose: The Alternative Leadership, Speeches, Articles, Statements and Letters, June 1939–1941* (Permanent Black, 1998)

Julia Boyd, -*A Dance with the Dragon: The Vanished World of Peking's Foreign Colony* (I.B. Tauris Books, 2012)

- *Travellers in the Third Reich: The Rise of Fascism, 1919–1945* (Pegasus Books, 2018)

Gregg A. Brazinsky, *Winning the Third World: Sino-American Rivalry during the Cold War*, (University of North Carolina Press, 2017)

Michael Brecher, *Nehru: A Political Biography* (Oxford University Press, 1956)

Judith Brown,-*Gandhi's Rise to Power: Indian Politics, 1915–1922* (Cambridge University Press, 1972)

-*Modern India: The Origins of an Asian Democracy* (Oxford University Press, 1985)

Jeffrey James Byrne, *Mecca of Revolution: Algeria, Decolonization and the Third World Order* (Oxford University Press, 2016)

James Cameron,

-*Point of Departure: An Experiment in Autobiography* (Grafton Books, 1969)

-*An Indian Summer: A Personal Experience of India* (Penguin India, 2000)

Alan Campbell-Johnson, *Mission with Mountbatten* (Jaico Publishing House, 1951)

Miranda Carter, *The Three Emperors: Three Cousins, Three Empires & The Road to War* (Penguin Books, 2009)

B.J. Chacko (ed.), *Sardar K. M. Panikkar. Shashtyabdapoorthy Souvenir* (Mathrubhumi Press, 1954)

Bipan Chandra et al., *India's Struggle for Independence* (Penguin Books India, 1989)

Jung Chang, *Big Sister, Little Sister, Red Sister* (Jonathan Cape, 2019)

John Charmley, *Churchill: The End of Glory: A Political Biography*, (Harcourt, 1992)

Lucy Chester, *Borders and Conflict in South Asia: The Radcliffe Boundary Commission and the Partition of Punjab* (Palgrave MacMillan, 2009)

Peter Clarke, *The Cripps Version: The Life of Sir Stafford Cripps, 1889–1952* (Allen Lane, 2002)

Sujit Choudhry et al. (eds), *The Oxford Handbook of the Indian Constitution* (Oxford University Press, 2016)

P. L. Chudgar, *Indian Princes under British Protection: A Study of their Personal Rule, their Constitutional Position and their Future* (Williams & Norgate Ltd., 1929)

Elizabeth Cooper, *The Harim and the Purdah: Studies of Oriental Women* (Century Books, 1915)

Ian Copland, *The Princes of India in the End Game of Empire* (Cambridge University Press, 1999. Published online in 2009)

Margaret Cousins, *The Awakening of Asian Womanhood* (Ganesh & Co, 1922)

Bhagwan Dass Dua & Mahendra Prasad Singh (eds), *Indian Federalism in the New Millennium* (Manohar Books, 2003)

Jarmani Das, *Maharaja* (Hind Pocket Books, 2008)

Amit Das Gupta & Lüthi, Lorenz (eds), *The Sino-Indian War of 1962* (Routledge, 2017)

Amit Das Gupta,

-*Serving India: A Political Biography of Subimal Dutt, 1903–1992, India's Longest Serving Foreign Secretary* (Manohar Books, 2017)

-*The Indian Civil Service and Indian Foreign Policy, 1923–1961* (Routledge, 2021)

Rohit De, *A People's Constitution* (Princeton University Press, 2018)

Anne de Courcy,

-*Margot At War* (Weidenfeld & Nicolson, 2015)

-*Diana Mosley: Mitford Beauty, British Fascist, Hitler's Angel* (HarperCollins, 2004)

Sharada Dwivedi, *The Automobiles of the Maharajahs* (Om Books, 2003)

Rosita Forbes, *India of the Princes* (E.P. Dutton & Company, 1941)

Michael Fisher, *Indirect Rule in India: Residents and the Residency System, 1764–1858* (Oxford University Press, 1998)

Yvonne Fitzroy, *Courts & Camps in India: Viceregal Tours, 1921–1926* (Methuen & Co Ltd, 1926)

Patrick French, *Liberty or Death: India's Journey to Independence and Division* (HarperCollins, 1997)

Jeremy Friedman, *Shadow Cold War: The Sino-Soviet Competition for the Third World* (University of North Carolina Press, 2015)

John Lewis Gaddis, *Strategies of Containment: A Critical Appraisal of American National Security Policy during the Cold War* (Oxford University Press, 2005)

K.M. George, *A Survey of Malayalam Literature* (Asia Publishing House, 1968)

David Lloyd George, *War Memoirs*, Vol. II (Little, Brown & Company, 1933)

Durba Ghosh, *Gentlemanly Terrorists: Political Violence and the Colonial State in India, 1919–1947* (Cambridge University Press, 2017)

Dalai Lama, *Freedom in Exile: The Autobiography of the Dalai Lama* (HarperCollins, 1991)

Yitzshak Gerberg, *The Changing Nature of Israeli-Indian Relations, 1948–2005*, PhD Dissertation (University of South Africa, 2008)

Hamilton Gibb, *Mohammedanism* (Oxford University Press, 1996)

Martin Gilbert, *The Churchill Collection* (Hillsdale College Press, 2013)

Rami Ginat, *Egypt and the Struggle for Power in Sudan: From World War II to Nasserism* (Cambridge University Press, 2017)

John Glendevon, *Viceroy at Bay: Linlithgow in India, 1936–1943* (Collins, 1971)

Vijay Gokhale, *Crosswinds: Nehru, Zhou and the Anglo-American Competition over China* (Vintage Books, 2024)

Melvyn Goldstein, *A History of Modern Tibet, 1913–1951: The Demise of the Lamaist State* (University of California Press, 1989)

Sarvepalli Gopal, *Jawaharlal Nehru: A Biography: 1947–1956* (Oxford University Press, 1979)

Leonard A. Gordon, *Brothers Against the Raj: A Biography of Indian Nationalists Sarat and Subhas Chandra Bose* (Viking Books, 1990)

Joel Gordon: *Nasser's Blessed Movement: Egypt's Free Officers and the July Revolution*, (Oxford University Press, 1992).

J.S. Grewal, *Master Tara Singh in Indian History: Colonialism, Nationalism and the Politics of Sikh Identity* (Oxford University Press, 2017)

Ramachandra Guha, *India after Gandhi: The History of the World's Largest Democracy* (Picador India, 2017)

Karunakar Gupta, *Sino-Indian Relations, 1948–1952: Role of K.M. Panikkar* (Minerva, 1987)

Bérénice Guyot-Réchard, *Shadow States: India, China and the Himalayas, 1910–1962* (Cambridge University Press, 2017)

Nisid Hajari, *Midnight's Furies: The Deadly Legacy of India's Partition* (Penguin Random House India, 2016)

David Halberstam, *The Coldest Winter: America and the Korean War* (Hachette, 2008)

Lezlee Brown Halper and Stefan Halper, *Tibet: An Unfinished Story* (Hurst Publishers: 2013)

Cicely Hamilton, *Modern Germanies as Seen by an Englishwoman* (Dent & Sons, 1931)

Selig Harrison, *India: The Most Dangerous Decades* (Princeton University Press, 1960)

Mohammad Hatta, *Mohammad Hatta, Indonesian Patriot: Memoirs* (Gunung Agung, 1981)

Edmund Heward, *The Great and the Good: A Life of Lord Radcliffe* (Barry Rose Publishers, 1994)

Rima Hooja: *Crusader for Self-Rule: Tej Bahadur Sapru & the Indian National Movement*, (Rawat Books, 1999)

Aya Ikegame, *Princely India Re-imagined* (Routledge, 2013)

James Jankowski, *Nasser's Egypt, Arab Nationalism, and the United Arab Republic* (Rienner, 2002)

Godfrey H. Jansen,

-*Zionism, Israel and Asian Nationalism* (Institute for Palestine Studies, 1971)

-*Militant Islam* (Harper & Row, 1979)

Robin Jeffrey,

-(ed.) *People, Princes and Paramount Power: Society and Politics in the Indian Princely States* (Oxford University Press, 1978)

-*The Decline of Nair Dominance, Society and Politics in Travancore, 1847–1908* (Manohar Publishers, 1994).

Anees Jung, *Night of the New Moon* (Penguin Books, 1993)

Triloki Nath Kaul, *Diplomacy in Peace and War: Recollections and Reflections* (Vikas Publishing, 1979)

Caroline Keen, *Princely India and the British* (I.B. Tauris, 2012)
Madhav Khosla, *India's Founding Moment* (Harvard University Press, 2020)
Mary Elizabeth King, *Gandhian Nonviolent Struggle and Untouchability in South India: The 1924–1925 Vykom Satyagraha and Mechanisms of Change* (Oxford University Press, 2020)
Robert King, *Nehru and the Language Politics of India* (Oxford University Press, 1997)
Krishna Kodesia, *The Problems of Linguistic States in India* (Sterling, 1969)
Balraj Krishna, *Sardar Vallabhbhai Patel: India's Iron Man* (Rupa Publications, 2005)
Raj Kumar, *Women and the Indian Freedom Struggle*, Vol. 6 (Pointer Publishers, 1998)
R. Nalenan, *Arnold Mononutu* (Gunung Agung, 1981)
K.V. Narayana Rao, *The Emergence of Andhra Pradesh* (Emescobooks:, 2017)
Prem Nath Bazaz, *Struggle for Freedom in Kashmir* (Kashmir Publishing House, 1954)
Swapna Kona Nayudu, *The Nehru Years. Indian Non-Alignment as the Critique, Discourse and Practice of Security (1947–1964)*, Ph.D. Dissertation (King's College, 2016)
P.R. Kumaraswamy, *India's Israel Policy* (Columbia University Press, 2010)
Shompa Lahiri, *Indians in Britain: Anglo-Indian Encounters, Race and Identity, 1880–1930* (Frank Cass, 2000)
Alastair Lamb, *Tibet, China and India 1914–1950: A History of Imperial Diplomacy* (Roxford Books, 1989)
Guy Laron, *Origins of the Suez Crisis. Postwar Development Diplomacy and the Struggle over Third World Industrialization, 1945–1956* (The Johns Hopkins University Press, 2013)
Deborah Lavin, *From Empire to International Commonwealth: A Biography of Lionel Curtis* (Clarendon Books, 1995)
Stephen Legg, *Round Table Geographies: Constituting Colonial India* (Cambridge University Press, 2023)
Sir Arthur Cunningham Lothian, *Kingdoms of Yesterday* (John Murray, 1951)
William Louis, *Ends of British Imperialism: The Scramble for Empire, Suez, and Decolonization* (I.B. Tauris, 2006)
Verney Lovett, *History of the Indian Nationalist Movement* (Murray, 1920)
Ben MacIntyre, *Colditz: Prisoners of the Castle* (Penguin Random House, 2023)
Tanvi Madan,
Fateful Triangle. How China Shaped U.S.-India Relations during the Cold War (The Brookings Institution, 2020)
With an Eye to the East: The China Factor and the US-India Relationship, 1949–1979, Ph.D. Dissertation (University of Texas, 2012)
Sneh Mahajan, *Foreign Policy of Colonial India, 1900–1947* (Routledge, 2018).
Livia Manera Sambuy, *In Search of Amrit Kaur,* translated by Todd Portnowitz (Chatto & Windus, 2023)
Philip Mason, *A Shaft of Sunlight: Memories of a Varied Life* (Vikas Publishing House, 1978)
Samuel Mateer, *Native Life in Travancore* (W.H. Allen & Co, 1883)
Mundapallil Oommen Mathai, *Reminiscences of the Nehru Age* (Vikas Publishing House, 1978)

Margaret MacMillan, *Paris 1919: Six Months that Changed the World* (Random House, 2003)

Paul McGarr, *The Cold War in South Asia: Britain, the United States and the Indian Subcontinent, 1945–1965* (Cambridge University Press, 2013)

John McLeod, *Sovereignty, Power, Control: Politics in the States of Western India 1916–1947* (Brill, 1999)

Alex McKay (ed.), *The History of Tibet, Vol. 3: The Tibetan Encounter with Modernity* (Curzon Press, 2003)

Stephen McKenna, *While I Remember* (George H. Doran & Company, 1921)

Roderick MacLean, *Royalty and Diplomacy in Europe, 1890–1914* (Cambridge University Press, 2001)

Robert McMahon, *The Cold War on the Periphery: The United States, India, and Pakistan* (Columbia University Press, 1994).

Sean McMeekin, *The Red Millionaire: A Political Biography of Willi Munzenberg, Moscow's Secret Propaganda Tsar in the West* (Yale University Press, 2005)

Alappat Sreedhara Menon,

-*Kerala and the Freedom Struggle* (D.C. Books, 1997)

-*A Survey of Kerala History* (D.C. Books, 2007).

Dilip Menon, *Caste, Nationalism and Communism in South India. Malabar 1900–1948* (Cambridge University Press, 1994)

K.P.S. Menon, *Many Worlds: An Autobiography* (Oxford University Press, 1965)

V.P. Menon,

-*The Story of the Integration of the Indian States* (Orient Longman, 1957)

-*The Transfer of Power in India* (Orient Longman, 1957)

Leonard Mosley, *The Last Days of the British Raj* (Weidenfeld & Nicolson, 1961)

Aloys Michel, *The Indus Rivers: A Study of the Effects of Partition* (Yale University Press, 1967)

Gail Minault, *The Khilafat Movement: Religious Symbolism and Political Mobilization in India* (Columbia University Press, 1982)

N. Miskovic, H. Fischer-Tine, N. Boskovska (eds), *The Non-Aligned Movement and Cold War: Delhi-Bandung-Belgrade* (Routledge, 2015)

Yu Ming-Shaw, *An American Missionary in China: John Leighton Stuart and Chinese-American Relations* (Harvard University Press, 1992)

Chaudhary Mohammad Ali, *Emergence of Pakistan* (Columbia University Press, 1967)

Ghulam Mohammad Bakshi, *Kashmir Today* (Bombay Provincial Congress Committee, 1946)

Penderel Moon,

-(ed.) *Wavell: The Viceroy's Journal* (Oxford University Press, 1973)

-*Divide and Quit: An Eyewitness Account of the Partition of India*, Vol. 2 (Oxford University Press, 1988)

Ottoline Morrell, *Early Memoirs*, (Faber & Faber, 1963)

Robin Moore, *The Crisis of Indian Unity, 1917–1950* (Oxford University Press, 1974)

Lucy Moore, *Maharanis: The Lives and Times of Three Generations of Indian Princesses* (Viking Books, 2004)

Jessica Namakkal, *Unsettling Utopia: The Making and Unmaking of French India* (Columbia University Press, 2021)

Bhola Nath Mullik, *My Years with Nehru: The Chinese Betrayal* (Allied Publishers, 1971)

B.R. Nanda, *Mahatma Gandhi: A Biography* (Oxford University Press, 1958)

Kalidas Nag,

-*Greater India* (The Book Centre Private Ltd., 1960)

-*Memoirs* (Writer's Workshop, 1991)

Konniyoor R. Narendranath, *Sardar Panikkar: His Life and Times* (Publication Division, Ministry of Information and Broadcasting, 1998)

Kunwar Natwar Singh, *The Magnificent Maharaja: The Life and Times of Maharaja Bhupinder Singh, 1891–1938* (Rupa Publications, 2012)

Jawaharlal Nehru:

-*Toward Freedom: An Autobiography* (Beacon Press, 1941)

-*An Autobiography with Musings on Recent Events in India* (Bodley Head, 1989)

-(ed.) *A Bunch of Old Letters* (Penguin, 2005)

Feriel Nissa Kissoon, *The Creole Indian: The Emergence of East Indian Civil Society in Trinidad and Tobago, c.1897–1945*, Ph.D. Dissertation (King's College, 2014)

William Jane O'Barr (ed.), *Language and Politics* (The Hague, 1976)

Daniel Oakman, *Facing Asia: A History of the Colombo Plan* (ANU Press, 2010)

Nicholas Owen, *The British Left and India: Metropolitan Anti-Imperialism, 1885–1947* (Oxford University Press, 2007)

Rita Paolini and Marco Elli, *Indian National Identity and Foreign Policy: Reevaluating the Career of K.M. Panikkar, 1894–1963* (Palgrave MacMillan, 2023)

Ayyappa Panikkar,

-*K.M. Panikkar* (Madras: MacMillan India, 1982)

-*Kavalam*, from *Pathumanippookkal* (Poetry at Midnight), translated by P. Ravindran Nayar (Folio Books, 2010)

Makarand Paranjpe (ed.), *Sarojini Naidu: Selected Letters, 1890s to 1940s* (Kali For Women, 1996)

P.K. Parameswaran Nair, *History of the Malayalam Literature* (Sahitya Akademi, 1967)

G. Parthasarathi (ed.), *Letters to Chief Ministers, 1947–1949*, Vol. I (Oxford University Press, 1998)

S.H Patil, *The Congress Party and Princely States* (Himalaya Publishing House, 1981)

James Foreman Peck, *A History of the World Economy: International Economic Relations since 1850* (Harvester Wheatsheaf, 1995)

Baron Jean Pellanc, *Diamonds and Dust*, translated by Stuart Gilbert (John Murray, 1936)

C.H. Philips (ed.), *Historians of India, Pakistan and Ceylon*, (Oxford University Press, 1961)

D. Nichols Pigache, *Café Royal Days* (Hutchinson Books, 1934)

Manu Pillai, *False Allies: India's Maharajahs in the Age of Ravi Verma* (Juggernaut Books, 2021)

Velu Ramon Pillai and Puthenveetil Govinda Kerala Panikkar, *Land Reclamation in Kerala* (Asia Publishing House, 1965)

Ben Pimlott (ed.), *The Second World War Diary of Hugh Dalton 1940–1945* (Cape Books, 1986)

Syed Sharifuddin Pirzada, *The Collected Works of Quaid-e-Azam Mohammad Ali Jinnah* (East and West Publishing Company, 1986)

Richard Popplewell, *Intelligence and Imperial Defence: British Intelligence and the Defence of the Indian Empire, 1904–1924* (Routledge Books, 1995)

Louis Porter, *Cold War Internationalism: The USSR in UNESCO, 1945–1967*, PhD Dissertation (University of North Carolina, 2018)

Tanguturi Prakasam, *The Journey of my life: An Autobiography* (Prakasam Institute of Development Studies, 1992)

Jean-Baptiste Preshant More, *Towards Freedom in Pondicherry: Society, Economy and Politics under French Rule, 1816–1962* (Routledge, 2023)

Sunil Purushottham, *Sovereignty, Federation and Constituent Power in Interwar India* (Duke University Press, 2020)

Srinath Raghavan, *War and Peace in Modern India: A Strategic History of the Nehru Years* (Permanent Black, 2010).

David Malone, C. Raja Mohan and Srinath Raghavan (ed.), *The Oxford Handbook of Indian Foreign Policy* (Oxford University Press, 2015)

A. Raghu, *Duty, Destiny and Glory: The Life of Sir CP Ramaswami Aiyar* (Orient Blackswan, 2014)

Barbara Ramusack,

-*The New Cambridge History of India, vol. III.6: The Indian Princes and Their States* (Cambridge University Press, 2004).

-*The Princes of India in the Twilight of Empire* (University of Cincinnati, 1978)

B.V.R. Rao (ed.), *The Constitution and Language Politics of India* (B.R. Publishing Corporation, 2003)

Nirupama Rao, *The Fractured Himalaya: India, Tibet, China, 1949–1962* (Penguin Random House India, 2022)

P.R. Rao, *History of Modern Andhra* (Sterling Publishers, 1984)

P. Rajaraman, *The Justice Party: A Historical Perspective (1916–1937)* (Poompozhil Publishers, 1988)

Jairam Ramesh, *A Chequered Brilliance. The Many Lives of V. K. Krishna Menon* (Penguin Random House India, 2019).

T.K. Ravindran, *Vaikkam Satyagraha and Gandhi* (Sri Institute of Social and Cultural Development, 1975)

S.A. Gowher Rizvi, *Linlithgow in India: A Study of British Policy and the Political Impasse in India, 1936–1943* (Royal Historical Society, 1970)

J.N. Sahni,

-*The Lid Off: 50 Years of Indian Politics* (Deep Publications, 1971)

-*Truth About the Indian Press* (Bombay Allied, 1974)

Kanwar Sain, *Reminiscences of an Engineer* (Young Asia Publications, 1978)

Priyasha Saksena, *Sovereignty, International Law and the Princely States of Colonial South Asia* (Oxford University Press, 2023)

Narendra Sarila, *Once a Prince of Sarila: Of Palaces and Tiger Hunts, of Nehrus and Mountbattens* (I.B. Tauris, 2008)

Anil Seal, *The Emergence of Indian Nationalism* (Cambridge University Press, 1968)

Tansen Sen, *India, China, and the World. A Connected History* (Rowman & Littlefield, 2017)

Adrian Sever (ed.), *Documents and Speeches on the Indian Princely States* (B.R. Publishing Corporation, 1985)

Mehtab Ali Shah, *The Foreign Policy of Pakistan: Ethnic Impacts on Diplomacy, 1971–1994* (I.B. Tauris, 1997)

Tsering Shakya, *The Dragon in the Land of Snows. A History of Modern Tibet since 1947* (Columbia University Press, 1999).

Phool Kumar Sharma, *Political Aspects of States Reorganization in India* (Mohini, 1969).

Farzana Shaikh, *Community and Consensus in Islam: Muslim Representation in Colonial India, 1860–1947* (Imprint One, 2012)

Akita Shigeru et al. (eds), *The Transformation of the International Order of Asia. Decolonization, the Cold War, and the Colombo Plan* (Routledge, 2014).

Karan Singh, *Heir Apparent: An Autobiography* (Oxford University Press, 1984)

Mohinder Singh, *The Akali Struggle: A Retrospect* (Atlantic Books, 1988)

Bhupinder Singh, *Public Pronouncements by His Highness the Maharaja Dhiraj of Patiala in connection with the Indian States Committee* (Spottiswoode, Ballantyne and Co., 1928)

John Allsebrook Simon, *Retrospect: The Memoirs of the Rt. Honourable Viscount Simon* (Hutchinson Books, 1952)

F.W.F. Smith, *Halifax: The Life of Lord Halifax* (Hamilton House Publishers, 1965)

Simon Smith (ed.), *Reassessing Suez 1956* (Ashgate, 2008).

Vincent Smith, *Oxford History of India* (Oxford University Press, 1920)

Warren Smith, *Tibetan Nation: A History of Tibetan Nationalism and Sino-Tibetan Relations* (Westview Press, 1997)

Reginald Sorenson, *My Impressions of India*, (Meridian Books, 1947)

Ian Stephens, Pakistan (Ernest Benn, 1967)

Klaas Stutje, *Behind the Banner of Unity: Nationalism and Anti-colonialism among Indonesian Students in Europe, 1917–1931*, Ph.D Thesis (University of Amsterdam, 2016)

G.V. Subba Rao (ed.), *History of Andhra Movement* (The Committee of History of Andhra Movement, 1982)

G.M.D. Sufi, *Kashir: Being a History of Kashmir from the Earliest Times to Our Own*, Vol. I (Light & Life Publishers, 1974)

Abidaa Sultan, *Memoirs of a Rebel Princess* (Oxford University Press, 2004)

Yorim Spoelder, *Visions of Greater India: Transimperial Knowledge and Anti-Colonial Nationalism, c. 1800–1960* (Cambridge University, 2024)

C. Stahn, *The Law and Practice of International Territorial Administration: Versailles to Iraq and Beyond* (Cambridge University Press, 2008)

D. Stoker (ed.), *Military Advising and Assistance: From Mercenaries to Privatisation 1815–2007*, (Routledge, 2008)

Rabindranath Tagore, *Greater India* (S. Ganesan, 1921)

J. Lee Thompson, *A Wider Patriotism: Alfred Milner and the British Empire*, (Pickering & Chatto, 2008)

Eve Troutt Powell, *A Different Shade of Colonialism. Egypt, Great Britain, and the Mastery of the Sudan* (University of California Press, 2003).

Harry Truman, *Years of Trial and Hope* (Doubleday & Company, 1956).

Barbara Tuchman, *The Guns of August* (MacMillan Books, 1962)

S.Y. Qureishi, *An Undocumented Wonder: The Great Indian Election* (Penguin, 2019)

C.J. Phillips & Mary Wainwright (eds), *The Partition of India, Policies and Perspectives* (Allen & Unwin, 1970)

Chaim Weizmann, *Trial and Error: The Autobiography of Chaim Weizmann* (Harper & Brothers, 1949)

Woodrow Wyatt, *Confessions of an Optimist* (HarperCollins Publishers, 1985)

Stanley Wolpert, *Shameful Flight: The Last Years of the British Empire in India* (Oxford University Press, 2006)

Roland Wild, *Ranji: The Biography of Colonel His Highness Shri Sir Ranjitsinhji Vibhaji* (Rich & Cowan, 1934)

Vanya Vaidehi Bhargav, *Being Hindu, Being Indian: Lala Lajpat Rai's Ideas of Nationhood* (Viking Books, 2024)

Juliette Veillier-Duray with Leonie Burunel, *Mahatma Gandhi* (Ganesh Publishers, 1928)

Jolita Zabarskait⊠, *Greater India and the Indian Expansionist Imagination, c. 1885–1965: The Rise and Decline of the Idea of a Lost Hindu Empire* (DeGruyter Oldenbourg, 2023)

A. Moin Zaidi & Shaheda Gufran Zaidi (eds), *Encyclopaedia of the Indian National Congress* (S. Chand & Co, 1976)

Philip Zeigler, *Mountbatten: An Official Biography* (Weidenfeld & Nicolson, 2001)

Taya Zinkin, *Reporting India* (Chatto & Windus, 1962)

Maurice and Taya Zinkin: *Britain and India: Requiem for Empire* (Chatto & Windus, 1964)

John Zubryzcki: *Dethroned: Patel, Menon and the Integration of Princely India* (Juggernaut Books, 2023)

Parliamentary Debates

Constituent Assembly Debates
Lok Sabha Debates
Rajya Sabha Debates

Collections of Official Documents

The Collected Works of Mahatma Gandhi, (The Publication Division, Ministry of Information and Broadcasting, 1958–1984)

Benegal Shiva Rao (ed.), *The Framing of India's Constitution: Select Documents*, (Indian Institute of Public Administration, 1966–1968)

Nicholas Mansergh & E.W.R. Lumby (eds.): *Constitutional Relations between Great Britain and India, Transfer of Power, 1942–1947*, (HMSO, 1970–1983)

Sir Maurice Gwyer & A. Appadorai (ed.), *Speeches and Documents on the Indian Constitution, 1921–1947*, (Oxford University Press, 1957)

Sarvepalli Gopal et al. (eds.), *Selected Works of Jawaharlal Nehru*, (Jawaharlal Nehru Memorial Fund, 1972–2020)

Durga Das (ed.) *Sardar Patel Correspondence 1945–1950*, (Navjivan Publishing House, 1973)

Madhav Khosla (ed.), *Letters for a Nation: From Jawaharlal Nehru to His Chief Ministers 1947–1963*, (Penguin, 2015)

Avtar Singh Bhasin (ed.), *India-China Relations 1947–2000. A Documentary Study*, (Geetika Publishers, 2018)

Records of the Office of Chinese Affairs, 1945–1955 Collection, National Archives (USA), in *Gale Archives Unbound*

S.R. Ashton, G. Bennett & K. Hamilton (eds), *Documents on British Policy Overseas, 1945–1950,* Series I, Vol. VIII (Routledge Books, 2014)

For A United India: Speeches of Sardar Patel 1947–1950, (Publications Division, Ministry of Information and Broadcasting, Government of India, 1967)

Foreign Relations of the United States (Office of the Historian, Foreign Service Institute, US Department of State)

Unpublished Sources

P. Velayudha Panicker, *A Sardar from Kavalam*

Diary of the Reverend George Woodford, United States Naval Archive

H.V. Hodson, *Autobiography*

Journal Articles, Newspaper Articles & Book Chapters

S.R. Ashton, 'Imperialism and Nationalism in South-East Asia', in Judith Brown (ed.) *The Oxford History of the British Empire*, Vol. 4: The twentieth century, (Oxford University Press, 1999)

Roger Nash Baldwin, 'The Capital of the Men Without a Country', *The Survey*, 1 August 1927, pp. 460–467

Tarasankar Banerjee, 'Sardar K.M. Panikkar' in R.C. Majumdar (ed.), *Historians and Historiography in Modern India*, (Institute of Historical Studies, 1973)

Kenneth Ballhatchet, 'Asian Nationalism and Christian Missions', *The International Review of Missions*, Vol. 46, No. 182, (1957), pp. 201–204.

A.L. Basham, 'Modern Historians on Ancient India', in C.H. Philips (ed.), *Historians of India, Pakistan and Ceylon*, (Oxford University Press, 1961)

Saul Dubow, 'Colonial Nationalism, the Milner Kindergarten and the rise of South Africanism, 1902–1910', *History Workshop Journal*, Vol. 43 (1997), pp. 53–85

Poul Duedahl, 'Selling Mankind: UNESCO and the Invention of Global History, 1945–1976', *Journal of World History*, Vol. 22, No. 1, (2011), pp. 101–133

'Een verblijdende Phase uit onze nationale beweging', *Indonesia Merdeka*, Vol. 3 (1925)

"Extract van de lezing van KM Panikkar getiteld 'the necessity of Asiatic Unity' gehouden op de Alg. Vergadering te Den Haag," Indonesia Merdeka, 4.3–4, (June-July 1926)

Michael Goebel, 'The Capital of the Men Without a Country: Migrants and Anticolonialism in Interwar Paris', *The American Historical Review*, Vol. 121, No. 5 (2016), pp. 1444–1467

Mohammad Hatta, 'Non-cooperation', *Indonesia Merdeka*, Vol. 8, No.4, July 1930

Maharaja of Alwar, 'The Princes and Dominion Status', *Asiatic Review*, Vol. 26, January 1930

Ramachandra Guha, 'Democracy's Biggest Gamble: India's First Free Elections in 1952', *World Policy Journal*, Vol. 19, No. 1, (2002), pp. 95–103

Karunakar Gupta, 'Hidden History of the Sino-Indian Frontier, 1947–1954', *Economic and Political Weekly*, Vol. 9, No. 18, (4 May 1974), pp. 721–726

V. Hardas, 'A Brief Life-Sketch', in N. Dixit (ed.), *Dharmaveer Dr. B.S. Moonje, Commemorative Volume*, (Centenary Commemorative Committee, Nagpur, 1972)

Robin Jeffrey, 'Temple-Entry Movement in Travancore, 1860–1940', *Social Scientist*, Vol. 4, No. 8 (1976), pp. 3–27

P.R. Kumaraswamy, 'K.M. Panikkar and Indo-Israeli Relations', *International Studies*, Vol. 32, No. 3 (1995), pp. 327–337.

John Last, 'The Prince of Wales' Trip to India in November 1921 was a Royal Disaster', JSTOR, 2 February 2022.

David Lelyveld, 'Three Aligarh Students: Aftab Ahmad Khan, Ziauddin Ahmad and Muhammad Ali', *Modern Asian Studies*, Vol. 9, No. 2 (1975)

William D. Rubenstein, 'The Secret of Leopold Amery', *Historical Research*, Vol. 73, No. 181 (2000)

William M. Matthew, 'India, Palestine and the Balfour Declaration', The Balfour Project

W.D. McIntyre, 'The Strange Death of Dominion Status', *The Journal of Imperial and Commonwealth History*, Vol. 27, No. 2 (1999), pp. 193–212

Joseph McQuade, 'Beyond an Imperial Foreign Policy?: India at the League of Nations, 1919–1946', *The Journal of Imperial and Commonwealth History*, Vol. 48, No. 2 (2020), pp. 263–295

Filmer Northrop, 'Asia and Western Dominance by K.M. Panikkar', *The Far Eastern Quarterly*, Vol. 14, No. 2, (1955), pp. 262–263

Guy Pauker, 'Panikkarism: The Highest Stage of Opportunism', *World Politics*, Vol. 7, No. 1, (1954), p. 10

Elie Podeh, 'The Drift Towards Neutrality: Egyptian Foreign Policy During the Early Nasserist Years, 1952–1955', *Middle Eastern Studies*, Vol. 32, No. 1, (1996), pp. 159–178

Barbara Ramusack, 'An Incident at Nabha: Interaction between Indian States and British Indian Politics', *The Journal of Asian Studies*, Vol. 28, No. 3 (1969), pp. 563–577

Margery Sabin, 'Ramananda Reviewed', *Economic and Political Weekly*, Vol. 51, No. 42 (2016), pp. 38–43

Hugh Seton-Watson, 'Asian Nationalism', *Encounter*, Vol. 1, (1956), pp. 1–18.

Michael M. Sheng, 'Mao, Tibet and the Korean War', *Journal of Cold War Studies*, Vol. 8, No. 3, (2006), pp. 15–33.

Percival Spear, 'Asia and Western Dominance by K.M. Panikkar', *Asian Review*, Vol. 50, No. 182, (1954), p. 166

Jehuda Reinharz, 'Chaim Weizmann: Statesman Without a State', *Modern Judaism*, Vol. 12, No. 3 (1992), pp. 225–242

L. Rushbrook-Williams, 'India Between the Conferences', *Foreign Affairs*, Vol. 9, No. 4, July 1931, pp. 624–637

Jadunath Sarkar, 'Review: Malabar and the Portuguese', Modern Review, Vol. 47, No. 1 (1930), p. 72.

Ornit Shani, 'The People and the Making of India's Constitution', *The Historical Journal*, Vol. 65, No. 4 (2022), pp. 1102–1103

F.R. Scott, 'The End of Dominion Status', *American Journal of International Law*, Vol. 38, No. 1 (1944), pp. 34–39

Fang Tien-Tze, 'An Assessment of Ambassador Luo Jialun's Mission to India, 1947–1949', *China Report*, Vol. 50, No. 3, (2014)

Vineet Thakur,

-'India's Diplomatic Entrepreneurism: Revisiting India's Role in the Korean Crisis, 1950–1952', *China Report*, Vol. 49, Issue 3 (2013), pp. 273–298.

-'An Asian Drama: The Asian Relations Conference, 1947', *The International History Review*, Vol. 41, No. 3 (2019), pp. 673–695

Leslie Wolf-Phillips, "Why 'Third World'?: Origin, Definition and Usage," *Third World Quarterly*, Vol. 9 (1987), pp. 1311–1327

Yan Jia, 'Subterranean Translation: The Absent Presence of Shen Congwen in K.M. Panikkar's Modern Chinese Stories', *World Literature Studies*, Vol. 1, No. 12 (2020), pp. 5–18

Electronic Sources

Seminar on K.M. Panikkar, Vol. I and Vol. II, Sahitya Akademi, 1994. Audio-tape recording SAK-226_1-AC, dated 21 June 1994. Available online at www.archive.org

ICWA International Conference on 'KM Panikkar and the Growth of a Maritime Consciousness in India', 23 March 2021. Available on YouTube: https://www.youtube.com/watch?v=VB5Z6195_Fk

A Selection of Works by K.M. Panikkar (in chronological order)

Books

An Introduction to the Study of the Problems of Greater India, (T.K. Swaminathan, 1916).

Indian Nationalism: Its Origin, History, and Ideals (Faith Press, 1920).

Essays on Educational Reconstruction in India (Ganesh & Co, 1920).

Imperialism in Practice and Theory (India Printing Press, 1922).

Sri Harsha of Kanauj: A Monograph on the History of India in the First Half of the seventh Century A.D. (D.B Taraporevala & Sons, 1922).

The Ideals of Sikhism (Sikh Tract Society, 1924).

An Introduction to the Study of the Relations of Indian States with the Government of India (Martin Hopkinson & Co., 1927).

(as Kerala Putra, pseudonym) *The Working of Dyarchy in India, 1919–1928* (D.B Taraporevala & Sons, 1928).

Malabar and the Portuguese. Being a History of the Relations of the Portuguese with Malabar from 1500 to 1663 (D.B Taraporevala & Sons, 1929).

The British Crown & the Indian States. An Outline Sketch Drawn up on behalf of the Standing Committee of the Chamber of Princes (King & Sons, 1929).

Federal India, with Kailas Narayan Haksar (Martin Hopkinson, 1930).

The Evolution of British Policy towards Indian States, 1774–1858 (Calcutta University Readership Lectures, 1930).

Gulab Singh, 1792–1858, Founder of Kashmir (Martin Hopkinson, 1930).

The Ring Fence System and the Marathas (Reprinted from the *Journal of Indian History*, Vol. 8, No. 3, 1929) (Calcutta, 1930).

Malabar and the Dutch. Being the History of the Fall of the Nayar Power in Malabar (D.B Taraporevala & Sons, 1931).

Indian States and the Government of India, (new edition of *An Introduction to the Study of the Relations of Indian States with the Government of India*) (Martin Hopkinson, 1932).

Caste and Democracy (L. & V. Woolf, Hogarth Press, 1933).

The New Empire. Letters to a Conservative Member of Parliament on the Future of England and India (Martin Hopkinson, 1934).

Inter-Statal Law: The Law Affecting the Relations of the Indian States with the British Crown (Sundaram Ayyar-Krishnaswami Ayyar Lectures, 1935).

The Indian Princes in Council. A Record of the Chancellorship of His Highness the Maharaja of Patiala, 1926–1931 and 1933–1936 (Oxford University Press, 1936).

His Highness the Maharaja of Bikaner. A Biography (Oxford University Press, 1937).

Hinduism & the Modern World (Kitabistan, 1938).

Origin and Evolution of Kingship in India (Baroda State Press, 1938).

Indian States (Oxford University Press, 1942).

The Future of South-East Asia: An Indian View (Allen & Unwin, 1943).

Imperial Organisation: Circulated as an Indian Preparatory Paper for the British Commonwealth Relations Conference, 1945 (Kitabistan, 1944).

The Strategic Problems of the Indian Ocean (Kitabistan, 1944).

India and the Indian Ocean. An Essay on the Influence of Sea Power on Indian History (Allen & Unwin, 1945).

The Basis of an Indo-British Treaty (Oxford University Press, 1946).

(as Chanakya, pseudonym), *Indian Constituent Assembly* (Book Depot, 1947).

A Survey of Indian History (National Information & Publication Ltd, 1947).

Regionalism and Security, with Vangal Thiruvenkatachari Krishnamachari et al. (Oxford University Press, 1948).

Population Problems (Indian Institute for Population Studies, 1950).

Chanakya (pseud. K.M. Panikkar), *Indian Revolution* (National Information & Publications, 1951).

The Principles and Practice of Diplomacy (Ranjit Printers & Publishers, 1952).

Asia and Western Dominance. A Survey of the Vasco da Gama Epoch of Asian History, 1498–1945 (Allen & Unwin, 1953).

The Founding of the Kashmir State. A Biography of Maharajah Gulab Singh, 1792–1858, new edition of *Gulab Singh, 1792–1858. Founder of Kashmir* (Allen & Unwin, 1953).

Convocation Address (Patna University Press, 1954).

Civil Services, History and Problems (University of Madras, 1955).

Geographical Factors in Indian History (Bharatiya Vidya Bhavan, 1955).

Hindu Society at Cross Roads (Asia Publishing House, 1955).

In Two Chinas. Memoirs of a Diplomat (Allen & Unwin, 1955).

Indian Doctrines of Politics (Harold Laski Institute of Political Science, 1955).

The State and the Citizen (Asia Publishing House, 1956).

India and China. A Study of Cultural Relations (Asia Publishing House, 1957).

The Afro-Asian States and Their Problems (Allen & Unwin, 1959).

Common Sense about India (Gollancz, 1960).

A History of Kerala, 1498–1801 (Annamalai University, 1960).

Problems of Indian Defence (Asia Publishing House, 1960).

A Survey of Indian History, third revised edition (Asia Publishing House, 1960).

The Determining Periods of Indian History (Bharatiya Vidya Bhavan, 1962).

In Defence of Liberalism. Issued under the auspices of the Indian School of International Studies (Asia Publishing House, 1962).

The Ideas of Sovereignty and State in Indian Political Thought (Bharatiya Vidya Bhavan, 1963).

The Foundations of New India (Allen & Unwin, 1963).

Studies in Indian History (Asia Publishing House, 1963).

Pazhassi Raja [The Lion of Kerala] (Sahitya Academy, 1963).

Essential Features of Indian Culture (Bharatiya Vidya Bhavan, 1964).

Hinduism & the West: A Study in Challenge and Response (Punjab University Publication Bureau, 1964).

Lectures on India's Contact with the World in the pre-British Period (Nagpur University, 1964).

History of Mankind. Cultural and Scientific Development, vol. VI: The twentieth century, with Caroline Ware and Jan Romein (Harper & Row: 1966).

An Autobiography, translated from the Malayalam into English by K. Krishnamurthy (Oxford University Press, 1977).

Portuguese Soldier, translated from Malayalam by Dr V. Haridasan (DAS, 2001).

Ministry of External Affairs Publication (internal use only):

A Tour in North-West China, 2 reports (New Delhi: Ministry of External Affairs, 1951), available at NMML.

A Report on Libya (New Delhi: Ministry of External Affairs, 1953), available at NMML.

Britain and the Arabs (New Delhi: Ministry of External Affairs, 1953), available at NMML.

Articles

'Louis Kossuth and the Hungarian Revival', *The Indian Review,* Vol.16, No. 5, 1915.
'India and the Imperial Cabinet', *The Commonweal,* Vol. 6, 13 August 1915.
'European War and Nationality', *The Commonweal,* Vol. 4, 27 August 1915.
'Some Economic Illusions', *The Commonweal,* Vol. 5, 1 October 1915.
'The London Money-market and the War', *The Commonweal,* Vol. 5, October 1915 and reprinted in *The Modern Review,* Vol.19, No. 3, 1916.
'The Claim of Imperial Citizenship', *The Commonweal,* Vol. 6, 15 September 1916.
The Exclusion of Indians from the Colonies, *The Commonweal,* 13 October 1916.
'Citizenship and Identity', *The Commonweal,* Vol. 7, October 1916.
'Indian Home Rule and Imperial Federalism', *The Commonweal,* 27 October 1916.
'Our Bookshelf—India and Imperial Reconstruction', *The Commonweal,* Vol. 6, 10 November 1916.
'The Problem of Education in the Colonies', *The Modern Review,* Vol. 21, No.1, 1917.
'The Illusions of Anglo-India. I: The Cult of Efficiency', *The Commonweal,* 5 January 1917.
'The Illusions of Anglo-India. II: Historical and Geographical Myths', *The Commonweal,* 12 January 1917.
'India's Place in the Empire', *The Commonweal,* Vol. 7, 12 January 1917.
'The Illusions of Anglo-India. III: Hypnotism and Hypothetics', *The Commonweal,* 19 January 1917.
'The Illusions of Anglo-India. IV: Social Myths', *The Commonweal,* 16 February 1917.
'The Educational Problem of Indian Nationalism', *The Modern Review,* Vol. 23, No.1, 1918.
'Problems of National Education in India', *The Asiatic Review,* Vol. 13–14, No. 39, 1918.
'Some Aspects of Nayar Life', *Journal of the Royal Anthropological Society of Great Britain and Ireland,* Vol. 48, 1918.
'Religion and Magic among the Nayars', *Man,* Vol. 18, 1918.
'Indian Agencies in England', *The Indian Review,* Vol. 20, No. 1, 1919.
'The Native States and Indian Nationalism', *The Modern Review,* Vol. 25, No. 1, 1919.
'The Interpretation of History', *The Hindustan Review,* Vol. XLV, No. 271, April 1922. Republished in a summarised version: 'What Indian History Means' in 'Indian Periodicals', *The Modern Review,* May 1922
'Europe and Asia', *The Modern Review,* Vol. 34, No. 4, 1923.
'The Past and the Present', *The Modern Review,* Vol. 36, No. 4, 1924.
'The Principles of Social Progress', *The Hindustan Times,* 31 December 1924.
'The Akali Struggle', *Hindustan Times,* 14, 15 and 16 January 1925.
'Militarism and Empire', *The Modern Review,* Vol. 39, No. 3, 1926.
'La tache de Lord Irwin nouveau vice-roi des Indes', *Europe Nouvelle,* Vol. 9, No. 434, 1926
'The Necessity of Asiatic Unity', *Indonesia Merdeka,* Vol. 4., Nos. 3–4, June-July 1926

Documents, 'Asia and Peace', *Indian Quarterly*, first published 22 August 1926 and reprinted by Panikkar himself in 1946. *India Quarterly*, Vol. 2, No. 2 (1946), pp. 192–195

'The National Movement in India', *Indonesia Merdeka,* Vol.4, No.1, February 1926

'The Psychology of the Hindu-Muslim Riots', *The Contemporary Review,* Vol. 131, No. 738, 1927.

'The Colour Problem in the British Empire', *Revue des Nations,* Vol. 1, No. 2, 1927.

'International Law Affecting Indian States', *The Indian Review,* Vol. 28, No. 9, 1927.

'The Reflex Action of Colonialism on Europe', *Revue des Nations,* Vol. 1, No. 5, 1927.

"'The Ring Fence System' and the Marathas," *The Journal of Indian History,* Vol. 8, No. 1, 1929.

'The Princes and India's Future', *Foreign Affairs,* Vol. 21, No. 3, 1943.

'The Indian States, Adjusting to Changing Times', *The Commonwealth and Empire Review,* Vol. 79, No. 80, 1945.

'Regional Organization for the Indian Ocean Area', *Pacific Affairs,* Vol. 18, No. 3, 1945.

'The Defence of India and Indo-British Obligations', *International Affairs,* Vol. 22, No. 1, 1946.

'Regionalism and World Security', *India Quarterly,* Vol. 2, No. 2, 1946.

'The Himalayas and Indian Defence', *India Quarterly,* Vol. 3, No. 2, 1947.

'The Himalayas and Indian Defence (continued)', *India Quarterly,* Vol. 3, No. 3, 1947.

'Problems of Indian History', *The Journal of Indian History,* Vol. 39, No. 1, 1951.

'India and China through the Ages', *The Asiatic Review,* Vol. 48, No. 174, 1952.

'The twentieth century in Asian and World History. An Inaugural Address', *India Quarterly,* Vol. 12, No. 3, 1956.

'The Government of India', *Current History,* Vol. 30, No.174, 1956.

'India Old and New', *The Indo-Asian Culture,* Vol. 5, 1956–1957.

'The Indian Version', *The National and English Review*, No. 150, 1958.

'Parties and Politics in India', *Current History,* Vol. 36, No. 211, 1959.

'Annual Day Address—Indian School of International Studies – 13 February 1961', *International Studies,* Vol. 22, No. 2, 1985.

'What Life Has Taught Me', *Bharatya Vidya Bhavan's Journal*, 1961 (reprinted on 5 January 1964).

Reviews

'Bismarck', *The Indian Review,* Vol. 20, No. 3, 1919.

'Dr. Slater on "South Indian Villages"', *The Indian Review,* Vol. 20, No. 7, 1919.

'A Passage to India, a Review', *The Hindustan Times*, 1 August 1924.

'History of Kerala by K. P. Padmanabha Menon', *The Modern Review*, Vol. 37, No. 3, 1925.

'Revolt of Asia', *Pacific Affairs,* Vol. 21, No. 1, 1948.

'Asia and the West by Maurice Zinkin', *India Quarterly,* Vol. 10, No. 3, 1954.

'The Middle East. A Political and Economic Survey', *The Indian Review*, Vol. 11, No. 1, 1955.

'A Study of History by Arnold Toynbee', *India Quarterly,* Vol. 13, No. 1, 1957.

'Democracy and Public Philosophy', *India Quarterly*, Vol. 13, No. 2, 1957.

<u>*Contributions to Volumes*</u>

'The Ruler of Bikaner. Soldier, Statesman, Innovator', in Laurence Frederic Rushbrook Williams (ed.), *The Great Men of India* (The Home Library Club, 1939), pp. 235–245.

'Guru Govind Singh. The Great Sikh Teacher', in Laurence Frederic Rushbrook Williams (ed.), *The Great Men of India* (The Home Library Club, 1939), pp. 483–491.

'A Universal Outlook', in K.M. Panikkar & Humayun Kabir, *Basis of Indian Culture* (Information Service of India, 1955), pp. 1–5.

<u>*Other Contributions*</u>

'Minutes of Dissent to the Report. April 17–20, 1947', in Benegal Shiva Rao (ed.), *The Framing of India's Constitution: Select Documents*, Vol. II (Indian Institute of Public Administration, 1967), 183–91.

'A Note on Some General Principles of the Union Constitution, May 1947', in Benegal Shiva Rao (ed.), *The Framing of India's Constitution: Select Documents*, Vol. II (Indian Institute of Public Administration, 1967), 534.

'A Further Note on Some Principles of the Union Constitution', in Benegal Shiva Rao (ed.), *The Framing of India's Constitution: Select Documents*, Vol. II (Indian Institute of Public Administration, 1967), 539.

Foreword to Dasharatha Sharma, *Early Chauhan Dynasties* (Motilal Banarsidass, 1959).

Foreword to Hermann Goetz, *Art and Architecture of Bikaner State* (Bruno Cassier, 1950).

Preface to K. M. Panikkar (ed.), *Modern Chinese Stories* (Ranjit Printers & Publishers, 1953).

Preface to Kunduri Iswara Dutt, *The Street of Ink* (Triveni Publishers, 1956).

Foreword to Jan Romein, *The Asian Century. A History of Modern Nationalism in Asia* (Allen & Unwin, 1962).

Foreword to Sunil Chandra Ray, *Early History and Culture of Kashmir*, 2nd ed. (Munshiram Manoharlal, 1970).

<u>*Official Reports*</u>

Report on the Indian Constitutional Reforms (Superintendent Government Printing, 1918)

Report of the Committee on Indian Students 1921–1922 (His Majesty's Stationery Office, otherwise HMSO, 1922)

A Collection of Treaties, Engagements and Sanads relating to India and Neighbouring Countries, (Government of India, Publication Branch 1929)

Report of the Indian States Committee (1928–1929) (HMSO, 1929)

Report of the All India States' People's Conference (AISPC, Bombay, 1939)

Report of the Indian Statutory Commission Presented by the Secretary of State for the Home Department to Parliament by Command of His Majesty (HMSO, 1930)

Indian Round Table Conference, 12 November 1930 – 19 January 1931: Proceedings (HMSO, 1931)

Report of the Indian States Enquiry Committee (Financial), 1932 (Government of India Press, 1932)

Joint Committee on Indian Constitutional Reform: Report (HMSO, 1934)

Bikaner Bulletin (1944–1948)

Report on the Administration of the Bikaner State for 1939–1948 (Government Press, 1948)

Asian Relations: Being a Report of the Proceedings and Documentation of the First Asian Relations Conference, New Delhi, March–April, 1947 (Asian Relations Organization, 1948)

Report of the States' Reorganisation Commission, 1955 (Manager of Publications, Government of India Press, 1956)

Leading Events in India-China Relations 1947–1962 (External Publicity Division, Ministry of External Affairs, 1962)

Report of the Committee on Emotional Integration (The Manager of Publications, Government of India, 1962)

Notes, Memoranda and Letters Exchanged between the Governments of India and China. White Papers (1954–1962), (Ministry of External Affairs, Government of India, 1960–1967)

Index

Acknowledgements

THIS BOOK HAS TAKEN FOUR YEARS AND A PANDEMIC TO WRITE. Sometimes I feel even that has been too little time for Panikkar to step out of the pages of this book.

I must thank the Panikkar family for being so kind and forthcoming about K.M. Panikkar's remarkable life, both professional and personal. It is never easy to write a biography about a man whose descendants are very much around, and there is always a certain hesitation in approaching tricky subjects, such as there are in all human lives. To Panikkar's youngest daughter, Radha Mohan and to his grandson, R. Madhavan Nair—it has been a privilege and an honour to record your memories. Thank you. My especial affection is for Ambika Nair, Panikkar's granddaughter, whom I first contacted as a potential source, and who has, in the course of writing this book, become a wonderful friend. If it had not been for her constant encouragement, her ready sense of humour and her patience in plying me with countless hot chocolates and comfort food while I fretted anxiously, this book would have remained stuck for a good while.

The bulk of this manuscript has been written and researched at the Prime Ministers' Museum and Library (PMML, but to me, it will always be NMML). Writing it in the carrel by the window upstairs has been a big part of my everyday existence for the last five years, as have been the walks in the grounds when my eyes hurt from looking at a computer screen all day. NMML is not just a library, not just an archive. For me, it has been a sanctuary. To Jyoti Luthra and the staff of the Manuscript Division, my gratitude is endless. It is a delight to work with archivists who know and love their work.

Thanks are not enough for the staff at the National Archives of India, both in the research room and in the Private Papers division. There have been several major changes in everyday functioning and requisitioning at the NAI, and the staff have kept research going fluidly despite the speedbumps and potholes of bureaucratic red tape.

My friends have propped me up with laughter, love and constant encouragement. I'm lucky to have the people I do—they are an unmixed blessing and I would not be the same without their presence in my life. Swati D'Souza (3000), Anumita Raj (coffee and cake!), Juhi Mendiratta, Mushtaq Salim, Tanvi Lal, Ambika Vishwanath, Amit Julka, Ankur Paliwal, Karishma Mehrotra, Sadhika Tiwari, Bhasker Tripathi, Pooja Pillai, Mythili Vijay, Dhrubo Jyoti, Nadia Nooreyezdan, Vandana Menon, Sudeept Maiti, Abhishek Upadhayay, Namrata Raju, Sumitha Kutty, Aanchal Malhotra, Pragya Tiwari, Teesta Guha Sarkar, Govind Deecee, Sneha Annavarapu, Vakasha Sachdev, Somya Lakhani, Medha Venkat, Abhishek Mehrotra, Amruta Byatnal, Saneet Chakradeo and Tripurdaman Singh—thank you.

Sam Dalrymple read the first draft of this manuscript as it was being written, long before I had the courage to show it to anyone else. His infectious delight in this story and the invaluable insights and comments he gave me are real gifts, both as a writer and as a friend. Thank you always.

Lakshana Palat, for being my sister in more ways than I can count, for the chaotic cake deliveries and travel plans, and for the happy simplicity of every day.

Deep Pal, for the sync of our relentlessly bad jokes, for the nights of good food and good Bollywood and for the wise and clear-eyed counsel you gave me during the early stages of writing this book. Thank you, favourite human. You are my family.

Saudamini Jain does not like being termed either patient, loving or steadfast, but her unwavering presence has helped me through 2024 in more ways than I can explain. Thank you, S. You're the best.

Anish Gawande, for the kind of unstinting love, presence and support across time-zones and timelines that I could only have imagined before I met him; for the constant cheerleading, the zany practicality and the solid friendship.

Deeksha Khanna and Zoya Wahi: for the laughter, the daily check-ins and the weekly *addas*, for Mowgli and Toff.

My undying thanks, especially to Janpath Online, for letting me occupy a corner of their office for weeks, while I hammered through the last, brain-frying edits of this book.

Khushi Singh Rathore, for the long walks around the grounds of Teen Murti to clear my head, for the constant encouragement and putting your foot down when I began digging too deep down a stray research rabbit-hole.

Samit Basu, for the daily giggles, the de-puffing and for being there through all the venting and ranting.

Kanishka Gupta has been my friend for as long as he has been my agent and for that, gratitude falls short. Thank you, Kan.

In Westland Books, I had the joy and relief of knowing that my editors believed in this story—enough to wait out an entire pandemic and more. Karthika and Ajitha, thank you for everything. There aren't words.

When this manuscript was given to Kushalrani Gulab to edit, everyone told me that it had been given to the best in the business. It was the truth. She held my hand through multiple panic attacks and gently yet incisively honed multiple drafts. Panikkar walks through these pages proudly because of her. Thank you, Bunny.

And finally, to my mother, who always encouraged me to follow my own path, who stands ready to fight the world (and me, on defeated days!) to see to it that my dreams come true. I love you, Ammi.